# LEADERSHIP GENETIC ENGINEERING FORMULA:

## Toward a Hybrid Culture of Good Governance, Peace, and Prosperity for All!

## VOLUME 2

Agola Auma-Osolo

Order this book online at www.trafford.com
or email orders@trafford.com

Most Trafford titles are also available at major online book retailers.



Printed in the United States of America.

ISBN: 978-1-4907-1502-5 (sc)
ISBN: 978-1-4907-1503-2 (e)

*Trafford rev. 06/09/2014*

Trafford PUBLISHING www.trafford.com

**North America & international**
toll-free: 1 888 232 4444 (USA & Canada)
fax: 812 355 4082

## DEDICATION

**To the Scientists of The African Mysteries System of The Grand Lodge of Luxor, in Ancient Egypt who are The Founding Fathers of this Discovery and Prime Minister Dr. Immohotep who together with Prime Minister Joseph put the discovery into Practice leading that Ancient Egypt into a Prosperous Nation of all Times.**

**And**

**To the American People and Government for their Institute for International Education (IIE) for my college education ; and National Science Foundation Fellowship for my professional training in International Law at The Hague Academy of International Law, The International Court of Justice, The Hague (1969).**

**Prof. Agola Auma-Osolo**
**Maseno University**
**Maseno—Kenya**

# Contents

## PART ONE



## PART TWO

### DEMOCRACY VERSUS UNDEMOCRACY: A Test for Leadership Conceptualization Contradiction Disaster

## PART THREE

## THEORY AND PRACTICE CONTRADICTION: A test for Leadership Disaster to Humaninty and as a Paragigm in Leadership Deterioration and Disintegration.

## PART FOUR

## THE GOALS, PROBLEMS AND STRATEGIES OF EAST AFRICAN NATION-STATES ON THE WORLD MARKET. A Test for The Spirit of Community Intergration in The East African Region.

**CHAPTER III**



**CHAPTER IV**



**CHAPTER V**

## PART FIVE

## LEADERSHIP AND WORLD PEACE: A Test for World Leadership's Concept of and Trust in a Lasting Peace

## PART SIX

## UNIVERSITY AND THE CULTURE OF PEACE AND DEMOCRACY DEVELOPMENT: A Test for Universities Efficacy as An Agent for Conflict Vaccination

### CHAPTER 1



### CHAPTER II



### CHAPTER III

**CHAPTER IV**



**CHAPTER V**

## CHAPTER III



## CHAPTER IV



## PART NINE

## LEADERSHIP AND MORALITY: A Test for Man's Mechanical Efforts to Create and Institutionalize Democracy and Good Governance

## CHAPTER 1

**CHAPTER II**



**CHAPTER III**



## PART TEN

## SOVEREIGN EQUALITY DEMAND, CARROT DIPLOMACY, HARAMBEE MYTH, TERRORISM AND WAR: A Test for Leadership Paranoia and Failure.

**CHAPTER I**



**CHAPTER II**

**CHAPTER III**



**CHAPTER III (a)**



**CHAPTER IV**

**CHAPTER V**



**CHAPTER VI**

## PART ELEVEN

## LEADERSHIP GENETIC ENGINEERING FORMULA: A Test for a Hybrid Culture, Good Governance, Peace and World Prosperity for All



## PART ELEVEN (A)

## HOW ANIMUS DOMINANDI VIRUS WAS ELIMINATED BY ANCIENT EGYPT USING THE AFRICAN MYSTERIES SYSTEM OF THE GRAND LODGE OF LUXOR'S METHODOLOGY OF CONFLICT VACCINATION

### CHAPTER 1



### CHAPTER II

## CHAPTER III



## CHAPTER IV

**CHAPTER V**



## PART ELEVEN (B)

## HOW A SIMILAR HUMAN DEFECT IS BEING ELIMINATED TODAY BY BIO-SCIENCE USING GENETIC ENGINEERING METHODOLOGY



## PART TWELVE

## CONFLICT VACCINATION FORMULA: A Path to a Hybrid Culture of Peace, Democracy and Good Governance and Accelerated Socio-Economic Recovery and Development in Africa and Total World.

# PART ONE

*"HE THAT RULES OVER MEN MUST BE JUST, RULING IN THE FEAR OF GOD.*

*AND HE SHALL BE AS THE LIGHT OF THE MORNING, WHEN THE SUN RISETH, EVEN A MORNING WITHOUT CLOUDS; AS THE TENDER GRASS SPRINGING OUT OF THE EARTH BY CLEAR SHINING AFTER RAIN."*

*(The Spirit of the LORD,*
*The God of Israel*
*The Rock of Israel.*
*II SAMUEL 23:2-4*
*THE HOLY BIBLE)*

*"MY PEOPLE ARE DESTROYED FOR LACK OF KNOWLEDGE: BECAUSE THOU HAST REJECTED KNOWLEDGE, I WILL ALSO REJECT THEE, THAT THOU SHALT BE NO PRIEST TO ME: SEEING THOU HAST FORGOTTEN THE LAW OF THY GOD, I WILL ALSO FORGET THEY CHILDREN."*

*(The Word of the LORD*
*Hosea 4:6, THE HOLY BIBLE)*

# A PREAMBLE

This Volume Two is an Omega of Volume One. Its sole purpose is to complete the marathon research expedition initiated in Volume One on the mysteries surrounding and being responsible for man's chronic failure in the leadership profession that has always (i.e., since Man's Creatuib period) plunged the innocent masses under that leader-into a sea of various acute agonies characterized by death, physical (body) injuries of diverse degrees, trauma and other psychological defects; and also destruction of property and the environment in a total contradiction to/with man's multi-potentials endowed to him by his Creator as so explicitly confirmed by the data gained from using an inter-disciplinary approach particularly from The Book of The Genesis, Chapter 1;26-31 as follows:

> ***"And God said 'Let Us make man in Our image, after Our likeness, and let them have dominion [authority] over the fish of the sea, and over the fowl of the air, and over the cattle, and over every creeping thing that creeps upon the earth." . . . .***

In the final analysis, this research expedition contained in both Volumes One and Two is succinctly an Etiology of the Leadership Failure endemic with a view to finding/providing a solution to the problem that has been terrorizing Humanity ever since the time of our Patriarch Adam and Matriarch Eve.

In Volume One, we sought to examine and analyze the phenomenon in a greater detail, using every data available beginning with the generation of our Patriarch Adam and matriarch Eva to our own. In this regard, we systematically showed its nature, role, dynamics and usefulness in both the Animal and Plant Kingdoms. We demonstrated its universal role among all species and how its role and significance naturally differ from one species to another.

In doing so, we proved beyond any reasonable doubt that the concept of this phenomenon, "Leadership", is a significant tool to every living species' survival; and that it is, therefore, very important to/for not only a Social Scientist but also to/for other Scientists, in their respective areas and fields of study, for understanding its role, goal and dynamics in not only human but also in all aspects of life.

Because of this very significant cause, it is unfortunate that certain Scientist such as those in Psychology tend to believe that the concept is no more of any value to man on the assumption that it has largely lost its value for the Social Science. Among them include, for example, Cecil A. Gibb who seems to comfortably believe so possibly on the strength of his enormous research work in psychology effective the 1940's.

But, unfortunately to his intention, his view is not shared at all by other prominent scholars who have also invested as much energy as his own in their respective research expeditions on the same leadership concept albeit in non-psychology areas of study. For instance, if Gibb's view had any reliable validity at all, his own contemporaries in social sciences such as Arnold S. Tannembaum in Sociology and Lester G. Seligman in Political Science would believe otherwise on the same issue. To the two, the concept is an irrefutable tool for one's understanding and explaining the role and effectiveness of any people and leader in their political system on how they manage their corporate affairs against disaster odds for the purpose of their survival.

In view of this fact, it is self-evident that the leadership concept is an indiscipensible tool to/for both Social Science and all other areas and disciplines of Science. Its value to Science is inelastic, inter subjective and spatio-temporal free in Science.

As a concept, it aids/enables a Scientist to understand the mysteries of its multifaceted meanings. For instance, in Science, one may be understood or referred to as a leading scientist in one's area of specialization on the strength of his/her discoveries and publications of the same; an institution may be said to be a leader or leading of/our of all other institutions in performance such as research discoveries, enrolment, games and athletics; etc. In social life, one out of all other members of an organization such as a nuclear family, may be said to be/ as a leader of that social organization. One may be identified as a leader of a club, fraternity, society, etc. And, in political life, one may be identified/said to be a leader of a political system, party, association or group. This fact holds true in Science from the Greek City States political life to our Modern 20$^{th}$ Century nation-states political life. In the latter political life, such a person who is identified as a leader of all others may be descried or characterized as a "president" or "prime Minister", having specific unique authority over all others and their affairs technically known or referred to as "executive powers" by which such a person or leader is expected by all others below him or under his/her domination/authority to authoritatively govern these others as so stipulated to him to do by the legal instrument of those people collectively agreed upon by them all. Such instrument is called a "constitution".

By such instrument, a Country's leader is empowered to authoritatively govern his people/country; to periodically seek election or yield the leadership to a new person who may turn out to be one who has successfully won the election in a free and fair electoral process; to safeguard and promote the sanctity of the life and property rights of every individual within/under his/her dominion; to ensure that justice is not only seen to be done but actually done to/for all regardless of gender, ethnicity, creed, race or any other forms of affiliation.

All this wisdom and knowledge cannot and will not become handy to a scientist from oblivion without the aid of this concept "leadership" as his guiding star or torch right through various challenging odds until he reaches to the mysteries of the truth he seeks to understand.

Because of this irrefutable empirical evidence, one must therefore rightly question the validity and reliability of Professor Cecil A. Gibb's argument that the concept has lost its value for the social science. The affore-going facts prove beyond any reasonable doubt that in Human life, leadership is a natural political affair management. It is a universal phenomenon found in every human grouping beginning from a nuclear family right up to all other social groups having a sublime political character first before one gets to the real politically oriented party, association, chapter, union and system (country).

This fact is naturally inherent in man. It arises from man's unique natural make-up (architecture or architectural design by which man was naturally made/created by his creator). This design is his biological constitution containing the purposes) by which man was thus created to do and the principles by which man was thus created to do and the principles by which man was thus expected to be guided in his daily life.

It is by virtue and strength of this biological constitution that man is therefore not only a homo politicus entity. Also, he is an entity of a host of other multi-potentials. Unlike all other members of the Animal Kingdom, man is a homo societicus in that he interacts with other members of his community; he is a homo communicatus in that he legibly and intelligibly communicates with his fellow community members; he is a homo economicus in that he transacts businesses with his fellow men in commerce and trade; he is a homo juridicus in that he prosecutes and adjudicates matters deserving such actions and puts the affected to justice in keeping with the Rule of Law and Justice, etc.

Consequently, out of all his counterparts in the Animal Kingdom, man is the only most fortunate, happy being. He is the only one that enjoys this unique opportunity endowed to him by his Creator as so explicitly evidenced by the data gained from an inter-disciplinary approach under The Book of The Genesis of The Holy Bible Chapter 1:26.

In view of this cardinal fact, leadership is neither man's creation nor a phenomenon of recent times. The data confirms that it is as old as mankind in the human history; and is, therefore, a spatio-temporal free (i.e), a universal and thus free from space and time conditions.

Its immense significant role and function to man in the human life lies in its capacity as a man's natural instrument for identifying man's problem and resources that must be exploited in order to provide goods and services needed as a cure or preventive measures of the problem in question or at hand.

In addition to this theological fact, another theological fact stipulates the following conditions under/by which one may be deemed a leader in society:

> ***"He that rules over men must be just, ruling in the fear of God. And, he shall be as the light of the morning, when the sun rises, even a morning without clouds; as the tender grass springing out of the earth by clear shining after rain" II Samuel 23:3-4, The Holy Bible*).**

However, in spite of its double-edged utility to Mankind, and qualification required of every one in leadership, most unfortunately this phenomenon never received man's prompt serious attention as a worthy subject for a study like other various phenomena were seriously treated. Unlike these other phenomena in which enormous man's energies were invested not only in BioSciences and Physical Sciences but also in both Social and Behavioural Sciences, this phenomenon received a marginal attention. Where it was considered at all for study as Thucydides tried to do at all in his study of the Peloponnesian War of 431 BC where the researcher's main interest and goal was merely to understand why the War ever broke out between the Spartan League and the Athenian Empire, given the fact that the two had been good neighbours for ages on the one hand and also the fact that the Athenian Empire was headed by an able wise leadership of Pericles on the other. In his amazement, Thucydides stumbled onto a discovery concerning Pericles that inspite of his renown name and image in the Mediterranean Region as a prudent leader, Pericles was obsessed with an aggressive instinct to an arrogant belief that

> "We [Athenians] are alone among mankind in doing men benefits, not on calculations of self interest, but in the fearless confidence of freedom. In a word, 1 [Pericles] claim that our city as a whole is an education to Greece"
>
> (Thucydides, by Livingstone, 1943, pp 113-114).

In his conclusion, Thucydides zeroed his satisfaction not from his efforts to understand what leadership is and is not; and what it can or cannot do. He did so in getting to know the actual root-causes of the War between Sparta and her good neighbor, Athens. In his own words, he concludes,

> "The real cause I consider to be the one which was formally not kept out of sight. The growth of the power of Athens, and the alarm which this [power] inspired in Lacedaemon made war inevitable" (Thucydides, by Crawley, 1951, p.23).

Thus, unlike the interest of this and the First Volume titled *WHY LEADERS FAIL*, Thucydides research efforts do not help any reader interested in understanding the phenomenon called "leadership".

Another study that could have answered this fundamental question not answered by Thucydides during the classical time is Niccolo Machiavelli whose book titled *The Prince* strikes the reader with a hope that one is going to understand what this leadership phenomenon actually is and how strategically useful it is at all to Humanity.

Unfortunately, Machiavelli's efforts is of no good consequences to the reader at all as it lacks the essence and significance of leadership to Humanity in keeping with the spirit and goal of science as Bio-Sciences and Physical Sciences have each demonstrated by improving

Humanity's standard of living using their respective discoveries and innovations. Unlike studies in these Sciences, Machiavelli's study in Social Sciences is but a tragedy to Humanity. It incites man against man by arguing that in order for one to become a leader, he/she has to use aggression and terrorism in the sense that this is the actual way the Roman leaders became emperors, expanded and maintained their leadership.

Because of this provocative argument in Machiavelli's study, The Prince, Machiavelli was globally adored; and his argument is still cherished up to today by some scientists in the Social Sciences, terming it as a "foundation" of the so-called Realist School in the Social Sciences without reflecting and considering the amount of havoc the study has caused to Humanity overtime, such as colonialism and imperialism that it encouraged to cause a global catastrophe to Humanity in Africa, Asia, South America and North America.

The critical acid test against Machiavelli's study and all those other studies of the same kind arises from this very consequence of the studies. For example, if the essence and goal of a study is to discover ways and means through and by which Humanity may be improved in a societal standard of living against all forms of insecurities, does Machiavelli's study do so? And if injustices to mankind is the essence and goal of Machiavelli's study, of what good is his study?

Therefore, in view of the fact that the cardinal essence and goal of leadership is that:

> ***"He that ruleth over men must be just, ruling in the fear [respect] of God. And he shall be as the light of the morning, when the sun riseth, even a morning without clouds; as the tender grass springing out of the earth by clear shining after rain" (II Samuel, 23:3-4, THE HOLY BIBLE),***

It is self-evident that Machiavelli's study lacks any essence and significance to mankind. Also, in this regard, it is also self-explanatory that the study is antithetical to the essence and goal of Science. And if so, then it must be pseudo-scientific. It does not fit and qualify as a scientific study for it is of no significance to Mankind.

In the same vein of this tragedy of Machiavelli's study in Social Sciences, another similar tragedy in the same Social Sciences which consequently constitutes a valid justification of our reason that "Leadership" phenomenon must be exhaustively studied afresh, is that in spite of the immense significance of Leadership to Humanity in its capacity as a man's indispensable natural tool that he uses to identify and exploit resources into goods and services that he needs in order to eradicate his insecurities around him and his fellow men, unfortunately, this Leadership phenomenon never received a satisfactory attention during the Classical Ages. It was not until the 20th century that the phenomenon began receiving any adequate attention. It was now put on the Social Sciences agenda as also an important item for study.

Albeit this turned out to be so in favour of the Leadership phenomenon as also a significant subject worthy man's effort as a study, the subject was treated solely as a secondary item in the Political Science and Social Sciences as a whole. In Social Sciences, it was treated as essentially a stuff of Political Science inherent in political life but not a matter related to or found in other spheres of Human life that were not purely political such as nuclear family, social groups, business organizations, etc.

Through such skewed and myopic assumptions, the Leadership phenomenon was naively perceived and understood as solely a concept attributed to a political role and function of one that was made to serve as a leader of all others in society, with a view to facilitating or doing all those duties that a society needs to be done in order for it to achieve its perceived goal. This goal may, e.g., be eradication of a society's problem such as a disease, poverty, famine, poor road net-work communication problem, illiteracy, aggression, etc.

But, in as much as all these facts are true in respect to the role and function of leadership in political life, the fact still remains that this is not all true. Leadership does not exist in political life alone. It also exists in other various sectors of life such as social, economic, scientific, etc.

In social life, leadership exists in nuclear family, social groups, etc. In nuclear family organization, leadership manifests itself in the role and function of a father who, in his capacity as head of the family, does all those functions also envisaged in a leader in political life. As a family leader, he provides food security and all other security means against diseases, poverty, famine, poor communication, illiteracy, aggression etc.

In economic life, leadership also exists in abundance. In profit-making business organizations, leadership is extremely honoured and used to mobilize and enhance all those resources essential for empowering the business to realize efficient and sound production and to also enable the business to achieve a comfortable profit. Otherwise, the business can easily close down its doors without such efforts. Hence the need for a good and effective leadership in economic life.

Similarly, in scientific organizations, leadership is also an essential asset because of its contributions to the development and growth of scientific programmes such as research projects etc that have always led man to extra-ordinary noble scientific discoveries and innovations for the good of mankind. Such discoveries are endless. They, however, include X-Rays, Polio Vaccine, Electronic Telecommunication, Tele Vision, Aeroplanes, Outer-Space, Antibiotics, Information Technology (IT),etc which could not have been possibly discovered for mankind's use had there not been leadership in scientific organizations to facilitate research efforts towards their discoveries.

And, in Education sector, the latter could not have otherwise managed to grow and proliferate throughout the World and to facilitate eradication of illiteracy had there not been a leadership ingredient in Education Sector. Thus, it was this ingredient that empowered the Education sector to eradicate illiteracy and promote literacy in the former's place. This is why Education Management is one of the core sub-disciplines in the Education Discipline.

In this regard, leadership is indeed a universal phenomenon in all sectors or spheres of life in society in its capacity as the engine that makes an organization function. It is universal in that man is not only a homo politicus but also a multidimential and multi-potential man. While he is a homo politicus, he is also a homo societicus, homo economicus, homo communicus, homo scientificus, homo diplomaticus, homo medicinicus, etc.

Starting with homo societicus first, empirical evidence overtime show that man is a social animal in that he contacts and interacts with his fellow man for various reasons befitting his social needs in life. He interacts with members of his nuclear family, extended family, peer groups, work-mates, etc for the purpose of his social good and satisfaction. Without this satisfaction, man cannot be himself. He becomes unhappy, withdrawn, lonely etc. These factors end up compelling him to search for one to interact with. On getting this someone to interact with, man becomes a happy man and no more does he feel lonely, withdrawn or socially naked. This is why he is homo societicus in life.

As a homo economicus, man is an economic man by virtue of his habitual economic activities in life. In order to survive, he has to look for food. He does so by every means available to him, all depending to his environment space in which he lives and must look and find the kind of food that he wants. If the environment space can only offer fishing, the man must also rely on fishing as his source of a living. Also, he has to do fish mongering with his fellow man whose means of survival may not be fishing by virtue of the habitat where he lives. If one is in an environment space where he must depend only of hunting wild animals and birds, then that will be that man's suitable economic source on his survival. And he may also use that to trade with his counterpart whose source of income is not hunting. In all, each man is an economic man by virtue of his efforts for survival in life.

Coming to man's homo communicatus potential, there is no doubt that, unlike all other members of the Animal Kingdom, man is the only species with a unique communication abilities that enable him to easily interact with his fellow man not only physically but also through various media of communication. Whereas other members of the Animal Kingdom do also have means and codes of communication between and among themselves, the fact is that their means are only biological. They are empowered to communicate biologically from their birth but lack a learned communication potential like man's. It is because of this unique advantage in man above all other members of The Animal Kingdom that make man is inventions unique above all other members in The Animal Kingdom.

As a homo Scientificus, man again has a unique superiority over all other members of the Animal Kingdom. Unlike them, man engages in Scientific and Technological discoveries and innventions for his survival. Ants, birds, bees, wasps and other members of the Animal Kingdom may have means of making sophisticated homes for themselves. However, all these abilities and achievements are a product of their in-born potentials. Each is biologically constituted to do so and no more at all. Their abilities are not learned as those of man arising from scientific research and discoveries.

And as a homo diplomaticus, man is by nature, a diplomat. He is endowed by his Creator this ability that he uses in his interaction with his fellow men. This ability is reflected and manifested in his use of persuasion to his fellow men in order for them to allow him have or get what he is in need of. In his efforts to gain love affair with a woman, he uses courtship or seductive diplomacy coupled with caressing with a view to stimulating a woman's sexual desire towards him. And in his efforts to gain friendship with strangers, man uses friendly sweet words with which to gain attention of the stranger and make this stranger interested in wanting to build a friendly relations with him. Although all this is a natural social phenomenon in private affairs, in public affairs man's ability as a diplomat is also in abundance in public offices most especially in those offices dealing with foreign relations. In addition to its being abundant in such public offices, it is also very much abundant in international relations particularly in matters of peace building such as peace treaties, accords, and pacts which are always the end-results of round-table-peace talks aimed at restoring peace after the latter has been disrupted by the outbreak of war.

And, as a *homomedicus*, man is also a healer of diseases. He heals himself and his fellow man whenever such a need arises. Hence the on-going proliferation of numerous health care centres, pharmacies, theatres for surgery, etc globally.

But, the key phenomenon in each of these man's abilities is none else other than "leadership". It is a key in human life in that it is by the presence of this ingredient in each of these abilities that man is fortunately able to realize his needs from each of these potentials.

In the final analysis, it is self-evident that in every society, leadership is very much universal. It is universal in that man is, by, nature, a homo politicus which is an inborn attribute or instinct which enables man to mobilize his fellow men and women into a pact unionis (a firm contractual union or partnership), with a view to using the same for the purpose of pursuing a common objective or goal that is beneficial for/to one's society.

But pactum unionis does not and cannot exist in oblivion. It works hand-in-hand with pacta subjectionis (i.e., a firm contractual agreement by the society to have or select one among themselves to act as their servant with a view to using him/her as a conduit through which they can channel their problems and wishes against these problems). On the strength of this pacta subjectionis each society member submits his/her loyality to him/her that may have been appointed/selected so that the latter may be able to effectively discharge his/her duties in accordance with the wishes and expectations of his/her duties in accordance with the wishes and expectations of his/her society members against the problems the society wants to be dealt with.Such a person is given an explicit authority to discharge those duties bestowed to him/her by that society for its good.

Whereas this is the fundamental need in and by every society, the perplexing paradox to mankind is that, since Antiquity beginning with the generation of our Patriarch Adam and Matriarch Eve, history shows that to-date, man has already bled a lot as a result of Leadership

Failure endemic. And, also that this agony continues to deteriorate overtime due to man's continued failure in Social and Behavioural Sciences to unlock the mysteries of this epidemic in the same manner that man's efforts in both Physical and Biosciences have managed to do, e.g., in discoveries and inventions of various means and ways for man's advancement. Because of this serious disparity between the achievement in both Social and Behavioural Sciences on the one hand and the achievement in both Physical and Biosciences on the other, man in both Social and Behavioural Sciences must now prove or show why his action should also be qualified as a science at all since anything scientific must be for the benefit of man's advancement as man's action in both Physical and Bio-sciences has proved to Mankind since Antiquity to today.

Accordingly, this book is a function of this concern. It is a product of my 40 years marathon concern and search for an answer(s) to mysteries surrounding the existing perennial epidemic of Leadership Failure in Political Life globally that have always evaded recognition of every past research effort albeit the latter's tireless rigor and determination to unlock these mysteries and then understand the actual reasons behind this Leadership Failure epidemic that has always plunged the Innocent Population into a sea of various disaster agonies. This include agonies of civil and international wars; various forms of genocide (i.e., one-sided and mutual genocide), exodus of displaced and refugee persons; various pathetic living conditions of these persons in terrible makeshifts exacerbated by harsh natural conditions such as bad weather, malaria parasites, malnutrition, hunger and thirst terror, long hours of walking in search of a safe haven, etc.

Vivid empirical evidences of this Leadership Failure epidemic and its horrors to Humanity and the Environment include, for instance, the World War II and its aftermath, and of the Cold War which terrorized Africa, Latin America and Asia more than the World War II did to them, by using its warring Capitalist Bloc headed by the USA on the one hand and the Communist Bloc headed by the Soviet Union (USSR) to hire and set their leaders into Civil Wars, political assassinations, coups d'etat and cessessions. The most terrible cases of this horror include the Korean Civil War of 1950/51 that led that Country into a break up into two separate countries of North and South Korea; the Chinese Civil war that led that Country into a break up into Mainland China and Island China (Formosa) in 1949; The Chilean Civil War that led to the assassination of a democratically elected President Salvador Allende of Chile in 1974; the forceful creation of the of Israel in 1948 with a total neglect of the sanctity of the human and sovereign rights of the Palestinian People who had permanently resided in the area for ages thus forcing creation of an endless bloody war between The Israels and the Palestinians ever, since 1949; and an endless confrontation between the Developed and Underdeveloped Countries in the United Nations General Assembly where the Underdeveloped Countries now opted to exploit their endowed Arab oil leverage to compel the Developed Countries who are the chief oil consumers to submit to their demands for the Palestinian rights to sovereignty and also to officially declare Zionism as racism—a demand that was recognized as a result of the UN General Assembly's decision to pass a resolution in 1975 condemning Zionism as racism, and also to invite the Palestinian Liberation Organization (PLO) Leader Yasir Arafat not only to address it but also recognized him as head of government and greeted him with sustained applause while limiting the time for Israel's response which was delivered to a virtually empty Assembly. Also, the Arab-African majority in co-operation with the Communist Bloc barred Israeli participation in non-political UN Educational, Scientific and Cultural Organization (UNESCO); expelled apartheid South Africa from its session because of the regime's racial practices after the UN Security Council had refused to take action against that regime; and consequently made the UN an alternative battle ground for the Cold War between the Capitalist and the Communist Bloc Leaders.

Today, prima facie evidences of the horrors of this Leadership Poverty epidemic to Humanity and the Environment include the most recently concluded civil war in Sudan in 2004 caused by the insensitivity of President Jaafer Muhammed al-Nimeri and his supporters to the rights of the Christian population in the Southern Sudan as compared to his sensitivity to the rights of his fellow Moslem population in the Northern Sudan which has consequently terrorized that Country so much through civil war and displacement of the innocent peoples from their habitual residences between the predominantly Islamic Northern Sudan headed by an Islamic regime based in Khartoum on the one side and the predominantly Christian Southern Sudan headed by the non-Islamic military wing, Sudan People's Liberation Army (SPLA) under the late Dr. John Garang, since the Country's independence in 1959 to the Sudan Peace Agreement in 2004.

Before 2004, Sudan had hardly been allowed by its Leadership to enjoy a comfortable peace and socio-economic development. All that it was allowed to enjoy was a daily harsh life of various agonies of bloodshed and hundreds of thousand loss of life and body injuries thus rendering that Country to being a maimed nation physically, psychologically, economically, politically, culturally, socially and spiritually.

But that is not all. The Northern and Southern Sudanese conflict based on religious disparity is not all. It is being worsened by another unsettled agony of the Civil War in Western Region, Darfur, where the African Union (AU) Peace Keeping Force has found it so difficult to bring down the Civil War that the International Community Leadership spearheaded by the USA President Geroge W. Bush, Jr., now believes intervention of the International peace keeping Force as being necessary in order to reinforce the All Peace Keeping Force. But, the Khartoum regime can hardly tolerate such idea. It is strongly opposed to the proposal thereby creating an endless inter-leadership tug-of-war on the Darfur Peace Question.

But, all the above is just a tip of the iceberg. It is just another typical example of numerous cases of a similar leadership poverty epidemic in Africa, Asia, Latin America and Europe.

In Europe, similar cases such as Bosnia and Chechnia abound. They are all classic examples of Leadership Failure caused by the same virus of global leadership epidemic—a fact which, therefore, constitutes a valid justification of this book's efforts to search for a viable remedy to this epidemic in order to set Humanity free.

Therefore, whereas the aim of the First Volume in this series titled Why Leaders Fail and Plunge The Innocent into a Sea of Agonies, was to unearth, examine and then provide the reader with the actual root-causes of this failure ever since the era of our Patriarch Adam and Matriarch Eve right up to our own era, as a first step in this marathon scientific expedition for the mysteries of Leadership failure endemic, the aim of this Second Volume is succinctly to systematically synthesize these root-causes into a coherent body of knowledge able to lead us to a genetic formula that would provide Humanity with an environment of a hybrid culture requisite for Good Governance and Democracy, which are, in turn, a mandatory *sinqua non* condition for any sign of socio-economic development and prosperity in every country such as the USA, UK, Japan, Germany Canada, Switzerland, Australia and Newzland today.

Because of this reason, this Volume is important in the sense that it seeks to discover/invent a unique methodology by which Humanity may now be able to break-through this existing perennial mystery of leadership failure epidemic which has always terrorized Humanity since antiquity to the present (2008). Hence, the book's title: Leadership Genetic Engineering Formula: Toward A Hybrid Culture for Democracy and Good Governance for National Prosperity.

In order to discover this formula, the book examines the ancient Leadership Genetic Engineering Formula used between the years 7000 BC and 5000 BC by the Egyptians of antiquity that enabled them to develop an extra-ordinary Hybrid Culture with a Hybrid Political Leadership second to none in the History of Mankind—a Culture and Leadership of unique excellence that empowered the Egyptian people of the time to advance to the highest heights of greatness in various areas of scientific and technological discoveries and inventions that even our own advanced technology today is unable to comprehend, e.g., in the area of mummification of human dead bodies to a level of being able to exist for centuries.

Accordingly, this book's goal is solely to do just that and to explain this formula in greater details so as to enable the reader understand and appreciate the efficacy and usefulness of the formula.

However, whereas this formula is thoroughly explained in detail in Part Eleven of this book, Leadership Genetic Engineering is a process by which a leader undergoes a mechanical metamorphosis of socio-psychological transformation from a leadership personality "A" to a leadership personality "B" for the sole-purpose of rehabilitating an apparent destructive leadership personality of obsessive appetite for corruption, dishonesty, self-glorification, arrogance against the Rule of Law and Justice, etc, to a constructive leadership personality of stern adherence to the Rule of Law and Justice and the Policy of **zero tolerance** against corruption, dishonesty, arrogance, self-glorification, etc critically detrimental to the spirit of socio-economic development.

As a rehabilition mechanism, Leadership Genetic Engineering is both a curative and preventive remedy against various leadership maladies characterized by dictatorial, fascist, militaristic, undemocratic, totalitarian and other tendencies (viruses) of Bad Governance. As a curative mechanism, it enables an unrighteous leader infested with such viruses to shed off such viruses through this process. And, as a preventive mechanism, it cushions a righteous leader from being infected with or acquiring such viruses due to one's prior awareness of their destructive effects on leadership.

In this regard, the ultimate goal of this Book is to unearth all those processes collectively known as Leadership Genetic Engineering highly essential for good leadership construction i.e as a way forward toward Good Governance which every country in both Africa and the rest of The World needs if it is to prosper. Because of its strategic importance to every country as the heart of each country's life and normal functioning (i.e peace and order), absence of Good Governance automatically leads to anarchy and civil strife (war) all way from a nuclear family organization structure to a nation-state and right up to a global organizational structure such as the United Nations, which has always proved a perpetual hostage to the Rule of Anarchy of the super powers' arrogance and selfishness by virtue of their notorious obsession with their constitutionally mandated absolute veto power monopoly in the UN Security Council having no regard to the rights and needs of the less powerful members of The United Nations (UN) in The International System, since the birth of the UN in 1945.

A clinical Diagnosis of the UN life since its birth to the present (2013) confirms this fact. The anarchical decision with respect to the Korean War of 1951 shortly after the UN's birth in 1945 and to all other sub-segment conflict cases involving these veto-power monopoly holders in the Security Council such as the current cases of Afghanistan and Iraq are individually and collectively prima facie proofs of this perennial hostage situation terrorizing the UN and also a proof of Bad Governance at the global organizational level.

In search for the answers to these mysteries, this book is divided into Twelve Parts; and each Part is also divided into several chapters.

Succinctly, in this Volume Two, Part I deals with the introductory task of the Volume with a view to explaining the nature of the "Problem" inherent in this phenomenon, "Leadership", and the reasons it warrants a meticulous study such as this one to be carried out and expose its actual mysteries; the "purpose" showing what this Volume Two is actually expected to achieve from this etiology of the problem; "methodology" showing exactly the steps and techniques the Volume seeks to employ in its efforts to achieve those objectives; and finally, the "Rationale" vividly showing valid justification of this Etiology and the extent of its possible usefulness or utility to Humanity and future research in Academia.

As a servant of this Scientific World and Humanity in total, PART II of this Etiology begins and thoroughly deals with the concept of Democracy and how this concept has now been enveloped and subdued by the "undemocracy" concept in Africa due to confusions among its users who often do not understand the two and therefore tend to confuse "Undemocracy" to "Democracy" by applying the former on assumption that they are actually applying the latter thereby subjecting those whom they are expected to govern by the concept and rule of Democracy to untold sorrows of the vices of undemocracy which include dictatorship;

totalitarianism; arrogance; arrests, detention and some times assassination of opposition for no justifiable and justified cause; looting of state coffers and all other acts of corruption aimed at filling one's stomach and pockets to the maximum at the expense of the poor dying hungry general public under his leadership.

Part III, on the other hand deals with the concept and contradiction of Theory and Practice in African Leadership with a main view showing the scope and toll of the disease of confusion among African leaders on the question of theory and practice relations. This Part III vividly shows where and how the contradiction and conflict between the two has always caused serious problems to both the same leader and the latters' subjects because of his own ignorance and carelessness regarding the difference and significance of the two for his own leadership survival in political life. As an illustration, it uses the case of Jomo Kenyatta as an example. Part IV, deals with the concept of goals, problems and strategies of Eastern African states as representative of all other African states in terms of how they manage to survive on a scarce World Market in the international system. Part V on the other hand deals with Leadership and World peace and tests for World Leadership Concept of trust and Lasting Peace.

Thereafter, Part V deals with the role of a university as a breeding ground of/for human excellence, and, to this end, seeks to understand what a university has so far done towards this end in alleviating conflict, poverty and other vices against humanity and human progress; and what university may therefore endeavour to do in assisting leadership training in keeping with its role as a centre of excellence in human development. As an illustration, it employs the cases of India and Africa where a Political Socialization process was effectively used by the leaders in order to rehabilitate and, therefore, liberate the victims of destructive myths as a beginning of a good way forward from the darkness of poverty, social hatred and conflict to the light of social togetherness, for a mutual national productivity and prosperity.

Part VII deals with the concept and significance of Neighbourly Love in Globalization as a reliable road map to a Hybrid Culture for World Peace. Part VIII deals with Political Socialization and its role as a contributor of political earthquakes against unethical (undemocratic) leadership in Colonial Africa as a lesson to Humanity and man's war against **abnormal politics**. Part IX deals with leadership and Democracy and how man eagerly seeks to institutionalize Good Governance for the good of Humanity. Part X examines Leadership paranoia and how it leads to leadership failure amd disaster.

Similarly, Part XI of the book deals with the real heart of the book. It dives deep into the clouds of the nous i.e the unknown knowledge and wisdom of Leadership "Genetic Engineering" with a view to bringing forth a real formula toward Good Leadership and Good Governance which was used by the Old Egyptian talents of The African Mysteries System of The Grand Lodge of Luxor (re-named Alexandria by Alexander The Great on the conquest of Egypt and total North Africa in the year 332 BC in order to plunder its amazing cultural and scientific glory next to none in those days) to create a Hybrid culture and a Hybrid Political Leadership that, in turn, empowered Egypt to accelerate in amazingly extra-ordinary heights of discoveries and innovations in Science, Technology and Philosophy which no man had ever dreamed of outside Egypt between 700 BC and 671 BC when the Assyrian leader, King Esarhaddon, conquered Egypt and enabled Assyria, Persia and other Asia Minor countries such as Macedonia and Greece to get to know this extra-ordinary glory of the Egyptian people, and began also to scramble for it as Persia under King Cyrus unsuccessfully tried to do but later succeeded by his son Chambyses Ii in 525 BC; and as Greece and Macedonia later came to do by toppling the Persians in Egypt and all North Africa in 332 BC and total Asia minor by 331 BC.

Accordingly, Part XII winds up this research expedition by discovering and explaining the real nature, scope function and usefulness of Leadership Genetic Engineering as a formula used by the Egyptians of Antiquity to create good leadership and good governance using The African mysteries system of The Grand Lodge of Luxor. In the final analysis, unlike all Part I to Part X which were generally a survey of various issues and problems in the art of Leadership, Parts XI and XII are the heart of this research expedition in that they lead to a discovery of what has always been evading Humanity and the latter's researchers. They are, therefore, a 2013 gift to Humanity by Science, thus, The Rationale of this Volume and the entire research expedition commenced by Volume One.

# PART TWO

## DEMOCRACY VERSUS UNDEMOCRACY: A Test for Leadership Conceptualization Contradiction Disaster

# A PREFACE

Democracy versus Undemocracy conceptualization contradiction is a serious perennial disease to mankind globally. It has caused to mankind such various untold sorrows of agonies from diverse disasters in political, social, economic, psychological, environmental (ecological), etc that an etiology of the mysteries of this disease is extremely necessary. In Africa, for example, the contradiction has proved the actual root-cause of the continent's endless civil strifes, poverty, various easily preventable and treatable diseases, etc. And the same problem also holds true throughout the World. Like in other Countries outside Africa, the problem is a perpetual womb in which viruses of continued disaster of socio-economic underdevelopment is embedded which therefore constitutes a valid justification of this Volume Two of our research on the mysteries of this disease.

Using the African continent case as a unit of analysis in this research expedition with a view to employing it as an explanatory factor to what we actually need to understand about the mysteries surrounding this disease inherent in Democracy versus Undemocracy Conceptualization contradiction, the outcome is very encouraging indeed.

First and foremost, the data shows a very flabbergasting paradox. For example it shows that whereas before independence, Africa had severely suffered various political tortures during the era of her colonial occupation; and whereas it was these tortures that finally led to the rise of a universal continental euphoria of Pan-Africanism continentwide against the existing undemocratic tendencies of this foreign occupation, the now liberated independent Africa also failed to pay heed and honour the concept of Democracy! Like its foreign counterpart, the newly independent African leadership also succumbed to the same disease of undemocracy virus that had also taken hostage the foreign leadership in Africa.

The euphoria of Pan-Africanism was/became so vehement and hostile to the foreign occupation of the continent that the occupier occupied relations gradually deteriorated to a point of no return. This hostile relations between the two automatically began to germinate into an acute cold war and eventually into a real hot war.

First, there emerged a situation of Africa's diasporan form of nationalism called "Pan-Africanism" hatched out in 1900 in London by a Trinidad barrister Sylvester-Williams, presently residing in the United Kingdom, with a collective support of some philanthropists British clergy and missionaries who had fortunately gained a first hand nasty experience of the undemocratic cruelty of their British colonial leadership to the colonized African in the occupied Africa.

With the support of these philanthropists Africa's sympathizers, Sylvester-Williams convened the first ever held Pan-African conference in 1900 in London. This action was later followed by a series of other conferences. The first of these was held in Manchester in1945. Others followed on later.

However, in general, Pan-Africanism's ultimate goal was liberation of total occupied African Continent from the existing scourge of European Colonialism and Imperialism which, by virtue of its inhumane leadership, was seen and believed to be totally naked of the true character and image of the Democracy based on a granite foundation of the Rule of Law and Justice stipulated under The Second Book of Samuel to the effect that:

**"He that rules over men must be just, ruling in the fear of God**

> ***And he shall be as the light of the morning, when the sun rises, even a morning without clouds; as the tender grass springing out of the earth by clear shining after rain". (II Samule, 23:3-4).***

Thus, according to both Continental African and the Diasporan African, the colonizer had neither a secular nor divine right to occupy Africa and subject its legitimate owner to a myriad of acute agonies of both psychological and physical sufferings that the Continent had already experienced and was still experiencing at the expense of an illegitimate owner dubbed as a "colonizer" or "colonial master".

From the diasporan African group, Sylevester—Williams was first/initially joined by Dr. W. E. B. DuBois and T. R. Makonnen from the United States of America. Later, the group coming from within Continental Africa. This later group was spearheaded by Dr. Kwame Nkrumah from the Gold Coast, now known as Ghana when as effective to the Country's attainment of her independence from the United Kingdom on 6th march, 1957), who in 1945 became a joint secretary to the pan-African Conference convened in Manichester City, the United Kingdom, in the same year (1945); Jomo Kenyatta (from Kenya Colony and Protectorate (now known as the Republic of Kenya effective the Country's attainement of her independence from the United Kingdom on 12th December, 1963); Julius K. Nyerere (from the then Tanganyika (now known as The Republic of Tanzania upon the Country's attainment of her independence from the United Kingdom on 9th December, 1961 and then uniting with her neighbouring Country of Zanzibar into Tanzania on 26th April, 1964.

But no sooner had this Manchester Conference ended than the Pan-Africanism mood against colonial occupation rapidly germinated into specific African nationalism in every occupied African country. And no sooner this developed than the anti-colonialism mood in Europe was now transplanted into The African Continent itself with Nkrumah as its torch bearer; who was later on followed by Kenyatta and Nyerere to intensify the colonial eradication mood in Tanganyika and Kenya which rapidly became the nucleus and a launching pad of anti-colonial war in the entire Colonial African Continent.

In a nut-shell, the Colonial Supremacy over Africa was defeated and overthrown with the Gold Coast (now Ghana) setting up the first leg in 1957 and thus becoming a model for all other occupied African Countries to follow suit.

However, in as much as all these anti-colonialism efforts were obviously logical and noble in that they enabled a foreign illegitimate leader to get lost and leave room for a legitimate leadership from an indigenious Africans themselves to take care of their welfare, the nagging questions abound against the same African leaders who had vowed that they were going to do better for their African people who had been being exploited and treated like dirt by the foreign leaders.

These questions include, for instance (1) To what extent have they honoured their vow? (2) What evidence do they have to demonstrate that they are faithfully committed to honour and respect their vow during their independence struggle as a prima facie evidence and valid justification of their hostile criticism and blame against their respective foreign leadership that the latter was naked of the true concept of Democracy in Africa? (4) Given the fact that these problems abound in their countries: civil strifes, abject poverty, malnutrition, increasing mortality from even easily preventable and curable diseases, increasing dependence on foreign donor community in order to make their respective countries' ends meet on condition that failure of which could lead them to a myriad of massive job retrenchment in the Civil Service, abhorring corruption in government by government officers including heads of state who paradoxically are expected, on oath, to be chief custodians of their respective national legacy, image and other resources among its fellow members of the International Community, what does the African leadership has to be proud of? (5), in view of these chronic multi-socio-economic and political ills now facing all African countries because of poor political leadership of their own African folks due to the latter's kleptocracy and other corrupt tendencies as so vividly supported by the on-going revelations of The Goldenberg Commission of Inquiry in Kenya initiated and carried out by The national Alliance Rainbow Coalition (NARC) Government under President Mwai Kibaki, who also became a hostage of the same kleptocracy because of his direct involvement in the AngloLeasing and Finance scandal followed by abhorring stealing of the December 2007 Presidential Election votes leading to ethnic mutual genocide in Kenya, what evidences do they have deeming or justifying them as good leaders to their respective peoples and countries worth any grain of repute, credit or distinction? (6) And, in this regard what does Science have in store to offer to this besieged African political leadership as a remedy to this global cancer to not only African leadership but also the leadership globally? Or they do not have anything for this cancer given the allegation by one of their own fellow prominent scientist and Nobel prize winner Dr. James

Watson to the effect that an African by nature is daft and is, therefore, no closer in intelligence to his counterpart of the Caucasian race (*Sunday Nation*, Nairobi, November 4, 2007)? Could this be the actual contributing factor to the perennial chronic civil war, abject poverty, and or myrad of other ills in Africa?

In view of these existing perennial difficulties terrorizing every African country due to the ineptitude and leadership poverty of their respective leaders, the purpose of this research expedition is to:-

(a) Carryout an Etiology (i.e, an in-depth clinical diagnosis) of the continent's problems with a view to identifying and meticulously examining their actual root-cause(s).

(b) Synthensize those rool-causes into some parsimonious body of knowledge for one's easier and quick understanding about Africa's problems and where these problems are coming from and why and by whom.
(c) Go back to the drawing board and identify a reliable remedy or solution to this myrad of problems in Africa.

Since the first objective and rationale of Pan-Africanism and African Nationalism of each occupied African country were to eradicate a foreign leadership because of the latter's being naked of (deficiency on) the concepts of Democracy, Peace and The Rule of Law and Justice, this book's first and foremost step is to test the same architect of this war against the foreign rule regarding this architect competence in these concepts both in theory and practice. Thus, this book shall want to show whether this architect was able to do better than his colonial counterpart whom he boastfully castigated as being empty, and, therefore, unfit to continue ruling Africa.

In this regard, this book is categorically divided into a total of VI Parts for the purpose of allowing each part to have a comfortable degree of freedom to exhaustively examine its won problem area in details in order to vividly illuminate the scope and possible remedy of each problem as meticulously and as bold as possible.

## CHAPTER I

# Introduction

### 1. Problem

Before her independence, Africa was saturated with a continental euphoria of Pan-Africanism and the demand "The White Man and His Colonial Rule Must Go Away and Give Room for Africans To Rule Themselves!"

By doing this, they argued that the White man's colonial rule lacked a correct concept of "Democracy"; and that this was exactly the reason they now wanted this foreign rule to get lost from Africa. But when this foreign rule tried to be stubborn and resist to abide by this African demand, its stubbornness was met with a civil rebellion ranging from verbal to a physical war, initiated by The Gold Coast (now-renamed Ghana) led by Dr. Kwame Nkrumah and his Bonvention People's Party (CPP) and Dr. J. B. Danquah and his United Gold Coast Convention (UGCC) party. This euphoria rapidly spread all over the Continent of Africa. In Kenya, it was first initiated by Kenya African Study Union organized by Harry Thuku in 1944. This later germinated into Kenya African Union (KAU) led by James Gichuru in 1946, which gradually metamorphosed into two parties the Kenya African Democratic Union (KADU) organized by Ronald Ngala and Masinde Muliro (June, 1960) and another party, the Kenya African National Union (KANU) organized by the same James Gichuru et al. (march, 1960). And, in Tanganyika (now re-named Tanzania), this euphoria was first spearheaded by Tanganyika African Association (TAA) organized in 1929 which later metamorphosed into a more powerful political party called "Tangayika African National Union (TANU) led by Julius K. Nyerere and another political party called African National Congress (ANC) headeded by Zubedi Mtemvu (1957) which later phased out in favour of TANU which spearheaded the euphoria against what they perceived as a white man's undemocratic leadership in Tanganyika.

In the final analysis, all these efforts aimed at achieving a common goal in Africa viz: eradication of the undemocratic colonial rule and replacement of this rule with an African democratic rule.

But, the nagging question now is: Has Africa now achieved this goal? Thus, does the continent have this mode of leadership?

But, given that most Africa has, ever since independence, been locked in endless recurrent conflicts characterized by leadership schisms, assassinations, coups d'etat, etc and given that the Continent is the poorest of all Continents, then what justifications does Africa have supporting its euphoria against the Colonial Rule? Does the continent actually understand the meaning and virtues of Democracy? Do African leaders know what is democratic and what is not?

## 2. Purpose

In view of these nagging questions, the purpose of this Part III in this book is to seek for answers to these questions with a view to establishing whether or not African leadership does know what is meant as "Democracy" and what is "Undemocracy" and if so/not, the corresponding consequences.

## 3. Methodology

In pursuit of these mysteries, this Part II of the book, first examines the concept of Democracy with a view to identifying the variance between the concept of undemocracy. Thereafter, it examines the manner in which Democracy as a concept was understood and used, by the colonial leadership and by Post-Colonial leadership (i.e, the African leadership) with a view to establishing which of the two leaderships did or did not conform with/to the true meaning and virtues of Democracy; and finally what may have been the outcome or consequences of such lack of understanding of the concept in its true form.

## 4. Rationale

This approach and results thereof is very essential if we have to understand the mysteries surrounding the continental African euphoria of "undemocratic colonial Rule Must Go!" and its justification.

## CHAPTER II

# Democracy Conceptualization Contradiction Disaster

A Case Study of Africa as a unit of analysis conceptualization of "Democracy" in Africa has always fallen on evil days. It has always suffered miserably mostly at the hand of the African leaders and their youth wingers who, based on their political behaviour overtime, never correctly understood the true meaning and virtues (or significance) to both themselves and to the general pulbic they are expected, under the oath of their offices, to govern and do so honestly to their satisfaction and happiness.

Instead of doing what they are expected under oath to do, they have always associated its meaning with that of what is not Democracy i.e "undemocracy", and for this very reason they have always tried to mix and then confuse the meaning of Democracy and that of undemocracy without understanding and appreciating the permanent mutual hatred and enemity between the two conepts as the permanent mutual hatred and enemity between sugar and salt, and between fire and water-entities which have agreed to permanently disagree from now up to the end of this universe.

In view of this confusion of the two concepts within the African leader-ship, what then is meant by the concept "conceptualization of Democracy?"

First and foremost, "conceptualization" is succinctly a process of understanding or knowing or trying to comprehend what one wishes to know, and possibly make use of it in whatever way one wants to do so.

This process or act is so essential in every one's life that without it, life automatically becomes so impossible and cumbersome that it proves no more worth living as one would now be totally incapacitated, an idiot, and, hence, a serious burden to others to take him around; to take him to toilet; etc. Thus, such life becomes extremely pathetic, a disaster and a costly life indeed.

However, "conceptualization" can be a very tricky, slippery and evasive puzzle if not handled meticulously. As a process, it is usually the root-cause of failures among human beings as well as in all living entities. This failure is usually caused by none other than lack of good, perfect or correct conceptualization of a matter, situation, problem or phenomenon. When one fails, in most cases, one would say, oh! Sorry, I misunderstood you or what I was to do right. Failing to do a thing right or correctly is not because one did not or does not want to do it right but simply because one misunderstood the thing or what he was doing and how to do it correctly or right. Those who usually refuse to hearken to correct conceptualization of Democracy or a situation are normally demagogues, autocratic and dictatorial persons.

But whereas no one would definitely want to look fool or dumb for not knowing the world around him or her, it is natural that every one has an inborn abilities to seek and know or understand about the self and what is actually around him or her. This ability is not restricted to adults only nor is it also restricted to the young only. It is universal to both the young and the adult; and it is also universal to both the sane and insane though this varies in degree between the young and the adult; and also between the sane and insane.

In the final analysis, every living entity has a relative degree of abilities to know or understand what is sacrosanct to/for its life; and in this regard, to differentiate a phenomenon, thing, problem or non-problem from one to another if it is to exist a peaceful, happy and successful life.

Accordingly, the concept, "Conceptualization and Practice of Democracy in Africa" is succinctly the manner in and by which Democracy as a political phenomenon is thus defined, understood or known in Africa as a first and foremost step in political life before one ever goes to the second step of trying to do for the people in his/her capacity as their leader. Thus, in order for one to prove a good, successful or effective leader, one has first to be able to understand what the art of leadership is all about by conceptualizing the meaning and usefulness of Democracy in terms of its merits and demerits; what would make one fail or succeed in leadership; what actions would satisfy and then please those that one leads and the actions that would not; and, if so, what would be the repercussions of each situation.

But leaders are also human individuals. Consequently, they are naturally bound to differ in their degree of intellectual understanding what a phenomenon such as "Democracy" is all about or means in political life. For this reason, the concept has suffered a great deal from conflicting multi-definitions and how to be used in political life of Africa. While some definitions may be correct and useful indeed, dictatorial, autocratic and cannibalistic leaders hardly see any of these differences. And due to the luxury of the monopoly of their equal sovereign supremacy endowed to each head of state world-wide which, therefore, fools them by empowering them to enjoy immunity from every prosecution while still in office, most leaders in and outside Africa usually assume that one's mode of leadership, in terms of policies and acts, is also democratic by every means. Consequently, no one is expected to question that leader's mode of leadership at all unless one wants to end up in police without or with false trial as was the rampant case throughout Africa, India, Asia and Thirteen North American Colonies, during the colonial era; and also is the case in most post-colonial regimes. In Africa, for example, where most every same and adult African fully co-operated with his or her nationalists in the fierce struggle for independence, these torture cells and detentions without or with false trial are the order of the day including massive embezzlement of state coffers, and bribery in the Judiciary, whereby both judges and advocates thrive so much on bribery that justice is a normal hot cake sale affair.

Because of this existing culture of confusion and corruption due to misconceptualization of Democracy in and outside Africa, a proper re-definition of the concept must be necessary as a remedy to save the situation.

This approach is necessary. In view of the prevailing cobwebs sealing off the mysteries of this concept of Democracy from man's proper understanding of it, this approach would be most cost-effective in getting to its true meaning, and the extent to which it is understood and applied in Africa.

Accordingly, the strategy in this study will be to first plough through the trails of select major African political leaders beginning with the first leaders at independence to the present.

Thereafter, we will analyze and assess the similarity between their level of understanding what "Democracy" means and their actual policies and activities using the meaning of Democracy.

In short, the ultimate objective of this study will be to show the degree at which these leaders' political actions have been really in keeping with their own understanding of what "Democracy" actually means in political life. But since most of them have proved a failure in their art of leadership, the objective of this study will be to clinically diagnose the mysteries surrounding and responsible for this failure.

In this regard, the aim of this Etiology is to drive deep into the subcutenous strata of those mysteries using a high power lens and examine the actual nature and character of these mysteries, beginning with the mode of colonial government which was expected to be the foundation on and from which succeeding African leaders' mode of leadership was to rest and emulate.

Thus, this study will seek to understand first and foremost why this colonial mode of leadership failed to honour and practice "Democracy" not only in Africa but also in every place where it ever tried to exist, e.g. in North America, India and the rest of Asia including South America. It will seek to get an in-depth understanding of all these mysteries as a prelude to its efforts to understand the root-causes of African political leadership failure. Specifically, it will endeavour to enter right deep into the depths of all underlying factors contributing to colonial leadership failure globally as a first step towards our understanding causes of African leadership failure. Since colonial masters were regarded to be not only masters of the peoples they had colonized but also masters of the actual meaning and usefulness of Democracy during their tenure as political leaders. But since these colonial masters also failed like their counterpart African leaders who took over the leadership from them upon independence, this study will, therefore, seek to understand reasons leading to the failure of these colonial masters given the fact that this concept of Democracy originated from/in the political culture of their generation in the 18$^{th}$ and 19$^{th}$ centuries caused by rivalry among individuals who bitterly resented abnormal economic profits (i.e, capital accumulation) through forced labour on being gained by factories and coal mines from women and children from poverty stricken homes.

This approach is necessary if one is to properly understand the genesis and cataracts of Democracy. The data on this rivalry between the advocates of the human rights of these poor women and children on the one hand, and the advocates of those who owned the means of production (industries, factories and coal mines) on the others, shows that the more these intolerable conditions prevailed, the more opposition and resentment accumulated in defence of the human rights of those poor women and children. Advocates of those poor women and children were philanthropists spearheaded by the Utilitarians, e.g., Jeremy Bentham (1748-1832) and John Stuart Mill (1806-1873); the Victorian English Poets, e.g, Alfred Tennyson (1809-1893) and Robert Browning (1812-1898); the Victorian Novelists, e.g., William Makepeace Thackery (1811-1863) and Charles Dickens (1812-1870).

But these philanthopists' criticisms from utilitarians, Victorian Poets and novelists were not ends in themselves. These forces became a stimulus to the genesis of the concept of

Democracy in opposition of the existing social, economic and political tendencies of undemocracy in the 18th and 19th centuries European life.

A vivid empirical evidence of this vehement force against the existing tendencies of undemocracy in Europe is reflected in the bitter sentiment of Matthew Arnold (1822-1888) who felt so disillusioned by the existing conduct of life in Europe that he bitterly lamented that

> ". . . the materialistic standard of an industrialized society of his time in Europe were completely incompatible with the great humanistic values inherited from Greece and the Renaissance. In his view, mid-victorian culture was beset by personal self-seeking and lack of social purpose and moral strength by aristocrats".

Because of this nauseating behaviour contrary to the humanistic customary values and beliefs inherited from Greece and the Ranaissance, Arnold also could not afford to spare the advocates of those who owned the means of production. Like other philanthropists he ridiculed them by calling them "barbarians"! on the grounds that they lacked a genuine social consciousness about the prevailing inhumane socio-economic and political conditions of the general public apart from only knowing how to exploit and maximize for themselves abnormal profits at the expense of the poor.

But all this cold war between the two antagonistic forces preceded the 20th century generation of the colonial masters who must, therefore, have had all the privileges of understanding the meaning and virtues and vices of Democracy and Undemocracy. Accordingly, although they came to fail in their art of leadership, it is self evident that all of them understood pretty well the concept, of Democracy in terms of its actual meaning, goal, glory and dangers in political life. And, that in view of their prior immense experience about the concept, they were expected to show a good example of a Democratic mode of governance to the colonial peoples that they did govern. Thus, they were expected to be teachers of these colonial peoples on how to govern better using Democratic principles gained from their intra-European political culture experience(s).

But now that most African leaders, since the advent of post-Colonial Africa Era, have failed a practical test in leadership, the purpose of this study is to understand the reason(s) of this recurrent failure as a prelude to our in-depth understanding those mysteries surrounding Leadership Failure globally and possible remedy to the cancer in question.

## (A) Meaning of "Democracy" Concept

The term "Democracy" succinctly means a sensitive rational mode of governance rich in justice. It is formed by a people through a structured popular election for the purpose of assisting them in the management of their affair for their common general good called "welfare"[1], against all adds of disaster. In this process a single operative principle is "Gentlemanship." By this principle, both winner and loser recognize and embrace each other with total dignity and gratitude for a competion fairly and freely done by each. This principle is abundant in modern USA, Canada and WEurope but very marginal in Asia and very critical in Africa where even a loser refuses to yield to the actual winner!

There are two distinct types of Democracy. One is a type of government in which the supreme power is vested in the people and exercised by them directly as in the ancient Greek City-States but which is no longer exercised in a Modern Civilization. This form of government is called "Direct Democracy". However, there is another type of governance in which the supreme power is vested in the people and exercised by them indirectly through a system of representation and delegated authority and in which the people choose their officials and representatives at periodically held free and fair elections. This type of governance is called "Representative Democracy[2]," and is the one now exercised in Modern Civilization.

Accordingly, in order for a country to be called or accepted as "Democratic" that country must prove that it has a government formed by its own people and managed by the same people, for their own welfare; and that it strictly adheres on those laid down conditions not only in theory (words) but also in practice (acts) at all times and costs. Short if this, that government can be thrown out and another one formed by the people using the same electoral process.

### (a) Governments which are "Undemocratic"

For this reason, all colonial governments in African, Asia, America, etc. which were managed by insensitive persons for their selfish good only were not "Democratic". Consequently they qualify as dominions of undemocracy. They qualify as such because they were unjust in that they all lacked free local participation. A genuine modern form of "Democracy" government is a representative form of government in which a constitutionally agreed upon number of leaders are periodically elected by their own local people called "grass roots". All elected leaders must be neither rigged in nor directly appointed by a head of state or body of persons as it often happens in various governments of Africa. They must be properly chosen by their own followers who shall, in turn, be the Center of power. Accordingly, any independent African Country whose government Ministers and other members of parliament become rigged in office but not properly elected as required by the Electoral Code of Conduct governing electoral processes under Democratic principles is automatically undemocratic (not "Democratic") although that country may be free from a foreign rule. This includes all other countries which are under the military rule through a military coup d'elat; those which condone "life presidency" during Presidency such as Malawi; and those which indulge in massive corruption in all sectors of government service including the Judiciary with a view to suffocating the Country to death as the case of Kenya during the 40 years rule of the Kenya African National Union (KANU) party (1963-2002).

### (b) Governments which are "Democratic"

Finally, a Democratic government is that government which permits full freedom to everybody who is sane and who is at least 18 years of age to participate in the political process; and must be a government which allows freedom of speech, press, religion, education, science and technology.

Example of such mode of governance is the existing regimes in all well advanced countries such as USA, Canada, UK, Russia, Japan, France, German, etc. All of them are succeeding democracies. In Africa, the only country which has shown a good example of a succeeding democracy is of course South Africa today after the minority white regime whose leadership had been contaminated by racism and other abnormalities. The Kenya of today is a failed Democracy under a new and rational leadership of President Mwai Kibaki government of The National Alliance Rainbow Coalition (NARC) party since Jan 2003, which started very well with the steam inherent in a democratic process but gradually fell out of the race because of the greed tendencies of most leaders in the helm of government thereby leading the Government into the domain of undemocracy. These greed tendencies were kleptocracy and disobedience to Justice.

### (B) Problem of Democracy During the Colonial Era (Effective Occupation to the late 1950's).

In my previous book, Cause-Effects of Modern African Nationalism on the World Market3 the data show the following mysteries:

(a) That the African Continent militarily fell under the Colonial Leadership by virtue of The Berlin General Act of March 1885 arising from The Berlin Conference of The Scramble for Africa-held in Berlin, which Germany Spain, Holland, France, Portugal and Germany were the . . . . with USA as an observer;
(b) That since then till independence, effective the late 1950's, Africa was under a horrifying madness of Undemocracy characterized by misrule and acute ineptitude totally unhealthy for the colonial people's wellbeing;
(c) That, absence of Democracy in Africa during the colonial era from 1885 till the late 1950's became an automatic womb in which and from which modern African nationalism and nation states were conceived and born;
(d) That it was not due to the colonial rulers' ignorance of the concept of Democracy that these rulers failed to apply it in their leadership of African colonies; and
(e) That all of them were fully and properly conversant with the concept and its consequences from their political experiences back home (in Europe from the 18$^{th}$ and 19$^{th}$ centuries and also from the American War of Independence in 1776.

From this research on three hundred years (the 1600s to the 1900's) of the European political experience, for example, it was also discovered that there were numerous political philosophers such as John Locke (an English man 1632-1704, Jean Jacques Rousseau (a French man 1712-1778), and many others whose common view about "Democracy" was that in the eyes of

God, all men were created equal regardless of their colour, creed or nationality including sex (gender)! Pg. 4.

It was also discovered from the American history records that it was this theocentric view which also became the main cornerstone of the American colonies' argument and excuse of their war of independence from Britain. The American colonies so successfully challenged their colonizer that they eventually gained their independence on the 4 July, 1776 using this excuse as their main weapon. Accordingly, political turmoils in both European and American experience of the time were not caused by any other factor other than by the spirit of dishonest of the colonial masters who could not honour and practice Democracy in their own homes Europe and in American colonies.

Further, it was discovered that it was the same factor of dishonesty also caused the rise of communism and socialism in Europe which later also filtered into other continents, such as Africa. Otherwise, Karl Marx and his philosophy of Marxism and Vladmir Lenin and his philosophy of Leninism could not have emerged in Europe by chance alone, had there been a true Democracy in Europe, although some of us who even do not know this would have the guts to abuse and criticize Marx and Lenin for advocating their respective philosophies. This reality also holds true in Africa. All colonies in Africa could not have began a war with their respective colonial rulers had these colonial masters dared to pay heed to the principles and virtues of Democracy; and to treat those colonies with mutual respect and dignity along the lines of those Democratic principles and virtues, fully known to all of them. From their own political philosophers, novelists, poets and other critics, during the 18th and 19th Centuries European political culture.

Knowingly or unknowingly, there are enough evidences proving that the colonial masters neglected these principles and virtues. They instead chose to believe in and practice all sorts of most inhumane acts <u>against Africans</u>. The Africans were, for example, regarded as half human beings. Accordingly, Africans were always denied suffrage as they were considered by the colonial masters as not qualified enough to warrant representation or participation of any kind in the political process. The Africans' attempts to resist this resulted into their arbitrary arrests and detention without trial. Also, Africans were denied to hold or apply for any white-colour job, or to use any recreational facilities such as restaurants, hotels, parks, swimming pools, schools, hospitals, churches, beaches as all these were restricted to <u>whites only</u>. In all, Africans were confined to a socio-economic and political helplessness and frustration. Obviously, such conduct by the colonial rule against Africans was totally incompatible with those principles and virtues of Democracy known to all colonial masters.

In my book mentioned above, I also discovered that in the same manner the colonial rulers were kicked out of North America in 1776 by the colonies because of these colonial negligence to honour and respect the principles and virtues of Democracy so were all other colonial masters also kicked out of Africa because of the same reason. By the end of the 1960s almost all colonies in Africa had achieved their freedom to have their suffrage and representation in the political process in accordance with the principles and virtues of Democracy.

## (C) Problems of Democracy

(i) Incogruency Between Leadership and Democracy

The arrival of independence in Africa, beginning with Ghana in 1957, was welcomed with the greatest joy and euphoria of celebrations. In independent Africa, one would, therefore, have hoped with this jubilation that the new African leaders would now do better for their fellow desperate Africans than their former colonial masters. For example, one would have hoped that there would be no more such arbitrary arrests without a just trial; no more interference in individual's freedom of expression, justice, etc; no more evils of corruption and other evils of Bad Governance.

On the contrary, a quick glance at what has been happening up to today in independent African politics, one is left with nothing to be desired at all. Although, all Africa is now free from the yoke of colonial leadership, it is possible to conclude that Africa has just changed hands from a foreign evil to a local evil in fact, to a worst one. The empirical evidence of this fact include the following:

(a) all African leaders who rescued Africa from the foreign evil with an aim of restoring Democracy in Africa summarily became victims at the hands of their fellow Africans because of the failure to respect and fulfill the aims of Democracy. According to our history records, the majority of these leaders were all summarily eliminated through assassination and other means. The rest were assassinated without cause other than due to the Cold War power struggle. These unfortunate victims included Patrice Lumumba of Congo (renamed later Zaire by his successor), Dr. Kwame Nkrumah of

Ghana, Ahmed Ben Mbella of Algeria, Samora Machel of Mozambique and others person who sacrificed all their time to fight for the African Freedom and dignity from the colonial masters and to sustain that freedom and dignity at all costs in the Community of Nations.

(b) Paradoxically those who took over from them began doing the opposite, worse than the colonial masters. These included Mobutu Sese Seko, Moise Tshombe, Daniel T. arap Moi, Jp, p Kenyatta etc.etc.

(c) Recurrent political assassinations, arbitrary arrests, police torture and detentions without any just trial abund in Africa. In Kenya, for example, many were victims of this. While some were assassinated, eg, Ronald Ngala, Gama Pinto, Tom Mboya, J. M. Kariuki, Argwings Kodhek; Bishop Alexandar Muge, Dr. Robert Ouko, etc; others were herded into police torture cells, detentions and other problems such as home confinement. These included Jaramogi Oginga Odinga, Josepoh Martin Shikuku, Raila Odinga, Kenneth Matiba, Charles Rubia, Koigi wa Mwere and many others.

(d) Harassment of the opposition is also rampant all over Africa. General and other forms of elections are only elections by name but not in real practical terms. Those who purport to have been elected during the elections do not get elected by their respective people as is expected under the principles and virtues of Democracy. Rather, they are craftly selected by the head of state through rigging elections.

(e) Such leaders normally do this in order to return their political assistants as partners in the looting of public funds and property. Such assistants are elevated to important government portfolios so that they may all again continue there habitual looting together as a team. As head of state in control of all state machinery funds, security, media, and personnel, his job is to do exactly this in order to remain in power.

(f) To achieve this goal, all presiding officers are either willingly or forcefully instructed by the head of state to exchange votes from the turns out to be the winner of the elections. This rotten political culture is rampant throughout Africa. It is the worst disease above the mightiness of the dangers of HIV Aids in Africa.

(g) Because of this obvious undemocratic electoral method, there is hardly one single African independent country which honours, respects and, therefore, practices Democracy in the strict test sense of the Democratic principles.

(h) In addition, disease of massive corruption is throughout Africa. The disease is so grandiose, contagious, and unchecked that a public service employee is naturally on two pay-rolls. A <u>written pay-roll</u> by which one is openly paid monthly in the form of a briber.

(i) This reality holds true in all public office; and is extremely worse among traffic polices on road, streets and highways who have now made it their habit.

(j) In fact, what these officers collect in a week from motorists, most especially from commercial ones, is so attractive to them that they would most likely die with whoever tries to challenge such acts.

(k) The same sentiment was noted in 1992 by the then President Daniel T. arap Moi of Kenya during his speech at Mbale, kakamega, a speech which was also replayed by the Kenya Television Network (KTN) evening news on 22$^{nd}$ October, 1992. The President confessed that to the Kenyans, but argued in defence of the culture by saying that after all, the on-going corruption in Kenya had neither started during his leadership nor was it limited to Kenya.

(l) According to him, socio-economic evil had, in fact, began during Jomo Kenyatta's regime; it was rampant in all Africa; and it began with Adam. The President, therefore, concluded by arguing that, his regime had, therefore, no case to answer with respect to the issue as this was a God given sin on earth.

(m) During the 1992 and 1997 General Elections in Kenya, the President used this strategy to buy the entire Country with colossal money so that the voters may vote him in as President of Kenya, as he had always done during all other election throughout his tenure as President effective 1978.

(n) Another extremely flabbergasting problem facing Africa which is totally antithetical to the principles and virtues of Democracy and which one would not have expected from such African leaders who contended to be better than Lumumba, Nkrumah and Machel by eradicating them from power using violence is <u>abnormal massive self-aggrandizement</u> by such African leaders.

(o) A scrutiny of most current heads of states in Africa one notes with shock an overwhelming wealth each has accumulated during his tenure of office. The most excellent example include, for example, the late President Mobute Sese Seko of Zaire, President arap Moi of Kenya and President M. Siad Barre of Somalia (before the latter was ousted in 1987).

(p) The problem is not limited to them alone as heads of state. It is a contagion all way below from their deputies and ministers right down to permanent secretaries and managing directors or executive chairmen who are the bona fide officers of their respective ministries and parastatal bodies respectively.

(q) This behaviour by a head of state obviously is abnormal as it is not in keeping with the cardinal philosophy of being mindful of other people's welfare coined and daily echoed by same Kenyan President Moi.

(r) It is, therefore, questionable why a colonial evil should be substituted with a worst one. This does not make any sense at all. No wonder in one single country such as Kenya several leading politicians such as the Bishop of Diocese of Eldoret (Rt. Rev. Alexander Muge), the Kenya Foreign Minister (Dr. Robert Ouko), and many Kenya legislators such as Tom Mboya, pinto, Argwins Kodheck, Ronald Ngala etc. could be assassinated simply because of their beliefs in and defence of Democracy in Kenya. Even when inquiries were lawfully instituted to bring the culprits to book, the heads of state of the time either threw out the findings or simply dismissed the commission before the latter had completed its investigation, thereby rendering the original objective of the inquiry and of kicking out the colonial rule in Africa totally hopeless and useless.

(s) Surprisingly, on realizing later that things were now becoming extremely hot from the opposition activities and statements in and outside Parliament against the evil of this strategy, the same President Moi became extremely worried. He summarily summoned all Permanent Secretaries (who are Chief Executive and Accounting Officers of their respective Ministries in the Civil Service) at the State House Nairobi on 7th April, 1993 and instrumented them to promptly initiate an immediate "Anti-Corruption" measure in their respective Ministries and root-out all those Civil Servants who are found to be corrupt.

(t) The President further stressed to them that from now on, this was to be taken as new government priority, and that it must be implemented with immediate effect in order to save the ailing Kenyan economy from collapsing.

(u) However, it is apparent from al this that any sane person would obviously see this Presidential directive strange. It is questionable how on earth culprit "A" could instruct and expect culprit "B" to take appropriate measure or action on culprit "C" given the fact that there is no difference between "A", "B" and "C" in their character. Given the fact that the whole system from top-bottom is saturated with the same evil, it is self-evident that "A", "B" and "C" do speak the same language and have a common culture. It is, therefore, questionable as to who of the three would blame whom.

(v) Accordingly, the directive is not rational at all. To call on Permanent Secretaries to initiate anti-corruption campaign policy and to possibly root out all corrupt Civil Servants from their respective Ministries since this would automatically not only mean asking them to commit suicide but also mean revealing his own participation in the evil that may also force him into his own suicide as is now being revealed by the findings on the same Moi and all members of his family, Cabinet, civil service, security, etc from the on-going proceedings of The Goldenberg International Commission of Inquiry at the Kenyatta International Conference Centre (KICC) in Nairobi confirming his direct involvement of the looting of Kenyan people's fixed and liquid assets in billions and billions totally unknown in the history of the World. What a pity to Kenya!

(w) Accordingly, such directives by President Daniel arap Moi to his top Civil Servants must, therefore, have been a big joke, a myth and a contempt of true Democracy and JUSTICE. This is exactly where and how African leadership always goes wrong, even at the simplest problem possible. It is a tragedy for which Africa is bound to pay dearly unless she, wakes up and seriously rectifies her leadership careless behaviour before everything falls a part completely.

### (ii) Consequences of Such Incongruency Between Theory and Practice of Democracy in Africa

The end-results of this incongruency between Africa leaders' understanding or knowledge of Democracy and how they actually use their understanding of Democracy in treating their fellow African followers in their respective political jurisdictions is very pathetic, and devastating to the socio-economic development of their own policies.

But this revelation on Moi's dirty dealings while in office as President of Kenya is just a tip of a huge submerged iceberg in the Ocean. Sooner or later other numerous revelations on the same Moi are yet to come out from already set-up and various other Commissions of Inquiry, e.g., on the murder of Robert Ouko; The Rt. Rev. Bishop Alexandar Muge; and many on other Kenyans who had to be murdered en mass through tribal clashes organized by Moi's regime; and more so, on those, eg. Raila Odinga, Kenneth Matiba, etc who were mercilessly herded into police cells and got so much tortured that some of them such as Matiba lost his nervous balance of his body for no normal reason other than an abnormal government reason that these victims had questioned Moi's concept and practice of Democracy and the reason why he was promoting corruption in Kenya.

This is the major reason (1) why each African Country has failed to maintain any steady growth in G.N.P., (2) why each African country has kept on undergoing recurrent domestic socio-economic recession; (3) why each African country continues to be faced with recurrent domestic political unrest; etc.

Also according to findings in various publications such as Ali—A. Mazrui, D. Austin, B. Decalo, P. Hannington, R. Lucknam, E.A. Nordinger, Claude E. Welch and also in my paper, "Objective African Military Control; A New Paradigm in Civil Military Relation" Peace Journal (1980) it is self-evident that most African Countries have experienced either a successful or abortive civilian or military coup d'etat and that the causal factor of these coups was African Leaders' own dishonesty to use the principles and virtues of Democracy in their treatment of those that they govern. In this respect, it is important to conclude in this study:-

(1) That although all African political leaders may not be that ignorant of what Democracy means, and although they may also know very well that it was the carelessness of European political leaders to apply Democracy in Europe and North America colonies that caused leadership miscarriage in Europe and North America, it is very apparent that what they know and preach about Democracy in Africa remain at the meetings. They do not apply it at all in their leadership.
(2) That it is because of their own carelessness in political leadership that they fail to put what they know about Democracy into proper use. But when they find themselves caught up in fire, they begin claiming that Africa was not yet politically ready enough for multi-party politics.
(3) And that Africa has always fallen on evil days partly because of its OAU's docility. Although article 3 of OAU Charter did prohibit OAU from intervening in Member States' domestic crisis, OAU Leadership proved all the time too weak to intervene in critically demanding time and famine and dispases kept on claiming innocent lives in thousands daily. Otherwise, one is left to wonder why outsiders such as UN, USA, UK and other sympathizers and volunteers should have come all way outside Africa to assist while OAU was no where to be heard of. This is another indicator of African leadership poverty, and a shame to Africa. It is, therefore, hoped that the new African Union (AU) formed a year ago (2003) will turn the history all around given OAU's failures.

## (D) Significance of Democracy for Africa as a Paradigm for Total World

**In the final analysis,**

Democracy is the only engine of a political culture which is capable of encouraging and nurturing a viable evolution and growth of a state in all walks of life for the betterment of the general public. It is the only one which is able to effectively tame a state's activities and attitude which may be against human and civil rights of an individual. By taming them, Democracy would sanctify (purify) them into a degree of perfection and holiness with a good hope and intentions of ridding a country's leadership from corruption and all viruses of Bad Governance that is detrimental to the day-to-day well being of the general public akin to those that Kenya has always suffered during colonial and post-colonial leaderships.

It is a political culture which does not agree with current mode of dictatorship and other autocratic tendencies in contemporary Africa which embrace suicidal assumptions that one is a "Life President" or is "Above-the-Law", in disregard of the wishes and welfare of the individual and general human and civil war against that type of Leadership. Such tendencies in contemporary Africa obviously do not respect the natural law. According to the natural law, it is only God who is above the law" But since even Jesus Christ, and all Prophets also confirmed publicly confirmed that they were below the Law it is therefore open to question why and how any sane political leader or religious leader who is just a mere creature of God and who goes to sleep, to toilet, to eat, to drink, etc on the dictates of the law of nature can claim to be above the law!! This is all absurd!! It is not only indicative of an individual's leadership poverty but indeed that individual's road to a political suicide subject to plunge the innocent general public into a sea of untold sorrows.

Unlike autocratic leadership which is very rampant throughout Africa, a democratic leadership is always sober, tolerant and accommodative to every critism. It encourages pluralism and plurastic undertakings so long as these undertakings are not injurious to society or individual rights. Most importantly, it encourages on accelerated scientific and technological creativities because unlike automatic dictatorial leadership, it is the only type of political leadership which is capable of controlling the state's apparatus which include security forces and all other civil servants from arrogant and corruptive attitude and other forms of malpractices at the expense of the general public. It is an antibiotic agent or device in and for every body politique interested in accelerating in advanced socio-economic development with minimum cost. An empirical examples include North America, Europe and Japan which accept to and adopt this Democratic path after having always failed in their socio-economic development through an autocratic dictatorial leadership. This recognition became a most reliable and cost-effective remedy to them against their existing social and economic stagnation.

Because of this attitude and character of an autocratic dictatorial leadership, North America and Europe had often been hostages of recurrent political turmoils. The only solution to such turmoils in Europe and North America, was for them to FIRST search in their hearts and mind a better form of government to adopt in order to put an end to this turmoil.

And as soon as the two continents accepted to follow a Democratic path obviously, their political turmoil ended. The end of this political turmoil in Europe and North America became a major blessing to those two continents. This end of the turmoil became a fertile soil for their socio-economic development. First, their science and Technology began to flourish and blossom to their highest level. And, second this growth in Science and Technology, in turn, generated resulted into a dynamic beginning of socio-economic development in both Europe and North America.

But, that was not all. Whoever wants to know how some nations become super powers, the answer is:

1. This is exactly the way North America and Europe became super powers on the World Market. The two continents have since then continued to control and dictate prices on the World Market simply because of their socio-economic power monopoly which they achieved through a Democratic leadership path. Without this path, they would still be as stagnant and doomed as Africa still is today inspite of lots of her enormous natural resources and liquid assets from both tax payers and foreign and which unfortunately always get wasted abnormally through lootings by the ruling elite and their hatred of Democratic virtues.
2. Unfortunately, in Africa, Democracy has not yet taken root properly. Most African leadership is against Democracy in favour of autocratic and dictatorial tendencies which have, in turn, continued to breed political unrest at home. This is exactly the reason why Africa remains stagnant in socio-economic development on the World Market. So, if contemporary Africa wishes to grow also and became recognized and respected as a credible and formidable socio-economic power on the World Market on

an equal footing with North America, Europe and Japan, Africa would also need to accept to follow the same Democratic path.

In order to do so, Africa must, first and foremost, be willing to accept to disentangle herself from her present autocratic dictatorial nepotistic attitude and behaviour in political leadership. Africa must reconcile with herself on this issue and be ready to build and sustain a sustainable democratic culture of openness, tolerance, integrity, honour and excellence in all her contemporary institutions and has to realize that this is the only path to socio-economic salvation and power on the World Market, if Africa also wishes to have this power on the market. Otherwise, Africa is subject to stagnate herself indefinitely in all walks of life, and to remain a pertual minor actor on the market for easier manipulation by North America and Europe who have accepted this salvation.

3. The unfortunate theory by the then minority white political leadership in South Africa marginalizing the ANC Leadership not yet mature and experienced enough to be given the chance to rule and that if African leadership were given such a chance it would not respect, honour and follow the Democratic path has proved false in the post apartheid leadership under ANC President. The fact is that even in Africa is most likely to take roots deeply once African Leadership comes to understand the virtues and vices of Democracy properly; and to also realize:

    (a) that it was because of the presence of Democracy in North America and Europe that the two continents became socio-economic super powers on the World Market today.
    (b) And, that Japan has also become another super power on the Market because of Japan's recognition and acceptance of the Democratic path in her political process. Otherwise, Japan would still be as socio-economically stagnant as Africa is today.

## (E) Conclusion

From the evidences documented above on the absence of Democracy in Africa and empirical consequences thereof, it is self-evident that whereas Conceptualization of in Democracy Africa has been misconceived as being an easy task, putting these principles and virtues of Democracy into practice has been a very slippery uphill task for the African leadership. This difficulty has risen from no where other than from African Leaders' own dishonesty and negligence to their own oath of office. What they preach has not been what they actually do in their respective leadership.

Like their colonial counterparts, African leaders do not seem to have had a good foresight on the consequences of their own dishonesty and negligence. But unlike their colonial counterparts, they have proved to be more inhumane in their leadership. What they do to their own fellow Africans is worse than what the colonial masters used to do. Unlike them, colonial rulers would not condone corruption and political assassination although they supported segregation or apartheid as is the case in South Africa. During the colonial time, efficiency, transparency and accountability were extremely respected and honoured at all times in both public and private sectors. Almost every undertaking in Africa was guided by those three cardinal principles. Quality was another cardinal principle in the colonial leader-ship. This held true in all health, education, roads, and other sectors, in conformity with the Code of Regulations which served as a bible for every sector of the Civil Service. This document is now just been stored on office shelves but hardly used or heard. But unlike in post-colonial Era today, administrative and managerial discipline in colonial Era was very scrupulous and admirable in deed.

No matter how little a service was it was a must that it had to be expected to be excellent. This is also the reason why African student who had to go through various rigorous educational stages of examinations, etc. was always superior to a white student. This used to be vividly evident during the English Competitive Examination in the entire British Empire. Most excellent marks such as "Distinction" and "Credits" were scored by Africans. So, one wonders why the same Africans should not do better in political leadership too, given the fact that Africans ought to have the same abilities to properly understand the true meaning, virtues and vices of Democracy in political life.

It is, therefore, a shame that most Africans have proved a failure as leaders in political life, both at home and in international organizations such as OAU though we have yet to evaluate performance of its successor (the African Union). Further, this problem should not be seen as being caused by selfishness or lack of professional advice from African intellectuals.

From history records on African leadership's relations with scholarship, numerous good Samaritans dons (think tanks) abound offering their intellectual service to leaders but all in vain from the leaders who claim that they are also political philosophers, learned, and therefore experts enough to handle their problems without needings the dons' assistance. The other excuse by the leaders is usually that the dons' advice is largely too foreign to be accepted or applicable in Africa.

On the tribal clashes genocide issue in Kenya during the 1991-92 period whose escalation claimed such an alarming tolls of deaths and treatable injuries in the Rift Valley Province, Kisii, and Coast Province that the Kenyan public had to appeal to the UN for assistance, various appeals entered the State House and The Office of The President calling on him to hearken to them without any positive response.

Later, it came to emerge from the Parliamentary record titled The Kiliku Report on The Tribal Clashes in Kenya that the genocide was actually a state architectural design to confuse the direction of the 1992 General Election and to make the said area an unenabling environment for any smooth elections particularly for the oppositions vi: the Forum for the Restoration of Democracy (FORD-Kenya) headed by Jaramogi Oginga Odinga (Chairman) and Masinde Muliro (Vice-Chairman); the Democratic Party of Kenya (DP) headed by Mwai Kibaki (Chairman) who is now from 2003-to present the President of The Republic of Kenya; and FORD-Asili headed by Kenneth Matiba (Chairman) and Thinge (Vice-Chairman).

From a politico-psychiartry, all such refusals by the Kenyan Head of State were not by accident other than by leadership arrogance, pride, and stubbornness coupled with excessive abnormal self-glorification which hold true to all African leaders and govern their actions and interactions with those that they purport to govern. Succinctly, it is these abnormalities which, in turn, drive most African leaders into a total confusion in recognizing the distinction between theory and practice and whether the two are indeed in keeping with the true theory and practice of Democracy.

In a nut-shell, most African leaders fail in their art of leadership not because they lack the wisdom and knowledge (know-how) from the intellectual community in their respective countries. They do fail simply because they cannot be counseled. They are habitually anti-scholarship and anti-professionalism. Because of such attitude, they stubbornly keep off every source for scholarship and professionalism. Consequently, they end up fumbling in their leadership work like a sickly incapacitated or an infant awkwardly trying to walk but falling over and over for lack of a walking strength or skills.

But, because they would not like to be seen this way, their strategy is to continue fumbling through their daily routine with the pretext that they actually know what they are doing and also that what they are thus doing is definitely correct and is totally in keeping with the principles and virtues of Democracy needed by the general public and the World at large. Also, the other strategy is to try to keep off both the intellectuals and the opposition. These two are normally kept at bay because they are regarded to be knowing and talking too much. If brought closer, they would definitely talk too much to the outsiders and the general public would mobilize a rebellion against the leadership. Hence the purpose and rationale of anti-scholarship and anti-opposition attitude among most African leaders. Any intellectual or opposition that is acceptable to the leadership of the day is normally a double edged knife which cuts on both sides i.e, a double agent who has a habit of eating from both the ruling elite and his own end. When he is with the ruling elite, he talks good of them in order to be given favours such as a cash bribe or a job bribe.

In Kenya, this has been a very favourite strategy by the then President Moi. Because of this strategy, Moi came to be popularly characterized as a "Carrot-President" i.e. a leader who regarded Kenyans as though they were as cheap as a rabbit to be silenced from criticizing mode of governance by using all sorts of bribery.

Although, in 1992, President Moi and his supporters of a one-party KANU mode of leadership eventually agreed to repeal the existing Kenya Constitution which had declared Kenya a de jure one-party Democracy, from that status to new status of multi-party Democracy, this change turned out a total gimmick. The change did not allow multi-party democracy to take root as the ruling KANU party continued to behave as Kenya were still a one-party Democracy.

All opposition parties were so much daily censured and harassed by the ruling KANU party security apparatus that the General Elections of 1992 in which the opposition felt that they had won turned out to be a total disappointment to all of them as the KANU regime security so hurriedly and secretly worked day and night on the last week of the Elections making preparations for the swearing in of President Moi at the State House that by the time the opposition woke up on a Monday morning, President Moi had already been sworn in at the State House as President of The Republic of Kenya.

But although the opposition tried to file an election petition to The High Court against the election and swearing in of Moi as President of The Republic of Kenya, the outcome was obvious. The petition was thrown out with costs.

Similarly, between January 1993 till another General Election in 1997, the Oppositions efforts and the Kenyan general public cries always fell on the deaf ears of the stubborn and totally unconcerned KANU party regime. Consequently, another political humiliation by KANU using its same old tricks of election rigging and tribal clashes to confuse and destabilize the election ground so that the opposition may not be allowed to have a fair and free election.

And when the results of the1997 General Elections were announced by the ruling KANU government obviously it was another repeat of the1992 election results. KANU and President Moi were to continue in power at all costs. Another attempt by the opposition to restrain Moi and his KANU party from the leadership system, that attempt also resulted into the same situation of 1992. The petition was thrown out with costs.

In the final analysis, although African leadership may act as accepting an advice but in most cases, this is done just in order to be seen as though one's advice is been listened to while in actual sense not.

An advice may be taken on the surface only but not inside. The Kenyan Constitutional repeal case explicitly confirms this reality in the African leadership.

But why do they behave as they do in such situations? Is it that they are ignorant of their actions in terms of what they are doing and what they should actually do?

In the case of Kenyan Constitution Repeal, again, as an example, it was true that the ruling KANU party and its torch bearer, President Moi, agreed to the repeal. But although they did so, they did so under pressure from the opposition and the International Community particularly the Diplomatic Corps accredited to Kenya and the Donors. The latter for example were so vocal to Kenya, by threatening that without the repeal no foreign aid would be released to Kenya, that President Moi and his ruling one-party KANU party was let with no other option but to bow down accept the repeal.

Further, most Kenyans were already too tired with KANU and the latter's one-party Democracy form of governance. Consequently they also added their fuel on the already burning fire in demand for a repeal.

Because of these multi-factors impinging on President Moi and his one-party ideals, obviously the pressure could hardly enable both Moi and his KANU party sleep soundly. They all knew that in the presence of one-party mode of governance, they are the lords in the Kenyan politics. But in its absence, they would automatically be no more lords. They would lose this golden opportunity because their habitual belief in and enjoyment of one-party Democracy mean minority rule and minority right would automatically wither away with the death of one-party democracy as a result of that constitutional repeal.

Because of this phobia, President Moi and his KANU 's one party Democracy supporters in Kenya were always nauseated by everyone talking in support of Multi-Party Democracy and the repealing of Constitution to Multi-Party Democracy that such a person whether Kenyan or foreigner was automatically regarded as an arch-enemy. One was regarded as such because any advocacy for Multi-Democracy to both Moi and KANU had always enjoyed under the patronage of One-Party Democracy of minority right and majority submission ever since Kenyan independence in December, 1963. Thus, the root-cause of bitterness and anger against every soul in and outside Kenya that was seen or heard promoting and advocating multi-party Democracy.

Whereas they supported the Democratic principle of checks and balances, this was only acceptable so long as the checks and balances duties were rested in The Office of The President under Moi, who could then check on and command the Judiciary, Parliament and his own Officers at both The Office of The President and at The State House, by using the carrot diplomacy to influence everyone of them to support his ideals whether virtuous or vice.

This attitude was the root-cause of the fierce disagreement that erupted between President Joseph Kasavubu and Prime Minister Patrice Lumumba of Congo immediately that Countrty achieve her independence in 1960. Whereas President Kasavubu demanded that he wanted to have control over the three branches of Government, Prime Minister was not in favour. And, when the President felt that he should get rid of Lumumba from the Prime Ministership, the latter received a 95% vote of confidence from the Congolese Senate in September, 1960 against Kasavubu's attempt to dismiss him.

In other words, the Democratic principle of checks and balances is normally not an acceptable thing to most African leaders whose ulterior motive is to monopolize both functions by themselves in their office. They do so because they believe that it is not that beneficial to them. It is only acceptable so long as the principal's serve the leaders' personal interests in looting state coffers and protecting the action from legal prosecution or any other side effects.

To this end, the above is an explicit picture of the dynamics of African leadership across the continent from north to South and from east to west without bias. Also, it is a universal depiction of fundamental fatal factors leading to recurrent leadership failures in the Continent.

But, this viruses are not unique to African leadership. The study reveals that it was also the root-cause of the failure of the colonial leadership during the colonial Era. And, that the Colonial failure must have, in turn, become the root-cause or simply a contagious disease permanently circulating in African leadership blood system that cannot allow them to succeed in their tenure.

Hence, the hope that Africa will see the need to go back to her drawing board and start all over again if she is to rehabilitate her mode of leadership.

# PART THREE

## THEORY AND PRACTICE CONTRADICTION: A test for Leadership Disaster to Humaninty and as a Paragigm in Leadership Deterioration and Disintegration.

# PREFACE

The Question as to who can prudently decide for whom with a high degree of confidence in a given organization has been a critical area of concern and inquiry from the time immemorial, dating as far back as the time of our Patriarch Adam. Our Etiology of this problem strongly confirms: (a) that in every type of organization, the latter's degree of enfunction is totally dependent on the degree of its member's trust and confidence in its leadership; (b) that both these trust and confidence are also dependent on the degree of compatibility between that leadership's ideals and deeds; (c) that this compatibility, in turn, totally relies on that leadership's rationality—its ability to prudently distinguish and analyze the difference between the two variables and the consequences thereof; and (d) that the leadership's failure to recognize and uphold this natural behavioural law will have no cure but self-deterioration and a possible total disintegration.

This reality is spatio-temporal free and holds true to every situation. It holds true at the individual level, nuclear family level, small group level, village community level, and corporate community level ranging from nation-states, regional organizations and right up to the global organization we have today called The United Nations.

At each level, the degree of enfuction of the entity involved is completely dependant on the existing degree of trust and confidence in its leadership coupled with the degree of rationality of the leadership. This enfuction relies on the leadership's ability to systematically analyze both the problems, the needs of the people under the dominion of its leadership and an appropriate strategy that must be used as a means or remedial measure to the existing situation. And above all, it has to see to it that it does so short of any bias generated by nepotism, or any other tendencies of undemocracy and partiality in contravention of the concept of justice explicitly documented. The Second Book of Samuel 23:3-4, which states inter alia that:

***"He that rules men must be just, ruling in the fear of God"***

*"And he shall be as the light of the morning, when the sun rises, even a morning without clouds; as the tender grass springing out of the earth by clear shining after rain"*

As will be noted in the succeeding pages of this PART III of Volume TWO on. Kenyatta's theory and practice as a unit of analysis in this Volume Two's efforts to unearth those mysteries surrounding and responsible for leadership failure endemic globally, theory and practice contradiction is the real oasis or womb in which all political and other societal man—made disasters are conceived and born. The contradiction always gives rises to leadership deterioration and disintegration in every society or community. This deterioration and disintegration of a leadership in any country is not caused by any other factor other than theory and practice contradiction of that country's leadership.

This contradiction usually leads to a fatal contamination of the concept of justice in a country thereby triggering national unrest and possible revolt against the leadership.

In Kenya today, every Kenyan has witnessed this reality resulting from the dishonesty of the leadership to try and rig the December 27, 2007 Presidential Elections results. This political disaster left to over 1,500 Kenyans dead, an unquantifiable number of people destroyed, so many injured Kenyans, and other untold sorrows of displaced persons restlessly running around in search of a safe haven, food, water, medicines and all other sorts of emergency humanitarian assistance.

An etiology of this disaster shows that most of the contributing factors were architected by Jomo Kenyatta's leadership which forced non-Kikuyu communities such as Kalenjins and Masais to accept his Kikuyu community members to settle on the land of those non-Kikuyu communities.

Therefore, all these non-Kikuyu communities quickly grabbed the opportunity of political discord in Kenya created by the Mwai Kibaki leadership of the Party of National Unity (PNU) because of PNU's tendency to steal the Presidential Election votes and declare himself as the winner of the Elections. They grabbed and exploited the opportunity to up-root the unwanted Kikuyus from their land who are also fellow members of Mwai Kibaki.

The critical fact here is that all this quagmire could not have emerged leading to blood shed of over 1500 death and unknown number of injuries and displaced persons. All this became a reality because of leadership theory and practice contradiction inherent in Toroitich arap Moi's leadership (since it was Moi whom Kenyatta used to force Moi's Kalenjin in the Rift Valley to give away their land for Kenyatta's fellow Kikuyu tribesmen to settle on if Moi was to continue serving as Kenyatta's Vice President), and finally in Kibaki leadership which was also seen as a Kikuyu leadership like that of Kenyatta for this forced settlement of Kikuyus on the Kalenjins' land without their consent.

# CHAPTER I

# Introduction

## A. Problem

In all organizations ranging from a nuclear family to a nation-state, the chances and degree of peace (stability) and progress in that organization individually and collectively rely on the nature and degree of the followers' trust and confidence in their leadership. And as will be noted in this study, this degree of trust and confidence also depends completely on the degree of consistency between their leader's ideals and deeds, i.e., what their leader says and promises them through various media and what he/she actually does.

Thus, the low the consistency between these two variables, the greater the chances that the degree of the followers' trust and confidence in their leadership will also be low; and the more this holds true among the majority of the followers, the greater the chances that both overt and covert actions (criticisms and campaigns) will begin to emerge and to multiply against that leadership with specific and clear intentions to either totally remove it from the decision-making machinery or to simply ignore whatever it says or requests them to do.

Failure to honour and maintain this consistency even by those who claim that they encourage the ballot, their ballot is not a ballot in the strict sense of the concept in Political Science. Some of them publicly announce to their followers that they are anti-corruption believers while in their deeds, they are the chief proponents of corruption of various forms. They announce general elections dates but they rig elections in order to maintain their positions. By so doing, they leave their level of honesty and consistency between their ideals and deeds wide open to question by the critics and the general public. Concomitantly, they become open to attacks and possible removal from their offices by the gun.

Absence of this consistency is succinctly a product of a low level of leadership rationality—its inability to prudently identify populous cost-effective developmental projects, i.e., inability (a) to meticulously analyse each project's gains and constraints; (b) to seek and prescribe sound solutions to such constraints; and (c) to do all this with a high degree of consistency and without any favourism.

This is precisely the reason why the Father of Philosophy, Socrates, concluded 20 centuries ago that an effective leadership is only possible from a philosopher king. Similarly, this is also the reason why Machiavelli chose to write The Prince to become a guide for his head of state whom he believed definitely needed to guide, short of which disintegration of that leadership was eminent.

Unfortunately, this problem has continued to evade recognition of scientists inspite of recurrent instability in all nation-states from generations to generations. Instead of addressing ourselves to this specific problem, some of us such as Robert Dahl tend to be concerned with petty issues such as Who Governs.

Inspite of its strategic relevancy to the study of politics, it is submitted that Dahl's concern is too myopic. It neither evokes fundamental questions related to why such governors fail in their leadership from time to time and from one country to another. Consequently, such studies tend to leave all of us dangling on a cliff of ignorance and despair—in a mist of confusions.

## B. Purpose

It is due to this total omission in the study of Politics that this Paper seeks to meticulously examine the Late Mzee Jomo Kenyatta's leadership in its capacity as the pioneer of the Kenya national leadership, i.e., as the first Chief Executive of that Nation, and a paradigm for our understanding of not necessarily the dynamics of political leadership in the emerging nation-states but of the consequences of such type of leadership in every organization.

## C. Methodology

To do this, this Paper examines and critically analyzes the relationship between Jomo Kenyatta's political theory and his political practices in Kenya since he entered politics as an example. It will be concerned with (a) the logical consistency between the political promises which Kenyatta outlined to his fellow oppressed Africans during the period of colonial rule and which he was determined to fulfill upon Kenya's rise to independence on one hand and (b) the policies and actions he put into real practice at that time on the other. When this is done, the Paper will then examine the implications of the consistency or inconsistency that exist between the two, in terms of their consequences on the level of progress in the national development in Kenya.

In order to achieve these objectives, the Paper is divided into three parts. Part I examines the theoretical aspect of Kenyatta's politics; Part II first examines the practical aspect of Kenyatta's politics in post-independence Kenya and then probes into the logical consistency between theory (Kenyatta's promises as seen in Part II) and practice (Kenyatta's actual policies and actions, as envisaged in the first section of Part III); and finally, Part IV compares and summarizes Parts II and III in terms of their inter-relationships and consistency, and then studies the implications of the degree of consistency that has been observed, as a paradigm, i.e., a breakthrough to our understanding of the real factors responsible for (a) the existing mounting problems of under-development in the emerging nation-states, and (b) inevitable poor progress in every organization with a low level of rationality at the leadership point.

## D. Rationale

This study is very important for both scientist and non-scientists mainly peace-keeping administrators and enthusiastics in that it clearly exposes most of the fundamental reasons why in various organizations (ranging from nuclear families to supra-organizations such as nation-states and World bodies) intra-organizational morale and stability are recurrently very low; and why and how rebellions or strikes often develop against the leadership.

Because of the space shortage in this paper, the Study selected only one leadership (Kenyatta's Kenya) as a specimen which was then intensively and meticulously examined with the following purposes: (1) To meticulously identify and confirm the real reasons why there were massive discontents in Kenya against Kenyatta's leadership and yet without this leadership—a leadership which successfully mobilized and triggered Mau Mau uprising against the British colonial rule in Kenya—Kenya might not have achieved her independence at that time (1963); and (2) To use these findings as a paradigm for our understanding properly the real reasons why, in various organizations, discontents against the leadership and leadership circulation abound. Hence the rationale and justifications of this study.

CHAPTER II

# Jomo Kenyatta's Political Theory as a Unit of Analysis

## A. His Birth

Jomo Kenyatta[1] was born and raised at Ngenda, Kenya, about ten miles northwest of what is now Nairobi. His father was Muigai, and his mother Wambui[2]. Although the actual date of his birth remains a mystery, for official purposes, the Kenya records place it at approximately 1898. His name was Kamau[3] and in August of 1914, he was baptized as Johnstone kamau in the Scottish Church Mission at Thogoto, in Kenya.

## B. His Political Theory

### (a) At an Early Childhood Stage

Kenyatta's poltical theory was first manifested neither verbally nor in writing, but in his observable activism and rebellion in childhood. In Kenyatta, for example, Jeremy Murray-

---

1 "Jomo" means a burning spear. "Kenyatta" was coined from the word "Kenyatta" meaning a beaded belt which his first wife, Grace Wahu, used to wear around her waist. Kenyatta later also began wearing a similar belt. On his return from Britain in 1946, due to his political activism, most children began to call him by the Kenyatta belt he wore. Thereafter, Johnstone Kamau, began to give room to Jomo Kenyatta.

2 Note that nominology in African tradition, especially among the "Bantu" in East Africa and traditional Egypt, places emphasis on one name only, though one might have been given two or more names by parents.

3 See Note 1, above

Brown[4] clearly shows that Kenyatta was a rebellious child who would stand firmly committed on his course of action despite external pressures. He adds that when Kenyatta was to be baptized, he refused to abide by the conventional dictates of the Church of Scotland Mission. Every child to be baptized was free to choose either a Biblical or colonial master's name, but only one Biblical name was allowed.

Contrary to this dictatum, Kenyatta stubbornly demanded to be baptized "John Peter Kamau". He chose John Peter over other Biblical names because both Peter and John were the leading figures among Jesus' apostles. When the Mission refused his request, Kenyatta decided to fool them in order to get his own way. He realized that peter meant "stone" and so he married the name John to the meaning of the name Peter, and, by-passing Mission regulations, he was finally baptized as "Johnstone Kamau". The Mission was indignant at the young boy's stubbornness and it took him many petitions and requests, but the future "Kenyatta" was eventually baptized according to his demands.

### (b) At Adult Stage

As the young boy began to reach maturity, Kenyatta's activism and stubbornness began crystallize into mature, concrete political attitudes, beliefs and systems. It was not until he was old enough to understand and critically evaluate the British colonial political system under which he lived that his political theory finally began to assume a concrete shape. This reality is borne out in his early writings, such as Facing Mr. Kenya[5], which clearly demonstrates the evolution of his political thoughts.

### (i) Conservatism & Anti-Colonialism

In Facing Mt. Kenya, Kenyatta's political theory is seen to revolve around two fused fundamental concepts: (a) conservatism and (b) anti-colonialism. Kenyatta bitterly accused the British colonial rulers in Kenya of using oppression and slavery on Africans, of usurping African lands and mineral wealth, of disrupting traditional African cultures and values, and of practicing discrimination in all public sectors, including education, employment, recreation, and all the other facilities and opportunities that, in the 20th century, are essential for man's

---

4 Jeremy Murray-Brown, Kenyatta (New York: E. P. Dutton and Company, Inc., 1973), p.63.
5 Jomo Kenyatta, Facing Mt. Kenya (London: Secker and Warburg, 1938).

basic needs. He also criticized the British colonial rule for its spontaneous alienation of Africans from their lands, and the subsequent loss of dignity and the sense of identity. The deprivation of the African people extended even to denying them rights to equal due process of law, which would have allowed them to fight the mistreatment received at the hands of the colonial regime. Karl Marx and Friedrich Engels would have labeled such attacks on the African ego as "swindlerism" or an organized attempt by the colonial powers to dehumanize the African and the latter's ego into a commodity.[6]

His bitterness against colonialism and imperialism; and his strong conservatism, particularly with regard to African traditions, are also evident in Kenyatta's pre-independence overt and covert political behaviours. His pre-independence activism is recorded by Jeremy Murray-Brown in Kenyatta. Kenyatta's political acts after his return from Britain in 1946 show that he was not only a political theorist, but also a practitioner. His enemy was colonialism and he aimed to destroy it as soon as possible and at all costs. It was this intense anti-colonialism/conservatism tension which eventually lead to and characterized Kenyatta's charismatic leadership from the late 1940's to the time of his arrest and imprisonment by the colonial rule in 1952.

### (ii) Kenyatta & Leninism

Kenyatta's political theory between 1946 and 1952 shows a fundamental positive correlation between kenyattaism and Leninism. At that time, Kenyatta emulated Vladimir Lenin's leap-over theory which suggests that one does not need to wait for the natural suicide of capitalism and the latter's evils before one resorts to a revolution against capitalism. Because Lenin had successfully used it in Russia in the 1919 Peasant Revulution, Kenyatta decided to also use it against the British colonialism and imperialism in Kenya. This is mirrored in all of Kenyatta's political conduct in Kenya before he was arrested. For example, applying Lenin's theory, he subjected both the proletariat and the peasantry in Kenya to an oath taking ritual so that he could be certain of their full individual political commitment to his strategy of immediate destruction of colonialism at all costs.

---

6 See Karl Marx, Das Kapital, trans. By S. Moore and E. Aveling, ed., (London: D. Torr, 1957); and Marx, Contribution to the Critique of Political Economy, trans by S. W. Ryazanskaya, ed. (London: M. Dobb, 1971)

Another indicator of the Marxist origins of many of Kenyatta's ideas is the fact that Kenyatta rationalized the legitimacy of using Leninian strategy of force against force and evil against evel or any other methods necessary to eliminate British capitalism and imperialism which were making life in Kenya increasingly intolerable for Africans.

### (iii) Kenyattaism & Peterism

In Kenyatta, Murray-Brown reports that Kenyatta vehemently denied leading the MAU MAU or even taking part in any oath-taking ceremonies. However, anyone who knows the Biblical story of how St. peter denied his knowledge of Jesus to Pilate's security forces could not fail to understand and appreciate why Kenyatta denied his knowledge of the MAU MAU and the oath-taking to the colonial security. Kenyatta's denial was spurred by the motive of self-preservation vis a vis the existing forces around him. It was a psychological defense mechanism but not a sign of cowardice. Otherwise, he could not have boldly fought to be christened "Johnstone" against the Mission's will.

### (iv) Kenyattaism & Democracy and Pluralism

Did Kenyatta's arrest and imprisonment by the British colonial rulers in 1952 have any significant effect on his "leap-over" theory, which he had taken from the writings of Lenin? This theory, which had been under development in his mind, did not weaken while he was in prison, and even though he was not permitted to utter any sensitive statements following his probation and release from prison in 1962, his political activism is still evident in most of his speeches, delivered immediately before and after independence was achieved on December 12, 1963. For instance, in his inaugural speech to mark the beginning of self-government in Kenya on June 1, 1963,[7] Kenyatta emphasized that, unlike the previous colonial government, the new one was going to be a government of and for everybody in Kenya. It would not be a government for the few privileged individuals, groups or classes, but one for all Kenyans. Kenyatta made it clear that even the opposition was part of the government according to the constitution and, as such, was entitled to an unbiased application of the due process of law.

7 Jomo Kenyatta, Harambee! The Prime Minister of Kenya's Speeches, 1963-1964 (Nairobi: Oxford University Press, 1964), pp. 8-9

Unlike the outgoing colonialist, Kenyatta made it clear that in spite of criticisms and disagreements between parties in a government concerning policies and action, the opposition party (which by that time was the Kenya African Democratic Union or KADU) was formally recognized by the Constitution, which not merely tolerated the second party, but actually encouraged it as an essential element for a healthy political process and a sound programme of nation-building. Thus whereas the colonialists did not tolerate criticism, Kenyatta allowed it. According to him, both his ruling KANU party and the opposition (KADU) party had a mutual responsibility in building Kenya. He argued that neither KANU nor KADU alone could successfully lead Kenya. It was only through their mutual efforts that Ujamaa (socialism) could be achieved in independent Kenya. Contradictory efforts were not only undesirable but practically suicidal. They were not in the best interests of either party of the entire nation.

### (v) Kenyattaism & the Genesis of "Harambee" Concept

Kenyatta's subsequent speeches in parliament between internal self-government day (June 1, 1963) and final independence day (December 12, 1963) show that his political theory began to develop from anti-colonialism and pro-conservatism into a more broad and complex scope. For instance, his attention and emphasis began to shift from anti-colonialism and pro-African tradition to a concern for the dangerous, divisive forces that might be generated by "tribalism" and racism. These were also viewed as diseases which would impede progress. In order to avoid this political blunder in the new nation, Kenyatta appealed to all Kenyans to stand "shoulder-to-shoulder" in the spirit of "Harambee", a united struggle against the common enemies of "poverty, ignorance and disease".[8]

The same sentiment is also reflected in three other Kenyatta speeches, one in Mombasa approximately one month after independence (February, 1964), one to the Meru Cooperative Union in August, 1964, and one in Githunguri, in September of 1964.[9] In all these speeches for instances, Kenyatta Promised his audience and the rest of the nation that as long as he had the mandate to rule Kenya, he was willing to accept and exercise his duties diligently. He then warned that there might be certain people or groups who perceived him as a Kikuyu prime minister, but that he was not prepared to accept any such label. Personally, he did

8 Kenyatta's Speeches in Parliament in July, 1963 and in June, 1964. Also, see Kenyatta, Harambee, p. 9.

9 Idem

not care whether a leader was a Kikuyu or a member of any other ethnic group; all that mattered was that the leader be a Kenyan. Thus, kenyatta's objective was not to favour any one single individual, ethnic group or class. The divisive colonial rule had been defeated and now no single individual, group, class or ethnic group was to be permitted to dominate the others politically, economically or in any other way. Every Kenyan was legitimately entitled to participate equally in the political process and to enjoy equal distribution of public goods and services without any discrimination or favoritisms. In kenyatta's own word, he promised the nation that:

> It is my wish to you that Africans
> of this country are now free. The period of
> European rule is past. We are now all citizens of
> this country. Since we Africans are (now) ruling
> our country, all of us should rule it together . . . . [10]

### (vi) Kenyattaism and the Concept and Value of "Unity" in Kenya:

Another fundamental precept of Kenyatta's political theory that was demonstrated in the three speeches mentioned above is his firm commitment to equal participatory rights and freedom for every Kenyan in the political process. By emphasizing unity as a pre-requisite ingredient in kenya's nation-building, Kenyatta showed himself to be aware of the inherent dangers of divisiveness. His assumption was simply that, without unity, there was no way Kenya or any other country would be strong. To him, it was immaterial whether or not each ethnic group retained its traditional culture and values as the masai have done, for all that mattered was that everyone must be willing to work with one another in the spirit of Harambee (socialism) for the sake of building the new nation of Kenya. From another perspective, Kenyatta's political theory at the twilight of self-rule in Kenya was that Kenya would definitely collapse and again be in a vulnerable position, in which colonialism and imperialism could grow, unless every Kenyan (individual and tribe alike) waived away some of their differences and ethnocentricisms and began consolidating their collective senses of oneness as a people of the same and one country, nation and common national interest and legacy of bitter experiences encountered from the harshness of undemocratic tendencies and practices of the foreign

---

[10] Kenyatta's Speech in Mombasa Stadium (February, 1964), to Meru Co-operative Union (August, 1964), and to a political rally at Githunguri (September, 1964). Also, see Kenyatta, Harambee, p.10

colonial rule which had so much terrorized, humiliated and reduced them to a second grade human being almost equivalent to a mere object such as a toilet paper that is only good to mankind whenever the user wants and is ready to use it. But immediately it has served him/her the purpose he/she wants, obviously the same poor object becomes obsolete and unwanted without any further value. Thus, the manner and condition in which the colonized African was treated by his/her colonizer. Even a fool and insane cannot forget this terrible and horrible experience.

Armed with this concept about the colonizer, Kenyatta warned every Kenyan to remember that although Kenya was now already independent from this unhealthy colonial leadership, the latter was not yet far away. It was still at/by the corner of Kenyan border ready to attack once again. It was at the door step to spy and quickly dash into Kenya to take advantage of the spoils of disunity and tribal schisms and to allow these disunity and schisms to take root and govern their daily thinking and undertakings vis a vis each other.

On this, Kenyatta did not miss strong words to put his sentiment across very effectively so that every Kenyan could get him correctly and seriously and do as he so wanted him/her to do in order to save Kenya once and for all from the hungry colonizer at the door steps salvating for a golden opportunity given to him by the stupid quarreling Kenyan. For example, he described the colonizer as a human predator whose meal was in the hands of the colonized. But, since this colonized (Africa and Kenya for one) was now liberated, the colonizer was terribly affected. He was now so much abnormally hungry that:

> Whether waking or sleeping—only think of ruling Africa. And when they sleep, a dream comes to them urging them to divide Africa, divide and then rule.[11]

### (a) On His call for Kenyan Unity to Serve as a Model for All Other African Sister States:

Kenyatta also warned that only through unity could Africa contain the attempts by foreigners to dominate their continent. He made it clear that this unity was to begin in Kenya. If

---

11 Kenyatta, Harambee, 1964, p. 18

Kenyans could unite, the new nation would provide a model that the rest of Africa could follow.

> If we Kenyans achieve unity, the whole world will respect us. We shall be the foundation and the shield of mother Africa.[12]

Thus, Kenyatta did not perceive Kenya's rise to independence solely as an end for the Kenyans; he saw it as the nucleus of Africa unity. Kenya was to be the stepping stone towards a united Africa and the more powerful the thrust of unity was in Kenya, the greater the chances were that the message would spill over the borders to all of Africa. Every living organism's growth must start from somewhere; in every life there is a beginning, a nucleus. So Kenya's unity was seen to be the starting point of African unity. If unity could not be achieved in the small nation of Kenya, how could one hope for continental unity?

**(b) On Racism or Apartheid**: The **Origin of His Suffering Without Bitterness Concept:**

One of the fundamental theoretical points emphasized by Kenyatta in his Independence Day speech was his position on the racial question popularly known as apartheid in the South African politics. Because Kenya's independence came about as a function of the struggle between Black Africans and white British settlers in Kenya, Kenyatta resolved to ensure that independent Kenya's position on colonialism was free of racism. Arguing that his position against colonialism had nothing to do with racial discrimination, Kenyatta remarked:

> Some people may say that—alas!—Kenyatta now is advocating a colour-bar. This is not so; I have no colour feelings at all. What I want is for us to be united, so that we can go forward and co-operate with the rest of the world. This is our goal.[13]

In his speeches in Mombasa, Nairobi, Thika, Embu and Githunguri, between February and September of 1964, Kenyatta frequently emphasized that he was not a racist. Addressing an audience in Nairobi in June of 1964, Kenyatta said:

---

12 Idem

13 Ibid

> Even though we were persecuted, we should not seek revenge. If people were unjust in their day, there is no reason why we should commit injustices.[14]

But, why did Kenyatta take such a stand vis-à-vis the enemy? Further, there was no doubt that Britain and other colonial powers in Africa were all against Africans and the latter's cultures and values, why didn't Kenyatta (and all Black Africans in Kenya) treat this enemy in the same manner the enemy had treated them? What was wrong with the "an eye for an eye" theory?

To Kenyatta, it was clear that this type of tit-for-tat theory would make a bad policy because it would indicate that those who were formerly persecuted were equally evils. If Kenyans were to mistreat the British nationals in Kenya, or hate Britain for her past colonial activities in Kenya, then Kenyans would not have brought in any positive change. They would have substituted an evil with another evil. As a result, Kenyatta resolved to make his fellow Kenyans to forget the past and the mistreatment they had unfortunately received at the hands of unthinking colonial rulers. Also, they resolved to concentrate on building their new nation. Kenyatta maintained that the past was now no longer relevant to the present and the future Kenya. But if his "suffering without bitterness" concept is a fact of life which should become part of the basis of political realism vis-à-vis colonialism, in the entire colonial world politics, does this also hold true between Kenyatta's ruling party (KANU) and Oginga Odinga's opposition party (Kenya Peoples Union, KPU) and other critics of the KANU party? And, if Kenyatta's Suffering Without Bitterness[15] has been made into the fundamental philosophy underlying political actions in Kenya on matters concerning the colonialists, to what extent does this hold true with respect to his degree of tolerance he granted his top critics? This will be exhaustively examined in Part II of this Paper.

### (c) On Foreign Relations

In the Swahili version of his independence day speech, Kenyatta emphasized that, under his leadership, Kenya would freely ally herself to either the East or the West all depending to her own will and wishes. Thus, Kenya was going to interact with any country that was willing. He also emphasized that, although Kenya had now become independent, Britain's friendship was still welcome as he personally wanted good relationships between the two countries to prevail.

---

14 Ibid, p. 18

15 Jomo Kenyatta, Suffering Without Bitterness (Nairobi: East African Publishing House, 1968)

The other important characteristic in his attitude toward foreign powers was that Kenyatta pledged that his Government would "never agree to friendship through any form of bribes". Of course, fine ideals; however, one now wonders the extent to which these ideals were put into practice. Further, Kenyatta maintained that "it is better to be poor and remain free than to be technically free but still tied on a string". A horse cannot choose to act according to its own dictates because it is fed by a master, whom it must obey. Kenyatta contended that Kenya was not prepared to live such a life and he promised that he was neither going to allow foreign nations, businesses or individuals to penetrate his young Kenyan government through the offers of foreign aid or other bribes nor to allow himself to be induced to perform favours or provide certain incentives in exchange of bribes or other favours. One might now ask, to what extent did Kenyatta apply his ideals and live up to his promises?

## CHAPTER III

# Jomo Kenyatta's Political Theory in Practice: A Paradigm in Leadership Failure Disaster to Humanity

### (A) Questioning Kenyatta's Political Theory

In Part I of this paper, we have noted a host of concepts, propositions and promises concerning Kenyatta and the emerging nation of Kenya. We have described Kenyatta's emphasis on unity as a prerequisite for successful nation-building. Also, we have noted Kenyatta's deliberate down-playing of racial differences and his emphasis on the importance of a lack of bitterness against the British for whatever harms they might have inflicted on him personally and the rest of Africans in Kenya. However, certain nagging questions arise with regard to the consistency of Kenyatta's political theory and his political actions after becoming the first Chief Executive of the independent Kenya. Particularly, one wonders the degree to which he actually kept his activities within the promises he made to his people. Thus, did Kenyatta keep his word in theory and practice[16], or was he just one of those men (leaders) whose words speak louder than their own actions?[17]

From a Behavioural level of analysis, it is submitted that, most African political practitioners are all a victim of Europhilia in thought, and deeds—a colonial psychosis arising from colonial classical conditioning among other various colonial mental tortures and brain-washing

16 Psalms, Chapter 69, Paragraph 1, Verse 2

17 Bernard Crick, Political Theory and Practice (New York: Basic Books, Inc., 1973), p.19

through schools, apprenticeship, etc. by the colonizers. This is explicitly borne out in Franz Fanon's book, Black Skin, White Masks[18], which places the blame for this phenomenon upon the type of education received by Black Africans. Further, as also noted by Leopold Sedar Senghor (First President of Senegal) African intellectuals and the intelligentsia, who are now national leaders in Africa, live in two conflicting worlds, "African" and "European." Most of them are strangers in their own (African) social settings. The more they deeply got involved in the Westernism (the Western way of life), the more they are now unable to understand their own people and the fundamental problems facing their predominantly black African citizenry. This reality is also confirmed by other African scholars such as Robert Muema Mbato (African, Kenya)[19] and non-African writers such as Colin M. Turnbull (non-African).[20]

Kenyatta is definitely one of those African intelligensia wearing these two conflicting cocoons and living between these two conflicting worlds. His actions since independence (December, 1963) will not fail to help us to examine and measure his effectiveness in carrying out the promises he personally offered his Kenyans at the dawn of independence. Below, we are going to witness whether the evidence refutes or supports the afore allegations made by Fanon, Senghor, Mbato, et. al. Then, we shall fairly evaluate the extent to which Kenyatta's political theory manifests itself in practice during his reign in the emerging Kenyan nation-state as a paradigm for our thorough understanding the level of leadership effectiveness in socio-economic development.

## (B) Findings: Kenyatta's Political Actions in Kenya

In his independence speech on December 12, 1963, Kenyatta first addressed the audience in English before he turned to Kiswahili. Having had the privilege of being one of the participants in that Uhuru (Independence) Day celebration, I noticed that Africans outnumbered both Europeans and Asians together by 100:1, and yet Kenyatta chose to speak in a foreign language first, as though his own African culture had no language worth respect and usage at that extremely historical occasion. A further examination of his speech on that Uhuru Day shows another intriguing phenomenon which reflects significantly on those allegations made by Fanon, Mbato and Turnbull. For instance, Kenyatta began his speech as follows:

---

18 Franz Fanon, Black Skin, White Masks (New York: Grove Press, 1967)

19 Robert Muema Mbato, "Identiry", Nairobi, Vol. 2, No. 3, 1969, pp. 31-34.

20 Colin M. Turnbull, The Lonely African (New York: Simon and Schuster, 1962).

> Your Royal Highness, Your Excellency, distinguished guests, ladies and gentlemen . . . .[21]

Who was this "Royal Highness"? Who was this "Your Excellency"? It is submitted that the "distinguished guests" at the celebration could have been Africans or other individuals from foreign countries who were invited as special guests. The "ladies and gentlemen" Kenyatta referred to could have been Africans or any other participants. The "Royal Highness" and the "Excellency" Kenyatta addressed could only have been the Duke of Edinburgh (husband of Britain's Queen Elizabeth) and Mr. McDonald (Britain's Governor General in Kenya), both of whom were there to represent the Queen at the Uhuru Day Celebration. In the entire opening address there is absolutely no indication of Kenyatta's concern for the realization of his nation's aspiration to sovereignty. Is it not a slur to African dignity to address the out-going colonial master first? Would not such a disregard or omission constitute empirical evidence to support these allegations by Fanon, Mbata and Turnbull? If we were to assume that there was no positive correlation between Kenyatta's conduct at the Uhuru Celebration and the criticisms made by Fanon and the others, we can look still further into Kenyatta's activities in the search for evidence that may either refute or support such allegation!

A further examination of the Uhuru Day speech unearths additional interesting phenomena. Kenyatta's speech focused primarily on the Queen's husband as though the latter were the only most visible key political figure at the occasion. In the Swahili version of the speech, Kenyatta repeated what he had done earlier in the English version. Thus, he was fully convinced that the first image worth addressing was the same colonial master who had initiated and baptized him with the Fanonian "White masks." The Swahili version of the speech began as follows:

> We are all grateful for the greetings from Her Majesty the Queen which the Duke of Edinburgh has read to us today. We ask him—when he returns to Britain—to convey our greetings to the Queen: tell her that, although we have become independent, we shall still remain her friends.[22]

Of course, it is nice to be polite to a guest, both friend and enemy alike in your own home or yard. It was equally polite to show that, in spite of the hardships Kenya had been subjected to

---

21 See Kenyatta, Harambee, p. 15

22 Ibid, p. 17

by Britain, Kenya had nothing significant to gain from seeking revenge. However, the fact that Kenyatta's focal point in both the English and Swahili versions of his Uhuru Day Celebration were both the Queen and her husband raises serious questions. Did Kenyatta consider them the most superior characters in the Independence Celebration drama? Does this attitude not render Kenyatta's perceptions and appreciation of Africa tradition, sovereignty and dignity also questionable? If the Kenya Independence Celebration was to mark the Restoration of the African sovereignty and dignity, which had been side-tracked into a perpetual adolescence by the British colonial rule, why did Kenyatta begin his address on such a momentous occasion by addressing the oppressor over his own consistents, the oppressed Africans he was now to lead? Who was the Star of the Play?

It is submitted that on many occasions prior to December 12, 1963, the British colonial elites (including the Queen) had played the leading role in Kenyan politics. They had been addressed with dignity and at times worshipped by Africans as though they were little gods. But the Uhuru Day Celebration was to be a turning point in the history of Kenya. It meant that African Sovereignty and Dignity were now to be the first priority to which Kenyatta and every other African nationalist was, therefore, supposed to address Africans first, before addressing any other sovereignties.

The fact that Kenyatta chose to uphold the British sovereignty was not an oversight on the leader's part. Rather, it was due to Kenyatta's own attachment to the white man's umbilical cord that he had to do so. Otherwise, he could have suffered acute dissonance. From a psychoanalytical perspective, such conduct is indicative of the conflict between Kenyatta's inherited black skin and culture on the one hand and his acquired white masks on the other, just as Fanon contends. It is also a function of the assymetrical dialectic of two values in which his white masks dominated over his black skin in Kenyatta's political life.

It might further be said that Kenyatta's circulatory system was injected with more white doses than black ones and that, consequently, he had no alternative but to behave as he did in order to maintain his own psychic balance. Any failure to do this, i.e., to recognize the image of the colonial elite as the superior character in the Uhuru Celebration Day ceremony, would definitely have been psychologically costly to Kenyatta. This reality holds true among all post-colonial African political leaders. E.g. Senghor, et.al.

But, to what extent do the above findings hold true in the remainder of Kenyatta's political life? As a political broker between Kenyan Africans on the one hand, and non-Kenyans on the other, where did Kenyatta concentrate his attention and interests? We have noted in his political theory (see Part I) that unity among the Kenyans was essential for both nation-building in Kenya and the unification of Africa, but to what degree did his political actions after independence contribute to African unity in and outside Kenya? How significant is the agreement between his theory and practice?

Data on Kenyan politics from December 12, 1963 to the time of his death in August, 1978, shows that, apart from Nigeria, the Ivory Coast and Ghana in the West, Egypt, Libya, Tunisia, Algeria and Morocco in the North; and Azania (South Africa) and Zimbabwe in the South, Kenya was claimed to be the most socio-economically progressive country of all African nations[23] as supported by her steady rise in her GNP and per capita income and by a higher level of urbanization in Kenya than one would find in her neighbouring countries of Ethiopia, Somalia, Tanzania and Uganda during that time. Also, it was alleged that Kenya's currency exchange rate at that time was far superior to those of Tanzania and Uganda currencies and that unlike Nyerere's socialist Tanzania and Amin's military Uganda, Kenyatta's Kenya was a capitalist country and, therefore, the only democracy in Eastern Africa.

On the other hand, serious nagging questions arise with respect to Kenyatta's political actions in Kenya between December 12, 1963 and his death (1978), regarding the promises he had made to the people of Kenya. In order to establish a clear correlation between Kenyatta's theory and practice, let us first examine the following: (a) Kenyatta's response to the call for African unity; (b) his political actions with regard to who controlled various key institutions in the country; (c) his conduct in the economic sector; (d) his response to his African critics in and outside Kenya; and (e) his view of the relations between Africans and non-Africans in Kenya.

In his speeches at the dawn of Kenya's nationhood, Kenyatta gave the impression that internal unity in Kenya would kill two birds with one stone. Thus, he assumed that this would increase the chances for a rapid nation-building and to this end, contribute to the future unification of Africa. Yet an examination of his perceptions of other ethnic groups in Kenya shows lack

---

23 See Donald G. Morrison, Robert C. Mitchell, John N. Paden and Hugh M. Stevenson, eds, Black Africa: A Comparative Handbook (New York: The Free Press, 1972)

of this positive correlation between his promises and his actions. For instance, in most of the key position throughout Kenya's major infrastructure, one finds members of Kenyatta's tribe (Kikuyu). What is perhaps most important to note is that, since independence nearly all key cabinet ministries (i.e., Finance, the Defense, Foreign Affairs, State, Attorney-General and Lands & Settlement Ministries) were held by a group of members of Kenyatta's tribe. The same phenomenon holds true with respect to all Kenya's Ambassadors to major world powers e.g., U.S.A, and U.K. to chairmen and managing directors of major parastatal bodies and substantive committees and boards ambassadorial personnel overseas, and Kenyans working in foreign embassies in Kenya. Not withstanding, over 50% of foreign grants and scholarships given to Kenya were re-routed to students from Kenyatta's tribe most loans and grants for economic development, which were supposed to be open to every Kenyan interested in business, were given to people from Kenyatta's tribe; most Provincial Commissioners, District Commissioners, and District Officers in Kenya were from Kenyatta's tribe; most key commanding officers in the armed forces (including the police) came from Kenyatta's tribe. Finally the Central Bank Governor, the Unviersity of Nairobi, which is the only seat of higher learning in Kenya and the Commander of the General Service Unit (GSU, Kenyatta's main security force) were all manned by men from Kenyatta's ethnic group. The same holds true with respect to development grants to Kenya from overseas were diverted to Kenyatta's district of Kiambu in particular and his own central province in general. Another intriguing phenomenon in the above profile is that approximately 85% of all the individuals mentioned were from Kenyatta's own township, Gatundu-kiambu, while the remaining ones came from the Gatundu—Kiambu periphery (Muranga, Nyeri, and so on). Either way, the people from both areas belong to Kenyatta's tribe and related tribes, such as the Embu and Meru, which are culturally similar and easily communicate with no difficult. These three tribes together represent one of the largest groups in Kenya, like the Abaluyia, Dholuo, Akamba, Nandi, Kipgsis and Masai.

A further examination of who is who in Kenyan economic sector during the reign of Kenyatta (1963-1978) reveals a host of other striking phenomena which, in turn, raise further questions about the consistency of Kenyatta's political theory and practice. For instance, the studies in the 1960's and 1970's show that in the Kenyan political economy, both political and economical sectors were controlled by the same individuals or families. In its study of the Kenyan economy after ten years of independence, To the point[24] note that there were

[24] To The Point, January 12 1974, p. 23

ten millionaires in Kenya: Kenyatta, Kenyatta's wife (Ngina), Mungai Njoroge (Kenyatta's relative through marriage) Njonjo (Attorney-General from Kenyatta's district), inter alias. The argument recurs in a slightly altered aspect in the Christian science monitor's study, who Controls Industry in Kenya?, William A. Attwood's study, The Reds and the Blacks, and in Colin Leys' study, Under-Development in Kenya: The Political Economy of Neo-Colonialism, 1964-1971[25]. How did Kenyatta, his wife, and their immediate associates become so wealthy in such a short time (1963-1968)?

The studies indicated above show that Kenyatta's ulterior motive in political life, had always been to use his political position as a means through which to obtain economic benefits. Ali A. Mazrui notes that:

> What is significant in [Kenyatta's politics] is [Kenyatta's] conviction that failure to prosper is an argument against a leader. As a socialist radical, [Bildad] Kaggia was urging a redistribution of land in Kenya to the poor. Kenyatta was suggesting that a person who had failed to prosper through his own exertions should not be advocating free things.[26]

Both Bildad Kaggia and Kenyatta had been jailed together during the colonial rule but because Kaggia later became disillusioned by the high degree of discrepancy between Kenyatta's political theory and practice, Kaggia demanded that Kenyatta honour his promises to the Kenyan people. For instance, since land issues had been the fundamental cause of the "MAU MAU" war against the British settlers in Kenya, and since in his Facing Mt.Kenya, and Kenya, The Land of Conflict [27], Kenyatta had indicated that African land and cultures were to be returned to, or left intact for their habitual African owners from whom the settlers usurped the land, Kaggia expected that after Kenya achieved her independence, those lands which had been taken by the European and Asian settlers would be returned to their rightful

25 A Working Party, Who Controls Industry in Kenya? (Nairobi: East African Publishing House, 1968); W. A. Attwood, The Reds and the Blacks, (New York: Harper and Row, 1967); Colin Leys, Under-Development in Kenya, The Political Economy of Neo-Colonialism, 1964-1971 (California: University of California Press; 1975)

26 Ali A. Mazrui, "The Monarchial Tendency in African Political Culture". In Marion E. Doro and Newell M. Stultz, Governing in Black Africa (Englewood Cliffs, N. J.: Prentice-Hall, Inc., 1970), p. 21.

27 Jomo Kenyatta, Facing Mt. Kenya (London: Secker and Warburg, 1938); Kenyatta, Kenya, The Land of Conflict (Manchester: International African Service Bureau, Pana-Service, Ltd., 1944)

owners. However, to Kaggia's surprise, no one received his land back! Kenyatta demanded that whoever wanted his land back must first of all pay for it. The axiom was simple: no money, no land! Thus, the possession of money was the sine quan on for land restoration or acquisition.

Kenyatta ridiculed and disgraced his exinmate (Kaggia) by publicly saying,

> [Kaggia,] we were together with Paul Ngei jailed if you go to Ngei's farm, he has planted a lot of coffee and other crops. What have you done for yourself? If you go to Kubai's [another ex-inmate-home,] he has a big house and a nice shamba. Kaggia, what have you done yourself? We were together with Kungu Karumba in jail, now he is running his own buses. What have you done for yourself?[28]

This argument between Kaggia and Kenyatta took place in 1965; but more recent studies on the land tenure question confirm that Kenyatta's objection to the distribution of land prevailed till his death in 1978.[29] Land which belonged to x before independence could only be returned back to x after independence if x had the money to buy back his own land. Otherwise, x had no right over it.

Another most amazing aspects of Kenyatta's political action was his demand that Africans must pay to buy lands that were formerly lost to white settlers, since Kenyatta knew perfectly well (1) that most of his own people who lost their land were too poor to buy the land without the benefit of loans, and also (2) that no one could get a loan without any substantial collateral or sound proof of ability to pay back the loan. Finally, numerous studies by scholars, the mass media and others collectively and individually show that Kenyatta's own possessions were considerable and that he had many avenues for getting them and the money. Another most intriguing finding by those studies is that Kenyatta was one the few heads of states from the developing countries who was on the CIA payroll[30]—a major contradiction between his pledge that he would never allow himself to be exploited by foreigners with bribes or any such corruptive incentives.

---

[28] From Ali A. Mazrui, op.cit., in Note 26 above. Also in East African Standard, Nairobi, April 12, 1965.

[29] Ngweno Osolo-Nasubo, A Socio-Economic Study of the Kenya Highlands from 1900-1970: A Case Study of the Uhuru Government (Washington, D.C.:University Press of America, 1977)

[30] See The Washington Post, issues between March 21-30, 1977.

Kenyatta's ambition to rapidly increase his own wealth can be set opposite his intentions to not allow people to reclaim their lost land and property. This is a significant evidence to prove the existence of the contradiction between his political theory and practice. His criticism of Kaggia is yet another indication of this; otherwise, it is certain that Kaggia would not have challenged Kenyatta with the demand that the lands be restored to their respective rightful owners.

Those who have dared to go further than Kaggia in their protestations against Kenyatta's political behaviour (e.g, Tom Mboya, Oginga Odinga, J.M Kariuki, Martin Shikuku, Ronald, Argwings Kothek and others) have been silenced or eliminated. Roger Mann, The Washington Post Special Correspondent in Kenya[31], noted in his analysis of Kenyatta's leadership in Kenya that Kenyatta's methods and motive were not only undemocratic and oligarchical, but also opportunistic. Together with his Gikuyu clique (mainly from the Kiambu District and commonly characterized as "Mount Kenya Mafia"), Kenyatta always shielded Kenya's leadership from non-Kikuyu tribesmen. For example, in his observation of the problem of succession (i.e., who was most likely to succeed Kenyatta to the presidency), Mannfound that,

> In the years that followed, the likely candidates to succeed Kenyatta were eliminated. Oginga odinga, Kenya's first post-independence vice-president (but then resigned because of his disillusionment with Kenyatta's policy) was jailed and his opposition party banned. Tom Mboya, Kenyatta's most likely successor, was shot dead in Nairobi by a Kikuyu (Kenyatta's tribe) gunman. Ronald Ngala, widely popular Cabinet Minister, died in a mysterious car accident. Finally, last year, J. M. Kariuki, a politician with mass appeal and open presidential aspiration was murdered.[32]

It is clear that the elimination of one's critics and possible successors was a significant contradiction to the promises that were made to the people of Kenya in Kenyatta's pre-and post-Uhuru speeches. Kenyatta had promised the Kenyan nation that his rule would be totally and completely different from the British rule which had excluded Africans from the political process and which had deprived them of the due process of law. Unlike its outgoing British government, Kenyatta's government was to fling open all the doors to all Africans. He alleged

---

31 See Note 32 below

32 Roger Mann, "Kenya Finds Succession in a Troublesome Issue", The Washington Post, October 24, 1976, P. A24

that he would welcome criticism from the opposition, and individuals and concentrate on a co-operative policy aimed at the problem of nation-building. He declared that without such criticisms, his ruling party (KANU) could not be effective. Thus, Kenyatta had initially viewed the existence of an opposition as a healthy input to the political process in Kenya.

But one is lead to wonder why Kenyatta had to depart from his political ideals given that he had suffered so much at the hand of undemocratic colonial rule in Kenya.

An analysis of Kenyatta's activities above suggest that his departure from this earlier line of action to a different one must have been a function of his realization that he had already solidified his political leadership position well enough not to worry about anything. Thus, Kenyatta did not just become a revisionist. Rather, the analysis shows that he became a deviant political theoretician highly possessed with most attractive enormous economic gains and political prestige attached to the office of the Presidency. Like his all counterpart throughout the developing world, Kenyatta became so flooded with riches coming from corruptive offers from inside and outside Kenya in return to his favours to the source of such riches and offers that he could not stomach criticisms from Kaggia, Odinga, Kariuki and other socialism advocates.

There is no doubt that this must have been the reason why his wife (Mama Ngina) and all other members of his family became millionaires within a very short time; why sharply observant leaders, such as Odinga and Joseph Murumbi, could not be allowed to continue as Vice-Presidents by Kenyatta; why he wanted the post of the President to remain within his Kikuyu tribe in order to protect the wealth he had already accumulated on a large scale; and why Kenyatta could not tolerate the existence and political ideals of his critics, e.g., Mboya and Odinga (Dholuo), Ngala (Giriama), Kodhek (Dholuo), Shikuku (Abaluyia), and even critics from his own tribe such as J. M. Kariuki. Kariuki became so disillusioned with Kenyatta's deviation from the promises that he at once began to intensify his relationships with non-Gikuyu tribes against Kenyatta's leadership which, to them, was no longer intolerable and acceptable.

Worried to the future of his Presidency amid these mounting critics, Kenyatta adopted a double-edged sword strategy—an elimination strategy designed to completely clean out every potential critic whether or not such a critic was of his Gikuyu tribe, e.g., J. M. Kariuki or from outside Kenya e.g., Idi Amin In Uganda. Both cases are evidenced by the facts that he brutally eliminated J. M. Kariuki (his own tribes's man) and he privately collaborated with Israel in the Entebbe invasion on 4th July, 1976[33]—an incident Kenyatta unsuccessfully tried to deny but which was finally confirmed by the media.[34]

Kenyatta's decision to extend his double edged strategy of elimination from his domestic politics to regional African politics by seeking to destroy the leaders of his own African neighbouring states such as President Idi Amin Dada of Uganda by collaborating with foreigners such as Israel is not an end in itself. It strongly confirms that Kenyatta was interested in protecting his presidency and massive wealth he, his family and associates had accumulated. Also, it suggests that he was a permanent hostage of "black skin"; "white masks" confusion—of which the latter seems to have been paramount to the former.

Otherwise, it is open to question why, in his capacity as one of the pioneers of Pan-Africanism (others being Web Du Bois, Kwame Nkrumah and Mackonen), Kenyatta could have encouraged the Entebbe invasion against his own sister African nation-state which, in conformity with the concept of Pan-Africanism, Kenyatta was expected to defend and protect against foreigners? And, the fact that he eliminated Mboya, Ngala and Kodhek in cold blood and put Odinga, Shikuku and others into detention throughout his presidency, it is obvious that Kenyatta's political actions did not conform to his political theory. The two were significantly contradictory—a leadership problem prevalent in all nations-states though the problem is extremely acute in the developing countries.

---

33 The Toronto Star, July 5-17, 1976. Also see Kenya Government Statement on "The Current Relations with the Republic of Uganda" (Washington, D.C.: Kenya Embassy, July 27, 1976)

34 The Washington Post, March 31, 1977, P.A1, A27

# CHAPTER IV

## Conclusions

In Part II of this study, we were concerned with the nature, scope and dimensions of Kenyatta's political theory before and immediately after the Africans of Kenya regained their sovereignty from the British colonial rule. In all, we noted that Kenyatta's political theory was vehemently anti-colonialism on the one hand and strongly conservative on the other. This duality is reflected in his two books, Facing Mt. Kenya and Kenya, The Land of Conflict, which he wrote while in exile in England. He was bitterly anti-colonial because of the usurpation of African land and the colonial attempts to disrupt African traditions, particularly with references to the Kikuyu female circumcision. His main objectives in an overthrow of the colonial rule would have been the following: to restore the usurped land to the rightful owners; to eradicate all forms of class distinctions and their causes; to see to it that everyone in Kenya had a right to the due process of law (a right previously denied to many by the colonial rulers); to eradicate all forms and causes of coercion which were being exercised by the colonial regime; and to govern Kenya within the framework of Harambee, a socialistic principle of all against the common enemies, i.e., hunger, poverty, ignorance, disease, opportunism, bourgeois oppression and so on.

In the final analysis it is evident that Kenyatta's political theory grew directly out of Leninism. Unlike Karl Marx and Friedrich Engels, whose political strategy against capitalism's oppression prescribed that primitive (pre-industrial) societies should accept imperialism first in order to give capitalism room to commit its inevitable, natural suicide, Kenyatta's judgment was that the Africans in Kenya had already suffered enough at the hands of the imperialists. Like Vladimir Lenin's attitude against the suffering mass proletariat Russians before 1917 Russian Peasant Revolution against the few filthy rich Russians, Kenyatta's attitude towards colonialism and imperialism was that the two were too oppressive to bear; and that Kenya was, therefore, unable to await such a natural death. By so doing, Kenyatta argued that it was high time for the oppressed African to take another route altogether and apply the most direct means possible. Emulating the leap-over theory used by Lenin in Russia in 1917, by Mao Tse Tung in China in 1949, by Kwame Nkrumah in the Gold Coast now Ghana between 1952 and 1957, by Fidel Castro in Cuba in 1959 and by Patrice Lumumba in the Congo now Zaire in 1960, Kenyatta decided to fight the evils of capitalism and imperialism right away by inflicting a heavy blow on the British colonial rulers in Kenya so that his fellow Africans would be free once again. Having succeeded against colonialism, Kenyatta's next step in his political strategy was to mobilize all Kenyans into a united front under the slogan of "Harambee", meaning togetherness in order: (a) to build their emerging new nation and (b) to help him in the unification of all Africa.

In Part III, we have attempted to examine the correlation between Kenyatta's political theory on the one hand, and his actions during and after independence on the other. In doing so, our fundamental goal was to measure the similarity between Kenyatta's theory and practice and to sue this finding as a paradigm for our understanding, explaining and predicting the ability of many key political leaders to initiate and enhance national development.

As a result of our investigations, we have noted that significant degree of inconsistency abound between a political leader's theory and practice. This is borne out by out findings on Kenyatta who at the eve of independence, gave several empty promises that he later on could not honour. These include his promise that he was going to restore usurped land to its rightful former owners; that he was going to welcome the opposition and other government critics as an essential ingredient for a healthy political process; that he would respect and uphold the due process of law; that he would not tolerate job distribution which was not based on merit or achievement; that he was not a Kikuyu leader but a national leader and therefore that all tribes were going to harvest equal shares of Kenya's independence; that African tradition and sovereignty were more important to him than foreign values an ideal which proved to be false in practice time between independence (December 12, 1963) and his death in August, 1978. His other problems include his decision to eliminate those he perceived as his political threats; his deviance from Pan-Africanism; and his alignment with Israel and other foreign powers against neighbouring sister countries are explicit ramifications of his significant degree of departure from his political theories. His boasts that during his presidency in Kenya, Kenya had nothing of value to gain from both Tanzania and Uganda boasts which caused the demise of the East African Community in 1977. As explained in Part II, there is no doubt that these and other Kenyatta's political actions collectively demonstrate a clear practical departure from his political theory. This is also the reason why many people during Kenyatta's leadership felt that Kenya was still "Not Yet Uhuru".

In the final analysis, Kenyatta's practices, seen in Part II of this Paper, and the contradiction between those practices and Kenyatta's theories as expressed in part I suggest that not all political leaders adhere to their theories in practice. Thus, Julius K. Nyerere's fourth assumption in "The Rational Choice", which suggests that African national leaders do not aim at replacing their "alien rulers by local privileged elites but to create societies which ensure human dignity and self-respect for all"[35] is definitely worth questioning. Our diagnosis of Kenyatta's political life in part II of this paper fails to support Nyerere's argument. It may hold true in Nyerere's Tanzania, but it definitely does not do so in Kenyatta's Kenya. As the data in Parts I and II confirms, there is very little sense of respect for the concepts of human dignity and self-respect throughout the developing world. Elimination of political oppositions abound in this world though it is also evident in highly industrialized world. In his study of this phenomenon in Kenyatta's Kenya, Roger Man discovered that Kenyatta's opposition and critics were eliminated from the political scene by (1) assassination, (2) disqualification (3) or elections would be called off when it was predicted obvious that Kenyatta or one of his favoured politician was going to lose the election.[36] From a Marxist perspective, this contradiction between Kenyatta's promises and hid actual political policy automatically suggests a fact that Kenyatta's revolution against colonialism had not yet reached maturity, i.e., it had not yet reached the quality of a genuine revolution of the proletariat. In Mao Tse Tung's words, it was simply "counter revolutionary front of world capitalism . . ."[37] Another important phenomenon in Kenyatta's leadership in Kenya is that although Kenyatta's attacks against colonialism and imperialism were complementary to the socialist revolution against capitalism and imperialism, Kenyatta's failure to focus his political activities in Kenya within his own political theory and promises to his people suggest that his behaviours were essentially of a "bourgeois-democratic nature "but not of a "proletariat-socialist nature"

---

35 Oginga Odinga, Not Yet Uhuru (London: Heinemann, 1967)

36 Julius K. Nyerere, "The Rational Choice", in Paul E. Sgimund, Jr., The Ideologies of the Developing Nations (New York: Praeger, 1974), pp. 11-128

37 See Roger Mann, The Washington Post, op.cit., Note 32 above. Mann's findings also hold in Kenyatta's recent cancellation of the 1977 elections in Kenya in fear of Odinga's increasingly growing popularity and chances of winning the election

This reality is borne out by his engagement in opportunism, capitalism and the elimination of those who criticized him or demanded that Kenya be transformed into a socialist society. According to his critics such as Odinga, in order to become a socialist state in which satisfaction and respect for the majority can be realized, Kenyatta's bourgeois-democratic revolution would first have to undergo a counter revolution; otherwise they argued that Kenyatta's Kenya was likely to remain a bourgeois democracy indefinitely. It is evident from the foregoing analysis that his rational choice was a contradiction of what he had promised his Kenyans at the eve of independence. However, the data clearly suggests that to Jomo Kenyatta, theory and practice meant two different things—a problem extremely antithetical peace, populous trust and a high degree of progress. As noted in my other paper "objective African Military Control: A New Paradigm in Civil-Military Relation, "Peace Research Vol. 17 (1980)[38], more than 60% of all independent African countries have already tested either a military or civilian coup. The same problem also holds true with respect to all countries in the Third World including USSR, China, etc.

An examination of the causal factor responsible for this problem shows that it is, by and large, this inconsistency between theory and practice that breeds coups and all other forms of political instability from country to country.[39] Similarly, in each organization including nuclear families, the degree of this inconsistency between what a leader says and what he actually does is always a disease—a terminal cancer to the public trust and confidence in the leadership.

And as also noted in Mary P. Nichols' recent inquiry into the actual essence of rhetoric,[40] it is submitted that no single leadership is free from internal instability no matter how rhetorically powerful that leadership may be unless its powerful rhetoric is accompanied by a high degree of consistency between its ideals and its deeds. In short, powerful rhetoric, military might, etc., at the disposal of any leadership are definitely not a reliable insurance against the fall of that leadership. The most reliable insurance for every leadership is succinctly a high degree of consistency between theory and practice of that leadership.

---

38 Mao Tse-Tung, On New Democracy (Peking: Foreign Languages Press, 1960); also, see Paul E. Sigmund, Jr., ed., The Ideologies of the Developing Nations (New York: Praeger, 1974), pp. 44-50

39 Agola Auma-Osolo, "Objective African Military Control: A New Paradigm in Civil-Military Relations", Peace Research, Vol. 17 (1980)

40 Idem

In the final analysis, like all living organisms, all organizations ranging from minute nuclear family to supra-organizations such as nation states and both regional and universal international organizations, are also governed by concrete behavioural laws. Some of these laws are specifically related to organization leadership, e.g., (a) the manner in which that leadership must conduct itself if it is to maintain a high degree of trust and confidence among members of that organization; and (b) what would happen in the event that this degree of trust and confidence is lacking. From our afore findings on Kenyatta's Kenya, it is submitted that there was low degree of populous trust and confidence in Kenyatta's actions in theory and in practice. Otherwise, his own closest associates, e.g., Kaggia, Odinga, Mboya, Shikuku, Kariuki and many other outstanding pillars of the rebellion against the British colonial rule in Kenya such as Kaggia (who together with Kenyatta suffered bitterly in the British colonial detentions) could not have totally differed with Kenyatta short of this high degree of contradictions between Kenyatta's ideals and deeds before and immediately after Kenyan independence (1963).

## References


Attwood, W. A., The Reds and the Blacks, Political Economy of Neo-Colonialism, 1964-1971. University of California Press, 1975.

Auma-Osolo, Agola, "Objective African Military Control: A New Paradigm in Civil Military Relations" Peace Research Vol. 17, 1980.

A Working Party, Who Controls Industry in Kenya? Nairobi: East African Publishing House, 1968.

Crick, Bernard, Political Theory and Practice. New York: Basic Books, Inc, 1973.

East African Standard. Nairobi: April 12, 1965.

Fanon, Franz, Black Skin, White Masks. New York: Grove Press, 1967.

Kenyatta, Jomo, Harambee! The Prime Minister of Kenya's Speeches, 1963-1964. Nairobi: Oxford University Press, 1964.

__________, Suffering Without Bitterness. Nairobi: East African Publishing House, 1968.

__________, Kenya, the Land of Conflict. Manchester: International African Service Bureau, Pana-Service, Ltd., 1944.

Mann, Roger, "Kenya Finds Succession is a Troublesome Issue", The Washington Post, October 24, 1976.

Marx, Karl, Das Kapital, trans. S. Moore and E. Aveling, ed. London: D. Torr, 1957.

__________, Contribution to the Critique of Political Economy, trans. S. W. Ryazanskaya, ed. London: M. Dobb, 1971.

Mazrui, Ali A., "The Monarchial Tendency in African Political Culture", in Marion E. Doro and Newell M. Stultz, Governing in Black Africa. Englewood Cliffs, N. J.: Prentice-Hall, Inc., 1970.

Mbato, Robert Muema, "Identity", Bursara. Nairobi: Vol. 2, No. 3, 1969.

Morrison, Donald G. et al, Black Africa, A Comparative Handbook. New York: The Free Press, 1972.

Murray-Brown, Jeremy, Kenyatta. New York: E.P. Dutton and Co., Inc., 1973.

Nicholas, Mary P., "Aristotle's Defense of Rhetoric", The Journal of Politics, vol. 49 No. 3, 1987.

Odinga, Oginga, Not Yet Uhuru. London: Heinemann, 1967.

Osolo-Nasubo, Ng'weno, A Socio-Economic Study of the Kenya Highlands, University Press of America, 1977.

**Psalms**

Sigmund, Paul E., Jr., ed., The ideologies of the Developing Nations, New York: Praeger, 1974.

The Toronto Star, July 5-14, 1976

The Washington Post, March 21-30, 1977

The Washington Post, March 31, 1977

To the Point, January 12, 1974

Tse-Tung, Mao, On New Democracy. Peking: Foreign Languages Press, 1960

Turnbull, Colin M., The Lonely African. New York: Simon & Schuster, 1962

# PART FOUR

## THE GOALS, PROBLEMS AND STRATEGIES OF EAST AFRICAN NATION-STATES ON THE WORLD MARKET.

## A Test for The Spirit of Community Intergration in The East African Region.

CHAPTER 1

# Introduction

## 1. Problem

In every community of living organisms, each organism is naturally duty bound to sustain itself in one way or another. Thus, survival is the fundamental goal of every organism. While by acting so, every organism also helps its community to sustain itself, [4] naturally, survival of the community results from spillovers only. The community goal is secondary as far as each organism's goal is concerned. The primary goal of every organism is to sustain itself.[5] Thus, the "self" concepts always forms the first priority of every organism in its community because the goal or values constantly sought by each are too scarce to meet its total demands. Because every organism seeks the same goal(s), and since these goal (s) are too scarce to find or get easily and cheaply from the community chances of conflicts occurring are significantly high.[6]

Similar goals and situations also exist in our International Community. However, knowing (a) what these goals are, (b) where they are,(c) when to find them,(d) how to find them, and (e) from whom a nation-state can possibly get them for its national survival collectively constitute the most fundamental problems, concerns and worries of every nation-state. In search for these goals on the World-market, nation-states consequently interact with each other across their national boundaries. But, these goals are too scarce to meet every nation-state's demands. Therefore, they are too difficult to find and get that cheaply.

Also, because nation-states are composed of individuals, every nation-state is a human being. But, all individuals differ in their attitudes, temperaments, bargaining styles and perceive one another. Therefore, nation-state differs in their attitude, temperament, concept of reality, inter perception, bargaining style and behavioural strategy on the world market.

Because of these universal significant intellectual and attitudinal variances among nation-state and the scarcity of the goals nation-states always seek on the World Market mixed with the amorphous and cephalous problem of that market, which, in turn makes it impossible for the market to strictly regulate and police over the conduct of each nation-state in the same manner each nation-state strictly does over the conduct of each of its nationals at home even punish that national for any violation of the law of the land using its juridical and other law enforcement machineries, reckless competition and conflict among Nation-state for these goals on the World market are also high. It is due to this very reason that nation-states' interaction on the Market is highly political and anarchical collectively posing a critical pathological problem of concern to each state.

And, since nation-state significantly differ in their attitudes, temperaments, interperception and conceptions of reality, they also differ in their bargaining strength,[7] and strategies towards the goals they seek of the world market. They may use pacific, coercive [8] or both strategies, all depending on each actor's strength and the magnitude of the conflict.

Those who opt for coercive to pacific strategy, always rationalize that strategy. They justify it as another inevitable, rational means of achieving the goal(s) that they would not otherwise attain unless the use such strategy (ies). Consequently, to date, pacific and coercive strategies are the two integral parts of the World Politics that each nation-state is naturally expected to use in pursuit of its milieu goal and in defense of its possesional goal, all depending on each nation-state's capacity vis a vis the capabilities of other nation-states who are competing for the same milieu goal or defending their possessional goal.

But, in view of this compex pathological problem on the World Market, do the East African nation-states (hereafter referred to as African nation-states) have necessary capacity with which to pursue what they seek from the World Market and to protect their dignity and heritage?

Further, given the fact that in his article "Babies Given Aids in Tests" which appeared in the Daily Nation, Nairobi, on 20th September, 1979, the nation Correspondent based in London, by Paul Redfern, shows a flabbergasting pathological problem on The World Market which, therefore, raises a series of more critical questions against strategic capabilities of African Nation-States and all other politically, socio-economically and militarily too weak nation-states to competently defend their possessional and milieu goal against their most aggressive and powerful counterpart on the World Market. Their weakness is vivid in their inability to defend their national Dignity and Human Rights enshrined in the Universal Declaration of Human Rights of the UN Charter Principles and Articles. Because of the seriousness of this revelation against the strategic strength of these African Nation-States to effectively defend their dignity and total survival on the World Market which is composed of Nation-States and Leaders of different attitude and morals, the following long quotation from Paul Redfern is therefore very necessary in order for the reader to capture fully the criticality of this danger facing the capabilities of the African Nation-States and their leadership on the World Market today:-

> "About 1,000 children in Kenya, Uganda and seven other sub-saharan African countries may have been unnecessarily infected with the HIV virus because of unethical medical experiments conducted by the United States, Belgium, France, Denmark and South Africa.
>
> This is because of experiments involving around 12,000 women in 15 different trials over the past two years. As well as the nine African countries, research was also carried out in Thailand and the Dominican Republic.
>
> Some of the women involved in the trial were given the AZT drug, which is known to cut the risk of transmission of the virus between mother and baby by two thirds, while others were only given placebo pills.
>
> The Guardian newspaper, which led on the story today following publication of the research in the New England Journal of Medicine, said that even some US scientist had condemned the experiments as "unethical," adding that the way the research was conducted "appears to contradict global guidelines which say that medical research in developing countries should always be conducted according to ethical standards 'no less exacting' than in the developed world, where placebo tests are strictly regulated.
>
> An estimated six million women in the developing world will be infected with Aids by the turn of the century, scientists predict. The guardian said that the researchers in the trials were "knowingly condemning some of the yet-to-be born infants to death by Aids".

But, this is not all. Although this HIV case may be a very devastating challenge to the competence of the African leadership to protect the health security and other goals of Africa and her African Peoples on the World Market which is, in fact, Goal Number One of every African Leader and nation-State on that Market, this case is just a tip of the iceberg. More serious cases abound between the Cold War Era (effective 1945) and the present Post-Cold War Era (2001). Prima facie empirical evidences of this reality include, for instance, the following:-

1. Numerous assassinations carried out against African leaders identified as being too bright, competent and tough in defence of the goals of Africa and her people and who are too difficult to be easily manipulated and used as a puppet to advance the interests (goals) of the Super Powers on The World Market. From the Cold War Era to the present Post-Cold War Era, these leaders are numerous. The list is endless of now (July, 2001). However, for the purpose of clarity, a few of these leaders include Prime Minister Patrice Lumumba who was unjustly put to an ignominious death on 17 January, 1961 by the enemy of Justice, Truth and Righteousness without any genuine cause, apart from being falsely assumed to be a threat to the mineral interests of Belgium and the anti-Communism Camp in the mineral-rich Katanga Province of the Congo Republic (now called The Democratic Republic of Congo); President Gamel Nassar of Egypt who was also unjustly murdered in 1958 for no any substantive genuine cause other than for being assumed to be leaning too much on the side on the Communist Camp against the interests of the Capitalist Camp in Egypt particularly in the Suez Canal; President Samora Machel of Mozambique who was also unjustly put to a similar ignominious death in 1986 for falsely being perceived as Enemy Number One of the apartheid policy of the Minority White Regime in South Africa and also for his goal to assist Nelson Mandela and the latter's African national Congress (ANC) whose goal was to dismantle that policy and the culture of Bad Governance of that regime from South Africa; Steve Biko, another most brilliant and dreadful Human Rights and Civil Rights African Leader who was similarly murdered simply because of his goal to achieve liberty and dignity of not only his Black People but also both Whites and the Mixed Race Peoples of that Country in his capacity as an advocate of Good Governance and Summum Bonum (i.e the Greatest Good or Happiness for all characterized by the virtues of Justice, Wisdom, Temperance and Courage); President Melchier Ndagaye of Burundi who was murdered in October 1993 together with several members for his newly constituted Cabinet shortly

after winning the Presidential Elections in that Country; and Presidents Juvenal habyarimana of Rwanda and Cyprian Ntaryamira of Burundian Government on 6 April, 1994 while landing at Kigali Airport to drop off President habyarimana from their last and final Peace Meeting in Dar es Salaam without any substantive act of intervention by the African Leadership to find out who actually killed them and for what reason(s) as a first step of identifying the actual root-cause(s) and remedy of the perennial catastrophe which has always devastated both Rwanda and Burundi ever since the 1950's, instead of leaving the matter to non-rightful persons who chose to cover up their sins by wasting resources on which hunting, arresting, prosecuting and wrongly convicting those who do not have any genuine cause for which to convict them and leaving out the actual criminals and evil-bearers. Although the UN did intervene, it too failed and cannot provide a solution to this catastrophe due to its negligence on the question of why those heinous murders had to be carried out at all against those three innocent Heads of State of Rwanda and Burundi and members of their Governments, and most serious of all, why the Arusha Peace Accord of August 1993 chaired by the Organization of African Unity in Tanzania had been and rendered totally useless and meaningless by those who were signatories of the Peace Accord and the shooting down of the plane in Kigali for the purpose of killing President Habyarimana, President Ntaryamira and his Burundian Cabinet Members, and all those on board.

2. Numerous Coups d'etat, e.g. the military coup d'etat of 1972 against President Kwame Nkurumah who had paradoxically emerged as the first and foremost Founding Father of African Nationalism, Freedom, Liberty and Independence on the one hand, and also The Founding Father of Pan-Africanism and African Unity on the other, simply because of his global goal to enhance and promote those Africa's Goals on the World Market, particularly with a view to achieving Global Recognition of Africa's Dignity and Sovereign Equality on the World Market from ex-Colonial Masters such as Britain and France and non-Colonial Masters such as the USA and Japan in accordance with the Principles of The Universal Declaration of Human Rights and Sovereign Equality enshrined in the UN Charter—Masters who, because of their overly pride and self-seeking Darwinism, could hardly stomach that at all; and the most recent coup d'etat in the UN Organization against UN Secretary General Dr. Boutrus Ghali in 1998 who was unjustly toppled from his post as a UN Secretarial Chief simply because of being supportive to the goals and wishes of African nation States and for refusing to

be susceptible to the influence and manipulation of the same Masters who, by virtue of their superior power, arbitrarily control The UN Security Council and its decisions on all issues affecting their interests such as the Rwanda, Burundi, Somalia, Sudan and Democratic Republic of Congo issues where current empirical evidences in those Countries show that the socio-economic dynamics or behaviour is now drifting away from the old Francophone market to a new Anglo-phone market in favour of the USA and other Anglo-phone manufacturers and manufactured goods to suit the interests of those dominant Super Powers who were against Boutros Ghali's continuation as the UN Secretary General.

3. Numerous Detentions against African liberation leaders such as the African national Congress (ANC) leader, Nelson Mandela, who was detained and jailed for a painful period of twenty seven (27) years in an isolated remote Roben Island Prison in the Indian Ocean till 1987 simply because of his ambitious goal to liberate his endangered country and people of South Africa and for organizing and leading ANC with which to dismantle apartheid policy and all other viruses of Bad Governance of Minority White Regime in Country—a goal which both that Minority White Regime and its associates in the socio-economic activities particularly from the Capitalist World who had heavily invested immensely in the gold, diamond and other mineral wealth of that country could not afford to accept to yield to without use of coercion by ANC and its Military Wind; the Kenya African Union (KAU) leader, Jomo Kenyatta, who was arrested and detained by the British Colonial Regime for a period of seven (7) years till 1961 for organizing and leading an anti-British Colonial Rule rebellion called "Mau Mau" in Kenya aimed at dismantling that Colonial Rule and restoring Freedom to the people of Kenya which according to Kenyatta and his Kenyan People, had been stolen or usurped from them by a foreign Colonial Rule which, at the same time, neither respected them nor was of any substantial use to their Human Rights and Civil Rights enshrined in the UN Charter; and finally the Tanganyika African National Union (TANU) leader, Julius K. Nyerere, who was also arrested and sentenced to jail in 1958 for his rebellious goal against the security of the British Colonial Rule using TANU jail but who agree to pay a fine in lieu of a jail sentence.

4. Numerous Bribery acts by foreign masters to earmarked African Leaders with a view to luring and using them to enhance and promote the goals of these foreign masters in Africa at the expense of the goals of the Nation-States of Africa. Prima facie evidences

include, for example, Joseph Kasavubu, Moise Tsombe and Mobutu Sese Seko of the Republic of Congo now called Democratic Republic of Congo who, because of such bribery in both cash and in kind, became so much wealthy and intoxicated by the source of such bribery that they were easy to be foolishly used by this source as a tool against their own national goal and leadership which often resulted into the assassination of their own Prime Minister, Patrice Lumumba, in 1961 for having been perceived by that source of such bribery as being a communist and therefore a real threat to the socio-economic and political security of that source particularly the Union Minere based in Katanga Province in the Eastern Region of that Country which belonged to the Belgium settlers; and Mobutu Sese Seko who, after the fall of both Kasavubu and Tsombe through natural death, became so much rich from such bribery coming from the same source due to the latter's acute Cold War with the Communist Camp in Africa and Total World that his wealth overwhelmingly exceeded the Gross Nation Product (GNP) of his own Country (Zaire) that he rules—a fact which also raise other serious questions against the competence and honesty of the African leadership to effectively defend Africa's goal today though the Cold War has now ended. It is this source which is the actual root-cause of bribery of the present culture of corruption and Bad Governance in entire Africa. It is this massive bribery by this source during the Cold War Era that planted corruption in Africa's Ecosystem. This bribery, in turn, bred lies, stealing, dishonesty, leadership mediocracy, intolerance and conflict throughout Africa. All this collectively generated a Culture of a Bad Governance which is now already a permanent virus in the attitude (theory) and behaviour (practice) of every African Civil Servant which is another serious concern against the competence of both the Security and the Law Enforcement Forces of every African Nation-State to defend Africa's Security and Sovereign Equality enshrined in the UN Charter.

5. Numerous Wide Spread Dumping cases on the African Markets and total African Ecosystem against the health security of the Peoples of Africa, the dignity of African national Leaders, and sovereign equality of African nation-States on the World Market Delinquency against African nation-States. These acts of delinquency include, for example the Dumping on the African Markets reject, substandard and obsolete manufactured goods such as bicycles, razor trades, vehicles, TVs, electrical items, medicines and many other manufactured items especially from non-European Countries which have already been proved unfit for the markets of their countries

lacking a liable life expectancy worth to one's effort of procuring them; Dumping of unsafe food stuffs such as corn, powdered milk, etc. which have been already declared expired or unfit for human consumption in their own counties of manufacture but which come to be dumped on the African Market or offered to African national leaders with false pretense as "Food Aid", "Food for Peace", "Food for Freedom" or "Food for Partnership" while the donor country knows very well that this food is not safe for human health security; Dumping on the African markets dangerous manufactured chemicals such as DDT etc. which has already been scientifically tested and proven too dangerous to the ecosystem by the country of manufacture; Dumping of absolete medicines such as the famously dreadful Depo Proverra and other contraceptives which have already been scientifically proven dangerous to the human use and therefore legally banned by the Court of Law in the manufacturing country but which have always secretly found ways to enter African markets and Total African Ecosystem to make huge profits from the African Nation-States, and irreparable injuries on their nationals without any protection from these dangers by their respective Political Leaders; and the Dumping of contaminated foods on the African Markets with false labeling as in the on-going case of falsely labeling of the mad cow meats whose carcasses have already been banned on all markets throughout the European Union (EU) hemisphere but which are paradoxically allowed to enter into the African market without any due regard to the health security by African leadership to effectively defend Africa's health security and other goals.

6. A One-sided Retorsion policy against Africa's goals e.g., the recent banning of the importation of the African fresh water fish particularly from East Africa (Kenya, Tanzania and Uganda) by the markets of the European Union (EU) hemisphere on the grounds that the fish was a health hazard to human consumption in Europe due to the chemical fishing means that was being used at that time by the fishing industry on Lake Victoria. To defend their policy, the EU markets argue that this is a kin to the same manner that the same EU had banned its mad cow meats on its markets. While this was a noble action on the EU's part, it is therefore open to question why the same EU could, at the same time, turn around and export the same banned mad cow meat carcasses to Africa markets with a deliberate view to selling them on these markets without any concern, sympathy or compassion for the health security of Africa and her Peoples! What a pity!! Is this not tantamount to murder? How different is it from the Nazi policy's goal that the Allies fought against in World War II who are

now the same key architects of the EU. And, whose of all, while all this World Market Delinquency was paradoxically allowed to go on by the unscrupulous EU Leadership and Peoples, the affected African Leadership and Peoples equally did a zero work by keeping quiet! What a pity to Africa's glory and dignity! How can they successfully claim for Sovereign Equality while they cannot have the courage to effectively defend their possessional goal and rights for mileu goal?

7. Alarming increase of Brain-drain of African Expertise from Africa into foreign Countries looking for greener pastures because of the negligence of the African Leadership which marginalizes and ignores the rare strategic national importance of these expertise in preference of foreign expertise whose remuneration is paradoxically too exorbitant for a poor African country to afford. Another paradox is that whereas they are too expensive, they are not professionally competent and also fully sympathetic and supportive to the goal of Africa and her people, as African expertise are on the questions of Africa's health Security, Leadership Security, Science and Technology Security, National Dignity Security, Professionalism Security, etc. Obviously this Brain-drain poses a serious nagging question against the competence and wisdom of African leadership who have always failed to recognize this problem as a real threat to their own national security and dignity.

8. Recurrent widespread student riots and rampage throughout Africa is another serious challenge to the African Leadership's ability and competence to maintain peace and stability at home as Africa's Goal Number One that every African Leader must seek and pursue at all costs in order for that leadership to attract foreign investors and investment into Africa to boost Socio-Economic Recovery and Development in the continent. Obviously, no foreign investor can afford to invest in a chaotic country in which the investment is likely to collapse due to this instability.

9. An absence of a Hybrid Culture in Africa which is a culture that is free from and resistant, resilient and robust to bribery, dishonesty and all acts of corruption and other symptoms of bad governance because of its firm belief in Theocentric Humanism Philosophy characterized by Holiness, Perfection (or Excellence) and Godliness and the Doctrine of Summum Bonum characterized by a belief in justice, wisdom, Temperance (or Compassion), Courage, Dignity (or Self-Love and Self-Respect) and Tolerance by every one in a Society which Africa is totally lacking and which she

should have as pre-requisite in order for her to not only achieve a needed enabling environment for a rapid socio-economic recovery and development, and to attract foreign investors into the Continent to boost her socio-economic recovery and development.

10. Acute Abject Poverty which has for years, tormented and agonized the overwhelming majority of the Peoples of Kenya and Total Africa and is now on an increase. Its impact is manifested in various ways, e.g their miserable per capital income of less than US $400 p.a.; poor health care; poor diet; poor housing (shelter); and unaffordable inflated costs fo child education; food stuffs,; medicines; etc. By virtue of this miserable poverty, most Africans cannot afford to live a decent life like their minority filthy-wealthy counterpart, in the same Continent. This is exactly the reason why these most poor are always psychologically forced to indulge into heinous illegal and health-hazard socio-economic activities such as brewing and drinking of poisonous brews. They are forced to do so with a view to inoculating themselves with such brews so that it may give them a possible relief from their day and night agonizing memories of acute poverty nightmares. Although this act has already proved to be too dangerous in Kenya in 2000 for having resulted into a total of over 137 Kenyans dead and over 500 in critical condition in hospital in a single week from drinking such brew, the fact is that most Kenyans are too poor to do without it. Most of them cannot afford the inflated cost of the legalized and safe drinks such as beer, whisky, gin, vodka, wine, etc whose cost has been deliberately inflated by the establishment (regime) on false excuse of socio-economic liberalization in Kenya and Total Africa as so demanded by the Donor countries who are also the same Super Powers who control the economy on the World Market and the Balance of Payment that all African Countries do not have and must, therefore, seek at all costs in order for them to survive.

11. Super Power Industrial Mafia on the World Market by which the socio-economically and militarily powerful Nation-States of the Industrialized World ruthlessly expropriate this leverage to hoard their economic advantage and discourage all attempts of both African nation-States and other socio-economically and militarily poor (weak) Nation-States aimed at creating their own industrial capability on the contention that such attempts could energize Africa and enable her to become equal with them and then begin to not only compete but also to interfere with their super industrial Mafia monopoly on the World Market.

12. Numerous shocking cases of International Terrorism against the security of the leadership and peoples of Africa such as the recent cases of Bomb blasts in both Nairobi and Dar es Salaam cities in 1998 causing untold havoc and sorrows not only to Kenya and Tanzania but also to the Entire African Continent—a situation which could again happen to Africa at will in future due to the strategic weakness of not only Kenya and Tanzania but also most African Countries which are still strategically too weak to protect themselves against such acts of terrorism as effectively as strategically powerful countries such as USA, UK, etc are each able to protect themselves and their destiny (goals).

13. Their inability to uphold their pacta sunt servanda enshrined in the normal functioning of the International System with respect to the Original and Vicarious Responsibilities which reach sovereign nation-state is expected by that System under International law to recognize and carryout at all times on the World Market. Numerous prima facie evidences of this problem abound. These include, for instance, the recent bomb explosions in Nairobi, Kenya and Dar es Salaam, Tanzania in 1998, which according to the International Law, Kenya and Tanzania each had the rights and obligations to prevent from happening. Otherwise, each was liable for or supposed to be charged for the offense of an Original Responsibility if it ever had a prior knowledge of the act and did collaborate with the actor(s); or to be charged for a Vicarious Responsibility if at al each neither had any prior knowledge nor collaborated with the actor(s). But the fact is that like all other African nation-states, both Kenya and Tanzania are so poor and too weak socio-economically, politically and militarily that they could hardly have had the necessary means by which to know in advance the intentions of those internationally sophisticated terrorists in the same manner the most highly sophisticated Super Powers such as the USA, UK, etc could have done. This is exactly another serious prima facie evidence against the security of all African nation-States on The World Market. Although they are entitled to the privileges and rights of sovereign Equality on the World Market, these litmus paper tests listed above totally disqualify that theory.

14. Acute Intra-and Inter-African Leadership Schisms, Assassinations and Detentions which has been rocking and tormenting the entire African Continent from the Colonial Era to the Post-Colonial Era—a situation which has had nothing to do with the Super Powers' political influence at all but which was solely an African leadership's

creation influenced by the obsolete pseudo-scientific geopolitical colonial theory of Survival of the Fittest gained from Charles Darwin and Niccolo Machiavelli and which, has often foolishly misled certain African leaders into a vain assumption that whoever was able to successfully influence the masses using every means necessary including use of terror and murder of one's opponent(s) wherever necessary automatically qualified to control the Political Scene of leadership for life. This is exactly the crazy and most suicidal theory which has, over the years, fooled most African leaders into numerous heinous assassinations, detentions and imprisonment of their own African colleagues. Vivid recent examples include, for instance, Paul Tembo of Zambia who had been President Chiluba's former Campaign Manager and Vice President but expelled from Chiluba's Ruling Party in June, 2001 and then foolishly murdered on Friday, 6 July, 2001 using such theory simply because of his resentment against President Chiluba's bid for a Third Term Tenure as Zambian President (Sunday Nation, July 8, 2001, p.7); Dr. Robert Ouko of Kenya who had been the Kenyan Foreign Minister in the President Daniel Toroitich arap Moi Government during his heinous assassination in 1988 for the same contagious virus of Acute Intra-and Inter-African Leadership Schisms, Assassinations and Detentions tormenting the continent ever since the Colonial Era. Vivid cases of detention of Oginga Odinga include that which was totally antithetical to the Original Goal of Uhuru (Freedom) struggle in Kenya against the British Colonial Rule; and that of Kenneth Matiba who was detained due to his opposition to the Single Party Mode of Democracy in Kenya. Other vivid cases include self-exile in foreign countries because of fear of their life if they dared to return to their own Mother Countries.

15. Inter-African nation-State War of Aggression continues to be another devastating virus against the security goal of not only the African Nation-States in the Eastern Africa Region but also in the Total African Continent since the Continent began to achieve her freedom from the Colonial Masters in the 1950's and 1960's. Vivid prima facie cases of this virus include, for instance, the on-going military invasion of the Democratic Republic of Congo (DRC) by the combined forces of Uganda, Rwanda and Burundi on pretext that they have a duty to do so for their own security reasons against their rebels alleged by the three countries to be hiding in the DRC between the said three invading forces and the combined forces of the DRC and the DRC's allies viz: Zimbabwe, Angola, Namibia, Chad and Mozambique. Another symptom of this virus is the invasion of Rwanda effective 1st October, 1990 by the combined forces

of Uganda and the forces of the Rwanda Patriotic Front (RPF) called the Rwanda Patriotic Army (RPA) on Uganda's pretext that she had the duty to do so with a view to aiding the RPF and RPA to liberate Rwanda from the unwanted Hutu Leadership of President Jevenal Habyarimana—an ill-conceived act which has so far resulted into more than two million Rwandese dead and a loss of property of unquantifiable value in Rwanda effective the day President Habyarimana's plane was shot down by the same invading forces while the said plane was landing at Kigali Airport in the evening of 6$^{th}$ April, 1994 to the present (July, 2001).

16. An intensifying Wide Spread Neo-Viking Thuggery manifested in various forms of viruses akin to the old Northern or Viking robbery of 8$^{th}$-10$^{th}$ century characterized by armed robbery mainly of the banking and other commercial institutions, residences, vehicles, etc. On the one hand; and the Mafia robbery characterized by corruptive demand for commissions from the goods and passenger transporters by both traffic police officers and touts popularly known in Kenya as "Manambas" and found at every highway bus stop. Both viruses are now so much institutionalized and entrenched in the African political culture that socio-economic and political security in the Continent is already in the Intensive Care Unit (ICU) requiring a major surgery to remove the viruses from the culture.

17. An Increasing Wide Spread of Unemployment throughout the Eastern Africa and the Total Continent arising mainly from the on-going ili-conceived policy of Employee Retrenchment which is consequently not doing the Region and Total Continent any good other than taking the matter from the frying pan and putting into the fire. In fact, a Clinical Diagnosis of the virus of the on-going Wide Spread Thurgery indicated in Problem No. 16 above shows that this virus is a function of this on-going feeble minded policy of Employee Retrenchment which has now increased and intensified both armed robbery and cunning robbery in the Region and the Total Continent.

18. Prevalent Institutionalized Culture of Corruption manifested in massive looting of public property in the form of cash money and fixed assets such as land, plots, buildings, farms, etc. for personal use paradoxically by the same Government Officials who are expected under oath to be the custodians of these properties—a fact which is, therefore, a serious acid test against the competence and legitimacy of Good Governance in Africa on the one hand; and also an acid test against Africa's

rightful claim or demand for Sovereign Equality on the World Market in view of this decaying Culture. A further Clinical Diagnosis of this looting mania in Africa shows the following striking revelation: Because of this mania, most African Government coffers are virtually dry. Most revenues from all forms fo taxes and the Donor Aid have already mysteriously disappeared. They cannot be easily traced. Even if they have to be traced, the law enforcement organ which is expected to sniff and apprehend the culprit for this crime is also a culprit of the same crime. Its only national option is to remain cool and pretend to be doing something good instead of trying to chase its own shadow and blood. This is precisely the reason why the Golden Berg case and similar cases all over Africa are simply mirages. They cannot be pursued. It is for this reason that on-going ill-conceived policy of Employee Retrenchment was hatched out as the only national choice by which to cut down national recurrent expenditures on personnel emoluments since the national coffer already lacks enough funds due to such left and right lootings by its own guardians. In the final analysis, the policy is not for the greatest good of Africa as it has been so alleged by its architects and builders. The truth is that it is a two edges word: First, it is to protect the coffer guardians by using the defenseless employee as a scapegoat and shield of these guardians against a potential public outcry and other acts of retortion against them demanding to know where the looted public assets went and also for an immediate return of these assets to the public coffer if these guardians prove unable to pay public staff salaries due to lack of funds. And second, it is to enable these guardians to sustain their tenure against the Opposition who are already another government in the waiting and very hungry for the take-over and a possible prosecution of the out-going coffer guardians. This is precisely the main root-cause of the on-going pathological climate now haunting almost every African nation-state leadership not only in the Eastern Africa Region but also in the entire Continent. And, it is also the same reason why most African Governments which are now in power are proving too difficult in handing over power through a free and fair elections; and the reason why assassinations, detentions, and coups d'etat continue to hound the Continent thereby making it virtually impossible for the Continent to effectively defend its possessional goals and also pursue its competitive goals on the World Market.

In view of all these eighteen acid tests militating against strategic capabilities of African Nation-States to defend their people's Human Rights such as their rights to good health and dignity in the International Community, the nagging question is thus:—**Do East African**

**Nation-States actually have necessary capability to do so? And do they have enough or reliable bargaining capacity to effectively compete with such most powerful and aggressive Nation-States such as USA, UK, Japan, France, Germany etc.on the World Market for the possessional and milieu goals they believe to be definitely theirs and most essential for their national survival and dignity in the International Community? If so, how can we explain this phenomenon with a high degree of parsimony, precision and satisfaction in our scientific World? And, through what behavioural law(s) or body of knowledge can this dynamics be explained, predicted and understood better than it had been done before by other research on the same subject?**

## 2. Purpose

In view of these nagging questions noted above, the purpose of this Paper is to clinically examine very meticulously the goals, problems and strategies of the East Africa and of the African nation-states on the World Market in terms of (a) what these goals are (b) similarities between their goals and the goals of other nation-states; (c) what strategies African nation-states use to defend or acquire such goals and why; (d) problems facing African nation-states in pursuit or defense of these goals; (e) how African nation-states manipulate and adapt themselves to such problems, and (f) the political implications of the interaction between these two major variables: the East African nation-states on the one hand; and the goals, problems and strategies of the World market on the other.

## 3. Methodology

This paper is divided into Six Parts. Part 1 examines contending theories in the Normal Social Sciences literature[9] on the subject matter. Part 11 gives a critique of such theories, and systematically re-examines the problem of using an inter-disciplinary approach which shall include Anatomy, Physiology and Ontology of The International System as a container of The World Market. It shall use this new and unique approach, in order to illuminate the reasons why and how nation-states behave as they habitually do on the world market vis-a-vis certain goals. Part III examines the relative strength of East African nation-states (hereafter referred to as the African Nation-States) on the World Market in order to determine whether they also really have any significant basis of bargaining power with their competitors. Part IV examines the problems facing African nationstates on the World Market resulting from their relative strength as compared to other members of that market. Also, it gleans from such experiences some useful behavioural laws which constantly govern the political atmosphere between African nation-states and other nationstates. Part V clinically diagnosis certain fundamental strategies which these African nation-states have always employed against certain anti-bodies internally. Finally, Part VI systematically synthesizes these findings into some parsimonious body of knowledge called Behavioural Laws through which the conduct of African nation-states in the East African Region and the Total Continent on the World Market for their survival may be properly understood with a high degree of precision and confidence.

CHAPTER II

# Contending Theories on National Goals on the World Market Re-Examined

## (A) Observation

### 1. First Observation: Historical Reality in World Politics

Under the Charter of the United Nations,[10] individual and collective maintenance of international peace and security; belief in and respect of pacta sunt servanda; promotion of international co-operation and fundamental principles of human rights; respect for the principles of sovereign equality; self-determination and territorial integrity among nation-states; and the like, collectively constitute the basic goals which every member of the international community not only ought to respect, uphold and pursue at all times but is naturally expected by all others to do so in keeping with the protocols, principles and rules on International Law. While nation-states may pursue other goals, they have to do so within the spirits of these rules.

Their rules are expected to contribute to, but not to conflict with or undermine these goals. Thus, every nation-state is bound to defend these goals at all times and at all cost. Failure to do so constitutes a potential threat to the principles and purposes for which the United Nations was created after World War II.

A similar idea is mirrored directly and indirectly in 100% of bilateral and multilateral agreements and treaties in international political life free of spatio temporal context. It exists in the Charters of e.g, the East African Community (1999),Inter-Government Authority on Development (IGDA, 1987) the Organization of African Unity (OAU, 1963), and the newly created African Union (AU, 2001), the North Atlantic Treaty Organization (NATO 1949), and the Warsaw pact (1951); and, in the Treaty of Versalles or the League of Nations Convent (1919), the Treaty of Westphalia (16480, the Treaty of Toresillas (1494), the Treaty of the first phase of the Peloponnesian War (421 B.C.)[11] and the Egyptian-Hittite Treaty of Non-Aggression (1284BC).

Whereas apart from a record on Egyptian-Hittite bilateral relations in which each party was duty-bound to legally recognize and live with each other in mutual peace and to aid each other during emergencies, we may lack any other accurate record of international politics before the Hellenic Civilization; and whereas, although our modern nation-states originated from the peace for Westphalia in 1648 AD, it is self-evident that based on our own empirical experiences of International Politics since the Treaty of Westpalia of 1648, these goals are perennial and extremely crucial for the survival of every nation-state. And, they are likely to remain the fundamental universal basis of our future International Politics beyond the year 2001. hence, the discovery and significance of this Research not only for Political Science but also for Science in total.

## 2. Second Observation: Contending Theories in the Normal Social Sciences Literature

In the Normal Social Sciences Literature, numerous contending theories abound anent national goals and strategies designed to help attain such goals and constraints against such strategies. For instance, Anorld Wolfer[12] notes (1) that nation-states pursue milieu goals, i.e., those values which they do not have and must, therefore, get from the world market by trading with other nation-states, e.g., equal trading rights and opportunities and other economic benefits. And (2) that nation-states strive to protect their possessional goals, i.e., values which nation states already have (e.g., territory, sovereignty, self-love and self respect, and the like) at all times and cost. Talcott Parsons, David Easton and other system theorists contend that every living entity performs four cardinal functions which constitute the basic goals of every political or social system: Pattern Maintenance, Adaptation, Goal attainment, and integration[13].

A similar finding but with a different approach is also held by Gabriel A. Almond and other structural functionalists.[14] To them, all political systems are similar in their input, output, functions and goals. Inputs consist of political socialization and recruitment, interest articulation, interest aggregation, and political communication; output consist of rule making, rule application, and rule adjudication. In order to achieve these goals effectively, every political system has some capabilities with which to pursue such goals. Each political system has also administrative capabilities (regulative, extractive and distributive), conversion capabilities (interest articulation, interest aggregation, rule making, rule application, rule adjudication and political communication), and system theorist Abraham Maslow [15] adds that all living organism have common aspirations; they all seek similar basic needs. These include security, self actualization, food shelter, love, and the like.

But, each nation-state has constraints (financial, intellectual or prudence, military, manpower, etc) which collectively militate against the effectiveness and efficacy of each nation-state's capabilities. Hence the purpose of part II of this paper below

## (B) A Critique <u>Vis A Vis</u> Those Contending Theories

It is reasonable to assume, based on the argument in part I, that the common, fundamental goal of every nation-sate is to defend and nourish itself at all costs. Also, it is plausible that nation-state are <u>rational</u> beings in that they prudently analyze their past experiences as means of acquiring their perceived goals or of protecting their possession goals.

By doing so, nation-states avoid risks and maximize their netgains. Also they have a concept of <u>pacta sunt servanda</u>, i.e, the ability to respect and uphold their mutual contract, agreement or treaty.

However, as fully documented in the problem statement of this this which, in turn, is the justification of the Clinical Diagnosis, it is essential to note that although every nation-state's basic goal is survival and, in spite of the fact that every nation-state will do anything possible in order to survive, it is doubtful that all nation-states use similar strategies vis-à-vis their possession and milieu goals. Any assumption which purports that nation-states are identical in their aspirations for goals fails to realize that nation-states are a kin to human beings in capabilities, mentality, and temperaments. They fail to realize that nation-states are essentially human beings and that they, therefore differ in their geopolitical, economic, military, social demographic, scientific and technological, and information gathering and deciphering capabilities[16] and most serious of mistakes, they fail to realize that due to amorphous and cephalous nature of the world market, the latter is too anarchical to ensure a high degree of Hobbes' <u>pacta sunt servanda17</u>

Numerous empirical evidences shows that due to the anarchical nature of the world Market, certain nation-state have a tendency to exploit their national capabilities for their own egocentric /self goals without regard to international law under chapter 1 of the UN xviii. To these nation-states, ultimo ratio (war) is also diplomacy by other means. Consequently, those Nation-States which are relatively weak on the world market find it difficult to either acquire most of those milieu goals they need for their own nations, or defend their possessional goals from external aggression by other bully nation-states.

The weak find it difficult to resist that strength of the other often pressed to act in ways which economically and politically benefit only those other bully nation-states. They feed the cow but do not milk it. It is milked by and for the benefits of those nation-State which are relatively strong on the world market[18]. In the final analysis, from the Anthropocentric Humanism it is the fittest that enjoys the fruits of the weaker's labour.[xx] The fittest decides who gets what, when, how and why. And above all, it determines the fate of the weak members of the world market.

It is plausible that such arguments could be spurious. However, this anarchical behavior is neither unique to nation-states, nor does it apply only to those species that charles Darwin studied. It is common to every species of the Animal kingdom. For instance, in every given species, the strength of each member of that species determines the status and power location of each member relative to other members.

Thus, it is strength which determines who is who in the system, and the power configuration of, the system. Within a group of every species, the survival of weaker members is always at the mercy of the stronger ones. Among the fish species, the powerful ones, such as sharks, dolphins, mud fish, trout, white fish, in turn, feed on less powerful species, such worms, fungi and the like. In the like manner, the most powerful ones such as lions, cheetahs, leopards, hyenas and the like feed on the less powerful ones such as rabbits, deer, monkeys, squirrels, wild pigs and the like.

Furthermore it is plausible that stronger animals are often carnivores; they have no other choice but to feed on other animals because their biological constitution conditions them to do so in order to survive. But, carnivores do not bother elephants. If carnivores must exist at the expense of the lives of other animals, why do they not feed on elephant? Carnivores never attack elephant, even when carnivores are very hungry, due to elephants' enormous physical strength, greater than every carnivores power. The obvious law therefore is succinctly that carnivores exclude elephant from their menu, not because elephants are not delicious; only because of the elephants' enormous deterrent power.

Another striking behavioural pattern among animals which resembles the behavioural patterns of Nation-States is that a species never seeks to act foolishly. If A is to exploit B, A's success in doing so will be highly dependent on A's knowledge of the relative capabilities of A and B. Thus, unless A is physically stronger than B, it is likely that A will dare to exploit B or make B act for the benefit of A. Another prerequisite is that, in order for A to attempt to exploit B, there must exist certain goals which A considers essential for its survival. A can use B as a means to achieve its goals only if A knows that by doing so A would benefit.

In other words, A would use B only if such exploitation was A's efficient way fo achieving A's goals. On the World Market, these three fundamental patterns of exploitation behaviour may be explained in the following three behavioural models:-

Model I: A may use B to acquire certain goals (x), possessed by a third party (c) as Israel used Kenya to rescue Israel hostages in Uganda since Israel could not successfully do it alone without the aid of one of Uganda's neighbours (Fig. 1).

Fig. I

| A ——→ | B ——→ | X |
|---|---|---|
| e.g., Israel | e.g., Kenya | e.g., Israel hostages in C (Uganda) |

Model II: A may use B to acquire goals (x) in B's possession, as industrialized nation-States use African and other nation-states to acquire raw material cheaply (Fig. II)

Fig. II

| A ——→ | B ——→ | X |
|---|---|---|
| e.g., the U.S | e.g., Zaire Democratic Republic of Congo | e.g., Uranium in B's (Congo's jurisdiction) |

Model III: A may use B to acquire certain goals (x) that are in B's possession, but A, for one reason or another, is unable or unwilling to expand the effort to make use of its own resources (Fig. III)

Fig. III

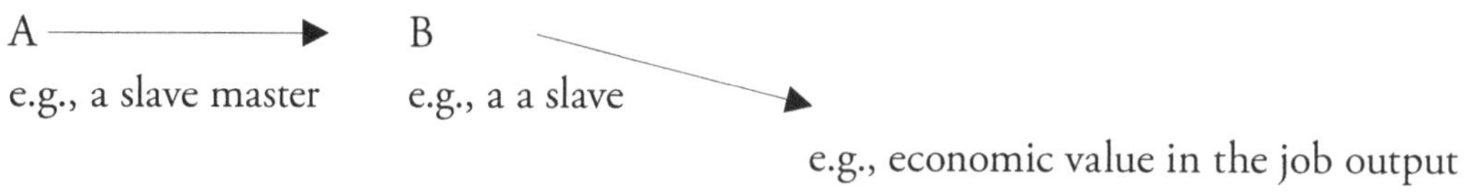


<u>Source</u>: Author's work-product (Dec. 2000)

Although non-human species do not often exploit each other along these indicated behavioural line, they also engage in exploitation. For example, carnivore exploit the lives of other animals which they use as their food. Also the dominant members(s) of a given species often grab economic and social values (i.e., food, shelter and sex) from the weaker member(s) of that species. However, in most species, the strongest male normally tries to usurp and monopolize all the female. Among the lions for example, it is normally the lioness which hunts. But once she has killed her prey, she does not get to enjoy the fruits of her labours. The lion often takes the prey from the rightful owner. Because of her inferior strength, the lioness always gives in to the lion. It is until the stronger (the lion) has finished eating and is well satisfied that he will allow the weak lioness and the young ones to eat the left-overs.

Similarly, in the same Animal Kingdom, with regard to sex, the strongest male has no more sexual desires than weaker males has. However, the strongest of all always monopolizes the females. This reality holds true among dogs, cats, cattle, goats, birds, and other species. Empirical evidence overtime shows that a bully male will always board females, and chase away other males in order to satisfy its greedy lust.

This behavioural law permeates and governs almost all members of the Animal Kingdom in below the Human Beings but mildly does so also among the Human Beings.

It is plausible that human behaviour can neither be equated with animal behaviour, nor be understood, explained or predicted with a high degree of parsimony, precision and confidence from an enthological context.

However, human behaviour is little different from other species' behaviour in the Animal Kingdom.[19] Empirical evidences drawn from the International System effective the Treaty of WestPhalia in 1648 shows that all Nation-States and all other species have a tendency to feel frustrated when either mentally or physically disturbed by others, hunger, thirst, sexual desires and so on. They all respond to threats; they all have the propensity to defend their pride, their territory, love, prestige, young and other possessional goals; and, they all are likely to seek and pursue certain perceived milieu goals such as food, territory prestige, water and love.

In this regard, it is one's strategic strength which determines one's position among other members for any given species. But, Nation-States are living human entities. Therefore nation-States, it is also national strength which determines a Nation-State's status on the World Market. The fittest Nation-States decide who gets what, when, how and why. They determine the fate of all weaker Nation-States. Consequently, not all Nation-States behave equally on the World Market, and not all successfully attain what they believe are their rightfull goals. Weaker nation-States are often the losers because of their inadequate bargaining power on the World Market. Weaker Nation-States such as African countries do not have the chance to defend their possessional goals or acquire those milieu goals which they seek as the fitter nations do. Like Congo in 1960 and Uganda in1976 when those African Nation-States were easily invaded by Belgium and Israel respectively without any sufficient degree of resistance from both Congo and Uganda due to their military weakness below the military strength of Belgium and Israel respectively, all African Nation-States are automatic victims of not only the capability superiority of the stronger Nation-States but also of their own weakness and lack of the zeal to eradicate or alleviate that liability in the International System due to their mismanagement of their own resources through corruption and civil strife. This is the fundamental constraint and reason why their goals and concerns on the world Market are not usually matters of much concern to the stronger parties.[20]

However, since African Nation-States are also living organisms, it is possible that they also hold their own survival at the top of their list of objectives and will use whatever necessary to attain that goal, as any entity always does. Hence, our purpose in the following Part III of this paper.

# CHAPTER III

# Two Broad Forms of National Goals and Their Problems and Behavioural Laws on the World Market

## (A) Basic Domestic Goals and Their Problems

To understand the goals, problems and strategies of the East African nation-state, we must first conceptualize the latter as living human entities composed of a network of interactions and an interdependence of parts, defined in terms of individuals. Also, we must perceive these individuals as a configuration of both formal political sub-systems (political parties, legislatures, cabinets, judiciaries, and the bureaucracy) and informal political sub-systems (social clubs, ethnic groups, nuclear families and other pressure groups). These sub-systems have their various functions, roles, norms, goals and strategies, all rooted into, and determined by the civic culture of the main system, the Nation-state. And, since as David Easton notes "every political system . . . is a set of interactions, abstracted from the totality of social behaviour, through which goods and services are authoritatively allocated for society,"[21] it is equally self-evident that the individual's behaviour in such a network are necessary to their Nation-States, in that they articulate their support for and their demands on the system.

But, if so, how do African political systems, in turn, aggregate, accommodate and satisfy these inputs?[22] In other words, compared to the most politically and socio-economically powerful Nation-States today such as the United States, Russia, the Peoples Republic of China, the United Kingdom, France, Japan and others due to their most amazing level of socio-economic development, per capita income, life expectancy, military capability and science and technology, do African Nation-States have the capacity to make binding decisions and the ability to implement those decisions on the World Market?

Compared to highly developed Nation-States, how much loyalty and economic support do African Nation-States receives from within and without their domestic jurisdictions to sustain themselves? What support do they, in turn, offer their citizens from the world Market? What are their common problems (constraints) and strategies against such problems?

It is generally accepted that he central concern of a polity is to mobilize its societal resources into goals (goods and services) for the members of its systems. However, it would be presumptuous for anyone to analyze the political behaviour[23] of any given African Nation-State in World Politics without fully comprehending its unique political history, on the one hand, and its relative bargaining strength on the World Market, on the other.[24]

Geographically, Africa is an amazing land mass of approximately 11, 700, 000 square miles situated in a winter problem-free zone. Because of this amazing God-given climatically advantage, it is ever-green all year round. However, in spite of these natural advantages which are totally non-existent in North America and Europe which dominate the monopoly of socio-economic and military superiority in the International System as of today (2000). Africa has very little arable land. The North is almost covered by the Sahara Desert, except only a small arable strip align the Southern coast of the Mediterranean Sea which is favoured by. In the South, the Kalahari (Namibia) Desert occupies almost the whole of Southwest Africa. Agronomically, most of Africa is barren.

Where the land is arable at all, it has poor, red soil; it is infested with carriers of malaria, sleeping sickness, bilharzia, and other tropical diseases; its science and technology are underdeveloped and other means essential for abundant socio-economic growth are lacking.[25] Because of these deficiencies and other symptoms of constraints in African Nation-States, most African Nation-States are frequently caught in a cobweb of socio-economic and hygienic problems. Some lack treated or safe drinking water, living instead on water from ponds, rivers or lakes. Some Nation-States, such as Senegal, must import their treated drinking water from as far away as France. Politically, contemporary African Nation-State; are significantly young compared to Britain, France, the United States Japan and the Soviet Union (see Table 1). Between 1900 and 1949, there were only two African Nation-States, Ethiopia and Liberia.[26] It was not until the 1950's and 1960's that African Nation-States began to form. Even though many of them are now independent, they have not yet reached a political maturation, i.e., a significant national integration and patriotism as found in the United States, the United Kingdom, France, Japan, the Soviet Union and the longer-established Nation-States. Consequently, the African Nation-States' foreign policy and status on the World Market still lack significant internal and external support by comparison.

**Table 1: Frequency Distribution of African Colonies Achieving Freedom from their Respective Colonial Rulers (1900-1978)**

| Year | Belgian | British | French | Portuguese | Spanish | Total |
|---|---|---|---|---|---|---|
| 1900-04 | 0 | 0 | 0 | 0 | 0 | 0 |
| 1905-09 | 0 | 0 | 0 | 0 | 0 | 0 |
| 1910-14 | 0 | 0 | 0 | 0 | 0 | 0 |
| 1915-19 | 0 | 0 | 0 | 0 | 0 | 0 |
| 1920-24 | 0 | 0 | 0 | 0 | 0 | 0 |
| 1925-29 | 0 | 0 | 0 | 0 | 0 | 0 |
| 1930-34 | 0 | 0 | 0 | 0 | 0 | 0 |
| 1935-39 | 0 | 0 | 0 | 0 | 0 | 0 |
| 1940-44 | 0 | 0 | 0 | 0 | 0 | 0 |
| 1945-49 | 0 | 0 | 0 | 0 | 0 | 0 |
| 1950-54 | 0 | 1 | 3 | 0 | 0 | 1 |
| 1955-59 | 0 | 2 | 15 | 0 | 0 | 5 |
| 1960-64 | 3 | 9 | 1 | 0 | 0 | 27 |
| 1965-69 | 0 | 4 | 0 | 0 | 1 | 6 |
| 1970-74 | 0 | 0 | 0 | 0 | 0 | 0 |
| 1975-78 | 0 | 0 | | 0 | 3 | 3 |
| x | 3 | 16 | 19 | 3 | 1 | 42 |
| Y | 3 | 20* | 21 | 5 | 5m | 54** |
| Proportion (%) | 100.00 | 80.00 | 90.48 | 60.00 | 20.00 | 77.78 |

X = Total number of colonies which are now independent

Y = Total number of African countries which were occupied as "colonies"

* = Three of which are Namibia (or South West Africa), South Africa (as universally perceived by Africans) and Zimbabwe (or Rhodesia).

| | | |
|---|---|---|
| + | = | Table excludes both Germany and Italy because the colonies they had occupied were removed from them by the Allies after World War 1. |
| ** | = | For details on frequency distribution of these countries among European Colonial powers, see the tables Appendix 1—below, and the General appendices. The tables show exactly which country was occupied by whom before independence. On the other hand, Chapters II-VIII show how these countries revolted against their respective colonial rulers. The chapters also show how group formation (political parties) became essential to African nationalist in the course of their interest articulation against the colonial rule. |
| M | = | Two of the (Ifni and Spanish Sahara) were ceded to Morocco in 1969 and to Morocco and Mauritania in 1976 respectively. |

<u>Source</u>: Author's work-product. Data computed from Appendix 1-1, of my book <u>Cause-Effects of African Nationalism in World Politics,</u> University Press of America, 1983

Socio-economically, Contemporary Africa is inchoate compared to highly developed nation-states such as the United States, the United Kingdom and France (see Table 2, below). The average income per person in independent Africa is 95.84% <u>less</u> than the average income per person in developed countries; the mobility rate per African is <u>lower</u> than that in the developed countries by 63.24%, the average literacy rate in Africa is <u>lower</u> than the literacy rate in the developed countries by 75.76%; and the average life expectancy in Africa is 54.72% <u>lower</u> than that in the more developed countries.

Due to these weaknesses, African average mortality rate is significantly higher than that of the developed countries by 83.81% per 1,000 births and by 58.33% per 1,000 population. And, between 1979 and today (2000), the situation is now extremely critical due to the emergence of Aids epidemic and sporadic Ebola and other infectious diseases.

Young and weak as they are on the World Market, how do African nation-states cope with stresses imposed on them from within and outside of their domestic jurisdictions? Can they really satisfy the needs of their citizens? Since the modern, highly informed African is likely to demand improved goods and services (education, housing, medical or health care, proper diet, etc), is it not possible that every African national leader is faced with heavier obligation than the decision-makers in the more highly developed Nation-States? Is it not also possible that leadership maintenance is more difficult in African nation-States than it is in the more highly developed States? Faced with this rough leadership situation, are African decision-makers competent enough to comprehend, analyze, and accommodate the demands imposed upon them? Can the essential consumer goods be obtained from their citizens or will the elites have to resort to repression of their critical nationals in order to deter those demands? Even if the sources of the disturbance were eliminated, is there any guarantee that those elites will be willing to satisfy the needs of their docile citizens? But, according to the data in Tables 1 and 2 above, there is no doubt that African Nation-States are still too poor and weak to compete effectively and with dignity on the World Market. Then, how do they successfully compete with the most powerful nation-States for scarce goods on the World Market? How do they avoid risks and troubles with those fitter nation-States?

In search for the answers to these nagging questions, let us now turn to Part IV here below.

**Table 2: approximate Xs of African and Outside World Socio-Economic Differences**

| Least Developed Countries | Per Capita Income* | Mobility Rate* | Literacy Rate* | Life Expectancy* | Mortality Rate | |
|---|---|---|---|---|---|---|
| AFRICA | $ | % | % | Years | Per 1,000 Births | Per 1,000 Pop |
| Algeria (North) | 660.00 | 37 | 28 | 53 | 86 | 15 |
| Ethiopia (N.E) | 100.00 | 4 | 7 | 38 | 84 | 30 |
| Senegal (N.W) | 315.00 | 5 | 10 | 44 | 93 | 24 |
| Ghana (West) | 394.00 | 42 | 25 | 48 | 156 | 22 |
| Kenya (West) | 209.00 | 42 | 25 | 50 | 54 | 16 |
| Zaire (Congo) | 172.00 | 12 | 12 | 45 | 104 | 21 |
| Lesotho (South) | 115.00 | 22 | 50 | 51 | 114 | 39 |
| Swaziland (S.E) ux | 382.00 | 35 | 36 | 44 | 149 | 22 |
| X | 293.00 | 25 | 24 | 47 | 105 | 24 |

| Highly Developed Countries | $ | % | % | Years | | |
|---|---|---|---|---|---|---|
| Canada | 5,680.00 | 80 | 99 | 73 | 15 | 8 |
| United States | 7,863.00 | 81 | 99 | 73 | 16 | 9 |
| Soviet Union {Russia} | 3,386.00 | 55 | 99 | 70 | 28 | 9 |
| United Kingdom | 3,871.00 | 65 | 99 | 72 | 16 | 18 |
| France | 6,512.00 | 52 | 99 | 72 | 12 | 9 |
| Japan | 5,117.00 | 70 | 99 | 73 | 10 | 6 |
| W. Germany | 7,336.00 | 75 | 99 | 71 | 21 | 12 |
| $X^{-u}$ | 5,681.00 | 68 | 99 | 72 | 17 | 10 |
| X | | | | | | |

*Means computed from Reader's Digest Almanac, The World Almanac, UNESCO, Statistical yearbook, and Official Associated Press Almanac, in combination. Because every source gives different data, this method was used deliberately to eliminate this incongruency.

**$X^{-u}$**

X Unweighted mean of the mean. This method was the only method I could use with maximum net gains because most African countries still lack complete census figures. Also, it was used in the D.C's measurement due to the habitual year-round immigration and emigration that always evade accurate census.

## (B) Basic External Goals and Their Problems

### (1) Their Socio-Economic and Military Weakness

Although African Nation-States, like every Nation-States in the World Community, enjoy equal sovereignty under Chapter 1, Article (4-6), of the United Nations Charter, their inchoate status on the World Market automatically weakens their rights to enjoy equal sovereign status with others. Their socio-economic and military weakness automatically are their serious constraints. This forces them to depend on powerful (industrialized) nation-States for economic and military aid. For instance, when Kenya wanted to deter Idi Amin Dada's Uganda in 1976 from what Kenya called "Uganda's provocation against Kenya" had to rely on assistance from the United States and Israel albeit the public humiliation Kenya had to suffer before other African Nation-States for having collaborated with foreigner(s) against her own sister African Nation-State, Uganda.

### (2) Their Parasitism

It is, therefore, evident that although African Nation-State are independent, they are inevitable victims of their own weakness on the World Market. They are independent in theory only; but in practice, they are parasites. Consequently, they are susceptible to the whims of stronger nations (to foreign subversion and to exploitation), i.e., they are potential victims of "neo-colonialism"[27] and the prevailing tensions between the Capitalist and Communist camps. They do not only occupy an extremely delicate position in the World Market; also, they lack any insurance against potential external vultures. This scientific realism is supported or attested by these prima facie empirical evidences. In 1960, Belgium <u>easily</u> invaded Patrice Lumumba's Congo (re-named Zaire); in 1975, Portugal <u>easily</u> invade Selou Toure's Guinea; in 1976, South Africa and some Western powers <u>easily</u> invaded Angola; in 1976, Israel <u>easily</u> invaded Idi Amini's Uganda; and in 1976, 1977, and 1978 "Rhodesia" f<u>requently</u> invade Mozambique.

In view of this scientific behavioural truth, it is therefore explicit that without adequate defense power from within African Nation-States, the latter are helpless against powerful aggressors. Their only recourse may be the United Nations.

### (3) Their Judgement Poverty

A further clinical diagnosis of this UN resource also shows another scaring constraints. Ever since the UN was formed in 1945, the only aid Africa has ever received from the United Nations is formal condolences and informal condemnations of the aggressor since no victim African nation-state has ever received any reparation, through the Untied Nations, other African nation-States, or on its own. Even now, majority African nation-States are totally <u>impotent</u> on Sierra Leone, Sudan, Rwanda, Burundi, Congo etc as they were on the "Congo Apartheid and Rhodesia Questions" in the 1960s-1980s. In the Rhodesian Question, for example, they pleaded to Britain for a military action against the "Rhodesia Regime" without using their prudent judgement to realize that due to cultural ties between the Rhodesians and the British, Britain could hardly do what they expected other than giving them verbal support only as under no circumstances could Britain take up arms against the Rhodesians, except in cases where such action could be of crucial importance for Britain's national interest. But, the Rhodesian issue was not a Britain's highest priority. Britain had very little and almost nothing to gain from African majority rule in Rhodesia. Therefore, it was of utter nonsense for African Nation-States to assume that Britain would militarily intervene in a situation whose optimum net-gains for Britain was absent or non-existent.

A similar poor judgement on the part of African leadership also held true in the Namibia and apartheid questions in South Africa. While all African Nation-States supported African majority in both Namibia and South Africa, their actions were limited to talk. They lacked a coercive capability to effect their wishes. Just as they expected Britain to take up arms against Ian Smith's Unilateral Declaration of Independence in Rhodesia, they also assumed that some other members of the World Community would take up arms against the apartheid regime Southern African for them.

In the final analysis, due to their judgement Poverty, an African Nation-State's chances of successfully defending its possessional goals and achieving its perceived milieu goals without external help are still very slim.

### (4) Their Self-Confidence Deficiency

The same problem also holds true in African Nation-States' internal affairs. In 1964 and 1969, Kenya had to appeal to Britain for military assistance against internal upheavals against Kenyatta's regime. In 1964, Tanzania also called upon Britain for a similar assistance. Gabon and the Congo (Brazzaville) called up on France for military aid during their internal troubles; and in 1976, Kenya called upon the United States for military assistance against Uganda.

Although, under Article 3 of the Charter of the Organization of African Unity, every African Nation-States is expected to keep from aligning itself militarily with non-African nation-States, most of them still maintain bilateral military alignments with foreigners. Nigeria maintained such a treaty with Britain until the Mohammed regime terminated it in the 1970's. With the exception of Guinea, most ex-French African colonies such as Ivory Coast, Gabon and Chad, maintain bilateral military defense treaties with Britain. Liberia has maintained a bilateral defense treaty with the United States for more than a century. Although under the OAU Charter, no African Nation-State was supposed to transact business with the apartheid regime in South African, many African Nation-States such as Gabon, Kenya Malawi, Lesotho, Ivory Coast and others did so.

And, although under the same OAU Charter, no African Nation-States is supposed to shy away from another African Nation-States wherever the latter is under foreign aggression, no single African Nation-State ever came to the aid of Mozambique and Zambia against the Rhodesian frequent military raids.

### (5) Their Inability to Quickly Discern Between an Enemy and a True Friend

Another crucial problem facing African Nation-States is that, because of their parasitic relationships with foreign Nation-States, they are unable to discern quickly and easily between a true enemy and a true friend. Because of this deficiency, they are automatically susceptible to external penetration and manipulation. The more easily penetrated and manipulated by external influences they are, the more they are susceptible to high levels of internal political instability, e.g, coups d'etats, assassinations, schisms, revolts, demonstrations and kickbacks as in the pathetic cases of Congo (1960) Mozambique, Angola, South Africa during apartheid, and Rwanda, Burundi, Democratic Republic of Congo, Somalia where peace solution has failed to firmly take root.

As of now, November 2000, approximately 100% of African Nation-States are now no longer miniature international systems as they used to be in the Cold War Era. During the Cold War, each African Nation-States was characterized by two ideological camps, Capitalism and Communism. Because of these dynamics, most African Nation-States experienced at least one or more attempted coup d'etat, assassination, schism, revolt etc. While such symptoms of political instability very rarely occurred in more highly developed Nation-States, which did not need to depend upon others for their nation survival, the fact that such problems are common in African and other developing nation-States (e.g., in South America), reveals that the internal political instability of weaker Nation-States is a function of their dependence on foreign economic and military aids (see Figure 1). As also indicated in Figure 1, every contemporary African Nation-State exists and functions within a conflicting, ideologically, international environment. They were caught between Externality A (Communism) and Externality B (Capitalism). Each Externality was heavily engaged in cultivating alliances on the World Market in order for it to consolidate its strength against the adversary.

Internally, every contemporary African Nation-State existed and functioned within the conflicting ideological problems that existed between an Internality x (a pro-elite faction which liked and supported the elite's domestic and foreign policies) and an Internality y the anti-elite faction, which due to the foreign influence, did not also want to see the African elite, e.g, Kwame Nkrumah, Patrice Lumumba, Idi Amin and others, in power. All those tough African leadership who could not prove as "Yes men to the Western Powers had to be eliminated as the cases of Lumumba, Nkrumah, Samora Machel etc.

Figure 1: Channels Through Which African nation-States Became Manipulated on the World Market by Communism-Capitalism Race for Allies During the Cold War

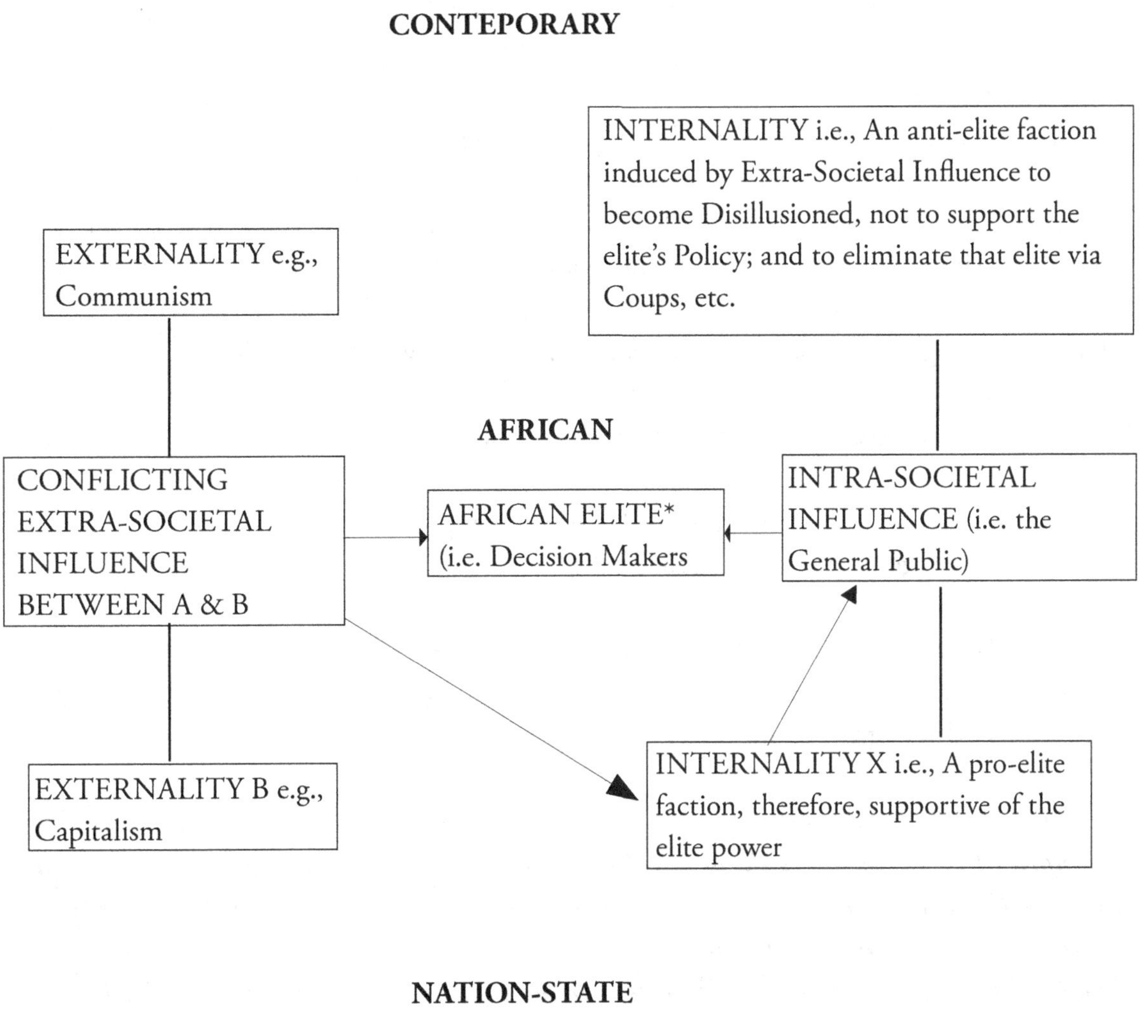

Key ⟶ Channels of Extra-Societal Influence and Impact on the African foreign policy decision maker.

_______ Permeable Membrane of the Nation-State

- The elite may start out as either a Communist, Capitalist or Anti-both ideologies. However, due to the increasing Communism. Capitalism race for allies, that Elite becomes an automatic target and, therefore, innocent victim of that race on the World Market as in the case of Congo (1960), Korea (1950), Chile (1974), Vietnam (1954-75), Angola and Mozambique (1976), etc.

Source: Author's work product-model synthesized from the entire paper.

The internal tensions between the Pro-Elite and Anti-Elite due to tension confronted every African nation-States. Consequently, the position of every African Nation-State on the World Market became extremely precarious and pathetic—a situation that was totally absent or non-existent in all self-reliant Nations States e.g, U.S, U.S.S.R., etc. This problem made it so difficult for African nation-States to effectively and successfully protect their possessional goals and acquire milieu goals on the World Market in the Cold War Era that by today (2000), it has more foreign aid loans to service (pay back) than they are able to do so or to even use in order to heal their wounds arising from the Cold War Era battle between the Capitalists headed by USA and the Communists headed by the Soviet Union.

A synthesis of these two major problems facing contemporary African nation-States on the World Market suggests the following four behavioural laws:-

## (C) Four Behavioural Laws Governing the Conduct of Both External and Internal Forces Against Contemporary African Nation-States on the World Market during the Cold War.

***Behavioural Law No. 1: During the Cold War Era, whenever, an African ruling Elite was noticed to be on the side of the Communist camp, the Capitalist camp would influence the Anti-Elite faction to take over that elite's government through a coup d'etat in order to disrupt the relationships between the Communist Camp and that Elite and then initiate a new relationship between the new government and its Externality.*** The justification of this Behavioural Law is that when Patrice Lumumba's, Kwame Nkrumah's, and S. Allende's regimes were destroyed along these lines by the CIA of the USA because the Capitalists camp (headed by USA) assumed that such regimes were becoming Communist[28] and would therefore help or enable USSR achieve Communism victory over Capitalism. However, the Communist camp also behaved in the same fashion whenever an African ruling Elite was seen to be on the Capitalist side, as this would contribute to the downfall of Communism.[29]

Behavioural Law No. 2: ***From the Colonial Era up to today, whenever a socio-economically powerful nation-state notices that its monopoly in an industry is likely to be threatened by the introduction of World Market in Africa by a far-sighted African Elite which might increase African productivity, employment, and, hence, independence, that Nation-State is likely to influence the Anti-Elite faction to uproot the existing Elite who is advocating that change.*** For example, Nkrumah's extraordinary idea to create a United States of Africa with a Supreme Command and a domestic industry and market, so that Africa would (1) no longer depend on the outside world and (2) minimize Africa's vulnerability to foreign influence, was summarily destroyed through the Capitalist camps influence on the late Ex-Emperor Haile Selassie 1 of Ethiopia, William Vacanarat Shadrack Tubman of Liberia, Mnadi Azikiwe of Nigeria and Felix Houphouet-Biogny of the Ivory Coast. These leaders were persuaded and hoodwinked to disagree with Nkrumah at the Addis Ababa Conference in 1963[30] by warnings issued by the Western powers that Nkrumah's ulterior motive was to become the eventual, sole ruler of Africa.[31]

Also, when Patrice Lumumba was found to be one of those able African elite members who desired to drive Africa into a mighty power and conceivably, had the ability to do so by virtue of his eloquence and his ability to reach people better than Moise Tshombe and Joseph Kasavubu and Mobuto Sese Seko could, Belgium and its NATO colleagues prejudiced Kasavubu, Tshombe and Seko against Lumumba.

When arrested and detained in Algeria in July, 1968, Tshombe uttered, "I am a victim of my popularity and the CIA," a statement that the U.S. Department of State strongly denounced.[32]

Similarly, on realizing that the cooperative aim of Tanzania and Zambia to build a railway between the two countries in 1968 would become another gigantic step towards industrial development in Africa and a reduction of Africa's dependency on the Capitalist camp, the latter denied the Tanzo-Zambian request for a loan to build the Tanzo-Zambian railway. Even when the two countries later decided to appeal to the People's Republic of China for the loan. The Capitalist camp continued to discourage them claiming that the plan was still inappropriate.[33]

Also, in 1956 President Gamal Abdul Nasser's request to the Capitalist camp for a loan to build the Aswan Dam had to be denied for the same reason. Had Nasser's appeal to the Communist camp not been positively answered, the Aswan Dam could not have been built.

***Behavioural Law No. 3:*** *In the absence of a strong Anti-Elite faction, a Capitalist or Communist Camp would maintain or establish its relationship directly with a ruling Elite. Each camp would influence the Elite directly. It would use technological aid, economic aid, military aid, or a compound of those aids. But, should the Elite refuse to accept this offer, that Elite would be publicly humiliated by that Externality*. Supporting Evidence: Having failed to influence Sekou Toure's regime in 1958, President Charles de Gaulle of France vehemently humiliated that regime publicly by removing all office equipments in Guinea. Telephone and electric lines were disrupted, offices were stripped and even the electric light bulbs were removed. Guinea's political machinery was unable to function normally until Ghana and the Soviet Union responded to Sekou Toure's appeal for help with massive financial aid and technicians.[34]

***Behavioural Law No. 4:*** *In a nation-state where there is both a strong Anti-Elite faction and a strong Elite, each being supported by either Communist or Capitalist camp, the camp which lacked influence on the ruling Elite would always attempt to influence the Anti-Elite faction against the Elite. In spite of its failures against the Elite, that camp would be forced to continue to do so until that Elite is either removed from office or lured to that camp's side*. Supporting Evidence: in spite of the enormous economic, military and technological aids Egypt had always received from the USSR from 1948 to 1977 against Israel, a U.S. protégé; and in spite of Egypt's prolonged hatred of the Capitalist camp due to that camp's Imperialism and Colonialism, the Capitalist camp continued to lure Egypt's ruling Elite until that Elite was finally drifted from the USSR to the capitalist camp in 1977.[35]

***Behavioural Law No. 5: In a political situation whereby there is total absence of a cold war between hostile camps such as the Communist Camp on the one hand and the Capitalist on the other in the International System during the Cold War, such hysterical antagonism between the said camps and the efforts to Elites of weaker States such as***

***African Nation-States today to change alliances and the efforts to even eliminate the stubborn Elite who does not want to be lured also ceases to exist.***

Supporting Evidence: As at November, 2000, no single African political Elite has been openly accused and castigated by his people or World Public Opinion that he was pamphlet or stooge to the Capitalist or Communist Camp as the case used to be during the Cold War when numerous African Leaders such as Moise Tsombe and Mobute Sese Sekou were vehemently accused by the entire World Public Opinion.

***Behavioural Law No. 6: Ina non-camp International System, the search for puppets is always silently done and minimal because of absence of need or gain.***

Supporting Evidence: In the Rwanda and Burundi cases to day between the mutually hostile Hutu and Tutsi tribes, research evidences show that while France sought to safeguard her foreign markets in those two countries through continuity of Hutu leadership, the USA supported the Tutsi tribe to take over so that the Tutsis may dismantle the existing Francophone Market and replace it with an Anglo phone one which could then be conducive to their commerce. Hence, the root-cause of the Rwanda Catastrophe of 1994-5 and continued hostility in these two countries in the Central African Region.

## CHAPTER IV

# Basic Strategies by which African Nation-States Withstand Actual and Potential Disturbances From Internal and External Environments

Every animate object has sufficient ability with which to defend itself against actual and potential sources of dangers to its survival. It develops biological defensive chemicals within its body against the invasion of foreign bodies, which are so microscopic that they cannot be observed with naked eye. It may develop observable defensive weapons (horns, thorns, a nasty odour as with skunks, sharp teeth claws poison, and so on). Or it may develop strategies with which it can rationally eliminate or evade its adversary. Such natural and totally involuntary strategies include the ability of a living entity to change colour as a mean of camouflage, as in the case of the chameleon. Such strategies evolve through the ages because of necessity, or can be acquired biologically, physically, or socially. Biologically, an entity can develop immunity against certain areas in African countries which are infested by malaria-carrying mosquitoes. Physically, an entity can discover artificial chemical that successfully neutralize and paralyze certain anti-bodies in its system. One can receive an anti-malaria inoculation and thereby artificially develop the immunity.

But in more complicated situation such as the treatment of polio, one must receive a polio vaccine discovered by Dr. Jonas E. Salk of the University of Pittsburgh in 1955, and Dr. Albert Sabin of the University of Cincinati in 1961 in order to be able to develop a biological immunity within one's body against poliomyelitis. Short of this dose or input, paralysis or death is automatic.

Similarly, in the International System, nationals of countries in Euro-America, where malaria-carriers are very rare, cannot easily survive most African nations unless they first receive anti-malaria inoculations or use anti-malaria pills as medically prescribed before they travel into Africa. While Euro-Americans must depend on man-made anti-malaria vaccine in order to survive in the African world; most Africans do not. Even though they are not vaccinated, and yet they habitually, comfortably and normally co-exist with malaria carriers. Socially, an entity may either create or emulate a defensive method of another entity against perceived odds for the purpose of its survival.

In this regard survival of the living entity can be used as an analogy to explain better the survival phenomenon of Nation-States on the World Market. While African Nation-States are still very poor and therefore, too weak to successfully compete with wealthy and, therefore, powerful Nation-States, each African Nation-State definitely has its own sufficient means of getting by within and outside of its domestic jurisdiction. Thus, each is reasonably competent enough in its own right to defend its possessional goals and to pursue its milieu goals without foolishly causing unnecessary quarrels with other Nation-States and thus jeopardizing its image (i.e dignity) sovereign equality, and chances of getting what it seeks from others on the World Market.

Further, whereas African Nation-States are also stilltoo weak militarily to combat more powerfulnations militarily; their most efficient strategies against the source of internal political instability are:—(1) Use of prostitutional diplomacy, i.e., oscillating from one powerful Nation-State to another for both national economic and military benefits; (2) Use of ideological diplomacy e.g., Pan-Africanism, Socialism, Non-Alignment, etc as a defensive weapon or mechanism; (3) Use of ex-Colonial bureaucracy with which to effectively convert the Intra-Societal demands into satisfactory consumer goods (goods and services to its citizens); and (4) Use of Rival Elimination, i.e., eliminating individuals who prove a potential threat to the existing regimes. In all those four ways, they may sue local, foreign, or both security and economic aids. In Kenyatta's Kenya, for instance, the likely candidates to succeed Kenyatta were eliminated. Oginga Odinga, Kenyatta's first Post-Independence Vice-President resigned because of his disillusionment with Kenyatta's policy), was jailed and his opposition party banned. This Odinga's demise was quickly followed by the demises of Tom Mboya, Kenyatta's most likely successor, who was shot dead in Nairobi by a Kikuyu (Kenyatta's tribe) gunman, Ronald Ngala, a widely popular Cabinet Minister, who was killed in a mysterious car accident.; and (J.M.) Kariuki, a politician with mass appeal and open presidential aspirations, was murdered in 1975 by Kenyatta's operatives.

Similarly, in Daniel T. Arap Moi's Kenya, all the above strategies have been emulated. In book, <u>Moi: The Making of African Statesman</u> (1998), Andrew Morton's comprehensive study of Moi's leadership since Moi took over this leadership from Kenyatta on 10$^{th}$ October, 1978 after the latter's death in the same year (1978), also confirms this reality.

And, this is not all. A list of other numerours evidence of this Rival Eliminatio strategy is endless. This list encludes, for instance, Tanzania's ruthless conduct in Zanzibar Election by the International Observations; Ivory Coast's ruthless conduct which proved as bollody as Tanzania Elections and which could hae possibly become too catastrophic had Ivory Coast masses not gone out in an anarchy in streets for the sole purpose of using mob-justice to drive out the ill-cultured military junta who had already staged a military coup d'état with a view to nullifying the election so that he may remain in power by force against the will of the people of Ivory Coast and the International Community.

In the final analysis, in spite of their prevailing weak status on the World Market, African Nation-States do also have a way of co-existing with their antibodies (see figure 2). <u>Internally</u>, each African Nation-State receives local tangible support (P) and intangible support (Q) from its citizens as a defense against the stress imposed upon the decision-maker (DM). In return, its citizens receive goods and services ($r^1$) in response to their demands ($d^1$).

<u>Internationally</u>, each African Nation-States offers certain services to some of the members of the International Systems (E) in responses to demands imposed on its decision-maker (DM) by E. For example, when in 1976 Kenya's assistance was requested during the Israeli Rescue mission of Israeli hostages, in Entebe, Kenya had to comply in order to fulfill the demand imposed upon it by an important external influence. Had Kenya been militarily and economically independent, as the United States is now, Kenya would definitely not have agreed to request. Therefore, by carrying out such functions inside and outside their domestic jurisdictions, African and other militarily weak Nation-States establish and maintain a political atmosphere conducive for their own existence. This is precisely why they have always resorted to bilateral military treaties with foreign Nation-States in contravention of the provision under their own OAU Charter before the African Union and its Charter were recently created; they welcome foreign aid; they collaborate with foreign Nation-States against

their own neighbouring African nation-states; they quarrel and speak ill of each other at International Gatherings as did Zambia, under President Kenneth Kaunda, when it spoke against President Idi Amin's Uganda at the Commonwealth Summit Meeting in London in June, 1977; sometimes they dissolve their treaties because they cannot stand each other, as Kenya, Uganda and Tanzania did in 1977 with East African Common Market; some of them trade with illegitimate regimes as Malawi, the Ivory Coast, Zambia and Gabon were now doing when they traded with the minority white South African regime against the will of other African nation-states and OAU. They break their own pacta sunt servanda in these ways and many other ways for their own survival.

Figure 2: Strategies of African Nation-States for Survival on the Anarchical World Market due to the latter's Amorphous and Acephelous Structure

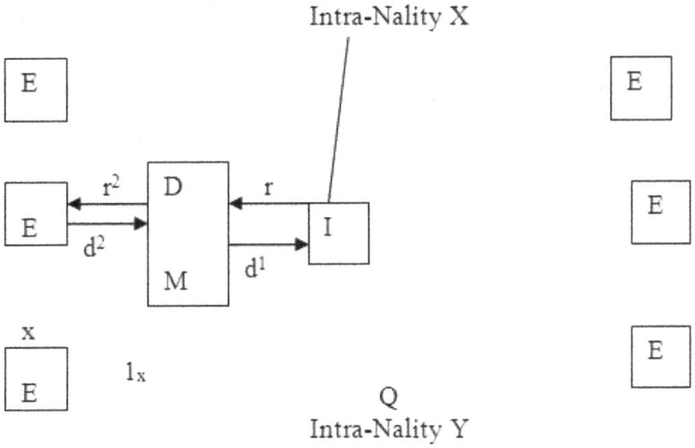


**Key**

| | |
|---|---|
| $d^1$ & $d^2$ | =demands |
| DM | =Decision-Maker |
| E | =Externality, i.e, foreign influence |
| I | =Internality, i.e, domestic or internal influence |
| P | =Tangible support (i.e, taxes) |
| Q | =Intangible support (i.e, loyality) $r^1$& $r^2$ =Response |
| . . . . . . | =Periodical group formation against the system |
| • x-x | =Permeable membrane of African nation-states because every nation-state is an open system in the International System |

Source: Author's work-product. This is precisely an iconic model. Its objective is to depict communication flow between an African Nation-State(s) and the outside world on the World Market, based as African nation-state, does not have or posses or control all that is necessary for its basic needs. Every Nation-State must interact with others in order to acquire those values very essential for its survival but which it cannot easily and cheaply get locally at home. For this reason, every African Nation-State, as well as other Nation-States on the World Market, is an open system, contained in a permeable membrane through which communication with the outside world continuously flows as indicated above, between the External Influences' and itself in pursuit of those needed basic values for the survival of all parts for the system, Nation-States. Likewise, the model is designed to show how an African Nation-State, like every other actor on the World Market, habitually reacts in response to certain anti-bodies from within and outside its environment in defense of its own survival. Thus, due to the fact that the World Market is essentially amorphous, acephelous and scarce in resources, the Market is highly anarchical. And the more the Market is anarchical, the greater it is too insecure and scarey for weaker actors such as the African Nation-State which therefore develops certain strategies against such threats from within and outside its borders.

CHAPTER V

# Conclusion

The aim of this Etiological effort has been to undertake a Clinical Diagnosis of the East African Nation-States as a representative of all African Nation-States with regard to their Habitual Problems; Strategies they usually use on The World Market; and above all the Behavioural Laws synthesized from their conduct which govern weaker states' conduct on that Market; and which one may therefore use in order to understand fairly well the actual dynamics of the Market and the International System as a whole. On the strength of this reality based on numerous prima facie evidences adduced in this it is self-evident that the East African and all other African nation-States are too weak politically, socially, economically and militarily to effectively compete on the World on the equal footing with their socio-economically and militarily most powerful counter part are on that Market. And, that because of this weakness, they are always easily susceptible and vulnerable to manipulation by their socio-economically powerful counter parts on the World Market. They are daily faced with a host of multi-difficulties that these counterpart do not have both at home and outside their borders (on The World Market).

But this is not and cannot be the end of the road for them. Like their sister African nation-states as well as all other Nation-States on the World Market, the East African nation-states are also living human organisms. Although they are less socio-economically and militarily advantaged on the World Market than their socio-economically and militarily most powerful counterparts are such as USA, Britain, France, Germany, etc, the natural fact is that they must do all that pertains to their survival. Accodingly, they are naturally duty bound to respond to the common behavioural law that governs and regulates all living entities including all nation-states in Biopolitics. For example, they are duty-bound by the inter-subjective Biological Consittution to:

(1) seek identical hierarchy of goals
(2) perform identical hierarchy of functions
(3) use similar hierarchy of strategies in pursuit and defense of those goals;
(4) and to succeed often if they have to exist at all.

In sum, they do engage in the following acts for skivival: Pattern Maintenance, Adaptation, Goal Attainment, and Integration. However, this does not mean that African and other socio economically and politically weak Nation-States on the World Market use the identical strategy(ies) that relatively powerful Nation-States habitually use on Market. Although African Nation-States are as equally interested in their national interest,[36] nation building,[37] and socio-economic development[38] on the World Market as all other nation-states are, the fact is that they are too weak to use war-by-proxy, kick-baked or other similar strategies which are commonly used by the most powerful Nation-States on the World Market.

Consequently, tbecause of their relative disabilities, their chances of successfully defending their possessional goals and competing for milieu goals on the World Market with their most powerful counterpart are significantly minimal. Their inability to successfully defend their possessional goals and to compete for milieu goals is explicitly manifested in their easy propensity to be lured and subjected to coups d'etat, political assassinations, schisms, terrorism corruption (bribery) foreign sub-standard manufactured goods, and massive strikes and revolts in their own boundaries not easily found in the boundaries of those most powerful Nation-States such as the U.S., Russia, Britain, Germany, France and Japan by those other relatively powerful acts on the World Market for the socio-economic and political advantages of such actors.

In the final analysis, in order for them to maintain this equitable co-existence with their counterpart on the Market, they can do so only by relying on The Behavioural Law of Elimination Strategy and The Behavioural Law of Prostitutional Strategy which counterpart neither use nor are governed by. In the former, most African Nation-States wipe out their internal political competitors and critics; and in the latter, they often cling on those powerful Nation-States like parasites and prostitutes behaviourally do with a view to getting foreign aid and other most essential goals which they do not have and cannot achieve on their own. In a nut-shell, African and other weaker Nation-States achieve their goals on the World Market by clinging to the most powerful Nation-States. Likewise, the latter achieve theirs by also doing the same to those weaker parties. In spite of its neo-colonialist and neo-imperialist effects, this symbiotic relationship between the two is the most common rational strategy used by all African Nation-States on the one hand and their socio-economically and militarily most powerful counterpart on the other in their individual defense of possessional goals and pursuit of milieu goals on the World Market.[39]

These multi-goals and strategies are the key determinants[40] of the dynamics of our International System not only between African Nation-States and their most powerful counterpart on the World Market today (2000). They are also the same determinants of the same International System throughout the life of the systems ever since its inception during the time of the Egypto-Hittite Treaty of Non-Aggression of 1284 BC up to the Treaty of Westaphalia in 1648 AD and right up to our time today (2000). It is the same behavioural law that determines the eufunction of this system.

Therefore although African nation-States may be faced with various constraints of not only other competing members but also of demanding rules called International Law, a Scarce Market, Different Foreign National Capabilities, National Interests and Aggressive Leaderships and Temperaments competing for the same goals on the scarce market, each African nation-state is also an inter-subjective member of the System and, as such, is also naturally governed by the same behavioural laws on the World Market and always honours them like every other Nation-State in the System. Failure to abide with this strategic behavioural law is an assured political suicide as the cases of Adolf Hitler Germany, Emporer Hirohito Japan Mursolin Italy, Saddam Hussein Iraq, Idi Amin Uganda etc.—nation-States which succumbed to their own political suicide because of their failure to recognize and abide with/by this strategic behavioural law on the World Market.

# PART FIVE

## LEADERSHIP AND WORLD PEACE: A Test for World Leadership's Concept of and Trust in a Lasting Peace

CHAPTER 1

# Introduction

## (1) Problem

From the Preamble of the United Nations Charter, one encounters these striking sentiments:

> ***We the peoples of the United Nations determined to save succeeding generations from the scourge of war, which twice in our lifetime has brought untold sorrow to mankind, and to reaffirm faith in fundamentals of human rights, in the dignity and worth of the human person, in the equal rights of men and women and of nations large and small, and to establish conditions under which justice and respect for the obligations arising from treaties and other sources of international law can be maintained, and to promote social progress and better standards of life in larger freedom and for these ends to practice tolerance and live together in peace and security, and to ensure, by the acceptance of principles and the institution of methods, that armed force shall not be used, save in the common interest, and to employ international machinery for the promotion of the economic and social advancement of all peoples, have resolved to combine our efforts to accomplish these aims. Accordingly, our respective Governments, through representatives assembled in the City of San Francisco, who have exhibited***

But, whose sentiments are these? From a psychiatric[1] level of analysis, (a) what do they mean to us? (b) What might have been their causal factor(s)? (c) what impact have they made on national foreign policy decision-makers most especially in our own generation with reference to World Peace and Tranquaility? And (d) If so, to what extent have they done so? But, given the fact that since the inception of the United Nations as a global body mandated to maintain and restore a durable World Peace effective that year (1945) to the present (2013), our adored World has never enjoyed at all, this peace any single moment. Instead, it has always been subjected to recurrent terrors of leaders obsessed with self-seeking national interests in a total disobedience and disregard to these sentiments of our Forefathers in their capacity as The UN Founding Fathers. In his own words, The USA President Ronald Reagan lamentingly vowed in 1980 that in defense of this World Peace, he would no more want to see the United States of America continue submitting to a world Leadership of mediocrity, which did not believe in this World Peace. In this regard, he sought and teamed up with the USSR President Mikhael Gorbachev to bring about this dream. They began this by first tearing down the Berlin Wall between East and West Germany as a beginning sign for this Peace in Europe, in commemoration of the 40th Anniversary of The Nomandy Landing by The Allies to root out the German forces and other architects of World War II. With his sense of discency and humor mixed with his dream for World Peace and Democracy, President Reagan sought to initiate and enhance a new sense of a totally new direction of World Leadershiip. In this regard, he sought to create an exemplary model of a leadership for all others World-wide—a leadership of and for optism, which in the final analysis popularized his image so much especially in Europe that every one there loved him and his concept of leadership.

But, given that this is the way of leadership each leader globally was to toe his/her leadership, the nagging mystery is (a) How far has this exemplary model held true? (b) How far did it realize the same goal of World Peace during his own tenure of office as President of the USA? (c) What new strategy(ies) of leadership did he put in place to realize his dream?

## (2) Purpose

The main purpose of this study is to examine and measure the style and degree to which foreign policy decision-makers have so far responded to our Forefathers' call for "None Use of Force as a means of settling international disputes"—a Call which was made at the end of World War II in 1945 as a result of the devastating destruction of both human lives and property by this war, a damage which, in turn, generated such a world-wide panic that the same victors of this war became psychologically forced by their own conscience to formulate this Decision calling upon all men and nations alike to accept and conduct their inter-state affairs within the framework of this Decision. It was a hasty and emotional but a very rational and cost-effective move for the succeeding generations to hearten to and sustain at all times and all costs using man's God-given talents in Science and Technology abundantly available today.

## (3) Rationale

This examination is necessary because ever since this call was launched in 1945, (a) implementation of it has remained a chalange (b) most key nation-state decision makers do not seem to recognize and appreciate the pairs of World War I and II—the pains that psychologically forced our Forefathers to initiate this Call; and (c) at least ten nation-states viz: US, USSR (now called Russia), China, UK, France, Israel, India, Pakistan, South Africa and Brazil have already gone to the extent of acquiring nuclear weaponry—a highly devastating power capable of destroying our Planet in a matter of seconds; and above all (d) even to-date (2013) with all highly advanced wisdom and knowledge in Science and Technology, implementation problem of this call has always evaded recognition of all peace-keeping researchers ever since the call was launched in the aftermath of the 2nd World War in 1945, albeit certain researchers have attempted to allude to it. Such peace researchers include L. Sohn, Cases on United Nations Law (1956); M.Rajan, United Nations and Domestic Jurisdiction (1958), W. Joshua, United Nations in the Congo 1960-1964 (1966); Agola Auma-osolo, "UN Peace Keeping Policy: Some Basic Causes of Its Implementation Problems and Their Implications", California Western International Law Journal, Vol. 6 91976); and same author, The Law of The United nations as Applied to Interventions within the Framework of Art. 2 Par. 7 of the UN Charter, (1969). Neither these nor any other studies focus on the problem directly and exhaustively.

It is, therefore, due to this omission in the existing studies on the problem that this study resolved to undertake the task accordingly. Hence the rationale and justification of the study.

NB: These methodology and findings arising from this study is a function of a marathon research expedition that commenced ways back in the late 1980s from a call to me in my capacity as The Administrator of The Kenya National Academy of Sciences (KNAS) by The USSR Academy of Sciences in Moscow to prepare for presentation a paper at The Soviet-African Scientific Conference on "International Peace, Co-operation and Social Progress" in Moscow, 23rd-26th June, 1986, organized by the USSR. Academy of Sciences (now re-named Russian Academy of Sciences) and The Institute of African Studies. The first Edition of this work was prepared and presented as a keynote Address to The Kenya National Seminar on

The Associated Schools Project at The Church of The Province of Kenya (CPK, now re-named The Anglican Church of Kenya, ACK) Language School Guest House on April 21-24, 1986 organized by The Kenya National Commission to UNESCO of The Ministry of Education, Science and Technology in Nairobi, because of the increasing climax of the heat of a terrible nuclearphobia from The on-going Cold War between the West headed by the USA and the East headed by the USSR (now-renamed Russia at the end of this heat). My idea and urge to do this was caused by my memory of an extra-ordinary contribution of the USA President Woodrow Wilson—a man who lost his dear life in his vigorous and tireless efforts between 1918 and 1919 in his capacity as a Socratic "Philosopher King" to bring together all different nations of the World of the time into one common Bond of Brotherhood and Sisterhood, i.e., "THE LEAGUE OF NATIONS", at the close of World War I in 1918 and a son of not only The United States of America (USA) but also a True and Dedicated Son of The Entire International Community who, by such unique leadership virtues, cared the least but, by and large, the HAPPIEST FUTURE of the Entire World Community, and who, in that regard, fatally collapsed at PUEBLO, Colarado, USA on the 25$^{th}$ day of September, 1919 in the cause of this straneous criss-cross-America stateman safaris campaigning for his American Community to accept this end and ratify The League of Nations Treaty. Also, my idea and motivation to do this was abundantly empowered and guided by my humble need to also give a Tribute and Heartfelt Appreciations to those Sons of The International Community for their exemplary contributions against the evils of *animus dominandi*, e.g. Marcus Garvey whose philosophy and doctrine of "Back To Africa" in the 1800s became a flabbergasting morning star", a Greatest Reawakening Light, to The Total World against the evil of racism and other untold evils of animus dominandi terrorizing the Africans of Diaspora in North America in particular but also The Concept of World Peace and Brotherhood in appreciation to our Almighty Creator's Divine Judgement to create man in His own Image but in different races as per His own Omniscience and Omnipotence; Barrister Sylevester Williams of Trinidard, whose residence in London empowered him to also light a torch of Pan-Africanism in 1900 aimed at eradicating colonialism and imperialism in Africa as an added asset to World Leadership against the vices of animus dominandi which was acting as enemy number one of World Peace and Order in The Continent of Africa; USA President Abraham Lincoln whose contribution to World Peace was manifested in his courageous suppression of slavery and slave trade yoke from the life of Africans of Diaspora, in the USA, who had been dehumanized and used as a donkey and a horse to provide free labour to his fellow white man in North America particularly on the cotton, tobacco, sugar and other plantations in the Southern States such as Alabama, Georgia, Louisiania, Texas, Florida, Mexico, etc—a noble goal indeed though it resulted into his assassination by the advocates of slavery, slave trade and the vices of animus dominandi against the concept and virtues of World Peace and Order to give glory to The Divine Creator of The Universe and The latter's Humanity and all other Creation; Kwame Nkrumah for his role as The Torch Bearer of This World Peace and Order from the hands of Sylvester Williams in London (a foreign soil) to the African soil in The Continent of Africa in 1951 and who laid down the seed of Colonial and Imperial Destruction in the Continent; Prime Minister Patrice Lumumba whose philosophy and doctrine in support of World Peace and Order is fully documented and envisaged in his book, "Congo My Country" where he cries vehemently for the need of inter-racial tolerance and solidarity to bring about an ever lasting martyrs living spirit of a Durable World Peace, that only a few understood while the overwhelming majority did not due to their obsession with euphoria of The Cold War—a reminiscent of man's instinct of animus dominadi against the concept and virtues of a Durable World Peace and Order, which in 1961 put this Prime Minister to a pathetic sad death and Congo to War; to President Vladimir Lenin, for his efforts to eradicate the vices of animus dominandi in Russia using the October Russian Peasants Revolution effective 1917 and fulfilled that goal using the Doctrine of Dr. Karl Marx outlined in The Communist Manifesto; to President Mao Tse Tung, who did the same on mainland China in order to liberate his helpless innocent Chinese masses besieged by the vices of animus dominandi of those who claimed to be endowed with the wealth of capital and the right by the will of The Divine Creator to terrorize and enslave the helpless malnourished poor masses for their own selfish ends without any due regard to the concept and virtues of World Peace and Order; to President Ho Chi Minh who did the same to get rid of this same yoke from the necks, legs and hands of his helpless malnourished Vietnamese in Vietnam; to Dr. Martin Luther King and Malcom X who became martyrs in defence of Human and Civil Rights of their besieged African Americans in the United States of America by the architects and brokers of white superiority and all other vices of animus dominandi against World Peace and Order; President Nelson Mandela, Chief Luthuli, Martyr Steve Bikko and The Most Rev. Archbishop Desmond Tutu who individually and collectively tirelessly sacrificed in South Africa in Defence for Human Rights against the animus dominandi vices from the bloody hand of apartheid regime of minority whites in the Country; and finally but not least to J. M. Kariuki, Dedan Kimathi, The Rt. Rev. Bishop Alexander Muge and Dr. Robert Ouko in Kenya who became martyrs of their righteousness against the same evils of animus dominandi that have over-time characterized the Kenyan political leadership ever since Kenyan independence on 12th December 1963 thereby putting the Country's leadership at odds with the concept of a Durable World Peace and Order as also witnessed by the appalling revelations out of The Goldenberg Commission of Inquiry Political Leadership—an extremely flabbergasting, pathetic and nauseating scandal any leadership had never been accused of before in the History of Mankind. Hence, the rationale of this Tribute to all those leaders who demonstrated without hiding within their hearts Justice wisdom, companion, temperance courage and dedication in the cause of their duties as leaders to fight against bad mode of Governance and Leadership and even lose their dear life on behalf of their fellow men and women faced by the scourge of the human instinct of animus dominandi, a natural disease to a Durable World Peace and Order for all.

## (4) Methodology

To do this, the study dives deep into the main stratum and roots of Our Forefathers' call—not necessarily to identify the reason(s) why the fact that since The Reagan Administration up to the present President George Bush Jr Administration in the same most powerful nation in the World today, leadership contradiction abound between theory and practice with regard to the fate of this world peace as also vividly manifested in the most flabbergasting action the Bush Administration has taken against Iraq without any due respect to the principle of Equal Sovereignty protecting Iraq as much as it also protects the USA, UK, Kenya, Ghana, China, Japan, France, India, Pakistan, etc in devoid of any iota of discrimination. USA purported that Iraq leadership of president Sadam Hussein posed a potential danger to the World Peace which leaders were expected to protect and that Iraq possessed dangerous weapons of mass destruction. When cautioned by other World Leaders in the UN Security Council and the General Assembly not to abruptly do so short of the UN participation, USA teamed up with the United Kingdom to disobey that caution; declared the UN as a body which had already out-lived its usefulness; and then stubbornly invaded Iraq and subjected the innocent Iraq people to a sea of unnecessary agonies of this invasion. To-date, men and nations are called upon to desist with immediate effect from the use of coercion as a way of setting international disputes; but, in the main, in order to show whether or not our Forefathers' Call was welcomed and honoured; and if so/not, the extent to which this call was accepted or ignored.

Again, in order to do all this, the study attempts to identify those empirical evidences or ramifications of the success or failure of our Fore-fathers' Call and those nation-states or persons strategically responsible for this success or failure of our Forefathers' Call.

Thereafter, the study attempts to critically analyze those success/failures with a view of identifying causal factors responsible for such success or failure of our Forefathers' Call.

But, as also noted by Y. Dror, Public Policy Making Re-Examined (1968), scientific investigations and findings must not only be ends in themselves or only serve as building blocks for theory-building or lectures in classrooms and at scientific conference and similar scientific forums as conventional research thus purports. In the main, in order to serve their scientific purpose effectively, they must also be useful to policy-decision-makers by providing them with viable solutions to existing societal problems in view of the fact that such problems can in no way be solved short of such scientific findings and recommendations from scientists.

It is for these and similar reasons that the Purpose and Methodology of this study collectively seek to identify and give some explicit and parsimonious line of actions which key foreign policy decision-makers in each nation-state ought to take against (a) this on-going deterioration of World Peace which has been caused by the present discovery of highly devastating nuclear weapons and (b) the proliferation of this highly dangerous weapons.

Hundreds of thousands lives and property of unquantified value have been totally destroyed by this reckless leadership, which had been castigated before in the same USA by the former leadership under Ronald Reagan. The Bush Administration and other coalition partners viz: The United Kingdom, Spain, Italy and Turkey thoroughly searched for these weapons they sought to remove from Iraq of Saddam Hussein Administration. But this search did not find these weapons. The investigators confirmed that Iraq had no such weapons. And that the Bush Administration erred. Consequently, the Director of the USA Central Intelligence Agency tendered his resignation to President Bush for that failure. But, resignation or no resignation no longer matters. Unquantifiable property in value have already been destroyed and some lives already maimed. How can such resignations pay for such senseless damages caused by mediocre leadership?

CHAPTER II

# Findings

## (1) A Psychiatric Diagnosis into the Sentiments of the UN Founding Fathers in the UN Chapter Preamble

By the nature of the Preamble sentiment, our Forefathers who created the United Nations in 1945 at the time World War II was just ending were the same Forefathers who had, also encountered the bitter holocaust of World War I from 1914 to 1919.

Consequently, from a psychiatric level of analysis, all of them were already fed up with the dangers of this recurrent war terrorism; and that by 1945, they were already too saturated with terrible panic and phobia of war arising from devastating damages on property and human lives.

Their bitterness is self-explanatory. It is an explicit ramification of their high degree of phobia and detaste against future wars. Further, a psycho-diagnosis of this bitterness clearly shows that our Forefathers had been so hard hit by the experience of those two wars that they neither wanted to see it again at all during their generation nor to see it happen to future generation(s). This precisely was the reason why they all decided to meet together and crystallize their sentiments into a public record for all future generations. Hence, the Preamble of The Charter of The United Nations.

With this in their mind, our Forefathers hoped that by synchronizing their bitterness against war into concrete prescriptions envisaged in the UN Charter Preamble for both their generation and future generations, they were definitely doing a noble service to Humanity. They hoped that based on our obvious day-to-day principle of "Prevention is better than

Cure", war must be prevented at all cost and time through co-operation and other amicable machinery other than through wars or arms race.

For this reason, our Forefathers prayed to all men and nations alike to re-evaluate their mode of conduct vis a vis each other on the World Market. They therefore prayed that their sentiments be equally accepted and shared with honour by future generations.[2]

But from our own experience to-date, have these sentiments brought forth good results? Have they been equally accepted and shared by our generation? If so to what extent and why?

## (2) A Fundamental Challenge to the UN Goals Effective 1945

A clinical diagnosis of what is happening today by the US to Iraq and Afghanistan; and between India and Pakistan, and Democratic Republic of Congo and her neighbours particularly Rwanda, Uganda and Burundi on the one hand: and another in 1945 to the present clearly confirm that our Forefathers hopes have fallen on deaf ears of our foreign policy decision-makers. This reality is borne out by numerous incidents of war and similar conflicts.

An autopsy of the League of Nations fatal problem of World War 1 (1914-1918) reveals that it was this deafness and self-seeking mentality of certain member-states of the League which gradually developed into World War II in 1939 and which, in turn, killed the League.

However, whereas it was a known fact to our Forefathers, that it was this disease which had become a terminal cancer to the League; up to now, this reality has not yet been recognized by most of our own foreign policy decision-makers. This reality is empirically supported by the out-break of the East-West Cold War immediately after the end of World War II (1945)—a war which, in turn, influenced both parties to engage into a vicious circle of arms race and the formation of regional military organization, namely the North Atlantic Treaty Organization (NATO) in 1949 headed by the US; and the Warsaw Pact in 1950 headed by the Union of The Soviet Socialist Republic (USSR). Like the US, blindness and deafness while invading Iraq without hearkening to the UN caution, the two parties to the cold war were also blind and deaf to the chance that their Cold War could become a terminal cancer to the UN; a fact which has always manifested in various conflicts in the UN that could have possibly killed the UN in the same way similar to self-seeking conflicts in the League of Nations also killed The League.

Additional empirical evidences proving that our Forefathers' call has fallen on deaf ears of World Leaders in their capacity as our foreign policy decision-makers begins with the following dangerous intensity of arms race between these super powers which have also continued to be used as a strategy by the dominating powers such as the USA, Russia, Britain, France and China which still control the United Nation's by virtue of their veto powers monopoly in the UN security council:-

As was also noted in 1986 by the Press, the discovery and deployment of the "Star Wars Plan" in the US arms race against the Soviet Union during the Cold War was not limited to the USA. Her allies were also gradually lured into the Plan by the USA. For instance Britain quickly signed up for participation in the Plan and others also followed suit albeit some fo them had first to sort out their respective problems at home over their role in the project given the fact that the USA President Ronald Reagan had also claimed three years ago (1983) that this Star Wars Plan would rid mankind of nuclear fear. Following the British Nyayo (foot steps), West Germany became the second country to sign this agreement with Washington giving its national firms participation rights in this $26b. research programme called "Strategic Defence Initiatives" (SDI).

This Bonn-Washington accord was signed in February 1987 following the Memorandum of Understanding on the SDI signed between Britain and the United States in December, 1985.

Immediately, USA lounged this SDI programme in 1986, USA also quickly initiated its NATO partners, including Australia, Israel, and Japan, to help in the programme. USA officials expected these agreements to be reached with Israel, Italy and Japan by the summer of 1986, a programme that was vigorously met in that very time.

But whereas these accords materialized intense debates emerged and continued indefinitely on whether the SDI which was to use high powered beams to destroy nuclear missiles in flight was possible and desirable.

All Western allies faced a similar dilemma. They feared that if they did not take part in the SDI, they would fall further behind in this high technology stakes. AT the same time, they feared that by so doing, they would be seen as promoting the arms race. European officials at a NATO meeting in West Germany in February, 1986, regarded the SDI unstoppable. The

Belgium Defence Minister, Fracois-Xavier de Donnea, felt it was very important for European firms to participate.

Whereas all Western allies decision-makers found it imperative to participate in the Star Wars Plan, they all faced opposing situations within their groups against the SDI. Consequently, most of them seemed to think that the Soviet Union was possibly right to dismiss claims made by the Reagan Administration which attempted to suggest that SDI programme would make nuclear missiles "impotent and obsolete". Agreeing with Moscow, they fealt (a) That this initiative would most likely take the arms race into space; and (b) that this SDI Plan might just be to shield the USA while leaving Europe uncovered. For this reason, the West German Defense Minister, Manfred Woerner, had in the proceeding year, proposed that Europe should build up its own anti-missile defence, using available technologies rather that colluding with, or totally depending on the USA Star Wars Plan.

In order to convince the Western European allies from such phobia, SDI Director, James Abrahamson, told NATO in February, 1986 that Washington was going to seek technologies to combat the short and medium-range missiles aimed at Europe as well as the long-range rockets targeted on the USA.

However, the allies found it difficult to succeed in selling this plan to the general public. This failure was, in fact, compounded by the USA refusal to commit any specific sum to foreign research contracts, although its officials estimated they could allocate several hundred million dollars.

In addition to this problem, attempts to classify SDI technologies as an official secret was surfaced in February, 1986 in Britain by the most enthusiastic supporter of the initiative. This revelation created a big embarrassment between London and Washington when a consultant hired by the USA Pentagon, Clarence Robinson, arrived in Britain to talk to military industries with little or no advance notice to draw up SDI areas for classification, but was refused security clearance by the British Defence Ministry. Although a USA London-based spokesman tried to convince Britain that Robinson's mission was not associated with the SDI but to a separate $ 250 million programme for USA co-operation with the allies in other arms fields, the USA finally had to apologize to Britain in order to appease the latter.

The SDI opposition in Britain felt that their national decision-makers might have secretly welcomed this opportunity to protect technologies of possibly lucrative civilian applications from classification for the sake of minor defence research contracts. SDI deals, handled by British firms so far totaled only about $1.4 million. However, according to Richard Ennals who had just resigned as a Researcher at Britain's London's Imperial College over British SDI involvement, the USA apology was obviously a sigh of relief on the British Government.

Unlike its British counterpart, the West German Government where the Christian Democrats Party (CDP) was minority partner, the Free Democrats Party did not only appear unconcerned towards the SDI. Also, it had pursed a more cautious line than Britain. It wanted a public agreement rather than the Secret US-British memorandum. It had stressed the commercial over the military aspects of the agreement thereby putting its Economics Minister, Martin Bangemann, in charge of the negotiations instead of its Defense Minister, Woerner, as President Reagan's Administration in Washington would have preferred.

Out of these initiatives, two accords were put in force, one covering Bonn's backing for West German firms taking part in SDI research; and the other, a framework regulating use of the technological development and innovation.

Next to West German, Italy became the third NATO ally to sign up for this SDI. Italy Defence Minister, Giovani Spadolini, indicated that Rome was negotiating an agreement with Washington inspite of a strong opposition to the SDI from the Italy's Communist Party, the largest in the West.

The only NATO allies which were constantly opposed to the Plan were France, Denmark, Norway, Greece and Canada. These allies did not accept government-level agreements. However, they argued that individual companies in those countries were free to bid for SDI contracts if they wanted to do so.

Outside NATO, Japan faced problems akin to Europe's, if not more. It took time to make up its mind whether to follow NATO's Nyayo (footsteps) or not. It is plausible that as a world leader in high technology, Japan had much to offer the SDI. However, as the only country which suffered nuclear attack[5], it was reluctant to become involved in anything related to strategic weapons.

Israel was quickly ready to join the SDI and promptly passed on to Washington its several proposals for Israel firms. However, according to its Defence Ministry official, no formal discussions existed yet between Israel and the US on joining "Star Wars".

In his Cold War Era study pertaining to the USA behaviour in the arms race vis a vis her behaviour in those other areas which are not for human destruction such as Agriculture and Health improvement of mankind, Lester R. Brown[6] noted that the two super powers (USA and USSR) seem to be more interested in their mutual scramble for both guns and butter; and that this contradiction between the surge for guns and the surge for butter had become the prime causal factor or the Era's world-wide starvation. Brown's findings and analysis are very sound. It is submitted that no sane political leader who is interested in boosting armaments budget can successfully deal with ecological deterioration and mounting debts that are undermining his economy. Whereas this has been so, for some countries such as the Soviet Union and the USA, their allies in the Warsaw Pact and NATO respectively, this did not prove so for the Less Developed Countries (LDC) such as Kenya and other African Countries. According to the needs of these LDCs in general and Kenya in particular, environmental decline and economic deficits, were obviously a greater threat to their national security than armed aggression. In Kenya and other Less Developed Countries, restoration and expansion of their national economies was their rational choice in the sense that they meant much more to them than armaments were to them. However, although these Less Developed Countries recognized and believed this, their paradox was that many of them could be easily lured into militarization and civil wars by the super powers through bribery. They could be easily used into this bribery deals as both pawns and a prime source of foreign markets for the super powers' low class manufactured goods as well as light weapons for civil strifes. Also, they were cheaply used as a source of raw materials for the super powers' domestic manufacturing industries[7].

It is, therefore, submitted that super powers which were expected to set a good example for the Developing Countries or LDCs were the same ones who were working the boat by bribing LDC leaders to engage in corruption and other acts of leadership Poverty. Their leadership capacity was bent largely on military and similar activities with a potential threat to World Peace and Security than on activities which were a potential threat to poverty, diseases, ignorance and all other symptoms of Leadership Poverty and World Disorder.

A further study of this problem by Prof. Brown of The World-wide Institute shows that the growth of the global military expenses over the last quarter of a century was much more steady and higher than the growth of the world economy. Between 1960 and 1985, the military expenses, for example, rose from US $400bn. to $940bn. While expenses on telecommunication and other programmes for human development fell significantly World arms imports in 1948 totalled $35b. as compared to $33b. for grain and other food stuffs[8].

But a meticulous scrutiny of the real causal factor(s) of these super powers' lust for arms race as opposed to programmes for human development during the Cold War reveals that the real causal factor is the ideological conflict characterized by the scramble for the spoils of World War II and the surge for dominance and monopoly over the World Market between the parties involved. Furthermore, when one examines the economic implications of this arms race problem between the Soviet Union and the USA, one finds that this problem has exhaustively sacked most of the energies and resources of not only these two super powers but also of the entire World. Also, one notices tha tthe innocent Developing countries or LDCs which were not a part of this when the Cold War between the two super powers started in 1945, accidentally also became a hostage of the problem and therefore began also paying a heavy price for a foreign problem which they neither understand nor had any share in.

To trust and appreciate the fact that these two super powers wasted most of their time and that of the LDCs in this senseless arms race, one has to look at Japan heights of greatness in socio-economic development. Japan which was barred by the 1945 treaty, after World War II from militarization automatically became the sole benefactor by virtue of enjoying a monopoly of non-participation in the arms race. Because of this monopoly, it began moving into an easy position of a World Economic Dominance. It immediately became a super economic power comparable to both Soviet Union and the USA. Unlike both the USA and the Soviet Union, Japan discovered that military power was no longer a dependable weapon in this nuclear age. Japan recognized that it was now the economic power but not military power that spoke loudest on the World Market. So by 1990, Japan easily proved that she was the leading World trading power. Therefore, with this Japanese experience, it is here hoped that Developing Countries or LDCs would also learn from Japan. And that they would understand that their main threat is not the invading armies but expanding deserts and other ecological problems such as shrinking forests; erosion of soils; the falling of water tables; deterioration of grasslands due to an on-going decrease in amount of rainfall from year to year; depletion of oil reserves and other energy resources such as coal; and finally, the gradual changes in climatic condition from year to year, that often lead to most of them to suffer a top poor harvest that they cannot therefore easily make their ends meet in order to enable those that they govern to have some food on their table.

Whereas this experience of Japan's impressive success was known to both the Soviet Union and the USA including their allies, it is questionable whether these two super powers did ever realize the dangers of their arms race and the benefits that they would gain by diverting their attention from arms race to this Japanese rational choice. In its study for the US budgetary expenses for 1987, "Reagan Proposes $994 b. budget" (Washington D.C. Thursday, February 6, 1986 also reported in The Kenya Times, Friday March 7, 1986) REUTERS noted that out of $994bn. US budget earmarked for 1987, a total of $311.6 bn. 933%) had been earmarked for military expenses[9]. A clear indicator and a major paradox of our World Leadership Poverty in both LDCs and the Developed Countries alike not fit for World Peace and Order at all.

Defending this budget, the USA Defense Secretary, Casper Weinberger, argued that peace was also expensive and, therefore, that it was imperative for the US to consider such alternatives; and that if the USA ever failed to keep the peace this way, they doubt the cost of their standard of living would become incredible[10]. Thus, according to the USA viewpoint, the USA had to do so otherwise its lifestyle would not be safe from communism—a lifestyle they hated so much that they would not like to see coming at their door-steps at all.

Hence, the paradox and tragedy of the arms race epidemic during the Cold War which has, in turn, laid down a critically dangerous foundation for International Relations today (2004). And although the USA Leadership today under President George Bush Jr. may contend that USA invasion and toppling of Iraq leadership was rational and well justified for it was aimed at removing and possibly containing the spread of dangerous nuclear weapons from/in the hands of irresponsible LDCs such as Iraq which may use it foolishly against others or else where on the globe, the fact is that all this is illogical and totally unreliable. Otherwise, why could the GA chief have resigned due to spearheading falsehood? The only logical reason of such invasion was in order to sustain a perpetual USA monopoly of armament superiority in her capacity as a World lone super power now that USSR is already dead. Hence the tragedy and paradox of leadership poverty today globally. If this assertion were spurious (i.e., not so) then why has USA Leadership and its allies in Iraq failed to prove otherwise??

## (3) Critique

Many theories and allegations on "arms race" as a "deterrence" abound. However, arms race alone is not, and has never been a reliable insurance against future international wars. From world history, nations and even nuclear families alike have fought with or without arms. Wherever and whenever they lacked arms, they fought with words, hence the concept "Cold War"

It is submitted that millions of years ago, men and nations alike did not have the present sophisticated weaponry. However, it is equally submitted that so long as these entities had the human nature characterized by animus dominandi (selfishness and the desire to dominate others), and existed in a world of resource scarcity, fighting was part and parcel of their lives. They fought either in defense of their possessional values or to acquire milieu values (those properties they wished to get but could not easily and peacefully get.) Such values included wealth, slaves, lovers, territory and the like. It is a well known fact that due to this human mentality coupled with resource scarcity, men have always fought. Even today, where sophisticated weapons are not available, men will always fight with feasts, teeth, legs (by kicks and many other bodily weapon(s) in defense or in each of certain perceived objectives).

From generation to generation, men and nations alike began to learn how to use stones, sticks, clubs, and so on as weapons. Further, they learnt how to develop more sophisticated weapons. In the Iron Age, they learnt how to develop and use spears, arrows, knives, axes, as weapons against their opponents. This aggressive weaponry innovation was further reinforced and increased by man's recurrent cold wars couples with man's inherent desire to dominate over others (animus dominandi).

So, the more men and nations alike competed for this dominance, the more they competed for weapon superiority; and the more they did this, the more they advanced in weapon invention. The game did not only become part and parcel of their foreign policy but also a vicious circle, a very expensive and annoying national task from year to year. In fact, it is the same disease which now occupies most of our foreign policy decision-makers' attention.

Consequently, the "Star War" (SDI) which is the present most superior weapon, is neither an end in itself nor a solution to arms race. Rather, it is just another new age or era of weapon innovation—a nuisance vicious circle phenomenon of "arms innovation" and "arms race'. It is only superior today in "The Nuclear Age" just as "Stones" were also superior during the "Stone Age"; as spears, arrows and axes were superior during the "Iron Age"; as rifles were during the "Rifles Age"; as Artillery were superior in the "Artillery Age"; as tanks were superior in "The Tank Age"; as Warships were superior in the "Naval Age"; as the atomic bomb was a superior weapon during the "Atomic Age"; and more so, as both RBMs and IBMs became superior weapons during the "Nuclear Age".

Therefore, the "Star Wars" weapon cannot and will not be the final or last stage of weapon innovation. Also, they cannot be a reliable deterrent weapon. So long as men and nations alike continue to negatively perceive each other and to be governed by this animus dominandi mentality, as they have always been doing from generation to generation, arms race is here to stay among men and nations alike until men and nations come to terms with how to control themselves against this animus dominandi mentality. But arms race and arms innovation have become a fertile area for economic profit makers and speculators.

Certain key foreign policy-makers are not only political leaders of their respective nation-states. Also, they are principle partners in armament manufacturing corporations[11].

Due to this animus dominandi mentality and man's lust for these enormous economic benefits inherent in armament production industry, arms race is most likely to remain a chronic pain in the neck. To be able to control it effectively, may require an honest collective struggle from all men and nations alike. Otherwise, any attempt to do so without this element is most likely to be futile.

## CHAPTER III

# A Strategy for a Durable World Peace, Co-Operation and Socio Economic Prosperity

### (1) A Call for an Honest Collective World-wide Responsibility and Commitment

### (a) An Overview

It is submitted that in order for Sudan to find a solution to its one two decade civil war, it used a roundtable conference in Naivasha, Kenya (2004).

However control of this chronic problem does necessarily require elegant roundtable conferences but not alone. In the main, it also requires an honest worldwide collective commitment and responsibility to the struggle of both men and nations alike. Otherwise, any attempt(s) to do so; short of this commitment will not only be futile but also a total waste of time. This is why most negotiations, e.g. Strategic Arms Limitation Talks (SALT) and many others before SALT have always been either less productive or just a total failure as the Somalia Civil War Talks, where the innocent general Somalis who effective 2008 continue being subjected to the rule of the jungle characterized by anarchical tendencies of different Somali Clan War-Lords each defending his parodual clan supremacy and other interested antithetical to the interests of other clans. The same phenomenon also holds true in many other African countries where peace has already proved a too expensive commodity second to none. In The Congo Republic, the Country remains in a shaky balance between peace and war ever since the country achieved its independence in 1960. The Congolese people have never rested from their leadership's terrorism which constantly looted the natural resources of the Country to such an extent that her wealth has been siphoned and harboured in foreign countries exceeded the gross national product. And, Liberia, Sierra Leone & Civil wars plus, in the inter-state war between Ethiopia and Eriterea remain another bothersome headache to Africa and Total World Community regardless of numerous roundtable peace conferences. Such conferences alone cannot answer the reason why both Prime Minister Meles Zenawi of Ethiopia could have sought joint effort of President Isayas Afeweki of Eritrea in order to root out President Mengitsu Haile Mariam from his leadership over Addis Ababa in 1991 and later begin to lock their horns in a devastating war across their common borders. If, Afeweki had agreed to give a hand to his friend Zenawi (who is also said as being AFeweki's blood cousin), on mutual understanding that after rooting out Haile Mariam to give way for Zenawi's leadership to take over Addis Ababa Capital, (1) Eritrea and Ethiopia would each be a separate sovereign state and (2) Badme village which both Countries were using as their main port and harbour could be given to Eritrea as a form of war-victory award. Conference alone cannot do this because they are not well equipped with requisite scientific tools with which to deal exhaustively with such puzzles caused by the mysteries of the human nature. Hence, the obvious recurrent sparks of conflict between the two warring parties.

But, why has man and nations alike failed to recognize this reality? What must, therefore, be done in order for them to do so?

### (b) The reasons men and Nations alike have failed to recognize this reality:

Several reasons have been identified as causal factors to man's failure to recognize our Forefathers' CALL against War(s). Such reasons include: the lust for wealth accumulation from arms race and armament production, animus dominandi, and the like. However, from a micro-diagnosis of the problem using an individual as a unit of analysis, it is submitted that the whole world is Filthy-wicked, From nuclear family to peer-groups, organizations and nation-states, wickedness abound. Hatred, lies, dishonesty, trickeries, corruption, misreporting, lack of genuine appreciations, misinterpretation, false accusations, exploitation, theft, robberies, embezzlement, and the like are a habitual order of the day everywhere albeit this may differ in degree from individual to individual and from nation-state to another. In the final analysis, Humanity is grounded on a wicked foundation characterized by a general indiscipline and irresponsibility.

Man's wickedness is neither new nor unique. It is as old as mankind. It has been the major target of attack throughout history by all religions, prophets, philanthropists, saints, and many others. This is precisely why religions were formed; and why Prophets, Saints and other Philanthropists emerged. The latter did not emerge by accident. Their aim was to assist Churches, Synagogues, Temples, etc. to free man from this vicious yoke of wickedness, albeit the general excuse has always been to enable man's soul enter the Eternal Life.

From the Old Testament, for example, we note that it was this wickedness which generated hatred, lies, dishonesty, etc. among the peoples and individuals of the time. For instance, it induced the wife of Isaac to lie to her husband (Isaac) that her son (Jacob) was indeed Isaac's elder son (Esau)—an action which created an everlasting intra-family feuds and divorce between Esau and Jacob. Similarly, it induced the Israel tribe to massacre many other tribes, e.g., the Gentiles, et. al. using obsessed illusions and myths that they were a "Chosen Children of God" as though the Gentiles and other tribes had not been created by the same God. Further, it induced the same so-called the "Chosen Children of God" to disobey their own Prophet (Moses) even when the latter was still busy emancipating them from the bondage of slavery in Egypt. Worse of all, it induced them to reject and revolt against not only their emanicipator (Moses). During the Days of Jesus after Moses, they also revolted against the teachings of Jesus Christ regardless of what had been prophesied to them in the Old Testament. Tamed by this power of wickedness, they had no choice but to commit Jesus to the Cross albeit they also knew well, from the teachings of John The Baptist, that Jesus was indeed the "Christ" and the "True Son of God" who, according to the prophecy, was to come and save them from this wickedness. And before Christ, we also note that it was the same wickedness which induced Herod's wife to exploit her daughter's dependency to her to have her own father (Herod) to behead John The Baptist who, became of the Biblical norms, was opposed to her mother marrying Herod, so that she (Herod's wife) may remain married to Herod.

It is plausible that such Biblical stories could be rhetorics to those still a hostage of darkness. Also, it is submitted that the contrast between our generation and that of the Old Testament is so vast that comparison between the two generations may not be logical. However, empirical evidences show that whereas before the birth of Christ, Socrates was sentenced to death simply because he was misunderstood and, therefore, falsely accused of corrupting children. In our own generation, Sir Thomas Moore, Patrice Lumumba, and many others have also been put to death through false allegations and witnesses. In addition, Rev. Dr. Martin Luther King, Rev. Malcom X, Steve Biko, inter alios have also been victims of such symptoms of wickedness. All this did not occur by chance. Further, they were all a function of societal wickedness free from spatial temporal context.

### (c) Submission

In view of these empirical evidences, it is submitted that wickedness is a terrible disease—a dangerous cancer rooted in mankind; and an enemy of peace, unity and progress within and among families, groups, organizations and nation-states.

Quarrels and wars whether explicit or tacit are all a function of this disease. Although the habitual scarcity of our Market from one generation to another may also be a contributing factor, from a psychiatric level of analysis, wickedness is the motor and generator of quarrels, wars and other forms for conflicts. In the absence of it, there is no doubt that conflicts on our scarce market would be easily settled peacefully and nobly.

Whereas it is plausible that all these elements are biologically rooted (innate). However, it is submitted that man is not born a thief, a liar, or dishonest. He becomes so only after he has grown up and become an intersubjective member of his/her society, ie. when he has become well cognizant of the world around him in terms of who is who; what is what; when to lie and when not to do so; and above all, who to lie and who not to lie. In view of this, wickedness is partially innate and partially learned. Society is the principal teacher (socializing agent) of each individual. It is a vehicle and promoter of this cancer.

Society's behavioural patterns (i.e., culture), is the motor for each member's mode of behaviour in that society. If it is corrupt, most of its members will equally be so. Thus, although wickedness is innate, wickedness is active only where conditions are permitting it. Otherwise, it is subject to remain dormant permanently. As corruptive parents or peer groups always breed corruptive children and members respectively, so are corruptive leaders most likely to breed corruptive followers. On the contrary, noble and scrupulous leaders are subject to breed noble and law-abiding followers in conformity with the Behavioural Law of "Like-Begets-like".

In conformity with this Behavioral Law, no scrupulous and noble parents can breed noble and scrupulous children if their society is infested with corrupt and arrogant children and parents. Children always behave to the tune of the majority of their society in order for them to feel comfortable and to be true members of their intersubjective society. If they do not do so, they are likely to suffer from dissonance. This is why anomie, inertia and child-rebellion abound in most rigidly conservative homes. Children and followers will always support their parents and leaders respectively only when they know that their parents' or leaders' behaviour is inter-subjective, i.e., universally shared by the majority of their society. This is why most white children in South Africa supported their minority white South African regime, and hated every indigenous African children as well as Indian and mixed children. They did so because they fully knew that this was what all their white parents wanted and believed in. This reality also held true with respect to religion and parents or society. All their offsprings were expected to be followers of the same religion and to speak their parental Afrikaana language and accent.

In a South Africa of the apartheid white minority rule, this phenomenon was a natural must because of natural law culturally conditioning offsprings to behave so in order to be deemed intersubjective members of their society. For example, let us take two English speaking children for example,—one from Britain and one from the United States and examine their accent. From observing the two, one is likely to note a significant difference in their accent albeit they are both English speakers. Their accent variance is not accidental; rather, it is a function of their social setting and cultural difference. In the final analysis, it is an explicit explanation as well as a ramification of the Behavioural Law of Like-Begets-Like which is also a kin to the Biological Law of heredity.

### (2) A call for a Comprehensive World-wide Education Programme or International Peace, Co-operation and Socio Economic Prosperity

Several empirical evidences cited above collectively confirm the fact that inspite of our high level of education, science and technology which our generation has acquired so far, we are still an ignorant generation of ourselves. Consequently, we are unable to control ourselves against arms race. Also, we are unable to properly understand these concepts of peace, co-operation and social progress. Serious of all, we have not only been negligent of our Forefathers' sentiments and worries documented in the Preamble of the UN on the question of future World Peace and collective responsibility against war(s). Also, it is equally submitted that we have been negligent of what Humanity is all about; of what we actually need from life; and of how to achieve these needs.

It is for this reason: (1) that our dishonesty, hatred and the search for evil deeds against our fellow men abound both at the individual and nation-state levels; (2) that certain key foreign policy-decision makers e.g., the current British Prime Minister, in the name of nation-states, are seen craving for nuclear and other highly sophisticated weapons from NATO on pretence that these weapons are essential for their national self-defence; (3) that as of now, at least 10 nation-states Russia, US, UK, France, India, Pakistan, South Africa, Israel and Brazil have already acquired nuclear capabilities; (4) that now our Planet is most likely to be soon saturated with this dangerous nuclear weapons; and (5) that our Planet is now doomed for a total destruction by the mighty of this dangerous nuclear power due to man's inborn wickedness.

In view of this failure, it is reasonable to conclude that what both Jean Jacque Rousseau (1712-1778) and Thomas Hobbes (1588-1679) observed and predicted about man's behaviour two centuries ago still holds true in our own generation. Also, it is submitted that what Rousseau recommended two centuries ago in his Emile but was not implemented or tested in the real world may be worthwhile for us to try.

In his Emile, Rousseau had suggested that in order for man to rid himself for animus dominandi mentality which, in turn, drive men and nations alike into quarrels and wars, a comprehensive re-education of society was necessary.

Although Rousseau's call may be too obselete by now, the essence of his call is important indeed. It is, therefore, possible that a comprehensive world-wide education on our Forefathers' sentiments and concepts may be a cost-effective ANSWER—a Rational Alternative. If honestly responded to by men and nations alike, it is quite possible that this programme would effectively enlighten men and nations alike on our Forefathers' sentiments and, therefore, promote the concepts of international peace, co-operation, human rights and social progress. It would enlighten our present national leaders who are our key foreign policy decision-makers on the importance of these concepts of international peace, co-operation, understanding, and human rights for our world social progress—concepts which seem to have not been understood properly.

It is plausible that, in the event of war or threat of war of aggression, the aggression is legally allowed, under Article 51 of the UN Charter, to seek military assistance from its regional ally(ies) or any other sympathizer(s) against the aggressor in case the UN has not yet decided on what to do or is against the aggressor in case the UN has not yet decided on what to do or is still looking into ways and means of settling the dispute between the two parties as Congo (now Zaire) did in January 1960 vis a vis Belgium war of aggression[13]. However, according to the sentiments of our Forefathers, the latter were totally against any use of force or coercion. This is precisely why they collectively formulated for us these prescriptions contained in the UN Charter. By doing so, they hoped that all of us and future generations would uphold, respect and make use of their recommendations for international co-operation, understanding, peace, human rights and the rights of peoples of all nations.

But, our Forefathers did not expect us to do this because they were the victors in the World War II. Rather, they wanted to do this because they were concerned about our well-being and that of future generations. From their personal fresh experience from World Wars I and II, they were now fully convinced that war was no better than a senseless and useless affair—a threat to humanity and its advancement. It was succinctly due to this reality that they earnestly called upon all men and nations alike to completely and finally decist from any use of force as a means of settling disputes.

Again, it is plausible that whereas our Forefathers were able to analize the existing world problem and to come up with these rational prescriptions embodied in the UN Charter for us, they were not as highly educated as we are today. Also, it is plausible that sophisticated as we are, we must, therefore, be in a better position to do better than our Forefathers did over forty years ago.

If this reasoning holds true, then it is submitted that Henry Kissinger's recent argument aimed at encouraging the US to forget the USSR's proposed reduction in nuclear armaments arguing that the USSR was simply bluffing, is totally deplorable Given that Kissenger has a Ph.D. degree which neither of our Forefathers did not hold, it is equally plausible that the level of his rationality vis a vis that of our Forefathers is questionable.

However, it is hereby hoped that with our level of sophistication in Science and Technology superior to that of our Forefathers in the 1940's,

(1) We will start doing better and rational, that whatever we have done in the past.
(2) Our discoveries and inventions in Science and Technology will now be better synchronized and converged into the areas of peaceful use, for human advancement, e.g., in health, life expectancy, etc. than in areas of self-destruction e.g., nuclear weapons and pollution.

CHAPTER IV

# Conclusion

With this in mind, it is, therefore, hoped that our huge annual budget each nation-state wastes on armaments and the like will no longer be a necessity. Such national budgets will now be diverted into various peaceful scientific and technological activities for peaceful ends e.g.:

## (A) Selected areas where funds wasted on armament and environmental pollution may now be wisely invested.

1. Present Research Struggle against Acquired Immune Deficiency Syndrome (AIDS), and other diseases now seriously facing the entire World.
2. Research and other grassroot self-help movements, e.g., in Chile and Santago where these countries are now busy collaborating with World Health Organization in a research struggle against alcohol problems, and the like.
3. Individual and collective national contributions to the present plight of refugees as in the present case of Tanzania where the latter is now granting land and citizenship to hundreds of refugees in Tanzania in order to help unfortunate persons to settle down and to become self-sufficient. Tanzania now hosts 179,000 refugees, i.e. 0.9% of the total population in Tanzania.
4. Cultivation of good self-discipline and attitude toward work in most developing countries where such important element of human power seems to be still very low.
5. Cultivation of better ways and means of helping poverty stricken countries such as Chad which tend to depend by and large on food relief's instead of practical agriculture development. (Chad seems to have realized this essence and is now shifting from food relief to actual dependable agricultural development).
6. Cultivation of better advises to developing countries in their economic endeavours in order to assist them expand the manufacturing facilities by switching from being

producers of commodities to being processors of commodities a strategy that is likely to assist them manage their own urban development challenges as also noted by the executive Director of Habitat, Dr. Arcot Ramachandran, during his address at the UN Congress in Sub-Saharan Africa[14].

7. Cultivation of very scarce resources into productive use as in the case of the Nile Delta in Egypt which inspite of its schistomiasis (Bilharzia) problems has now been exploited for proper and productive agricultural use by Egypt.
8. Present mounting efforts by scientists to unlock the secrets of herbs for the advancement of humanity.
9. Efforts against world population explosion, etc.
10. More Exploration into peaceful use of nuclear energy e.g., in medical and surgical areas, in food technology areas, etc,
11. Exploration into safe disposal of nuclear energy waste before any full-scale use of nuclear energy is recommended or initiated at all.

Thus, huge sums of funds being wasted on armament would now be diverted to these peaceful and meaningful research problem areas in order to enable us:

(a) to expand our frontiers of scientific knowledge; and (b) to improve on our present standard of living and life expectancy.

In doing this, man would now no longer be an inevitable potential enemy of his fellow man. Man's common enemy no. 1 would now be poverty, ignorance, diseases and the like. These could now become our universal principal targets to which our funds previously earmarked for armaments would now be spent.

But all these activities cannot possibly be carried out effectively without first re-educating the entire World Community on them. So the most fundamental question that we must now examine carefully is: How can our World Community be re-educated? With what means? Is it by the use of schools, from what level of schools and by which other institutions?

## (B) Some Institutions that may be Mobilized to Promote These Concepts World-wide

A succinct and candid answer is that the programme must be part and parcel of every Government's education policy. It must be a world-wide policy priority.

Secondly, it must be a formal (structured) programme required in every school beginning with primary level. Children must be given a better chance to grow up with this idea crystallized in their mind that war is an evil and, therefore, undesirable.

In view of this, it should also be world-wide priority Government policy that every community beginning with nuclear family should assist schools in socializing children on the concept of war and the concept of international co-operation, understanding, peace, human rights and the rights of other peoples.

In Kenya, we already have a National Students' Science Congress Programme jointly funded by the UNESCO and the Kenya Government and managed by The Kenya National Academy of Sciences on behalf of the Kenya Government. The programme has been covering biological and physical sciences disciplines only. The programme is now looking into the possibility of also incorporating social and behavioural sciences disciplines.

It would, therefore, be equally cost-effective if we could also incorporate these concepts of International Co-operation, understanding, peace, human and rights of other peoples in our National Students' Science Congress activities. Whereas The Kenya National Academy of Sciences may be delighted to do so, would the USSR Academy of Sciences, the US National Academy of Sciences and other Academies be equally willing to do this? What about Schools, Colleges and Universities throughout the World? Are they equally prepared to do this? It is submitted that he Papacy and all other spiritual leaders have tried to help; however, empirical evidences show that their contributions have been insignificant indeed. They have not been impressive at all, given that thousands of lives and property are being wasted daily by the hungry gun allover the planet.

The only Spiritual Leaders who have attempted to do this with total commitment and responsibility in our own generation have been Rev. Martin Luther King, Rev. Malcolm X., Rev. Desmond Tutu, Rev. Jessie Jackson and Rev. Masinde Muliro (a man who contributed significantly in the Kenyan uprising activities against the British Colonial rule). All others have been too dependent on political leaders who, according to our Father of Philosophy (Socrates) do not seem to be informed well enough both in mind and at heart. Instead of being the breeders of peace some of these Spiritual Leaders have been found to be significant breeders of inter-church hatred, factionalism and conflicts which are indeed significant indicators of a high level of animus dominandi mentality of these Spiritual Leaders. Empirical evidences of this behaviour include the on-going apartheid situation in South Africa; Catho-Protestant conflict in Northern Ireland; Inter alios[15].

Now that we are already aware of our own shortcomings and the latter's causal factors, it is here hoped that all leaders[16] would re-evaluate their attitude and reverse their gears accordingly in support of this new struggle against arms race and all other forms of animus dominandi.

It is submitted that the Mikhael Gorbachev-Reagan nuclear missiles accord (1987) is a commendable significant achievement for us all; a significant contribution to world peace today; and a sound source for our hope and expectation for a calm bright future. However, how many times has humanity witnessed treaty abrogations? How come The Peace of Westphalia (1648)—the most outstanding peace treaty in the history of inter-European politics "which put an end to the great Thirty Years War of religion and marked the acceptance of the new political order in Europe"[17]—did not last that long before it was equally abrogated by its own signatories? In view of this reality,

1. Used here not in the tradition sense of the treatment of mental disorder but in a behavioural sense meaning an inquiry into the causal factors of the subject's behaviour in decision-making. See Agola Auma_Osolo, "A Retrorespective Analysis of UN Activity in the Congo and Its Significance for Contemporary Africa", Vanderbilt Journal of Transnational Law, Vol. 8, 1975 pp. 468-473; and Agola Auma_Osolo, Cause-Effects of Modern African nationalism on the World Market, University Press of America (1983) on political behaviour of Nkrumah, Kenyatta and Nyerere, vis a vis colonialism and imperialism in Africa.
   This will be our methodology throughout this study in order to expose and analyse those real causal factors (independent variables) of war which have always evaded recognition of both scientists and policy decision-makers from generation to generation.
   See also, Margot Mayne, Peace on Earth: A Peace Anthology, UNESCO, Paris, 1984.

3. See, for example, Auma_Osolo, "UN Peace-Keeping Policy: Some Basic Causal Factors of Its Implementation Problems and their Implications" California Western International Law Journal, Vol. 6, 1976 pp. 349-357. Arnold Simon, Beyond Repair (The Urgent Need for a new World Organization). Collier-MaCmillan, Canada, Ltd., 1972 and Robert J. Art and Robert Jervis, International Politics (Anarchy, Force and Imperialism), Little, Brown & Co., Boston, 1973.
4. See for instance the Associated Press, "Reagan's Star Wars Plan Attracting more US Allies" London, Monday, March 24, 1986 and The Daily Nation, Nairobi, Tuesday, Nairobi, Tuesday, March 25, 1986.
5. At both Nagasaki and Hiroshima in World War II.
6. Lester R. Brown, State of the World (1986). Brown is the President of World-wide Institute and Director of the study.
7. See for example, The Sunday Nation, 15th June,1986; and Agola Auma_Osolo, Cause-Effects of Modern African Nationalism on the World Market, University Press of America, (1983).
8. Lester R. Brown, op. cit. note 6.
9. The Kenya Times, Friday March 7, 1986.
10. Idem.
11. Lister R. Brown, op.cit. notes 6 and 8.
12. Elizabeth Farnsworth, "Chile: What was the US's Role?", Foreign Policy, (1974); Robert Art and Robert Jervis, International Politics: Anarchy, Force and Imperialism, Boston, little Brown & Co. Ltd. (1973); Robert Art and Kenneth N. Waltz, eds., The Use of Force: International Politics and Foreign Policy, Boston, Little Brown & Co. Ltd, (1971); and Samir Amin, Accumulation on a World Scale, A Critique of the Theory of Under-development. Monthly Review Press, New York (1974); and The Kenya Times, Friday March 7, 1986.

    According to both theorists (particularly Hobbes), man is, by nature, an irrational and selfish animal. Due to this innate mentality, man will always crave for more wealth, glory and love. Since everyone is doing the same, and due to scarcity of all such values from the environment, competition and conflict among men and nations for these values abound. Hence the theory of "survival of the Fittest" by Charles Rober Darwin (1809-1882). And as Darwin also noted it, due to this "Survival of the Fittest" mentality among men and nations alike, there is always a tendency the fittest party to exploit the weaker party for the fittest's own good. They may use them as slaves, colonies, puppets or in many other forms. For further details, see Agola Auma-Osolo,

"Rationality and Foreign Policy Process", The Year Book of World Affairs 1977, pp. 260-263; and Agola Auma-Osolo, Cause Effects of Modern African Nationalism on the World Market, University Press of America (1983) esp. Chapter II.

13. Also, see Agola Auma-Osolo, "A Retrospective Analysis of the UN Activity in the Congo & its Significance for Contemporary Africa", op.ct., note 1; and Articles 1, 2 and 51 of the UN Charter.
14. The Kenya Times, Tuesday, March 11, 1986.
15. In South Africa (Azania) all institutions from nuclear families to churches, schools etc, white children and adults alike are deliberately and forcefully taught to hate all Africans and other non-whites (Asians and half-casts). To make it worse, the Dutch Reformed church in South Africa is the principal socializing agent. It is the breeder and promoter of this hatred popularly known as "apartheid". The Dutch is like one side of the coin. So, what one does is automatically condoned and endorsed by the other.
16. Meaning political, economic, spiritual, intellectual, inter alios. The call is to all leaders because (a) the task requires collective efforts from all sectors of life; and (b) both political and economic simple medicine against self-destruction.
17. J. L. Brierly, The Law of Nations, Oxford University Press, 1963 p. 5

# PART SIX

## UNIVERSITY AND THE CULTURE OF PEACE AND DEMOCRACY DEVELOPMENT: A Test for Universities Efficacy as An Agent for Conflict Vaccination

CHAPTER 1

# Introduction

## 1. Problem

This topic poses three exhaustive mutually exclusive fundamental problems which must be first and foremost dealt with and understood thoroughly well before we dare to embark on the real purpose or objective of the topic.

These problems are:

(1) understanding the meaning and role of a university to humanity
(2) Understanding the meaning and role of a Culture of Peace to humanity; and finally
(3) Understanding the meaning and role of a Culture of Democracy to humanity.

## 2. Purpose, Methodology and Rationale

In this regard, in Part II of this paper let us, therefore, first begin with what each of those three concepts means and what it is expected to do to humanity. Thereafter, Part III will deal with the Substantive Area of Inquiry; Part IV with Conflict Vaccination cum Cultural Engineering and Expected Results; Part V with the Efficacy and Reliability of Conflict Vaccination cum Cultural Engineering; and Part VI with Conclusion of this research exercise.

In this research expedition, from Parts I to VI, our sole fundamental purpose is:-

1. To save Humanity from the scourge of perennial massacres, genocide, espionage, terrorism, landmines, and all other symptoms of the existing culture of No-Peace and No-Democracy characterized by rampant conflict at both national and international

levels in the same spirit Dr. Jonas E. Salk and Dr. Albert Sabin saved Humanity from the scourge of the killer polio disease in 1953/54 and 1955 (respectively;

2. And, to, therefore boost (accelerate) our Social and Behavioural Sciences also into those unknown horizons of the needed wisdom and knowledge as both Dr. Salk and Dr. Sabin did to their Biosciences albeit polio may not be as much destructive to Humanity as Conflict is which is not only destructive to Humanity but to both Humanity and Property en mass as the case of Hiroshima and Nagasaki atomic bomb havoc in 1945.

However, for the benefit of those who may not be fairly conversant with polio vaccine discovery by these two giant scientists, whose contribution to Humanity is akin and a prelude to our own intended Conflict vaccination cum Cultural Engineering, the following short account on their wok is very necessary.

In order for the two to achieve the needed polio vaccine for humanity, both had to go through thick and thin. And, before they could do so, every odd was against them and their efforts, e.g. their own fellow scientists who were interested in descriptive other than in problem solving research.

But, in spite of all these constraints, our giants could neither rest nor bow down to leave every stone unturned. They were determined to continue unperturbed until they got to the real bottom of those unknown horizons of the needed wisdom and knowledge for the cure of the polio disease.

Because of their fixed determination, they refused to be silenced or satisfied with what their colleagues such as Dr. Jacob Heine(a German born doctor, 1840) and Dr. Karl Landsteirner (an Austrian immunologist 1902) were interested in which was purely a description of poliomyelitis as the root-cause of polio.

The two (Dr. Salk and Dr.Sabin) were adamant that although such on-going Science in theory building, in the final analysis, it actually lacked any significant tangible consequence to and from Humanity and Science which were already endangered by the presence of this killer disease. And, they stood firm until their fixed determination proved them right by bearing the needed fruits for both Humanity and Science (i.e., polio vaccine discovery)! But how did they manager to do so?

Seriously concerned with polio manace to Humanity that had existed for ages, and being filled and, therefore, motivated by the spirit of Neighbourly Love which their Country (USA) had demonstrated in the post-World War Era in order to save desperate Europe which had now been severly devastated by both World Wars I and II (1914-18 and 1939-45 respectively) using a comprehensive recurrent and development emergency humanitarian assistance, THE MARSHALL PLAN, many Universities arose in a battle against that menace. For example, a team of three (3) Harvard University bacteriologists in USA arose in 1949 against the threat namely Dr. Hohn F.Enders, Dr. Fredrick C. Robbins and Dr. Thomas H. Weller. This team managed to develop and put in place a practical way on how to grow polio viruses outside a human body. Its work consequently made it practically possible for Humanity to begin producing large quantities of viruses that man desparately needed to make vaccines against polio-phobia. And, four years later (about1953-55), on the strength of the research efforts by Dr. Jonas. E. Salk of the University of Pittsburgh (USA), the vaccine was declared "safe" and "effective". (The World Book Encyclopedia, Vol.15 p.55). Similarly, on the strength of further research efforts by Dr. Albert Sabin of the Univeristy of Cincinnati (USA), the vaccine was finally confirmed reliably effective as an Oral Vaccine! Hence, the unique significance of the role and contribution of the University to Humanity.

In the final analysis, and as will also be noted in my other publication, "Role of Neighbourly Love in Disaster Management", International Journal of Disaster Management and Risk Reduction ( IJDMRR), vol.3, No.2 (2011) (pp.164-174), their discovery became a remarkable New Chapter not only in Biosciences but also to Humanity against the man killer polio. And in as much as polio was brought to its knees by the determination of those two giant scientists so is also our good hope that conflict is apt to be brought to its knees by our collective determination reflected in this Paper. This is the Motto of this Paper albeit the anti-Salk and anti-Sabin political scientists may not be positively moved by it.

In this regard, it is hoped that both the University and entire World Leadership will also emulate the noble roles of:—(1) President Frankline D. Roosevelt, himself partially paralyzed by polio, who immediately recognized the urgent need to support the crusade by founding the Georgia Warm Springs Foundation in 1927 and devoted it exclusively to caring for polio patients and by also establishing the National Foundation for Infantile Paralysis in 1938, which is today called National Foundation, to finance intensive polio research which assisted both Dr. Salk and Dr. Sabin in their discoveries of their vaccines for Humanity; and (2) The Harvard University which also saw the same need to support the crusade against polio by growing polio viruses outside the body which, in turn, became the foundation of the making of the needed vaccines by both Dr. Salk in 1953/54 and also Dr. Sabin in 1955 of the University of Pittsburgh and the Univeristy of Cincinnati respectively (for further details, see The World Book Encyclopedia, Vol. 15, 1973, pp. 55-3), so that we can also bring the existing killer Global Conflict disease to its knees.

CHAPTER II

# A Conceptual Definition

## 1. A University and its Responsibility to Humanity

On the strength of definitions gained from dictionaries, encyclopaedia and our own experience as veteran members of The Academia, a university is succinctly a center for higher learning and advanced research in Science and Technology.

Because of its inherent dual responsibilities, a university's purpose is to unlock the mysteries of life and total universe for the benefit of the humanity by increasingly enhancing the latter's scope of understanding of the life around it and thus enabling it to improve and advance in its standard of living. It is expected to do so using its various disciplinary approaches, which include Physical Sciences, Biosciences, Behavioural Sciences, Social Sciences and Arts.

As also noted from history records,[1] this has been the normal traditional function of a university effective the beginning of man's civilization in Mesopotamia ways back in 7000 BC where the Sumerians first discovered:

(1) the essence and significance of such a centre to be responsible for such dual duties;
(2) the essence and significance of the Ziggurat[2] to unify them and synchronize their community affairs by cultivating a culture of peace and democracy which would provide them with an enabling environment for their collective gains and advancements in food security, shelter security, political security, health security, spiritual security, literary security, art security, and other categories of security man needs in life; and
(3) the essence and significance of not only a sufficient support but actually a maximum and mandatory support to their centre for higher learning and scientific research by

their Ziggurat whose need was seen as most critical by virtue of its role as a fountain of the science and technology they seriously needed for their development.[3]

This realism also holds true with regard to all other ancient centers of civilization such as the renown African Mysteries Systems of The Grand Lodge of Luxor[4] located in northeast Egypt now called "Alexandria" where these dual responsibilities of advanced learning and scientific research flourished; enhanced the advancement of civilization in Egypt; and attracted Socrates, Herodotus, Hypocrates and other Greek scholars including other foreign scholars of the time to come to Luxor for the exposure.

Further, the fame of these African Mysteries Systems of the Grand Lodge of Luxor did not only attract many foreign scholars. Also, it envied them so much that this envy attracted the Greek King, Alexander The Great to invade it in 332 BC and plunder all its library treasure which he then carried away with him to Greece and placed them under the free use of his tutor Aristotle, who, in turn, converted their authorship to his own without even knowing their actual original author as books of that time were always anonymous for the purpose for security of the writer.

Because of this enormous intellectual advantage plundered from The African Mysteries Systems of The Grand Lodge of Luxor by Alexander The Great.

1. Alexander's leadership fame enhanced significantly throughout the Region at the expense of the decline of the Egyptian supremacy[5].
2. Greek Empire expanded from Macedonia and Greece to as far southwest as Libya in North Africa; to as far north as the Caspian and Black Seas and as far east as the Indus River in West India and also far up to the Himalaya Mountains in North India.
3. His tutor, Aristotle, got a free advantage of being an author of books on various disciplines he actually had not written.[6]

Drawing from the above account of what humanity has been able to benefit from the ancient centers of advanced learning and scientific research not only in Mesopotamia and Egypt but also in Asia, China, Japan, India and others, and also drawing from our own experience of what our universities actually do in our own generation, there is no doubt that as a center inherent with such important dual responsibility, it is also the duty of each university to assist humanity in a cultural engineering with a view to facilitating or bring about a Culture of Peace and Democracy—a culture of an enabling environment for an accelerated socio-economic development at both national and global levels.

But then, what is this thing called "A Culture of Peace" and a "Culture of Democracy"? which the University is expected by humanity to bring about for it? What is each of them in a simplest term?

## 2. A Culture of Peace

By the concept a "Culture of Peace", we hereby simply mean a culture in which there is no presence of political conflicts. And, by the concept "political conflict", we also hereby simply mean a situation between two or more parties e.g. political leaders, political parties or countries (nation-states).

A political conflict falls into two exhaustive and mutually exclusive categories or types namely:

(a) a verbal political conflict, and
(b) A physical political conflict

The two are exhaustively defined as follows in (A) and (B); and both also fall into two scopes marked (C) below:

### (A) Verbal Conflict

### 1. In a Political Setting

This type of political conflict is also referred to, understood or known in the diplomatic circles as "cold war". It may exist between political leaders, (i.e., inter-leadership schism or cold war); between political parties (i.e. inter-party cold war); between leaders of the same political party (i.e., intra-party leadership schism or cold war); or between politically independent countries called nation-states (i.e., international Cold war).

Therefore, the on-going inter-political party verbal conflict between Kenya African National Union (KANU) and the Opposition Political parties in Kenya today such as the Democratic Party of Kenya (DP) on the issue of the Presidential Election Results of 1992 and 1997 on the one hand, and on the current burning controversial issue of the Constitutional Review on the other are just a few of the prima facie empirical evidences of the "Inter-Party Verbal Political Conflict or Cold War.

Similarly, the on-going verbal political conflict between Simeon Nyachae and President Daniel T. arap Moi within political Party KANU on the question of corruption and other elements of Bad Governance in Kenya on the one hand, and also the on-going verbal conflict between Oloo Aringo and Raila Odinga within the National Development Party of Kenya (NDP) on the controversial issue of the on-going interfication of the inter-party co-operation between KANU and NDP to which Aringo and other NDP members are opposed on the other, are succinct empirical evidences of intra-political party verbal leadership conflicts without actual physical confrontation between the parties thereof.

And finally the euphoria of capitalism—communism Cold War between the western nation states headed by the USA on the one hand and the Eastern nation—states headed by the then the Union fo Soviet Socialist Republic (USSR) on the other also constitutes another prima facie empirical evidence of international verbal conflict which has wrecked and tormented the international system for over two decades since the end of World War II, albeit this cold war is now over.

## 2. In a Religious Setting

A verbal conflict may be political or religious. Whereas a political conflict is characterized by those empirical examples or evidences stated above, a religious conflict is characterized by religious issues and tensions such as:

1. The Caste System in India institutionalized and constantly promoted by Hindu fundamentalism ever since the 7th to 6th Century BC against those other Indians who refused to accept, recognize and worship a cow object as their sacred god[7]—The main and sole reason why that culture of the touchables and untouchables rivalry was initiated and institutionalized in India which, consequently resulted into:-

    (a) India being subjected to perennial untold sorrows of a perpetual culture of religious tensions; and

(b) India becoming a prima facie model for what Frantz Fanon calls the "Wretched of the Earth".[8]

1. The other existing horrifying cultural practices in the same country of India promoted by the same Hindu Fundamentalism e.g.,

    (a) The Purdah System[9]—i.e., an institutionalized system in which husbands must be recognized and treated as gods by their wives.
    (b) The Devadasis system[10]—i.e., an institutionalized system in which most beautiful girls must be identified throughout India and then brought and subjected to the Temple as Temple Sex Girls (also called Temple Prostitution Girls) on the false pretense that they must do so in the service of religion and god.
    (c) The Child Marriage System[11]—i.e., also an institutionalized child marriage by which a little girl of less than ten is forced to marriage, and when her husband dies then she must remain a widow forever throughout her prime life.
    (d) Cruel Woman Dowry System[12] by which women must pay a price for a husband, and a husband is free to disown her and get another dowry from another girl whenever he so wishes and the first one must get lost at once. The husband may keep on moving from one wife to another and thus, getting richer and richer from Woman Dowry as such wealth is not refundable. Whenever it may be refundable, the husband coins a master plan to eliminate his wife so that he is not forced by her parents to refund the Woman Dowry.

In view of this nauseating culture knowingly institutionalized by the Hindu Religion in India, there is no doubt that Fanon's conclusion is totally right.[13].

### 3. In a Social Setting

Also, a verbal conflict may be purely social. This type is characterized by a social tension which often arises from time to time between football teams such as the perennial rivalry inherent between Gor Mahia and AFC Leopards Football teams in Kenya where each team always claims to be superior to the other and would wish to be recognized as such in Kenya for no other cause other than pure social prestige. The same paranoia for prestige between teams holds true all over the world, e.g. in the United States of America, the United Kingdom, Germany, France, Russia, Italy, etc. It is a global realism.

## 4. In an Economic Setting

Unlike the above 3rd type, which is motivated by social prestige, the Economic Verbal Conflict arises from the scramble for the monopoly for huge economic profits. It arises from economic rivalry between companies engaged in a common or similar trade or business.

Besides this type of inter-company rivalry, which is the scramble between the Haves and the Haves-Nots, Economic Verbal Conflict also arises between the Haves and the Have-Nots. A vivid example of this is, for example, a nauseating economic situation which engulfed England in the 18th and 19th Century caused by the mad scramble for riches by the *nouveaux riches* which engaged the literary class in England so much of what was going on in England that one of the English poets (Matthew Arnold, 1822-1888)[14] vehemently lamented:-

i. That the materialistic standards of an industrialized society of his time in Europe were completely incompatible with the great humanistic values, inherited from Greece and the Renaissance[15].
ii. And, that the mid-Victorian culture was now beset by so much personal self-seeking and lack of social purpose and moral strength by the aristocrats that this rich class was essentially "barbarians".
iii. To him, they lacked social consciousness about the prevailing inhumane socio-economic conditions of the "Populace" (the general lpublic) even though in contradiction they knew how to maximize only profits at the expense of the poor.
iv. In this anger and bitterness, Arnold further called them names as "Philistines" because they neither understood nor cared about culture in its humanistic terms".
v. He called them "Industrial bourgeoisie" who thought only of power and riches and saw in the external signs of change proof of spiritual advancement and who each valued himself not on what he was but on the number of railroads he had constructed."

A further autopsy of the 18th-19th Century mid-Victorian culture of economic rivalry as a vivid illustration of the economic verbal conflict category reveals to us the following nauseating symptoms:-

i. Ridiculing his existing culture in England, Benjamin Disraeli (1804-1881) wrote in his novel, Sybil; or Two Nations[16], the like most other European nations of the time, England was a nation of two distinct nationalities (or socio-economic classes).
"... Between whom there was no intercourse and no sympathy; who are as ignorant of each other's habits; thoughts, and feelings, as if they were different planets; who are formed by a different breeding, are fed by a different food, are ordered by different manners, and are not governed by the same laws ... the Rich and the Poor".[17]
ii. Men and women from poverty stricken homes or families were herded into coal mines and factories by those who owned the means of production where they were forced to work long hours for subsistence/meager wages.[18]
iii. Like these poor stricken men and women children of six and seven years were also herded into coal mines under ground twelve hours a day; forced to open and shut ventilation doors; and to be harnessed "like dogs to a go-card" to haul coal-wagons.[19]
iv. When the nobles pressured Parliament to protect these poor little children from the existing nauseating situation and Parliament accepted to do so and passed the 1833 Factory Act setting down various restrictions on women and child labour abuse plus their working hour,

    (a) Vehement resentments erupted against this Factory Act from the advocates of Individual Rights, Survival of The Fittest and the Rights of Free Market.
    (b) Using his unique position in Parliament as a powerful orator and statesman, John Bright (1811-1889) for example, vehemently argued that this legislation was the most injurious and destructive of the best interest of England and the liberty of the subject and the freedom of the contract.[20]

v. Although Parliament went ahead to implement this 1833 Factory Act and revised the Freedom of Free Market rights to fit into this Act and further passed other Factory Acts such as the 1842 and 1846 Acts aimed at reinforcing the goal of the 1833 Factory Act,[21]

(a) This child abuse corruption continued under cover through secret plans corruptly designed by Factory owners and coal miners. It was due to this corruption that heated uproar engulfed both England and total mainland Europe thus providing a fertile breeding ground for the germination and multiplication of both Utilitarian[22] and Socialist[23] throughout Europe in an economic cold war against the nouveaux riches[26] who had now turned the Culture of amazing Victorian Legacy into a Culture of decays and maggots!

(b) Phobic of this new formidable force arising from this uproar at home caused by the rise of these Utilitarian and Socialist philosophers,

    (i) The architects and promoters[27] of this culture decay resolved to move this virus from Europe to Asia and Africa.

    (ii) In Africa, this action was further corruptly legitimized by the so-called Berlin General Act of March 1885 by which these architects and promoters of the culture decay chopped Africa into colonies which they shared among themselves for their own economic plunder.

    (iii) As an unfortunate embarrassment and disgrace to the University (The Academia)[28], the Berlin General Act and its outcome were also hailed by the Scientists and Scholars of the time using their pseudo-science. to legitimize the Act, and to encourage the parties to his Act on the grounds that their action was legitimized by virtue of their Individual Rights, Survival of The Fittest Rights and Free Market Rights[29]

    (vi) However, this pseudo-scientific advice brought neither a lasting joy to the parties of this Act nor a scientific credit to those pseudo-scientists as:

        (a) This ill-advice soon manifested in a wide spread of bloodshed from the conflict between the proponents of the culture of inhumane colonial policies and the proponents of the culture of African Nationalism and demand for Africa freedom which intensified between the 1950s and the 1960s all over Africa[30].

        (b) The same phenomena also manifested itself in India much earlier thereby resulting into India Independence in 1947[31].

Turning our telescopes and microscopes from this Economic culture of inhumane colonial policies to the Economic Culture of slavery and slave trade which was also a culture motivated largely by no other ends other than economic gains, what do we also see or find from the history of human civilization?

Like the horrors of the above findings gained from our autopsy of the global inhumane culture of colonialism and imperialism, the autopsy for the global culture of slavery and slave trade also shows the following horrors:-

1. Africans in Egypt (before Egypt was later occupied by the Arabs immediately after the death of Mohammed in 632 AD) waged imperialistic wars in the region and colonized the first human civilization of Mesopotamia, in the Fertile Crescent as well as India; and enslaved the Jews for some centuries whom they used as a primary source of free labour, and whose life and total security was at the disposal of the slave master should any slave attempt to disobey to provide this free labour to the master.
2. Athens and Sparta individually waged imperialistic wars, colonized other City States and acquired slaves even before the Poleponnesia War (in 541 BC) for the same economic gains witnessed above in the case of the ancient Egypt.
3. Alexander the Great, King of Macedonia (336-323 BC), also waged imperialistic wars colonized Greece, the Persian empire and Egypt between 332 and 323 BC; and, did not only plunder all library from the African Mysteries System of the Grand Lodge of Luxor in Egypt and re-named Luxor "Alexandria" but also acquired uncountable number of Africans as slaves whom he took with him to Macedonia for sale to those who sought a source of free labour.
4. The Roman Empire waged wars by which it did not only colonize most of Europe and Asia effective 27 BC. till the time of Niccolo Machiavelli Era in 1469-1527 AD but also withheld uncountable number of slaves plundered from all conquered region.
5. Even before the white man found Africa an easy prey to be converted into colonies to provide Europe with free industrial raw materials (e.g., minerals, hardwood, rubber, cocoa, etc) in the $19^{th}$ century, the same white man, in a collusion with the Arab slave traders, had already plundered Africa for slaves whom they first chained to each other and then herded them down like animals into the slave ships waiting for them in various ports along the sea coast to take them away for sale in Arabia, Europe, West Indies and North America.
6. Whereas those enslaved Africans who were taken to Arabia and Europe were basically used as primary source of free domestic labour, those taken to West Indies and North America were subjected to a hostile culture as a primary source of free hard labour on

tobacco, sugar, cotton and corn plantations—a so much hostile hard labour culture that when this situation was recently depicted as a play on American televisions in the late 1970s, acute tension flared all over the United States between the Black Americans and White Americans and could have caused untold havoc between the two sides had the Federal Government and especially the National Association for the Advancement of the Coloured People (NAACP) not promptly intervened to water down the increasingly formenting racial tension in the country.

7. To appreciate the seriousness of the racial tension in both North America and West Indies rooted in the nasty inhumane culture of slavery and slave trade in those two parts of the earth surface, every significantly powerful political leader thereof who attempted to bring a remedy to this culture hardly survived long. Fore example President Abraham Lincoln was assassinated in 14th April 1865, President John F. Kennedy was equally assassinated in 1962; his younger brother Robert Kennedy was assassinated on 5th June 1968; Rev. Malcolm X and James Meredith were assassinated in the same year of 1966; and the Civil Rights Leader and President of the NAACP Dr Martin Luther King Junior was also assassinated on 4th April 1968 for no other significant cause other than for the purpose of eliminating the potential or real roots of remedy to that malady—a problem which similarly affected Gandhi who was also assassinated by his own Indian country when he was seen that he was becoming a potential or real root-cause of the remedy to the existing culture of the caste system (or the touchable versus untouchables) in India institutionalized and promoted by fanatic Hinduism effective the 5th Century BC.

Now that we are fairly well conversant with the characteristics which collectively constitute the "Verbal Conflict", let us now shift our gear from that category to another category called a "Physical Conflict" in (B) below:-

### (B) A Physical Political Conflict

Unlike its counterpart (the Verbal Conflict),the Physical Conflict category includes all cases of conflict characterized by (a) actual physical body contact between the parties to the conflict, (b) actual shed of blood between the two and (c) actual acquisition of the enemy's property by usurpation (use of physical force) in conformity with Charles Darwin's axiom of "Survival of the Fittest".

Prima facie empirical evidences to apprise us better on this category and its characteristics include, for instance, the following:-

1. All armed wars of aggression for territorial conquest carried out throughout human civilization as also already noted above in the cases of:-

   (a) Egypt against Mesopotamia that did not only cripple the Sumerican civilization in the Fertile Crescent but also placed Mesopotamia under Egypt's dominance and proceeded right up to India to do the same to India.
   (b) Alexander the Great (King of Macedonia) who waged wars and colonized Greece, Asia Minor, Persia and Egypt.
   (c) Athens which attempted to do the same in the Aegean Region using The Peloponnesian War (431-404 BC) but then failed to achieve its goal due to Sparta's military might;
   (d) Nazi Germany under Adolf Hitler which in World War II brought about untold sorrows in our civilization during our own generation by subjecting 4 million German Jews and 6 million Germany Gypsies to mass genocide (though the latter have not been lucky enough to have anyone to advocate for them). In that War and in World War 1, Franco-Prussian War (1870-71), Anglo-French War over Egypt (1881-82). The Hague Conferences (1889-1907), etc. German's real objective was to conquer entire Europe as her pre-requisite for conquering the whole world in keeping with the Geopolitics pseudo-scientists' theory of the Heartland which contended that whoever conquered and possessed Europe would obviously be declared the conqueror, master and ruler of the whole world—a false science which not only misguided Hitler and the latter's Nazi Germany to fail but also fooled Hitler into self-annihilation and made Germany to be conquered and then divided into two (East Germany and West Germany) including her capital of Berlin, though this division has now been amended by bringing back the two Germany halves into one Germany and the two Berlins into one Berlin.
   (e) The recent Rwanda catastrophe[32] which erupted effective 6 April 1994 that ended up with a death toll of over 1 million is another good model of a physical bloody conflict; and also a good example of a physical bloody conflict caused by pseudo-science and the greedy culture of political leaders salivating for power after power using Professor Hans Morgenthau's parsimonious analysis.

(f) The on-going physical conflicts in other parts of Africa such as Sudan, Sierra Leone, Somalia, Ethiopia, Eritrea, etc where the African Union (AU) which is mandated by its African Members-States to facilitate peace and order whenever and wherever these peace and order are disturbed, is entangled into so much serious cobwebs of difficulties from both the parties to the conflict and its own Member States that it cannot just achieve its peace objective. In the case of Rwanda catastrophe[32], for instance, the AU's predecessor Organization of African Unity (OAU) had already managed to bring to the Negotiation Table in Arusha both parties to the conflict namely the majority Hutus (under their political party umbrella of the Movement for Development of Democracy or MDDD) on the one hand and the Minority Tutsis (under their political party umbrella of Rwanda Patriotic Front or RPF). The two had mutually agreed in Arusha in August, 1993 on these important key points:-

i. To mutually end their long-term conflict which had already devastated their country ever since 1959.
ii. To collectively reinforce this cessation of their mutual hostilities:

1. By dismantling the existing Hutu dominated Government
2. By Replacing that Government with a new Joint Transitional Government of National Unity composed of all political parties which was expected to last for only two years and then an election is called to usher in a new government leadership.
3. By dismantling the existing Army and replacing it with a newly created Joint national Army composed of the former army officers and officers drawn from the RPF's military organ called Rwanda Patriotic Army (RPA)
4. By mutually agreeing to forget their mutual hostile past and begin afresh to forge a new reconciliatory path leading them to a new life of Rwandese nationalism and patriotism.

   To OAU's surprise, all this became a mirage chase in the hot sandy deserts. This Peace Accord was trampled underfoot by some of the signatories to the same Peace Accord who preferred to resort to Charles Darwin's theory of Survival of the Fittest, and Machiavelli's theory of "Lionism" other than wasting their time on what they seem to have viewed as a "useless and worthless Accord"!

(g) Besides Rwanda, the Somali case in Africa also still poses another serious acid test of the AU's efficacy as a reliable continental Africa peace-keeping instrument. Like the Rwanda case, the Somali conflict case remains unresolved because of the same existing culture of Darwinism and Lionism that is haunting all African countries which also collectively constitute the AU political culture and its chronic headache.

(h) Because of this culture of self-seeking, Members States are unfortunately misguided by both pseudo-science and erroneous understanding of the concepts of Domestic Jurisdiction, Sovereign Equality and Territorial Independence. The case of Somalia has dragged on for years without any genuine sign of a total peace-settlement ever since Somalia drowned in a civil war in 1987-88.

(i) Since then that country remains somewhat stateless, amorphous acephelous and in a state of anarchy governed and promoted by the culture "War-Lords" and clanism!

## (C) Scope Of Conflict

In the preceding paragraphs, our purpose has been to understand the concept "conflict" in terms of its two types or categories namely"—(1) Verbal Conflict and (2) Physical Conflict—a task which we have now already exhausted.

Therefore, in the following paragraphs, our purpose will now be to further understand conflict in terms of its scope.

Conflict falls into two exhaustive and mutually exclusive categories of scope: (1) a large scope and (2) a small or limited scope.

### 1. A Large Scope Conflict

A conflict of a large scope or scale is a conflict which is very wide spread such as the Peloponnesian War (431-404 BC), One Hundred Years War (1337-1453, The Thirty Years' War (1618-1648), and World Wars I and II (1914-18 and 1938-1945 respectively). Although such a category refers mainly to those conflicts which may be beyond national boundaries, bloody national conflicts of a holocaust scope such as the recent Rwanda Catastrophe (1994) also falls within this category by virtue of its intensity and extensity resulting in over 1 million people dead.

## 2. A Small Scope Conflict

However, a conflict which is limited to just a small area or scale such as tribal clashes in some parts of Kenya which began in 1992 particularly in the Rift Valley and Coast Provinces and are still being witnessed in those parts or sections of the Country but are very much limited to those small scale areas, automatically fails to quality as a large scale or scope conflict. Consequently, such a conflict is comfortably classified as a "Small Scope Conflict", though it also involves bloodshed.

Up to this point, we have been labouring to understand the concept of a "university", and the concept of the "Culture of Peace".

But, since our Terms of Reference in this Paper is to examine "The University" and "The Culture of Peace and Democracy", our final task now is therefore, to define also the remaining third concept "The Culture of Democracy".

## 3. A Culture of Democracy

A culture of Democracy is a culture in which there is no presence of viri which are dysfunctional anti-thetical or detrimental to the normal functioning of the body politique. These include, for example, corruption; inter-leadership schism, opportunism, innuendoes and assassinations; expropriation of office at all levels; embezzlement of public coffer and other public assets such as land, houses, etc by misusing of one's office to do so with total impunity and disregard to his actual Terms of Reference and Oath of Office; use of lies to mislead the general public with a view to soliciting support which may be in terms of votes during the election or issues in which one is involved and cannot honestly get any support due to his poor image or qualifications not suitable for the vote or job he or she is seeking from the general public; misuse of public resources on foolish elephant projects and other programs without listening to profession advice so timely provided to the leader; formulating and implementing inhumane policies such as the colonial policies which were misguided by pseudo-science of the time such as the apartheid policy during the minority white regime era in South Africa which was similarly not only misguided by pseudo-science but also misguided by the Dutch Reformed Church[33] which like the Catholic Church in Mozambique[34] also used Jesus Christ's Teaching such as His Sermon on The Mountain and The Ten Commandments to hoodwink and fool Africans to accept but not to rebel against those inhumane policies; exploitation of the poor as the cases of poor men, women and children in the 18th and 19th Century England and entire Continent of Europe who used to be herded into coal mines and factories by those who owned these mines and factories where they were forced to work under intolerable working conditions—a situation which, in turn, generated a widespread uproar all over Europe and promoted the rise of Utilitarian Philosophers such as Jeremy Bentham, John Mill, John Stuart Mill, et. al. and also the rise of Scientific Socialists such as Karl Marx, Frederick Engels, Vladmir Lenin[35] et. al. as a formidable force in defense of these oppressed poor families against coal mine and factory owners all over Europe.

In the final analysis, any country which has a culture of any of the above symptoms is definitely a country without a Culture of Democracy. A Country with such symptoms is a country with a culture of Bad Governance. And, a culture of Bad Governance is a culture, which practices False Democracy. It is a culture which, according to Prophet Isaiah,[36] is in a perpetual darkness with all its people covered by thick darkness. In the words of Thomas Hobbes,[37] (1588-1679) it is a culture of wolves but not of genuine human beings. And, in the words of Chinua Achebe[38], it is a culture of things already falling apart!—a culture of the "Wretched Earth"!

These sentiments about our dented World Culture from all ways back to the time of Prophet Isaiah in the 7th Century BC period right up to the generation of Achebe in the 20th Century AD which is also our own generation, are not all. In the 18th and 19th Century AD, Charles Darwin also called it a culture of the "Survival of the Fittest"[39] which in the simplest words means a "Culture of Man-Eat-Man"!

In fact, this is the actual reason why Frantz Fanon concludes that our Earth is indeed wretched![40] It is wretched in that all those symptoms of Bad Governance enumerated above hold true in every country today. Each Country would not hesitate to boast to another or others that it is a democratic country. It would not accept or tolerate any criticisms from within or without that it is not democratic as each assumes that it is a government of the people by the people for the people—a total myth which cannot stand any acid test.

Obviously, this is the common and universal argument by every country. Each country tries to hand on this argument with a view to legitimizing its form of governance.

Also, this is the common and universal argument found among even those ex-rebel leaders and governments which after ascending to power through the use of bloody violence quickly rush to all over the world seeking recognition of their new regimes.[41]

The paradox of all this is that even those leaders and governments who know very well that those new leaders and governments neither merit nor qualify for recognition and also for admission to Regional, Continental and Universal International Bodies because of having used an illegal method of leadership succession, always fail to exercise their mandate[42]. Their inaction or failure to do so is definitely a suspect.

An examination of their failure, in fact, reveals that while some are civilian leaders who came into power using the ballot as a right tool for leadership succession, some of the them (and possibly most of them) are not.

They are akin to the illegal new leaders in the sense that they also came into power either through a bloody coup d'etat or civil war using the gun or rigged elections which individually and collectively constitute illegal means.

Exactly, this is the reason:

1. Why Prophet Isaiah's prophesy that our earth is in darkness and that all of use are covered by thick darkness still stands and badly needs University's prompt intervention;
2. Why Chinua Achebe's lamentation that things are indeed falling apart globally must also be paid heed to by the University
3. Why Fanon's lamentation that the Earth is wretched and is under the mercies of Black Skin and White Masks totally in capable of improving this anomaly also deserves a serious attention from the University.
4. And, why this study is, therefore, significant at this forum and at this point in time for Humanity in Africa and entire World.

## CHAPTER III

# A Substantive Area of Inquiry

Now that we are fairly well apprised and literate enough on:—(1) the meaning of "University", (2) the meaning of a "Culture of Peace", and (3) the meaning of a Culture of Democracy" which collectively constitute the topic or Theme of this research, our pending burning question now which actually constitutes our real Terms of Reference is "Then, what should the University's responsibility be to humanity with regard to the "Culture of Peace and Democracy"?

## (A) Expected University's Responsibility to Humanity

### 1. An Overview (A Prelude)

From our conceptual definition of a University as a concept, we have noted that, by nature, a University is a centre for these two tasks and goals-

i. For higher learning and advanced research in Science and Technology; and
ii. For the benefit of humanity's advancement in the latter's standard of living in both Africa and total World.

In view of this inherent dual responsibility of a University to humanity, then it must be self-evident that our University needs now to arise and shine through this existing darkness in order to fulfill its natural mandate to humanity as the latter's radiant. It should do so since it has an inherent unique mandate and capacity by which to unlock those mysteries of life and the whole Universe that have always blocked Global Peace and Democracy to flourish.

In other words, our University has an inherent monopoly of tools with which to assist the needy humanity, which does not have these tools.

And, since humanity lacks these tools, it is totally unable to cultivate and bring about this Culture of Global Peace and Democracy on its own which it desperately seeks to have but lacks the necessary capacity.

But then, what should the University do given that it has the monopoly of tools for this task?

## 2. The Sumerian Model

During our conceptual definition of a University and its role noted in Part II of this research, we noted inter alia the following role of the University even as far back as the period of the Sumerian Civilization in Mesopotamia at around 7000 BC:-

i. The Sumerian People always used and relied on their University to forge a co-ordinated and progressive culture in the Fertile Crescent of Mesopotamia, which no other peoples had ever dreamt of before. The consequences of the Sumerians' reliance on their University as their only alternative productive means, this turned out to be a job well done which later also attracted many foreign countries such as Egypt, Asia Minor, Persia, etc. To come to Mesopotamia to learn and emulate this strategy for their own advancement in their respective countries.
ii. Also, these Sumerians had a strong faith in God whom they believed to be their Creator and Giver of all life, food, water, and talent security. Accordingly, they held that it was up to one to do good to God and be blessed; or to do evil to Him and be damned; and that it was necessary to cultivate science and technology by which to do good to this God, the Creator.
iii. By doing so, they forged out what they called "Zuggurat" as a people's community centre charged with the co-ordination and governance responsibility of their secular activities and also as a people's centre for worship.
iv. Management of this Ziggurat was, by and large, left in the hands of the "Think Tank" (which later grew into what we now call University) whose duty was to give scientific and technological guidance to all Sumerian people in various activities. This is the reason why they managed to create for the first in the history of mankind, an all-important network of canals, dams and dikes and controlled the flooding of rivers

and to irrigate the land using Tigris River and Euphrates River. They invented, for the first time, a potter's wheel, a sailboat, use of baked bricks, how to construct an arch and also a vault—an amazing remarkable civilization achievement which they could not have otherwise achieved without their faith in and dependence on their Think Tank (University). This is exactly the reason why Socrates had to conclude that every Republic definitely needs "The Philosopher King" to succeed to such a remarkable level! (of the Sumerians in Mesopotamia).

v. In the other words, their life was embraced in and guided by their belief in the divine order of things on the one hand and also in Science and Technology on the other in order for them not to offend their God in their performance.

vi. This fame of the Sumerian productivity and creativity attracted so many foreigners that their northern Semitic neighbours called the Akkadians became over jealous. Consequently, in 2340 BC these Akkadians adopted the Sumerian culture by which they were able to accelerate so much in their political and socio-economic development that they managed to become the first world's empire; and to acquire and govern all Mesopotamia—a remarkable progress indeed!

vii. However, in 2180 BC, these Akkadians also succumbed to other envious neighbours called the Guti who descended on them from the Zagros mountains in what is now called Iran, and took away all that these Akkadians had also plundered from the Sumerians plus any other wealth they had developed using the Sumerians progressive culture of science and technology.

viii.But by 2060 BC., the Sumerians again emerged under the leadership of Ur-Nammu—a lover of science and technology which he believed was <u>the only</u> source of a happy and progressive life.

ix. Ur-Namimu who, in Jurisprudence, is the world's first law-giver, recognized and taught his Sumerian people to believe in social justice and maximum protection of the poor. To Ur-Nammu, the poor has as much equal protection rights just like everyone else! Thus, the genesis of The Fundamental Principles of Human and Civil Rights now embraced by the UN and our total Civilization today.

x. Drawing from the lessons of the good work of the Zuggurat as a servant of the people charged with the responsibility of providing food security, health security, peace security, intellectual security, food security, art (aesthetic) security, etc, before the enemy invasion by the Akkadians in2340 BC, Ur-Nammu created the first ever elaborate and impressive Culture of Peace and Democracy of the time, though this legacy was later destroyed by the foreign invasion in 1750 BC.

xi. When Babylon took over the ruminants of the Sumerian culture in Mesopotamia in 1750 BC under a very wise King called Hammurabi, this King also appreciated and fully relied on the role of the University just as Ur-Nammu had done way back in 2060 BC (320 years ago) e.g.,

(a) Hammurabi followed the footsteps of Ur-Nammu in the art of Governance.
(b) He re-organized Mesopotamia according to how he scientifically understood leadership should be exercised for the good of all people but not for the leader's own selfish ends and his cohorts as it is the culture today in many African regimes and total World regimes.
(c) To do that for the people, Hammurabi first established a very strong central government and closely regulated the economy without sitting too far away listening to falsehoods, innuendo's and encouraging corruption and inter-leadership schism, opportunism, and gossips as is the common practice in the Continent of Africa and globally today.
(d) "Hammurabi issued the earliest major written law code in existence today",[44] which inter alia "called for a just treatment of his people, but which also imposed harsh retributive punishments on trasgressors",[45]
(e) According to this famous Hammurabi code, "if a person accused another of a serious capital offence and could not prove his charges, he was put to death"[46] i.e., he/she had to be hanged for his/her own malice or mischief!
(f) By this consecutive leadership appreciation of the role of the University in Mesopotamia beginning from the Sumerians, to the Akkadians and also to Babylonians under Hammurabi, we also note the following most impressing and encouraging outcome:-

(i) That in Babylon, Babylonians became the best mathematicians of the ancient world before the Greeks overcame them.
(ii) And, that they also became the best astronomers.[47]

xii. Like the talented and University caring leadership in Mesopotamia by the Sumerians, Akkadians and Babylonians, the leadership in Egypt also recognized the essence and significant of a University as a pre-requisite for the advancement of a society and humanity in total, e.g.

(a) "As in Mesopotamia, the task of controlling the river's overflow and installing irrigation systems necessitated a common effort that in turn called for a more highly organized society".[48]

(b) Drawing from these significant lessons on the need for a Culture of Peace and Democracy left behind by both Ur-Nammu in 2060 BC and Hammurabi in 1792-1750 BC, the Egyptian leadership and the Hittites' leadership in 1284 BC jointly agreed[49], for example:-

   (i) to mutually cease their war by signing the only Non-Aggression Pact known in the ancient Near East; and also the first peace treaty ever recorded in our Ancient and Present Civilization.
   (ii) to mutually recognize and respect each other's spheres of influence;
   (iii) to mutually aid each other during emergencies, e.g during floods, foreign invasion, famine, etc.
   (iv) and, to mutually affirm this pact by "marriage of a Hittite princess to the pharaoh.[50]—an amazing achievement in the history of Diplomacy!

   (a) In as much as the Ur-Nammu and Hammurabi individually valued the significance of the role of the University for their leadership success, Alexandar the Great also did the same! Cognizant of this value of the role of a University, and on realizing that there existed some valuable library and books at the African Mysteries Systems of The Grand Lodge of Luxor, from which he could benefit for his leadership successful expansion, he moved very fast to the target with a sole vicious aim: to practically plunder all of it; and to place it under the care of his tutor, Aristotle, whom he instructed to use it for the enrichment and advancement of the Macedonian culture.[51]

xiii. Also, drawing from these ancient fruitful lessons enumerated above, former mutual enemies of the Cold War, namely the Eastern Block headed by USSR on the one hand and the Western Bloc headed by the USA on the other, consistently relied on their Universities as a source of the needed tools and type of military for their national security against their mutual enemy[52].

xiv. Even today, after the Cold War ended, USA still retains a total of 16 Universities as her Resource Centres. These are:-

- Columbia University
- Duke University
- Johns Hopkins University
- Michigan State University
- Ohio State University
- Tufts University
- University of Denver
- University of Iowa
- University of Minnesota
- University of North Carolina
- University of Pennsylvania
- University of Southern California, Los Angeles
- University of Washington
- University of Winsconsin—Milwaukee and Marquette University
- Yale University.[53]

xv. While these Centres' responsibilities to their national leadership may be confidential for the purpose of their Country's national security, the fact is that their linkage with their national political leadership could also serve as an important useful tool to provide the leadership with proper professional guidance on a cultural engineering with a view to transforming their country from the existing culture of conflict and false democracy to a Culture of a Lasting Peace and Genuine Democracy which would indeed be congruent to the existing meaning of a government of the people by the people for the people.

## 3. Methodology for Creating a Culture of Peace and Democracy

In the preceding paragraphs of Part III (A-1) above, we have successfully endured all hardships of the dark jungles and hot deserts relying totally on the grace and mercies of historians and their published research work with a sole view to discovering the needed answers to our puzzles on how our humanity has actually been able to sustain itself throughout its civilization from ancient times to the present in the absence of a Culture of Peace and Democracy—in a Culture of man-eat-man society[54]; in a Culture of the Survival of the Fittest[55]; in a Culture of the Wretched of the Earth[56]; in a Culture of Wolves[57]; in a Culture of nauseating Corrosion and Decays with everything falling apart[58]; in Culture of total darkness where people appear, from their attitude and behaviour towards each other, to be completely covered by thick darkness![59]; and in a culture of the Gun Smoke and Robin Hood The Robber! For instance:-

### (a) Hammurabian Methodology

From the above account on Hammurabi, we have noted with appreciation, the efforts of Hammurabi who saw a serious need to formulate a Containment Methodology using the knowledge and wisdom of his University to enhance human security and thus rehabilitate the existing bloody Wretched Culture into a Culture of Peace and Democracy—a culture of The People by The People!

Using the talents of his University, Hammurabi constructed 3200 line-code of ethics by which he sought to rehabilitate the decaying culture of his people in Babylon. The most admirable noble achievement useful for us in this research is his Seriousness of Purpose in dealing with wicked persons in Babylon whose motive was to destroy the whole culture because of their selfish wickedness.

For instance, Hammurabi made it very crystal clear to his Babylonians that wheres the sole objective of this code of ethics was to enhance dignity and justice of each person in Babylon, this protection did not give room to a person to do whatever he or she wished as this could be injurious to other people. It was not a license for one to do malice to another!

Accordingly, Hammurabi warned them that whereas everyone was free to do whatever one wanted such as accusing one another for the purpose of seeing to it that justice is done and protected at all time; however, the accuser must also be prepared to prove his or her case beyond any reasonable doubt against the accused. Otherwise, the accuser must also answer for any accusation without any prima facie evidence(s). In order to strengthen this rule, Hammurabi declared that a pay off for such false accusations through slanders and innuendo's must be death. The false accuser must be hanged!

Nota Bene:-

(1) A preventive formula also emulated by King Darius of the Medes Kingdom in the case of his presidents and satraps who had collectively accused Daniel falsely to their king causing the King to throw Daniel into the den of fierce hungry lions but whom this

King later also threw himself in to the same den on discovering that they had actually lied to him against Daniel. The amazing miracle of all this drama to the King and which must also be a fundamental lesson to our humanity today is that although these lions were too hungry, they completely refused to eat the innocent Daniel but at once ate all those false accusers and rumour-monger even before they landed at the bottom of the den! (Daniel 6:24).

(2) And, a preventive formula which could also save Africa and entire World against the existing rampant culture of rumour—mongers, innuendos, false-accusations and similar mischief's if emulated and made an intergral ingredient of our Culture and Civilization globally by all Governments in and outside Africa on a prudent guidance of The Univeristy (The Academia)!

Because of this meticulous strict policy of Hammurabi, the Culture in Babylon was streamlined. The root-causes of cultural corrosion and decay in Babylon were put at bay. The general public was easy to be governed; the number and frequency of corruption and other forms of civil cases were significantly contained or reduced; the chance of criminal cases were significantly contained or reduced; the chance of criminal cases arising from the presence of cultural corrosion and decays was also reduced; and the Babylonians now began to enjoy and live in a new virtuous Culture of Peace and Democracy which nobody had ever experienced before or expected to see in Hammurabi's Babylon—a culture with a stupendous enabling environment in which each sane and able individual can easily live and make a full use of his of her God-given talents and other potentials to the maximum for the betterment of his standard of living and for the benefit of his nation and national leadership in toto! (A lesson that could be very useful to Kenya and entire Africa and The World)!

In the final analysis, in order to eradicate the existing virus or roots of cultural corrosion and decay which had wretched our Cultures globally for generations after generations, it is now a high time that our University takes time to reflect on Hammurabi Methodology and its merits. It would be cost-effective for us to emulate Hammurabi as so shown in (b) below.

### (b) Post-Hammurabian Methodology

After Hammurabi era, there has been a series of other efforts by Humanity to device, invent or discover a reliable methodology with which to adjust and sustain itself to/against recurrent turbulence of rampant perennial conflicts without any success toward that end. These efforts include, for instance:-

i. Development of the International Understandings through peace treaties and pacts, e.g. the first ever renown treat in the history of International Relations called the "Egypto-Hittite Treaty" of Aggressive (1284 B.C.) establishing a specific sphere of influence for each party to the Treaty sealed with a mutual pledge by each party to aid each other during emergencies and further strengthened by a marriage of a Hittite princess to the Egyptian Pharaoh—an act which became the foundation of all ideals of peace treaties and pacts in International Relations up to our modern times (see for example (iii) (8) below).
ii. Development of International Defence Organizations or Alliances, e.g.,

    1. The Delian Military League of 478/77 B.C. which was formed by numerous Greek city-states on the island of Delos under the guidance and leadership of Athens immediately after their war victory against the Persian aggression led by King Darious, with a view to enabling themselves (the city-states) to maintain an explicit military preparedness against foreign aggression—an act which also laid the foundation of all military pacts and ideals including those of our modern times such as NATO (1949), Warsaw Pact (1951), etc.
    2. And The Concert of Europe—an ad hoc system of diplomatic conferences of European great powers which came into being in1814 AD with a view to holding meetings to seek a peaceful solution to conflicts wherever the latter occurred or was suspected occur in any part of Europe ever since The Concert's inception till the outbreak of World War 1 in 1914; and which later metamorphosed into the League of Nations in 1919 and finally into the United Nations in 1945.

iii. Development of various Modern Approaches to Peace, as a result of unbearable injurious lessons of World War 1 and World War II, e.g.,

    1. Efforts to use Peaceful Settlement of Disputes as so stipulated under Chapter VI of The UN of The UN Charter.
    2. Efforts to use Collective Security as so stipulated under Chapter VII of The UN Charter.
    3. Efforts to use the Balance of Power as a means, e.g. Uni-polar, Bi-polar, Tri-polar, Multi-polar, etc.

4. Efforts to use Disarmament and Arms Control as possible alternatives.
5. Efforts to use Preventive Diplomacy as a means, e.g., tacit/explict bargaining and negotiations; fixed point/shuttle diplomacy; cordial/threatening diplomacy; face-to-face/telecommunication diplomacy; etc.
6. Efforts to use Grand Debates or For a at the UN General Assembly and the Security Council as so provided under the UN Charter.
7. Efforts to use The International Court of Justice based at The Hague as per The Statute.
8. Effort to use International Conventions and pacts such as the Brian-Kellogg Pact (also called The Pact of Paris) of 1927 and more so The International Convention on Genocide of 1948 and The recent Arusha Peace Agreement of August, 1993 as a solution to conflicts and genocide.
9. Efforts by the League of Nations (1919-1939) and the UN (1945-the present) to use the Mandate System and the Trusteeship System as a solution to a durable global peace and security.
10. Efforts to use Economic or a functional approach as a rational means towards a harmonious integrated global peoples and cultures of a durable peace and security.
11. Attempts to use cultural, scientific and technological exchange or transfer programmes between the most developed nations and the developing nations, e.g., through Peace Corps; and between the most developed nations and their counterpart as in the on-going space-technology collaboration between USA and Russia even before the end of the Cold War as a way of forging out a means for a cultural of a durable global peace.
12. Efforts to develop and use International Law which up to now lacks an enforcement means.
13. The on-going efforts towards formation of continental unions such as the European Union and African Union as another possible rational means.
14. Efforts by other quarters calling for a global government which, could possibly integrate all multiplicities of existing peoples and cultures into a new organisms of one global people and culture as a possible insurance or guaranteed for a permanent global law and order.
15. And finaly the on-going ambition by the International Community to strongly enforce International Law and Justice against Crime Against Humanity by using Rome Statute Through the International Criminal Court (ICC) based at the Hague.

## (B) A Balance Sheet of All Peace Efforts as at 2013 AD

Inspite of all those glittering efforts by mankind empirical evidences on our Balance Sheet of World Peace and Security as at the year 31st August 2013, confirm beyond any reasonable doubts:

(1) That all humanity's attempts and efforts, no matter how noble and serious they may appear to be, have failed and more will continue to fail to put conflict to a permanent stop or significant reduction.
(2) And, therefore, that it is high time that humanity begins to seriously seek another alternative(s).

Hence, the purpose of Part IV below.

CHAPTER IV

# Conflict Vaccination Cum Cultural Engineering Methodology

## 1. A Conceptual Definition

Unlike the Hammurabian Methodology which was essentially a methodology of Containment also called Prevention, Conflict Vaccination which is also called Cultural Genetic Engineering, is not a preventive methodology. Rather, it is a curative methodology aimed at destroying conflict viruses called "conflictus" (sing.) or "conflicti" (pl) inherent in the body politique which like the poliomyelitis virus of the polio disease is now normally destroyed by Dr. Salk's and Dr. Sabin's polio in the affected human body so as to save that body's life. Its application and efficacy lies in or enshrined in the rehabilitation capacity of our conflict-saturated culture by re-educating it from society to society on the concept, essence and significance of Peace and Democracy to humanity. It calls for and enables each person to be born again, i.e., to discard one's old wicked inner person saturated with conflict viruses and to acquire a totally new pure righteous inner person conducive for a Culture of Peace and Democracy to take root.

As a curative methodology, Conflict Vaccination aims at setting each individual free from his old virtuousless inner-person and refilling him with a new virtuous inner person through a systematic structured comprehensive Peace and Democracy Education—a process which is also commonly referred to by lay persons as Civic Education albeit Civic Education generally refers to structured political socialization, i.e., political education one's political rights and duties, e.g. in elections and voting for candidates.

In Conflict Vaccination cum Cultural Engineering, an individual is normally the focus of attention, i.e., a unit of attention. This unit of attention may be an individual political leader, or a simple individual adult voter, or child provided that individual is a members of the target (society).

Thus, Conflict Vaccination lacks any discrimination based on gender, age or profession. It is totally impartial or blind to such values or classifications.

Conflict Vaccination's fundamental goal is succinctly to cleanse or transform the existing corroded culture of Bad Governance and Rampant Conflict to a pure culture of Good Governance and Peace free from rampant incidents of conflict.

Like Genetic Engineering Methodology whose sole goal is to obtain a high breed seed capable of giving better yield than an ordinary non-high breed seed is capable of doing by mechanically manipulating that ordinary seed for this very purpose, Conflict Vaccination's sole goal is also to obtain a high breed Culture as a prerequisite for Peace and Democracy to take root—a Culture capable:-

(a) of giving a better socio-economic yield by mechanically manipulating an existing Culture of No peace and NO Democracy for this very purpose; and
(b) of reproducing high breed societies of virtuous future cultures free from the Darwin's attitude of Survival of The Fittest and Machiavellism—an attitude of man-eat-man culture. By the concept "better socio-economic yield", we hereby mean various productive positive results which do not and cannot possibly be realized in and from a Culture of chaos which is a wretched culture without any enabling environment which is conducive enough for productive socio-economic development as the present case in Somalia and Southern Sudan where agriculture and other meaningful socio-economic activities have always been disrupted and hampered by the existence of a perennial civil war in those two Countries motivated by Darwinism and Machiavellism.

## 2. Its Application and Tools

As a curative technique through a teaching, learning, cleansing and rehabilitation process, Conflict Vaccination cum Cultural engineering uses various tools, These tools include:-

(a) **Elite Conflict Vaccination:** which is a re-education of the Elite's on the concept, essence and significance of Peace and Democracy with a view to:-

i. Apprising that leader on both tangible and intangible advantages of this process to his leadership, e.g., making his people or country peaceful enough for him to govern them very easily.
ii. And, enabling that leader to also re-educate other leaders and the general public commonly called the "grass roots" on the concept, essence and significance of Peace and Democracy.

Nota Bene:

- This process is also called VERTICAL CONFLICT VACCINATION.
- The process is an Elite Cultural Engineering, etc as socializing agents (tools). Although TVs, Radios and Pamphlets may also be good teaching vehicles or tools, they may not be as best as Conferences, Seminars, Cabinet Meetings since Elite's hardly have enough time to sit and listen to electronic media programmes though they normally love listening to prime news during news time.

**(b) Mass (Grass Root)** Conflict Vaccination: which is a re-education of the general public on the same concept, essence and significance of Peace and Democracy to them in terms of socio-economic development of their own life or families and also their country.

However, unlike the case of Elite Conflict Vaccination whereby the use of electronic media for Conflict Vaccination in not as productive as the use of Conferences and similar method, Grass Root Conflict Vaccination would do better using electronic media since most grassroots or persons do not and cannot easily make it to Conferences, Seminars, etc. They lack the necessary means.

However, most grassroots, especially hard-core followers of leaders such as radical youth-wingers, etc always love physically seeing and listening to their leaders addressing and telling them in political rallies what should be done or should not be done more than hearing all this from radios and television or reading these declarations from daily newspapers etc. Because of this important snag, political rallies convened and addressed jointly by Political Leaders to re-educate their public on the concept essence and significance of Peace and Democracy to the life of entire World, would definitely be the best Conflict Vaccination Tool.

## 3. Its Efficacy

By Elite and Mass Grass Roots Conflict Vaccination cum cultural Engineering, we hereby mean two processes vix—(a) Top-Down-Top Conflict Vaccinationand (b) Sideways Conflict Vaccination. These two are defined as follows:-

### (a) Top-Down-Top (Vertical)

By Top-Down Top Conflict Vaccination cum Cultural Engineering, we succinctly mean a Vertical Process aimed at:

(i) First cleansing or rehabilitating Political Leaders from their old dented or virtuousless inner-persons of a Culture of Bad Governance and Civil Strife first and then re-filling them with a totally new pure or virtuous inner-persons of a Culture of Peace and Democracy through an intensive and extensive re-socialization process and dynamic psychoanalysis on the merits expected from this re-education to their Leadership Security or tenure as a first and foremost pre-requisite step before moving on to the next step of Mass Grassroots Conflict Vaccination cum Cultural Engineering process.

(ii) After first cleansing/rehabilitating Political Leaders as so prescribed in (a) above, the same Leaders may then also be used as reliable agents of Conflict Vaccination to similarly re-educate or rehabilitate their followers and total mass Grassroots from their old dented inner persons of a Culture of Civil Strife and Hate with a view to refilling them with totally new pure inner persons of a Culture of their own (i.e., of those already rehabilitated Leaders). By so doing, each Leader and Grass roots would be expected to be thoroughly exposed or re-educated on the concept, essence and significance of a Culture of Peace and Democracy. By virtue of their political positions in society or country, Political Leaders are obviously the most influential and, therefore, the best and effective vehicle or agents of Conflict Vaccination to the General Public. Since what they tell their followers is normally listened to very keenly and is usually carried out by their followers especially radical youth-wingers and advisers, Conflict Vaccination cum Cultural Engineering would be much more cost-effective and bear a lot of fruits by using Political Leaders as a vehicle in this process than any other tool or agent.

(iii) While the Political Leaders (or Elites) are still engaged in the process of cleansing their respective grass roots, and although they may be doing a commendable job, grassroots could also be a very reliable and productive tool of Conflict Vaccination cum Cultural Engineering process Mass Grass-roots, especially hard core youth-wingers, churches, schools, colleges, Universities, Non-Governmental Organizations (NGOs), multi-national and national business companies, etc would be an additional indispensable tool for this cause. Each of them would be very much productive if empowered by their respective political authority to use their jurisdiction and powers to promote Conflict Vaccination cum Cultural Engineering to those under their jurisdiction and powers, in the same manner Minority White Regime in South Africa successfully used its State apparatus and the Dutch Reformed Church[60] to promote apartheid system against Majority Blacks in that Country; and the Hindu fundamentalists[61] used their overwhelming population majority advantage in India to institutionalize and promote a somewhat permanent caste system in India against those Indians who refused to accept and worship a cow as their God thereby forcing them into a state of miserable poverty, diseases and other untold sorrows such as being referred to as half-human beings and, therefore, the UNTOUCHABLES! Worst of all, when their national hero Mahatma Gandhi tried to dismantle this system, he could no longer be viewed as their national hero but a virus possibly worse than an AIDS Virus. They summarily gunned him down in the same way (i) Abraham Lincoln was gunned down by his own American people though they were very much cherishing and glorifying him; (ii) Nelson Mandela was imprisoned for 27 years in South Africa by Minority White Regime when he was viewed as a real threat to the apartheid culture in that Country which the Regime adored and possibly worshiped; and (iii) Patrice Lumumba, Kwame Nkrumah, Samora Machel and Sekom Toure-were also done away witht by those enemies of a Culture of Peace and Democracy in Africa and total world.

### (b) Sideways (Horizontal) Conflict Vaccination

By Sideways Conflict Vaccination cum Cultural Engineering, we hereby mean:-

(i) Cleansing humanly horizontally from one place to another, and from one country to another, as already prescribed above in Part III (A) (2) 9a)-(b) and by re-educating them on the concept, essence and significance of Peace and Democracy to humanity world-wide using both political leaders, mass grassroots, all state apparatuses, multinational corporations, local business companies, churches, NGOs. Tourism and tourists, Schools, Colleges, Universities, etc. as important vehicles.

(ii) Encouraging systematic global Elite Class interaction for Conflict Vaccination cum Cultural Engineering cause.

## 4. Expected Results

From the foregoing intellectual safari through hot deserts and thick jungles of darkness and other difficulties, we sought to dissect and overhaul these deserts and jungles with a view to discovering or getting answers on:—(1) what a University is; (2) what should be its role to humanity vis a vis this jungle and its existing perennial threat to global Culture of Peace and Democracy; and (3) what is meant by this Culture of Peace and Democracy.

Parts I-IV of this Paper have been able to do just that. Accordingly, this Part IV (C) is expected to provide a succinct parsimonious assessment of what humanity would benefit from this dose of Conflict Vaccination <u>cum</u> Culture of Engineering.

In this regard, the following constitute inter alia some basic expected results of the dose:-

**(A) If this dose were recognized and put in place (i.e. administered to the ailing Global Culture), it would yield the following good results:-**

1. A High Breed Culture for a genuine Global Peace and Democracy would be realized.
2. The existing wretched Culture of Civil Strife (characterized or marred by rampant massacres and genocide); and Bad Governance and Bad Leadership (also characterized by leader schisms, innuendo's, coups d'etat, assassinations, leaders expropriation of office and misuse of public assets and other resources for their personal ends at the expense of the general public who are the actual owners of these resources, etc) etc would be dismantled and eradicated from the face of the Earth to give way and room for the germination of a High Breed Culture of Good Governance and Good Leadership—a Culture of a Virtuous Global Humanity.
3. A Global joy for a Culture of Peace and Democracy would emerge flourish and triumph on Earth.
4. A New Global Culture of Accelerated Socio-Economic Growth and Development would now emerge and flourish for the good of humanity as:-

(a) There would now be no longer room for a Caste System Culture in India of The Touchables versus The Untouchables conflict that is haunting India today.

(b) There would be no longer room for a culture of international terrorism, arms race, cold and hot wars, injurious drug trafficking trade barriers, etc, as we see them today.

(c) And, there would now be no logner room for rampant riots e.g. by students and discontented nationalist in various parts of Africa, Asia, and total World as we see them today every now and then.

**(B) In the final analsysis,**

(1) The Earth would now have a chance to be at Peace!

(2) Humanity would now have a chance to change its gears and direction from a point fo self-destruction through wars to a point of self-development by now saving and utilizing its scarce assets and other resources for that purpose instead fo using it for self annihilation as it has been habitually doing before.

(3) The University would, therefore, have now well executed its pending mandated responsibility to humanity and accomplished its overdue job expected form it for ages by humanity effective the era of Hammurabi

(4) And, as a curative dose,

(i) Conflict Vaccination cum Cultural Engineering Methodology would definitely make everyone to be born again (i.e. discard his or her old virtuousless inner person and replace it with a totally new virtuous inner person which is conducive for the needed Culture of Peace and Democracy in Africa and entire World). This is the heart or main ramification of its efficacy and reliability as a curative dose.

(ii) It would consequently enable both developed and developing economies to interact with mutual respect and dignity for the well being of each other.

(iii) And, existing injurious trade barriers, etc., deliberately created by developed nations to hurt their counterpart by using these barriers to assist themselves to socio-economically grow at the expense of the developing nations by way fo dwarfing these developing nations as also noted in the following lamentation over this selfish situation by Cabinet Minister Nicholas Biwott of The Trade, Industry and Tourism Ministry in Kenya would also be eliminated by the capacity of this Conflict Vaccination cum Cultural Engineering dose:-

"I attended the recent WTO (World Trade Organization) summit in Seattle, (the United States) and many developing economies came up with proposals that did not auger well with the American entrepreneurs"

". . . When the Americans realized that African, Asian and other South American nations had come up with their own ideas about how world trade should be co-ordinated in equal terms, they staged demonstrations around the summit venue and the police had to be called to restore calm so that the summit could proceed."[61]

CHAPTER V

# Efficacy and Reliability of Conflict Vacciantion Cum Cultural Engineering Dose

Throughout the Animal Kingdom, every member of the Kingdom naturally seeks and believes in only those ideas, plans, strategies, laws or principles which work or can work. Whichever does not or cannot work is neither good nor desirable at all. It is summarily pruned, weeded out and discarded and then a new one is sought at once.

Because of this natural given, Humanity has advanced significantly in various discoveries and innovations in both Science and Technology through various tests and re-tests of their findings, methodologies and the tool(s) it seeks to use in its efforts to achieve its goal(s). Both Physical and Bio-Sciences disciplines have been very particular and successful in doing this.

Unfortunately, both Behavioural and Social Sciences have lagged very much behind their counterpart in Academia because of their less utilization of this natural given. This is the fundamental reason and rationale why many endless questions always arise and sometimes squabbles too between scientists questioning each other as to whether and how the recommended methodology would work.

In this regard, as to whether Conflict Vaccination cum Cultural Engineering methodology can or would work is indeed a welcome valid question and concern because there is no need to waste our valuable time on useless recommendations which do not work, cannot work and will not work. Also, we do not need to waste our valuable time on myths which cannot be scientifically tested and prove true in the real world.

In view of this realism, it is necessary to confirm beyond any reasonable doubt that the recommended Conflict Vaccination cum Cutlural Engineering methodology would definitely work; and also that it is reliable based on (1) the prima facie empirical evidences of lessons drawn from the cases of India, South Africa, The Thirteen American Colonies, 19th Century Europe and the Colonial Africa (above); and (2) the following additional in-depth Clinical Diagnosis cases of India, South Africa and The Ancient Israel.

## 1. India

### (A) The Cases of A Culture of The Untouchables and The Touchables in India: A CLINICAL DIAGNOSIS

In the words of John Moniz[62] who was born in India in 1959 lived, studied, worked and carried out an amazing intensive and extensive clinical diagnosis fo India, we encounter the following nauseating clinical diagnosis findings of symptoms about India which Mahatma Gandhi sought to eradicate from that Country's virtuousless culture using Conflcit Vaccination cum Cultural Engineering methodology:-

1. "Before proceeding further, let us make a survey of their (Indian's) living conditions. The life of an untouchable was one of utmost humiliation; they had to live outside of society. They were denied entry into any public place such as schools, hospitals, hotels and transport. They could not draw water from public wells and were served the leftovers. Worst of all, was the denial of their right to worship. They were kept away from the temples. They were reduced to the level of non-persons . . . ."[63]
2. "There existed a hierarchy even in the practice of untouchability. There were some whose touch rendered the rest unclean. Others whose mere sight caused pollution. And, there were still others who polluted the atmosphere just walking on the public street. Thus, the system had reduced a large number of Hindus to a level lower than that of beasts".[64]
3 ". . . . A very large number of them now eat carrion and garbage and the leavings from the meals of the higher caste people. Their houses, separated from the cast people's dwellings, are hovels hardly fit for human habitation".[65]
4. "it is a deplorable fact of Indian society that for a long period, the status of women was misconceived. They were held in respect on the one hand and subject to many kinds of suffering on the other. The system of child marriage, the dedication of the girls to

temples, the dowry system and self immolation (Sati) of the wife upon the death of her husband, had made woman a slave in a male dominated society. Above all, she was considered a child-producing machine and an object of pleasure . . . ."[66]

5. ". . . . In such a dehumanized society, Gandhi began his 'crusade' for the cause of untouchables."[67]
6. ". . . . Liberating the low-caste meant making 'non-persons' into human persons . . . ."[68]
7. "As a first step in liberating the low-caste:

    (a) Gandhi <u>identified</u> himself in their suffering . . . .
    (b) Gandhi himself became a low-caste by choice
    (c) He also wanted every Hindu to become a <u>Harijan</u> . . . . The process (of liberating the untouchables) (which) can be accelerated (only) if every Hindu would deliberately shed (off) his superiority and in practice become a <u>Harijan</u>
    (d) "He adopted an untouchable child as his daughter."
    (e) "He was wedded to the cause of untouchables long before he was wedded to his wife."
    (f) "He allowed himself only the minimum of clothing like the untouchables were allowed."
    (g) "He swept and worked with them."
    (h) "His identification with them was one of perfect human solidarity."
    (i) "The system of untouchability was disliked by Gandhi even as a boy.

        — "He told his mother that she was entirely wrong in considering physical contact with an untouchable to be sinful."
        — "The similar attitude of his wife made him disagree with her to the point of separation."
        — "He preferred rather to work for the untouchables than remain with his wife."

    (j) "The cause of low-caste people, for him, was more important than his food"
    (k) "He would live without food but not without continuing the fight for them."
    (j) "Gandhi was ready to atone for the sins committed against the untouchables to the extent of making an expiation through his own person".[69]

## (B) Reasons for Gandhi's Personal Intervention Using Conflict Vaccination cum Cultural Engineering Formula (Dose)

1. Gandhi personally intervened to fight against the existing nauseating culture of untouchability in order to re-educate the general public all over India and the whole world on this existing major disease.
2. Immediately he recognized limited success of the Hindu-renaissance leaders, he resolved to directly attack the root-cause of this culture decays and corrosions by himself alone.
3. Whereas he accepted human classes or classifications based on professional division or labour, he taught his Hindu nation that this classification did not mean a caste-system which had been initiated and promoted ever since 500 B.C. by the Hindu religion. he, further taught his Hindu nations that such division of labour had no God-given right to establish a connotation of superiority—inferiority syndrome in India or anywhere in the World.
4. In this regard, Gandhi emphasized to them that such division of labour system was healthy for the normal functioning of a nation as opposed to the existing Caste-system of the touchables versus the untouchables war which was, in the final analysis, a real socio-economic, political and spiritual terminal cancer to India.
5. Succinctly, Gandhi called this division of labour classification a system of varnasramadharma aimed at the smooth running of India in the same way it does all over the World. And, he fully succeeded winning their understanding of this missing wisdom in their life.
6. Gandhi further realized that he could better win this war through mass media.
7. Consequently, he initiated a weekly magazine called Harijan for this cause.
8. Important of all, he called on the University and all centres for learning and research to pay heed to the following revelations:-

    (a) He asked them to look in the Hindu Scriptures where the issue of untouchabes and untouchability was spoken of, and interpret for themselves the meaning of such verses.

    (b) He argued to them that no such verses ever existed in the Hindu Scriptures and that these ideas or notions of untouchability and untouchables were a man-made plague disease meant to kill the Indian Hindu Nation.

(c) He further re-educated them on the fact that as these notions of untouchables and untouchability never existed in the Hindu Scriptures, then it was crystal clear that they were "a deliberate device of Satan"; "a gross injustice to the Hindu Community and Religion; and a devilish mischief to humanity."[79]

9. In this regard, Gandhi called on his Hindu nation to accept it as an utter sin to regard anyone born in Hinduism as polluted or untouchable since no one include the temple spiritual leaders had a warrant or mandate from God or anywhere to treat any human being no matter how poor or sick he/she may be, look or appear to be in public, as "untouchable"!

(a) In addition to this written appeal to the literature class in India, through the weekly Harijan magazine, Gandhi also conceived another idea. He decided to dismantle this nauseating culture of the untouchability in Hinduism by:- directing the lowest class of the untouchable labeled as satyagrahas to be allowed to have access to the temple
(b) And, also by fasting "to the point of death for their cause".[71]

10. Gandhi gave due importance to the formation and the uplifting of the low caste people:-

(a) by aiming at transforming their old inner persons through renouncing their old bad habits, fear and artificial inferiority complex mechanically created and planted in their psyche (psychological life) by the disciples for evil called the "touchables" in India;
(b) by encouraging them to shake and wash off this stereotype complex through self-purification's of ones's life and to begin to be conscious and proud of whatever responsibility they possessed or they would be given by the nation;
(c) and, by inviting them to the temple and offer their sacrifices in a worthy and honorable manner like every one else such as the touchable Hindu believer.

11. Finally, Gandhi made these untouchables a most stupendous proud people for the first time in their life history. Obviously they could not believe their ears and their eyes of what they were hearing and seeing from their National hero Gandhi. For instance,

they could neither believe not just understand what kind of a man he was when he echoed:-

"You, too, have to bring your own sacrifice to the altar and that that consists in the strict observance of the laws of sanitation—internal and external . . . ."[72]

## (C) Outcome of Gandhi's Intervention Against a Culture of Anti-Peace and Anti-Democracy in India Using Conflict Vaccination Formula (Dose)

Whereas this batter was too taxing, tedious and dangerous, Gandhi obviously was a too special species of the Human Race to be deterred. In spite of the psychological and physical difficulties he encountered, his stamina, motivation and will yielded the following amazing results not to and for him per se but to and for (1) these once considered as untouchables by their own Hindu religion brothers and sisters in the eyes of God, (2) the whole nation of India and its dignity in the World and (3) the entire Humanity and God Its Creator:-

1. The crusade covered all India and became one of the greatest victorious socio-economic and spiritual mass movements in the history of mankind.
2. Throughout India, it forced the door of all public facilities opened for the untouchable people. These facilities included schools, hospitals, temples, water wells, and all public utility places.
3. For the first time in the history of these untouchables, the latter began to see and enjoy <u>inter alia</u>:-

    (a) the public utilities which had been kept away from them by their own brothers and sisters because of the latter's virtuousless inner persons; and their human dignity which was now restored to them by the efforts of Gandhi, their national hero and their man of virtue.

4. And, for this successful crusade, Gandhi won the title of 'FATHER OF THE NATION'[73].
5. This successful crusade, in turn, became a great lesson to Gandhi's Hindu nation, e.g.,

(a) His nation now came to understand the essence, concept and significance of the basic dignity of a person and human rights and equality among all people regardless of gender, race, religion, nationality, or birth.
(b) His nation now came to understand and appreciate the sovereign rule of the law of love which had been lacking in that Country of rages especially among the so-called "the touchables".
(c) His nation now came to hate injustice, inequality and any form that was against God's creation especially of the human nature—though this dream was disrupted by his assassination.

(6) Like their National hero, India began to believe that the World would not have pauperism if each person restrained himself or herself from theft and the false inciting notion of Survival of the Fittest, Individual Rights and Free Market which is a sense are more inciting to people to become grabbers, thieves, robbers and potential and actual murderers of their fellow men and brothers in search of wealth after wealth.
(7) In sum, although Gandhi was assassinated before 100% of his crusade's goal had been fully realized, his unique noble efforts to Humanity in India is an exemplary justification of the efficacy of Conflict Vaccination cum Cultural Engineering in India against this dented virtousless culture of Bad Governance and Civil Strife—a culture of no Peace and no Democracy—because of Gandhi's unique personal courage which the University should also emulate now to assist Humanity globally as Gandhi thus did to his Hindu Nation in India, and has consequently taught us how to use this Conflict Vaccination cum Cultural Engineering as a reliable tool for this cause.

## 2. South Africa

### (A) A Case of a Culture of Apartheid in the Former Minority White Rule in South Africa: A CLINICAL DIAGNOSIS

As also noted by Leonard M. Thompson who carried out a very thorough clinical diagnosis of the nature of the apartheid disease in South Africa published in his book, Politics in the Republic of Africa,[74]

(1) Apartheid's succinct fundamental aim was to keep the majority Black people in South Africa at arms' length. They were to be kept away from possible contact or interaction

with their minority White counterpart of the same Country. Just like the untouchables predicament in India, they were also looked upon as untouchables, contagious disease carriers or skunks!

(2) These minority whites migrated to that Country and settled there by the use of the gun and Charles Darwin's inciting theory of Survival of The Fittest (published in 1859) which incited them to use that gun for the sake and in defense of their settlements and their white race which, according to Darwin, was the most favoured race. What a pity to Science! by the injustice of pseudo-Scientists such as Charles Darwin!

(3) Armed with this mad Darwinism fever, minority White families and their white dominated and controlled regime was totally wild against every Black person that came to sight. A mere presence of a Black person in a public place such as a cinema (or movie), bus stop (or station), cafeteria (or hotel), school, hospital, church, train, football ground, etc especially those designated as reserved white public places, that Black person was automatically a persona non grata—a criminal who must be arrested at once and charged in a Court of Law for trespass.

Before that was done to him, he had to be first tortured as a first prior lesson to this affected Black person.

(4) In the other words, during the apartheid period in South Africa, a Black person was viewed by the white community in that Country as a stinker, a second class human being next to a striking black-and-white looking little animal in North America called a skunk—an animal no person would ever want to come into contact with because of its nasty nauseating oduor (smell).

Like their untouchable counterparts in India, Black Africans in South Africa lacked both human and civil rights in their own mother Country as they could neither be allowed to enjoy nor be expected to show their face in such facilities apart from those ragged low class facilities reserved specifically for Blacks only.

(5) From Thompson's diagnosis of the roots of this malady, we note with shock that his was not just by accident. Also, it was not a function of the state apparatus because of dirty politics which governments are often accused of whenever something goes wrong in a country. According to Thompson:-

(a) Intensity and extensity of apartheid was a function of Cultural Engineering exercise by the spiritual leaders of the Dutch Reformed Church in that Country.
(b) Using this Cultural Engineering exercise, these Dutch Reformed Church leaders mechanically and systematically vaccinated every white child and adult into:-

(i) **lackphobia.** i.e., a fear against everyone who was Black in that Country by recognizing him as a real threat to the survival of the white man and woman in South Africa.
(ii) **Black Containment**, i.e., a belief that a Black man was a real threat and disease to the white man and woman and that it was, therefore, mandatory for every Black man and woman, and that to be kept at arms' length by the white community at all costs and at all time.

(6) As a result of all this ill Cultural Engineering in South Africa motivated by Darwinism as well as Lockism, Smithism and Rousseauism, South Africa slipped into a total darkness. It became so much a wretch country that intervention from whatever source was necessary to save it from that thick darkness.

## (B) Reasons for Nelson Mandela's Intervention Using Conflict Vaccination cum Cultural Engineering Formula (Dose)

1. In a nut-shell, the Clinical Diagnosis findings encountered in (A) above constitute valid reasons which prompted intervention by Nelson Mandela, Oliver Tambo, Steve Bikko, John L, Dube, S. P. Bunting, Robert Sobukive, Winny Mandela, Mbeki and other African nationalists under the umbrella of African Natinal Congress (ANC) party and others under different umbrellas such as The Communist Party.
2. The sole objective of this intervention was not actually to eliminate their white counterpart as the Dutch Reformed Church leaders had purported to teach the white community in and outside the Country. Its sole purpose was to eradicate the existing roots fo a Culture of anti-Peace and anti-Democracy in South Africa.
3. To do this, Mandela and his associated under the said umbrellas resorted to Conflict Vaccination cum Cultural Engineering used by Mahatima Gandhi against the caste system culture in India before Gandhi was assassinated. And, by emulating Gandhi, Mandela brought about the following outcome to South Africa.

## (C) Outcome of Mandela's Intervention Agaisnt a Culture of Anti-Peace and Anti-Democracy in South Africa Using Conflict Vaccination cum Cultural Engineering Formula (Dose)

1. Mandela's achievements in his noble crusade against the apartheid disease in South Africa significantly outweigh his painful difficulties and failures he encountered during the crusade.
2. Although he was imprisoned for twenty seven painful years in a solitary jail on a small island called the Robin Island, the fact is that:-

    (a) He re-educated the entire Country to the concept, essence and significance of Peace and Democracy as a first and foremost ingredient for a healthy non-racial nation in South Africa where both Black and White Communities would live in a flourishing Love, Peace and Unity and thus set up a good foundation for the next generation.

    (b) To do this effectively, he had to resort to Conflict Vaccination cum Cultural Engineering methodology by which he vaccinated both Balck and White against Conflict.

3. Recognizing and appreciating the significance of Mandela's Conflict Vaccination crusade in that Country, the World Community arose in support of him to the extent that:-

    (a) By 1988, that Country'smost difficult and stubborn President P. W. Botha had no other alternative but to bow down to the Will of The People all over the World and accept that he and his culture of apartheid were wrong, inhumane and evil against Humanity.

    (b) And, although Mandela's ascendancy to the Presidency as president fo South Africa was largely a function of the efforts of President B. W, De Klerk who facilitated the germination of a Culture of Peace and Democracy in that Country after taking over from Botha, the most important fact here is that by Botha accepting to release Mandela.

        (i) This initiative became the beginning of the beginning of the roots fo a Culture of Peace and Democracy in that Country.

(ii) Botha had successfully recived an enough DOSE of Conflict Vaccination cum Cultural Engineering.

(iii) And, Mandela's Conflcit Vaccination cum Cultural Engineering had indeed worked on both Botha and Botha's minority White apartheid regime—a fantastic development in our Civilization.

4. On gaining victory against apartheid, Mandela reinforced his application of Conflict Vaccinationcum Cultural Engineering with a Peace and Reconciliation Commission—an agent created by Mandela's ANC Government with which to vaccinate both Black and White Communities with a view to eradicating the roots of apartheid culture in that Country.
5. And, in view of this realism, then it must also be self-evident that our Conflict Vaccination cum Cultural Engineering Methodology proposed above in Part of this Paper-

   (a) Will, in no doubt, also successfully work!
   (b) There is a Good Hope!

## 3. Israel

### (A) A Case of a Culture of Iniquity and Abomination in Israel During the B.C. Time: A CLINICAL DIAGNOSIS

Disappointed and angered by man's culture fo stubbornness and abomination which had put the Earth to such a wretched state that everything was now falling apart because of a culture misguided by naked soulless notions of Survival of the Fittest, Individual Rights and Free Market Rights without regard to man's concept of the Humanism legacy inherited from the Sumerian and the Ur peoples' civilization created in Mesopotamia 7000-5000 BC ago,

1. God has often been compelled by this wrath to commission several Prophets with a view to re-educating man on this concept of humanism.
2. By doing so, God has often sought to remove the existing evil culture and replace it with a culture fo righteousness and humanism—a culture which would be congruent to what President Daniel arap Moi of Kenya always refered to in his addresses to the Kenyans as a cultue of people who are mindful of other people's welfare!

3. And, in the words of David Reagan who has done a most impressively extensive and intensive Clinical Diagnosis of this problem, Reagan apprises us:-

   (a) That "God often use drama to get people's attention. For example, He told [Prophet] Isaiah to go barefoot and naked for three years (Isaiah 20;2ff) Yes, Isaiah was the original streaker!
   He used an unconventional method to get people's attention. The message was graphic and clear: Repent or be stripped naked like Isaiah."[77]
   (b) That Prophet "Jeremiah was told to wear a yoke on his neck to emphasize God's message that King Zedekiah should submit to Nebuchadnezzar (Jeremiah 27)"[78]
   (c) And, that Prophet "Ezekiel was called on to act many times. On one occasion, the Lord told him to pack all his bags and carry them around Jerusalem in the sight of the peope as a sign that if they did not repent, God would send them into exile (Ezekiel 12)"[79]

4. And, also in the words fo Prophet Micah, we encounter this astonishing revelation about the dented nature of the Culture of the Ancient Israel which is also a true representative of our dented Global culture today.

   "Hear this, you heads fo the house of Jacob
   and rulers of the house of Israel,
   who abhor justice
   and pervert all equity,
   who build Zion with blood
   and Jerusalem with wrong.
   Its heads give judgement for a bribe,
   Its priests teach for hire,
   Its prophets divine for money;'
   And yet they lean upon the Lord and say
   "Is not the Lord in the midst of us?
   No evil shall come upon us." (Micah 3:9-11)

**(B) Reasons for God's Intervention Using Prophets as His Agents for Conflict Vaccination *cum* Cutural Engineering Formula (Dose).**

1. As Also noted by Reagan and particularly the Prophets, it was because fo the man-made virtuousless culture of no-Peace and no-Democracy which has put the Earth and her peoples into a so much thick darknes and rampant scramble for personal gains at the detriment of another person that:-

    (a) There is no more any room for a man and woman of virtue, honesty, sincerity and a good humble heart to another other than a plenty of room for a man and woman of a man-eat-man society!
    (b) There is no more any room in our Culture in which each person is able to be contented with what he/she has (Luke 3:11-14) or to use his position as professor, doctor, poltical leader, accountant, lawyer, Judge, cook, driver, clerk, administrator, priest or preacher, etc to do justice to another most especially to that most desperately needy person and humanity as a whole in his or her capacity as a child fo God. Our culture is wretched.

2. If parents, children and everyone else in his or her position did just that which is righteous to another and also to oneself an total Humanity (no matter how little that would be) in order to save those who are in captivity obviously then,

    (a) Our Humanity would be rescued from the existing pangs of the existing Wretched of the Earth, Survival of The Fittest and Total Thick Darkness!
    (b) All potholes, ups-and-downs and crooked roads would be eliminated globally.
    (c) And, all Humanity would definitely be filled and continous refilled with a bliss of overlasting Joy and Peace globally.

3. If each fo us globally cared to reflect on John The Baptist's candid self-evaluation and honesty in his responses to the Pharisees who sought to know from him in what name or capa;city he was doing what he was doing by teaching and baptizing people—a work which, according to these interrogators, was supposed to be a work of a Prophet or Christ (Luke 3:15-17):-

    (a) Each of us would become another John The Baptist—a virtuous person!

i. Each of us would become a Maker of this desired virtuous Way of a Joyous Future Generation(s) which is:- a generation of a culture which is pure and righteous totally free from those evil attitudes for "*TOA KITU KIDOGO*" (TKK) i.e Swahili language word meaning "bring something small" in English language) now commonly practiced not only in Kenya and Nigeria but all over Africa, and elsewhere too globally.

ii. And, a generation of a culture which is also pure, righteous and totally free from all those abnormal acts of Totenism, Cannibalism, Use of Dead Persons Spirits called (Amayembe) and devil worship which is now prevalent all over the Earth with most devil worshippers such as diviners misusing it to hurt the life fo other persons due to envy, jealousy and innuendo's—acts which individually and collectively constitute the tap roots of the existing global culture of no Peace and no Democracy especially in the African Continent.

**(C) Outcome of God's Intervention Using Prophets as Agents of Conflict Vaccination cum Cultural Engineering Formula (Dose)**

The realism of all this is that as a result of Israel's disobedience to God's message brought to them in good faith through the said Prophets, Israelis lost the battle in that:-

1. They were all exiled to Babylon.
2. Their King Zedekia was exiled also to Babylon where he encountered untold sorrows of tortures, e.g.,

   (a) All his family members were wiped out; and
   (b) His both eyes were plucked out, and he remained blind till he was finally killed.

3. Their Kingdom of Judah which was the only one now remaining also died in the same manner their other Kingdom of Israel had fallen.
4. Had they paid heed to these Prophets as agents of Conflict and Cultural Engineering.

   (a) They would have avoided this painful punishment.
   (b) Their Kingdom would possibly have been the Greatest World Power today had they not been hard headed and hard hearted.

## 4. Colonial Africa

### (A) A Case of a Culture of Colonialism and Imperialism in Africa and other Colonially Affected World, e.g., India, 13 North American Colonies, etc. (CLINICAL DIAGNOSIS).

A further prima facie empirical evidence of man's failure as a political leader is also vividly supported by the following psychiatric diagnosis of three selected nationalists who emerged in Africa during the Colonial era-nationalists who could not otherwise had any valid and reliable reason to emerge at all as rebels against their Colonial Regimes in Africa had those Regimes, been cautious enough about their leadership's true rights and obligations which was to serve all equally regardless of colour, creed or gender in Africa.

### 1. Kwame Nkrumah (1909-1973)

Kwame Nkrumah was born into a goldsmith family in a small village called Nkreful in the Gold Coast (now Ghana),1 As also noted in Chapter v-2(b-2), a psychiatric methods as used in this study does not mean the treatments of a mental illness as the term is conventionally used. Rather, it means a complete inquiry into the life history of the individual in order to illuminate those strategic factors responsible for his behavior and died in 1973. Inspite of the fact that his actual birthday is not certain, it is believed to on a Sunday, September 18th, 1909.

Thus, "Kwame" means a son born on Saturday. In this autobiography, he frankly states that until some time after birth, his mother had given up all interest in him as she had believed him to be dead.

At an early age, Nkrumah was a shrewd, bold and pramagtic boy. As the only child in his household, he was very much loved by his mother. Because of his father's continual absence from home on his goldsmith enterprises, in Half Assini (some miles away from Nkruful), Nkrumah spent most of his time with his mother. It could, therefore, be said that he knew his mother more than he knew his father and she knew the child better than the father did.

Nkurumah first went to a Roman Catholic School in his village. Of his parents, it was only his mother who was a Roman Catholic convert: on the other hand, his father was neither a Roman Catholic convert nor fond of any other religion. Therefore, with the help of Father

George Fischer, a Roman Catholic Priest of German origin, Nkrumah was eventually baptized (initiated) into the same church with his mother. It was through his mother's influence that Nkrumah attended school.

Again, as the only child in his household, Nkrumah was raised with tender lover and much attention. Consequently, he hated caning at school, since he was not accustomed to it at home. In addition, he was so possessive and shrewd that he, on one occasion, beat a policeman who attempted to reprimand one of his half-brothers for mischief on the beach: and, on another, forced the lover of his half-sister to leave their compound. Nkrumah also tells us in his autobiography that because of hi possessiveness, he never felt comfortable when his father came to sleep in the bed he shared with his mother.

In his own word, Nkrumah says "several times he tried to explain to me that he was married to my mother, but I told him that I also was married to her and that it was my job to protect her" 2. After his eight years of elementary school, Nkrumah became a pupil-teacher for one year at Half Assini. A year later, in 1926, he was recommended for training at the Government Training College in Accra by the principal of that college. This became another stage in Nkrumah's life history.

As a rurally raised child, Nkrumah was at first bewildered by city life. Shortly after, he was stillmore bewildered by his father's death. It was in this period of great tragedy that he met Dr. Qwegyir Aggrey, one of the first Africans with a high standard education, and, in fact, the first African to be offered a respectable post as an Assistant Vice-Principal of the newly founded Prince of Wales College at Achimota.

-Expressing his deep admiration for Dr. Aggrey, Nkrumah narrates:

> To me, he seemed the most remarkable man that I had ever met and I had the deepest affection for him. He possessed intense vitality and enthusiasm and a most infectious laugh that seemed to bubble up from his heart and he was a very good orator.[3]

It was because of Dr. Aggrey that Nkrumah, for the first time, became aware of and began to develop his sense of nationalism. In his own words, Nkrumah narrates,

> "It was through him that my nationalism was first aroused. He was exteremely proud of his colour . . . ."[4]

Consequently, on learning that Dr. Aggrey had suddenly died in New York, where he had gone for a short visit, Nkrumah was so angry that he fasted for three days: and hitherto, decided to acquire as much education as Dr. Aggrey had done.

While still at Achimota, Nkurumah was only interested in his class work but also in other competitive activities, e.g., sports. Although he hated drill, which he had to attend at 5.30 every morning, he was very keen in inter-college sports, especially in short-dash relays. Besides sports, he was also very good at amateur dramatics.

Even as a Catholic, Nkrumah strongly hated the Roman Catholic Church mandatory regulations, such as regular church attendance. It was because of his shrewdness that he was summarily appointed prefect during his senior year. At the same time, he also began to take up other activities. He helped to establish the Aggrey Students' Society, to act as a speech-making forum in memory of Dr. Aggrey. He was so much involved that he was once warned by the "Method" instructor, Mr. Herbert (thereafter Lord Hemingford) that he was at Achimota to be taught and not teach.[5]

Nkrumah graduated from Achimota in 1930 and thereafter begun to teach at the Roman Catholic Junior School at Elmina, where he was loved by many children. While at Elmina, he helped in founding the Teacher's Association with the aim of trying to improve and protect the teachers' rights against the administration. A year later, he was promoted to head teacher of the Roman Catholic Junior School at Axim, and he also helped to found, inter-alia, the Nzima Literature National Society, the Society through which he met Mr. S. R. Wood, Secretary of the National Congress of British West Africa, who later happened to be Nkrumah's personal master in the Gold Coast political history. In Nkrumah's words, "this rare character first introduced me to politics. He knew more about Gold Coast political history than any other person I have ever met and we had many long conversations together"[6] In fact, it was this same person that recommended Nkrumah to Lincoln Univeristy, Pennsylvania, for further studies.

In 1934, Nkrumah was transferred to teach clergy-trainees at the Roman Catholic Seminary at Amissano near Elmina. White at Amissano, he developed the idea of becoming a Jesuit, but later decided not to, since he planned to go to U.S. for further education.

Nkrumah also tells us that his nationalism was later revived by the articles in The African Morning Post. Written by Nnamdi Zikiwe from east Nigeria and Wallace Johnson from Sierra Leone.

In 1935, Nkurumah left to continue his studies in the United States, while in London, en rout to New York, Nkurumah encountered news from his home:

> . . . . and on the plackard, I read: I read: 'MUSSOLINI INVADES ETHIOPIA'. That was all I needed. At that moment, it was almost as personally. For the next few minutes, I could do nothing but glare at each impassive face, wondering if these people could possible realize the wickedness for colonialism, and praying that the day might come when I could play apart in bringing about the downfall of such a system. My nationalism surged to the fore; I was ready and willing to go through hell itself, in order to achieve my object.[7]

Nkurumah proceeded to New York and finally reached Lincoln University. AT Lincoln, he took part in freshman oratorical contest and won a second place gold medal. He also joined several organizations, one being the Phi Beta Sigma Fraternity of Lincolin. He graduated in 1939 with a Bachelor" Degree in Economics and Sociology.[8]

In the 1939-1940 academic year, he was recalled by the Theology Professor to return to Lincoln as an assistant lecturer in philosophy. As a result, he read Kant, hegel, Descartes, Schopenhauer, Nietzsche, Freud, inter alios.

In 1942, he was awarded a Bachelor of Theology degree by the Lincoln Seminary, and a Master of Science degree in Education by the University of Pennsylvania.

In 1943, he was awarded a Master's degree in Philosophy by the Universtiy of Pennsylvana, and tentatively began to prepare himself for his doctorate degree examination.

In 1945, he successfully finished his required course work and preliminary examinations for the doctorate of Philosophy Degree. At Lincoln, he was honoured as the most outstanding Professor of the year by the University magazine, The Lincolnian. And before leaving Pennsylvania, Nkurumah helped in setting up a number of programmes such as the African

Studies section, the African Students Association of America and Canada, and a newspaper called the African Interpreter.

Furthermore, he endeavoured to acquaint himself with many political organization such as the Republicans, the Democrats, including other organizations, such as the National Association for the Advancement of Coloured People. Of all his ten years in the United States expecially at Lincoln, 1945 seems to have been the initial stage, in that it marked period in which he fully understood politics both in theory and practice. After receiving his Master's Degree in Philosophy in 1943, Nkurumah continued to reinforce his knowledge of political philosophy with the works of Hegel, Karl Marx, Friedrich Engels, Lenin and Mazzini; and, as it will be envisaged in the following paragraph, it was indeed the written political ideas of the people inter alios, which influenced him in his revolutionary attitude.

Previously, he had just met with C.L.R. James, one of the leading members of the Trotskyiets, through whom he came to understand how the underground movement works. Thereafter, upon reading the works of other political philosophers, he was very much moved particularly by Karl Marx and Lenin. In his own words, he comments:

> "The writing of these men did much to influence me in my revolutionary ideas and activities, and Karl Marx and Lenin particularly impressed me as I felt sure that their philosophy was capable of solving these problems"[10] However, he stresses that, ". . . of all the literature that I studied, the book that did more than any other to fire my enthusiasm was Philosophy and Opinions of Marcus Garvey, published in 1923, especially Garvey's "philosophy of 'Africa for Africans' "and his "Back to Africa" movement".[11]

Nkurumah's political philosophy is first envisaged in his writings, of numerous articles, pamphlets and books. Thereafter, it is also evident in his political career, first as an organizer, and reconcilliator, and finally as leader of the first Black nation to restore its sovereignity and political independence south of the Sahara.

Among the writings, we first come across his pamphlets entitled "Toward Colonial Freedom", in which he vehemently attacks and demands from the colonial powers an immediate recognition of the rights of the colonial peoples of Africa over their land and its resources; over their humanity and manhood. In fact, upon examining his book, Neo-Colonialism, the last stage of Colonialism, we are struck with the same political attitude. The quest for complete restoration for the African Sovereignity has remain at the heart of his politics. As he puts it, "seek ye the political independence first, then all others will be given unto thee"; it has always been his conviction that until achieves her political huru first, she will obviously have an exceedingly hard time in protecting her Sovereignty and political independence.

In addition, Nkurumah unceasingly preached about African unity. The quest for a United States of Africa was another substantial goal on his agenda in political life. To him, African unity was the shield for the defense of African sovereignity. Without this unity, Africa is, in Nkrumaha's analysis definitely apt to fall prey to hungry external poor vultures. Like Patrice Lumumba.[12] Nkrumah prophetically believed that division is but a political suicide of Africa.

In his practical experience in politics, Nkurumah organized a series of meetings and conferences in his attempts to bring Africa together. As we can also witness from the history of the Pan-African movement, Nkurumah was the real heir to that task.

As soon as he reached London in May of 1945, he registered at the London School of Economics to acquire his doctorate degree in "Logical Positivism", and also took a vital part in the Pan-Africa Congress which convened in Manchester in the same year, arranged by W.E.B. Du Bois, George Padmore, C.L.R. James, inter alios.

At the conference, Nkurumah served as a joint-secretary with George Padmore, the only man that he had previously known in England because of Padmore's numerous sensitive articles. We also come to learn that it was Nkrumah who resumed Du Bois' responsibility over the Congress and thereafter transferred it from foreign soil to African soil in 1953.

Even before that, we also note that immediately after he reached London, he became a member, and, thereafter, vice-president of the West African Students' Union—an organization deliberately designed to: first, help new African students in London to find accommodations and college registrations; second, to agitate and pressure the British and French colonial offices for better conditions in their colonized mother countries in West Africa; and thirdly, to act as reconciliator between African students and landlords whenever the two were to odds.

With reference to his duties in Pan-African movements, it is also interesting to note that of the two declarations made to the colonial powers by the Manchester conference in 1945, one was written by Du Bios and the other by him. In these declarations, it was expressed that colonial peoples must be free. The declarations,

> . . . . asserted the determination of colonial people's to be free and condemned the monopoly profits alone. They made a stand for economic democracy and appealed to colonial peoples everywhere . . . to awaken to their responsibilities in freeing themselves and saving the world from the clutches of imperialism.[13]

In addition, it was Nkrumah, inter alios, who helped to set up the West African national Secretariat at 94 Gray's Inn Road, London, designed to promote African affairs with particular reference to West African colonies in their plans for self-rule from the British and French regime. In his capacity as secretary-general of the Secretariat, Nkrumah established the New African, a monthly publication designed to propagate the Secretariat's political work and goals: Its motto was "For unity and Absolute Independence". Until the Kenyatta-Makonnen publication, Pan-Africanism, took over, The New African made a series of political preachings on African Unity and Nationalism vis-a-vis.

Shortly after, Nkrumah was requested to organize a West African National Conference to be held in Lagos in October of 1948; however, the conference to be held in Lagos in October of 1948; however, the conference did not materialize. Before getting back to Africa to put his revolutionary political philosophy into practice, Nkruma first served as Chairman of "The Circle", one and above all, the vanguard of the student groups under the auspices of the West African National Secretariat, whose aim was to train themselves in how to begin revolutionary activities in Africa against colonialism. It was at this time that he received Ako Adjel's letter from the Gold Coast, requesting him to take on the job of general secretary of the "United Gold Coast Convention".

Fully aware of the political situation in the Gold Coast, and the policy he was going to follow, Nkrumah accepted the job, on his safari home, he was fully armed with the policy that he intended to follow; and quite sure of the quarrel that was likely to take place between him and the Danquah's group. It happened indeed.

On the 14th of November, 1947, Nkrumah left London with only one suit, a newspaper in one hand a brief-case in the other, for Takorodi in the Gold Coast, destined for what he called a mission "to so the seed of Pan-Africanism". Upon reaching the Gold Coast, he found Alan

Burns' administration, the British colonial rule (1941-1947), which Nkrumah defined as "a great political awakening". Burn had appointed some Africans (chiefs and non-chiefs) to the Executive Council as opposed to previous colonial administrations. The African intelligentsia strongly opposed the system, and tentatively began to devise some opposition to the system.

On the other hand, Dr. Danguah (one of the vice-presidents of the UGCC) supported Burns and was therefore, nominated by the joining Provincial Council of Chiefs to represent them to the Burns and Legislative Council.

But it was not unitl Dr. Danquah and his brothers were pronounced in the alleged murder of their brother, Akyea Mensah, which had been committed immediately after their father's death (Nana Sir Ofori Atta), that Danquah withdrew his support from the Burns Constitution in demand fro a new one. Therefore, Nkrumah was hired to take over the U.G.C.C.'s program, to include the Northern Territories and Trans-Volta/Togoland, which he had left out in the former U.G.C.C. Constitution.

Shortly after the Christiansborge incident (parafic demonstration by the ex-servicemen, denouncing high prices on imported merchandise) Nkrumah was arrested along with five other leaders of the UGCC, viz: Danquah, Ofori Atta, Akufo, Ako Adjei and Obesebi Lamptey, on March 12, 1948, by the new colonial administration of Gerald Creasey.

After his release from prison, Nkrumah came to encounter strong harassments from the UGCC Working Committee. The Committee removed him from his general secretariship because he was considered both a potential menace to the Convetion and the only beneficiary (i.e., in popularity gaining) of the Convention.

The fact that Nkrumah had, inter alia, established the Ghana College for students who had been expelled from their schools because of their demonstrations of the Big Five's apprehension, and the "Cropper" printing machine for the Accra Evening Newspaper, made him so popular that he was consequently accused by Danquah and other UGCC members of having become popular because of those achievements!

On the 12th of June, 1949, Nkrumah consequently announced his own political party, the Convention People's Party (CPP), largely supported by young people; and a few days later, he Resigned from the UGCC.

It is here, in the creation of the CPP, that we vividly come to Nkrumah's political philosophy at high tide. Whereas in the UGCC he had been firmly restrained from carrying his total revolutionary movement ideas and objectives he had carried with him from England, by the Big Five, in CPP, he now had complete freedom of expression and the execution of his objective plans. It was at this time that he mobilized his revolutionary political might vis-à-vis the colonial rule in the Gold Coast. For instance, unlike the UGCC constitution which demanded "self-government within the shortest possible time", the CPP constitution adopted the pragmantic demand for "self-government now". In his own words, Nkrumah declared:

> The time has arrived . . . when a definite line of action must be taken if we are going to save our country from continued imperialist exploitation and oppression. In order to prevent further wrangling between the C.Y.O who are ready for action, and the Working Committee of the UGCC, who are out to suppress this progressive youth organization, the CYO has decided on a line of action that will be consistent with the political aspirations of the chiefs and the people of the country".[14]

At the same time, Nkrumah introduced and heavily expounded his concept of "no-violent positive action"—Gandhi's political strategy in India in the 1940's. When summoned before the Ga State Council to define the concept, Nkrumah states:

> I described Positive Action as the adoption of all legitimate and constitutional means by which we could attack the forces of imperialism in this country. The weapons were legitimate political agitation, newspaper and educational campaigns and, as a last resort, the constitutional application of strikes, boycotts and non-co-operation based on the principle of absolute non-violence, as used by Gandhi in India.[15]

And, at to when Positive Action was to be put into force, Nkrumah has this to say:

> The final stage of Positive Action . . . would not be called into play until all other avenues for obtaining self-government had been closed. WE would first study Coussey Report. If we found it favourable, all well and good; if not we would put forward our own suggestions and proposals. If these were rejected then we would invoke Positive action on the lines already explained.[16]

On meeting with R.H. Solway, the Colonial Secretary, in the Gold Coast, Nkrumah touched on the concepts of justice and representation. In his own words, he uttered:

> We, the people, believe that our requests for the election of a constituent assembly is reasonable and just. We willnot accept half measure. The report fo the Coussey Committee, a committee on which the rank and file of the people were not represented, is a mater that concerns us all . . . if our request is not given consideration, then I have to tell you that a Positive Action will continue.[17]

But, it did not take long before Nkrumah's Positive was put in force:

> All the store were closed, the strains were stationary, all Government services had closed down and the workers were sitting at home. The whole economic life of the country was at a standstill. Public meetings were forbidden, and all party letters were opened and censored.[18]

Consequently, Nkrumah was arrested and sentenced to three years in prison at James Fort Prison. However, while still in prison, he never ceased to communicate with his surviving party comrades, nor did the latter stop continuing their party operations. Because of the party's strength, a general election was finally called for the 8$^{th}$ of February, 1951. In that election, the CPP came out with a sweeping victory (22, 780 votes out of 23, 122).

As a result of this victory in the 1951, and general election, Nkrumah was released on the 12$^{th}$ of February, 1951, and summarily asked to form a new government. And on the 10$^{th}$ of July, 1953, he delivered his motion, "The Motion of Destiny", to the Legislative Assembly, in which he expounded his poltical philosophy to the British colonial Government, saying: "The right of people to decide their destiny, to make their way in freedom, is not to be measured by the yard stick of colour or degree of social development."[19]

With reference to his political stand on African Unity, Nkrumah had been marked for his active role in both England and Africa. After Du Bois' withdrawal from its organizational responbilities, it was Nkrumah who took it over, and in 1953, transferred from London to Kumasi, in the Gold Coast. Nkrumah's aim was to promote unity among West African countries, as a first step towards African unity. On the 18$^{th}$ of April, thus immediately after the Gold Coast had been declared de facto state of Ghana, with Nkrumah as its first Prime Minister in 1957, Nkrumah against called for another Pan-African Congress, which convened in Accra.

This was the first time that the Congress was attended by all independent African states.[20] The purpose thereof was to petition the colonial powers to grant self-rule to African Independent countries. Unlike all other Pan-African Congress, the Accra Congress was radical and pragmatic in its declaration to the colonial powers. With Nkrumah's encouragement, the Congress petitioned for dates to be named on which these colonies would have their independence restored, so that they could also join their sister-countries into a United States of Africa. And, above all, in the 1963 Addis Ababa Conference, Nkrumah, together with his Casablanca groups, urged for an immediate political unity of external "vultures".

## 2. Jomo Kenyatta

Until his return to Kenya from Europe in 1946, Kenyatta's real name was Jonstone Kamau Ngugi. On his return to Kenya in 1946, he became popularly known as Jomo Kenyatta (Jomo meaning the "Burning Spear" AND Kenyatta meaning a "beaded belt", which, his first wife, Grace Ahu, he began wearing on his return from overseas).

Kenyatta was first educated at the Church of Scotland Missionary School near Nairobi where he spent the first five years of his education.

After the Church of Scotland Missionary School, Kenyatta first worked as an interpreter in the Supreme Court under the British colonial rule in Kenya. Shortly afterwards, he joined the Nairobi Town Council Water Department, as a pipeline measure, meter reader and employees' supervisor. AT the same time, the Gikuyu Central Organization (GCA) had just been formed with a vehement ideology against the British colonial rule, which, to the Gikuyus, had arbitrarily usurped their land against their will. Furthermore, the (GCA) had now developed an unavoidable attitude against British dominance. It demanded some political change, or simply, an egalitarian style. Membership was an honourable symbol of one's convictions and dedication to one's people—one's pride in carrying out one's rightful duty in denunciation of the arbitrary and, therefore, undesirable foreign values. Thus, the pride of one's culture despite the effects of social change. In the modern sense, it could be termed as the quest for preservation of one's cultural dignity, political independence and sovereign equality among nations.

For many years, the GCA was faced with harassments from the British colonial regime, especially through the District Officer, District Commissioners and also by the Provisional Officer for the Central Province. Besides, party leadership was another factor.

As there was only a meager number of persons (mainly at high school level), party leadership and effective articulation for better results were several incentives for party factions and violence. It was, however, not until the end of World War II that a considerable number of people were eventually convinced to join the movement.

By the influence of his colleague, Kangethe, following the Kahuhia Meeting (in Gikuyu in 1928, Kenyatta was convinced to join the Association in the following year (1929) as its new Secretary-General. As a government rule, Kenyatta had to give up his government post prior to joining politics.

As to why Kenyatta was asked to take the party's administration must be explained. He was asked to do so precisely because of dissatisfaction and quarrels among and between the party leaders.

After assuming the new post as the Secretary-General of the GCA in 1929, Kenyatta revived the collapsing Association and reconciled the quarrel between the Kiambu and Fort Hall politicians. Prior to his administration, the Association had been known as the Central Gikuyu Association (CGA): but now, the Association's name was changed to "Gikuyu central Associaton" (GCA), meaning a Pan-Gikuyu political association designed to liberate the Gikuyu land from the British colonial settlers.

To mobilize his people, Kenyatta introduced a cultural monthly journal, Muigwithania (a Gikuyu concept, meaning the "Reconciler"). It was published in the Gikuyu language with Kenyatta as its first editor. After the first nine issues, he was succeeded by Henry Mwangi Gichuru in March, 1929, who also became the Acting Secretary while Kenyatta had been commissioned to go to England by the GCA.

On his trip to England on the 8th of March, 1929, Kenyatta was commissioned by the GCA to plead the case of his Gikuyu people before the Colonial Secreatry about the Gikuyu farmers' land that had been arbitrary appropriated by the white settlers.

Kenyatta returned to Kenya in the fall of 1930. Shortly afterwards, he went back to London on the 22nd of May, 1931. Kenyatta returned to London with Parmenas Githendu Mukeri, a teacher-graduate of Makerere College in Uganda Prior to their departure, on April 28, 1931, the two swore before the Gikuyu elders and other members of the GCA at Pumwani, Nairobi, that they would take the Gikuyu's grievances to the Colonial Secretary, particularly to the Parliamentary Joint Committee on Closer Union in East Africa against further deliberate attempts to alienate Africans from their land and cultural dignity. At the same time, the two men swore that while en route, they would never reveal their secret to anyone, until they reached London.

Before returning to Kenya, Kenyatta visited Moscow and decided to study there. Consequently, he took two and half years to study at the University of Moscow and returned to London in 1936, where he took his post-graduate studies in Anthropology at the London School of Economics. Under Profesor B. Malinowski, Kenyatta completed and thereafter published his thesis: Facing Mount Kenya.[22] a dynamic study and defence of his Gikuyu culture against foreign contamination.

In his book, he critisized the European writers who could not understand that hhis people are not "Kikuyu" as the English put it, but "Gikuyu".

Secondly, he vehemently criticized the missionaries who could not comprehend and hence, appreciate the Gikuyu's tradition of clitoridectomy (female circumcision) which is customarily designed to make a female symbol of adult-hood after child-hood—the condition sine qua non of the Gikuyu tribal law, religion and morality. In a sense, Kenyatta's motive was to articulate his Gikuyuism against the foreigners who, under the myth of St. Pauls's journey's sought to invade Africa to disrupt the Africa traditions.

While in England, Kenyatta also worked on an English farm, and then got married to an English woman, Edna Clarke, a second wife, before he married the now "Ngina" Kenyatta, a daughter of a Gikuyu chief, popularly known as "Mama Ngina".[23] He also took a very active part in the Pan-African Congress organized by Dr. DU Bois in Manchester in 1945.

At the end of the Congress, Kenyatta, T. R. Makonnen and Dr. Peter Millard remained in Manchester to organize the Pan-African Federation while George Padmore, Peter Abrahams, and Kwame Nkrumah returned to London. It was at this time that both Kenyatta and Makonnen established a magazine called Pan-Africa in Manchester to serve as the organ of the Pan-Africa Federation-a magazine that has been able to exist to the time of this writing.

Kenyatta's relationship with the British colonial regime in Kenya began to deteriorate because fo four incidents: (1) his resignation from the government and eventual enrolment in the GCA; (2) his first trip to London to plead his people's case before the Colonial Secretary against the white settlers in Kenya; (3) the second trip to London to appeal both the Colonial Secretary and the Joint Committee on Closer Union in East Africa against any unification in Africa that would, in turn jeopardize the African cause; and (4) his active participation in the Pan-African Congres, in Manchester, 1945. Consequently, on his return to Kenya in 1946, and his subsequent resumption on the presidency of the Kenya African Union on 1st June, 1947, Kenyatta began to be watched closely. To the settler, Kenyatta was both a real threat and a dangerous activist. However, he actively took part in the new organization and managed to unite the GCA and the KAU members who had never been able to work together until he returned from London.

The KAU developed broader grievances than those of the GCA. In addition to land grievances, it also complained about the Kipande (passes) and demanded more representation in the Legislative Council.

He was soon joined by other politically minded men such as Oginga Odinga (a Luo, Tom Mboya (half Luo and half Luhya), Paul Ngei (Akamba), James S. Gichuru (Kikuyu), and foremost, Peter Mbiyu Koinange (Kikuyu).[24]

When MAU MAU became both extensive and intensive, Kenyatta was confronted with what to do next. Consequently, he once uttered a Gikuyu curse: Kura Na Miiri Ya Mikongoi (to be driven into oblivion) in denunciation of MAU MAU's name in the former's violent killings.

However, on the 18th day of April, 1953, Kenyatta was arrested and sentenced to seven years' imprisonment by the British regime in Kenya for managing MAU MAU which, according to the British colonial regime was "a terrorist and dangerous organization in Kenya". Responding to the Magistrate (Ransley Thacker, a retired Supreme Court Judge), Kenyatta said:-

> None of us would condone the mutilation of human beings. We have families of our own. If you think that in working for African rights we have turned Mau Mau, you have been misled.

We feel this case has to strangle the Kenya African Union-the only African political organization which fights for the rights of the people.[25]

The advocate D. N. Prit, Q. C., acknowledged the true threat of MAU MAU, but was unable to prove the involvement of Kenyatta and the other six accused in the movement.

While he was still in jail at Lodwar (a remote semi-arid areas in the northern region of Kenya), the Kenya African National Union was formed by James Gichuru, Oginga Odinga, Tom mboya, et, al., in March of 1960. On his release on August 15,1961, Kenyatta was automatically recognized as the leader of the new political party, the Kenya Africa National Union (KANU).

He entered the Legislative Council in January, 1962, as leader of the opposition against the Kenya African Democratic Union (KADU) Government, under the leadership of Ronald Ngala and Masinde Muliro. In 1963, he won an overwhelming majority during the general election and summarily drove the nation to independence on the 12$^{th}$ day of December, 1963, with himself as the first Prime Minister of Kenya.

Immdediately after Kenya's freedom, Kenyatta introduced his philosophy of Democratic African Socialism: a belief in "rapid economic development and social progress for all our citizens "which he paradoxically honoured theoretically but not practically due to his selfishness and continuously mounting repression he felt against his competitors.

In this philosophy, Kenyatta (formally addressed Mzee in Swahili, literally meaning "the old one" and politically, the "most honourable") analytically emphasized six basic human needs, vix:1) Politically equality; 2) social justice; 3) human dignity, including freedom of conscience; 4) freedom from want, disease and exploitation; 5) equal opportunities; and 6) high and growing per capita incomes with equitable distribution—the needs that only his family and immediate associates had the rights to enjoy thoughout Kenyatta's leadership. Besides, he warned that whereas the term socialism is also common among the East European countries, African socialism was replica of the European socialism, but rather an African creation in total. It was African in that it was of the African subsistence, specifically destined to convey the African ideas and personality. On the other hand, it also entails the African flexibility, and, therefore, a capability for "incorporation of useful and compatible techniques from whatever source provided that it was guided by these three principles:-

1. It must be drawn from the African tradition meaning political democracy and mutual responsibility);
2. It must be adaptable to the new and rapidly changing circumstance; and
3. It must not rest, for its success, on a satellite relationship with any other country or group of countries.

On foreign relation, Kenyatta, like Nkrumah, strongly emphasized the policy of non-alignment—a political ideology designed to protect the African political dignity and sovereign equality among the nations against foreign quarrels in which Africa has no profit. On the Madaraka Day, June, 1965, Kenyatta warned:-

> For over forty years, I fought and sacrificed my active life so that this country could get rid of the yoke of colonialism and imperialism. Many sons and daughters of our land have suffered and she bled so that our children may be born free. You can, therefore, understand my personal feelings about the future. How can I tolerate anything that could compromise or jeopardize the promises to our children. Let me declare once more that as Head of your Government, I shall fight with all my strength anymore, or group of any country, that will be termed to undermine our independence. This pledge remains true whether such forces should come from within or from outside Kenya.[26]

Kenyatta was occasionally sought for advice on African Unity questions; and personally played a very vital role in the founding of the Organization of African Unity. On becoming Kenya's Head of State in 1963, he has since played many roles in inter-African relations. For instance, he organized and presided over an OAU mediation Committee about the Angolan Crisis in 1975.[27] Inspite of the numerous prevailing accusations against him on the question of succession elimination (e.g., of Tom Mboya, Ronald Ngala, J. M. Kariuki, e.t.c) in Kenyan politics[28], the United States CIA payroll participation in World Politics[29], participation in the Entebbe plot against Amin's Uganda[30] Karafu, i.e., a Swahili name for Clove(s) now popularly used in East Africa meaning smuggling and similar forms of corruption through which

Kenyatta sought to satisfy his lust for Capital Accumulation during his presidency, and failure to return the colonially occupied land to the owners[31] as he had promised before Kenyan independence[32], Kenyatta's development of national consciousness against the British colonial rule was significant in the development of Kenyatta's nationalism and the drive to self-rule.

It is empirically true and correct that it was not only Kenyatta who played a significant role in Kenya's nationalism and cultivation of self-rule. Apart form him were, for instance, Peter Mbiyu Koinange-another Gikuyu nationalist who had to hide in Britain during the Kenyatta's MAU MAU Trials in Kenya, so that if Kenyatta were sentenced to death by the British colonial court in Kenya, so that would be able to revive the same drive for the Gikuyu's land from the colonial occupation: Oginga Odinga and Tom Mboya—both Luo nationalists in Kenya without whom Kenyatta would definitely have been done away with by the British colonial authority, since Gikuyu nationalists and chiefs has already submitted a signed petition to the British colonial authority requesting that authority to eliminate Kenyatta completely: Ronald Ngala and Muinga Chokwe from the Coast; James Osogo, Clement Were, Clement Ochwada, Masinde Muliro and other Abaluyia from the Western Region; to name but only a few.

It is also true that Kenyatta's acts in Kenyan politics ever since independence to his death in August 1978 constituted a significant contradiction with his own political theory.[33] However, the correlation between Kenyatta's nationalism and goals on the one hand, and Kenyan nationalism and goals on the other before independence is significant indeed, since both sought self-rule from the British colonial rule.

### 3. Julius K. Nyerere (1922-1999):

Julius K. Nyerere, popularly known as Mwalimu (a Swahili word, meaning "the teacher"), was born in Butiama, Tanganyika (now Tanzania). Like both Nkrumah and Kenyatta, Nyerere's exact date of birth is uncertain. However, it has been supposed to be March, 1922, for official purposes. It was raining heavily the day of Nyerere's birth, and thus the name, "Kabarage", meaning an ancestral spirit who lived in the rain. Nyerere took the name Julius when, at the age of twenty, he was baptized into the Roman Catholic Church.

He was born to Nyerere Bunto, Chief of a small Zanaki Tribe, and Mugaya, Bunto's 18th wife. Although he was a chief's son, Nyerere's family lived on a subsistence budget because the family's chieftainship designed to economically serve only the British capitalists in Tanganyika.[34]

Nyerere was first educated at the Roman Catholic Boarding School in Musoma, where he studied, inter alia, Swahili and English. It was at Musoma, that he was introduced to Roman Catholism. In 1936, Nyerere took the Tabora Governement School Entrance Examinations on which he scored a First Division that qualified him for admission to that School in 1937.

At Tabora, Nyerere came into conflict with the British prefect system which granted the prefects special priviledges and allowed them to discipline other boys. For example, one time, to the headmaster. Nyerere became more infuriated when the headmaster sided with the prefect and forced Nyerere to discipline the same boy by caning him. Consequently, when Nyerere later became a prefect, he successfully fought for the abolition of prefect privileges. Thereafter, he became popularly known in the school as a reformer.

In January 1943, Nyerere joined Makerere College in Uganda, which was by then the sole centre of higher education in East Africa.

At Makerere College, Nyerere continued his political radicalism and activism by joining the Makerere Debating Society and helping to organize the Catholic Action Group and Tanganyika African Welfare (TAWA). He later disbanded that TAWA in favour of forming a new organization called the Makerere chapter of the Tanganyika African Association (TAA).

Nyerere twice entered the East African literary competition and won first prize both times, the second time utilizing John Stuart Mill's ideas vis-à-vis the subjection of women and by applying these ideas to African tribal society.

In 1945, after achieving his Diploma in Education, Nyerere was offered two teaching jobs—one from the government at Tabora and the other from St. Mary's School (a White Father's Missionary School) in Tabora.

While still entangled in a dilemma about which position to accept, he received an intimidating letter from the government school detailing the advantages of teaching at a government institution. Upon receiving this letter, Nyerere was furious. In relation against such coercion from the British colonial rule, he promptly accepted St. Mary's offer. At St. Mary's, he met the

Reverend Richard Walsh, who later became very instrumental in his interest and admission to the Univeristy of Edinburg, in Scotland.

However, while still teaching at St. Mary's, Nyerere delved into a new areas fo activism. He became a government price inspector, but later resigned in frustration because of the government ignored the violations he reported. Thereafter, he helped to organize a co-operative store in an effort to combat the monopoly of Indian Merchants in Tabora, and in the periodic discussions Nyerere, Andrew Tibandebage, and other friends and regarding Tanganyika affairs, Nyerere's devotion to his countrymen and their education was exemplified the night classes Nyerere held to teach English to the adults in Tabora. All these acts were definitely sold remifications of Nyerere's national consciousness, albeit at a low tide at that time.

With the help of Father Walsh, Nyerere obtained a scholarship to attend the University of Edinburg, where he studied British History, English Language, Moral Philosophy, Political Economy, Special Anthropology, Constitutional Law, and Economic History. He studied these subjects despite the fact that the Colonial Office, upon granting his scholarship, had intended Nyerere to study biology.

With regard to the effects of his studies at Edinburg, Nyerere tells us that: "(1) read a great deal. I had plenty of time to think. My ideas of politics were formed completely during that time. It was my own evolution, but it was complete."[35]

After Edinburg, he resume his teaching at Pupu, near Dar-es-Salaam, in 1952. However, as he himself tells us Nyerere's political philosophy dates right back to his time at Edniburg. It was Edinburg and most specifically during his first years teaching after Edinburg, that his political ideas became mature and real. At Edinburg, as well as his first years of teaching upon his return from the University, Nyerere had his first contact with different political ideas.[36]

Practically speaking, however, it was not until 1953 that he began to put his political theory into practice. Early that year, he did not only have definite theoretical political organization in his mind, as Thomas Patrick Melady puts it in his Profiles of African Leaders (1961)[37]; also he had some definite practical political ideas.

As a result, between 1953 and 1954, Nyerere was confronted with another dilemma: whether to continue teaching or to enter politics.

At the same time, he was offered the prestigious position of "District Officer" by the governor of Tanganyika; but, he categorically refused the offer, as he felt that it was now his duty to organize and lead his people from the colonial bondage.[38] Soon after, he accelerated his activities in politics as President of Tanganyika Africa Association, which was later renamed the "Tanganyika African National Union" (TANU).[39]

TANU sent Nyerere to the United Nations Trusteeship Council in New York City in 1955 to give his oppressed African people's views on the demand for Tanganyika's independence.

A second appearance at the United Nations Council and other speeches on independence between 1955 and 1958 caused Nyerere to become very popular with the British Colonial Administration. In 1958, the British Colonial Government, therefore, charged Nyerere with sedition. He was convicted and paid the fine instead of serving his sentence. It will be seen how this gesture on the part of Nyerere paid dividends.

Lord Twining was governor of Tanganyika until 1958. In early years, he had a healthy racial pattern in the country. But later (it is suspected the British Government was behind this move), Twining encouraged the United Tanganyika Party (UTP) to obstruct the growth of TANU. UTP wanted to lead the county into a multi-racial pattern with its politics based on racial proportions as opposed to non-racial integration.[41] Turnbull's appointment brought criticism from Dar-es-Salaam and London, due to his reputation of toughness against the MAU MAU in Kenya. However, Turnbull, because of Nyerere's gestures, regarding the sedition conviction, bettered relations between the Government House and political leaders in his first nine months. During his time, 1958-1959, Nyerere had become a full-time TANUworker. In the elections, TANU gained support of the African masses, and many Asians and Europeans.

Nyerere and his colleagues gained the Government's confidence; and the elected officials, for the first time, ignored the racial question entirely. The African representatives advocated retaining reserved seats for the Minorities.[42]

Nyerere proposed some changes in the Legislative Council, including increasing its membership. He said of this change, "a solution containing the barometer of feeling within the cobweb of the constitution; the way opened when experience is gained to establish full internal self-government and then independence.[43]

Due to Nyerere's wisdom, who became Prime Minister in May of 1961, and his colleagues' quite self-confidence and willingness to negotiate on issues such as integration, the British Government was favourably impressed with the success of non-racialism in Tanganyika.[44] Political speculators, at that time, viewed independence for Tanganyika as coming in1965. But through Nyerere's non-violent and non-hate policies towards peaceful racial unity, he and TANU "earned' independence for Tanganyika on December the 9th, 1961.

Nyerere had strong positive views on racial equality in the new independent refused to allow the Black African to use descrimination in reverse. He also understood the fears of minority groups. Despite the injustices committed within the African states during colonization, Nyerere showed deep and far-sighted understanding of racial problems. He believed that the African can afford to be "generous suffering was expected to be a good lesson to Africa on the true concept of more patience and understanding of fears and prejudices of the former 'ruler' than they understand themselves".[45] He further believed that the minorities fear through actions and words.[46]

Nyerere was much keen to see it that fellow Americans, Europeans, and Asians consider themselves as Tanganyika, not as separate entities. Of this racial Asians consider "Unity is our best weapon"[47], and "TANU is going to prove that you can have a democracy in rural society in Africa and have it happily . . . . In Tanganyika, the Asians and the Europeans have decided to trust us; in other territories, Tanganyika, the white settler minority has finally realized the advantage of coming to terms with the native Africans.[48]

In the elections of 1962, Nyerere became President of Tanganyika Republic with a 97% vote.[49] Nyerere was considered to be a modern man with the desire to turn his backward nation into a modern democratic society.[50]

In January of 1964, after the political revolution in Zanzibar and the overthrow of the Arab regime there, Nyerere and his government were threatened by a mutiny of the military. Even when concessions were made, the mutiny continued.

As a last resort, Nyerere called in the British troops which responded immediately. Nyerere in speeches after the uprising, called for his country's forgiveness for calling upon the British. But the incident, which showed his government's impotence when under attack, was an unfortunate lesson.[52]

In April of 1964, the Zanzibar People's Republic entered a union agreement, in which Nyerere became President of the United Republic of Tanganyika and Zanzibar (or Tanzania). Politically, it appeared that Zanzibar's eastern and communist leanings were moderated bythe unification.[53]

During this period, Nyerere accused the United States' Government of a plot to take over Tanzania. Articles on the subject indicate theories about the attempt to overthrow Nyerere's government and many people were suspect. The uprising put Nyerere in a very insecure position due lack of proof conviction of the instigators.[54]

Nyerere had a well-developed philosophy regarding the aims of foreign and non-alignment due to the power thus gained by the "giving" nation. This was the reason why in 1967, a nationalization programme was instituted barring aid from West German and other capitalist countries. Nyerere took this position rather than to agree to terms of no trade with East Germany[55]. In 1968 saw Nyerere out of political necessity, taking a more and more immoderate course. On May 3rd, 1968, quite contrary to his moderate policies, Nyerere had a law rammed through his judiciary, making it nearly impossible to criticize the government.

"The Newspaper Ordinance of May 3, 1968, empowers the President to ban any newspaper if he consideres it to be in the 'national interest.[56] His target was The Standard, a London-based English newspaper. The Minister of Defence and Justice, Rashidi M. Kawawa, claimed that "capitalists were using newspapers . . . in an attempt to subvert the nation . . . We cannot allow our Socialists ideas to be polluted by imperialist anti-people propaganda". Nyerere and his government which would allow him to close down that paper.[57]

"Nyerere, Bantu Socialism' is a pragmatic rather than dogmatic variety".[58] Nyerere had always admired the political philosophy and practice of the late President of Ghana, Kwame Nkrumah, and the late Congolese Prime Minister Patrice Lumumba; albeit his own philosophy and practice were far less radical.59 Nyerere's moderate position was influenced by the late Prime Minister Jawahrlal Nehru and by the late Mohandas Gandhi.

Nyerere said, "I have learnt to be a moderate through observing the inflexible behaviour of the Europeans".[60] Nehru stood for co-oepration with British officials. For India, the British colonial office developed a clear policy of training native Indian officials; In Tanzania, the fundamental problem around the time of independence was lack of enough trained native African officials to take over British position.[61]

His book, Ujamaa—meaning "family-hood"—describes Nyerere's socialism. His philosophy delved into Africa's traditional past which had socialistic practices as a rational base for his Tanzanian government. Nyerere impressed the observer as a man deeply committed to his peopleand having a great concern for their welfare. And as Melady once described theleader, "Nyerere speaks words with shocking power of ultimate truth . . . sees a basic problem with a pure, balanced sense of reality."[62] Nyerere is a man who lives by his beliefs.

Nyerere contended that socialism was a humanistic attitude of the mind. Under socialism, people are to be taught to care for each other's welfare. Distribution of wealth makes socialism different from capitalism.[64] A socialist society will care foran individual provided that he is willing to work and not hoard his wealth.[65] A man will reap his fair share of what he sows. Work and socialism go hand in hand. A man has no right to expect anything from a society to which he contributes nothing. In turn, that society must give the individual an opportunity to work.[66] The tenant of capitalism must be rejected: Since individual ownership of land and use of land as a commodity[67] is totally un-African.

Therefore, in accepting socialism as the "Rational choice", "and in rejecting the capitalist attitude of mind which colonialism brought to Africa, we must reject also capitalist methods which go with it.

One of these is the individual ownership fo land for accumulation of wealth over wealth."[68] in regards to income, an "individual must demand only that return for skilled work in proportion to wealth or poverty of the whole society".[69]

With the adoption of the Interim Constitution in July, 1965, Tanzania became a one party state.[70] The fundamental rationales behind the one party system were, *inter alia*. That: TANU had, ever since Independence, received the overwhelming national support; TANU had never had any viable position; a two-party state would mean a lack of party organization and a lack of enthusiasm of the people for fighting poverty; and, a two-party system would allow for the protection of the undeserving leaders, in Tanzania.[71] All these ideas were Nyerere's political creation.

Nyerere was also credited with the political creation of the Arusha Declaration on February 5$^{th}$, 1967, designed to set down TANU's policy on socialism and self-reliance. As a national policy, designed to many Tanzanians who could not understand English, it was written in both Swahili and English. The declaration's nine fundamentals axioms were:-

1. All human beings are equal
2. Every individual has the right to dignity and respect
3. Every citizen is an integral part of the nation and has a right to take equal part in government at the local, regional, and national level
4. Every citizen has the right to freedom of expression, of movement, of religious belief, and of association within the context of the law
5. Each individual has the right to receive from society protection of his life and property held according to law.
6. Each individual has the right a just return for his labour
7. All citizens together all natural resources of the country in trust for their descendants.
8. In order to ensure economic justice, the state must have effective control over principle means of production.
9. It is the state's responsibility to intervene actively in economic life of the nation so as to prevent the exploitation of one person by another or one group by another; and so as to prevent the accumulation of wealth to an extent which is consistent with existence of classes society.

And, in January of 1977, Nyerere showed a full satisfaction with the achievements and progress of the Declaration after ten years. In spite of the problems the Declaration had encountered in the course of its implementation, Nyerere's prediction was that with such ten-year experience, TANU was likely to do better if those encountered mistakes could be avoided; and if more leadership will and prudence would be injected into the future implementation.[72]

A futher examination of Nyerere's idea of Ujama (i.e socialism) shows the following elements of internal expectations:-

1. An absence of explanation, since every man, able to work, expects a just return for his labour performed with incomes from different types of work not grossly divergent. Only those for whom the state cannot provide a market for their labours shall be dependent.

2. Peasants and workers must equally control the major means of production and exchange, based upon equal opportunity and freedom.
3. The Government must be democratic since it is chosen and led by and for the peasants and workers themselves.
4. Everyone must believe in a practice socialism.[73]

Externally, Ujamaa advocated a policy of self-reliance which initially had a profound effect on Tanzania's foreign policy though this had to be abandoned later due to its most powerful competing capitalist forces from the already established capitalist world which was no more a match to the new weak Socialist World. In general, Nyerere's Ujamaa rationale was to turn Tanzania into a warring machine against colonialism Imperialism, Capitalism, Individualism, Poverty and Oppression. The struggle aimed at moving the people from Poverty into Prosperity. While money through taxation was not enough for this struggle,[74] Tanzania could afford the imperialistic baits attached to foreign aids. According to Nyerere, the private investments encouraged perpetual dependence upon others for funds endangers Tanzania's independence and ability to choose its own political polilicies;75 Industrialization at this time meant inviting in foreign investors (capitalists which consequently threatened Tanzania's sovereignty and policies of socialism.[76] But since Tanzania could not compete in the world market for goods to export; so the policy of "import substitution" was the only possibility. Goods which Tanzania was importing needed to be substituted with goods produced in Tanzania.[77]

To Nyerere, money was a result but not a basis for development.[78] Tanzania was very fertile land with sufficient rainfall, so agriculture should become the basis for its development. Domestic and exported crops were seen as Tanzania's future. If the production of crops could be increased, this could mean more food and money for each Tanzanian.[79] Men and "loiters" in Tanzanian villages needed to be asked to put forth hard work. Women were not supposed to more than they could afford.[80]

Better results could be achieved only if hard work was combined with intelligence and knowledge and passed onto the peasants for their farming, etc.[81] Technologies and educators were due to their monopoly of the know-how, expected to work in the villages to help the people increase the quality and quantity of their produce.

According to Nyerere, self-reliance was possible only if:-

1. The land is used for the benefit of the whole nation;
2. TANU sees to it that the country produces enough food and cash crops for export; and tools, training and leadership are made available for farmers to learn modern methods;
3. The peoplelearn and believe in self-reliance so that they become self-sufficient in attaining food, serviceable cloths, and good housing, since work brings pride, laziness scorn.
4. Good policies based on self-reliance are combined with socialism: to prevent exploitation; to bring fair distribution of national wealth; and to maintain independence and freedom without dependence on the countries, either financially or politically; and
5. Leaders can realize that good leadership means that every leader ought to learn and be trained in government policies so that the policies can be understood and implemented better.[82]

Apart from his Ujamaa policy under the Arusha Declaration, which became one of the fundamental bases of Nyerere's political leadership reputation, Nyerere's political realism anent the Pan-African Movement gained him an additional world-wide recognition.

While he wanted and vigorously sought to see Kenya, Uganda and Tanganyika (before the latter became federated with Zanzibar to form Tanzania) become federated into a unitary political system in the early 1960's Nyerere later realizes that due to the fact that every African nation-state was now a sovereign state itself with its unique problems, Pan-AFricanism could not a reality at that time.[84] He further realized that every Pan-Africanist, as well as the idea of Pan-AFricanism itself, was caught up in a dilemma of two alternatives: either to accept the fact that the Pan-AFricanism demanded supra-African consciousness or to overlook that fact and to, instead pay one's attention to the prevailing problems affecting one's nation in nation-building and socio-economoc development.[85]

While Nyerere realized this psychological tension among other problems now facing most Pan-Africanist because of the prevailing contradiction between their propensity toward a supra-(continental) loyalty and their propensity toward a parochial (national) loyalty, he believed that although Pan-Africanism demanded a supra-African consciousness and loyalty it is also demanded that every one of the nations of Africa. He believed so because developing any one part of Africa could also help Africa as a whole. Consequently, he strongly believed that within each African state, it was necessary "to promote a feeling of nationhood to avoid internal conflict and further dis-unity"[86] Each state devised a constitution and political structure appropriate to its own history and its own problems:.[87] A country needed to expand its own revenue through development. Competition for foreign dollars forces nations to fulfil obligations, regarding poverty, etc. to its people and not devote adversely affect the development of pride in Africa. This needed to be guarded against.[89]

On the other hand, Nyerere noted that while it looked rather impossible to achieve unity through nationalism, unity could be possible if these conditions prevailed:-

1. If African states remained optimistic that fifteen to twenty years from now then that unity could be possible.[91]
2. If African states accepted or were willing to agree on one psychological fact tha t loyalty between nations and leaders along with co-operation and understanding of the other's problems were highly essential for any viable unification among nations.
3. If African nations were willing to deliberately move toward unity, whether that move were essentially function or not. A co-operation along the lines of economic development, trade and economic institutions were very important. However, political union is necessary or else economic integration is likely to remain highly limited.

   Political union and economic integration do not necessarily have to coincide. The exampleof the Tanganyika-Zanzibar union shows that countries benefit by growing together. African unity will have a meaning only when that unity exists both in theory and practice-when Africa itself chooses a policy of "good neighbourliness".[92]
4. If African State Sovereignty is will or ready to be surrendered to a new body for Africa to move forward. The unity and solidarity of African states which the OAU initiated in May, 1963, must be strengthened and the spirit of the Charter honoured in a positive action for Africa to make progress.[93]

Nyerere advised that all African sovereign states needed to keep the goal of unity in sight because without this positive action at all times, that goal would be diverted.[94]

And although he deplored the collapse of the East African Community in 1977, and the on-going rampant civil war and intra-African war such as the on-going war in Zaire, he contented that African Unity would one day be achieved as nation-states in Africa were achieved.

## (B) Reasons for the Rise of Nkrumah, Kenyatta and Nyerere in the Development of African Nationalism and Patriotism Against Colonialism and on the World Imperialism Market

1. From Nkrumah's Biography, we note Nkrumah being needed back in the Gold Coast (now Ghana) by his people to re-organize the United Gold Coast Convention (UGCC). We also note Nkrumah him-self wishing to become a charismatic as Dr. Aggrey. And we see him vowing to fight against colonialism whenever he turns from overseas.
2. From Kenyatta's biography, we note Kenyatta being asked to take over the position of Secretary-General of the collapsing Gikuyu Central Association (GCA) in 1929; and thereafter the Kenya African Union (KAU) in 1947, and Kenya African National Union in (KANU) 1963. (He drove his country to self-rule in December of 1963).
3. And from Nyerere's biography, we also note him being essential to Tanganyika successful rebellion against the British Colonial authority. He preferred a missionary teaching position to a government job. After one year after his return from Edinburgh in 1952, Nyerere categorically refused to continue his teaching profession. Instead he diverged to politics against the British colonial rule in Tanganyika and finally hdrove his country (Tanganyika) to independence in 1961.
4. These revolutionary behaviours against the colonial regime were not unique to Nkrumah's Gold coast, Kenyatta's Kenya and Nyerere's Tanganyika. They were universal throughout the African continent. Anti-colonial politics in Nkrumah's Gold Coast, Kenyatta's Kenya and Nyerere's Tanganyika are collectively an empirical paradigm of the development of African nationalisms throughout occupied African countries.
5. This phenomenon is synthesized in Model I. As also indicated in Model I, our autopsy of colonial rule shows that the trouble with the rule first began with its own inherent (internal contradictions.
6. Motivated by the lust of capitalism, the colonial rule was automatically forced to implement European imperialism against the colonized African peoples. In Africa, it applied the same model in its imperialistic policy and administrative style which capitalism had failed to apply in European hemisphere especially England, against both European children and women in factories and coal mines. Like their helpless counterpart in Europe vix; both European woman and children, who had been exploited by capitalism until they were fortunately rescued by both Parliamentary

Laws and other anti-capitalism forces, e.g., Utilitarianism and Communism, the occupied Africans in Africa were also subjected to forced labour.

7. However, unlike those European and women and children, Africans were subjected to worse coercive measures.
8. These measures are enumerated in model I. The axiom governing those measures was simply this: "Your Work or You Die!" Also, in cases whereby African land was usurped and either allocated to European white settlers or declared a "Crown Land" by the colonial rule, this phenomenon is explained by Model 1:
9. Definitely, such conditions did not exist in the case of capitalism vis-à-vis European women and children, But, the fact still remains that both Africans on the one hand, and European women and children on the other, were subjected to similar tortures caused by capitalism. Otherwise, it is highly questionable why a normal individual—condition which he/she would not personally like to have imposed upon him/he in the real world.
10. It was due to these intolerable conditions that the Utilitarians, Communists, English Parliament and the African nationalists such as Nkrumah, English Parliament and the African nationalists such as Nkrumah, Kenyatta and Nyerere fought ferociously against capitalism. Or else, anti-capitalism and anti-imperialism in Europe and Africa would not have come by accident.
11. But, the fundamental questions at issue at are: (10 Why Nkrumah, Kenyatta and Nyerere? (2) Why did other Africans before these men do it? These similar questions are examined in the next chapter, VI.
12. In our laboratory, it will be the same subjects, namely, Nkrumah, Kenyatta, and Nyerere, as a paradigm of African nationalists, who first developed national consciousness before the rest of the African peasantry, agasint the colonial rule. In this Study, Nkrumah, Kenyatta and other African nationalists during and after Nkrumah's time are referred to as the Nkrumah Group; those African nationalists before Nkrumah's time are identified as the Pre-Nkrumah Group.

### (C) Outcome of African Nationalists 'Rise and Intervention Against A Colonial Culture of Anti-Peace and Anti-Democracy in Africa Using Conflict Vaccination cum Cutlural Engineering Formula (Dose)

1. The above-noted achievements by those three African nationalists particularly that of Nkrumah in the Gold Coast from 1952 to 1957 became not only an amazing

exemplary lesson of African political against Colonialism and Imperialism in Africa but also a very significant eye opener inspiration to every African in a hostile anti-Peace and anti_Democracy Colonial Regime in Africa—a culture which, for many years, had been characterized by a total disregard to African human right resulting into an acute awe and timidity in most every African due to torture and harassments by the Colonial masters who often forced them to leave their own regular workto do manual work for those masters without any pay.

2. Because of this Nkrumah's inspiration, the whole African Continent arose with a vehement demand for their Freedom and Democracy like fire racing through the dry bush land or a space craft zooming through the outer space with an amazing mighty power.
3. And, within a matter of three years or so (from 1957), the entire Continent was alredy free from the Colonial Rule and the latter had already been put to shame and forced to free back where it had come from—thus also further confirming the fact that man is indeed a habitual failure in political leadership.

## CHAPTER VI

# A Comparative Analysis of the Above Three Clinically Diagnosed Cases

### (1) Findings

A comparative Analysis of those three cases (above) leads us to the following conclusion:-

**(a) It significantly supports:-**

i. Prophet Isaiah's prophecy that the earth is indeed in darknes and its people are covered by a thick darknes requiring immediate intervention (Isaiah 60:1-5).
ii. Thomas Hobbes' view that because of the existing amorphous and acephelous nature of the International Community in which there is no central body and law above those of sovereign nation-states with which to regulate and punish these States for any violation, certain individuals, nation-states and giant private business or religious entities were just like wolves doing all sorts of injustices to others with total impunity.
iii. Achebe's conclusion that such anarchical conduct and self-seeking attitude have put our International System to so much conflict and shame that our global culture is now so corroded and rotten that almost everything is just falling apart from one corner to another in the system.
iv. And, Fanon's observation that the earth was indeed so much wretched that any good Samaritan's intervention now to save it from the decay would be very much highly appreciated.

**(b) It also supports:-**

i. Gandhi's prudent and courageous decision to use Conflict Vaccination cum Cultural Engineering Methodology in India in order to eradicate the existing rotten culture of untouchability and thus to save that Country from falling apart. Using this dose, he sought every one to be born again; discard his old inner person and get a totally new clean inner person.
ii. Mandela's decision to use the same Vaccination dose in order to eradicate the existing rotten culture of apartheid and thus save that Country from falling apart. Also by using this dose, he sought everyone to be born against, discard his inner person and receive a totally new clean inner person.
iii. And, Prophets Isaiah, Jeremiah and Ezekiel whom God commanded to use the same dose in order to eradicate the existing decaying culture in Israel and Judah characterized by various inhumane behaviour and attitude and devil worship—a situation God wanted all Israel and Judah to be cleansed of i.e. to be born again by discarding his old inner person and receiving a clean new inner person with the aid of the Prophets using a similar dose.

**(c) In addition to Gandhi, Mandela and the Prophets each of whom used this** Vaccination dose in order to achieve his goal, a comprehensive in-depth survey of the history of our Total Civilization from that of Mesopotamia in 7000 BC to the present (2013) also confirms that all revolutions against human rights violations and other injustices throughout the Civilization used a similar type of Conflict Vaccination cum Cultural Engineering dose. For example:—The Peloponnesian War (431-404BC) against Athens' war-mongerism virus which had to be paralyzed by Sparta in order for Athens to toe the line of Peace and Democracy. The French Commune Revolution (1793), against their boastful King Louis XVI whom they had to guillotine in 1793 as a lesson to future leaders for claiming that he was above the law and that the state was him and vice versa (L'etat c'est mois; et je suis l'etat)! The Religious Revolution leading to The Peace of Westaphalia (1648), The Glorious Revolution in England (1653-58, 1688-89).

The Rise of the Utilitarianism and Communism against Capitalism and the latter's colonial and imperialistic evils against the poor in Europe (19$^{th}$ Century). The Bolshevik or the Russian Workers' Revolution between the Have-Nots (the Proletarians) against the Haves and the latter's evils of Capitalism which are colonialism and imperialism in Russia (1917). The American Revolution by The Thirteen American Colonies against the oppressive stubborn British King George III (1776), The Indian Revolution for independence 91949). The American Black Revolution under the leadership of their principal white American advocate President Abraham Lincoln against slavery and other inhumane conditions imposed upon them by their white American brothers and sisters which was eventually brought to its knees by Lincoln's Emancipation Declaration/Policy (1860-1863). The Vietnam Revolution also aimed at eradicating the virtuousless culture of Capitalism in that Country (1970s) and The African Revolution throughout the Continent from Lagos to Mombasa (in the West and East respectively) and from Cape Town to Cairo (in the South and North Africa respectively) against the evils fo Capitalism viz. Colonialism and Imperialism (1950s-1960s).

(d) The Analysis further shows that short of this Conflict Vaccination cum Cultural Engineering dose which apprised the oppressed and helped to mobilize them against the existing roots of injustices, obviously none of these Revolutions would have succeeded or materialized to eradicate the existing culture of human rights violations and other forms of injustices in those Countries.

(e) In this regard, the efficacy and reliability of Conflict Vaccination cum Cultural Engineering Methodology recommended in this Paper is hereby supported.

## (2) Conclusion

In sum,

(1) **Aprior**; the University may, up to now, have a valid reason to be patted on the back and to receive a standing ovation for its commendable job well done in Science and Technology discoveries and innovations for humanity's benefits/advancement. Nobody should or can doubt that at all. However, from another lens or side of the coin, it must also be bold and honest enough to accept the fact that it has a valid case to answer to humanity in view of the fact that whereas it controls the monopoly of total know-how in both Science and Technology, it has unfortunately betrayed its client, (the humanity). It has betrayed humanity in the sense that it has failed to be faithful fully using all its monopoly of the know-how as Hammurabi and the University of his time successfully did by doing just that in Babylon in order to successfully maintain a virtuous Culture of Peace and Democracy in that Country.

Because of this perennial professional negligence by our University, obviously, billions of human life and unquantified property have been lost through civil and global wars, terrorism, assassinations, massacres, genocides, drug traffickings, and Bad Governance globally.

(2) Aposteriori, it is, however, not too late for the University to change its gears and fulfil its expected mandated responsibility to humanity using every means necessary such as those means stated above.

In this regard,

(a) Conflict Vaccination, which also means Cultural Engineering, would be a reliable tool for this cause.

(b) As already noted in those Parts 1-IV of this Paper, Conflict Vaccination cum Cultural Engineering is succinctly a curative methodology with sufficient capacity to cleanse or rehabilitate our existing wretched world Culture of Bad Governance and Instability and then transform it into a Cleansed World Culture of Good Governance characterized by the presence of significant elements of a virtuous Culture of Peace and Democracy different from the elements of the present type of a virtuousless Culture which falsely claim that its governments are governments of the people by the people for the people while in reality this is not so. In Charles Darwin's view, the present governments are governments of the fittest but not of the week, e.g. the poor. Succinctly, they are not governments of the weak, by the weak for the weak! The weak have no room.

In Thomas Hobbes' view the present governments are governments of wolves by virtue of their inhumane conduct and policies vis a vis the poor. And finally in Prophet Isaiah's words, all are governments in a thick darkness whose peoples are also covered by the same thick darkness.

(c) These problems, therefore, collectively constitute the reason and justification why the University should now no longer waste any more time but to immediately intervene and rescue humanity from this threatening and dangerous virtuousless Culture to humanity by dismantlingand replacing it with a virtuous Culture of Peace and Democracy using our recommended remedy called Conflict Vaccination cum Cultural Engineering—a culture of a rich enabling environment for:—(i) an accelerated socio-economic development and also (ii) an accelerated development in Science and Technology through discoveries and innovations becaue of the presence of this virtuous Culture of Peace and Democracy world-wide.

## Foot Notes

1. For example, Walter Wallbank, Alastair M. Taylor and Nels M. Bailkey, Civilization: Past and Present, Chicago: Scott, Foresman and Co. (1962); and Diane W. Darst, Western Civilization To 1648, McGraw-Hill's College Review Books, New york, (1990); and John B. Harrison, Richard E. Sullivan, and Dennis Sherman, A Short History of Western Civilization, 7th Ed. Same publisher, (1990).
2. A double-storied tower built by the Sumerian in Babylon around 500 BC. It was composed of a Temple at the top for their religious rites to their Creator whom they valued very much as a giver of rains, good harvest and as their salvation against floods from the Tigris and Euphrates Rivers encompassing or surrounding their Crescent Fertile Land. And, a Palace at the bottom for their king whom they also designated as their chief priest through whom they appealed or prayed to their God for poretection against these floods which periodically ravaged their land through those two surrounding rivers. See for example, Darst.
3. Because of these dual expected functions of the Ziggurat, everyone was expected to be part and parcel of this Ziggurat, which to each of them was also, called "The People of The Local Deity". Also, see, for instance Darst, ibid., pp. 16-18, specifically p. 17.Idem.
4. See also, George G. M. James, Stolen Legacy: The Greeks Were Not the Authors of Greek Philosophy, but the People of North Africa Commonly Called the Egyptians, New York: Philosophical Library (1954); Herodotus, The Histories, Baltimore: Penguin Books (1966) Book II, esp. pp. 139-142; Yosef Ben-Jochanan "Africa's Contribution to World's Civilization, in Agola Auma Osolo et.al.eds., New Frameworks in African Studies and Research, Milwaukee Winsconsin (1972); and Auma-Osolo, Cause-Effects of Modern African Nationalism on the World Market, Lanham: University Press of America (1983) p. 56.
5. In Egypt, he was declared their Pharaoh and also accorded divine honours reserved only to Egyptians. At this time, Greeks neither knew these honours nor were the Greeks accustomed to them.
6. Even though, it is debatable how any one scholar would be an authority on various disciplines and author authoritative books on each discipline! In view of the fact that this is not possible in our own generation, how then did Aristotle manage this?

7. See for example, John Moniz, No Greater Service: Mother and The Mahatima, Bombay: Saint Paul Society (1997) Better Yourself Books, Bandra, Mumbai, 400 050, India, pp. 79-99.
8. Frantz Fannon, The Wretched of the Earth, New York: Monthly Review Press (1966).
9. John Moniz, op.cit, p. 79
10. Ibid.pp.84-85
11. Ibid. pp. 81-88
12. Ibid. pp. 79-80
13. Frantz Fanon, op.cit.n.8.
14. An English poet, critic and educator
15. Walbank, et. al., op. cit. n.1., pp. 590-91. Also, see Auma-Osolo, Cause-Effects of Modern African Nationalism on the World Market, op. cit., n. 4, pp. 24-25.
16. A British politician, author and twice a Prime Minister (1968, and 1874-1880). 17.Benjamin Disraeli, Sybil; or Two Nations, London: Longmans, Green and Co., Ltd, (1926) pp. 76-77.
18. Wallbank, et. al., op. cit., n. 15, pp. 491-92.
19. Idem
20. Idem
21. idem
22. The Utilitarian Political Philosophers included, for example, (1) Jeremy Bentham (1748-1832), A Fragment of Government, London: I. Payne (1776) and Introduction to The Principles of Morals and Legislation, London: I. Payne (1789); (2) John Stuart Mill (1806-1863), On Liberty, London: J. W. Parker (1859), The Representative Government, London: Oxford University Press (1861); and The Subjection of Women London: Oxford University Press (1869) and many others who collectively pressured to Parliament to take prompt action against both factory and coal mine owners whose aims and conduct were antithetical and harmful to the general public and also a disgrace to the Victorian Culture gained from Greece and the Renaissance.
23. The Socialist Political Philosophers included mainly Karl Marx 91818-1883) Das Kapital, London: D. Torr 91958) and The Communist Manifesto, London: J. E. Von Burghard (1948) written together with Friederich Engels (1820-1895).
24. The Victorian Poets included for example, (1) Alfred Tennyson (1809-1892) and Robert Browning (1812-1898) whose bitter writings on the issue are contained in Wallbank et al op.cit. n. 18, pp. 489-90.

25. The Victorian novelists included, for instance, (1) William Makepeace Thackeray (1811-1863) and wrote Vanity Fair (1848); and (2) Charles Dickens in whose books Oliver Twist, The Bleak House, David Copperfield, etc., Dickens vehemently attached the nouveaux riches and ridiculed them for their sick obsession with riches at the expense of the poor in poor slums and prisons.
26. The nouveau riches (or the rich class who owned all means of production) who then lured their respective governments to cover them in their colonial expeditions in Africa. They created companies such as British East Africa Company, British West Africa Company, etc under the umbrella of their British Government. Others in France, Belgium, German, Spain and Portugal did the same and received their government protection in return for commissions to their government from economic gains looted in Africa as well as India—a situation which according to Jawahrlal Nehru called "plundering", see Nehru, The Discovery of India, London: Meridian Books, 1946), p.
27. Idem
28. See for example Dr. Henri Brunschwig (Director of "Ecole Practique des Hautes Etudes" in Paris) who claimed that such activities especially by his country of France were legitimate. His writing on this is "French Exploration and Conquest in Tropical Africa from 1865 to 1898" in L. H. Gann and Peter Duignan, eds, Colonialism in Africa 1870-1960, London: Cambridge University Press (1969) Vol. 1.
29. Idem. Argument drawn from the provocatively inciting philosophy of John Locke, Two Treatises of Civil Government, London: A. and J. Churchill (1690), Charles Darwin On The Origins of Species by Means of Natural Selection: Or, The Preservation of Favoured Races in the Struggle for Life, London: J. Murray (1859); and Adam Smith, The Wealth of Nations Dublin: Whitestone (1776).
30. Auma-Osolo, Cause—Effects of Modern African Nationalism on The World Market, op. cit, n. 15.
31. Jawahari Nehru, op. cit, n.25
32. Auma-Osolo, The Rwanda Catastrophe: Its Actual Root-Cause and Remedies to Prompt A Similar Situation in Rwanda, Nairobi: ICPCRIA (1995).
33. See for example, Leonard M. Thompson, Politics in the Republic of Africa, Boston: Brown and Co. (1996) and Auma-Osolo, Cause-Effects of Modern African Nationalism on the World Market, op. cit.no. 4, p. 79.

34. See also, Samora Machel, Establishing People's Power to Serve the Masses, Toronto, Canada: Toronto Committee for the Liberation of Southern Africa (1976) and also Auma-Osolo, op.cit. n. 34, pp. 67-68.
35. Vladimir Lenin, Imperialism: The Highest Stage of Capitalism, New York: International Publishing Co. (1939), State and Revolution, New York: International Publishers (1932), etc.
36. Isaiah 60: Verse 2 in The Holy Bible
37. An English Philosopher (1588-1679) and author of Leviathian, London (1651).
38. A 20th Century Nigerian novelist and author of Nigerian novelist and author of Things Fall Apart, London: William Heinemann (1958); A Man of The People, New York: John Day Co. (1966) and others.
39. An English naturalist (1809-1882) and author of On The Origins of Species by Means of Natural Selection: On The Preservation of FAvoured Races in the Struggle for Life op. cit. n. 29.
40. Also like Chinua Achebe, a 20th Century Nigerian novelist and author of The Wretched of The Earth, New York: Monthly Review Press (1966), Sutides in a Dying Colonialism, New York: Monthly Review Press (1967), Black Skin, White Masks, New York: Monthly Review Press (1967), etc.
41. Because the Earth and its people are covered by a thick darkness as so thoroughly prophesized by Prophet Isaiah in a mighty way (740-690BC), such actions are not surprising. In fact they are scientific evidences in support of Prophet Isaiah's prophesy—a man of God who had to go to every painful length to advise his people of Israel to repent of their sins and be cleansed by God. Yes, this is also clear empirical evidence in support of our call for Confict Vaccination cum Cultural Engineering which is the fundamental object of this paper.

    For more details about Prophet Isaiah and his efforts to bring about Cultural Engineering in Israel using the most painful and difficult means no ordinary man could have possibly managed to bear, see for example, David Regan, The Master Plan, Making Sense of The Controversies Surrounding Bible Prophecy today, Eugene, Oregon: Harvest House Publishers (1993), p. 35.
42. They cannot exercise their mandate to reject regimes formed illegally through illegal means because they are also a hostage of the same handicap prophesied by Prophet Isaiah in Idem. This is also an added prima facie evidence in support of our call for Conflict Vaccination cum Cultural Engineering worldwide.

43. For further detailed account on the productive methodology and efforts of the Sumerians who forged out the roots of human civilization in Mesopotamis ways back before the 5th millennium B.C., see for example, DArst, op. cit., n.1
44. Darst, ibid., p. 21
45. Idem
46. Idem
47. Idem
48. Ibid., p. 22
49. Idem
50. Idem
51. Also, see for example, George G. M. James, The Stolen Legacy, op. cit. n. 4
52. In addition to what each already had at home, they also shared and divided between them Jewish German Scientists after Germany's defeat in World War II 91945). This is also how the USSR and USA were able to develop first atomic bomb and later thermo-nuclear power. Scientific contribution by Dr. Edward Teller and Dr. herman Khan in the USA are an empirical example of how significant the Unversity role can actually be to a nation and the World as a whole if we all agree world-wide on eradicating this existing global Culture of Bad Governance and Civil Strife to bring about a new Culture of Peace and Democracy as Dr. Edward Teller (1908) brought to our Civilization and Atomic Bomb which no person had ever dreamt of; and Dr. Jonas E. Salk (1953) and Dr. Albert Sabin (1955) also brought to our Civilization Polio Vaccination discovery which had been tormenting humanity for centuries.
53. This is an excellent example in our own generation on what each Country or Nation must do in order to utilize its University for the good of nation-development beginning with eradication of the present culture of rampant conflict and bloodshed and replacing it with a new needed Global Culture of Peace and Democracy as a relief to the existing sorrows of genocide, massacres, civil strife, terrorism, etc.
54. Explained better by what is in Notes 55-59
55. As per the Philosophy of Charles Robert Darwin, op. cit. n.29 inciting interracial tensions and self-annihilation.
56. As per the findings by Fanon op.cit. n.8
57. As per the findings by Hobbes, op.cit. no
58. Also as per the findings by Achebe, op. cit. no. 40
59. As per the prophecy of Prophet Isaiah ways back in 740-690 BC cited under no. 41 above. In fact, this is not all. A further Clinical Diagnosis of the sickness of our

global Culture reveals more most shocking symptoms then the symptoms we have already encountered above regarding India. For example, in Africa alone, the following sickening symptoms are prevalent all over the Continent: (a) Cannibalism by which certain cultures e.g., the Abagisu in Eastern Uganda have a standing traditional condition that theymust eat the first born male of each parent family standing before that family is declared as an inter-subjective member of its society; and to accept human flesh eating as a delicacy. This is true in certain parts of Kisii, Tesso and the Chunyi sub-tribe of the Mijikenda Group found in the Coast Province (in Kenya) and among the Khekhe tribal people in southern part of Tanzania. (b) Totemism by which certain cultures domestically keep or tame wild reptiles and other animals such as leopards, as their sacred items for the purpose of naked night running, witchcrafts and sorceries. This realism was witnessed recently and also broadcasted on the radio concerning the strange Batabi culture of the late former President Julius K. Nyerere during his traditional funeral service in his billage home in Butiama where the mourners and other funeral service attendants from over the world vividly witnessed this flabbergasting experience of devil worship in which these tamed and worshipped animals went around the grave crying and yelling for the soul of their departed son. (c) Contagious Divinition e.g., Ju Ju in Nigeria and other countries in West, East, Central and South Africa by which the so-called diviners maliciously misuse religious use the original intention and purpose of divination in Africa traditional religions which was toaid humanity to overcome natural distasters such as drought and famine during such catastrophes. These malicious diviners misuse such powers as contagious agents by which they bewitch innocent people by either psychologically vaccinating them with madness, misfortune, foolishness, hopefulness, utter stupidity, poverty, confusion, family unrest and all other kinds of psychological and physical human abnormalities. And (d) Evil Spirits of already dead persons which in Uganda, Kenya and Tanzania are commonly called Amaembe (or Maembe) by which their owner secretly keeps them for a destructive purpose of hurting or destroying those persons or families that he or she hates or envies due to their impressive achievements in life. These dead persons' spirits are heads usually extracted from persons who had proved very crafty and cunning during their life time. These dead persons are exhumed and their heads chopped off by a magician who then mechanically transforms them into Amaembe for this destructive purpose.

In summary, the above and other similar malicious activities of Lucifer, the Satan, collectively constitute valid reasons why The Earth is Wretched; is covered by darkness; and, therefore, calls for immediate Univeristy's intervention.

60. Thompson, op. cit. n. 33. The Dutch Reformed church case in South Africa is not in isolation. Many other churches including schools, parastatal bodies, private companies throughout Africa and elsewhere get bribed to do worse than that, e.g., assist in elections where they are not ethically and morally supposed to do so. This is one of the reasons why qualified candidates are always left out if they have no money to bribe such institutions and voters; and also the reason why the World is still so wretched that no Culture of Peace and Democracy can hardly survive in such conditions.
61. Leornard M. Thompson, Politics in the Republic of Africa, Boston, Massachusetts: Little Brown & Co., (1966).
62. John Moniz, No Greater Service Mother and the Mahatima, Bandra, Mumbai; India: Beter Yourself Books (1998).
63. Ibid, p. 77
64. Idem
65. Idem
66. Idem
67. Idem
68. Idem
69. Idem
70. Idem
71. Idem., p. 75
72. Idem
73. Idem
74. Thompson, op.cit. n. 33
75. Daily Nation, Nairobi, Wednesday, August 18, 1999, p.7
76. David Reagan, The Master Plan, Eugene, Oregon: Harvest House Publishers (1993), p. 35.
77. Idem
78. Idem
79. Idem
80. Philip too, "Biwott's Plea on Barriers", Daily Nation, Nairobi, Tuesday, (December 14, 1999), p. 14.

# PART SEVEN

## NEIGHBOURLY LOVE IN GLOBALIZATION AS A RELIABLE ROAD MAP TOWARD A HYBRID WORLD CULTURE: A Test for Efficacy of Conflict Vaccination.

# A PREFACE

This Chapter tests for the "Neighbourly Love" concept in the Globalization process which is now accelerating at an amazing momentum in this Age than it ever did in the previous Ages as a reliable means for the development of a Hybrid World Culture for Humanity. It applies an interdisciplinary approach because of its indepth (comprehensive) high power lens above a unidisciplinary approach. And, by doing so, it shows that the concept is not only relevant and significant but also a **core** ingredient requisite for development of a Global Hybrid Culture of Holiness and Perfection rich in abundant lasting mutual peace and prosperity for all akin to that of Ancient Egypt extra-ordinary food, health, wisdom and security which flourished surpassing all other Countries of the time. Also, it shows that as a human process it is unique to man in the latter's capacity as a homo societicus, Globalization cannot thrive to such a Culture in absence of this mutual neighbourly love vertically and horizontally globally. And, that unlike non-human species such as the carnivorous which must explore and feed on their fellow herbivorous, and the big fish on their fellow small fish in keeping with their biological command, man is not commanded to do so to his fellow man. He is only commanded to explore, know, love, mutually interact and build a harmonious relations with neighbour(s) globally for their mutual good as empirically evidenced by various human activities globally by explorers, missionaries, tourists, Governments (Nation-States), inter-Governmental and Non-governmental entities, and others since Antiquity to the Modern Time. While economy may have been a powerful determinant of every culture and dynamics of man's society; however, this chapter shows that man has always been hoodwinked by Capitalism passion of man's greed, dishonesty, robbery, murder, lies, false doctrine and apostasy, devil worship, and other lusts. Due to such lusts, Mankind today is besieged by economy-centred mutual terrorism between the Haves and the Have nots, thereby misleading both Political Economists and Political Realists to assume that life is indeed a man-eat-man situation based on Who is The Fittest over Whom. But, a re-test of such assumption using primary sources of data such as The Holy Bible on how and why is man actually commanded by his Maker to relate to his fellow man, the data shows totally the opposite. Man is commanded by God to love but not to hate and terrorize his fellow man for any purpose. He is mandated to have dominion over all other Members of The Animal Kingdom and the Members of The Plant Kingdom for his food and other purpose(s) but not to do so to his fellow man (Gen 1: 26-31). Therefore, man's inhumane passion for his selfish ends, as has always been the Capitalism tendencies, is not only against a healthy end of Globalization inherent in the Command but also a total insult to God Himself. Such persons are deaf and blind to His stern warning against evil acts that may appear only good for one's body but not for one's soul (Rev.21:8). Hence, the sine qua non role of the concept of Neighbourly Love to this Age of Globalization if we are to achieve a Global Hybrid Culture of Holiness and Perfection for Summum Bonum (i.e., the greatest good for all).

CHAPTER 1

# Introduction

## (1) Definition of Neighbourly Love and Globalization Concepts

### (a) Neighbourly Love

Neighbourly Love is a living phenomenon and concept genetically and etymologically derived from the second of The Lord God's Ten Commandments enshrined in *The Holy Bible*, for example under Mathew 22:39. And, as will be noted in details in Part III of this chapter where the concept is exhaustively operationalized and explained in depth regarding its genesis and significance to man's life and the Total Humanity globally, Neighbourly Love succinctly means one's love for one's neighbour. Thus, it is a mutual love between and among all men and women alike both at home and across one's borders and right up unto the far ends of the globe horizons.

Its sole purpose is to create a Global Hybrid Culture of Peace, Love and Unity as a *sine qua non* road-map toward an accelerated tempo of an extra-ordinary global political and socio-economic productivity and recovery from the existing skewed tempo of a global imbalance between the minority filthy wealthy (i.e, the Haves) and the overwhelming majority miserably poor (i.e, the Have-nots) at the expense of the poor which has consequently given birth to perennial recurrent climate of wars between the two at all levels of Humanity *viz* at the nuclear family, village, national and international levels. In the final analysis, the concept entails a mutual love among all peoples within the frame work of *pacta sunt servanda* (i.e., firm commitment in theory and practice towards each other). This love is rooted and guided by one's philosophy of Theocentric Humanism and its double-edged cardinal virtues of Perfection and Holiness, and is reinforced by one's Doctrine of *Summum Bonum* (i.e, a belief in the greatest satisfaction, happiness and good health for all) because of the Doctrine's emphasis on the virtues of Justice, Wisdom, Temperance and Courage for each individual person to recognize, honour and practise in his/her life as was empirically witnessed in the Ancient Egypt during the days of the Pharaoh's Leadership. It was this philosophy and doctrine which jointly rehabilitated and transformed Egypt from a culture of klelptocracy, survival of the fittest and other symptoms of socioeconomic and political barenness to a Hybrid Culture which, in turn, empowered that country to rise up to an extra-ordinary heights of political and socio-economic achievements above all neighbouring countries' achievements in the Region (The Mediterranean and Asia Minor). Also, it was due to this achievement particularly in food security that Egypt began to attract an inflow of the hungry immigrants as refugees fleeing these menace from their acute famine and poverty stricken mother countries in the Region in search for a safe haven and food security in Egypt. These refugees included Abraham and his wife Sarah and in the later generations, the same phenomenon was also repeated by Abraham's grand son (Jacob and his Children).

But, Egypt did not achieve these extra-ordinary heights of food security, health security, etc by chance. It did so using this concept of "Neighbourly Love" as its mandatory seasoning ingredient in all its life.

In this regard, Neighbourly Love is the antidote of Neighbourly Hate caused by malice, envy, greed, false-hood, aggression, arrogance, robbery, bribery, self-glorification and all those viruses that always lead to inter-personal and inter-national conflicts and the destruction of innocent human life and the environment.Anyone with this Neighbourly Hate attitude is saturated with an air of anarchy, survival of the fittest attitude and aggression habitually craving for someone to have a quarrel with for even a trivial matter.

Such a person normally does so in order to release his/her abnormal steam of hate to his/her fellow individual, and always looks for a scape goat for his own faults in order to off-load his/her psychological hate trauma (furry). Like a night-runner (or wizard) who must go out into the night to madly run around naked in darkness terrorizing his/her innocent neighbours using a deadly weapon as a purpose of cooling himself down by releasing his/her psychological furry onto the neighbours' homes, a possessor of this Neighbourly Hate trauma is indeed a very dangerous person. He is a murderer. And if put in a place of power, such a person automatically slides into a terrible monster. He/she becomes either autocratic or totalitarian; and rules the subjects as simple objects to be seen but not to be heard. Further such person's character is either constantly or recurrently moody often issuing hostile outbursts aimed at not necessary guiding but actually frightening and reducing the subjects to a serf status worth not to be heard but only to be seen supporting the leader's egocentric selfish ends. Consequently, should such a person rise to power of leadership in any given country or organization, the outcome of his leadership is bound to be a catastrophic disaster as he/she cannot manage to live and work in harmony and mutual love and respect with anyone who is not a sychophant, ready to praise this leader in a godly fashion using psalms and hymns as though that leader were a god. And, the more the sychophants do so, the more such a leader is usually obsessed with glory and misled to reward them with various bribes of political titles, and public property looted from state coffers and other sources. If these psychophants are not readily available, such a leader wastes no time. He uses his office machinery to create them; and also to eliminate every critic that may try to arise and oppose his/her intolerable leadership style and policy by crushing each of them through murder or long detention with or without trial. Also, such a person is always paranoid because of his inferior qualifications below others who he, therefore, does not want to take over the position from him.

Thus and hence the distinction between the meaning, nature and dynamics of concept of "Neighbourly Love" on the one hand and the concept of "Neighbourly Hate" on the other.

### (b) Globalization

Globalization, like Neighbourly Love, is also a living phenomenon and concept in that it is a living process. It is as old as mankind though it is now amazingly accelerating with a more extra-ordinary momentum in our own Generation, than it did during the Ancient Generation. And, inspite of its current amazing speed, it's status and character as of now is none other than a function of centuries of mankind's tireless efforts to bring it about, initiated by Ancient Age explorers who vigorously and fearlessly began to do so in order to break the existing yoke of the jungles and cobwebs of ignorance and stupidity from hindering man to know better his World around him. This crusade began with the ancient Egyptians over 4000 years ago followed by the Minoans, Phoenicians, Greeks, Romans, Chinese, Vikings, Venetians, Spanish and finally the Portuguese, documented in Part II of this paper below.

Conceptually, Globalization is a spatio-temporal free process of man's efforts to gain access to all points and corners of the Universe by breaking and transversing various difficult horizons of barriers hindering his aim, rights and efforts of meeting, understanding and gaining mutual friendship with his fellow man yonder there; and also of understanding his total World around him for the purpose of dominating and exploiting it for the well-being as he is so commanded to do by his Creator under Chapter 1:26-30 of The Book of The Genesis in *The Holy Bible*.

Empirical evidence(s) show, to the satisfaction of the naked eye, that albeit the dynamics of the Ancient man's efforts were seriously challenged, frustrated and hindered by the absence of an advanced Science and Technology that man's efforts of the Modern Age now easily and comfortably use against such obstacles that would have blocked his amazing accelerating momentum of Globalization we have today, our Ancient man did all that he could possibly do under such strenuous circumstances by piercing and breaking through the existing difficult jungles and cobwebs into the horizons of the unknown world he sought to know. These amazing advantage of the Modern Age man above his Ancient Age counterpart include, for example, Electronic Media, Aero-transport, Telecommunications, etc which are totally a monopoly of the Modern Age man compared to a totally bare-handed Ancient Age man though the two obviously share one thing in common which is the Will and Desire to understand the total Globe around them and use it for their individual well-being as so mandated by God.

## (2) But what is Man?

By the grace of God envisaged under Chapter 1:26-31 The Book of Genesis in **The Holy Bible**, man is commanded to be a multi-dimensional creature—a too powerful living entity above all other entities in both Animal and Plant Kingdoms. Unlike them, he is a *homo societicus* in that he is able to seek and interact with his fellow man (men) in various ways/forms. Also, he is a *homo economicus, homo communicaticus, homo scientificus, homo technologicus, homo diplomaticus, homo educaticus, homo spiritus, homo juridicus, homo medicinus, homo philosophicus, homo poeticus*, etc. But in order to enable all these potentials to yield fruit for him, man is also a *homo politicus being* in that he is able to create *pacta unionis* with his fellow men by collectively transforming themselves into a corporate body or organization. And also, he is able to create a *pactum subjectionis* with his group members by agreeing to appoint one out of themselves to serve them as their group leader.

These two phenomena are biologically and socio-politically restricted to man only as all other creatures are barred by God from these potentials. By such multi-capabilities, man is able to mitigate against various problems facing him such as natural and human—made disasters using both unilateral, bilateral and multilateral humanitarian assistance from both at home and his neighbours outside his borders.

As a result of this reality, man is indeed not only a creature but also a creator various wonders by the grace of his Creator. Secondly, he is not just a solitary village man confined to his village island but **indeed** a global man empowered by his Creator to seek, interact and transact his businesses with his fellow neighbours and vice versa across their borders for the good of their mutual well being.

## (3) Problem

But whereas the Modern Age man today has all such Scientific and Technological advantage over his counterpart of the Ancient Age with which to exploit and effect Globalization as much as he wants and in whatever direction, he so desires, is that all? Is it enough for the Modern Age man? These and other nagging questions abound directly staring into our face with impunity. For example, is the Modern Age man able to realize the on-going Globalization euphoria bare-handedly by simply relying on such sophisticated scientific and technological means/tools alone unless such advantage is seasoned and blended with another ingredient? Even with such sophisticated tools, at his disposal, how possible is he going or able to successfully effect Globalization amid rampant perennial civil and international disharmony and social disorders that have always made such efforts in the past totally impossible by not only hindering but also, in fact, terrorizing and severely paralyzing such efforts or tearing apart and turning the entire Globe into dens of hostile pockets of "Enemy" against "Enemy" as in the cases of North Korea *versus* South Korea; Mainland China *versus* Island China (Taiwan); Israelis *versus* Palestinians; the Banana *versus* The Orange in Kenya today arising from the Constitution Referendum question between the "Yes" against the "No" hostile groups; numerous similar cases throughout the Globe as also evidenced by the increasing blood-lettings in Darfur Now Western Sudan, between the two warring Enemies and the *catastrophes of terrorism versus terrorism today.*

In other words, given the fact that the on-going Globalization is marred with rampant poverty, conflict, etc, what essential conflict and poverty resistant ingredient(s) must also be put in place today as an added asset to the advanced Science and Technology that the Modern Age man has for the process? Would "One's Love for One's Neighbour" suffice? If not, what could be a re-liable added asset so that a healthy Globalization process may be satisfactorily realized for mankind today? A healthy process toward a Global Hybrid Culture of perfection and holiness?

## (4) Methodology

### (a) Existing Methodological Deficiencies in Normal Social Sciences

In addition to those nagging problems documented in The Problem Statement (above) methodological deficiencies in Social Science Research. Their traditional reliance on Machiavelli-Darwinist prescription which is for destructive ends other than human welfare has alwaysled to heinious disaster against its own success and chance of advancing in discoveries and innovation akin to those prestigious horizons of honour already now being enjoyed by its counterparts in Biological and Physical Dominion(s) because of their reliance on discoveries.

Its most problem has always been its emphasis on the assumption that Scientific Truth and Spiritual Truth are but two exhaustive and mutually exclusive (or independent) islands (phenomena) in Human Life; that the two neither resemble nor have any assistance to each other as RELIABLE MUTUAL TOOLS for a researcher's satisfactory understanding and explaining reality; and that the two are therefore permanent enemies.

Because of this problem in the existing social Science research, the same problem has also led to other multi problems to Mankind in the latter's efforts towards Globalization. It has always misled Mankind to Global disasters arising from dangerous prescriptions claimed that whoever would manage to conquer the Heartland and its peripheries(i.e, Europe and the Seas) would be deemed the sole Master of the whole World. This provocative claim so much incited Mankind into various man-made disasters. These included Franco-Prussian War (1870-71), Anglo-Prussian War (1880/81), World War I (1914-1918), World War II (1938-1945) and The post-World War II Cold War between the Capitalist and The Communist War Lords. Also the claim led to untold sorrows of leader-assassinations, civil wars and irreparable misuse of national resources for such wars in all Developing Countries for the national interest of those two War Lords that these developing countries have up to today remained victims of dependency and underdevelopment in the International System at the expense of these two War Lords as also detailed in Professor George B. N. Ayittey's book, Africa Betrayed, Scholarly and Reference Division, St. Matrin's Press, Inc. 175 Fifth Ave. New York, N.Y 10010 (1992).

These havocS were a function of Publication by Alfred Thayer Mahan (1840-1914); Harold and Margaret Sprout; Sir Halford John Mackinder (1861-1947) influenced by the provocative writings of Charles Robert Darwin (1809-1882); and Niccolo Machiavelli (1469-1527) as the pioneer. This problem has now been inherited by the School of Realism as evidenced by the school's doctrine of "National Interest" defined in terms of "Power" as the ultimate essence, goal and dynamics of International Politics. According to the School's understanding and belief of the relations and interactions among sovereign political entities called Nation-States, which actually are the sole dominant actors in the International System, it contends that such entities do not meet for any other objective such as national brotherhood, sisterhood for mutual benevolent goals. They do so solely for selfish national interests defined in terms of power. And that this is why they are also justified to fight in order to protect such interest(s) as all others such as the Roman Empire also did in the past. It, therefore, leads nation-states and their respective policy makers and implementors alike to scramble for power which he calls as the essence of politics. Hence, the tragedy of the School against man's positive concept and aim of Globalization on the one hand, and a valid justification of the criticism against it, as the other.

### (b) Purpose, Methodology and Justification

In view of this epistemological and methodological dangers and other deficiencies inherent in the existing methodology and aim which have over time proved non-productive to man's long-time desirous efforts to bring about a healthy Globalization, the Purpose and Methodology of this Paper is to prove the Normal Social Sciences' myth wrong by showing beyond any reasonable doubt that an interdisciplinary approach is more reliable than traditional reliance on unidisciplinary approach because of the former's high power lens able to bring to the surface all that a researcher seeks to see and examine for one's research purpose. Unlike its unidisciplinary approach counterpart, the interdisciplinary approach is able to drive deeper into the lowest strata of the problem and shed more light on it for a better visibility than what a unidisciplinary approach is able to do, for the reasearcher.

In this regard, this Paper, therefore, treats each as a reliable tool with which to prove that the command "To Love One's Neighbour" is definitely not only relevant but also very significant to Mankind in this Age of Globalization. It is relevant and significant in that without it, growth of every social organism, (e.g., nuclear family) and process such as Globalization is bound to be malnourished. And because of this natural given truth that mutual love is the essential nutrition ingredient for every human relations, man's effort(s) toward a healthy Globalization today is headed to a worst result akin to the recent Tsunami and Katrina, Charly and Wilma hurricane disasters in Asia and North America respectively and the 8th October 2005 earthquake unless such effort(s) are nourished with mutual love as per the Command.

But in order to do justice to Science, the Paper first and foremost employs a Nosology of Globalization (i.e., a scientific classification of a phenomenon). Accordingly, it operationalizes Globalization into two exhaustive and mutually exclusive forms viz: and Ancient Age Globalization and Modern Age Globalization. For this purpose, Part II of this Paper first provides a Clinical Diagnosis of the trend at which Globalization has grown or developed through man's ingenuity effective the Ancient Age to the Modern Age, with a view to giving a clearer Balance Sheet of this Globalization process between the two Epochs in terms of their virtues and vices. Thereafter, Part III of the Paper then provides a substantive relationship between "Neighbourly Love" and "Globalization" as *Independent* and *Dependent* variables respectively.

CHAPTER II

# A Balance Sheet of Ancient and Modern Modes of Globalization

## (A) The Ancient Age Globalization Efforts

As already indicated in the Introduction Part of this Paper, Globalization process is as old as Mankind. It began with our Forefathers in Ancient Age, and has always managed to manouver and outlive all harsh hurdles from Antiquity to the Present as so documented here below beginning with the Egyptians:-

(1) *The Egyptians'* justification as the *Founding Fathers of Globalization Initiative* is manifested through the efforts of their explorer, Honnu, who lived over 4000 years ago, and sailed as far South to the Land of Punt on the Red Seacoast of Somaliland where they discovered the land very rich in gold, ivory, incense trees, and the myrrh which they already knew and used at home in Egypt for embalming their dead. The key important discovery here for the purpose of this research is that these Egyptian explorers did not only find a treasure of economic wealth for themselves to take with them home but also a treasure of love from the inhabitants of The Land of Punt which, in turn, motivated them to venture further into this first leg of Globalization phenomenon. The second key important discovery in this research to be underscored is the Egyptian interest in creating and sustaining a harmonious Neighbourly Relations with its neighbours as also empirically witnessed in their development of an Egypto-Hittite Treaty of Non-Aggression in 1284 BC between Egypt and Babylon. In this regard, the concept of Neighbourly Love must therefore be as old as Mankind—a fact which has become the foundation of international law and international relations in the history of mankind. Next, were (2) *The Minoans* who lived on the Island of Crete about 1400 BC. By virtue of their ecosystem, they culturally became habitual fishermen and sailors by trade. Consequently, they

explored the whole Mediterranean world and understood it pretty well for their well-being. Hence, the significance of their efforts to the beginning of Globalization during the Ancient Age by the help of these Minoans. The third were (3) *The Phoenicians* who lived around 1400 BC. Because of their barbarian life-style coupled with envy against the Minoans' progressiveness on the Island of Crete due to their art of trade as fishermen and sailors, Phoenicians invaded Crete with an aggressive aim of usurping the Minoans of their legacy. On succeeding to do so, they transversed through The Strait of Gibraltar and entered the Atlantic Ocean and further voyaged northwards to England and then Westwards, Southwards and Eastwards to Arabia and India looking for knowledge and more knowledge about their World around them. Hence their contribution also to this phenomenon of Globalization during the Ancient Age. *The fourth (4) were The Carthagians* who lived in Carthage on the northern tip of Tunis. By nature of their ecosystem, they explored Africa as far South as Cape Verde. In 500 BC, they sailed under their able sea captain, Manno, who on reaching Cape Verde was so confused by the strange wildlife he saw there that he went on capturing and taking home male and female apes (though the male ones escaped from him) on assumption that they were some sort of human beings. Hence, the significance of these Carthagians efforts as also an added significant contribution to Globalization phenomenon in the Ancient Age. The *fifth (5) were The Greeks* who, under their great adventurous leader, Alexander The Great, (King of Greece and Macedonia), they traversed into a new world south of their Country. They did so first by the aid of students who hailed from various parts of Asia Minor but mainly Greece, Ionia, and Macedonia. Prominent of them all included Thales (640 B.C), Pythagoras (582-500 B.C), Socrates (469-399 B.C.), Plato (427-347 B.c.), Aristotle (384-322 B.C.), etc. who traveled from their home countries of Greece and Macedonia to seek higher education in Egypt where such virtue was uniquely available during those days at The African Mysteries System of The Grand Lodge of Luxor located at the present city of Alexandria in the northern tip of Egypt. At this Centre of higher Learning, these students, like all others, first enrolled as "mortals" (i.e., those who had not attained the inner vision (i.e., undergraduates in our modern University classification); then later on advanced to "The Intelligences" grade (i.e., those who had now attained the inner vision of knowledge and wisdom, i.e., graduates); and then after that to "The Creators or Sons of Light" grade, (i.e., true spiritual consciousness, i.e, (postgraduates in our modern form of education). A significant lesson gleaned from these students' efforts in this Globalization process is that they did not only learn wisdom and knowledge. Also, they carried with them a new legacy to their home countries such as the philosophy of "MAN KNOW THYSELF", etc. which, in turn, helped significantly to enrich their countries' wisdom and knowledge but for which each of them was unfortunately punished very severely.

A good example of this is Socrates who was executed in 399 B.C. on false accusation that he was corrupting the Greek children and putting the Greek culture and gods to ridicule by promoting a foreign Theocentric Humanism Philosophy of *holiness* and perfection and the Doctrine of Summum Bonum (i.e., the greatest happiness for all) from North Africa in opposition to Greece's traditional philosophy of Anthropocentric Humanism and the Doctrine of Summum Malum (i.e., the greatest evil to all). The two were architectured and promoted by the anti-Socrates-"Sophists"-who loved cunning, deceit and false accusation as their professional way of life as opposed to-**Socrates' professional way of life grounded and governed by the tenet of Justice, Prudence, Temperance (Self-Restraint) and Courage disciplinary virtues which have now grown and developed into our present Granite System of Justice globally most particularly in Developed Countries such as US, UK, Germany, France, Japan, etc.** All this and much more is also supported by George C. M. James' in-depth research on this Globalization phenomenon during the Ancient time in his masterpiece contribution to Science titled *Stolen Legacy: The Greeks Were Not The Authors of Greek Philosophy But The People of North Africa Called Egyptians* (1954:17-27). After these students, there arose Greece's most famous adventurer and leader named Alexander The Great who, acting like a tornado or hurricane, did not only traverse from his home country of Greece and Macedonia in the southern tip of Europe but also carried with him the fame of his culture to the unknown worlds in Asia where he is said to have broken the Legend of a Gordian Knot of a Phrygian King in a temple that had defeated many men to undo. The knot carried an oracle that whoever succeeded to undo it would rule all Asia. And, because of this very reason, Alexander was successful in taking Persia and adding it to his dominion of Greece and Macedonia; and also moved his capital to Babylon. Hence, another key contribution to the beginning phase of Globalization in the Ancient Age. *The sixth (6) in line were The Romans* who quickly followed the early Globalization trail of ancient exploration motivated by the appetite for what early explorers were gaining from such endeavours. During and with the courage of their leader emperor Julius Ceasar, they also traversed the globe as far up as Ceylon now called (Srilanka) in Asia and to Cochin in China. Hence their contribution too to the early development of Globalization that has transcended to us today. *The seventh (7) after the Romans were The Chinese* who also explored deep inside the East just as the Phoenicians, the Greeks and the Romans were also doing so, in the West. During the 100 BC, China even sent ambassadors far a field in search of trade and allies. For example, China sent its greatest Chang Chien who traveled in 138 BC from Peking across the Gobi desert to Barkul and also across the Tien Shan mountains to Bactria which is now called "Iran". Through Chang Chien, China learnt for the first time much about Europe and India. Soon after, the Caravan trains began carrying foods, silks and spices from China to India which were later sold to Arabs who also, in turn, sold the same to European merchants. Hence the beginning of a political cancer that gradually and finally crippled the Roman Empire through barbarian invasions of Europe from the north called "North Men" or "Sea Men". *The eighth (8) were The Vikings* who were descendants of the tribes that had settled in the Scandinavian peninsula. Like the Chinese, they too explored the entire region where they lived and transformed it into what is called today "Norway". Using their most terrifying ships called "Vikings Boats", under the command of Bjarni Herjulfsen, Leif Ericson and Thorfinn Karlsefni, the Vikings sailed, discovered and settled far north in the Faeroe Islands. They later moved to Iceland and finally to Greenland. And at about 1000 AD, they reached the northeast Coast of North America and settled in Newfoundland as so empirically supported by the ruins of their settlement discovered in the 1960's. *The ninth (9) in line of Ancient Globalization efforts were The Venetians from Venice in North Italy* who could not allow themselves to be left behind in this attractive phenomenon of Globalization due to its confirmed luxurious trade in Chinese and Indian beautiful wares. Under their able leader Nocolo Polo, (father of Marco Polo), sought to also capture the trade and its impressive gains from these wares. He sought to do so by first understanding its direct source instead of having to go through a third party as most merchants did. Nicolo Polo succeeded in getting this source by first getting in contact with the messengers of Kublai Khan, the Mongol emperor of China, who finally brought Nicolo Polo to Kubai Khan. The two (Khan and Nicolo Polo) then became good friends. On returning back to Venice, Nicolo Polo again went back to the Emperor. This time he did so with his son, Marco Polo who became one of emperor Kublai Khan's most trusted servants. In the course of his duties at the Court of emperor Kublai Khan, the young Marco Polo traveled throughout the emperor's empire. When he returned to Venice, he published his famous book, *The Adventures of Marco Polo*, which, in turn, became a source of inspiration for later many explorations and discoveries such as those of Christopher Columbus, who was now led to believe that the quickest sea route to the spice-land of India could be found in the West across the Atlantic Ocean. Thus, the key motivating factor to Columbus' engagement in the sea voyage across the Atlantic that led him to discover the North America in 1492, in lieu of the quickest sea route to India that had been his main goal. *And finally (10), the Portuguese who* like the previous explorers were equally enthusiastic in also knowing new horizons of the World around them most particularly the sea route to India. They did so ways back even before Spain through Columbus Sea voyage. Empirical evidence shows that through their own fellow Portuguese man called Prince Henry the Navigator, (1394-1440) Portugal had already discovered lots of awareness about the outside world as far South as the present-day Ghana. And, also that after the death of Prince Henry the Navigator in 1460 AD, they had already sailed as far South as the Cape of Good Hope in 1487-1488 by the efforts of Bartolomeu Dias. This spirit was finally achieved by Vasco da Gama who left Lisbon in 1497 and sailed to the Cape Verde Islands and then to the Cape of Good Hope from where he further sailed to St. Helena Bay and then to Malindi on the east Coast of Africa which is now Kenya. In spite of difficulties and other untold sorrows of explorations, Vasco da Gama was so firm and faithful to his original goal of the mission that he was not willing to give itup. He loved his goal so much that he is recorded to have vowed to himself that:

> "Until I find information of which I have come to seek, to Portugal I do not return" (The World Book Encyclopedia, Vol. 6, p.348)

But due to amazing neighbourly welcome, love and other assistance that Vasco da Gama received from men and women of Malindi on landing at the port, Vasco da Gama enthusiastically sailed and reached India as he anxiously wanted to do.

And, with such achievement for his Portuguese people, many Portuguese ships followed suit using da Gama's route. In doing so, they also discovered the Spice Islands which became an added asset to Portugal's efforts to understand better the World around them for the purpose of using such knowledge for their well-being.

Infact, they strictly guarded the route by making it so much secret to themselves that Portugal grew overwhelmingly rich from the profits gained from the spice trade and became one of the most interested European colonial seekers and beneficiaries at The Berlin Conference for The Scramble for Africa from November 1884 to March 1885.

After Vasco da Gama's successful efforts to find the information about the Global World Portugal was living in, another Portuguese with a similar adventurous mind emerged. This was *Ferdinand Magellan*, who like Christopher Columbus, argued that he could still find and get this sea route to India via the West.

But since he could not find support from Portugal, as the latter was already convinced with Vasco da Gama's achievement, Magellan turned his request for sponsorship to Spain as Christopher Columbus had also done in 1492.

This untiring initiative led Magellan to enable mankind to triumph further in breaking through the mysteries of the pending horizons of the unknown world of the Globe. Magellan discovered the Continent of South America and the existence of the Sea route through the West across the Atlantic and into the Pacific Ocean. These names "Pacific" and "Magellan Straight" the latter connecting the Atlantic Ocean, to the Pacific Ocean are both names of his own making.

Magellan was killed in a fight shortly after reaching the Phillippines where he had tried to appease two rival Philippinos groups. And the expedition was taken over by his lieutenant Juan Sebastian del Cano who steered the voyage from the Philippines via the Cape of Good Hope around South Africa right up to Spain with a victory of Magellan's sea-route to the East Via the West across the Atlantic Ocean then to the Pacific Ocean and back again to the Atlantic on the way back home (Spain).

## (B) The Modern Age Globalization Efforts

Man's Ancient efforts noted above did not become ends in themselves. They became a real womb in which Globalization phenomenon we see to day was actually conceived and born. Small and insignificant those efforts may appear due to their deficiency in sophisticated scientific and technological tools or equipments akin to what is available to us today in our modern Age, the fact is that they laid down a granite foundation on which present Globalization process rests comfortably and functions.

However, unlike this Ancient Globalization process whose dynamics was by and large motivated and guided by none other than economic ends, the modern form of Globalization is characterized by a dynamics of a host of many ends. These multi-ends are manifested in multi-activities which are *totally alien* to those of the Ancient Globalization.

Unlike the Ancient Globalization's single economic goal, the modern form of Globalization is motivated by a host of political, social, cultural, scientific and technological goals.

The Economic activities of Modern Globalization are more globally oriented/focused than economic activities of Ancient form of Globalization. It is characterized by not only trade between individuals as it used to be perceived during the past epoch but also trade between and among sovereign political entities called "Nation-States" bilaterally and multilaterally through Regional Continental and also Universal bodies on the one hand, and also between and among non-sovereign entities called Transnationals such as Multi-National Corporations, (e.g. General Motors, Coca Cola, Firestone, International Telephone and Tele-Communications, International Business Machines, Rank Xerox, Kodak, Safaricom, Celtel, etc) and also non-governmental entities (or NGOs) such as The International Red Cross, etc.

Like Economic activities of the Modern Age of Globalization as compared to Economic activities of the Ancient Age, the political activities of the Modern Age of Globalization are also a new phenomenon. This new dimension in Globalization came about as a result of the emergence and rise of nationalism and patriotism followed by the rise of independent sovereign political entities called Nation-States effective 18$^{th}$ and 19$^{th}$ Centuries in Europe followed by Asia and Africa in the 20$^{th}$ Century. The striking phenomenon of this dynamics in the Modern form of Globalization is that it seeks and promotes Globalization by virtue of the need of each nation-State to have other Nation-States as friends either as *an ally* in defense military alliances such as North Atlantic Treaty Organization (NATO) or as *a partner or Member* as in the case of African Union (AU), The United Nations (UN), etc, so that one may be able *to sustain* its national interest by successfully defending its possessional values (legacies) *and also pursue* and successfully get milieu goals (or values she does not have at home) with the assistance or support of friends in the International Community. Again, like Economic activities, Political activities are in the form of *bilateral* and *multilateral relations* resulting into a Global net-work of international relations transversing the entire Globe from the North Pole to the South Pole and vice versa; and from the East end to the West end of the Globe and vice versa—a totally new phenomenon very much unheard of during the Old Age of Globalization.

Social activities today whose dynamics are another added energy to the modern form of Globalization that were not present during the Ancient form of Globalization, include, for example, Global relations and interactions among Nation-States in various leisure undertaking such as International Athletics, Olympic Games, Foot-ball, Boxing, Tennis, Volleyball, Basketball, Hocky, Cricket, Track, Beauty Contest, Performing Art Contest, etc.

Cultural activities which is also a new dimension of man's global activities now enhancing modern Globalization include mainly Tourism, in which individuals transverse their home Country borders into other countries purely for leisure purpose and to learn more about foreign peoples and their cultures—a phenomenon that was not part and parcel of the Ancient mode of Globalization.

Scientific and Technological activities are also a new phenomenon totally unique to the modern Age from of Globalization. This phenomenon is empirically evidenced in the areas of co-operation in scientific and Technological research such as various on-going joint-research between and among scientists from two or more Nation-States to find a cure to the on-going HIV/AIDS endemic. Also, numerous joint-research expeditions are under way today in outer-space exploration between scientists from the Untied States and other Nation-States; and also among scientists of the European Union (EU) members.

Presence of these multi-cooperations in the Modern Age is a multiplier effect to Globalization process. It is an added oil on fire in that these entities are an energizer/catalyst to the process in the modern form of Globalization.

## (C) Virtues and Vices of Globalization

From the Ancient to the present Age, Globalization process is characterized by the following virtues and vices:

### (1) Virtues

Globalization opened the World to interaction among peoples and cultures through communication links such as the internet, telephones and many forms of mail systems. In addition, the modes of transport between and among peoples, countries and continents are now faster and efficient to the extent that travel and transfer of passenger, goods and services across Continents can be done within hours unlike in the past when this would take months with greater risks.

Also, it has opened up avenues for interventions from benevolent Nation-Sates and organizations especially in response to humanitarian emergencies which have significantly helped to avert wide spread disasters that would otherwise have resulted to heavy casualties and deaths. Massive supplies of foods, drugs and clothings during earthquakes, floods and droughts in many parts of the world have helped to save lives, simply because of the emergence of this Globalization in our life.

But, that is not all. Its additional significant virtues include promotion of the advancement in the fields of Education, Science and Technology which have, in turn, led to the discovery of significantly useful knowledge now globally used to harness nature for the benefit of Mankind by creating policies to mitigate against and to adopt to natural and human disasters. This knowledge include modern methods of farming hence leading to high agricultural output, medical appliance, and drugs for treatment of dangerous disease such as polio, HIV/AIDS, etc, and also cultural exchanges to promote harmony among various nationalities. Also in spiritual area, *The Holy Bible* for example, provides evangelical examples of Globalization both from the "beginnings" even upto the return of The Lord Jesus Christ.

From the Spiritual perspective, *The Holy Bible*, for example, is immensely rich in prima facie empirical evangelical examples of Globalization right from the "Beginnings" even upto the time Return of The Lord Jesus Christ.

Under Genesis 1:28, The Lord God commanded Adam and Eve to fill the earth and subdue it, through exploitation of the abundant resources at their disposal. And, under Mathew 28:18-20 and Mark 16:15-20, The Lord, on the other hand, gave the great commission to His Disciples when He commanded them to go and preach the Good News starting from Jerusalem (Home), then Judea (neighbour) and to the whole World. Good News involved what He taught (To love God and To love one another); Healing the sick from diseases; and Deliverance of the afflicted from all forms of satanic oppression and poverty. A further inquiry into the meaning and significance of THIS COMMANDMENT simply reveals that we should do so in order that we may be one Globally even as He and The Father are also One in Heaven! (John 17:21-22) if we are to live and enjoy the abundance of glory and joy He gave to each of us freely while He was physically present with us; and to go forth and skip about like calves from the stall" (Malachi 4:1) without any worry or concern about The Obvious Forthcoming Tormenting Day which is of course not for the righteous and obedient children of God but solely reserved for the arrogant and every evil doer obsessed with carnalities (Revelation 20:14-15 and 21:8).

**(2) Vices**

Globalization vices are manifested in man's greed for power and materialism (two twins of capitalism)—a poison that has always proved a causal factor to unfair competition for the earth's scarce resources using the latter's scarcity as valid excuse for unfair acts globally resulting into untold sorrows of the war and refugee agonies. Early explorers opened a global way for every kind of merchant to engage in a healthy fair trade with who ever they wanted.

Unfortunately most of these 'traders' were not honest but resorted to extortion, piracy and theft hence polluting the sources which collectively constitute the true character of the on-going nature of capitalism which is the womb in which both colonialism and imperialism, slave trade and slavery, and various other kinds of vices came to be conceived and born globally in a total contravention of God's Commandment documented under Genesis 1:26-30.

Under this Commandment, God mandates Mankind to take dominion over and make use of only non-Human Members of the Animal Kingdom namely animals, fish, birds and insects including all Members of the Plant Kingdom for the purpose of its food *inter alia*. But under no circumstance(s) and also no where did and does God, in His capacity as the Creator of Heaven and Earth and all living and non-living things therein, ever mandate any member of Mankind to also take dominion over another member of Mankind for the purpose of colonization, slavery, slave trade, or for any other purpose short of a just work or labour that one is to be paid for in the form of wages, as is unfortunately alleged boastfully by Social Darwinians unless one is motivated by an evil mind and pseudo-science which collectively mislead Science from truth, its sole goal. From both Scientific and Spiritual inquiries, no such truth exists except among the non-Human Members of the Animal Kingdom whereby the carnivorous are mandated to feed on their fellow herbivorous; big fish such as the Nile Perch and Mudfish are also mandated to feed on the little fish; and non-grain eating birds also called birds of prey such as owls and hawks are equally mandated to feed on their fellow small birds. But, either way, at no single time are they seen killing their own kind for the purpose of food Does this mean that these birds are more intelligent and law-abiding than man? But since this is not the case, what then must have gone wrong with man?

Hence the paradox of the ongoing perpetual conflicts and insecurity between the Haves and Have-nots all over the World and man's temptation in all sectors of life including inside the Church and other places of worship to habitually engage in a apostasy, falsehood and lies and all other symptoms of satanic culture against Humanity and human efforts aimed at bringing about a Hybrid Culture of Holiness and Perfection for the betterment of mankind as it used to be the case in the Old Egypt during 5000-2000 BC *characterized* by extraordinary presence of food security, health security, knowledge security etc aimed at creating an enabling environment for *Summum Bonum* (greatest good for every individual at both leadership and grass-root level).

Obviously all these glory that every Egyptian enjoyed in the Ancient Egypt would not have come about by accident if it were not because of their respect and dedication to their Almighty God on the one hand, and also their respect and dedication to their own genuine mutual love among themselves on the other hand in conformity with their own Theocentric Humanism philosophy of Holiness and Perfection and the doctrine of *Summum Bonum* that called for every individual from top-bottom and vice versa to be guided in all their undertakings by the virtues of Justice, Wisdom, Temperance and Courage.

In view of these solid empirical evidences, one is definitely assured of abundant glory and joy in life whenever one's act(s) are deemed holy and perfect before one's Creator and community at large. But *this is only possible when one is* driven by Theocentric *Humanism philosophy and the Doctrine of Summum Bonum* and not by carnalities of greed, envy, lies and all other forms of dishonesty of Anthropocentric Humanism philosophy and the Doctrine of *Summum Malum* advocated and taught by the Sophists in the Ancient Greece and Macedonia and by the Patricians (now metamorphosed into Mafia gangsters) in the Ancient Italy of the time.

In such a case, one is subject to lead oneself into untold sorrows, of suicide, since these vices are clear empirical evidences of man's disrespect and disobedience to God's stern warning documented in *The Holy Bible* under Revelation 20:14-15 and 21:8. Also, they are true ramifications of man's need today to pay heed to the Command for Good Neighbourliness if Globalization today is to lead this Generation to a Global Hybrid Culture of holiness and perfection as a Granite Foundation for a lasting global peace and prosperity for all as so documented below in Chaptert III of this paper.

CHAPTER III

# Significance of Neighbourly Love Concept to this Age of Globalization

## (1) A Preamble

In order for Globalization to successfully take root and thrive abundantly in this age, it needs first and foremost an enabling environment characterized by a lasting peace and security vertically and horizontally.

*Vertically,* the International System needs a sufficient ingredient(s) of mutual harmony founded on the existing Fundamental Principle of Human Rights (1948) between its leaders and its grass-roots (those being led). And, *horizontally,* the System also needs a sound side-ways mutual harmony first between and among its leaders themselves alone on the one hand; and secondly between and among its grass-roots themselves, alone on the other.

This *Vertica*l and *Horizontal* sound mutual harmony must be totally free from any corruption (influence) by one's religious, political party, national, racial, gender, or other affiliations or inclination(s).

But any lasting mutual peace, and security is not always easy to come by. It cannot just come about overnight from oblivion, nothingness or a vacuum. It first needs a reliable enabling environment which is succinctly a good fertile and watered/irrigated soil in which to germinate and luxuriantly grow into a healthy evergreen shady tree for all nationally and internationally; *locally* and *globally.*

But what is this fertile and well-watered soil and what is it made of? And, how can it be achieved to facilitate success of the on-going globalization process in this Age?

## (2) Its Genesis

The real genesis of the concept of Neighbourly Love is the Lord Jesus Christ's Sermons on the relationship between man and his Creator on the one hand; and also between man and his neighbour, on the other. These sermons are the source.

In Chapter 5 of The Gospel according to St. Matthew in *The Holy Bible*, He makes it loud and clear to all *that the concept of love is the key ingredient for a peaceful co-existence between man and his God; and between man and his neighbour*, (both nearby and distant ones). The same also holds true in Chapter 13:31-35 of The Gospel according to St. John. And that whereas it is a human tendency to love only one's friend and hate one's enemy, this habit is a disservice to Globalization. It does not go well with a positive successful proliferation of Globalization.

According to the Lord's Command, it is prudent and holy to love both friend and enemy alike so

> "That ye may be the children of your Father which is in heaven: for He makes His sun to rise on the evil and on the good, and sendeth rain on the just and on the unjust". (Matth 5:45).

A meticulous Clinical Diagnosis of The Lord Jesus' command reveals both scientific and spiritual facts of life. For example, in justifying why we all need to shy away from hate but love all friends and non-friends, relatives and non-relatives, fellow citizens and non-citizens, fellow gender sex and non-gender sex, etc., The Lord Jesus *scientifically* proves *that when it rains it does so to and for all both evil and good, and that when it shines, it also does so to and for both without any discrimination.*

Accordingly, the on-going Globalization euphoria is not for only one race, one colour, one creed, one gender, one socio-economic or political status. The truth is that *it is for all without any discrimination.* Short of this scientific and spiritual truth is a total falsehood, vanity.

But this truth that The Lord Jesus is edifizing the Total World on is not only *spiritual* but also *scientific*. It is also scientific in that *it is supported by not only spiritual truth but also empirical truth*. For example, whenever it rains or shines, it does not do so for either the rich or the poor; the short or the tall; the fat or the thin; the healthy or the unhealthy; the white or the black; the yellow or the red; the foolish or the smart *but for all!* The Lord God faithfully provides goods and services to all equally and also equitably, all depending on one's individual needs, and The Lord God's Judgement.

This is the *scientific* as well as *spiritual* justification for the supremacy of the Command that

> *"Thou shalt love the Lord thy God with all thy heart, and with all thy soul, and with all thy mind". (Matthew 22:37).*

On the strength of this prescription that one cannot and will never get in his life elsewhere other than from The Lord God, one is, therefore, justified to try up and down to live by and do as this First and Foremost Command thus calls globally. But the more one fails to do so, the more our concept and process of Globalization is bound to lead our Total Humanity to jeopardy.

But this love for one's Creator is neither an end in itself. It is the genesis of the beginning of one's concept and love for oneself and one's world around him beginning with one's nearest to the farthest neighbour.

It is because of the greatness and significance of this scientific and spiritual truth that The Lord God Jesus Christ strongly emphasized that whereas

> *"This is the first and greatest commandment"*

> *". . . . . the second [commandment] is like unto it, Thou shalt love thy neighbour as thyself". (Matthew 22:39).*

On *re-emphasizing* the significance of these two Commandments of one's love for one's God, and one's love for one's neighbour, The Lord Jesus vividly clarified that:

> *"On these two commandments hang all the law and the prophets" (Matthew 22:40; Lev. 19:18).*

But how and why does both the law and the prophets hang on these two commandments? A simple answer is that: Whereas the goal of every good law is to mitigate against all sources of evil by promoting love and peace and order between and among neighbours in society so is the goal of a true prophet, unless the law and prophet in question is evil in conformity with the natural law which states that "Evil begets Evil"; "Good begets Good", "Perfect begets Perfect", "Justice begets Justice" "Injustice begets Injustice", and "Holy begets Holy"!

Therefore, if the goal of a good law and a true prophet is promotion of not only peace and order but also Humanism between and among neighbours in a society which also means the same thing as "promotion of love between and among neighbours", then it must be self-explanatory and self-evident that "One's love for one's neighbour" is definitely a second-to-none pre-requisite ingredient or road map to a lasting peace in society. It is the most necessary nucleus for development of a *Hybrid Culture in that society ready to lead it to an amazing accelerated* socio-economic development and prosperity as was the same case in the Ancient Egypt (5000-100 BC).

But if so, then it must also be self-evident and self-explanatory that the same ingredient is a second-to-none pre-requisite for success of Globalization in our Age. It is a sine qua non panacea that Humanity now definitely needs in today's Globalization if man is to successfully achieve this needed extra-ordinary goal.

## CHAPTER IV

# Conclusion

In the final analysis, all the above facts prove beyond any reasonable doubt that "One's love for One's Neighbour" is a *sine qua non* ingredient for not only the development of a *Hybrid Culture* of Perfection and Holiness in a Society as a necessary road-map to an accelerated socio-economic recovery and development for the well-being of each individual in that society *but also for the success of a healthy Globalization in our Age*. It is a *sine que non* ingredient in that it is indeed the nucleus of such success. It is a mandatory requirement if such a process is to firmly take root and bear *Summum Bonum* globally.

One's love for one's neighbour is the healthy (fertile) ground (soil) needed for a *Hybrid Globalization* to thrive. Without it, the process is doomed to failure. It is vulnerable to inevitable rampant incurable political malady characterized by hate, envy, jealousy, greed, self-seeking tendencies against the Rule of Law and Justice, false accusation, dishonesty, lies, recurrent blood-lettings, and other symptoms of a systemic disorder and malfunctions that have always characterized and subjected Mankind to untold sorrows of wars both at the *national* and *international* levels. An Etiology of the ailing Kenyan political life today shows that this is also the root-cause of recurrent leadership failure in Kenya plunging The Innocent Kenyan into a sea of agonies, eg. abject poverty, tribal clashes, *abnormal corruption*, devil worship, child abduction and *traffic by wolves hidden in sheep coats.*

Thus, the tragedy of Globalization in our Age if the Command is not hearkened to by all. It is not only an anti-biotic pill but also a panacea of all existing socio-economic ills against Humanity aimed at transforming the currently accelerating Globalization from being a threat to an extra-ordinary opportunity for bridging the existing socio-economic gap between the Haves and the Have-Nots globally.

This recipe may be better appreciated using the following empirical evidence gained from the Lord Jesus Christ's Sermon, ***like a mustard seed which is naturally the least of all seeds but usually grows into a mighty safe haven tree for all birds of the air to come and happily and joyfully lodge in its branches thereof, and for the animals of the bush to also come and enjoy its comforting shade thereof without any discrimination whatsoever as per the command of their Creator*** (Math 13:31), ***so shall Globalization, which also began as a little idea as a mustard seed over four thousand years ago in the mind of a few individual Egyptian explores in search of the unknown outside Egypt and Asia Minor students in search of higher education in Egypt, also be able to grow and develop into an extra-ordinary mighty global safe haven environment for all races, nationalities, gender and classes of Mankind.***

But this cannot simply come about by a simple mathematical equation. It requires first and foremost a serious *pacta sunt servanda* (i.e. a firm commitment) by each individual person, government and country. Each must be touched by the virtues of *Summum Bonum* (ie, the greatest good for all) namely: Justice, Wisdom, Temperance and Courage and then thoroughly search one's heart so that one may faithfully and cheerfully accept and embrace this command of good neighbourliness as one's Granite Foundation and Road Map in this Age of Globalization for a *Summum Bonum* of this and the future generations as was also the original spirit and will of the Founding Fathers of the United Nations Organization in 1945 vividly document in the Preamble of The UN Charter.

Therefore, with this Command at our finger tips as our individual corporate policy or road map in life, our endangered Humanity is bound to rejuvenate from the on-going perennial soulless Globalization which has, for thousands of years, been a *hostage of the contagion* of pandemic poverty, inequality, conflict, various diseases, and other symptoms of unbearable conditions of living among the have-nots thus legitimizing these Have-Nots to ferment a socio-economic war against their Haves counterpart and vice versa.

Hence, the need for each individual person, organization, country and its government and general public to cheerfully and seriously recognize the significance of this Command as a sine qua non stimulant for *Summum Bonum* in this age of globalization is urgent. Since any failure by one to do so is also subject to spill over into another's failure, like an Epidemiologist, one has to be primarily concerned with both containment and eradication of a contagious disease.

In this regard, the above is obviously the needed rational choice with an optimum net-gain(s) against the contagion of the dangers of the existing soulless Globalization in our Generation.

Succinctly, this is the longest-awaited Age that, from the remotest antiquity to the present Age (spearheaded by explorers, missionaries, traders, statesmen, scientists, etc) man has always dreamt, pondered and talked about, strenuously laboured for, using various means to discover and understand so that he may be able to know, associate and interact with his fellow foreign neighbour from the North Pole to South Pole and vice versa; and also from the East end to the West end of the Globe and vice versa. Throughout this strenuous toil, man has always been guided by no other reason other than a search for a healthy relation that would be for his mutual benefit with his fellow foreign neighbour. i.e, a Hybrid Global Community.

At this most amazingly advanced level of our Civilization compared to that of our Forefathers during the Ancient days, our Age is, obviously an Age in which man and his Global neighbour are highly enlightened about each other's potentials and needs and also on total World around them. In this Age, man is empowered to exploit and develop his mutual enabling environment by loving his neighbour with a view to creating unity with this neighbour (as even our Lord Jesus Christ and The Father are also One) using the lessons the Lord personally taught us while He was with us during those Three Years before He was taken back on high by The Father from us. This is necessary so that our Humanity may be able to enjoy the glory of its *Summun Bonum*, i.e, a joy of abundant peace, and prosperity which the present soulless Globalization neither has nor is able to offer to the majority poor (the Have-Nots) as it abundantly does to the minority rich (The Haves). It is necessary for this Globalization process of the present Age to do so *because* apart from the "Haves" whom it has always favoured at the expense of the "Have-nots" by empowering the former to lavishly live in a perpetual wealth and happiness while the latter are miserably languishing in abject poverty, hunger and other forms of a hopeless life, obviously there exists a tremendously dangerous intrusive volcano in the life and attitude of the overwhelming Have-nots. The latter's daily life is miserable, shuttered and full of anger and hate against their counterpart. It is beset with perpetual abundant miseries and sadness arising from their oppression, poverty, illnesses and other untold sorrows which are a reminiscent of the on-going Globalization which the latter unfortunately does not seem to notice and discern its possible consequences.

This socio-economic imbalance and its miseries which is against the Have-nots is not an end in itself. It is a real danger to our civilization in that it is an oasis of a real intrusive volcano whose symptoms of chronic conflicts history has always witnessed between the Haves and the Have-nots globally in the form of civil wars, strikes, mutinies, coups d'etat and revolutions. Though this may seem unmanageable, the Have-nots may, because of their increasing temperature of relative deprivation caused by the greed and arrogancy of their habitual mutual enemy (the Haves), be driven by a temporary insanity to cause a catastrophe due to such unbearable frustration. They may opt to rush for this Age's advantage in thermonuclear capability as a rational solution against the Haves in order for them to balance the simple arithmetical equation with the source of their miseries (the Haves). But, because of the latter's obvious chronic stubbornness over the Ages, and unless Globalization of the present Age now arises and recognize this potential danger, the universe is at risk. It is sitting on a live atomic bomb simply because of man's inability to read and discern the signs of this danger using the natural mandate bestowed upon him by his Maker which are explicitly documented under Chapter 1 versus 26-31 of The Book of The Genesis in *The Holy Bible*, and also St. Mathew 5.45 and 22.37, 40; St. John 13:31-35; and finally The Leviticus 19:18 in The Same.

For the purpose of gaining an in-depth comprehension and significance of the seriousness of this threatening situation inherent in the culture and behaviour of our current Age of Globalization if a prompt measure is not taken to curb it, the following similar case in Ancient Age of Globalization that exploded in Egypt because of the arrogance, of the Haves (the Extra-ordinary affluent Egypt) against the Have-Nots (the starving innocent Children of Israel who had fled their famine-ravaged Mother Country in search of food security in Egypt beginning with Abraham and Sarah to Jacob and his Family) is a significant lesson for one to learn from.

An Etiology of the Egyptian case between the Haves and the Have-nots shows root-causes which are also reminiscent of the Globalization culture inherent in our Generation characterized by arrogance and defilements of God's Commandment by the Haves in their inhumane treatment of the Have-nots.

> ***"He that rules over men <u>must be</u> just, ruling in the fear of God." (II Samuel 23:3).***
>
> ***"And, <u>he shall</u> be as the light of the morning, when the sun rises, <u>even</u> a morning without clouds; <u>as</u> the tender grass <u>springing</u> out of the earth by clear shining after rain" (II Samuel 23:4).***

The case of Kenya today is a fresh epitome of this situation where a few who are fortunately blessed by God *to serve* each Kenyan in their diverse official roles in Government and private sectors do not do so as so mandated under oath. Instead, they mercilessly abuse that blessings by looting the country's wealth for their own selfish use as so witnessed in the recent two epic scandals of the Goldenberg and Anglo Leasing and Finance successfully following each other between a short span of 1991 and 2002—scandals that have not only shocked Kenyans and non-Kenyans globally but also terrorized and dilapidated Kenyan economy thereby driving majority Kenyans into a state of acute poverty, hunger and a sense of utter hopelessness and helplessness. The Have-nots in Kenya cannot make ends meet apart from easily succumbing to death due to the existing *culture and attitude of the don't care Haves controlling the centers of socio-economic and political power at the expense of the Kenyan tax payers.* The Haves' behaviour has led into the development of a strange abnormal culture in Kenya. Personal files in offices, for example, are deliberately hidden by officers until one produces a bribe for the file to be produced. In the area of justice, the *guardians of Justice corruptly sell it to criminals* thereby making the criminal look like a victim and the victim look like a criminal thereby ending with the victim in jail at the benefit of both the guardian and the actual criminal. This epidemic is not limited to the Judiciary or the Bench but also to the Bar (Advocates). In the famine-stricken areas, some relief foods and medicines donated by benevolent donor agencies and individual persons are also hidden and secretly sold by those in the centers of power thus not only depriving the desperately hungry and sick of such relief but also forcing such unfortunate suffering Kenyans and their livestock to succumb to an immediate death thereby putting God and His gracious blessing to the Haves to an utter ridicule.

Similarly, the findings on the Egyptian case also shows the same abuse of God's grace and blessings. It shows that it was because of Egypt's *disobedience* of God's Commandment enshrined in *The Holy Bible* under Genesis 1:26-31 on the one hand; and defilement of the blessings that God had graciously bestowed upon it and its leadership under The Pharaoh which had fortunately enabled the country to rise up to an extra-ordinary heights of all sorts of wealth above all other Countries of the time, on the other, by not only enslaving but by also subjecting the innocent hungry Children of Israel, in their role as the Have-nots in the Country, to unbearably terrible conditions which both the Pharaoh and his Egyptian subjects could not have tolerated, *that consequently put God to an ignominy and wrath.* The two acts were so ignominious to God that He had to appear to Prophet Moses and command him to immediately get hold of his elder brother Aaron and collectively go to the Pharaoh and demand that he immediately releases to them the crying innocent Children of Israel; and then take them out of Egypt to liberty in the lands of Canaan.

The findings further show that when the Pharaoh tried to prove too big and obstinate to the Command, obviously because of his country's immense glory of wealth and power acrued from such blessings, God decided to teach him an unforgettable lesson that he was absolutely nothing before His Creator. God inflicted to him and his Egyptian Country such a series of punishments in the form of pestilences that both the Pharaoh and his country could hardly resist anymore. He finally humbled down on his knees in submission to The Almighty God's Supremacy.

These pestilences included a plague of blood that polluted all sources of water leaving no chance for any one to get water. This was quickly followed by a series of other punishments in the form of various plagues of hail storms and floods all over Egypt; swarms of insects (flies, locusts and army worms) and frogs; boils, chicken and small pox diseases; death epidemic of cattle, horses, camels and asses; a three days darkness all over Egypt; and a death pandemic of all Egyptian first-born sons beginning with the Pharaoh's sons.

Short of such empirical ignominious acts of the Egyptian Pharaoh and his Wealthy Country against God's Commandment coupled with their abuse of His blessings graciously given to them free of charge which had consequently elevated them to such amazing heights of prosperity above all other Countries and the latter's leadership of the time, there exists no any other known prima facie cause that could have put God to such a wrath to punish them that far in defence of these Children of Israel given the fact that both these Children (*the oppressed*) and the Egyptian people (*the oppressor*) were equal creatures of God deserving equal treatment from their Creator.

Hence the justification for a compelling need for the present Age of Globalization to critically reflect on the seriousness of this Egyptian case with a view to using it as a (prima facie) lesson for its proper understanding and eradicating the defects in the existing culture characterized by man-eat-man society motivated by Darwinism. This attitude of survival of the fittest needs a comprehensive panel beating to a new character of Good Neighbourliness, *because of the latter's inherent mighty power seriously needed to develop for our Humanity a Hybrid Culture of abundant peace and productivity that would usher in Summun Bonum (i.e., the greatest happiness) for both the Haves and the Have-Nots, and to thus quickly bridge the existing socio-economic and political imbalance of a great rift valley between the two with a view to transforming them into Equal partners and Children of God.*

This action is essential because, on the strength of the Egyptian pestilences lesson, it may also be possible that the on-going HIV/Aids pandemic globally could also be a function of our own failure to learn from that lesson and use it as a road map for our Age mode of Globalization. The case of Kenya is an epitome of the same ignominious behaviour globally. It is an epitome in that the Haves in both the Developed and Developing Countries have also contravened and are still increasingly contravening the same God's Commandment enshrined in our mandate under Genesis 1:26-31. They have defiled His blessings graciously granted to them, that led them to such heights of wealth above all others, by subjecting the Have-nots to a slow death (as also evidenced above in the case of the conduct of the Haves against the Have-nots in Kenya and the rest of the World).

Therefore, as it was in the case of the most extra-ordinarily wealthy Egyptians against their fellow Innocent Poor Children of Israel in the Ancient Egypt that consequently put God to anger and severely punished that Country, it could also be possible that this existing similar ignominious behaviour today all over the Globe by the extra-ordinarily wealthy against their fellow Have-nots on the one hand, and the existing HIV/Aid endemic including other pestilences of civil wars, earthquakes, hurricanes, terrorism, bird flu, famine, etc. *on the other, are related*. It is possible in that, like in the case of the Ancient Egypt, the seriousness of this appalling behaviour in the present Age of Globalization could have equally put God to a wrath and led Him to put our Generation to the on-going HIV/Aid endemic and other pestilences as a warning. Obviously, these pestilences cannot be accidental acts. They may be serious reminders to this Generation to arise and change the course of the culture and attitude of its Globalization vis a vis the Have-nots in the latter's capacity as Innocent Crying Children of God seeking Salvation from the Creator against the arrogance of the Haves.

In the final analysis, this Command is a sine qua non guide to our goal and direction of our Globalization process. The latter is bound to put on a totally new garment. And on the strength of this, the New Globalization would flourish in abundance of Faith, Continence, Wisdom, Power, Patience, Simplicity, Innocence, Chastity, Cheerfulness, Truth, Good Mutual Understanding, Concord, and Charity for a Global *Summum Bonum* (i.e., the greatest happiness for all) short of any discrimination based on one's race, religion, gender, etc. as is the case in today's culture of Globalization. But, failure for the present Globalization to recognize the magnitude and significance of this Command, the chances are that its dynamics is bound to remain ill-focused and perpetually driven by the vices of Perfidiciousness, Incontinence, Infidelity, Pleasure, Sadness, Malice, Lust, Anger, Lying, Foolishness, Pride, Hatred, Corruption, False Accusation, and Murder whose final end is bound to be a more serious punishment to man today than the on-going chronic disasters such as HIV/Aids pandemic, Terrorism, Civil Wars, Hurricanes, Earthquakes, etc.

And as the Lord God reproves the inconsiderate arrogant and selfish shepherds under Ezekiel 34:1-31 in *The Holy Bible*, also, "woe" be unto the Haves who cunningly and arrogantly enrich themselves at the sweat of the Have-nots but, in return, absolutely care the least about the latter's miserable sufferings from acute poverty, hunger, diseases and other pathetic living conditions.

In this regard, borrowing a leaf from the famous memorable words of the late American Civil Rights Leader, Rev. Dr. Martin Luther King, in his lamentation and earnest prayer for racial equality and social justice and for his Black American Community before his assassination for the same cause in 1968, to have a change of heart and attitude from its existing culture of Neighbourly Hate characterized by racism against its fellow Black American Community so that one day the two communities may sit down side by side together as Brothers and Sisters in peace and harmony for the betterment of their Beautiful Great Mother America, **similarly**, it is here also hoped that The Haves shall like-wise now have a change of heart and attitude from their existing global culture of Neighbourly Hate characterized by their belief in and practice of the survival of the fittest arrogance and exploitation against their fellow Have-nots; and begin to welcome and embrace their Have-not Neighbours on equal footing in the spirit of a Global Neighbourly Love for the betterment of their Beautiful Great Mother Earth Planet.

Thus and hence the serious need and significance of the Neighbourly Love ingredient in Globalization today for *Summum Bonum* (the good health of our total Humanity and Global Environment).

## Bibliography

### The Holy Bible

Adar, Korwa Gombe and Rok Ajulu, eds, *Globalization and Emerging Trends in African States Foreign Policy-Making Process: A Comparative Perspective of Southern Africa*, Hampshire, Ashgate, (2002).

African Forum on Strategic Thinking Towards The Earth Summit and Beyond, *Sustainable Development, Governance and Globalization*, World Summit on Sustainable Development, Johannesburg (2002), The Heinrich Boll Foundation (publishers), Nairobi, Kenya (2002).

Alare, Alari, "Corrupt Leaders Made Me Githongo Says", *The Standard*, Nairobi, Kenya (Monday, October 17, 2005), p.6.

Amin, Ash and Nigel Thrift, *Globalization, Institutions, and Regional Development in Europe*, Oxford University Press, Oxford. (1996).

Antermicael, Berhanykun, *The OAU and The UN*, Africana Publishing Co. N. Y. (1973).

Art, Robert J. and Robert Jervis, *International Politics: Anarchy, Force and Imperialism*, Little, Brown and Co., Boston (1973).

Auma-Osolo, Agola, "A Retrospective Analysis of the UN Activity in The Congo and Its Significance for Contemporary Africa", *Vanderbilt Journal of Trans-national Law*, Vol. 6 No. 2 (1975).

_______________, "UN Peace-Keeping Policy: Some Basic Sources of Its Implementation Problems and Their Implications", *California Western International Law Journal*, Vol. 6, No. 2 (Spring 1976).

_______________, "Rationality and Foreign Policy Process" THE YEAR BOOK OF WORLD AFFAIRS 1977, London Institute of World Affairs, London (19770.

_______________, "Objective Military Control: A New Paradigm in Civil-Military Relations" Journal of Peace Research, No. 1, Vol. XVII, (1980).

_______________, *Cause-Effects of Modern African Nationalism on The World Market*; University Press of America, London (1983).

_______________, *The Law of The United Nations As Applied to Intervention Within The Framework of Article 2(7) of The UN Charter: The Problem of Domestic Jurisdiction*, North Carolina University, Chapel Hill (1969).

_______________, *The Rwanda Catastrophe*, ICPCRIA, Nairobi (1975).

_______________, *The Institute of Conflict Vaccination in Africa: A Path to a Hybrid Culture for Peace, Democracy, Good Governance and Accelerated Socio-Economic Recovery and*

*Development in the Continent*, ICPCRIA, Nairobi; Maseno University, Maseno; and Western University College, Kakamega (May 24, 2005).

Austin-Sparks, "*That They May All Be One, Even as We Are One*", Vol. One, Manila 1964 Meetings, Emmanuel Church, 12000 E. 14th St. Tulsa OK 74128-5016 USA.

Barnes, H. E., *The Story of Punishment: A Record of Man's Inhumanity to Man*, The Stratford Co., Boston (1930).

Baylis, John and Steve Smith, eds, *The Globalization of World Politics: An Introduction to International Relations*, Oxford University Press, Oxford, (2001).

Bienen, *The Military Intervenes, Case Studies in Political Development*, Russell Sage Foundation, New York (1968).

Burke, Edmund, *Emancipate Your Colonies*

Clegg, Stewart R., Eduardo Ibrrcolado and Luis Bueno, eds, *Global Management: Universal Theories and Local Realities*, SAGE Publications, London (1999).

Darst. Diane W., *Western Civilization To 1648*, An American BookWorks Corporation Project, McGraw-Hill Publishing Company, New York (1990).

Dougherty, James E. and Robert L. Pfaltzgraff, Jr., *Contending Theories of International Relations*, J.B., Lippincott Company, Philadelphia, (1971).

Elias, Taslim Olwale, *African and the Development of International Law* Dordrecht Kluwer Publication (1988)

Erb, Guy F. and Valeriana Kallab, eds, *Beyond Dependency: The Developing World Speaks Out, Overseas* Development Council, Washington, D. C. (September, 1975).

Feis, Herbert, *The Diplomacy of The Dollar 1919-1932*, The Norton Library, W. W. Norton & Company Inc., New York (1966).

Heron, Richard Le, *Globalized Agriculture: Political Choice*, Pergaman Press, Oxford (1993).

James, George G. M., *Stolen Legacy: The Greeks Were Not The Authors of Greek Philosophy But The People of North Africa Commonly Called The Egyptians*, Philosophical Library, N. Y. (1954).

Keegan, Warren J., *Global Marketing Management*, Prentice-Hall, Englewood Cliffs (1989)

Kirkbride, Paul, ed., *Globalization: The External Pressures*, John Wiley & Sons, Ltd, Baffins Lane, Chichester, West Sussex P.O. Box 19 IUD, England (2001).

_______________, and Karen Ward, eds, *Globalization: The Internal Dynamics*, John Wiley & Sons Ltd, Baffins Lane, Chichester, West Susses, P.O. Box 19 IUD, England (2001).

Kowalewski, David, *Global Establishment: The Political Economy of North/Asian Networks*, International Political Economy Series, St. Martin's Press Inc., Scholarly and Reference Division, 175 Fifth Ave., NY 10010.

Leys, Colin, *Underdevelopment in Kenya, The Political Economy of Neo-Colonialism*, University of California Press, Berkeley, California (1975).

Lo, Fu-Chen and Yueman Young, eds, *Globalization and The World of Large Cities*, U.N. University Press (1998).

McCormic, John, *The Global Environment Movement*, John Wiley, NewYork (1995).

Mebrahtu, Teame, Michael Crossley and David Johnson, *Globalization, Educational Transformation and Societies in Transition*, Symposium Books Oxford (2000).

Meigs, Cornelia, *The Great Design: Men & Events in The UN From 1945 to 1963*, Little, Brown and Co., Boston, Massachusetts (19640.

Moskowitz, Milton, *The Global Marketplace: 102 of The Most Influential Companies Outside America*, MacMillan Publishing Co. New York (1987).

Mureithi, Franics, "Middle East: Beware Britain and US", *The People Daily*, Nairobi, Kenya (October 27, 2005) p.7.

Nabutere, Dani W., ed. *Globalization and The Post-Colonial African State*, AAPS Books, Harare, Zimbabwe (2000).

Onyango-Obbo, "The Tears Never Dry Up for Africa", *Daily Nation*, Nairobi, Thursday April 14, 2005.

Pink, Arthur W. and Luther C. Peak, *The Golden Age: A Treatise on One Thousand Year Reign of Christ on Earth*, The Evangelist Press, 1014 South Ervay Street, P. O. Box 33, Dallas, Texas (1950).

Pirages, Dennis, *The New Contest for International Relations: Global Ecopolitics*, Duxbury Press, North Scituate, Massachusetts, (1978).

Reagan, David, The Master Plan, Making Sense of The Controversies, Surrounding Bible Prophecy Today, Harvest House Publishers, Eugene, Oregon 97402 (1993).

Sauper, "Hubert, *Darwin's Nightmare* (A VEDEO DOCUMENTARY, Belgium (2005).

Schelling, Thomas C., *Arms and Influence*, Yale University Press, New Haven, Connecticut (1966).

Simoni, Arnold, *Beyond Repair, The Urgent Need for a New World Organization*, Collier-Macmillan, Canada, NewYork (1972).

Spanier, John, *Games nations Play: Analysing International Politics*, Praeger Publishers, N. Y. (1973).

Stiglitz, Joseph E., *Globalization and Its Discontents*, W. W. Norton and Company, N. Y. (2003).

Wallbank, T. Walter, Alstair M. Taylor and Nels M. Bailkey, *Civilization: Past and Present*, Scott, Foreman and Company, Chicago (1962)

*The World Book Encyclopeadia.*

# PART EIGHT

## POLITICAL SOCIALIZATION AND THE RISE OF POLITICAL EARTHQUAKES IN COLONIAL AFRICA: A Test for a Detestable Leadership to Mankind.

## CHAPTER 1

# Introduction

### (1) Observation

In every group of people or society, community and country, the rise of a new idea, philosophy, doctrine or ideology always also leads to the development of a new phenomenon. This phenomenon may be for or against the welfare of those people, society, community or country. The rise of new scientific and technological discoveries and innovations in the $18^{th}$ and $19^{th}$ Europe led to the development of the Industrial Revolution for the welfare of not only Europe but also to a total mankind globally. Also, the discovery of the Polio Vaccine by a joint effort of Dr. Jonas E. Salk and Dr. Albert B. Sabin led to development of man's eradication of polio threat to mankind.

But, on the contrary, the rise of machiavellism from Niccolo Machiavelli (1469-1527) followed by the rise of the Survival of the Fittest doctrine from Charles Robert Darwin (1809-1882) also led to the development of a dangerous situation in Europe. It gave rise to inter-tribal rivalry in Europe with each tribe bent on overshining and overpowering the other in socio-economic and political power accumulation at the expense of the other. Succinctly, each sought to colonize others for that cause. This rivalry caused various bloody wars in the continent. These included, Napoleonic War, Anglo-Prussian War, Franco Prussian War, and World War I and II.

But the more it became apparent to the contenders that such a crusade could not materialize in Europe, the move then had to shift their interest from intra-European Colonization to African Colonization. Hence the Scramble for Africa as a solution.

The Imperial German Chancellor, Otto von Bismarck, prudently saved Europe from this quagmire. He promptly convened the Berlin Conference for the Scramble for Africa from November 1884 to March 1885 under his Chairmanship where each party to the conflict was invited, And, at the end of the Conference, each was granted a clean bill of rights to take possession of every country occupied before the Conference. Thus, legal colonization of Africa by the colonial powers.

However, although each colonial power's interest in Africa was basically to seek and exploit the continent's natural and human resources for the self, a systematic comparative analysis of the advantages and disadvantages of the Colonial Leadership to Africa in terms of its positive and negative contributions to the socio-economic welfare of the Continent with a view to identifying the reason why Africa had to revolt at all casts against the Colonial Leadership in demand for self-rule, the following striking revelation(s) comes to the surface in support of positive contributions:-

To the surprise and enjoyment of Africa, the Colonial Powers introduced and availed to the continent an immaculate civilization characterized by a myriad of socio-economic and political facilities. These included schools, health centres, churches as centres of worship of a True God as opposed to traditional centres of cults and hand-made object gods, road and railway net-works, telephone and telecommunication net-work, etc. In the British Colonial Leadership, there existed a Governor assisted by a host of other government officers ranging from the Provincial Commissioner (PC), the District Commissioner (DC), and several chiefs charged with management of local matters.

The Governor and his team constituted an Executive Branch of Government in each Colony in Africa and was responsive to the King or Queen back at home in the United Kingdom. Also, there existed a Legislative Council charged with Legislative matters peculiar to each Colony. And, finally, there also existed a Judiciary headed by a Chief Justice and assisted by Judges of High Court and Magistrates of Lower Courts.

Obviously, all these immaculate structures and their respective functions constituted a political socialization vehicles for a new wind of change in the traditional Africa. They led to the development of a new Civilization in Africa characterized by a dignified culture of No Tolerance to Kleptocracy, Nepotism, Dishonesty, Professional Poverty, and all other virtues and practice of Bad Governance. This culture emphasized efficiency, honesty, trust, and transparency and accountability in both public and private centres of work. It created a healthy professional culture for the function of any civilized country. For example, employment, admission to school, treatment at health centres, administration and processing of the candidates' examination were all conducted in good faith governed by an atmosphere of free and fair spirit short of a bribe, or any other element of prejudice as so widely experienced today in the independent Africa under an African Leadership which is itself the chief culprit of the vice, as recently witnessed in Kenya. This include, e.g., successful grand scandals of Goldenberg International during the Leadership era of President Daniel Toroitich arap Moi (1978-2002), followed by The Anglo Leasing and Finance during the Leadership of President Mwai Kibaki (2003-to the present); other worst ones also include Kibaki's red-handed involvement in the December 27, 2007 Presidential Election Results Fraud that resulted into untold sorrows of ethnic mutual genocide in Kenya between the pro-fraud group spearheaded by supporters of the President's Party of National Unity (PNU) and the anti-fraud group spearheaded by supporters of Honourable Raila's Pentagon of The Orange Democratic Movement (ODM) opposition party.

The mutual genocide between the two groups became so alarming both in and outside Kenya that Kenya was almost running into a dead end: Had the International Community not rushed into the country with necessary emergency humanitarian assistance and a stern threat to President Kibaki's regime to yield at once to H.E. Kofi Annan led Negotiation's demand for a power-sharing Formula between PNU and ODM, the prospect for Kenya's future was almost running to a halt. By the time this mutual blood shed was stopped, over 1,500 Kenyans had died; uncountable number injured and displaced from their habitual homes; and lots of property of unquantifiable value destroyed with fire or other means.

Therefore, given such nasty situation Africa has always undergone since independence to date at the hands of its own independent leadership; and also given the fact that Africa did enjoy a lot from a myriad of wonderful benefits during the colonial power's leadership, the nagging question one must ask is why did Africa have to revolt in search for self-rule from the Colonial Powers? What could have influenced Africa to do so? Did Political Socialization have any contribution to the development of this situation in colonialism Africa against the Colonial Powers?

## (2) A Nagging Question

But, given a myriad of all these immaculate benefits or advantages Africa received and enjoyed from the Colonial Leadership in the Continent, why then must she have revolted at all against the Leadership? What could or may have contributed to this reaction in demand for self-rule? Succintly, what could Political Africa's psychic?

CHAPTER II

# Political Socialization and its Effect on Colonial Africa

## 1. What is Political Socialization?

Political socialization is precisely a process through which the individual acquires political cues (orientations) from his political culture right from his parents at birth, nuclear family members, peergroups, and other sources (both informal and formal such as school, religious institutions, etc), using his inmate and acquired motivation energies. From the general socialization theory, we know that man is basically a dependent entity. Unlike all other members of the Animal Kingdom, which are born with well-developed skills, e.g. swimming, walking, etc., man is born practically ignorant and, therefore, practically dependent. To improve himself, man must, therefore, recreate his ignorant self into an advanced self with a host of both internal and external agents. **Internally**, the individual is a sum total of several biological organs whose co-ordination is extremely necessary for normal functioning of his body; **externally**, he is a single social organ whose social behaviour, developement and maturation depends and is largely determined by his social setting. To be a Luo, sue generis, one must be born of and raised by a Dholuo family in a Luo social setting. But, becaue one has to remake one's social self, man is equipped with a biological mechanism (i.e. motivations) constitutionally designed to enhance the making of his social self. With the aid of this internal agents, man endeavours directly and indirectly to become **somebod**y in his social setting. For instance, if born in Kenya but in a Luoland, he voluntarily and involuntarily learns first and foremost his local language *(Dholuo)*, food *(chiemo)*, food-acquisition and eating have its, marriage system, etc. Consequently, he finds himself not only an inter-subjective member of the world of his society but also an active participating member in and of that society[2].

Therefore, political socialization theory succinctly means that every individual learns the political culture of his society, in order for that individual to become a participating member of his inter-subjective political society.

But, it should also be noted meticulously that, that individual **may** or **may** not be possessive of his society. That is to say, he may or may not appreciate his society, and therefore feel fully or not fully supportive and defensive of his society. In all, however, his behaviour significantly depends upon the degree of congruency **between** his expectations and those of his society. If his expectations and the values (e.g., authority) of his society do not concur, that individual is most likely to resort to negative responses against authority. He may become revolutionary or simply anomic against it. But, if his expectations and his societal values do concur positively, that individual is likely to develop a positive political attitude towards authority in his political system, and may go all ways to do so even if it requires him resorting to suicide action to defend his society and its values (legacy).

That the individual can develop a positive attitude toward his system and authority and, therefore, defend them to any length possible, Stewart and Desjardins note that in the 19th century French nationalism, Lazare Carnot (a French nationalist) cried:

> Oh, France, oh my fatherland, oh great people, truly great people! On your soil, I had the happiness to be born. Only in death could I cease belonging to you. You encompass all the objects of my affection: the achievements to which my hands have contributed, the upright old man who sired me, the family without a blemish, the friends who know the depth of my heart . . . . [3]

And, that the individual may also develop a negative attitude towards his political system and its authority or leadership, Westby and Braungart note in their study of the American youths during the height of the Vietnamese War in the late 1960's that

> While the young generation leaves home to take life at school, for more elaborate socialization, tensions inherent and, therefore generated by the generation-gap, result in various reactions of partially autonomous youth cultures. Systems, which are run by the old generation, automatically become the target of organized attack by youth wings[4].

## 2. Objective

To this end, the aim of this paper is to examine the actual impact (effects) of Political Socialization on the African Political Culture and Attitude towards their respective Colonial Authority in Africa as a paradigm or stepping stone of our understanding of the universal impact of Political Socialization in Political Life World-wide. Specifically, it examines:

1) How, by the grace of this Political Socialization, the Continent of Africa was saved from her scourge of the Undemocratic Colonial Bondage and finally led it to Full Freedom and Membership in the Community of Free Nations on the equal footing with her former Colonial Masters.
2) And, how, by virtue of the same grace of Political Socialization, the Continent cannot and will not be saved from her Existing Undemocratic Culture of Bad Governance and other multi-socio-economic and political woes because of the same culture that she has and on which all her people/children are now being socialized right from childhood to adulthood which is now their foundation and basis of undemocratic behaviour and life in total and which is, therefore, obviously detrimental to their own chance of gaining a socio-economic recovery and development for their collective national prosperity and good health.

In this regard, and in order to achieve this double-edged objective, this Paper employs a Psychiatric Approach, by which to expose, identify and analyze those strategic factors responsible for the development of an African national consciousness against a foreign Leadership in Africa that was considered/found to be lacking the concept and virtue of Democracy. Unlike the conventional Psychiatry, our approach is not a treatment of a mental disorder. **Its sole aim is to identify casual factors of certain behavioural pattern but not to change those patterns, as conventional psychiatrists normally do**. It is an etiology of the actual root-causes of man-made-disaster cases such as hostility, and the like.

## 3. Hypotheses

(1) The more Africans became politically socialized by the Colonial Regimes through various formal and informal socializing agents on the Political Philosophy of Human Rights and all other sacred virtues sacrosanct to man's Summum Bonum (i.e., Greatest Good or Happiness in life), the more they become clearly aware and cognizant of

the evil of those Regimes' undemocratic policies, leadership attitude, behaviour and treatment to the colonized.

(2.) The more this Great Awakening developed and spread all over the Continent by the grace of Political Socialization, the more the Continent produced charismatic leaders against those Colonial Regimes and the latter's undemocratic tendencies.

(3.) And, the more our hypotheses in Nos. (1) and (2) holds true, then the chances are that the independent continent will encounter a similar political earthquake(s) and tornado(es) because of the following tendencies of her Regimes:

(a) Her own negligence or failure to learn from the past lessons of mass revolution in resistance against Colonial Regimes' undemocratic tendencies; and

(b) Her leaders' dangerous option to deviate from their original noble aim against Colonialism by pursuing suicidal undemocratic policies characterized by single party and fake multi-party dictatorship saturated with ugly rampant **institutionalized corruption and other forms of financial mismanagement**, leadership schisms and assassinations, abject poverty and diseases, dishonesty at all levels of Government and Bad Democracy which have often forced or compelled some Donor Community Members to either withhold or catergorically discontinue further aid unless and until such undemocratic policies and tendencies are corrected, eradicated or significantly improved.

## 4. Findings on Colonial Africa

### Finding No. 1 (The Role and Impact of Sociolization in General)

As a result of the scramble for Africa by the Colonies' Seekers, the following tangible socio-economic and political phenomena (i.e., interactions and development developed and emerged all over the Continent as an explicit empirical ramification/symptom(s) of the actual impact (or effect) of **Political Socialization in the Colonized Africa by the same Colonizers** (Colonial Powers/Regimes):-

**Table 1: Symptoms of Social Change in Africa as a Result of the European Scramble for Africa for Capital Accumulation on the World Market:**

Pre-Colonial Africa and Cultural Values (Legacies) before March 1885

1. Traditional religion and customs, e.g., Emisambwa, Juju, Orthodox Christianity, e.g, Egyptian Coptics, etc.
2. Traditional chiefs and headmen with the title from top-down to the chief's title: Muruka, Mulango and Kujeje.
3. Traditional languages, i.e. Luhya and Luo, Dholuo, etc.
4. Traditional political systems, i.e. Mumia Empire, Ghana Empire, Mali Empire, etc.
5. Traditional judicial systems.

Colonial Africa (after March 1885):

1. Introduction to Europeanized Christianity and other Euro-centered myths such as European names forced on every African to take as a mandatory rites of passage to Salvation during Church baptism,
2. Introduction of European languages, e.g. English, French, Portugues, Spanish as mandatory medium of communication in offices, school, and health centres.
3. Introduction of European customs and other beliefs (marriage registration).
4. Replacement of traditional rulers with warrant chiefs.
5. Introduction of Euroepan education, e.g. who "discovered" Mt. Kenya, River Niger, etc. as well as other similar non-isomorphic (unscientific) knowledge with a view to stupidfying the African to live in Eurocentric myths, falsehoods and superiority complex (disease) called "Europhialia".
6. Introduction of forces assimilation, especially by the French, Belgium and Portugues colonial rules, in their respective colonies, in order to maximize Europhilia at the expense of the African personality, culture, and dignity on the World Market.

**Post-Colonial Africa (the Independence Era)**

1. Change from Colonial Authority to African Authority.
2. Practice of European Christianity, e.g. use of English names and "Christmas tree" in some African homes.
3. Practice of colonial language, e.g. English and French as their official language.
4. Practice of European tradition, e.g. use of wigs in Courts by African judges in African Courts.

5. A change from traditional to "warrant rulers", e.g Presidents and Prime Ministers, instead of Kabaka, Omwami, Chiefs and Kings.
6. A change from Euro-American multi-party politics to one party politics, e.g KANU in Kenya: TANU in Tanzania, etc.
7. A change from civilian rule to military rule
8. A change from one or single party politics of undemocratic tendencies to multi-party politics toward Democracy Institutionalization.

**Finding No. 2 (Advantages Africa gained from Colonial Powers)**

As a result of the Europeans' scrambe for Africa for capital accumulation on the World Market, most post-colonial African countries accepted and still use English, French and Portugues as their official and principle medium of communication in and outside Africa, e.g., in the meetings of the Organization of African Unity (OAU) and the United Nations (UN). Also, in addition to European Christianity, which now ranks highest over both traditional African and other religions in Africa, the mobility rate, literacy, income per capita, communication and other products of industrial revolution, likewise increased significantly as a result of the Scramble for Africa. Thus, the more Africa changed from their traditional religions and other beliefs to their colonial power's religion; from their customs to languages; from their traditional rulers and kings to the warrant chiefs created by the colonial powers; from their humanistic political philosophy to European revolutionary political philosophy, such as that of Rousseau, the Utilitarian, Scientific Socialist (e.g., Marx and Engels, Marx and Lenin)—a philosophy they acquired by interacting with the colonial powers both at home and in Europe, especially during both World War 1 and World War II: and finally, from their high illiteracy rate and subsistence economy to high literacy and per capita income, the more they understood the weakness and fallaciousness of their colonial powers. And as it will be noted hereafter,

1. the more the Africans came into contact with Europeans both at home and abroad, the more they became politically socialized;
2. the more they became socialized, the more they became militant and mobile, to influence the Africa peasantry to fight against their "cruel" colonial ruler; and
3. the more they influenced the grass roots, the more nationalisms developed among the Africans and influences against their common enemy (the colonial powers).

Table 2 below tests for the above indicated assumption with a specific focus on the following variables: (a) *population increase*: (b) *expenditure on education and the mobility rate in Kenya in East Africa,* and *the literacy rate in Nigeria in West Africa* (both ex-British colonies until December 12, 1963 and October 1, 1960, respectively);

**Table 2: Some Empirical Statistics Evidences of African Social Change on the World Market due to Colonialism Before Independence:**

**1. Population Increase in Kenya:**

| | 1948 | 1960 | Net Increase (%) | | |
|---|---|---|---|---|---|
| Africans | 5,251,120 | 6,264,000 | 1,012,800 | = | 20 |
| Arabs | 24,174 | 38,600 | 14,426 | = | 59 |
| Asians | 97,687 | 174,300 | 86,613 | = | 89 |
| Europeans | 29,660 | 67,700 | 38,040 | = | 128 |
| Others | 3,325 | 6,100 | 2,775 | = | 83 |
| | | | X | = | 76 |

**2. Money Spent on Education in Kenya: ( in dollars)**

| 1935 | 1958/9 | % Increase |
|---|---|---|
| 170,000 | 6,721,848 | 3,854.03 |

**3. Mobility Rate Via Sea and Air in Kenya**

**Immigration**

| | 1961 | 1962 | = | % Increase |
|---|---|---|---|---|
| Europeans | 51,477 | 59,144 | = | 14.90 |
| Africans | 4,376 | 6,020 | = | 37.57 |
| | | X | = | 26.24 |

**Emigration**

| | 1961 | 1962 | % Increase | |
|---|---|---|---|---|
| Europeans | 56,745 | 60,023 | = | 5.78 |
| | 4,703 | 5,938 | = | 26.26 |
| | | X = | 16.02 | |

## 4. Educational Proliferation in Nigeria

**Number of Schools**

| Type of Schools | 1959 | 1963 | % Increase | |
|---|---|---|---|---|
| Primary | 15,620 | 15,090 | = | 3.40 |
| Secondary | 718 | 1,245 | = | 73.40 |
| Teacher-Training | 309 | 266 | = | 13.90 |
| Technical and Vocational | 25 | 31 | | 24.00 |
| | | X | 28.68 | |

**Male Students**

| Type of Schools | 1959 | 1963 | % Increase | |
|---|---|---|---|---|
| Primary | 1,756.380 | 1,771,644 | = | 0.90 |
| Secondary | 48,730 | 151,807 | = | 211.50 |
| Teacher-Training | 20,760 | 24,586 | = | 18.40 |
| Technical and Vocational | 7,250 | 7,250 | = | 0.00 |
| | | X | = | 5.77 |

**Female Students**

| Type of School | 1959 | 1960 | % | Increase |
|---|---|---|---|---|
| Primary | 1,019,559 | 1,124,738 | = | 10.30 |
| Secondary | 17,479 | 60,072 | = | 243,70 |
| Teacher Training | 5,723 | 7,753 | = | 35.50 |
| Technical and Vocational | 248 | 298 | | 2.40 |
| | | X | = | 72.98 |

Source: For data on Kenya, see: Colony and Protectorate of Kenya: East African Statistical Department. Kenya Unit Statistical Abstract. (1960) (Nairobi: Government Printers, 1960), pp. 28-29; Also Junod and Resnick; The Handbook of Africa (New York: New York University Press, 1963), p. 151: and Yearbook and Guide to East Africa, 1964, A. Gordon-Brown, F.R.G.S., F.R.Hist., ed., for Union-Castle Mail Steamship Company Ltd. (London: Robert Hale Ltd., 1964). P. 45.

N.B. Note a significant increase of European population in Kenya as compared to that of non. Europeans.

For data on Nigeria, see: Barclays Bank D.C.O., U, 1967-8, London: Thomas Skinner and Company, Ltd., 1969), p. 285.

As also noted in Table 2 above, the data on Kenya and Nigeria shows that:

1. More Europeans came to Kenya between 1948 and 1960 at the rate of 128% than non-Europeans. Therefore, it is self-evident that this immigration influx into Kenya enables Africans to interact with and know or learn more from Europeans and undemocratic and other inhuman tendencies or nature of the latter's Colonial Authority in Africa.
2. In Kenya, expenditure on education increased by 3854.03% between 1935 and 1958/1959.
3. In Kenya again, African mobility rates to and from Kenya increased by 31.92% while the Europeans rate increased only by 10.34% between 1961 and 1962.
4. Finally, in Nigeria, educational development, especially at the high section level, increased significantly. (Therefore, the more education proliferated in Nigeria and

the rest of the African colonies, the more the colonized Africans obviously became articulate enough to know and protest the legitimacy of the undemocratic colonial rule).

Writing on traffic increase in Nigeria as well as other West African countries as a result of World War II, and the dynamics of Capitalism, Imperialism, and Industrial Revolution in Europe, the Barclay's Bank, D.C.O., stated in 1969 that:

> "since the war, there has been considerable expansion both in road mileage and in traffic using the roads. The mileage of bitumen trunk roads increased from 2,688 to 7,509 between 1959 and 1963. The estimated total mileage of roads in 1965 was 49,428 of which about 7,509 were tarred, and 41, 919 gravel or earth."[5]

From this observation, it is equally self-evident that by the end of World War II, most West Africans had already advanced significantly, especially through education, extensive travel, interaction with Europeans in Africa, and through many other new aspects of life such as Christianity. And the more they were **exposed** to the European way of life and political philosophy, such as the quest for sovereign equality, the quest for Political Independence and Freedom, **inter alias** which every mature and normal individual or group of persons in a given territory has or have the inherent right to fight for, the more they **realized** their legitimate rights and duties to struggle for the same values. Therefore, it is most likely that it was indeed the same social change phenomenon which significantly contributed to the development of African nationalism vis-à-vis the colonial powers. In other words, once most Africans understood the European democractic political philosophy and culture in terms of a political party structure and processes, mass-mobilization techniques, etc., they obviously could not wait any longer before putting these ideas into practice, against their foreign oppressor.

But, ideas alone are not enough, even if they are shared by many people. Like a peasantry which can hardly develop itself into an organization without the presence of leadership, so an idea without leadership is totally meaningless and useless. It is like an empty automobile without a driver. In order to eliminate a perceived problem or achieve a desired objective, a people needs both an idea and the leadership to carry it out. A leader's presence is essential to synchronize different ideas and functions of his people or group towards a perceived goal. For this reason, no occupied African people could possibly have managed successfully to get rid of its oppressive colonial rule, no matter how well informed that people was on the European political philosophy and culture. For them to successfully regain their freedom from the Colonial Rule, they must have had some leadership with which to synchronize their respective interest articulations for freedom. Or else, it is doubtful that their independence today would have materialized or just come about by magic (i.e. by chance) alone.

In the following Section B-2, we will subject the above concerns to an empirical test with the aid of the data from our Psychiatric Model on Nkrumah, Kenyatta and Nyerere simultaneously in their unique capacity as Original African Leaders in Contemporary African political life.

**Finding No. 3 (A Psychiatric Findings on Three Original African Leaders viz:Nkrumah, Kenyatta and Nyerere):**

With the help of this Psychiatric Model, we seek to understand how these three original African political leaders were politically socialized; and why they, therefore, became revolutionaries against Colonialism. The effect of their political socialization and activism is supported by the emergence of independent African nation-states.

From our psychiatric data on Nkrumah gleaned from his Autobiography,[6] it is evident that it was not until Nkrumah came into direct contact with (1) the first notable African intellectuals, such as Dr. Quegyir Aggrey, whose intellectual personality impressed Nkrumah so much that Nkrumah vowed he must, by all means, also become like Aggrey; (2) the writings of both classical and contemporary political philosophers, such as Kant, Hegel, Descartes, Marx, Schoppenhauer, Nietzsche, Freud, Marcus Garvey, Lenin, Gandhi, **inter alios**; (3) the racial confrontation in the United States which he had personally experienced while a student in Pennsylvania from 1935 to May, 1945; and (4) the international Black intellectuals in Europe, such as Dr. W.E.B. Dubois and George Padmore from the United States and the West Indies respectively (the architects of the Pan-African movement), that he was able to develop this unique personality, different from other African intellectual elites before and after him.

We do not, however, come across his authentic political activities until we come to the time he went to Lonodn in May of 1945. AT that time, we find him deeply involved in the **West African Student Union**—an organization deliberately designed to help new African students in London and, above all, to make petitions to the Colonial Office for better conditions in West Africa: and, in the **Pan-African congress as a Joint Secretary with Padmore**—an organization deliberately designed to train the members and other participants in how to begin revolutionary activities in Africa against the colonial regimes. Thereafter, we find him attracted to the African intelligentsia back in the Gold Coast; and being summoned to come home to re-organize the United Gold Coast Convention (UGCC) which was almost dead because of disharmony among the intelligentsia who once formed it.

But, unlike all other African political philosophers before him, why did Nkrumah conceive the idea that Africa must be free and finally united into a United States of Africa? Is this not evident in his preaching for political independence as the first priority for Africa's security? Why, then, did he develop this attitude?

Again through our examination of his life history, we discover three main personality attributes that Nkrumah was brought up to possess **vis:-**

(1) lovable and loving; therefore, likely to be possessive (protective);
(2) admire; therefore, likely to be ambitious and industrious; and
(3) critical of traditional Catholic authoritative rules; therefore, likely to be innovative (trans-traditionalist).

**In the first attribute**, we note that Nkrumah grew up as the only child in his household. AT the same time, we also note that because of his father's continual absences from home, Nkrumah spent more time with his mother than he did with his father. From this inference, we may, therefore, hypothesize that **as the only child, Nkrumah would grow up with more affinity to and love for his mother than he would for his father**. In addition, we may also hypothesize that, **he would be more possessive toward his mother and she towards him than he would towards his father**.

The data about Nkrumah's early age suggests that Nkrumah's political **possessiveness** and **protectiveness** over the people of his own kind are rooted in his childhood. For instance, he was so fond of his mother that the latter's bed would not be shared with his father. When his father insisted that he had to sleep in that bed because he was the father, Nkrumah refused him and categorically warned him that even if he was married to her, he (Nkrumah) was also married to her. The third and fourth evidences that added more proof to the idea of

Nkrumah's possessiveness and the latter's bearing on his future politics are indicated in the incidents when he beat a policeman on the beach because the latter tried to reprimand Nkrumah's half-brother; and when also Nkrumah forced the lover of this half brother to vacate their home.

In the latter case, Nkrumah was too young and, therefore, too ignorant of love affairs. He, therefore, erroneously assumed that the strange young man was definitely an aggressor, and, therefore, undesirable. So, Nkrumah's attitude of "hands off from those that I know and love" (an indicator of possessiveness) must have grown from his childhood days. This fondness was further increased by another love he received from both his half-brothers and sisters. He tells us in his Autobiography that he was personally surprised when his half-brothers decided once that it was he that had to sit in the new toy and drive it around for testing!

Therefore, it was due to this personality attribute which Nkrumah acquired while still a young boy, through parental care, that eventually came to be developed into a more dynamic scope through his direct contacts with contemporary political philosophers mentioned above; and above all, Nkrumah's personal experiences with colonial maltreatments of the colonial peoples of Africa before he went abroad for further studies; and, the racial problems he encountered in the United States.

In the Second attribute, it is also noted from Nkrumah's Autobiography that on seeing Dr. Aggrey, he was so impressed by the latter's personality that on hearing that Dr. Aggrey had died suddenly in the United States, he was very angry and fasted for three days. In addition, he vowed that he would become the second Aggrey and accomplish what Aggrey had promised to the people of the Gold Coast! That he was very fond of Dr. Aggrey's intellectual personality, can be proved by making reference to his statement, "it was through him that my nationalism was first aroused. He was extremely proud of his colour . . ."! More so, we also learn that Nkrumah played a very vital role in setting up the Aggrey Students' Society in memory of Dr. Aggrey.

At another time, we also see him so much interested in George Padmore, a stranger he had never met before except through sensitive articles that the latter had occasionally written against colonialism, that on his return to London for further studies at the London School of Economics, he never hesitated in writing to Padmore for the latter to await him on Nkrumah's arrival in London. However, Nkrumah's anticipatory socialization (i.e., deliberate ambition)[7] that he must become the second Aggrey is well proved by his scholastic achievement while in the United States.

Because of this burning Anticipatory Socialization, Nkrumah sought to accomplish what Aggrey might have done had Aggrey lived long enough.

Consequently, regardless of his extenuating financial situation, he was able to achieve two Bachelor's degrees from Lincoln University (1939) and Lincoln Seminary (1942); two Master's degrees from the University of Pennsylvania 1942, Education, and 1943, Philosophy); and, except for a dissertation, to complete all requirements for his Ph.D. degree. On his arrival in London, we see him still curious for all additional doctorate program apart from the research he had gone to London for in partial fulfillment of his doctorate degree at the University of Pennsylvania. <u>And as an organizer</u>, Nkrumah is seen in a good number of organizations!

As also noted above, Nkrumah was one of those that organized the Aggrey Students' Society; while still a teacher at Elmina, he helped to found the Teachers' Association to protect the teachers from the administration; and while at Lincoln, he was very instrumental in seting up various program such as the African Studies program, the African Students' Association of America and Canada, and also the newspaper, called **African Interpreter.**

Also, we see him interested in knowing the nature and functions of political organizations in the United States, such as the Republican Party, the Democratic Party, the national Association for the Advancement of Coloured People (NAACP) the means by which he was able not only to fight against Colonialism but also to meet some of the Trotskyite members from whom he learned all about underground operations, against Bad Governance and the latter's evils against Human Rights and Freedom.

It was, therefore, due to his long-lived possessiveness and this powerful influential personality attribute he had acquired in his past life experience that on his arrival in London in 1945, Nkrumah was found politically and administratively capable-qualities which qualified him for the positions of Vice-President of the West African Student Union in London, and, thereafter, Joint-Secretary with Geoge Padmore to the Pan-African Congress in Manchester in 1945.

Nkrumah's love for both Aggrey and Padmore, inter alios, is significantly related to the development of his national consciousness, political leadership, political goals, political strategies and ideology against Colonialism because a number of studies have proved that child-peer intimacy plays a significant role in the development and direction of the individual's political personality. Talcott Parsons, for example, suggests that peer groups automatically become the most important agent for the child's political development, especially at the highschool level. At this level, both parental and teachers' influence over the child begins to diminish, giving way to peers' influence;[8] James S. Coleman, in his study of American adolescent culture, also stresses that peers begin to replace the parental role as of an early adolescent age; and Dawson and Prewitt, in their synthesis of Political Socialization also conclude that peer groups are not only the important agents of learning but also the most influential during adolescence and adulthood unit; an individual's political maturation[9].

With reference to the function of the degree of intimacy between child and peer in the former's political development, Dawson and Prewitt stress that:

> "In addition to a high level of interaction among the members, peer groups are characterized by highly personal and emotionally involved relationships. We know that political socialization, like other kinds of socialization, is facilitated by emotional strength of interpersonal relationship. Those groups and individuals with whom one is most deeply involved have the greatest impact upon the development and stability of one's political self."[10]

It is, therefore, no wonder why Nkrumah developed such an ambitious political attitude against the Undemocratic Mode of Colonial Authority. Even if some critics do not agree with this conclusion, other studies, e.g. by Darwin Cartwright and Alvin Zander (1960) also indicate that membership in a group(s) plays a great part in determining what and to what extent the individual in that/those groups will learn, see, experience or think about[11].

More importantly, the degree of the individual's intimacy with members of his group(s) subconsciously and consciously become the backborne and a motivating force in the development and direction of that individual's political personality. In Cartwright and Zander's words, "an individual may act like other members of this group because they are attractive to him and he like them[12] . . . ." So, in view of these important studies, there is less doubt that Nkrumah's later political behaviours was a consequence of his fondness for Aggrey and others personalities such as Padmore, DuBois, among other, who he did meet and interacted with during and after his adolescence but in Africa and overseas particularly the USA and the United Kingdom.

In the third and final personality attribute, we have seen that in his youth, Nkrumah was very opposed to authoritative regulations of the roman Catholic Missionary School that he first attended; especially; the School's demands for regular church attendance. Again, we have also noted above that while at Elmina, he and other teachers organized the Teacher's Association vis-à-vis the Roman Catholic Junior School Administration. In London, we have also seen him involved in similar revolutionary activities with "The Circle" against the Colonial Regimes in Africa. And upon his return home to take over the UGCC as its Secretary-General, Nkrumah in seen to be more radical and innovative than the rest of his UGCC staff members.

Furthermore, we see him being blamed and accused by his UGCC colleagues, such as Danquah, of his radicalism and pragmatism. Thereafter, we see his colleagues trying to remove him from the UGCC secretaryship that rest of the peasantry so much that the latter had to request him to help them to form another political party, the CPP, outside the UGCC, which they had always believed to be a political party and yet essentially a socio-economic pressure group designed to serve the interests of the Gold Coast intelligentsia.

Then, we not only seen immediate emergence of Nkrumah's new political party, the Convention People's Party (CPP), followed by Nkrumah's immediate resignation from the UGCC and his subsequent victory with the CPP over the UGCC during the General Election, even while Nkrumah himself was still in jail. Nkrumah is then recalled from jail by Charles Arden Clarke, then the Governor of the Gold Coast, to form a new government, with Nkrumah as the government's new Prime Minister—the first African politician to liberate his people from the foreign rule.

The intriguing question that remains to be asked is, what kind of a figure was this Nkrumah that could manage to do what other AFricans before and during his time had not been able to do, such as bringing this unusual renaissance to the people of the Gold Coast, Africa, and the world at large?

Succinctly, why and how was Nkrumah able to restore the lost sovereignty to the people of the Gold Coast (now Ghana)—a restoration which also influenced the entire African Continent to fight for each nation's sovereignty against its Colonial Rule?

Unlike most Africans before and during his time (before independence), Nkrumah was a charismatic leader. His charisma permeates his whole life. For instance, while in London **en route** to the United States, he recollects in his Autobiography his perplexion:" I heard an excited newspaper boy shouting (in London) . . . . He grabbed a bundle of the latest editions from a motor van, and on the placard, I read: MUSSOLINI INVADES! **That was all I needed! At that moment, it was almost as if the whole of London had suddenly declared war on me personally. My nationalism surged. I was ready and willing to go through hell itself . . . . in order to achieve my objective**[13]." Further, our Psychiatric data on Nkrumah throughout his life history up to the time he became the first Prime Minsiter of the Gold Coast in 1952, shows that Nkrumah's charismatic leadership was also enhanced by his childhood experience; the fascinating personalities (e.g., Dr. Aggrey, Dubois, Padmore, C.L.R. James, etc) he directly associated with; the fields of study he explored while in London and the United States; his academic qualifications; his overwhelming interest in the functions and processes of political and other organizations; and above all, his personal interest in organizing his own political groups.

However, it was not until Nkrumah reached London that his political radicalism became a reality. We note that while in London, he associated with those notable international Black intellectuals such as Dr. Du Bois and Padmore, who, because of their involvement in Pan-African movements, therefore, ignited and fanned Nkrumah's active participation in politics. They influenced Nkrumah because they themselves were also strongly against colonialism and other forms of oppression by one people over another. It was due to his interaction with them in London and Manchester that Nkrumah realized the time was now ripe for him to put his charismatic leadership into practice against colonialism; and, it was due to such interaction that he became so active that on his return to the Gold Coast, he could not stand the UGCC's lukewarm stand against Colonialsim.

Unlike the less charismatic and less revolutionary experienced UGCC members, such as Danquah, Nkrumah was fully armed with both charismatic leadership and revolutionary experience. This is why, unlike Danquah's UGCC party policy which called for "self-government within the shortest **possible** time," Otherwise, such significant variance in party policy-strategy could not have occurred by chance alone; his disagreement with the rank and file of the UGCC over the party policy **vis-à-vis** colonialism in the Gold Coast was not the only product of his past political experiences. Other empirical results of his past experiences include his introduction of Mahatma Gandhi's principle of "non-violent positive action" in the Gold Coast against the oppressive British colonial rule: his ceaseless attempts to create a "United States of Africa"; **inter alios**. In view of these empirical evidences in the cause of the development and style of Nkrumah's leadership in political life, it is self-evident that **one's political attitude and behaviour must be directly proportional to one's past political experiences**.

Therefore, in order to comprehend why Nkrumah's policy towards the West, especially the United States and the colonial powers, was very vehement and authoritative, we must not ignore the importance of his past experiences. For instance, because of his frame of reference, Nkrumah became critical of the American society on the grounds that, regardless fo their religious beliefs and Lockeanism, the American society still suffers from Marxism. Thus, so long as class and colour struggle are still encouraged in the United States, and so long a the latter still continued to collaborate with the Colonial Powers in political blocs such as the North Atlantic Treaty Organization (NATO) and more so in overseas commerce, particularly in the colonized countries, while the latter continue to be suppressed and maltreated by the respective Colonial Powers, as in the case fo apartheid in South Africa which was too undemocratic that even other whites inside and outside South Africa could no long tolerate its policy and conduct. Nkrumah was left with no other alternative but to begin right away mobilizing his African followers against what he perceived to be the common enemy, i.e. Undemocratic Colonial Leadership in the then Gold Coast and in the entire Continent of Africa.

The same attitude also held true in a host of other African intellectuals who proliferated all over Africa as a result of the following social changes in Africa:-

(1) The replacement of illiteracy with literacy, Gemeinschaft with Gesselschaft, agrarian with industrialization; Kaund ruralization with urbanization; pede-mobility with auto-mobility; subsistence economy with complex commercial economy; mouth-to-mouth communication with a complex mass media; inter alia; and
(2) The replacement of the "Warrant Chiefs" by new political leaders, such as Jomo Kenyatta (Kenya), Julius Nyerere (Tanzania), Chief Albert Luthuli (South Africa), Marehemu Patrice Lumumba (Congo-Kinshasa), Joshua Nkomo, Robert Ouko and N. Sithole (Rhodesia and thereafter, Zimbabwe), harry Nkkumbulaa and Kenneth Kaunda(Zambia), J. Chiwanuka and Milton Obote (Uganda), Nmandi Azikiwe and

Abbakka Tafewa (Nigeria) and Sekou Toure (Guinea), Nelson Mandela (South Africa) among others.

(3) Like Nkrumah, these African nationalists have always used their past experiences in their political dealings with the colonial powers. A flashback in the wake of their life histories also strikes us with intriguing policial strategies with which these political figures fought against Colonialisms in their Mother Country/land in spite of the tortures which they had to encounter in their struggles for Africa 'Huru' (an independent Africa). Some of them were thrown in jail for years; some were restricted to their homes without any visitation, privileges or mail circulation.

However, the common denominator in their individual political activities **vis-à-vis Colonialism is the struggle for and the belief in a restoration of a total African sovereignty and dignity, in World Affairs from the Colonial Rule**. It is this common goal which now permeates the foreign policy of every self-ruling African nation today. But as to why it was not possible for other African intellectuals prior to the above-named persons (hereafter referred to as "Pre-Nkrumah" and "Nkrumah" groups, respectively) to fight for independence in Africa, is one of the crucial questions to be examined in the following paragraph.

As we have noted from the previous paragraphs, Political Socialization through education plus other past experiences contribute a great deal in shaping the political philosophies of the contemporary political leaders. Thus, while **all three portraits were of intellectuals, they had also met several political thinkers and practitioners either diretly or indirectly; and they belonged to a number of organizations; and they had a reasonable amount of apprenticeships**. Secondly, when we examine their activities in terms of what they did prior to becoming active radicals against colonial rule, we also note each portrait with a number of accomplishments. And when we clinically diagnose these accomplishments, we find them significantly political. For instance, Kenyatta's book, **Facing Mount Kenya**[14] is basically a political reaction against the Colonial damage done to the Gikuyu culture.

Turning back to our Psychiatric data on Nkrumah, we also note that due to his negative experience with the British Colonial Rule in the Gold Coast, Nkrumah believed that "he who restricts the freedom of others can never be free himself.! Thus, Nkrumah's concerns were to question the white man's myth of superiority and the right to govern the rest of Mankind. Towards the white Americans, he argued that they would neither be free nor righteous until they recognize The Human and Civil Rights of the Black Americans; and, towards the European Colonial Powers, he also argued that they similarly never be free until they fully recognize the Human Rights of the Colonial Peoples, whose lives, land, and other property were at stake. Although Nyerere and Kenyatta has, in the early 1960s, shown a somewhat similar political attitude in their interaction with the West, the two came to differ in their attitude. Nyerere over whelmingly shifted toward the East, especially the People's Republic of China; while Kenyatta tried to drift to the West. To understand this phenomenon, it is necessary that we first examine their past political experiences.

Although both Kenyatta's and Nyerere's past experiences are not as rich as Nkrumah's, our Psychiatric Approach shows that **both Kenyatta and Nyerere were first educated at home and then in Europe**. It also tells us that **both played vital roles in bringing about the Independence of their respective countries.** But, they did not major in the same fields of study. Whereas Kenyatta was, by and large, interested in Anthropology, Nyerere was interested in a host of fields, **viz:** British History, English, Moral Philosophy, Political Economy, Special Anthropology, Constitutional Law and Economic History.

In spite of the fact that we have no definite proof as far as whose political philosophy he was strongly interested in while at Edinburgh, Nyerere's Political Philosophy and Behaviour are semiotically piece and parcel for our Laboratory. Based on these two variable, we find that Nyerere's political attitude was more inclined toward the East than it is to the West. For example, in 1965, when Ian Smith unilaterally declared Zimbabwe independent under the Rhodesian minority white rule, it was only Nyerere out of all East African national leaders that vehemently threatened Britain that Tanzania was ready to pull out from the British Commonwealth of Nations unless Britain took an immediate step to bring down this illegitimate regime in Zimbabwe. Since then, Nyerere never ever excused Britain for the latter's failure to act prudently in accordance with the majority interest of the African people in Zimbabwe. The more he developed this strong negative attitude towards Britain, the more he also attempted to project the same feelings towards other Western powers, especially the NATO powers. This phenomenon was inevitable simply because whatever affects one or two members of any one given defense bloc is apt to affect some or all members of that bloc.

This reality is empirically supported by the then existing relationships between NATO and the Warsaw pact; e.g., any member state of any one of these blocs was **ipso facto** an enemy of the other bloc. Similarly, so long as Nyerere envisioned the United States as one of the members and a principal figure of NATO, and as long as the United States continued to support Britain in the United Nations on issues which according to Nyerere strongly affected the vital interests of the African nations. Nyerere was psychologically forced to maintain the same negative political attitude of mistrust towards the United States, along with all other NATO member states.

It could, however, be wondered as to why, unlike Kenyatta, Nyerere should politically behave in the way(s) he did towards the West and yet throughout his training, he spent most of his time in West institutions.

From our Psychiatric data on him, we find that he was first trained at the Roman Catholic Boarding School at Musoma, Tanganyika (now Tanzania), then Makerere University College in Kampala, Uganda, from whence he obtained a diploma in Education. Thereafter, we see him in Britain at the University of Edinburgh, where he read a multitude of subjects, such as British History, English, Political Economy, Moral Philosophy **inter alios**. After this, he returned to Tanganyika to resume his teaching job.

But no sooner had he taught for a year than he decided to quit teaching and enter politics. Again, the data shows that before he went to Edinburgh, he rebelled against the British Colonial demand that he must teach at the Tabora Government School. On returning from Edinburgh, he again rebelled and absolutely refused to accept the post of District Officer which the Governor had planned to offer him so as to restrain him from political activities against the British Regime in Tanganyika. Like our Psychiatric data on Nkrumah, our Psychiatric data on Nyerere failed to show that Nyerere had ever been in the East European countries before Tanganyika attained her independence in 1961 to have thus influenced him into the Socialism philosophy he came to adapt on becoming President of Tanzania.

Another significant similarity between Nkrumah's political development and that of Nyerere is their fields of study. Like Nkrumah, Nyerere followed some courses in Philosophy and Political Economy. However, unlike Nkrumah, Nyerere did not get quite so involved with the Philosophy. This is why the two leaders' political philosophy and roles on the African Unity question and other questions were not significantly similar, e.g. on the "Biafra" issue, and the issue as to whether or not Africa should adapt a unified model that of the USA and become a United States of Africa.

But, on the other questions such as the question of the restoration of Africa's UHuru, the two figures are obviously significantly similar. Like Nkrumah's stand against Colonialism and Imperialism (as also evidenced in Nkrumah's radical action against Belgium in thE Congo Crisis of (1960), Nyerere's stand was permanently against Colonialsm and Imperialism. This is empirically proven in his radical action against Portugal in Mozambique, Guinea BIssau and Angola before those three countries restored their sovereignity in 1975 and 1976 respectively. His Nkrumah-like radicalism is also shown in his support of the African Liberation Forces against the Ian Smith regime.

All this similarity in their political revolutionary Behaviour against Colonialism and Imperialism in Africa after both Nkrumah and Nyerere had returned to their respective countries suggests **that the fields of study Nkrumah and Nyerere took while overseas travel, sui generic, their own ability to synthesize reality, etc, collectively enhanced Nkrumah and Nyerere in their later crusade against Colonialism**. Nyerere's and Nkrumah's decisions to enter politics right after their return from overseas studies while they had respectable educational qualifications with which to get equally respectable and highly paid jobs also suggest that their overseas, oppressive Colonial Rule in their countries that had no respect or any other positive regard for Democracy, Human Rights and all other values that are universally deemed sacred and, therefore sacrosanct for the Dignity and Survival of every person, people, community, society or country.

Like Nkrumah, Nyerere believed in Socialism as the only **rational choice** for a rapid socio-economic development[15]. Like Rousseeau, Marx, Engels, Lenin, Mao, Ho Chi Minh, Castro Cabral, Machel, Neto and other socialists, both Nkrumah and Nyerere believed Capitalilsm the fundamental source/cause of socio-economic inequality and exploitation of one man by another. It is this belief which consequently formed the basis of and guided Tanzania **Ujamaa** policy since independence in 1961 in and outside Tanzania; and it is the same idea that Nkrumah had also wanted to impelement before he was overthrown in 1966—which together with the Congo coup of 1960 immediately after Independence laid a foundation of Undemocratic means of Leadership Succession.

It is, of course, evident that Nyerere's political interpretation of African Socialism was basically African **sui generis**; however, as Leopold Sedar Senghor noted, African Socialism was reinforced by the East European Socialism. The present African socialism is a combination of both traditional African socialism and the contemporary East European Socialism. The latter was co-opeted into the former simply because of its unique qualities of Technology that African desperately needed for her socio-economic growth.

But as to why Nyerere's political attitude would differ from that of Kenyatta when both of them were more extensively trained in a European social setting than Nkrumah require another thorough study.

Kenyatta showed a very unique and moderate political attitude towards the West as compared with most African political leaders, such as Nkrumah, Nyerere, Odinga, Lumumba, etc., and yet he was, surprisingly enough, one of those who were bitterly punished by the colonial rule. Unlike Nyerere and Nkrumah, Kenyatta was imprisoned for almost nine years (Nyerere nine months, and Nkrumah three years) with all his residence and other property either destroyed or confiscated until after his release in 1963. It was not until he became a strong prospective Prime Minister of Kenya that he got the property back and also received some compensation for those which had been completely destroyed. However, unlike his contemporaries, Nkrumah and Nyerere, Kenyatta's political maturation through Political Socialization while still overseas was significantly de-revolutionized (i.e., tempered) by the prevailing forces in England, where he lived most of his time in Europe. For example, from our psychiatric data on his political development, we note five main heuristic factors, viz:

(3) While in Britain, he married an English woman;
(4) During his wedding, he was cordially welcomed to an Anglican Church there (in Britain) for matrimonial services and was treated as an equal, a phenomenon which could not have been tolerated by the British White settlers had the service been held in Kenya;
(5) While still in Britain, he discovered that not all English people were in favour of colonies, and that most of them were very sympathetic to the colonial peoples' plight;
(6) On his return to Kenya, he discovered that because of his white wife, most whites in Kenya did not like him at all, since to them, interracial marriage was between Black and White regarded as a direct humiliation and insult to the white race; and,
(7) On becoming President of Kenya, Kenyatta became a victim of a centripetal force between two schools of thought under Oginga Odinga (Eastern-minded) and Tom Mboya (Western-minded) respectively.

Kenyatta's first four experiences (above) suggest why he came to appreciate and to be fond of the English regardless of the white settlers' parochial attitude in Kenya. On the other hand, the fifth suggests that as soon as Kenyatta's Vice President, Oginga Odinga, resigned from Kenyatta's Government, Kenyatta's political attitude was so affected that he (Kenyatta) had to begin to re-evaluate his political position. But, Odinga resigned because of Kenyatta's significant inclination toward Mboya's rhetoric ideals and the Western influence on Mboya, especially from the United States. And it was on the basis of this schism between Kenyatta and Odinga that the latter began to organize his own political party. The Kenya People'sUnion (KPU) in opposition to Kenyatta's single party regime under Kenya African National Union (KANU) which could not tolerate any opposition or movement toward Democratic Institutionalization in Kenya.

But, to deter Odinga's movement, Kenyatta first scrutinized Odinga's strength. Having realized that it was the Communist countries on which Odinga's economic power depended, Kenyatta was, therefore, left with no other partner except the West. Consequently, through his political rhetoric aids, particularly Mboya, Kenyatta has, since his clash with Odinga, always been identified with the West more than he has with the East.

Furthermore, it should also be noted that, because of the long-lived relationships between Odinga and Russians, dating as far back as the last half of the 1950's, when Odinga was Vice President of KANU against the British Colonial Regime in Kenya, it is only the West that Kenyatta trusted as his potential asylum—the base from which he continually drew all reinforcements against his adversaries in and outside Kenya. And in order to maintain his Presidency in Kenya, he saw deterrence of Odingaism and his other rival powers as the only solution.

This is precisely why, in November of 1969, Kenyatta ordered Odinga's house arrest of eighteen months, even without trial. Besides, before this incident, Odinga and all other KPU members had been deliberately disqualified from the 1969 General Elections—a political strategy designed to contain Odingaism. The same Kenyatta strategy of elimination was applied to Mboya, Ngala, Argwings-Kodhek, J. M. Kariuki, Martin Shikuku, and other key actors in Kenyan politics whom Kenyatta believed to be potential threats to his presidency.[17]

Therefore, inorder to accurately understand the contradictions or paradoxes in Kenyatta's political activism, attitude change, and his foreign policy in post-independence Kenya, the above psychiatric data on his is essentially important. Otherwise, it would definitely have been difficult to answer any question or **to systematically explain and predict why Kenyatta's policy in and outside Kenya was significantly different from those of Nyerere and the late Nkrumah, in spite of their similarities of overseas travel and their common experiences of oppressive Colonial Rule** which was too naked of Democracy and other moral values which are sacred to every civilized person, society, etc.

Because of this change of political attitude in Kenyatta, it is also possible to predict that Nyerere's policy would likely also remain constantly cautious against the West until/unless:

(1) Britain nullified her asylum towards Kambona:
(2) Britain toppled the Smith UDI (unilateral Declaration of Independence);
(3) The United States restrained her support to Britain in and outside the United Nations in matters which directly affected African lives: and most importantly.
(4) Until all the NATO members refrained from direct collaboration with the then Southern African and "Rhodesian" minority white regimes in foreign trade, investment, recreation and other enterprises.

Also, it was likely that Nyerere could similarly alter his attitude towards the East, especially the People's Republic of China, unless the latter's political behaviour in Tanzania remained absolutely constant. That is to say, if at all it was known to Nyerere that the Chinese, who have built the Tanzo Zambian Railway for him and President Kenneth Kaunda of Zambia, were also engaged in some "leukemia diplomacy" (a visible fatal threat against Tanzania) then Nyerere would have definitely been left with no other choice but to vehemently, break off relations with them (the Chinese).

### B-3 Importance of the Nkrumah Group vis-à-vis Colonialism on the World Market:

One of the fundamental questions reaised in Section B2 above, was: "Why it was not until the Nkrumah Group initiated the struggle against European Colonialism and Imperialism after the 1930's that Africa Huru (i.e. Freedom) became a reality; and Why the Pre-Nkrumah Group could not do it?

To answer this and similar questions accurately and systematically, our Psychiatric Approach and Histology are again essential.

Prior to the post-1930's, there was only a meagrer number of Africans on the World Market with a higher level of Political Socialization through education and complex world experiences as compared to a large number of such Africans in the post-1930's. Before the 1930's most of them could be found only in the Gold Coast and Nigeria (especially Accra and Lagos cities) while only a very handful or minute number of them could be found in East Africa, Central Africa, etc. This variance was due to two significantly different political philosophies employed, e.g., by the British Colonial Rule in those regions.

In his Nationalism in Colonial Africa,[18] for example, Thomas Hodgkin erroneously contends that Britain used "Benthamism" in her West African colonies, and "Burkeanism" in her East African colonies for self-government, while under Burkeanism, Britain sought to conserve East African for an indefinite Colonization and Imperialism.

Our finding on the British Colonial Policy shows that Benthamism was not used at all. In East African, Britain used Lionism (a Machiavellian or dictatorial policy) because of the physio-climatic conditions highly conducive to the white man's existence; but unlike in East Africa, in West Africa, Britain used Foxism (a Machiavellian cooptation policy) partially because she considered West Africa a "white man's grave" due to great heat, malaria and sleeping sickness detrimental to the Whites and other non-Tropical residents, and partially because of the presence of a very strong African political leadership there. Either way, both universal and high education were strictly controlled because every Colonial Regime, especially those of Belgium, Portugal, Spain and Britain did not want to see many Africans highly educated as this would enable them to know the sins of their Undemocractic Colonial Leadership. Influenced by Machiavellianism, which taught the Colonial how to successfully acquire and keep colonies under control by keeping them ignorant through daily different tricks, all Colonial Regimes were very cautious of any Africans becoming too highly educated. Even in West Africa British Colonies, not many Africans were totally free. In fact, in his study of the causes of Pan-Africanism West Africa, George Padmore notes that up to 1930, in British West Africa, which was the most highly educated region of all colonial Africa, not every educated African person could easily get employment.[19] Also, he notes that it was due to this job discrimination against qualified Africans in West Africa that many of the West African intelligentsia began to get involved in the Pan-African movement. They joined the movement in order to use it as the bargaining vehicle with the Colonial Regime against the job colour bar. They felt it necessary to do so because: (1) none of them could be offered jobs equivalent to their professional qualifications; (2) their grievances against such discrimination could not be accommodated, aggregated or tolerated by the Colonial Rule (3) their less educated white counterparts would easily be offered supervisory jobs over highly educated Africans; and (4) even those of the African intelligentsia who were fortunate enough to be offered reasonable jobs, their wages were always lower than those of white employees holding inferior positions.

Based on my own experience in the British Colonial Rule's philosophy and practice in East Africa, all administrative and other well-paid jobs were confined to the whites, **but not because of their merits**. It was a common practice to find high school African graduates under the supervision of a primary school graduate or a dropout white officer with a salary more than 300% large than his academically superior African counterpart. Also, it was a common practice in East Africa to have a white high school drop-out receiving salary amounting to 400% or more higher than that of every African employee with a Univeristy degree (especially the Bachelor's degree, which was the highest degree any African could possibly be allowed to achieve in the Colonial Era). It was with this job discrimination against the African intelligentsia that the pre-1930's African interest articulations were obviously concerned—all over the Continent but not only West Africa.

In his Pan-Africanism or Communism.[20] Padmore further notes that in the Fifth Pan-African Congress, which was held in New York City in 1927, job discrimination in Africa was one of the major isues on the World Market which the delegation was greatly concerned with. At the Conclusion of Congress, the complaint against job discrimination in Africa became one of the vehement appeals in the Delegation's Resolution to the Colonial Powers. The appeal proclaimed, **inter alia**. That while it was necessary to yield to the Africans their legitimate right of expression to the Colonial Governments directing their affairs, it was also equally necessary for those Governments to recognize that qualified Africans should be treated equitably; and (2) that based on their professional qualifications, Africans should be appointed to reasonable positions related and congruent to their merits. The Resolutions, for instance, specified that African students of Jurisprudence should be appointed judges without any discrimination.

While African job discrimination was one of the critical situations of the time prior to the post-1930's, the African literacy rate discrimination was another factor of major concern. In fact, the latter became one of the major grievances that the New York Conference of 1927 embodied in its Resolution to Colonial Powers, calling upon those Powers to extend both primary and technical educational facilities also to the African children.

**Hence, the more Africans became educated in number in the post-1920's the more a great number of them realized what their elders in the pre-1930's had failed to understand**. Through higher education, many of them came to understand different political concepts. They came to understand how important it is for a people to determine their own destiny rather than being told what to do by foreigners. They came to understand how important the Principle of Human Rights and Civil Liberty was to Europeans and many other peoples. Consequently, they came to realize how necessary it was to mobilize their people against a common enemy in search of their sovereign equality and dignity. The quest for "Self-Rule!" soon became the dominant slogan across the Continent. As a result, political parties began to mushroom throughout Africa. Otherwise such political phenomenon could not have come about by accident such of the evils of the Undemocratic nature of the Colonial Leadership that was naked of this virtuous moral values sacred to every human being world-wide and at all times.

In the final analysis, the main reason why Africa did not claim its self-rule until after the 1920's was precisely because of a lack of sufficient education and Political Socialization in the pre-1930's. That is to say, it was not until after the 1930's that most Africans became well exposed to the Western political philosophy and culture. Some of them came to acquire this Political Socialization knowledge through educational institutions; others through the two World Wars. As a result, it was these two groups (the post-1930's African intelligentsia and the World Wars African veterans), which collectively became very instrumental in implementing revolts against Colonialism.

While the intelligentsia group became very instrumental in forming political organizations, planning political strategies and mobilizing the peasantly, the World Wars African veterans became very instrumental in forming military organizations, planning military strategies, and recruiting the peasantry into military combats against the Colonial Regimes. For instance, Generals Dedan Kimathi, "Cairo," and "China" in Kenya played a very vital role in the MAU MAU war against the British Colonial Rule in Kenya. Prior to that time, (in the pre-1930's), there had not been many Africans with such courageously aggressive personality attributes to initiate any challenging political or military force against Colonial Regimes in Africa although the pre-1930's Africans had potential political ideas, but since they were limited in the opportunity to exploit and develop these ideas through educational institutions and direct contacts with the Outside World and in the Colonial Rules' home-countries as the post-1930's Africans (hereafter identified as the pre-Nkrumah group) did not obviously have sufficient skills with which to effectively fight against the Colonial Rule to accept Democracy Institutionalization in Africa. As a result, it was not until the Nkrumah Group deployed their acquired skills from Political Socialization process that the mission against the colonial powers became possible, inevitable and real.

The Nkrumah Group's superior (effective) political skills and organizational ability over the Pre-Nkrumah Group's political skills and organizational ability are empirically evidenced by its devastating over and covert revolutionary acts and the political party formation phenomenon which began immediately after the 1930's against Colonialism arising from their unique type and content of Political Socializaton. It is empirically true that the first African political party to be experienced on the Continent of Africa was organized in 1897 by the Gold Coast intelligentsia; however, this was not a political party in the strict sense of the word. Rather, it was only a loose association of some learned Africans in the Gold Coast, whose main purpose was basically socio-economic (i.e., to maximize their personal socio-economic needs). More specifically, its members' main purpose was to organize a collective-bargaining instrument with which to effectively articulate their job-discrimination grievances to the British Colonial Rule in the Gold Coast. From then on, there is hardly any tangible political grouping until the post-1930's, when we note a significant proliferation of many African political parties all over the Continent.

The most intriguing attributes about this new and unique phenomenon of Africa political parties on the World Market are that each of them was organized by a group of African intellectuals; and that, whereas the pre-1930's African political organizations were, by and large, simply socio-economic political associations, the post-1930's African political organizations were strictly speaking political parties with well-defined rules of the game, political goals, strategies, and a motto (i.e. ideology). For instance, while the former were mainly concerned with job attainment above political needs, the latter were chiefly concerned with a struggle for political power and the restoration of African Sovereignty.

A further inquiry into the causes of the difference between the Nkrumah Group on the World Market also supports our findings above. For instance a diagnosis of the 18$^{th}$ and 19$^{th}$ Century Europe shows emergence of Capitalism; theories of individualism, laissez-faire and survival of the fittest; and the emergence of Industrial Revolution which, in turn, bred multiplicity of desires for the fruits of Industrialism in and outside Europe e.g., the North American Colonies. From World History, we note the quest by European nations, especially France,

Germany, Britain, Holland, Portugal and Belgium, to satisfy these desires. Also, we note the quest for colonies first in Europe by Napoleon, and then Africa by France and Germany, later followed by other colonial powers such as Britain—all virtually competing for a balance of power in Europe, but, by and large actuality struggling for economic power in Africa and anywhere else they could possibly find it.

Because of this econo-political anxiety among the colonial powers, the African pre 1930's political groupings also focused its goals on economic values such as job acquisition and land restoration short of any political interest for Self-Rule of Democracy Instituionalization goal.

Unlike that group, the post-1930's African political group focused its goals on political values, such as Self-Rule. This metamorphosis in goals perception between the two groups or generations is also shown by more radical reactions against the Colonial rule by Africans of the post 1930's era. For instance, Nyerere stubbornly refused to accept the position of District Officer, yet it was the highest and rarest post in the Colonial Administration to be given to an African. In spirt of its prestige, Nyerere turned it down and joined politics, to fight against the colonial Authority! This phenomenon would definitely not have happened in the pre-1930's World Market era.

Unlike in the post-1930's World Market era, in the pre-1930's World Market era, the well-being of the economy was the major goal. Whereas the Gold Coast Aborigines' Rights Protection Society was mainly concerned with better employment opportunieis for the Gold Coast intelligentsia, other parties, e.g., the Young Gikuyu Association, were concerned largely with the restoration of the Gikuyu Land from the British white settlers, who had usurped the land from the Gikuyu people in Kenya.

Further, while the pre-1930's African interest articulations were not political, their politics were only latent. Their politics increased their thermal heat after they had metamorphosed into the post-1930's political stage. It became a reality as a result of a high increase in the literacy rate all over Africa. Also, this phenomenon was invevitable because of the experiences and appraisals gained from the Second World War by the African war veterans. Apart from the increasing rate of literacy and national consciousness in Africa against Colonialism, after World War II, Colonial Powers were confronted with the problems of socio-economic Reconstruction at home to such an extent, that they hardly had time for Colonial problems. The more they shifted their attention from Africa to Europe, the more the Africans (especially those who had already discovered the meaning of the principle of self-determination through their schooling) filled the political vacuum.

It is plausible that this turnover could have also been possible had the war occurred in the 1920s. However, most African educated persons of the time had been so indoctrinated by the Colonial Powers on the World market that it is indeed hard to believe that this would have been inevitable. This argument is supported by the names Africans acquired and embraced in the pre-1930's political era in Africa. For instance, in the Gold Coast, we find that at least every intellectual had to adopt and be known by a Colonial name if he/she wanted to succeed in the Colonial System. Consequently, the Gold Coast intelligentsia carried Colonial names such as: Dr. Joseph W. de Graft-Johnson, Dr. James Mensah Satbah, to name but a few. In French, Portugese and Belgian Colonies, any African who wanted to succeed in those Colonial Systems was expected to transmute himself into an European, though the black skin was to be left intact. In some cases, the Colonial Power created certain bleaching chemicals for black skin, e.g. Bu-Tone, which Africans especially women in and outside South Africa, are still expected to use in order to become human beings. Failure to adopt Europeans names and to bleach one's black skin was a disgrace to oneself, and a hindrance to success in the Colonial System. While the African naminology role was charged to the Churches and Missionaries, the African skin bleaching chemistry duty was assigned to the Colonial pharmacies and beauty shops, throughout Africa. In Churches and Missions, Africans were deliberately cheated and tricked into adopting Colonial names. They were coerced not to question the authority as if they were simple creatures without their own traditional names[21]. Also, through the Colonial chemistry, white pigmentation was expected of all Africans.

Through such classical conditioning, most Africans were irrationally led to believe through Political Socialization that the only way to paradise was to substute their traditional sense of self with strange "selves." But, the more Africans were conditioned in this way, the more Colonialists kept themselves busy filling their granaries with African wealth at the expense of the fooled!

However, as already noted above, it was not until after the 1930's that there appeared some significant changes in Colonial Africa on the World Market. Because of the increase in African literacy, many Africans began to realize the fallacy and, therefore, the illegitimacy of the Colonial Rule which was confirmed as being naked of any Democratic values that were sacred and sacrosanct for the Dignity and Prosperity of an African. Some educated African groups began to do away with their own Colonial names and other values. For instance: Kwame Nkrumah dispensed with "Francis," Jomo Kenyatta dispensed with "Jonhson," Oginda Odinga did away with "Adonijah;" interalios of course including this author later in 1969 who had to do away with "Dixon Edward" in order to be also free!

Therefore, as soon as the administrative vacuum occurred in African political life as a result of the exhaustingly bitter experiences of World War II, these ambitious individuals began to react without haste in order to fill the vacuum. In view of these facts, it was not until Africa had gained a sizeable number of educataed people in the post-1930's Colonial Era that she politically became fully aware of herself. The post-1930's Africa came to realize that because she was, by nature, equal to other nations in the Grotian and Verttelian terms, it was essential for her to fight for her own Self-Rule, and Sovereign Equality and Dignity.

To this end, a social transition from illiteracy; from a subsistence economy to a market economy; from mouth to mouth to a technological communication media; from foot—mobility to auto-mobility; and so on, among other symptoms of social change, Consciousness. It was the development of this national consciousness through "Political Socialization" in the post-1930's that Africa got the genuinely political goals ofthe post-1930's. Africa group sought to achieve that the pre-1930's group was unable to conceptualize and do which distinguishes the two groups in the development of African Nationalism as a rational means toward democracy Institutionlization in Kenya and all over the African Continent—a task that had evaded recognition of both the colonial Leaders and the Pre-Nkrumah Group respectively.

But the fact that pre-Nkruma Group did not have education opportunity, a situation which, therefore, made them unable to restore Africa's sovereignity and dignity from the Colonial powers on the world Market before the Nkrumah Group (the post 1930's group) does not necessarily rule out their Africanism vis-à-vis colonialism. Also, it does not mean that the pre-1930's Africans were feeble-minded. Every record on Africa's reaction to Colonialism in the 19th century confirms that every African king, chief and common person in the village retaliated against Colonialism. They defended their land and peoples from becoming a prey to Colonialism and imperialism. This reality is indisputable. Due to the lack of comprehension of the Colonial languages and motives behind the Colonial treaty proposals pressed on them, every African traditional leader found himself, his dominion and his people victims of his own ignorance and the deceitful Colonial hunter. Had the Africa of the pre-1930's been as educated as the Africa of the post-1930's, it is evident that no African chief or king would have even allowed the Colonial hunters and fishermen to step on his soil without subjecting the motives of the stranger to a thorough scrutiny. In addition to the African literacy problem in the pre-1930's, returned of Africans, e.g., the Creoles in Sierra Leone, were another factor contributing to African defeat. In Sierras Leone, Creoles sided with the British against the native Africans.

A third factor causing African defeat was the lack of sophisticated logistics among Africans against the well-prepared colonial hunters. Thus, every African country was willy nilly vulnerable to the hunter because Africa relied on spears which could not match the superior guns of the enemy. Such were, inter alia, some of the prime reasons why the pre-1930's Nkrumah Group came to defeat. In fact, the Tanganyika case study which shows radical retaliations by African chiefs also shows that African leaders always became victims of their own grievances whenever they tried to petition the colonial rule to stop maltreatment of their African peoples. Therefore, while the Pre-Nkrumah Group lacked: adequate literacy and theory of the political world around them; sophisticated logistics and war material equivalent to those of its colonial enemy; an extenuating and exhausting world situation such as World War II; and anti-Colonial sentiment World Body such as the U.N. today; and an informed and anti-Colonial sentiment in the Colonial mother-coutnry as also noted about England, the Nkrumah Group of the post-1930's Colonial Era enjoyed and benefited from the presence of all these things.

Thus, the Nkrumah Group was able to become effectively articulate, not only because it was more literate and informed than the pre-Nkrumah Group, but also because the time had come for the Colonial defeat. It came up at the time when the Colonial situation had already significantly changed against the Colonial Powers, e.g., by the two World Wars which had made Germany drop out of the colonial race, leaving Britain and France (the only surviving major Colonial Powers) extremely exhausted economically because of Germany's selfish and gluttonous ambition for more colonies in Africa and Europe after 1900. After World War 1, its effects and the establishment of the League of Nations in 1919, based on Woodrow Wilson's Fourteen Points, containing, inter alia, the Mandate System, and the Principles of Self-Determination and Human Rights of the Non-Self-Governing Peoples, the surviving Colonial Powers had to modify their Colonial policies toward their Colonial peoples—a new wave/wind of change towards a possible Democracy Institutionalization in Kenya and the Total Africa.

This situation was further reinforced by the World War II experiences and the establishment of the United Nations and the Trusteeship to enforce the UN Charter and tasks which had been left pending by the League.

Consequently, when the Nkrumah Group came upon the political scene to fight Colonialism after World War II, Colonial time was quickly running out. The colonial powers were already standing on their toes, busy pondering at the exits because of the prevailing rought political tornado and earthquake that stood at the door starring against them in favour of the Nationalists. Unlike its counterpart, the Nkrumah Group exploited the existing World situation. Although the colonialist was still touchy, the Nkrumah Group was able to set up political parties to fight against Colonialism. With more learned and experienced Liberation Fighters, the Nkrumah Group parties employed powerful political strategies, gained from World Political Theories, e.g. Gandhi, Christian and Fabian Marxists, Marx and Engels, Lenin and Mao, to use against Colonial restrictions on African party activities. For example, Nkrumah's Gandhian style or strategy of Non-Violence in the Gold Coast became one of the most instrumental ways and means of getting by in the midst of his hostile enemy (the British colonial regime) in the Gold Coast.

The relationship between the World Political theorists' ideas and Nkrumah Group's politics in World Affairs today is also reflected in their principles and policies of Socialism, Non-Alignment, Pan-Africanism, Humanism, Sovereign Equality, etc. against the Colonial powers.

(1) In sum may in view of these, viz: emergence of these African retaliations and political groupings (parties) against the Colonial rule in Africa; and proliferation of nation-states in Africa between 1956 and 1968. **then our hypotheses on the impact of political socialization in Africa are supported.**

But, although some "scholars" have argued that it was "the white man's burden to come to Africa to civilize the heathens," the validity of this assertion is now open to question. Furthermore, given these burden(s) which Africans encountered from the Colonial Rule, the Africans' retaliations against this Rule and the emergence of contemporary African Nation-States, it is also questionable whether Colonialism was planted in Africa as a result of inter-European quarrels or because of the white man's burden! But, given that it were a "white man's burden to civilize the heathens," why, then, did African nationalism emerge against Colonialism? Secondly, if it were not the nature and goal of Colonialism which instigated

African nationalism and the proliferation of the contemporary African Nation-State what other valid factors might have encouraged the rise of African nationalism?

From both content Analysis and a Longitudinal Approach of African nationalism above, our psychiatric findings support the assertion that it was strictly the cruelty of the Colonial Rule in total, characterized by, e.g., African land usurpation, forced labour inflicted upon Africans arbitrary taxation of Africans, coercive replacement of traditional African rulers with "warrant chiefs," repressive imprisonment of some African traditional rulers and politicians, deliberate mutilations of innocent Africans, inter alios, which consequently precipitated African hostilities and African nationalism in total. Had there not been this mode of Bad Governance characterized by: Colonial brutalities and miscalculations vis-à-vis Africans, it is submitted that African retaliations and political parties, among other ramifications of African nationalisms, could not have erupted by chance alone. It is, therefore, possible that Africa could still have been under the Colonial Rule, had the latter's policy not respected the Africans' sacred virtues of self-love and self-respect, in World political life, as the Colonial Rulers had defended and protected their own oppressed women and children against Capitalism and Imperialism at home in the 18th and 19th Century Era of Industrial Revolution and the emergence of Capitalism.

**Test for Hypothesis No. 3:**

**(A) Hypothesis**

The more Africa produced charismatic leadership through Political Socialization, the more she intensified her resistance to the Colonial discriminatory policy which were deemed antithetical to Democratic virtues.

**(B) Findings:**

Above, we have noted that the post-World War II era was an era of both intensive and extensive riots in Africa, e.g.,

(a) the Christianborg riot in the Gold Coast (now Ghana) in 1948
(b) the Mau Mau xeno-phobia in Kenya in the 1950's; and
(c) vehement political speeches by African charismatic leaders;

(i) Nkkumbula (Northern Rhodesia, now Zambia): and
(ii) Nkomo (Southern Rhodesia)

**Test for Hypothesis No. 4:**

**(A) Hypothesis:**

The more Africa produced charismatic leaders through Political Socialization, the more Africa political parties were formed to fight against the undemocratic Colonial Authority.

**(B) Findings:**

The data below shows an interesting fact of the proliferation and metamorphosis of political parties in Africa—from 1880 to 1975. However, much emphasis here will be devoted to the 1941-1975 political parties because of their genuine political implication, i.e., the quest for self-rule (see Table 3 and Test for Hypothesis No. 5 below).

Table 3: Proliferation of African Political Parties Against Colonialism on the World Market As a Symptom of A Resuscitation Plan toward Democracy Institutionalization in Africa.

| | | No. of New Political Parties | Total Political Parties Formed | No. of Ctrs. With New Pol. Parties | % Increase | |
|---|---|---|---|---|---|---|
| | | | | | Parties | Countries |
| (a) | 1880-1885 | 0 | 0 | 0 | 0 | 0 |
| | 1886-1890 | 0 | 0 | 0 | 0 | 0 |
| | 1891-1895 | 0 | 0 | 0 | 0 | 0 |
| | 1896-1900 | 1 | 1 | 1 | 100 | 100 |
| | 1901-1905 | 0 | 1 | 0 | 0 | 0 |
| | 1906-1910 | 0 | 1 | 0 | 0 | 0 |
| | 1911-1915 | 1 | 2 | 1 | 100 | 100 |
| | 1916-1920 | 1 | 3 | 1 | 000 | 000 |
| | 1921-1925 | 2 | 5 | 2 | 200 | 200 |
| | 1926-1930 | 2 | 7 | 3 | 000 | 150 |

| | | | | | | |
|---|---|---|---|---|---|---|
| | 1931-1935 | 4 | 11 | 4 | 50 | 133 |
| | 1936-1940 | 2 | 13 | 2 | 50 | 50 |
| (b) | 1941-1945 | 14) | 27) | 12 | (700 | (600 |
| | 1946-1950 | 30)91% | 57)1177% | 25)1220% | (214 1046 | (208 |
| | 1951-1955 | 40) | 97) | 22 | (133 | (88 |
| | 1956-1960 | 69) | 166) | 33 | 173 | (150 |
| | 1961-1965 | 1 | 167 | 1 | 1 | 3 |
| | 1966-1970 | 1 | 168 | 1 | 100 | 0 |
| | 1971-1975 | 0 | 168 | 0 | | |

a= period of political associations (limited political parties), basically oriented towards **socio-economic goals** and only for few Africans (mostly intellectuals) in Africa

b= period of **Mass** political parties, with specific **political goals** and for the good of the majority of Africans in Africa.

**Source:** Author's work product. Data computed from Appendices all parties Africa-wide.

As also noted in Table 3, there was absolutely no single party in Africa between 1880 and 1895. This, therefore, means that when Africa was colonized as a result of the General Act of the Berlin Conference of March 1885 for the Scramble for Africa in 1885, there was no such thing in Africa as nationalism as we see it today. Surprisingly, between 1896 and 1900, we see only one country with one political party: (the Gold Coast Aborigines' Rights Protection society) organized by Joseph W. de Graft-Johnson et al, in 1897, "in order that they might oppose more effectively the promulgation of legislation that threatened to deprive the inhabitants of the Gold Coast of their land." However, it was not until 1911 and 1920 that the number of political parties steadily increased from 1 to 3.

But with reference to Figs. 1 and 2 below, 14 new political parties emerged in 12 countries between 1941 and 1945; from then on, both numbers began to increase tremendously, e.g., between 1946 and 1950, thus after World War II, 30 new political parties were formed in 25 countries; between 1951 and 1955, 40 new political parties were formed in 22 countries; between 1956 and 1960, 69 new political parties were formed in 33 countries; yet, between 1966 and 1970, only one new political party (the parti de 1' Unite et due Progress National du Burundi, 1961) is seen to have been formed by a Burundian nationalist, Andre Nugu.

Hence, it must be evident that Political Socialization was a major contributing factor to the development of political parties in Contemporary Africa toward Democracy Institutionalization, which is a subject of this Study in this Paper.

**FIG. 1: an Increase in the total Number of Africans Political Parties as a Symptoms of the emergence of African Nationalisms on the World Market (1920-1978):**

**Figure 2: An Increase in the Number of the New African Political Parties as a Symptom of the Emergence of African Nationalisms on the World Market (1921-1978):**

Computed from Table-3 and raw data by this author.

**Test for Hypothesis No. 5**

**(A) Hypothesis:**

The more political parties were formed with the assistance of charismatic leaders, the more goal-orientation was shifted from the socio-economic to the political (i.e., the quest for self-rule) in Africa.

**(B) Findings:**

1. From figs.—1 and 2 and Table—3 above:

(a) 91% of the total new political parties were formed between 1941 and 1960 at the rate of 1177% increase (also see Table—4 below).
(b) 58% of forty-one Africa countries regained independence by 1960.

2. In Table—4 below, it is also noted that while 92% of the total number of new African political parties (167) were formed between 1941 and 1975. 98% of the total number of (41) newly independent countries to date restored their self-rule!

**Table 4: Increse in Total Number of Independence African Countries as a Result of an Increase in African Political Parties on the World Market (1880-1970): As a Symptom of Resuscitation Plan toward Democracy Institutionalization in Africa.**

| Year | Total No. of New Political Parties | % Increase | Total No. of New Ind. Afr. Countries | % Increase |
|---|---|---|---|---|
| 1880-1910 | 1 | 0.6 | 0 | 0.0 |
| 1911-1940 | 12 | 7.2 | 1 | 2.4 |
| 1941-1970 | 154 | 92.2 | 40 | 97.6 |
| Total | 167 | 100.0 | 41 | 100.0 |

**Note:** In Table 4 above, it is supported that the rate of new independent African nationstates is related to the rate of new African political parties formed throughout Africa between 1880 and 1970. Between 1941 and 1970, for example, 92% of the total new African political parties were formed. In the same time bracket, 98% of the total African countries to date restored their self-rule.

6. A Preliminary Concluding Statement:
In view of these statistical evidences above, it must, therefore, have been these political parties through which the might and reality of African nationalism was intensified with a view to facilitating a Resuscitation Plan of Path toward Democracy Institutionalization in Colonial Africa.

But, with the aid of a thorough analysis of the dynamics of International Politics, it is noted that the Principle of Self-Determination, which states:-

(1) that each people has the right to enjoy a government exclusively its own; and
(2) that the only legitimate type of government is National Self-Government, was extensively preached in Europe from the late 19th Century on, especially during World War 1 by Woodrow Wilson, **et. al** Further, it is also noted that unspecified number of Africans (e.g. soldiers during both World War 1 and World War II, and students—Jomo Kenyatta, Julius Nyerere, and Leopold Sedar Senghor) had visited Europe for a period of not less than one year. It is, therefore, most likely that these Africans were exposed to this political philosophy while in Europe. But, the most revolutionary African politicians against Colonialism were foreignly trained intellectuals, e.g. Jomo Kenyatta, Julius Nyerere, Leopold Sedar Senghor, Kwame Nkrumah, **inter alios**.

Therefore, (1) their foreign travel, inter alia, became an additional contributing factor to their ability to organize African political parties by which this Principle of Self-Determination was extensively explained to the peasantry by this intelligentsia. But, Carlton J. H. Hayes also notes that, "since the eighteenth century, the idea that each nationality should cherish its distinctive language and culture and should constitute an independent polity, has been advanced by intellectual and political leaders in one country after another and has been accepted and acted upon by the masses of mankind"[22] and (2) the proliferation and metamorphosis of African political organizations, e.g., from KAU to KANU in Kenya, because of the organizational ingenuity of the post-1940's African nationalists and intellectuals, must also be a valuable indicator of the might and reality of the emergence of African nationalism against undemocratic tendencies of the Colonial Rule and Policies.

CHAPTER III

# Finding on Independent or Post-Colonial Africa

## Finding No. 1 (Africa in General: An Amazing Paradox of the Struggle for Self-Rule) from Dictatorial Colonial Leadership

Throughout the post-Colonial or Independent Africa has suffered terribly at the hand of Dictatorial Leadership akin to that of the Undemocratic Colonial Leadership Consequently; the Continent has never enjoyed any stable Peace and Democracy or Democratization as originally intended during her struggle for Self-Rule from the colonial Regime(s) which she vehemently blamed and accused of Democratic Poverty that lacked all those sacred virtues and values sacrosanct to the Summum Bonum (i.e., the Greatest Good and Happiness) of her African Peoples viz: Human Rights and Freedom.

Over 75% of the total Continent's independent countries have had or experienced at least one or more successful or abortive bloody military or civilian coup d'etat, political assassination, civil war, rigged election leading to unethical or illegal leadership succession, etc—a behaviour which is obviously totally antithetical and incongruent to/with the Continent's original aim! During her efforts to get rid of what she deemed or considered and accused of Undemocratic vices.

Obviously, this is not an end in itself. It is an explicit amazing paradox to the entire Continent and all her Peoples who vividly know or remember this truth that they (and all their already departed loved ones) shed blood for during the hostile Colonial Regime which unfortunately paid no heed or attention to their sacred virtues and values on which they were also paradoxically unable to acquire and believe in during their Political Socialization introduced and promoted by the same Colonial Authority.

But, this is not all. It is just the beginning or the floating top/tip of the Ice Berg mountain.

Let us now come to a micro-case of Kenya pathological case as a paradigm of this amazing paradox in post-Colonial (Independent) African Biopolitics (political life).

## Finding No. 2.(A Case of Kenya: Another Amazing Paradox of The Struggle for Self-Rule from an Intolerable Dictatorial Colonial Leadership)

In a micro-case of Kenya, for example, the problem of democratization in general and Democracy in particular is yet to be re-examined. The problem is so much at its threshold (climax) that it has now forced the Instrument of Government, (The Constitution) which, in all respects, has No Case to answer at all on the problem of Democracy and Democratization, to under go a major surgery (or Reform) as a scapegoat for the real culprit and root-cause of the on-going socio-economic and political agonies in the Country.

But a Constitutional Reform alone without a reform of heart (one's total Culture and Attitude) most especialy in the Kenyan Leadership, is a total waste of time and scarce resources because it is not the existing Constitution which is defective, tainted of dented but the total Culture and Attitude of all Kenyans characterized by rampant institutionalized tribalism and nepotism in devoid (or total disregard) of merit which, in actual sense, urgently need an immediate major surgery to remove this existing trauma (impurity) from it. But of what danger is this trauma to the Kenyan body politique?

This trauma is a dreadful contagious virus to the normal functioning of every body politique. It manifests itself in various symptoms, e.g., massive institutionalized corruption at all levels of government; lack of transparency and accountability; maximum absence of honesty and regard for professional excellence and other index of professional Ethics; leader's disregard of Human Rights and all other sacred virtue sacrosanct to the individual's Greatest Good and Greatest Happiness in life.

And, as will be noted below, because of this trauma, the concept and level of Justice in the Country is very much questionable. And, this is the main reason why Kenya and her African sister nation-states are often grilled by the Donor Community on the degree of their honest commitment to Democratization as a right path to Good Governance, Stable Peace and Accelerated Socio-economic Healing and Recovery as a pre-condition of getting Financial Aid or simply being denied that Aid.

But, as will also be noted here below, it is not just these Aid Donors alone who are very unhappy and displeased by the manner in which the Kenyan Government is handling or treating this question of Democratization and Justice in the Country which is a sirequa non path to a Durable Peace and Socio-Economic Stability and Recovery in Biopolitics.

On the question of Justice, the Law Society of Kenya, for example, has recently pointed out vehemently that:-

> "it is not just the IMF (the International Monetary Fund) that wants radical change in the Judiciary (of Kenya) . . . (they) too want a fresh bench that is not tainted with allegations of corruption, inefficiency, and-unprofessionalism.[23]

And, on the problem of Justice and Merits in appointement of Judges in their capacity as the Administrators of Justice in Kenya, The Society further laments that:

> ". . . . It is not through a process initiated by the Judicial Service Commission (JSC) as stipulated . . . . The appointment (of Judges) are effected through the lobbying by various interest groups to the President, who directs the JSC to ratify the appointment"[24]

And also that

> ". . . . This is no criteria used to determine the work ethics and professional standards that one should demonstrate before appointment."[25]

In other words, whereas the Kenyan Constitution vests Executive Authority in the President, and the Law making to Parliament, unfortunately the same Constitution does not give Judicial Authority to the Judiciary. By not so doing, it subjects the fate of Justice to the whims and wishes of the President who is just a politician and, therefore, uses it politically for his own self-seeking objectives, contrary to Juridical Morality and Moralism.

But this problem in the Administration of Justice is not limited to the Judiciary. The Bar of Kenya is also a hostage of the same disease/vice. Many cases of professional suicide in the Bar abound involving lawyers who habitually lure and then cheat their clients by not paying them their insurance compensation payments agreed upon in Court. A current classic empirical evidence in support of this from the Daily Nation editor:-

> "A Court has ordered the arrest of a lawyer convicted four years ago of stealing Kshs. 52 million from deceased prison warders."[26]

Disenchanted by the existing trauma symptoms in Government especially the ramp;ant mismanagement of Justice, public Assets, Public Health, and all other affairs affecting the life of the general public, the Parliamentary Group and the National Executive Committee of the political parties affiliated for change (NAC) are no more sleeping or smiling. They are in arms with the Government demanding for a totally new blood in a new Government; they want the Government in power now to explain why the Constitutional Review should not be ready before the end of this year to facilitate the forthcoming General Elections; and they are totally against any extension of the life of the present Parliament. Thus, they are totally fed up and hostile against the trauma and also the pathetical manner in which the Government is treating it. They believe that the Government is not that serious and honest against this trauma.

In Public Administration, we also note this alarming situation which confirms the criticality of this trauma in the country:

> "Detectives have moved into Kenyatta Hospital to investigate a 124 million scam . . . ."
>
> "This is the fourth rip-off to rock the highest hospital in East Africa in the recent past . . ."27

A much more detailed clinical diagnosis of the degree of this trauma's danger to Kenya body politic shows a hell of problems in the Financial Management. The Public Accounts Committee of Parliament is now demanding the Government to answer why a loss of Kshs. 900 million was incurred by the Cereals and Sugar Finance Corporation (CSFC).

It is further demanding what the government is now doing about: these and other various critical cases embarrassing and crippling Kenya:-

(1) the loss of Kshs. 22 billion used as loans to bail out 13 parastatals;
(2) Conclusion of all Goldenberg cases which have caused delay in conclusion to the swindle of Kshs. 5.8 billion;
(3) The loss of more than 200 million on 1987 All Africa Games;
(4) The fate of Kshs. 71 million advanced to a M/S Computer applications Ltd. CAL) and associates for unsupplied software;
(5) Why the Electoral Commission spends Kshs. 20 million yearly.[28]

Turning our microscopes and telescopes to the Country's source of labour force, and the manner in which it is being treated by the Government, we also note other various disenchantments which are of no good for a normal functioning of the Country as a body politic.

Primary and Secondary School Teachers are in arms demanding for their outstanding salary they were promised in the advent of 1997 elections. And, the Kenya National Union of Teachers (KNUT) is already out to defend its members. The Health Care Staff are also in arms demanding for a better salary. And, some are already opting to migrate abroad looking for greener pastures; to name but only a few cases of discontent against the Government and Country as a body politic.

All this add up to a sum total of a critical political culture in Kenya which if left untreated is likely to wreck Kenya's future. Through Political Socialization, this and the future generation will not and cannot be different or free from, this pathologically sick culture. It is an extenuating situation Kenya should not afford to ignore if she is to recover socio-economically and politically.

CHAPTER IV

# Conclusion

## (1) Conclusion

In the preceeding chapter the latter vividly shows the concept and significance of Political Socialization (1) to political life (man) in general and (2) to the Peoples of Africa in particular during the Colonial Era; and more so, during the present post-Colonial (or Independent) Africa as a reliable paradigm (explanatory factor) of political socialization in Biopolitics (political life).

Succintly, it shows: (1) that it was through this Political Socialization that the African peoples, throughout the Continent, became cognizant or aware of their actual sacred and inalienable virtues such as Human Rights, Liberty and Freedom which every Country's regime or leadership must honour, respect and promote at all time and place if that leadership is to survive at all; (2) that the negligence of the Colonial Leadership to pay heed, recognize and make use of this fundamental cardinal fact led it to slide into a political suicide not only in Africa but also all over the World, e.g., in the then Thirteen American Colonies, India, Parkistani, etc; and (3) that it is also due to the same reason that the post-Colonial (or Independent) African leadership is continuously encountering vehement political earthquakes and tornados forcing some leaders to slide into the same catastrophe of political Leadership decay and death as the Colonial Regimes/Leaderships did. (To date, many of them have already been forced to leave office unceremoniously).

And, with regard to the present Independent African Leadership's political future, the Paper further demonstrates in Part II (B), in particular, the following heuristic phenomena as the most tangible or explicit root-causes of the Leadership's own potential danger likely to lead it into a political suicide akin to its predessor (the Undemocratic Colonial Leadership) due to its lack of learning and making use of Lessons gained from past experiences and Political Philosophies.

(1) The Leadership is still pre-occupied with a dented and tainted political culture and attitude which is totally naked (devoid) of Democratic Attire.

(2) The Leadership harbours, embraces, nurtures, fosters and uses, at wil, with total impurity, a hostile attitude against Democracy and every effort of democratization aimed at bringing about a hybrid political culture which is the only sinaqua non means to Democracy and a durable Peace for every people, nation or country seeking or determined to recover from its existing socio-economic wretched situation of massive abject poverty, etc.

(3) This dangerous Political Leadership Culture could easily wreck the Continent beyond repair including the Continent's original goal it conceived through Political Socialization and which it used in its Revolution against the Colonial Leadership which, according to the Continent, was too undemocratic and intolerable for her people to continue living under it.

(4) A more serious potential danger of this type of Leadership is that, through Political Socialization as well as General Socialization, the present generation most especially the youth, is most likely to pass over its taintend anti-Democracy attitude to the future generation thereby making the future situation more precarious and intolerable than the present.

(5) In view of this danger in (4) above, it is self-evident:—(a) that the Continent and all her Peoples are already at the cross-road in that they are already a much more endangered species than they were before during the colonial Regime's Era; and (b) that this is now no longer due to the Undemocratic Colonial Leadership's tendencies other than the continent's own negligence manifested in her Leadership's deviation from its Original Wisdom and Knowledge about the meaning and significance of Democracy and Good Governance gained during the Colonial Leadership Era through Political Socialization.

## (2) A Resuscitation Plan

In this regard, the only medicine or cure to this potential threat or danger to Kenya in particular and the Continent as a whole is a call for an immediadte major surgery on this critically ill Political Culture and Attitude of all their People in general and the Leadership in particular in order to remove off leukemia trauma manifested in their anti-Democracy tendencies and other symptoms of Bad Gvoernance.

This should be the most rational and cost-effective Path or Paradigm to a successful Democracy Institutionalization in Kenya in particular and the Continent in general in order to avoid the already increasing potential danger of Political Earthquakes against their respective body politic.

By pointing an accusation finger to the Existing Constitution (in its capacity as The Instrument of Government from which the Coutnry and Government draws legitimacy and Sovereignty) as a real culprit and therefore the real cause of the on-going socio-economic and political maladies in Kenya is totally unfortunate and therefore very deplorable. It is unfortunate and very deplorable in the same that the following synopsis of the Clinical Diagnosis of a Constitution will definitely demonstrate beyond any reasonable doubt that the instrument is an unfortunate scapegoat; and that the real criminal or sick needing a major surgery is something else:

**A Constitution and Its Virtues and Excellence in Political Life:**

A constitution is an architectural design, plan or formula that each people, community, nation, country or institution which is free and ready to govern itself naturally needs and must have to assist or guide it on how to govern itself and its total affairs. It is a people's foundation stone from which its people draws legitimate ways and means of acquiring and distributing goods and services to the citizenry; setting up a governmental structure and specific rules authoritatively empowered to perform those specific duties aimed at facilitating smooth achievement of the main goal of government which is authoritative acquisition and allocation of goods and services to the citizenry according to each one's need; providing and safeguarding the sanctity of every individual freedom rights and liberty which are sacrosanct virtues for each citizen's happiness and satisfaction in his/her capacity as a genuine intersubjective member of his/her virtual society, community, nation or country, and formulating and managing governmental control machinery called "checks and balances" on "who should occupy what position in government?" "who should do what, when and how?" and "who should be rewarded or punished for what purpose, how and when?"

In the final analysis, a Constitutional is expected to be a people's leadership manual, map, guide, path, way and compass that is needed and must actually have and use at all times if is has to succeed; to be safe; to reach its destination, to achieve its perceived goal/objective in life. It is the oasis from which all legitimacy of one's authority, independence and sovereignty flows and it is also drawn.

But a constitution is just a manmade, artifact. It is not a self-executing entity. It's work and success depends entirely on the nature of the total culture and its significance?

A culture of a people is their total ways of life. It includes their level of knowledge and wisdom, beliefs, morals, customary norms or laws, opinions, religious beliefs, and above all, their attitude toward work, i.e. their customary ways of doing things from time immemorial. If their culture is a corrupt or lazy one, obviously, their attitude toward work must also be corrupt or lazy. But if their culture is a hybrid one, their attitude toward work and conduct will definitely have to be descent, righteous and totally hybrid oriented. A hybrid culture naturally and automatically enhances excellent work and accelerates productivity and prosperity for all. Professional ethnic in a hybrid culture is very high ensuring high efficiency and excellence. In this regard, accountability and transparency in a hybrid society is automatically assured all across the society due to the presence of a universal hybrid culture from the top (elite) right up to the bottom (grassroots). At all levels of a hybrid society, corruption, laziness, dishonesty and diseases which are inherent in a filthy Culture and Filthy Leadership are totally alien unheard of and a flabbergasting and nauseating thing or behaviour. Everyone in a hybrid society thinks and strives for excellence, good name, good image, and good dignity. In that society, Perfection, Holiness and Godliness is one's order of the day. Parents, schools, religious institutions, peer groups, etc are all a product and advocate of excellence, justice, righteousness and compassion by virtue of their attitude generated/created by the theocentric nature of their society's hybrid culture an Constitution. In this respect, a constitutional Review becomes instrumental or good to the people the Review is expected to serve only if it is mindful of Summum Bonum (i.e., The Greatest Good or Happiness for all) as the ultimate basis and goal of the nature of the people's culture and objective which that people actually seek to gain from the New Constitution.

Accordingly, the on-going Constitution Review in Kenya is already questionable and a possible total failure because it is not the existing Constitution that has a case to answer but the people of Kenya themselves and their total culture characterized by an abnormal attitude of dishonesty and disobedience to their own existing Constitution and all forms therefrom; acute tribalism and personal jealousy and envy manifested in their individual rampant destructive quest for quick self-aggrandizement at the expense of all other Kenyans; acute hate and bloodthirst against those who appear to be too righteous and critical against Corruption, Bad Governance, Nepotism, Espionage, Terrorism, Genocide, Managerial Poverty, Professional Mediocracy and Suicide, etc. To call a spade a spade, it is not the Existing Kenyan Constitution which is sick or ill, deformed or disabled but the Kenyan people themselves and their total culture, attitude and behavioural patterns who, therefore urgently need an ambulance to an Intensive Care Unit (ICU) for an immediate major surgery and not the Constitution per se! Short of this, like the existing Constitution, the New Constitution will not and cannot, on its own, miraculous bring about Summum Bonum in Kenya.

In the final analysis, this Paper is significant in that it explicitly and exhaustively express all these hidden anomalies against success of the on-going Constitution Review but unfortunately invisible to the many as also noted by Prophet Isaiah at 60.2 in the Holy Bible.

1. Also see, for instance, Robert D. Hess and Judith V. Torney, The Development of Political Attitudes in Children (Chicago: Aldine Publishing Company, 1967); Herbert H. Hyman, Political Socialization, A Study in the Psychology of Political Behaviour (New York: The Free Press, 1969); David Easton and Jack Dennis, Children in the Political System, Origins of Political Legitimacy (New York:McGraw-Hill, 1969); Jack Dennis, Political Socialization Research, A Bibliography (Beverly Hill, Calif.: Sage Publications, 1973); and Kenneth Prewitt, Educational and Political Values, An East African Case Study (Nairobi, 1971).
2. Also see Peter Berger and Thomas Luckman, Constraction of Social Reality (New York: Doubleday, Inc., 1966), Chps. II and III.
3. H.F. Stewart and Paul Desjardins, eds. French Patriotism in the Nineteenth Century, 1814-1833 (Cambridge University Press, 1923), p. 5.
4. David L. Westby and Richard G. Braungart, "The Alienation of Generations and Status Politics: Alternative Expectations of Student Political Activitism", in Roberta S. Sigal, ed., Learning About Politics: A Reader in Political Socialization (New York: Random House, 1970), pp. 476-489).
5. Barclays Bank, D.C.O., West African Directory, 1967-1968 (Lonodn: Thomas Skinner and Company, Ltd., 1969), p. 285.

# PART NINE

## LEADERSHIP AND MORALITY:
## A Test for Man's Mechanical Efforts to Create and Institutionalize Democracy and Good Governance

## CHAPTER 1

# Introduction

### 1. Problem

A priori, this chapter seeks to cast more light on "Leadership" and "Political Morality" concepts with a view to providing an in-depth explanation and understanding of their actual identity; role; dynamics; and above all, their significance or usefulness to man in Biopolitics (i.e., Political Life). Aposteriori, to use this explanation as a first and foremost stepping-stone, eye-opener, paradigm or lead-star to one's in-depth understanding and measuring the capacity/ accuracy of their strategic usefulness/utility to a least democratic country such as Kenya which is or may be seriously interested in seeking to know or understand a proper, better or cost-effective way or means of Institutionalizing Democracy (i.e., achieving Democracy Institutionalization) for the benefit of the Kenyans.

In this regard, obviously the following crucial question may equally be very instrumental as a useful path to that unknown wisdom and knowledge needed to bring about Democracy and Good Governance.

What is "Leadership"? and What is "Political Morality" What is their respective strategic roles or usefulness in life in general and to man in particular? And, above all, what is their correlation with respect to their individual and collective usefulness to man towards Democracy Institutionalization in a Country such as Kenya?

## 2. Definition and stategic usefulness of leadership to man in life

### (A) Definition of Leadership as a Concept

The concept, "leadership" is derived from a noun word "Leader" meaning a person, somebody or something that leads; which is also derived from a verb word "to lead" meaning to guide, show, direct, conduct, channel, start, etc. as to teach someone to know what one does not know and may not have otherwise known on his/her own; or to lead someone or oneself from the known to the unknown or from an undesirable situation to a desirable one as in the case of Plant Kingdom whereof a tree or plant has to lead or direct its branch(es) and leaves from the dark position toward the source of sunlight and its roots from the dry to where it can get water and minerals from the soil for its survival. The examples are endless.[1]

But, as pertains to its usefulness, "Leadership" is indeed undisputable indispensable biological ingredient found in all forms and at all levels of life from the Plant Kingdom right up to the Animal Kingdom due to its naturally inherent strategic usefulness and capacity as a tool to each living entity for the latter's management of itself and its all business or activities requisite for and sacrosanct for its eufunction (i.e., its normal functioning and survival)[2].

However, in spite of this strategic usefulness or importance of Leadership phenomenon to every living organism in life for this entity's survival, the most amazing and somewhat embarrasing paradox to the Academia today is that its true or actual identity and scope of its strategic role in life, in total, have not been exhaustively and properly or clearly exposed and made well known[3]. Its idenity and scope of its strategic role are still too obscure. They are still a dim, mystery to not only the social scientist but also to the same political leaders who do use it as their trade and always scramble and even maim or totally kill each other for it as their main souece of income.

But, as will be note in-depth in this Chapter), Leadership is not only an improtant tool in political life per se due to its strategic usefulness for management of one's political affairs nor it is only limited to that life as it has always been erroneously assumed in pseudo-science by using bereft paraphernalia or methodologies.

Contrary to such misleading wisdom and knowledge in Normal Social Sciences, this Paper will endeaviour to prove beyond any reasonable doubt that there still exists lots of unknown mysteries and wisdom about this Leadership phenomenon which is, therefore, a critical challenge to the Academia in particular and Mankind in general.

It is going to prove that this phenomenon is governed by the law of nature in the sense that it is biological.[4] It is biological in that it is innate, And, it is innate in that it is a biochemical component or constituent part of the whole biological compound inherent in that whole compound naturally inherent in each and every living organism which, in turn biologically constitutes or makes up the total anatomical and physiological component of that total being or organism.

Because of this universal functional role biologically bestowed upon it by the law of nature in every living entity with a sole view of assisting and enhancing the survival of that entity, Leadership obviously plays a very strategic and important role second to none in every member of both the Plant Kingdom and the Animal Kingdom.

This reality is empirically manifested in the manner that each member of the two Kingdoms naturally and practically manages itself and its total affairs amongst its other community members in terms of its self-perception and self-control or self-management on the one hand; and in terms of its perceptions and interactions with its fellow counterparts in the community on the other.

### (1) Leadership in the Plant Kingdom

In the Plant Kingdom,5 a Botanical diagnosis shows that each plant or species naturally behaves, acts or directs itself and its total acts in a manner which is individually and collectively sacrosanct to those requirements or conduct sacred or requisite to its eufunction (i.e., systemic normal functioning and livelihood or well-being needs).

These needs include, for example, respiratory security, food security, health security, etc. And, in the respiratory security, needs, for example, each species normally conducts, directs, manage or simply leads itself in a strategic manner expected to enable and enhance it to easily and properly breath in and out as it is biologically or naturally constitutioned to do in order for it to also enhance its proper metabolism without which that plant or species is subject to wither away and perish (normal functioning of this system) without which that plant or species would have to die.

Similarly, with respect to its food security, each plant or species is also biologically empowered, i.e. constitutionally required to conduct, manage or simply lead itself and all its acts in a strategic manner that will enable it to receive food, e.g., sunlight which it must get from the sun using its stomata embedded in its leaves; and to also receive water and minerals which it must get from the soil using its various types of roots, e.g., tap root, etc.

In both these cases (the search for air and food), the concept and role of self-leadership is real and crucial indeed. For example, the plant must lead its branches into a right direction where its knows and believes very well that it will definitely get sunlight using these leaves. Also, the plant must lead its roots into the right direction and place in the soil where it knows and believes very well that it will get the water and minerals it needs for its survival using these roots.

Thus, unless a plant or species is able to lead itself in manner which it knows and believes to be strategically sacrosanct to its needs for its livelihood, obviously that plant or species is doomed. It will not and cannot survive at all. It automatically dries up or withers away and dies in conformity to this natural law: Whoever fails to lead oneself in a manner which is sacrosanct to those sacred needs requisite for its survival automatically and summarily perishes.

In view of this naturally given ability, leadership does not exist in political life only as it has always been erroneously assumed and understood because of using pseudo-scientific paraphernalia/methods or bereft means . . . It is a universal phenomenon inherent in both political life and all other aspects of life (i.e living entities) in the universe. Without it, life would be naturally impossible. No member of the Plant Kingdom would exist.

Also, since the Animal Kingdom depends on this Plant Kingdom for its survival as a source of its vitamins and minerals food (vegetables) and oxygen (which plants breathe out in day time and breathe in carbon dioxide in night time), it is also self-evident that no species of the Animal Kingdom would survive without it. The end of death of the former would also mean the end or death of the latter in the universe (life). And, in this regard total life would be kaput!

But, now that we have unlocked this mystery of the concept "Leadership" to our satisfactory understanding it in terms of its true nature and strategic role in the life of the Plant Kingdom, what is its strategic role and significance in the life of the Animal Kingdom? How does it function? Is its nature and function the same as its nature and function in the Plant Kingdom? And, what is the correlation between "Leadership" and "Morality"? Can Leadership function in absence of Morality? If so or not, why? What would be the consequences?

### (2) Leadership in the Animal Kingdom

In as much as Leadership naturally exists and functions in all members of the Plant Kingdom (as so explicated above) by virtue of its biological mandate[6] bestowed upon it by the law of nature (i.e Natural Morality), Leadership is equally an indispensable biological ingredient in the Animal Kingdom life by virtue of its strategic role or mandate bestowed upon it by the same Natural Morality for the survival of this Kingdom.

Like its sacred role in each member of the Plant Kingdom, its role in each member of the Animal Kingdom is equally so sacred for the acquisition of each member's needs for survival that failure to do so is tantamount to suicide of that member.

However, whereas its role in the Plant Kingdom is strictly biological and not as easily observable as its role is in the Animal Kingdom, the role in the latter Kingdom, is both biological and physical.

(a) Biologically, Leadership plays a similar role in both Plan Kingdom and Animal Kingdom in that, in the same manner it does in the Plant Kingdom, in the Animal Kingdom, Leadership also enables each species or member to behave in a manner which is deemed sacrosanct to those biological needs requisite for the survival of the said species.

For instance, like the species in the Plant Kingdom, each species in the Animal Kingdom has also to breathe in and out (though in a different manner peculiar to each species is in question); eat and excrete what is no more needed by the body; reprocreate as so constitutionally mandated by its law of nature; and seek security sacrosanct to its total survival.

But all these are not by accident. They do not come about or happen from oblivion or by chance alone. Each species is biologically conditioned by the law of nature to organize, conduct, synchronize, discipline or direct itself towards those ends which are sacred to and for its survival. Hence, the role of Leadership in the Biological World/Life.

In all, each species is indeed a leader of both itself and its total affairs. Its Leadership is rational and purposive. It is rational in that the species is definitely in a full command of its decisions. It knows and understands very well what it wants in life and how to get what it actually wants. This goal may be milieu (outside its reach). In this case or in order to get it, the species will behave in certain ways that it believes to be strategically good or cost-effective to achieve that goal. Or the goal may be possessional (inside its reach). In this case, the species will behave in certain ways it believes to be strategically good or cost-effective to protect that goal, e.g., territorial space, etc.

Each species is a self-leader in that unless it does morally organize itself in a proper manner that is sacrosanct to those needs, it cannot get them. Similarly; unless it leads itself and all its affairs in a manner which is sacrosanct to the eufunction (i.e., normal functioning of its body as so constitutionally required by the law of nature, then that species is obviously doomed. It is subject to perish. It will not last that long. Hence, the positive correlation between biological leadership in the Animal Kingdom and biological leadership in the plant Kingdom.

(b) And, Physically, each member of both Plant and Animal Kingdoms naturally leads itself and all its acts by synchronizing these acts as rationally and sacred as it is constitutionally mandated to do by the law of nature governing all members of that species in the Plant Kingdom or Animal Kingdom (1) toward those needs which are deemed essential for its survival and (2) away from those needs that are deemed to be either not essential or harmful to its security and total life.

In view of these prima-facie facts, each member is a bona fide leader of both the self and its total activities. For the purpose of survival, each naturally leads itself and all its aspirations or desires in a manner it rationally understands and deems would cost-effectively enhance but not jeopardize its security and total survival.

In this regard, like in the Plant Kingdom, in the Animal Kingdom, Leadership manifests implicitly and explicitly in the following two ways:-

(1) Out-reach i.e., In those ways that are meant to direct the species towards those ends in fulfillment of its desire, theory, etc. due to absence of a potential danger or threat.
(2) Temperance i.e. In these ways that are meant to prevent or restrain it away from those harmful ends due to the presence of a potential danger or threat regardless of one's burning desire(s) or need(s).

In the final analysis, Leadership is indeed a natural necessity. It is a necessary tool inherent in each member of the Animal Kingdom as well as in each member the Plant Kingdom. Prima facie evidences adduced in the preceding paragraphs above collectively support this axiom (natural truth)

One of the significant variances of this axiom between the Plant Kingdom and the Animal Kingdom is that whereas in the former the behaviour of leadership is not easily observable using naked eye, in the Animal Kingdom, this phenomenon is easily observable most particularly in the manner each species, e.g. man behaves or physically moves himself in pursuit of what he desires or needs in life for his survival.

In a retrospect, this is a clear acid test for the presence of a Leadership ingredient in the Animal Kingdom; and also a test of the manner and ability that this ingredient enables and enhances a species to rationally lead itself and its total business in order to sustain its livelihood without which this species would not live any more.

### (B) A Retrospective Analysis

In a retrospect, it is self-evident, from the above new facts about the pending mystery about Leadership phenomenon in life, that there still exists a lot of wisdom or insights about the phenomenon than it is now presented in the Normal Social Sciences literature. And as a concept, it is also self-evident, from those facts, that as a concept, "Leadership" has to-date, indeed suffered a great deal of misinterpretation on the one hand; and superficiality on the other, generally arising from use of pseudo-Scientific paraphernalia or methodologies.

From a proper scientific analysis, the concept is obviously as old as mankind and the Total Creation by virtue of the fact that it is biologically governed by the law of nature. It is the foundation stone on which every living entirely rests and relies for its survival. It is the engine, guide or guidance, the teacher, etc naturally required by every living organism for the latter's successful acquisition of its needed milieu goals, objectives or values and for protection of its possessional values at hand, e.g., territorial space, etc.

In view of this natural fact, any people, society, community, nation or country without a Leadership is not only a disadvantaged amorphous and cephalous entity but also a most doomed one. It is doomed in that it is without guidance toward a promising prosperous future. Such a society is naturally a misguided and confused entity in that it lacks a teacher, guide, arbiter, keeper to authoritatively police over and harmonize its inter-personal behaviour, activities or interactions especially conflict and other forms of disagreements using every political morality means available.

In the final analysis, Leadership is the first and foremost essential ingredient every people, society, community, nation or country needs if it is to meaningfully have a prosperous and happy life.

But from the time immemorial to the present, beginning with our Patriarch Adam, empirical evidences show that a variety of Leadership has emerged overtime as follows:-

(1) The "Átrophied traditional primary-group identifications" succinctly known as "Paramodial Leadership" found and used in a traditional nuclear family, Church, village, community, etc. and characterized by face-to-face interaction between a leader and those that he leads; and extremely very rich in morality and moralism as a basic foundation of their survival in life in that every member found tampering with or violating its Moral Values or Principles is severely dealt with as in the case fo the Hammurabian Law formulated by Hammurabi (1955-1913 BC).
(2) The Theocentric Leadership which emerged by the will of God beginning with our Patriarch Adam to Noah, Moses, King Saul, King David, King Solomon, right up to King Zedekia of Israel (1050 BC 587 BC thus till Israel and Judah were destroyed) and also including the Egyptian Pharaoh who were each placed in Leadership theocentrically and to theocentrially serve the purpose of God as God's agents on earth anointed to serve God's people for their betterment by strictly adhering to God's Commandments; failure of which always resulted into a severe punishment to those Leaders as in the murder case of King David who had killed his servant Uriah in order to usurp Uriah's wife, (2 Samual 11:14-24, 12:9 and 24:15; and 1 Chronicles 17:1-2, and 22:6-10); And, also King Ahab and King Zedekia in particular who received the

severest punishment of all other Leaders in Israel Kingdom and also Israel and Judah Kingdoms.

(3) Self-Seeking Ledership which emerged by the will of man through various ways and means of man, e.g., (a) By Foregn Conquests, e.g. by Alexander The Great of Greece and Marcedonia (355-323 BC) AND Charlemagn (i.e., Charles The Great) of the Frankish Kingdom who, through such conquests by force became King of the Franks (768-814 AD) AND emperor of the Romans (800-814 AD) though he did, of course, bring about the emergence of Medieval Civilization in Western Europe that he occupied and ruled (i.e. Austria, Neustria, Alemannia, Burgundy, Aquitiane, Saxony, Bavaria, Lombardy, Brittany, Carinthia, Papal States, Spoleto, Spanish March, Corsica and the Balearic Islands); (b) By Hereditary, e.g. the present Queen Elizabeth II of Great Britain (1926-present) who was inscrolled on the throne on 6th Feb., 1952 at the age of 25 years as a result of her father's death (King George VI) on that date, (c) By Internal Conquests, e.g., President Idi Amin Dada of Uganda, President Mobutu Sese Seko of Zaire, etc who use their paramilitary means to stage bloody coup d'etat as their rational shortcut choice or means of Leadership Succession in order to enrich themselves at the expense of the overwhelming majority poor languishing in abject poverty agonies; (d) By Elections as in the case of Prime Minister Tony Blair of Great Britan, President George Bush of the USA and President Thabo Mbeki of South Africa today who ascended to their leadership by a genuine popular vote of their respective country voters guided by existing or standing Moral Principles purposely designed to govern every election and who, therefore, enjoy the Popular Will of their People's Majority; and finally (e)By The Least Morality-Led elections e.g President Mwai Kibaki in Kenya as a prima facie model of majority of the present African Leaders— who ascended to leadership through morally questionable means such as election riggings thereby putting majority voters to wrath and total discontent against their right of being in office.

But a further synthesis of this Leadershp phenomenon, particularly the present one, reveals that the phenomenon further falls into the following various heuristic sub-phenomena viz: (1) Authoritarian Leadership e.g., the Fascist Leadership of Benito Mussolini of World War II Italy (1883-1945)[8] whose aim in leadership was to use an iron hand to forcefully transform Italy into a great empire but instead failed terribly to do so by leaving Italy at his death in 1945 already fully occupied by foreign armies. Such a leader is generally a soulless person. He is usually evil, and blood-handed who likes to rule and live by murdering oppositions and any one that dares to question him and, his policy and mode of leadership. This mode of Leadership is also manifested in the dictatorial leadership of Joseph Stalin (1878-1953)[9] who also killed every one that opposed his leadership and policy; (2) Hero Executive Leadership which emerged with President Charlese de Gaulle of France (1890-1970)[10] by virtue of his stupendous role as an outstanding French patriot, soldier, and statesman of the 1900's because of his shrewd leadership that successfully steered France against Germany in World War II and later lead that Country into a Socio-economic and political recovery immediately after World War II; designed an amicable liaison with the still fresh France's enemy (Germany); became a symbol of France to both French men and people world-wide; and thus transformed France into one of Europe's leading nations. The same mode of Leadership is manifested in the strong executive leadership in Germany by Chancellor Konrad Adnauer (1876-1967)[11] who, due to his shrewd leadership stabilized West Germany Politics and thus put the Country into a heavy gear towards a speedy socio-economic A final acceleration and recovery after the World War II than his own counterpart in East-Germany was able to do in spite of the still freshly prevailing agonies of odds from the just ended World War II. A final vividly illustrative example is these two other World War II heroes viz: President Franklin D. Roosevelt of the USA (1882-1945)[12] the only American president to serve four consecutive terms (1933-1945) and earned a hero executive leadership for very successful leading the USA through its worst depression and worst war the World had ever experienced before; and Sir Winston Churchill (1966-1974)[13] who became one of the greatest world statesmen, and reached the height of his fame in history as a heroic prime minister of Great Britain during and after World War II because of his personal courage, magical words and faith in victory. Consequently, his mere sight cheered everyone. The other two empirical examples of a Hero Executive Leadership type are Presidnet Abraham Lincoln of the USA (1809-1865)[14] who proved in his Leadership tenure as a truly greatest leader of all times because of his extraordinary insighit capacity to detect/predict the implications of an act, e.g., that the breakout of Civil War in America could utterly destroy the concept and foundation of Democracy and Independence (freedom) America had laboured so hard to set up as a paradigm/model for all other nations striving toward that end if that Civil War is allowed to go on unchecked and contained in advance; and also due to his extraordinary ability to express his intentions, plans policies and goals so explicit and vivid that each American easily adopted as if it were his or her own.[15] Pseudo-Executive Leadership is manifested in deliberate deviations from its institutional prescriptions and descriptions by deliberately ignoring the laid down rules of separation of powers; and thus usurping and hoarding into its office the powers of other branches of government especially the Judiciary so that in the Leader's capacity as the Chief Executive, he may directly dictate at will to the judges whether to dismiss a case of convict the accused regardless of his being guilty or not. Also, in his capacity as the Chief Accounting Officer of the Nation (Republic), such an Executive has a tendency to expropriate his office by misappropriating public funds and other assets as he so desires on the false belief that he is legally above the law and nobody can, therefore, prosecute him in any Court of Law or impeach him for doing so; thereby impoverishing the country and people he is expected to lead. Because of this tendency, such Leadership could also be adequately identified as an "Oligarchical Leadership" whose aim is not actually to lead others but to use them for his self-aggrandizement by looting the national assets at will[16].

This pseudo-Chief Executive mode is not a myth, not a theory or hypothetical. It is real and prevalent in most African countries where the original aim of nationalism and national uprisings against Undemocratic Colonial Authority during the colonial Era was to eradicate the existing Bad Governance which was not sensitive to Democracy and Human Rights, and replace it with a Good Governance which had that sensitivity but which now (in Post Colonial Leadership) has paradoxically turned out to be much worse than its predecessor. Obviously, this is the paradox which, therefore, constitutes or legitimizes the Purpose and Rationale of the next Chapter on the questions:—"What dis Political Morality"? "And what is its significance to Leadership vis-à-vis Democracy Instituionalization in a country such as Kenya as a paradigm for other African Countries' efforts towards the same goal".

CHAPTER II

# Definition and Strategic Role and Usefulness of Political Morality to Man in Life as a Vehicle Towards Democracy Institutionalization

## (A) Definition of Political Morality

As a concept, "Political Morality" is derived from the general concept "Morality" which means ethical wisdom and knowledge of moral science, qualities, discourse (or instruction) sense, and truth which, in turn, simply means one's good conduct and good sense of duty in keeping with one's societal moral principles, doctrine or system of moral behaviour, or philosophy of a people, nation or country that every member thereof is expected to know, uphold and practice at all times and places as a guide of his/her conduct for the function of his/her people, nation or country.

Thus, in each a people, nation or country, there always exists a system of moral behaviour or conduct and normal[17] to them although this may be looked at as abnormal, silly, embarrassing, primitive, idiotic etc by certain outsider who, by chance, do not actually intelligibly understand it and the people concerned.

But, the fact is that the architect of this belief system naturally and normally hold it very highly as being normal, sensible, rational and inalienable to them. To them, it is a Master Key to their daily life by virtue of its strategic importance (or usefulness) to them.

Its strategic importance is manifested in the way it enhances for them an internal community cohesion; peace; collective responsibility; their uniqueness from all other outsiders; and their ability and swiftness to successfully mobilize themselves vis-à-vis every foreign aggression, to successfully work together as a corporate body in any task needing such action for their survival, e.g., during marriage and death ceremonies, disaster and disease out-breaks, etc.

It is obvious that without the presence of this universal belief system, doctrine, norms, customs, or culture to tie each member to his own community and its values, no such internal cohesion and the spirit of corporateness is possible in any people, community, nation or country.

A vivid empirical evidence of this reality is borne out by the case of the Eskimos who, by nature, live a typical animal life in Greenland and its environs because of the severest cold weather of the Arctic Region. Because of this harsh situation that no Kenya, German, British, Zimbabian or Australian can possibly withstand at any single time of their life as the Eskimos have naturally and happily done without any hurdle(s) or qualm(s), these brave begins conceived and adopted a unique formula of developing a culture and moral values which they believed to be sacred to them and also sacrosanct for their survival as a people in that terrible weather. This culture was for example: (1) to build and live in temporary iceberg-built igloos (which, by nature, are totally anti-heating or fire); (2) to live on completely uncooked or raw foods as typical animals mostly on seal fats which they knew would also metabolically keep their body temperature as constantly warm and normal as their seals and other preys habitually do by metabolically using their fatty bodies to withstand against this harsh weather in the area; and (3) to happily live solely by hunting and fishing in this daily snow and frozen environment as the said situation could not and still cannot allow them up; to day to plant and harvest any crop in the area.

Whereas such a terrifying life canot be tolerable to any other human being(s) not only because of the impossible nature of the weather but also because of the harsh or most scary culture and morality of these Eskimos, the fact is that all this is easily and happily tolerable to the Eskimos. It is tolerable to them because of their honesty and firm commitment to their own unique culture and moral values which they themselves happily and wisely constructed; and which they all collectively hold so sacred to them and sacrosanct for their survival that nothing else which is short of this culture morality can make them any happy.

In the final analysis, it is definitely their Doctrine of their Culture and Morality which has always sustained and kept them cohesively together and victorious as an Eskimo people, community or nation on equal footing with other peoples, communities or nations on Earth regardless and irrespective of their deadly challenging odds in the area. By all means, these Eskimos are consequently as happy as every other human beings.

But the most nagging question now is: What formula do these Eskimos apparently use to keep themselves perennial victors against so peculiarly harsh odds that no Kenyan, German or Angolan can ever manage while these Eskimos are neither that educated or civilized as the rest of the World is?

This question obviously leads us to the wisdom about "socialization" and "Political Socialization". Socialization is a vehicle or process that facilitates continuity overtime of the cultural values and all beliefs of a people from one generation to another.

Therefore, if, as we have already noted above in our definition of the concept "Morality," that this concept truly means moral, ethical, and acceptable behaviour to the society concerned, then it must also be true that it is the duty of that society to see to it or to facilitate (or ensure) that continuity of its moral values and all other values that collectively constitute its total Culture continue internally at all times.[17]

Thus, it is the Society's duty to ensure that its Total Culture and Moral's therein are Moralized[18] (i.e interpreted symbolically and perfectly to its members from one generation to another and the non-compliants are morally disciplined, and put right using both instructional and rehabilitation means of rewards and punishment). Further, it is the duty of that Society to assume the role of a Moralizer19 (i.e., one who moralizes others or a situation with a view to making moral reflection to the masses by virtue or way of vividly explaining the moral meaning of its Culture and Moral Values in conjunction with the social rules or laws of the land that every one is expected to know and apply in one's all acts and interaction with one's fellow Community or Society members.

In the final analysis, like in the Eskimo Society, in every Society such as Kenya, it is a naturally inherent duty of Kenya and all her leaders to assume the role of a Moralist and ensure that all Kenyans are moralled (i.e., are fully made cognizant, aware and equipped with the required Moral Standard (i.e., moral values that are sacrosanct for the eufunction of Kenya which is requisite for the normal socio-economic and political functioning and recover for the well-being and prosperity of all Kenyans but not just a few as it is the case in Kenya today.

But all this cannot come about by chance alone. It cannot be possible in Kenya unless the entire Kenyan Leadership and all Kenyan public alike willingly accept to believe in and practice Moralism[20] (i.e., all have a moral attachment or commitment to their sacred norms and values that govern them and thus sustains their well-being in life).

Without this moral commitment or attachments, obviously every effort of and through Socialization and Political Socialization toward a Hybrid Culture is already a sum-zero game. Thus, both the Leadership and the General Public have to agree to be genuine and honest Moralists[21] so that both may individually and collectively ensure that each Kenyan from the Leadership right up to the led (Grass-roots), each Kenyans behaviour and responsibility in life in general and in office or place of work bestowed upon him or her is in conformity to the social values and rules governing his terms of Reference; and is also in conformity with the General Will and Expectations of his/her Country but not in conformity with his/her own selfish egocentric lusts of grabbing public assets in order to get rich quickly at the expense and suffering of the entire Country's Population.

Whereas, these two concepts "Morality" and "Moralism" have not been understood fairly well by both scientists and Laymen alike; and whereas the most reknown work which could be deemed as purely scientific on the two, emerged from the work of a French Sociologist Emile Durkheim (1858-1917) in his classic book Le Suicide (1897) whose objective was to clinically study the actual causes of suicide from all countries world-wide that had statistics on suicide[22].

But although Durkheim's findings on suicide may not have helped much in amplifying vividly on the concepts of "Morality" and "Moralism," his findings are significant in that they proved that suicide behaviour normally emanate from one's lack of respect and love for the Moral Values of one's family, society, community, nation or country. Similarly, an individual who chooses to do an awful thing like suicide to himself or killing others without due regard to their feelings and sorrows and to the standing norms, rules or law of his or her society vis-à-vis that suicides is obviously amoral; and that he is, therefore, regarded as an undesirable member of his/her society community group or organization.

Durkheim is quite right because this is also exactly the reason why in most African cultures, as well as in Christian tradition, a suicide victim is never given a full moaning, funeral and burial rites as is normally given to normal deaths.

Like Durkeim, the first reknown Scientist on the subject matter before him is the Austrian physician Sigmund Freud (1856-1939) who argued that one's super ego (i.e., the superior disciplinary force which in this Study means "Morality" and "Moralism") has a natural mandate to police over the acts and aspirations of one's ego (i.e. the executive force that contacts the outside world of reality for the satisfaction of one's needs and which must, therefore, be checked at all times by the super ego lest it goes overboard into the dangerous foreign territory and cause trouble).

## (B) A Retrospective Analysis

In view of these facts noted in Chapter II (A) above on the concept of "Morality" and "Moralism" and their strategic utility to man, it is self-evident that "Morality" in particular is a very instrumental tool to man in life in that it serves as an external brake system to every individual's aspirations and acts with a view to preventing and minimizing unnecessary dangers to society caused by reckless individuals who may not be well equipped with their own internal brake-system (Morally and Moralism).

Further, it is also self-evident that each people, community, society, nation or country also naturally has its own biological constitution which authoritatively mandates it to encourage automatic socialization with a view to nurturing and fostering continuity of this brake-systems from one generation to another. And, that failure to do so would automatically result into systemic corrosion, decay and eventual death of a people, community, society, nation or country as Sodom and Gomorrah (Gen. 18:20, 21;19:24-28) did due to its lack of such brake-system.

And, as we also scientifically confirmed as early as the 1920 by a Swiss psychologist Jean Piaget (1896-) learning of one's Morals and total Culture is a natural reality and is spacio temporal free. In each people, community, society nation or country, one first begins as "a moral" and then gradually develops into a Durkheimain State of "moral", i.e., a stage of full cognition and respect of the moral values of his/her people, community, society, nation or country which the latter deems and hold sacred to them because of the naturally inherent significance of these values to them as a magnetic agent that holds all of them together into a cohesive people, community, society or country without which they cannot survive as such.

Obviously, this empirical evidence constitutes a biggest blow to Durkheim's contention that:— Morality is basically a matter of one's respect for fixed rules, laws, norms or customs and the authority behind them but is not necessarily of a rational calculation of the benefits and harm in concrete case that thus make one be deemed or become morality conscious attached, addicted or commited.[23] Whereas he is very scientifically correct: (1) that, morality is generally associated with the contention that if one did what was not considered good by all other members of his/her society, community or country, this would be tantamount to punishment and that this generally become the motivating force in certain individuals to accept morality merely for the sake of doing so to avoid punishment of humiliation; (2) that from one people to another, there is a wide degree of variance as to what rules or nature of rules that normally arouse moral respect, punitiveness, and sense of duty and finally (3) that while Western societies tend to divorce morality from religion, this is factually wrong since empirically, many people derive their morality and moral values from their relationship with God.[24]

He, however, concluded that all this is not centered on human—welfare consequences. Thus, according to him, one's moralism is not concerned with the benefits or harms to one's community as the Utilitarians had thus contended.

Obviously, this assumption must be tantamount to a devastating blow against Durkheim as a scientist and Durkheimism as a belief in his work. Various prima facie empirical evidences confirm beyond any reasonable doubt that in all life, in general and in Scientific and technological life in particular, everything and every act or action is conceptualized, understood; and more so respected by virtue of its function or utility. As the virtue of the eye is to see and its excellence is to see well, so is the virtue and excellence of every belief such as Moralism is to qualify one into being an inter-subjective member of his or her society, community or country. He becomes an acceptable member by virtue of his or her virtuously excellent behaviour by which he is judged or calculated in human-welfare consequences. This is exactly the most critical pot-hole in Durkheimism.

In every nuclear family, example, it is an empirical fact that each member of that family unit is measured in terms of its <u>goodness</u> or <u>values</u> to the family unit. And, that quality is also measured in terms of that member's ability to provide happiness and joy to the family unit.

This is exactly the empirical reason why a child is normally characterized as "a good child" or "a black ship" of the family (i.e., one who is deviant to the family norms or rules by doing what is not of any good or happiness to the family). This is also the reason why a child may be referred to either "moral" or immoral".

In all these cases, it is not, therefore, the question of one simply accepting to conform to one's family moral rules (morality) for the mere sake of doing so without any value or goodness of doing that as so erroneously assumed by Durkheim although may be deemed that it is highly celebrated by some scientist in the Academica. This revelation of most critical lpot-holes in his work obvious disqualifies Durkheimism beyond any reasonable doubt.

Whereas like his predecessor French sociologist Auguste Comte (1798-1857) who died barely one year before Durkheim was born in 1858, Durkheim and his Durkheimism emphasized **Positivism**, (i.e. that every one's research must be governed or based solely on empirical investigation of factual realities) other than on **spiritual** or **theological** (i.e., supernatural) and **metaphysical** (i.e., abstract) investigation and explanation; now, there is no doubt that his work and Durkheimism in total must be deficient of this same positivism dose that he sought to cherish and promote above **theology** and **metaphysics**.

In such circumstances, the conflict between his assumptions and conclusions on one hand; and his belief in positivism on the other obviously augers as terrifying complexity. His claim with Comte of Positivism as the only authentic Science above Theology and Metaphysics in that this is the only means to one's better understanding of reality is not only amoral but also an atheist path to scientism aimed at exalting the self to **omni-competence, omniscience** and omnipotence likely to create and widen not only cynicism of scientism supposed to revere and worship. And, why if its sole objective is succinctly to abide by the norms or rules of Scientism but not necessarily to assist man with the greatest happiness that man so expects from it? Why then is Sociology still deficient as a cure to societal ills? In a nut-shell, what would be its Moral Obligation to man? Without this **moral obligation**, what would be its value in life?

In their response to these fundamental questions, all Utilitarian such as David Hume (1711-1776), Jeremy Bentham (1748-1832), James Mill (1773-1836), John Stuart Mill (1806-1873)[25] individually and collectively confirmed that the virtue and excellence of a thing or individual are manifested in the usefulness and degree of goodness (i.e., quality) of that thing or individual. And that anything or any individual who lacks this usefulness to the people, community, society, nation or country is definitely deemed by the latter as being of no good and, hence obviously redundant! They further noted that every where in life, anybody who is considered bad or undesirable by his/her people is normally declared so because of the fact that he/she lacks moral value or utility to them. Similarly, any thing or item that is deemed valueless, is automatically put away or simply put out of existence. This is a universal phenomenon world-wide and thoughout all generations.

Hume, in particular stressed that whether or not one believes in God and the existence of God, the fact still remains that every human being naturally possesses some in-born virtuous characteristics of behaviour which are deemed morally agreeable and useful to one's people, community, society, nation or country.

Hume called these behavioural characteristics "Benevolence[26] (or good will) which, according to his Successors, such as Bentham, James Mill, John Stuart Mill, et. al. In the school of Utilitarianism, also conceptualized as "Compassion" which individually and collectively mean the same thing as "Good Morals" or Morality (in short).

But this prima facie empirical evidence from this Utilitarian Philosophers is not the only devastating acid test against Durkheim's erroneous assumption about this Morality phenomenon and its role to man in the socio-setting.

The Utilitarian evidence is also supported by the spirit of Theocentric Humanism Philosophy and the Doctrine of Summum Bonum of The African Mysteries System of The Grand Lodge of Luxor[27] which existed as far back as 7000 BC-3000 BC in what is today known as Egypt. Whereas Theocentric Humanism Philosophy emphasized that in life, one must live and function within the framework of Perfection, Holiness and Godliness if he/she is to attain happiness and love in one's Community, Society, Nation or Country. Thus, one must be guided by these three behavioural principles and must use them in practice at all times as his indispensable torch to happiness and prosperity and interactions with his/her fellow members of the Community, Society or Country in life.

But this is not all. To successfully realize this happiness and prosperity, one's belief or commitment to Theocentric Humanism Philosophy must also be reinforced by his belief in the Doctrine of Summum Bonum (i.e., the Greatest Good or Happiness for all). Thus, like a giraffe, which always sees and aims very high, a leader must also do the same. Thus, his aim in life must be to strive for the Greatest Good for all members of his/her community, society, nation, or country but not himself and his cohorts, as is now the habitual practice in Africa today where life appears to be slowly drifting into a Sodom and Gomorrah. Foolish life of devil worship and self-seeking men without hearkening to the consequences (Isaiah 2:1-22).

But, further, how can a leader attain this Greatest Good or Happiness for all? By what magic, formula or means?

According to The African Mysteries of The Grand Lodge of Luxor, one has to rely on not only Summum Bonum as a doctrine but by and large on its meaning which is: Justice, the virtue and excellence of Prudence (or Wisdom), Compassion and Courage. By relying on Justice, one is subject to be always free and fair without leaving any room for unethical or immoral values in his interactions with others; by relying on Prudence, virtue, one is subject to be excellent in one's all undertakings without giving room for professional mediocracy and poverty; by relying on Compassion, virtue, one is subject to be honest and mindful of other people's welfare; and to rely on Courage, virtue, one is also subject to fear no evil or any unrighteousness but to protect and sacrifice one's own life for what is righteous at all times and at all costs without any damn fear.

And, as an a priori stepping stone to one's better and proper understanding of Morality in general and Political Morality in particular in the art of Leadership in Political Life which is our next task in Part II (B) of this paper (below), our understanding of the virtue and excellence of both Theocentric Humanism Philosophy and the Doctrine of Summum Bonum is a first and foremost a necessity.

These Spirit and main emphasis of this Philosophy[6] and its Doctrine was that no one whether be a people, community, society, nation or country can possibly survive or accelerate in its socio-economic and political development unless both its leadership and all people in the country believed in and actually practiced Justice, Wisdom, Temperance and Courage. By doing this, one's community or country is assured of evolving into a Hybrid entity with a Hybrid culture which, according to this Philosophy and its Doctrine, was an essential prerequisite dose or path to Democracy Institutionalization, which is, in turn, also another essential pre-requisite dose or path to a comfortable durable peace and socio-economic recovery and prosperity for the benefit of that Country.

But the two strongly warned on the following condition to be borne in mind by every people, community, society or country. They warned that naturally, each individual in life is born totally ignorant of the world around it; and that individual is not able and cannot possibly tell right from birth what is virtue and what is vice. Accordingly, they emphasized that one can only do so (i.e, distinguish this variance) when he/she is moralized (i.e., educated or socialized) on the two. Because of this condition, the two, therefore, recommended that instead of relying totally on the individual to develop into a moral and useful being to his/her society community or country, Moralization (i.e, a genetic cultural engineering) on him/her was a first and foremost necessity. It was a necessity in that it would contain or prevent any chances of that individual from sliding into Immoralism (i.e, a belief or path into becoming a dangerously destructive monister in and against his/her people, community, society or country).

In the final analysis, the findings and emphasis of Theocentric Humanism Philosophy and its Doctrine of Summum Bonum are significantly useful indeed for the essence and significance of Socialization, Political Socialization, Moralization and Moralism to a people, community, society, nation or country in life if the latter is to accelerate in socio-economic and technological advancements as the Old Egyptian Community did in all these endeavours before Egypt was invaded and Macedonia under King Cyrus and Alexander The Great in 5225 BC and 332 BC (respectively) and carried away all this stupendous wealth to their own mother Countries.

Further, their findings and emphasis on the one hand, and those of the utilitarianism on the other are significantly congruent since both are concerned with the usefulness of one's character and behaviour in and to one's society which is quite logical and rational with regard to what every people, community, nation, society and country habitually and customarily do in their social setting. Also, it is on the basis of one's usefulness that one is normally conceptualized and judged whether good (moral) or bad (immoral) by others in his/her society. This reality and realism holds true not only on earth but also in Heaven.

On the strength of this important finding, we will now majestically move on to part III (C) of this paper below to examine our last and final double-edged question: which is:-

"If so, then what is 'Political Morality' And of what significance is it to man in life in relation to the 'Leadership' question which we have just tackled herein above in II (A) and (B) above?

## (C) Political Morality and Its Correlation with Leadership in Biopolitics.

Above (in II (A) and (B) of this Paper on the concept, function and usefulness of "Morality" in general social life), we have proved and confirmed that the concept is an indispensable component or ingredient of the social life in the sense that it is sacred and sacrosanct for the normal functioning and total survival of every people, community, society, nation or country in the latter's capacity as a Social entity which must also interact with other Social entities in the Community of Nations for survival.

In this regard, then, "Political Morality" must also be a strategic component or ingredient of political life sacrosanct for the normal functioning and total survival of every people, community society, nation or country in the latter's capacity as a Political entity.

And, since any absence of a "Morality" dose, ingredient, input or seasoning in a social life is tatamount to a social pathology of that social entity; it, therefore, also follows that any absence fo a "Political Morality" ingredient, dose, input or seasoning in a political life must also be tatamount to a political pathology of that political entity.

A political pathology is a political disease characterized by a variety of symptoms. These include, for example, Bad Leadership or Governance manifested in dictatorial policies and attitude, massive institutionalized corruption at and in all Branches of Government; looming country-wide abject poverty; various preventable and curable diseases; malnutrition; high infant mortality rate; inadequate health care facilities and medicines in spite of the presence of policies lying idle on shelves and cupboards unable to be attended to; rampant practice of management by crisis; looming abnormal use of state coffer to bribe for political support in order for a leader to continuing in one's political office; rampant conflict of various forms and at various levels; prevalent armed robberies of financial institutions, automobile owners, and homes; flabbergasting expropriation of one's office to misappropriate public assets for self-aggrandizement and with which to acquire sleek inter-cooler cars, etc at the expense of the general public which is, in turn, left hopelessly poor and even unable to pay salaries to its civil servants; hardly impassible road-net work all over the country forcefully keeping oneself in the public office by rigging the election or using public security to sustain the intention on the one hand, and by simply using nepotism to put and keep oneself, relatives and friends in office with total impunity in disregard of merits requirements and the law regulating recruitment, acquisition of jobs and promotions; and more so, total marginalization and disregard of the

Rule of Law and Justice thus justifying the contention that it should not be just the Existing Constitution in Kenya which is defective that requires reform but the people themselves and their total culture who are actually morally too sick requiring an immediate ambulance to an Intensive Care Unite (ICU) Hospital for a major surgery.

The actual meaning of all these pathological symptoms is succinctly that one's Leadership and total body politik is no more normal. It is abnormal in that it has lost a normal, healthy direction of Good Governance and moved into an abnormal, unhealthy direction as opposed to a normal, healthy direction in Political Life?

Obviously, an abnormal unhealthy direction is one which is characterized by those pathological symptoms noted in the immediate preceding paragraphs of this Paper. They are, in a nut-shell, manifested in an abnormal financial mismanagement promoted by a deliberate total lack and disrespect of the spirit of Transparency and Accountability on the one hand, and a deliberate total lack and disrespect of the concept of Democracy and Spirit of Self-Love and Self-Respect, on the other.

On the other hand, a normal, healthy direction is obviously one which has no such pathological problems found in the counterpart. Unlike its counterpart, the normal, healthy direction is a direction of a Leadership which is equally normal and healthy both in theory and practice. That is to say, what the Leader promise his people, community, society, nation or country is exactly what he actually does. He is, in other words, a true Political moralist who believes in, practices and teaches Political Moralism to his people that he leads to emulate him.

In this regard, as a Political Moralist expected to teach his people what moral values, are, then obviously, a Leader must be committed and guided by Political Moralism. Thus, he must be endowed with a natural gift of good political morals. And he must believe in Political Moralism. This is the only way he can also successfully convince all his people to have good political morals like him. **He must be able to set a good example in words and deeds (in theory and Practice) for his/her people, Community, Nation, or Country to emulate and to be proud of. He should be a reliable symbol and source of his/her peoples' pride and Dignity both at home and outside World of International Relations.**

But if he is of bad morals, obviously, then, he cannot make or expect his people to be what he is not. Thus, the Theory of Like-Begets-Like.

In this respect, then Political morality is an extremely crucial dose for every Leadership in order for his Country and the latter's political culture to acquire and have a morally acceptable values that are healthy, normal and conducive for all investments needed to accelerate socio-economic healing and recovery in his Country.

In other words, no country like Kenya which is so much wretched socio-economically can possibly get healed and recover from her existing socio-economic maladies without first and foremost get a healing and recovery from:-

(1) **Her Leadership's Deficiency in Good Political Morality**
(i.e., absence of the principles, rules, laws, doctrine, philosophy or ideals governing a normal and healthy body politik in order to accelerate that body politik in its socio-economic development and all efforts aimed at that goal); and

(2) **Her Leadership's Deficiency in Political Moralism**
Absence of a cardinal belief, addiction or commitment to one's Political Morality and its ideals for benefit of his Country and Prosperity of the people therein).

Accordingly, with this Political Morality at its finger-tips, such Leadershp is obviously assured of an accelerated socio-economic and political success for one's country and the people therein; and above all, one is also certainly assured of uninterrupted long tenure of one's political career because of these indisputable stupendous achievements for one's country and people which, in turn, succinctly means an automatic free key, license, passport or visa to office in every election. In all, this is the only Path to Democracy Institutionalization in any body politic. It is a reliable renaissance for a genuine Democracy Institutionalization for a young Country such as Kenya yearning for such goal for the Greatest Good of her People.

CHAPTER III

# Conclusion

## (1) Summary

From Part I to Part III of this research expedition, the effort has been to clinically diagnose: (I) the concept "Leadership" (see part II) and the concept "Political Morality" (see part III) in terms fo their meaning and their strategic usefulness to mankind in Biopolitics; (2) the reliability and accuracy, and the unreliability and inaccuracy or anomaly of the previous researchers on the subject matter; and above all, (3) the correlation between (Leadership" on the one hand, and "Political Morality" on the other with specific reference to their mutual or non-mutual usefulness to man in Political Life; and the reasons why.

In all, we have noted with significant satisfaction that Leadership is indeed an essential ingredient in life in the sense that without it, a nuclear family, a people, community, nation or country is essentially amorphous (i.e., disorganized, disjointed and, therefore, unstructured), and cephalous (i.e., headless, without any one to lead and help organize everyone into a cohesive entity for a common corporate goal or objective, e.g. food security, health security, external or foreign security, etc).

Further, we have also noted with the same satisfaction that "Morality" in general and "Political Morality" in particular are essential ingredients in the social, political and all sectors of life. Inasmuch as in the social life, no social entity can live or survive in the absence of this "Morality" ingredient (or dose) ; similarily, in the political life, no political entity can possibly live or survive in the absence of this "Political Morality" ingredient (or dose). **Succinctly, each is a harmonizing agent to its life because it serves as an antibiotic agent against any anti-body virus such as corruption, dishonesty, nepotism, abject poverty, professional poverty (mediocrity and negligence), tribal (ethnic) conflict, election rigging, Memorandum of**

**Understanding Dishonesty, management by crisis, and many other symptoms of Moral Decay in an Undemocracy.**

We *further* noted that whereas all these existing socio-economic and political woes in Kenya and most other African Countries are collectively a reminiscence of this Undemocracy syndrome or disease endemic in Africa; and that all these pathological problems are essentially man-made which could, therefore, be eradicated mechanically by the same man which is its architect and builder. And finally that in order for man to successfully do so is to, first and foremost, agree to form partnership with Science and use the latter's prescription against the existing socio-economic and political maladies.

To call a spade a spade, man must agree to use a scientific method to reform himself first in his capacity as a leader, and then make himself an exemplary model to all that he leads. To do so successfully, he has to: (1) Completely take off his present filthy and unrighteous attires of Political Immorality and Immoralism (characterized by his disobedience to his own moral values and other rules embodied in his National Constitution on the one hand; and in his Religious Beliefs on the other which collectively command him to respect his fellow man and serve him as so expected of him by his Terms of Reference and Oath of Office during the Inauguration); and (2) put on a completely new attire of Political Morality and Moralism (characterized by his obedience to his own moral values and other rules embodied in his National Constitution on the one hand; and in his Religious Beliefs on the other which collectively command him to respect his fellow man and serve him as so expected of him by his Terms of Reference and Oath of Office during the Inauguration).

Obviously, in a least democratic country such as Kenya, there is no any other magic above this Resuscitation Plan, if it is genuinely serious in its efforts toward Democracy Institutionalization, and also serious in realizing that goal.

Accordingly, any other effort(s) such as the on-going Constitutional Reform or Review in Kenya today is not only bound to be a futile exercise but also a funds-wastage since it is the existing Constitution which has any case to answer but solely the People of Kenya themselves and their sick culture of self-aggrandizement, institutionalized corruption and nepotism at the expense of the majority poor who who actually have a serious case to answer. Concomitantly, even with a very superb and glittering New Constitution dressed and coated with gold and diamonds, obviously this New Constitution will similarly not bring about Democracy and

Good Governance in Kenya. The present disgusting immoral culture behaviour at all levels of Public Offices is subject to continue unabated. In this regard, the on going Reform is, therefore, subject or bound to achieve nothing of a significant value to the Kenyans, in spite of the colossal time, energy and funds wasted on it so far. In a nut-shell, The Existing Constitution has no case to answer.

## (2) Succinct Recommendation/A Resuscitation Plan Toward Democracy Institutionalization in Biopolitics in general and Kenya in particular.

(a) General Recommendation

In a retrospect, in conformity with the virtue and excellence of Science, it is here now hope (1) that the following remedial measures will be taken into a serious consideration and used as a possible Logical Path to Democracy Institutionalization not only in Kenya but also in all other African Countries where perennial leadership crisis has always persisted un abated since the beginning of post-Colonial Leadership era; (2) that it hearkened to meticulously and scrupulously, these measures shall accordingly fulfill their intended obligation as a Resuscitation Plan to the user(s); (3) that, in the final analysis Kenya is subject to realized an amazing renaissance towards the expected Democracy Institutionalization goal.

(b) Specific Recommendations

(a) Whereas a Leader is normally and faithfully expected under his Oath of Office to adhere and do just that as so spelled out in his Terms of Reference, The Oath of Office, The Constitution and The Expectations of his People, obviously it is his sacred duty to do so.

(b) He should be a True Moralist who is able to teach his people more about Morality and Moralism; and above all, the significance of the two to The Nation.

(c) He should faithfully reveal his true self and all his aspirations or policy which collectively constitute his clear identity to his people, and above all, carry them out practically other than abandoning or absconding them by just heaping them on his Office shelves, and in cupboards, or draws at the mercy of cockroaches and cobwebs as is the practice today.

(d) He should show, by examples, to those that he leads the meaing of Benevolence to the neighbours, if he actually expects the same from neigbours.

(e) He should demonstrate what sacrifice actually is by practicing it himself as a paradigm to his people that he leads.
(f) He should practice Summum Bonum and its inherent virtues: Justice, Wisdom, Compassion and Courage against every form of temptations towards corruption, disorganization of the opposition aimed at disabling and making them totally hopeless and ineffective in their capacity or role as an anti-biotic pill against undemocracy and other forms of Bad Governance, etc.
(g) He should develop and have at his finger-tips a far reaching insight, honesty and dignity in all his acts, in his capacity as a true Chief Executive guided by Summum Bonum (Justice, Wisdom, Compassion and Courage) manifested in the Leadership of various men such as Churchill Roosevelt' Lincoln, Otto Bismark, Patrice Lumumba, Konrad Adenauer, Charles de Gaulle, Nelson Mandela, John Kennedy, etc who qualified as hero Chief Executive because of such Leadership qualities guided by Summum Bonum.
(h) He should be an initiator or learn how to initiate a new path towards a new Political Community and Culture of a hybrid nature which is free from corruption, election riggings, lies, all forms of dishonesty in one's Leadership ostensibly aimed at self-aggrandisement and get-rich quickly evil motive at the disadvantage of the entire nation likely to slide it into massive abject poverty, acute poor health state, poor eduction facilities, poor road-net work saturated with dangerous pot-holes to motorists, etc; and many other symptoms of national poverty, wretchedness, hopelessness, helplessness and easy susceptibility to foreign enemy.
(i) He should be one who is able to offer his people good hopes which are sensible, practicable and affordable but not infested or loaded with a bunch of lies and hopelessness that cannot be realized in the real world of one's national financial abilities.
(j) He should be one who is able and willing to do all these six cardinal duties if he actually seeks to achieve Democracy Institutionalization during his Leadership for his peoples and he is leading.
(k) In other words, a Leader must prove that he is able to do all these tasks by virtue of his role as a Leader.
(l) The Leader must play the role of a Political Moralist in as much as a parent plays the role of a Moralist to his/her children.

(m) And, to do, all these successfully, a Leader has a duty to be as committed to Political Moralism as a prent is always committed to Moralism with a view to bringing up moralled children.

(n) He should be one Loves, gains satisfaction and constantly rejoices in one's the people he leads who actually bestowed on him the Authority of his office but not one who boasts over one's wealth amessed through blantant theft from the same people who actually are his employer and payers of his salary.

(o) And, as a Father of The Nation, he is deemed or expected to set a good, dignified example of genuine honesty, love, unity but not a spirit of dishonesty, disunity and other evils on one hand; and reliance on use of state coffers to disstablize the opposition through bribery, intimidations, assassinations, and other undemocratic and immoral acts.

(p) Finally, he should be one who commands sufficient technical competence due to his professional expertise of what he is promising his people; and must also have a command of a sufficient information influence due to this logic of what he is talikg about. Thus, he should avoid being just a parrot talking almost nonsense.

## (3) Justifications of this Resuscitation Plan

The above provided Action Plan prescription is very much sound and logical. It is sound and logical in that:-

(a) Leadership alone in devoid of Political Morality is as suicidal as an acephelous society or people without Leadership. It is as useless and dangerous as a beautiful golden highway city without traffic lights or regulation. It cannot alone Lead one to Democracy Institutionalization.

(b) Both Leadership and Political Morality are naturally co-ingredients that each people, society, community, nation or country naturally needs and must always have in order for it to have a better future.

(c) These co-ingredients are the most essential antibiotic doses requisite for every wretched country such as those in Africa that are already a perpetual host of/to massive contengious viruses viz. abject poverty, various diseases, ignorance, and a myriad of other agonies. The presence of the two is critically important if a country, nation or people is to achieve and accelerate in socio-economic healing and recovery.

(d) But there are two types of Leadership and two types of Political Morality viz. "Good Leadership" and "Good Political Morality" on the one hand, which are co-instrumental to the people concerned; and "Bad Leadership" and "Bad Political Morality" on the other which are co-suicidal to the people concerned.

(e) Therefore, having a "Naked Leadership" and a "Naked Political Morality" which are not instrumental to the people they are supposed to serve is as equally suicidal as having "No Leadership" and "No Political Morality" at all.

(f) This is so due to the fact that it has always been because of the absence of the two co-ingredients (Good Leadership and Good Political Morality) in most African countries that has made Africa a perpetual host of those multi-agonies.

(g) In view of these facts, this Resuscitation Plan is obviously significant. It show how this unfortunate situation has always been allowed in Africa to germinate, grow and spread unchked all over the Continent, the implications and adverse effects of this negligence; and what could, therefore, be done in order to successfully contain or eradicate the actual root-cause of this negligence and set the Continent free.

## Foot-notes

(1) This approach has been used exhaustively in the author's on-going volume 1 titled Leadership Genetic Engineering (which as a thorough clinical diagnosis of Leadership success and failures from partriarch Adam generation to the present in the author's book titled WHY LEADERS FAIL.

(2) Idem.

(3) Even in Primary reference books such as encyclopaedia, apart from The International Encyclopaedia for Social Sciences, this very important subject is non-existent at least all of them. But where it has been examined, all this has been limited to human life in the Animal Kingdom only.

(4) Ibid., op. cit. N.1 above

(5) Idem

(6) Idem

(7) International Encyclopaedia for Social Sciences pp. 107-108

(8) The World Book Encyclopaedia vol. 13, pp. 807-808.

(9) Ibid., vol. 18, pp. 648 (a)-648 (d)

(10) Ibid., vol. 5. pp. 80 (b)-80 (c)

(11) Ibid., vol. 1, pp. 51

(12) Ibid., vol. 16, pp. 412-421
(13) Ibid., vol. 3, pp. 425-425
(14) Ibid., vol. Pp. 275-289
(15) Robert Michels' Political Parties, A Sociological Study of the Oligarchical Tendencies of Modern Democracy, Dover, N.Y. (1959)
(16) The International Encyclopaedia for social sciences pp. 483-494
(17) Agola Auma-Osolo, Cause-Effects, of Modern African Nationalism on the World Market, University Press of America, London (1983), chap. VII, particularly pp. 116-117
(18) See also The Oxford English Dictionary
(19) Idem
(20) Idem
(21) Idem
(22) World Book Encyclopaedia vol. 18, pp. 460
(23) The International Encyclopaedia for Social Sciences pp. 497-498
(24) Idem
(25) Auma-Osolo, op. cit. N. 17
(26) The World Book Encyclopaedia vol. 9, pp. 386
(27) George G.M. James, The Stolen Legacy, The Greeks Were Not the People of North Africa Community Called the Egyptians, philosophical Library, New York (1954)
(28) This Conclusion is drawn from the following analysis and facts on the subject in question:
(29) The concept "Conflict" and the latter's inherent dynamics and problem to Kenya today is as old as Mankind including the Total Creation. Theologically, it is first manifested in a situation of discord between God and God's archi-angel (Satan/Lucifer/Blair) in which Satan was consequently casted down to the Earth from heaven by God because of God's wrath against Satan's disloyalism and disloyalty to God; in a situation between God and Adam in which Adam was ejected out of the Garden of Eden into the scarce wilderness because of God's wrath against Adam's negligence/disobedience to God's commandment; and also, in a situation between God and Cain in which Cain got a curse from God because of Cain's murder of his righteous brother (Abel) and for his ruddiness to God on Abel's death question.

And, from a Behavioral and Social Sciences Approach, "Conflict" is succinctly a situation of discord, disagreement, disharmony, displeasure, etc. between two or more entities. These entities may be animate or inanimate. In the animates, conflict occurs in all members of the Animal Kingdom as well as those of the Plant Kingdom. And, in the inanimate, it also occurs between entities or things whenever they do not match, rhyme or agree in size, colour, sound, shape, weight, kind, taste, etc.

However, in as much as Conflict embraces all these multi various meanings or phenomena, this Study shall limit itself to the Conflict pertaining specifically to intra-and inter-personal discords only. But since these two phenomena also embrace various kinds of Conflict such as social Conflict (e.g., marital conflict), economic conflict (e.g. marktet price conflict), biological conflict (e.g., red blood cell—versus white blood cell conflict), academic conflict (e.g. author conflict), etc., this Study shall, therefore, restrict its focus to the political conflict per se with a particular attention to the manner in which it occurs in Kenya; how it is normally conceived and managed; and the problems inherent in the total process, as a pardigm of thid epidemic in the entire African Continent.

In the final analysis, this Study is expected to be significant to both Scientists and Policy-Makers a like in the sense that it is going to use an in-depth meticulous clinical diagnosis of all types of Conflicts in Kenya ranging from **Intra-Kenyan Political Conflicts** generated by various viruses such as intra-and inter-political party and ethnic discords to **Extra-kenyan Political Conflicts** generated by misunderstandings between Kenya and her neighbours including all other members of the Interantional Community iside and outside Africa. Also, it is going to synthesize the findings therefrom into some coherent parsimonious body of knowledge (statements) through which one may easily understand better the meaning, dynamics and problem "Conflict" on the one hand, and how and why man has been unable to contain it on the other, as a pardigm of Conflict in Political Life.

# PART TEN

## SOVEREIGN EQUALITY DEMAND, CARROT DIPLOMACY, HARAMBEE MYTH, TERRORISM AND WAR: A Test for Leadership Paranoia and Failure.

## CHAPTER I

# Introduction

### (1) The Problem

A people of the Luhya tribe in Kenya called "Samia" located in Samia District, Western Kenya, have a traditional saying that "okhuba Nolia Akhuya Mao Nobona" (i.e., whoever feeds you beats your mother while you helplessly watch). Of course this belief is neither limited to Samia People alone nor to other all Kenyans only. It is a universal belief throughout Africa; and as a human relations phenomenon, it must also be a belief of all World Communities.

Accordingly, taking into account the on-going contentions and counter-contentions between the Developing Countries and the Donor Community today regarding conditions for receiving aid from the Donor Community, it is evident that this debate is being precipitated by this universal belief. On the strength of my research findings gained from Kenya, Uganda, Tanzania, Ethiopia, Sudan and Djibout (1985-1993) on the subject during my tenure as an international civil servant and thereafter, it is apparent that all Developing Countries which, due to their weak socio-economic standing on the World Market have therefore to depend on the Donor Community for foreign aid in the form of grants and soft-loans which include foodstuffs, fertilizers, military hardwares, and technical assistance, are often worried that by so depending on such aid, their sovereignty, independence, territorial integrity, self-love, self-respect and self-pride are automatically endangered on the World Market among those who do finance and feed them. Accordingly, each is uneasy with those conditions attached to the aid by the Donor Community which include Structural Adjustment which calls for reduction of civil service staff; devaluation of local currency; introduction of Multi-Party Democracy in lieu of the One Party Democracy, Privatization of State-controlled economic institutions in order to facilitate checks-and-balances; devolution of power to avoid misuse of power, removal of inefficient corrupt key personnel and the like in order to stimulate efficiency and a productive socio-economic growth and development of their respective countries to be meaning sheer harassment and interference in the internal affairs of Developing Countries by Donor Countries using their AID as a carrot.

To these beneficiaries of the Donors' Aid, their general sentiments over the issue is simply that the Donor Community is not being fair to them. They are concerned that although they need this Aid, their right to Equal Sovereignty in the International System is not being respected as required by the International Law governing this right and the total system.

Because of this contentions tug of war between the two, obviously the health of the International System must be seriously affected. Its eufunction is questionable; and must, therefore, be addressed in order to establish mysteries surrounding the tug of war and their implication to the mutual relations between the two parties for the health security of the system.

## (2) Purpose

In view of this delicate nature of the relations between the Aid Donor Community on the one hand, and the Aid Beneficiary Community on the other which does not seem to be conducive to the normal functioning of the International System, the purpose of this Chapter in this Volume Two is to systematically examine their respective positions of these contentious issues and their implication(s) to the system.

## (3) Methodology

Since the nature of the Donor Aid Beneficiary Community is not as <u>cohesive</u> as that of the Donor Aid Community whose members know and interact with each other for the purpose of collectively managing their Aid and setting up conditions they want to govern their Aid for purpose(s) known to themselves, this study will focus on Africa as a unit of analysis. Africa will be used as a representative of all those who benefit from Aid.

The data will be from both primary and secondary sources. From the primary source, the data will be drawn from my own research sexperince in Afirca as follows: (1) during my tenure as an Assistant Program Officer whith US AID, Kenya based in Nairobi (Jan 1980—March 1983) from where I gained a first hand experience on Donor Community theory and practice with regard to their Aid dynamics and goal; and an international civil servant with the Desert Locust Control Organization from Eastern AFrica (DLCO-EA) based in Addis Ababa Ethiopia and composed of seven member Arican Countries viz: Djibouti, Eriteria, Ethiopia, Kenya, Somalia, Sudan, Tanzania and Uganda; and (2) in my capacity as a social scientist of the African heritage and permanently living in Kenya as a Kenyan national. And, from the secondary source, the data will be drawn from various types of the literature viz: books, journals, monographs, news papers, etc.

# CHAPTER II

# Sovereign Equality Rights

## (1) Definition

Sovereign Equality is a concept drawn from the concept sovereignty which inter alia means one's freedom from an external control, rule, dominion or authority. Thus, the concept is born from the concept sovereignty as follows:-

### (a) At the Individual Level

At the individual level, sovereign equality concept succinctly means one's right to exist in life on equal footing with all others with respect to his right to life and security as a human being. Even a slave who is supposed to live and work for his slave owner/master, the fact, which is natural and factual universally, is simply that like his master, he also has the right to life as his master does. The naturality and naturalism of this fact is borne out by another fact that both the slave and the slave master are governed by the law of nature architected by God Himself in His capacity as Creator of the total Universe which includes both that slave and his master. Governed by this law of nature, both the slave and the slave master unconditionally respond to the common demands of this law. For example, each is demanded by this law to do the same thing in order to survive. Each must breathe, eat, sleep, excreate, drink water, seek social love and respect by interacting with others, etc. However, in all these respects, each (the slave and his master) is naturally required by the same law to love oneself so much that every perceived source, of interference, risk, danger or disaster to one's life or survival is automatically not accepted at all. Each is naturally mandated by his Creator as so stipulated in The Book of The Genesis under Chapter 1:26-31 to do all those that pertains to protection and enhancement of one's survival as follows:

> ***"And God said "let us make man in Our image, after Our likeness; and let them have dominion over the fish of the sea, and over the fowl of the air, and over the cattle, and over all the earth, and over every creeping thing that creeps upon the earth". (verse 26)***
>
> ***"So God created man in His own image, in the image of God, he created him; male and female created He them." (verse 27)***
>
> ***"And God blessed them, and God said to them, Be fruitful and multiply, and replenish the earth, and subdue it: and have dominion over the fish of the sea, and over the fowl of the air, and over every living thing that moves upon the earth." (verse 28)***

A retrospective analysis of this data gained from an interdisciplinary approach shows beyond any reasonable doubt that God is the actual source of the concept of each person's right to life on equal footing with every one else. This source is recognized and used universally by every human being not only in social life but also in science. In Theological and Jurisprudence Science, for example, it is intersubjectively used with an emphais that before God, all men are equal regardless of race, gender, nationality, or creed. And in Administration of Justice, the law requires that each person must be treated equal. From The Second Book of Samuel in The Holy Bible this realiy is supported by God's command that:

> ***"He that rules over men must be just, ruling in the fear of God". (II Samuel 23:3)***
>
> ***"And he shall be as the light of the morning, when the sun rises, even a morning without clouds; as the tender grass springing out of the earth by clear shining after rain". (II Samuel 23:4)***

In the final analysis it is self-evident that sanctity to life and man's right to it is mandatory and universal. It is sacred emanating from God. It is neither man-made not man-given. It emanates from The Creator of man and total Universe. It is mandated to him not by man's justified right but by the grace of his Maker who made it so. And, it is therefore mandatory and universal in that it is inherent to all mankind regardless of race, creed, nationality, gender, or other statuses one may possess in society. This therefore simply means that by equal sovereignty right of man, each human being has equal rights to air, and all that are naturally accorded to him or her by the grace and wishes of his or her Maker.

On the strength of this reality with regard to the concepts of equality and equal sovereignty of every individual in life, each individual is entitled to equal civil and human rights in one's society, country or nation-state. Accordingly, as long as one is 18 years old or above, one is automatically qualified under his Country Constitution to cast his vote for a political candidate of his choice without any prejudice. And by the grace of God and Constituional Rights of one's Country, one's vote is equal to the vote of the other person. A woman's vote is equal in weight to the weight of a man's vote. A slave's vote and that of his master are also equal in weight.

Consequently, the concepts sovereignty and sovereign equality among people simply mean that all people are equal and must therefore, be accepted, treated and ruled or governed on equal weight of justice. Hence, the significance of the two concepts in terms of what each leader must do at all times as a leader to those he leads in order to sustain his Leadership.

### (b) At the Community Level

At the community level, sovereign equality is as significant as sovereign equality at the individual level. This reality is supported/ and emanates from the fact that community is a sum total of the same individuals (men and women) having and enjoying this right directly from the Law of Nature governed by The Greator of Total Universe who grants such rights to whoever He wishes to do so at will and at His own discretion.

In a nut shell, sovereign equality at a community level ranges from the rights of a nuclear family to peer groups, and finally to large and small formal organizations such as church, school, health centres, political party and nation-state or country. In each corporate entity, each member always wants recognition, love, fair and just treatment. Formal and informal norms are always found to be in place for the sole purpose of enforcing this sacred right of every individual member; and also for the purpose of punishing any wrong doer found contriving the norm. In Kenya, for instance, the Country has in place a National Constitution and various other laws and by-laws including Codes of Good Conduct which every Kenyan is expected to recognize and abide with in one's undertakings; failure of which one is right away arrested and arraigned in court for appropriate prosecution.

All political structures and norms in every Country have a common goal. They are to enforce every one's recognition and respect of each other's rights to life, property, business, etc provided that such rights are legitimate and is not a potential danger to the Country's survival.

And, in International System which is a sum total of all independent nation-states, multi-national corporations, individuals, etc, all nation-states (which are the principal actors in the System) have a clean bill of rights to this sovereign equality principle. This principle is one of the key fundamental principles of International Law aimed at protecting each nation-state's freedom from all external interferences in its domestic jurisdiction unless a matter which is domestic is understood to be loaded with a potential danger to World Peace and Security. It is because of this exception that grants the International Community Leadership the right of intervention in domestic matters that this leadership often intervenes in an internal matter of a Country whether with or without the consent of that Country.

An empirical evidence is borne out by the recent case of the International Community's intervention in Kenya during inter-ethnic genocide arising form the Presidential Election fraud in December, 2007. No matter how vehement the Kenyan Government under President Mwai Kibaki reacted by refusing to allow any foreign intervention by claiming that the Kenyan matter was solely internal and did not need any foreign interference, the International Community Leadership forced its way into Kenya so as to stop the on-going ethnic mutual genocide and to bring the two principlals of the conflict namely President Kibaki and his Governing Party of National Unity (PNU) and the Opposition Party of Honourable Raila Odinga and his party of Orange Democratic Movement (ODM) to a round table negotiation.

It was by this courageous efforts of the International Community Leadership (having a strong support of the then USA President (George W. Bush, Jr) that Kenya was thus fortunately saved from the quagmire.

The International Community Leadership's act was fully in keeping with International Law provision which inter alia states under Article 2 paragraph 7 of the UN Charter that although each UN Member State is at liberty to its right of domestic jurisdiction, this does not mean total freedom and exeption. This warning is as follows:-

> *Nothing contained in the present Charter shall authorize the United Nations to intervene in matters which are essentially within the domestic jurisdiction*

> *of any state or shall require the members to submit such matters to settlement under the present United Nations Charter; but this principle shall not prejudice the application of enforcement measuers [by The International Community Leadership] under Chapter VII (emphasis added).*

This reality is exhaustively documented in Agola Auma-Osolo, "A Retrospective Analysis of United Nations Activity in the Congo and Its Significance for Contemporary Africa", Vanderbilt Journal of Transnational Law, Vol. 8 No. 2, Spring 1975, p. 460.

In view of this empirical evidence, sovereign Equality rights of a people, Country or Nation-States can only be recognized and upheld whenever that right does not pose a potential danger to peace and security in the International Community. The Kenya case is a prima-facie evidence of such a problem. This is why the International Community Leadership waived Kenya's right of Sovereign Equality in order to save not only the Country from ethnic mutual genocide but, in the main, in order to save peace and security of the entire International System. It was argued particularly by the US President, the former UN Secretary General (H.E. Kofi Annan who headed the Peace Negotiation as Chief Negotiator) that Kenya was a host of various UN agencies such UN Environment Programme (UNEP), UN Habitat, UN Development Programme (UNDP); and thus it was very imperative to stop mutual genocide to spill over these UN facilities. Hence, a valid added asset to the legitimacy of the International Leadership's intervention. It was a most cost-effective prudent decision having enormous dividends.

## (2) Universal Demand For Sovereign Equality Rights

In Africa, each Government often assumes that its Country's Sovereignty is being endangered by external forces. In the Republic of Kenya, for example, complaints and warnings abound by the

Government authorities to Foreign Governments to respect the Kenyan Sovereignty to cease from interfering in the Kenyan internal affairs; and to stop dictating to Kenya on what to do and on what is right or wrong, as if Kenya were incapable and incompetent to prudently know and judge as to what was right or wrong for her national interest. This hostility was very vivid during the former leadership of President Daniel T. arap Moi.

For example, in the Daily Nation of Friday, August 6, 1993, the then President Daniel Toroitich Arap Moi vehemently complained about some diplomats accredited to Kenya for having constantly violated Diplomatic Conventions by associating themselves with subversive activities in Kenya against their diplomatic protocols. He then warned them to watch out as his Government was no longer going to tolerate such behaviour. In his own words, then then President emphasized, "We are a Sovereign State and the democratization process should not mean being bulldozed or dictated to by outsiders. We will not accept it". (Daily Nation, 6/8/93 pg. 1).

But no sooner had the President's warning lasted a week than the Diplomatic Corps accredited to Kenya reacted to the warning. As per the subsequent Daily Nation of Friday, August 13, 1993. for example, the German Ambassador Mr. Bernd Mutzelburg, defended his fellow Ambassadors accredited to Kenya by saying that whatever they were doing in Kenya was justified because: (1) they were doing so on behalf of their respective governments; and (2) the role of Kenyan Government on the question of Human Rights in the Country had not improved so far, with specific reference to the rights for opposition parties in the Country. The German Ambassador further argued that the climate was still saturated with intimidation, threats, and bribery all of which were totally antithetical, inhospitable and non-conducive to the Kenyan people's enjoyment of Human Rights expected in Kenya by the Ambassadors' respective governments. He emphasized that "There cannot be a good government where those in power do not enjoy legitimacy conveyed to them by free and fair election; do not allow channels for criticism and dissent; do infringe upon human rights and freedoms; do not believe in separation of powers; fail to promote an efficient civil service independent from political parties; and finally refuse to accept mechanisms for their own removal, if the people so wish." And then cautioned that "wherenever and whenever there is no lawful and peaceful means to change a government, those who have been excluded from power are inevitably frustrated and conflicts often result", thereby forcing those in power to abdicate such power.

Also, no sooner had a week also passed after this reply to. The President by the Diplomatic Corps in Kenya than the Kenyan Foreign Minister, Mr. Kalonzo Musyoka, intervened in defence of The President on Kenyan sovereignty issue. In as per the Sunday Nation of August 15,1993, Mr. Musyoka accused the Diplomats in Kenya of being biased against KANU leaders and for maintaining close links with the opposition against the KANU Government by using such links to implicate the KANU Government officials in unfounded scandals. [And the Foreign Minister also warned the Diplomats to keep off from Kenya's Internal Affairs as Kenya was a Sovereign State capable of managing its affairs on its own including its democratization process without needing foreign assistance].

In spite of these warnings [and other efforts by the Kenya Government to fend off what Kenya purports to be foreign interference in Kenyan Domestic Jurisdiction, the European Community (EC) which is now European Union (EU) held a closed-door meeting with the Foreign Minister and registered their complaints over what they considered as Kenyan Government's continued breaches of Press Freedom (see Daily Nation of August 26, 1993). On 24 August 1993, Denmark significantly reduced its Bilateral Aid to Kenya citing the Goldenberg Scandal, Corruption in the Government and continuing Clashes in the Country (see Daily Nation of 25 August 1993). And on 25 August, more Donors viz: USA, Canada, Germany and Sweden also joined Denmark threatening to cut off their Bilateral Aid to Kenya (see Daily Nation 25 August, 1993).

These new drastic cuts of the AID to Kenya by the Donors obviously disturbed the Kenyan Government so much that the latter had to also respond with an equal tough Official Policy Statement in the Kenya Broadcasting Coroporation News Commentary of Thursday 26 August, 1993. [In the Statement, the Government expressed its serious concern and dismay over the Donors' tendency to continue using their AID as a tool with which to harass Kenya and all other Needy Countries using lame and unfounded excuses while Kenya, for one, had already accepted and begun implementing all Donors' conditions, although such Conditions have, in the end, turned out to be very painful and expensive experiences to the Peoples of Kenya. And on Saturday August 28,1993, the Government expressed its serious dismay and concern over Ms Kerry Kennedy's allegations against Kenya on Tribal Clashes in Molo claiming that these allegations against Kenya on Tribal Clashes were totally untrue and malicious. This bitter contention by the Kenyan Government against the Donor Community has once again been echoed by the Government in its response against the most recent UK Report on Tribal Clashes in Kenya by Lord Davide Ennals of the House of Lords. In a strongly worded statement, the Report called it "outright lies and further efforts to hoodwink the international community from the fact that peace now prevails in Molo, Londiani and Burnt Forest." (Daily Nation, Sunday October 10, 1993).

## (3) Findings

But what is Sovereignty? For what use is it in political life, most particularly to Developing Countries? Where does justice lie between the two contending parties (The Kenya Government and the Diplomatic Corps accredited to Kenya) on the issue of Sovereign Equality? What lessons do we learn from this situation? Is it in keeping with our symbiotic world in which all live and need each other to improve for our future generation for national development particularly in Kenya, Africa and in the rest of the Developing World?

### (a) Sovereignty and Sovereign Equality

Sovereignty is the supreme, [absolute, and uncontrollable] power by which every independent state governs itself. A Sovereign State is a State which is independent and which is, therefore, absolutely free to manage its domestic (internal) affairs without any interference from external forces such as foreign governments, individuals, groups of individuals, business companies and corporations, etc. Further, a Sovereign State is a State, which is also absolutely free to manage its own non-domestic/foreign (external) affairs without any interference from those external forces cited above. Such external affairs include entering into all various types of contractual agreements and other activities with other Sovereign States, e.g., treaties, conventions, and to initiate and conclude war with any other Sovereign State or States. Such activities may be <u>bilateral</u> (i.e.) between two states) or multilateral (i.e. among three or more states).

Accordingly, it was this unanimous desire among the founding fathers of Sovereign States at the Peace of Westphalia (1648) three centuries ago that each State shall be free to maintain its freedom, and to manage its own domestic and external affairs without any external interference that became the fundamental root-cause of what we now know as "Sovereign Equality Rights Between and Among Independent States".

In the final analysis, by this concept of "Sovereign Equality of Independent States", we hereby mean that Kenya, USA, India, UK, Japan, Nigeria, Togo, Cambodia, Vietnam, Newzealand, etc., are all equal. All are on equal footing in the Community of Nations, and on The World Market, regardless of their differences in socio-economic status (development). In the United Nations General Assembly, Security Council, etc., all have equal voting power. Before the International Court of Justice or any other World Juridical Body, all are also on equal footing. None is superior to the other.

### (b) The Law of Sovereign Equality for Independent States

But, in order to safeguard this mutual understanding between and among Independent States, it was deemed necessary to have a tangible protective mechanism against the would-be bully/aggressive States against weaker States. Accordingly, the Law of Sovereign Equality was conceived and enshrined in International Law to safeguard such rights between and among States. This Law is universal and is envisaged in every convention and treaty between and among independent States effective the first ever lived treaty in Internaional Relations called Egypto-Hittite Treaty of Non-Aggression of 1284 BC between Ancient Egypt and Babylon.

This term "Independent State" must not be confused to include the States of Alabama, Michigan, Connecticutt, Massachussetts, Illinois, North Carolina, Georgia and other States in the United States of America. In the USA, each is independent only internally but not externally. This is why each cannot enter into treaties nor conventions with other States such as Kenya, Malawi, India, UK, Japan, and all those other Soverign States which are independent both internally and externally. In North American Continent, the only independent Sovereign States are The United States of America and Canada.

### (c) The Law of Domestic Jurisdiction for Independent Nation States

Whereas by The Law of Sovereign Equality, all Sovereign States are equal and must, therefore, treat each other as such at all times and places, The Law of Domestic Jurisdiction, on the other hand, presupposes the fact that "This is my home therefore nobody else but I alone is allowed to decide for my home as to who gets what, when, how and why". This is why under Article 2 of the UN Charter, neither a UN Member State nor the UN itself is allowed to intervene (interfere) in matters which are deemed to be essentially within the domestic jurisdiction of another Member-State of the UN. Also, this is why neither the African Union nor its Member-States is authorized to interfere/intervene in Somalia, Liberia, Congo, and all other African Independent States currently under civil turmoil. (Art. 3 of OAU Charter).

In other words, the aims and functions of The Law of Domestic Jurisdiction are complementary and supplementary to the aims and functions of the Law of Sovereign Equality and vice versa. In short, both Laws mutually assist each other to safeguard the interests, freedom, and personality of each independent State among it counterparts (States) on the World Market.

### (d) Universality of Sovereign Equality and Domestic Jurisdiction Concepts

These two concepts of "Soverign Equality" and "Domestic Jurisdiction" are not abstract ideals per se. Nor are they restricted to States and Political Life only. They are real and universal phenomena in our social setting. In every society, for example, each individual, family or business company is a sovereign in its own rights in that each is free to make its own decisions in life. Each is free to decide what to do, when, how and why. Each individual, group of individuals, or business company is free to decide who to deal with without any external dictates.

Similarly, each entity is free to handle its own affairs without being dictated to by external forces as to how and when to do it. Thus, each entity has natural rights over its domestic jurisdiction.

However, in spite of this natural rights and justice inherent in every living organism, such rights areonly justified so long as they do not infringe on the rights of another organism. Otherwise, one's natural sovereignty and natural justice rights automatically cease to be valid once they transpass into another individual's natural sovereignty and natural justice. In this case, one's domestic jurisdiction rights ceases to hold because of the said violation. And, the problem now becomes an inter-individual issue solvable only by the norm and machinery established by the Society of the said individuals. For example, purchasing and using a TV is one's natural domestic jurisdiction rights. But if that TV is stolen and later found in another's home, the matter is automatically deemed societal settleable only by their Society's machinery. A thief's ownership rights over the stolen TV or any other property automatically ceases to exist as soon as it is established that the TV is a stolen property.

Accordingly, these two concepts of "Sovereign Equality" and "Domestic Jurisdiction" are not unique to States and Political Life alone. They are universal throughout mankind and are spatio-temporal free (i.e., they are not limited to specific time or space at all).

## (4) A Comparative Analysis

Sovereign Equality Demand in Kenya is neither new nor restricted to Kenya or to Africa. As we will note in details here below, the Demand is a common phenomenon among all Less Developed Countries because of their poverty and military inferiority on the one hand, and their misunderstanding of the position and good intentionon of the Developed World on the other.

It is of course submitted that in our own generation, for example, we have witnessed Panama being invaded and its President captured and taken away to USA to be tried in US Courts; we have witnessed Uganda being invaded and its President driven out of Uganda by foreign forces; in Iraq, we have witnessed an execution of its President Saddam Husein and the bombardment of Iraq Capital of Baghdad by foreign forces and being dictated by the same forces to eliminate and destroy all her nuclear potentials; we have witnessed Cambodia, and many other South American independent states forced to behave in ways contrary to their own liking; in Korea, we have witnessed various political activities including civil war which ended up in splitting Korea into two parts (North Korea and South Korea); etc.

In view of these numerous empirical evidences, it is evident that the issue is not unique to Kenya. It is universal throughout the poverty stricken peoples of the Less Developed Countries. And that whereas under International Law with specific reference to "The Law of Domestic Jurisdiction of States", each State has the natural rights to be left alone to manage its own affairs without being dictated to by foreigners; and that. Because certain powerful States have failed to honour this pacta sunt servanda on the World Market, critical Soverign Equality Crisis have erupted unnecessarily forcing weaker States such as Korea, India, China, Vietnam, Germany, etc., to break into pieces, under the dictates of those most powerful States.

Further, it is equally noted that the Kenyan Government and all other ex-colonial African Governments are still too sensitive about ex-colonial powers because of Coloniophobia. Kenya and all other ex-colonial countries still have fresh memories of painful wounds inflicted on them by the colonial powers as a result of Charles Darwin's theory of "Survival of the Fittest" which he expounded in 1872 by arguing that, in life, there is a natural tendency in every species for the most powerful member of the species to dominate over the less powerful ones. They still remember that it was this Darwinian theory which paved the foundation and justification of Joseph Chamberlain's ridicule of smaller (weaker) nations in 1904 because of their misfortune in the midst of powerful nations. In his irritating words, Chamberlain glorified Darwinian Survival of the Fittest theory to justify his claim that "The day of smaller nations has passed away"; and that "The day of empires has come to swallow those little nations".

In view of these realities, any argument against foreign interference by Kenya and all other LDCs may be justified. Unless guided by maximum prudence, foreign interference by most Developed Powerful States have throughout history proved extremely frightening to Less Developed and Less Powerful Countries. The present situation in Somalia, where foreign intervention has proved less prudent, with regard to the Sovereign Equality Rights of the Peoples of Somalia may be a vivid example of this critical Sovereign Equality phobia perpetually facing the Less Developed Countries in Politicl Life.

But, the pending fundamental question now at issue is "Is all that true? Do all these allegations hold true when re-tested against the Law of Human Rights? To what degree has Kenya, and all Developing Countries, which because of their overwhelming socio-economic poverty and backwardness, been able to benefit from the Donor Community? Has this benefit been because of Bad Will or Good Will from the Donor Community?

### (a) The Law of Human Rights

From all that we know about life, every coin has two sides. Accordingly, although the argument against the Donor Community in matters which are deemed to be essentially within the domestic jurisdiction of an independent state may be valid, it is also not valid when the law of human rights in that state is deemed to be at stake. If activities of an individual, or state or company are deemed to be injurious to the interests of other individuals, states or companies in the social setting, then the human rights of the actor is automatically deemed unjust, and therefore illegal. Such activities are only just and legal when they recognize and respect the welfare of other actors (individuals, states, or companies) in the social setting.

Because of the natural fundamental duties inherent in the Head of State in his/her capacity as the Supreme Lord Protector of the socio-economic endowment of the state, the happiness of each individual in that state (both citizen and foreigner alike) lies totally in the domain of the Head of State who is, therefore, expected to encourage and excell it at all costs and at all times not only for the benefit of his/her peoples but also for the benefit of that Head of State. It is his/her paramount duty to do so because the more the peoples are happy, the more that Head of State will be also happy. And the more the majority of the peoples in the state are in this way, the greater the chances that the Head of State and his/her Government will be secure from criticism and capture the propencity by the critics to remove him/her from power.

Accordingly, when the foreign diplomats and their respective governments intervene in internal matters of their host country such as Kenya on the issue of Human Rights, and provided that such intervention is deemed to be in good faith, then, under the Law of Human Rights and Sovereign Equality of Individuals, such intervention is just and judicious. In Panama, for example, the USA intervention and the capture of the President of Panama was deemed just and judicious because it was aimed at destroying the root cause of intoxicating drug traffic into the USA. And the foreign intervention in African and other developing countries by calling on them to accept Multi-Party Democracy is also justified in that scientifically, for every life to come about, interaction/union between a positive (+) entity and a negative (-) entity is required. The interaction of the two always results into the desired life. This reality holds true in both natural and physical sciences.

In political life, a Ruling Party's job is to govern; while the job of the opposition is to police/oversee whether or not the government is governing the people well i.e., whether it is doing the right thing which is for welfare of the nation in total but not for only a selected few. Hence, the balance-of-power and good governance.

Accordingly, it is this Natural Checks and Balances mechanism and good governance inherent solely in a Multi-Party Democracy *ONLY* which constitutes a *SOUND* objective and Rationale of Multi-Party Democracy and which also justifies Foreign Donors' intervention in the domestic affairs of the Developing Countries. Their intervention is in good faith as it is aimed at bringing about Good Governance. Peaceful co-existence between the Governing Party and the Opposition, and long tenure of the Head of State.

It is healthy and consistent with our *SYMBIOSIS WORLD* and the *NOBLE* Spirit *OF* 'Good Samaritanism and 'Brotherhood' which encourages 'Those who have' to mercifully and generously give to 'Those who do no have'. It is a kin to our Kenyan noble HARAMBEE spirit initiated by our'Hayati' States President Jomo Kenyatta. Let all of us treat it as such because we mutually need each other. Both Donors and Donees (Beneficiaries of Donor's Aid) cannot afford to live and function without the other. This *SYMBIOSIS* is mutually *CRUCIA*L for each of them. Whereas the LDC's should be understanding to their Donors' petition for transparency and accountability with emphasis on proper management of the Donors' Aid and other Public Funds. It is also important for the Donors' Aid Beneficiaries to also take note that the Donors have always recognized the LDC's Peoples and Equal Sovereignity right; and that it is through this channels of understanding that AID has always been granted to them. If it had not been due to this *GOOD WILL* plus the Donors' concern for these Countries' repute and dignity; it is doubtful that such AID could have been initiated by the Donor Community. It is solely because of this concern for the repute and dignity of the Developing Countries' Peoples that the AID became essential and a yearly part and parcel of the foreign policy of the Donor Community for which all the Developing Countries and all of us who also benefit from such noble assistance must be most grateful and proud of in our bodies and souls.

But since independence to the present day, to what extent has Kenya, Africa and all other Developing Countries benefited from the Donor Community? Are these benefits a ramification of GOOD WILL or BAD WILL of the Donor Community?

### (b) Empirical Evidence of Donor Asistance to Developing Countries (LDCs)

Empirical evidence of the Donor Community's noble goodwill to Africa abound in millions of US Dollars, British Sterling Pounds, German Marks, Canadian Dollars, Japanese Yen, European Community Units (Euro) among other hard currencies ever since the country's independence.

As will be noted in my book, 'EXTERNAL DONOR ASSISTANCE TO KENYA', published by USAID/Kenya in June 1982, the data clearly confirms that from 1971 to 1980 alone for example, Gross Official Development Assistance to Kenya from both bilateral and multilateral contributions rose from US $73 million in 1971 to US $412 million in 1980. Between the two years, Kenya's Aid increased by 563% at a compound growth rate of 21.2% p.a. From a micro-economic analysis, Kenya benefited from this Overseas Development Assistance a net income of US $68 million, and this kept on increasing yearly. By 1980, the net receipts had grown to US $396 million, i.e., 585% increase within the 10-year bracket at a compound growth rate of 21.7% p.a. for Kenyan Socio-Economic Development.

Another very interesting data to reckon with justifying the Good will of the Donor Community to Developing Countries such as Kenya is that of all Overseas Development Assistance, most of it tends to be bilateral and are largely grants but not loans. Between the years (1971-1980) under review, 82% of the Donor Assistance came from by lateral Donors while only 18% of them were from Multilateral Agencies. Also, 60% of all the aid was in form of grants as compared to only 40%, which were in the form of soft loans.

## CHAPTER III

# Conclusion

From the above data, it is self-evident that the Good Will of the Donor Community to Developing Countries is extremely impressive. In this regard, a word of wisdom from the Donors such as the World Bank and the IMF to Aid Beneficiaries should be embraced without much ado. Obviously no soul without such Good Will would dare to assist as much as the Donors have so far done to Africa and the rest of the needy Developing Countries in their National Development. Their word of wisdom on the question of Human Rights and Good Governance should, therefore, not be misconstrued to a potential threat to the Sovereignty and Dignity of the Aid Receipients.

Accordingly, the on-going Sovereign Equality complaint by the Aid Receipients is a function of unfounded sound cause. It is obviously a function of misunderstandings and misconception on the part of the Developing Countries for reasons not related to the Donor Community's Good Wisdom to them to liberalize their economy and to embrace the Fundamental Universal Principles of Human Rights, enshrined in God's command that "He that rules over men must be just . . ." documented in the II Samuel 23:2-4.

The overwhelming empirical evidences in Parts I-III of this book do confirm that such complaints are not justified. They are precipated by a host of unrelated spurious root-causes. Such causes include mythical African traditional beliefs noted in Part I of this book; and the Developing Countries' insecuritophobia arising from the now existing exposed socio-economic scandals. Such scandals are of different shapes and magnitude. The worst ones include the Goldenberg, Anglo Leasing and Finance, etc., which tend to pose frightening potential threat to implicated Government Authorities. Unfortunately, exposure of such scandals by the opposition is now being erroneously blamed on the Donor Community because of the Donor Comuunity's advocacy for Multy-Partism and Good Governance.

Like Nature which has two opposite sides of the same coin viz life and death; positive and negative; good and bad; health and sickness; peace and war; friend and enemy; conducive and unconducive; lovel and hate; pleasant and nauseating; enabling and threatening; constructive and destructive; welcoming and unwelcoming; pretty and ugly; encouraging and discouraging; friendly and hostile; etc, each of these variables which collectively are a subject of this Part Eleven of the book also does the same as follows:-

## 1. Reality, Universality and Universalism of Sovereign Equality Rights Demand

This demand[1] is not new. It is as old as nationhood and international relations concepts which emerged as far back as the era of both regimes of the Ancient Egypt and Babylon, in the 1280's BC. In its efforts to repel off and firmly contain Babylonian aggression through which the latter sought to steal the Egyptian extra-ordinary scientific and technological legacy that Egypt had managed to achieve due to its invention of a Hybrid Culture of Democracy and Good Governance, Egypt successfully pressurized on Babylon to recognize and respect its sovereign rights, political independence and territorial integrity for the sake of their future mutual peace between the two.

In this regard, the two parties entered into an Egypto Hittite Treaty of Non-Aggression in the year 1284 BC in which the Hittites and their Babylonian Leadership firmly confessed to their counterpart in Egypt that they would now no longer repeat their previous attempted theft against Egypt. And, that as a guarantee to their firm commitment, they were also ready to enter into a tangible pacta sunt servanda with their counterpart (Egyptians) according to the latter's choice. Accordingly, the Hittite King agreed to offer his own daughter to marriage to the Egyptian Pharaoh as that security, with the understanding that if Babylon ever again repeated its previous act of aggression, it would compel the Egyptians to kill the Hittitian King's daughter as a pay off. In this regard, both parties firmly agreed to cease their war; to recognize and promote their mutual sovereign equality rights; and finally to aid each other during emergencies. The Hittite's daughter's marriage to the Egyptian Pharaoh was a deliberate intent to seal this pact[2]. Hence, the genersis of the Law of Pacta Sunt Servanda in International Law as an extention of the Law of Contract in Municipal Law initiated by God Himself in His Pact with our Patriarch Adam in which Adam agreed with God that he would do X but notify on condition that if Adam did only X as so agreed on; Adam would surely live and proper immensely but if Adam defied the terms, and did Y also, he would surely die[3].

The Scripture further tells us that on defying such bilaterally mutual agreement with God and did both X and Y as commanded not to do so, Adam surely landed himself into a serious trouble with God who, after having exhausted His concept of Natural Justice by allowing Adam to answer to God's reason as to the reasons whey he dishonoured the pact and finding Adam guilty of dishonesty, sentenced Adam to a punishment commiserate with his weight of offense, a punishment that also become a natural curse to Adam's seeds (from his generation to our own and future generations to come). Hence, the genesis of the virtues and vices of man's persistent sovereign equality rights demand globally.

As a virtue, it is expected to act as a people's reliable protective mechanism for their both **possessional values** (i.e., their political independence and territorial integrity, culture, natural resources, and all other legacies pertaining their heritage, which collectively give them a sense of national self-love, self-dignity and self-respect on the equal footing with every other peoples in the International system); and **milieu values** (i.e., those scarce values which they do not have handy at home but which they therefore must go outside their borders and find them for their survival). Vivid empirical evidences of this demand as a virtue abound in our life at both individual (man to man) level; and international (nation-to-nation) level, e.g., the Egypto-Hittite Treaty of Non-Aggression (1284 BC) whose commitment by the two parties (Egypt and Babylon) provided for them a very attractive (enabling) environment for each of them to not only happily co-exist but also engage in various international activities such as mutual self-defence in event that one was threatened by an external enemy; bilateral trade and commerce across their national borders; etc. And, their mode of peaceful co-existence and interaction is the same mode that characterizes out international relations today in the Internaional systems. Whenever this mode happens to be tampered with thereby posing a potential threat to peace and security, the all members of the International system are always and means of restoring the peaces and security so that the latter may collectively provide an enabling environment for them to securely interact and transact their affairs without any danger of fear of the same. In this regard, effective Egypto-Hittite Treaty in 1284 BC, obviously uncountable numbers of treaties, pacts, accords and other bilateral and multilateral agreements have been realized Egypto-Hittite Treaty and the atter's objectives. Example of this include the Peace of Westphalia (1648), the Treaty of Versailles (1919) and the Treaty of San Francisco (1945) in which the contacting partices reiteracted the same objective of Non-Aggression as that of Egypto-Hittite Treaty of Non-Aggression (1284 BC).

But, on the contrary, as a vice, Sovereign Equality Rights' Demand has a habit of misleading and thus putting one into a serious trouble with one's fellow partner(s) as it did to our patriarch Adam of misleading him to dishonour his Pacta Sunt Servanda with God thereby consequently putting both himself and all his seeds in a perpetual horrible difficulty.

Whereas the above prima facie empirical evidence of this demand as a vice between Adam and God is essentially of an inter-personal but not, of an international nature, numerous empirical evidences of this phenomenon at an international level abound and are as equally serious as that of Adam. And a list of these evidences is very endless, as also evidenced by our World History records.

A few of these include, for example, the following wars that have been caused in our own generation by wreckless self-seeking leaders who had no sense of their responsibility to Pacta Sunt Servanda with their fellow men in their capacity as a custordians of their peace and security a part form being a lover of their own self-glory and leadership megalomania.

**(a) Prussia Germany (1870-1945)**

Obssessed with its own wreckless national sovereign rights and interest, Prussia-German Leadership hardly paid a damn to the rights and survival of every non-Aryan German in Europe as to it, all these non-Aryan Germans, were no better than a pollution to German blood purity, who must therefore be driven both out of Prussia-Germany and much far away. Hence its goal to colonize the entire Europe in its various consecutive wars, eg. World War I and II (1914-1918 and 1938-1945 respectively). In each of these wars, Germany's fundamental goal was to do just that. Other goals pertaining to socio-economic matters were essentially serendipities. Aryan German blood purity protection was Prussia Germany's ultimate goal. This was the reason why all German Jews, Gypsies Germans in Germany had to be annihilated by the Nazi Regime. Their elimination claimed 4 to 6 million deaths using concentration camps during World War II between 1938 and 1945.

**(b) USA versus Iraq (2003-2004)**

Obsessed with its own wreckless national sovereign rights and interest as Prussian German had also done between 1870 and 1945 thereby plunging the innocent into a sea of various agonies, (as also evidenced by the lamentation of The UN Founding Fathers contained in The Preamble of The UN Charter), the USA under President George Bush's leadership deliberately refused to pay heed to the decision of the UN Security Council directing that no invasion of Iraq must take place until such a time that the UN Security Council shall have confirmed beyond any reasonable doubt that Iraq definitely had those dangerous weapons of mass destruction that were being alleged against that Country.

Defying this UN Security Decision, the USA President Bush argued that time to invade Iraq had already run out and also that USA had all the sovereign rights to do whatever USA deemed fit to do for the sake of its national interest. In this regard, President Bush declared that, since, to him, the UN seemed to have already out-lived its usefulness for which it was created by The Founding Fathers in 1945, it was now up to the USA to go it alone and invade Iraq for the sake of USA national interest whether the UN Security Council liked it or not.

But, whereas such argument could have proved the President right had he found the alleged weapons, the flabbergasting revelation is that none of the needed weapons were ever found after the invasion and a thorough search by the USA security authority in collaboration of the UK armed forces.

In addition to this embarrassing failure, to-date both the USA and the latter's coalition forces from UK, Turkey, Parkistan, Spain, Japan, south Korea and the Philippines have encountered numerous deaths, bodily injuries and unquantified property destruction in Iraq a senseless cost that could prudently have been avoided had a meticulious caution been needed to.

And, because of this embarrassing revelations in Iraq, none can now predict with a reasonable degree of confidence whether or not the same Presidnet Geroge Bush and his Republican Party would ever attempt to do so again were they be offered another leadership chance.

### (c) Sudan Civil War (1959-2008)

Also like the wreckless self-seeking leaderships of both Prussia Germany in 1870 to 1945 and the USA under President George Bush Jr. in 2003-2004 which could hardly be advised by anybody because of its megalomania and paranoia character, the Sudanese Leadership could hardly hearken to any friendly advice from every source, who sought to counsel that leadership against its megalomania and paranoia tendencies to the lives of its own citizens in both Southern and Western Sudan who are basically African by race and Christian by religion as compared to the Northern Sudanese who are basically Arab by race and Moslems by religion, but whose lives the Governement is determined to protect.

This Sudanese Government has always done this ever since that Country achieved its independence on 1st January, 1959. But, although Kenya has been able to persuade and bring to a Peace Agreement with its perennial foe, SPLA of Dr.John Garang, last month (June, 2004), all previous efforts always fell on Sudanese Government's deaf ear. These efforts included those by the former USA President Jimmy Carter; the former Anglican Church Archbishop, His Grace George Caren; The Roman Catholic Pontiff, Pope John Paul II; the former Kenyan President Daniel T. arap Moi, and many other World Statesmen.

As a result of this perpetual refusal by the Sudanese Leadership on the grounds that it had all rights under the Law of Sovereign Equality to do so as the matter was essentially within its own Jurisdiction and protected by the Law of Domestic Jurisdiction enshrined in The UN Charter under Article 2 paragraph 7, the refusal subjected millions of innocent Sudanese to a sea of irreparable agonies.

For instance, in its abhorring report on this situation titled "Threat of Genocide Brewing in Darfur", **the East Africa**[4] reported as follows:-

I In Darfur, which is now the battlefield of Civil War in Western Sudan after that in Southern Sudan ended last month (June, 2004), is where non-Arab African communities are now the target of attacks by some 20,000 Janjaweed militias.

II These Militias are emerging from Arab nomadic tribes aimed at exacerbating terror in Darfur by annihilating, every African Sudanese in sight.

III Amnesty International based in London holds these militias responsible for the massive human-rights violations being suffered by hundreds of thousands innocent Sudanese civilians in Darfur.

IV These Janjaweed militias are not acting on their own. They are fully backed and sponsored by the Sudanese Armed Forces.

V Human Rights Watch, based in USA, maintains that Darfur is witnessing a campaign of "ethnic cleansing" promoted by Sudanese Government against three African communities located in the Darfur area.

VI The European Humanitarian Aid Office, maintains that its persecution has so far left some two million people, or a 1/3 of the Darfur population (32 million) in a situation of grave danger. According to this Aid Director, Constanza Adinolfi, due to this danger,

(a) Between 750,000 and 1,000,000 internally displaced peoples are now spread all over Sudan as refugees.
(b) 110,000 of them have crossed the border into Chad as refugees

VII Liz Hodgkin, spokesman for Amnesty International research also confirmed a systematic and well-organized pillaging and destruction of villages which led to the forced displacement of the rural population of the Darfur.

VIII Kenneth Roth, Executive Director of Human Rights Watch (HRW), stressed that Darfur is not seeing just a mere problem of spontaneous ethnic conflict but on acute ethnic atrocities against African populations sponsored by the Arab-financed Khartoum Government aimed at cleaning the region of three targeted African ethnic communites viz: the Fur, Masalit and Zaghawa by 20,000 or so Janjaweed, militias coming from Arab nomadic tribes whose arms and uniforms are provided by the Sudanese Government.

IX Also, Jan Egeland, Co-ordinator of the UN Emergency Aid, estimated that US $236 million or so needed for the rest of the year to attend to the urgent needs of the communities of Darfur and the refugees in the neghbouring Chad, particularly for (i) food (ii) medicine (iii) housing (iv) agriculture (v) portable water (vi) sanitation (vii) education (viii) protection of human rights.

X Jan Egeland, further estimated that there were also:-

(i) 1,000,000 internally displaced people
(ii) 150,000 refugees in Chad
(iii) 700,000-800,000 to be severely affected Africans in Darfur by the end of this year.

XI The USAID Administrator, Andrew Natsios:

(i) Predicted a death toll to the tune of over 320,000 people arising from this acute problem; and announced a USA pledge of US $1888.5 million for humanitarian aid.

(ii) The UN Secretary General Kofi Annan had alerted the UN Commission for Human Rights in April, 2004 that the genocide was brewing in Darfur could result into a situation akin to that of Rwanda of 1994.

XII James Morris, Executive Director of the UN World Food Programme (WFP) lamented that:

(i) The Khartoum Government was deliberately creating obstacles for the international agencies and non-governmental groups (NGOs) for providing aid to the affected victims in Darfur.
(ii) Oxfarm, Britain-based humanitarian group was the only NGO which had received Khartoum Government authority to work in Darfur
(iii) The Khartoum Government should be made to provide improved security environment in Darfur in order to allow unimpeded humanitarian activities, and to create an enabling security situation in Darfur to able refugees to return back to their homes of domicile.
(iv) The said Government ought to do so by first and foremost disarming the Khartoum Government sponsored Janja weed militia groups in order to stop the on-going violence and insecurity complex to refugee returnees in Darfur.

## (d) Kenyan Leadership (1963-2008)

Whereas Kenya achieved her Independence effective 12$^{th}$ December,1963 from the United Kingdom (UK) through a shed of blood in the Civil War called Mau Mau between the Freedom Fighters on the one hand and the UK Colonial Authorities, with one fundamental aim namely to remove a dictatorial and undemocratic foreign regime and then replace it with an indigenous regime that would be sensitive to the people's democratic rights and needs, realization of this cardinal goal has been a perpetual night mare.

### (i) Jomo Kenyatta

He spearheaded the Country's governance from independence in December 1963, till his death in October 1978, left the Country in an acute problem of Kenyattaphobia. Throughout the Country, majority Kenyans lived in this acute fear by virtue of Kenyatta's leadership magalomania by which Kenyatta did everything with a jovial impunity with the excuse that, as head of sovereign country, he had an unquestionable rights to do whatever he did. His Vice President, Mr. Oginga Odinga, who had been his principal king maker during the pre-independence period would not be spared either. Whenever Odinga tried to correct him, the latter summarily silenced him by every means Kenyatta could think of which included putting him into a house-arrest, and banning him from participating in Kenyan politics. Mr. Joseph Murumbi who had succeeded Mr. Odinga as Vice President in 1966 hardly completed six months. Kenyatta Leadership megalomania and paranoia tendencies forced Mr. Murumbi to resign within six months of his tenure.

Another prima facie evidence of unbearable Kenyatta's ledership magolomania and paranoia is the case of Tom Mboya's assassination, in mid 1969. Mboya who had proved to be a very adorable spokesman for Kenyatta leadership against his fellow Luo man, Odinga against whom both Kenyatta and Mboya had allied together to silence from the political scene would not be spared either by his own ally (Kenyatta).

Immediately Kenyatta sensed that Mboya was secretly trying to cunningly encroach on his Leadership seat, Kenyatta swiftly brought him down using a third party immediately Mboya returned to Kenya from his USA trip.

In addition to both Odinga and Mboya, Pio Pinto and JM Kariuki were also gunned down in 1965 and 1967 respectively as a function of Kenyatta Leadership paranoia i.e, Kenyatta's fear of them on the grounds that they might overshadow him and therefore, snatch the leadership from him. This is exactly the reason why Kenyatta never allowed any election and opposition parties to take root.

**(ii) Daniel T. arap Moi**

When Kenyatta suddenly passed on in October, 1978 in Mombasa where he had gone for a brief rest, and Daniel T. arap Moi took over as President of The Republic, overwhelming majority looked at the succession as a God-given good omen in the sense that it was going to be a source of an over due sigh of a relief to the Country from Kenyatta-phobia generated by Kenyatta Leadership megalomania and paranoia by which he had so much terrorized Odinga and all oppositions in Kenya that Odinga in particular could hardly walk well due to his confined house-arrest by Kenyatta.

But, to the surprise of those who were anxiously waiting for this good omen, there was no sign of this. Every tap and all other sources of water relief remained as dry as they had ever been throughout Kenyatta Leadership. Instead, all that they could hear was "Harambee" yellings and "Nyayo" choruses day after day and year after year.

And, whoever tried to question in defence for one's rights one was taught such a rude lesson that one would never forget and dare to ask that question again. Also any political leader whom Moi did not want in Parliament because of his philosophical stand against corruption and all elements of Bad Governance, Moi made sure that such a leader was removed either during the elections or by assassination.

Using elections as a weapon, Moi hatched out various techniques of eliminating those leaders he never wanted because of their critical stand against his corrupt mode of governance. The two most famous techniques were (i) Secret Exchange of Ballot Boxes by which he eliminated such undesirables by way of secretly replacing actual ballot boxes of such persons with pre-prepared ballot boxes containing fewer number of ballots for the undesirable candidate but with a winning number of ballots for the desirable candidate(s). This process was carried out at the Counting Centres or while on the way (en route) from the voting stations to the Counting Centres by the police and returning officials on the instruction from President Moi. Immediately this exchange of Ballot Boxes was effected, genuine Ballot Boxes were promptly rushed to the District Commissioner whose duty was now to supervise their immediate destruction in order to cleverly conceal evidences.

But no sooner had this method been discovered and condemned by Kenyans, Moi hatched out a new other method as a weapon. He hatched out at *Mulolongo* by which voters were required to stand at the back of their preferred candidates in an Indian file (one line). However, this *Mulolongo* was none other than a repetition of Moi's cunning method aimed at eliminating those political candidates he did not want to cause him headaches. Whether one received the greatest number above the other candidates but was not in good books with Moi, such a candidate was automatically disqualified. The District Commissioner (DC) who was normally the returning officer would simply be ordered by Moi to announce the failure as the actual winning candidate. And, using such presidential absolute power, the DC always did so with total impunity. He would bestow the winner's majority vote to the Moi's losing candidate and then compel the victim to concede to the decision. But whenever, such a victim dared to file a legal suit in an Election Court assuming that he/she would get a just redress, the hurdles before him/her turned out to be so more expensive for the petitioner than what the latter could easily manage. Usually such petitions were cleverly floated and thrown out by corrupt judges on the instruction from President Moi himself. Hence, the genesis of Judicial corrosion and decay in Law Courts, in Kenya.

But, when questioned by the International Community Donors and Human Rights Agencies regarding this and other injustices, Moi's response to them was none other than a copy right of Kenyatta's response quoting the principle of Sovereign Equality Rights. And, when the Diplomatic Community also tried to question this, some were reported back to their home governments that they were interfering in Kenya's domestic affairs and, in this case, their actions were, therefore a violation of their Diplomatic Obligation.

And, when the Donor Community threatened Moi Leadership by withholding foreign aid from Kenya, in attempt to rehabilitate Moi Leadership from corruption, election rigging bribery in the Judiciary, and other Bad Governance Culture, Moi Leadership hardly hearkened to such corrective actions. Hence the genesis of Moi Leadership magalomania and paranoia—a psychiatric syndrome by which transformed him into a demagogue leader ready to kill if necessary for no any wrong done as he did to his Foreign Minister Dr. Robert Ouko for no reason other than that Ouko questioned him and his lieutenants regarding the accelerating speed of corruption and its possible damage on Kenyan image abroad particularly among the Donor Community Members which could consequently force the Community to withhold their aid to the country.

Apparently, it was the same two viruses of Leadership megalomania and paranoia that influenced Moi during the 2002 Election from seeing reality. Moi became so confused by these two viruses that he could not recognize that his choice of Uhuru Kenyatta was going to fail him and his KANU party. Because of his leadership magolomania, he went a head like a mad dog and forced in Uhuru as a winning candidate while everyone kept on telling him over and over no. And, whoever tried to do so, automatically became his enemy. Hence, the reason why Raila Odinga, George Saitoti, Kalonzo Musyoka, Fred Gumo, Joseph Kamotho, and many other strong pillars of KANU had to pull out and join the then opposition party National Alliance of Kenya (NAK) headed by Mwai Kibaki in his capacity as Chairman of Democratic Party of Kenya (DP), Michael Wamalwa Kijana in his capacity as Chairman of FORD Kenya; Charity Ngilu, in her capacity as Chairwoman of Social Democratic Party (SDP), and Paul Muite as Chairman of Safina.

Thus, had it not been due to Moi Leadership megalomania and paranoia, which influenced his thinking so much that he hardly listened to any constructive advice from every source, obviously, with Raila and all his National Development Party (NDP) members, KANU would have won with an overwhelming landslide. Hence, the root-cause of KANU failure in the 2002 General Elections.

**(iii) Mwai Kibaki Leadership (2003-present)**

Similarly, like in Moi's leadership succesion from Kenyatta in October, 1978, Mwai Kibaki's Leadership succession was met and greeted with an euphoria of a thunderous jubilation and a stupendous hilarity. Every Kenyan was obsiously very thirsty hand hungry for a sign of relief they had been yearning for four decades (from 1963 to 2003).

And, when Kenyans listened to Kibaki's inauguration speech[5] in December 2002 in which the newly elected President was now vowing to initiate a **Zero Tolerance War policy** against corruption and all forms of graft in the Country; to provide at least 500,000 new jobs every year; to provide a free Primary Education to every Kenya; to quickly complete the Constitutional Review; and finally to see to it that all stolen money by Moi regime is recovered from wherever it may have been hidden, they all went crazy with joy. Every one felt that this was now their time to be happy. They perceived Kibaki as their man who was going to give them the relief they had always been awaiting. Some cried with tears flowing down their cheeks because of the joy they had been longing. As one of those who were right next to the Dais where the swearing in was taking place, I attest to this fact that all Kenyans at the Park were full of joy for that memorable day at The Uhuru Park, Nairobi.

But, the nagging question now is: Has this Son of Good Omen fulfilled his promises that triggered automatic flow of tears at the Uhuru Park during the Inauguration in December, 2002?? And, given that the whole Country went into an euphoria of hilarious jubilation to welcome Kibaki to the Republic's Top-most seat of Leadership at The State House, why now is his NARC Government faced with an acute schism, quarrels and dirty-name-calling both within his Cabinet Ministers Groups? Why did he abruptly reshuffled his entire Government and created a new Government of National Unity thereby scrapping of his original coalition Government that was economically lean and esily affordable than this new too a monster establishment that was not economically viable for a Country that had yet to rescucitate a dying economy that was almost collapsing due to the devastating acts by the previous KANU

Regime? And, why did he secretly carryout the reshuffle without a proper prior consultation with other Chairmen of the parties that constituted the Coalition?

From January, 2003, all Primary Schools ceased to be a school fee paying institutions. Fees were scrapped off by the new Kibaki Government except in Government Boarding Schools where a child was required to pay for boarding and lodging only. But in Day Schools, tuition fees and other were waived, and taken over by the Government in fulfillment of President Kibaki's promise during his Inauguration Speech.

However in order to answer other questions pertaining to schism, quarrels, etc, the following Clinical Diagnosis of Kibaki performance since his inauguration in December 2004 to the present July, 2004) is very much necessary.

(1) In his article titled "Using MOU's To Paint Others Black"[6], Professor Kivutha Kibawana, who was one of those Kenyan politicians right inside the opposition during the KANU Regime since the advent of a Multi-Party Political Tornado against Moi's Pro-One Party attitude, exposes the following as being the root-cause of the explosion in the NARC Government and which must have obsiourslу led President Kibaki secretly and quickly remove the initial coalition type of Governance and replace it with a Governement of National Unity during his Reshuffle on 30th June,2004. He reveals that:

   (a) That the main stubborn issue generating the on-going schism, quarrels, etc within the Cabinet revolves around the failure of President Kibaki to honour his contractual obligation to The Two Memoranda of Understanding (MOU) mutually entered into by Kibaki in his capacity as Chairman of his Democratic Party (DP) of Kenya and other opposition political parties viz: (Liberal Democratic Party of Kenya (LDP); and the National Alliance (Party) of Kenya (NAK).
   (b) That it was because of Raila Odinga's political ingenuity, that enabled Raila to convince his political bed fellows to decamp from KANU to the opposition immediately he confirmed that President Moi would not agree to hand over KANU Governance to Saitoti-Raila-Kalonzo-Mudavadi-Awori-Ngala-Kamotho group.

(c) That the political merger between LDP and NAK political parties gave birth to a new offspring, The National Alliance Rainbow Coalition (NARC) which consequently managed to defeat the Moi sponsored KANU Uhuru project in the 2002 Presidential Elections and form the Coalition NARC Government.

(d) That in their first negotiation held in The Nairobi Club on power sharing, the said stakeholders in the NARC mutually agreed on the following lean structure of governance:-

- NAK was to supply the presidential candidate and then Vice President upon victiory (for Michael Kijana Wamalwa); Second Deputy Prime Minister (for Charity Ngilu); and Third Deputy Prime Minister (for Kipruto arap Kirwa).
- LDP was to get a Prime Minister (for Raila Odinga); Vice President (for Kalonzo Musyoka); First Deputy Prime Minister (for George Saitoti); and Senior Co-orindating Minister (Moody Awori).

(e) That this Nairobi Club Pact was finally sealed at the Hilton Hotel by The Big NARC Light called The Summit Members viz: Kibaki, Wamalwa, Ngilu, arap Kirwa (for NAK Party) on the one hand and Odinga, Saitoti, Awori and Musyoka (for LDP) on the other.

(f) That in this Pact, these Big NARC Eight mutually agreed to share power on a 50-50% basis.

(g) That it did not attach a list of names fo key leaders onfear that other ethnic communities would not support NARC in the Elections.

(h) That this MOU equalized NAK and LDP and the two mutually formed a de facto transitional NARC leadership.

(i) That by virtue of this rational process, MOU was a reliable legal document in all respects of pacta sunt servanda governing treaties, convenants, pacts, accords and other legally binding contractual agreements in our civilization.

(j) That it was succinctly on the nature and strength of this MOU that on appointing senior Government officers, President Kibaki prudently balanced the regional representation; degree of election support; and the fidelity to the MOUs.

(k) And, finally that whereas this is the reality leading to NARC victory against KANU, "*if the MOU route is no longer available, Mr. Odinga will look for another route. Kenyan politicians will henceforth carefully scrutinize any pacts they negotiate so that such settlements don't become political dynamite?*

(2) Like his predecessors (Moi and Kenyatta) and like President George Bush in USA, with regard to their wreckless leadership megalomania and paranoia in their quest for sovereign equality rights—tendencies which could not allow them to see the light and hearken to constructive advice—the Kibaki Leadership is also a hostage fo the same. For example, he has adamantly refused to hearken to his fellow signatory members of the MOU thereby igniting an irrevisible dynamite explosion in the Country. Also, he has refused to honour his other various pledges to his fellow Kenyans. Such pledges include Delivery of a New Constitution by 30th June, 2004; Provision of at least 500,000 new jobs yearly; and a satisfactory freedom of assembly, association and expression.

(3) As a result of his shocking leadership conduct contrary to the good expectations of the Kenyans across the Country, numerous disturbing concerns abound and are increasing daily regarding the President's real intention and direction. People are wondering what might have gone wrong. And whether they were wrong in their judgement for voting for NARC or whether there is some devilminded friend of the President, who because of their closeness he/she is using that opportunity to confuse and mislead the president into wrong directions contrary to the President's own rational wishes. A vivid evidence of this seriousness is borne out by the following concerns (A-J) from different quarters of the Country:-

(A) In order to avoid this headache, the President secretly reshuffled NARC Government and transformed it from a Coalition Status to a Status of National Unity by co-opting some opposition members in its recent article titled "NARC taken to task over Pledges" the Daily Nation of 6th July 2004 report that.

(B) "Muslim leaders yesterday asked the Government to honour its pre-election pledges. The Secretary of the Council of Imams and Preachers, Sheikh Mohammed Dor; the Chairman of the unregistered Islamic Party of Kenya, Sheikh Mohammed Dor; an official of Muslims for Human Rights, Mr. Ahmed Awadh, and others accused the Government of reneging on the promises.

(C) They asked donors to with hold aid until the Government demonstrated seriousness in fighting corruption and providing a new constitution".

(D) Also, in his speech marking the US Independence day (4th July, 1776) in Nairobi, the US Ambassador William Bellamy, equally criticized President Kibaki's mode of handling the wrangles in his NARC government, the recent reshuffle without proper consultations with other leaders of parties responsible for formation of the National Alliance Rainbow Coallition (NARC) Governement particularly Honourable Raila Odinga (Chairman of The Liberal Democratic Party of Kenya, LDP); the battle against corruption; acute poverty forcing most Kenyans to live on one dollar (Kshs 78) per day while a few flourish in stolen wealth; the on-going statement in the Constitution-making process which have collectively thrown Kenya into the on-going destructive political demonstrations looting and property destructrion by the "Saba Saba" political activists all over the Country.

(E) Further, the US Ambassador laments that although the Kibaki Government had initially shown a promising good hope of fighting corruption by setting up necessary machinery, what was happening thereafter, left the Country and foreigners alike wondering whether there was any political will on part of Government to fulfill the promised pledge. In short, he made it clear and loud that the Kibaki leadership had let everybody down.

(F) Thereafter, pressure mounted on the Kibaki Government forcing the latter to remove ministers and any other officials implicated in the Kshs. 7 billion Anglo Leasing and Finance Company Scandal in order for these ministers to allow a thorough and genuine investigation to take its course.

(G) Led by seven Western Missions accredited to Kenya, USA, UK, Canada, Germany, Switzerland, Sweden and Norway including Japan, and the European Union (EU) composed of 25 Member-States called on the President to begin to seriously take prompt action against such potholes in his leadership.

(H) Regarding corruption, they called on him to effect necessary corrections of the proven tax procedures in procurement which had misled the Government into massive payments to a ficticious company such as Anglo Leasing and Finance thereby showing evidence of abuse of national security contracts.

(I) In this regard, they called for a swift implementation of the Government's Action Plan for Enhanced Financial Management including the Integrated Financial Management Information System, and they objected to the Government's abortive attempt to remove the Anti-corruption agency headed by John Githongo from the Office of The President.

(J) Finally, they also called for President Kibaki to quickly appoint a strong director for the Kenya Anti-Corruption Commission (KACC) as part of its measures to effudicate corruption in the Country[7].

But, given the fact that President Kibaki cannot be President and at the same time be Minister and Permanent Secreatary of every Ministry of Government, the nagging question at issue is who was the Minister of Finance and what was his role so far in this Anglo Leasing and Finance business?? Did he know it at all? What did he know and what did he do to assist his President in the latter's policy of zero tolerance war against graft which he pledged to all Kenyans and the World at large on the day of his swearing in as President of The Republic of Kenya, in December, 2002?

The Kenya's Parliamentary Public Accounts Committee (PAC) composed of Mr. Omingo Magara (MP, South Mugirango) discovered from their investigations of the matter that: (1) Finance Minsiter, David Mwiraria, (a) was, infact, well briefed on the deal and (b) should, therefore, be held responsible for the Kshs. 2.7 million passports scandal; (2) All Ministers of Ministries involved in the passports deal with Anglo Leasing and Finance must be held responsible, i.e Minister for Home Affairs and Minister for Internal Security (3) All Permanent Secretaries of the said Ministries must be shown the door and that they should no longer be allowed to hold any public office. These were Mr. Joseph Magari (Finance); Mr. Joseph Oyula (Financial Secretary, Finance); and Mr. Sylvester Mwaliko (Office of The President and Ministry of Home Affairs). But what could be the meaning of all these episodes? What lessons should one learn from them? These episodes are not ends in themselves. They are a ramification of an acute radicalization in Kenya proving that Kenyans are now no longer politically immature or impotent as they used to be perceived in the era of Kenyatta-Moi regimes. According to the US Ambassador, they are clear indicators of Kibaki Team risking credibility". Whereas by expanding the Cabinet in the new Reshuffle dated Wednesday 30th June, 2004 from . . . . to . . . . Ministries may have been aimed at altering the existing balance of power in his decision makign which had earlier been based on three major pillars of Kibaki's Democratic Party of Kenya (DP), Musikari Kombo's Ford Kenya and Raila Odinga's Liberal Democratic Party of Kenya (LDP) which had collectively constituted a National Alliance Rainbow Coalition (NARC) Government, and which was, therefore, giving him much headache particularly from the LDP party, Kibaki reshuffle was a dangerous act morally and economically. Morally, it was a blatant breach of contract these three big whigs had entered into during the election quest to oust the KANU Regime from power and which successfully empowered them to root out KANU and replace the latter with their own NARC coalition party.

Economically, the reshuffle was an unnecessary excessive burden on the dwingling economy which had been terrorized so much by the out-going KANU Regime that it does not have that strength to reliably carry out such a very financial load. Its strength could worsen beyond repair should the Donor Community's threat materialize and then cut off the aid as so warned already.

Psychologically, the reshuffle is none other than a function of Leadership paranoia and megalomania. As a paranoia, it was a result of Kibaki's fear of the in-elastically powerful LDP's stand on the Memorandum of Understanding (MOU) that sought to have Kibaki honour its inherent pacta sunt servanda; but which Kibaki would not wish to honour. And as a function of a leadership megalomania, the reshuffle was aimed at showing the LDP that the latter had no power but Kibaki to decide and do whatever he wanted to do without having to be told by LDP or any one else.

## FOOTNOTES

(1) As will be noted in various publications on the concept "sovereignty" human demand for sovereignty over its territory is not limited to political rights. It also encompasses all natural resources called biodiversity (i.e, a variety of living organisms and how they behave to protect their genes, species and their ecosystem diversity since they are the main source of raw materials used in agricultural, medical and industrial innovations that make them essential and critically needed for sustainable development. For further details on this line of thinking, also see Vicente Sanchez and Calestous Juma, eds, Biodiplomacy: Genetic Resources and International Relations, Acts Press, African Centre for Technology Studies, Nairobi, Kenya, 91994).

(2) Diane W. Darst, Western Civilization to 1648, An American Book Publishign Company, New York (1990), p. 29

(3) See The Genesis in The Holy Bible, Chap. 2

(4) The East African, No. 504, June 28-July 4, 2004, p. 10.

(5) Mwai Kibaki's Presidential Inaugural Speech.

(6) Kibutha Kibwana, "using MOUs to Paint Others Black, The Daily Nation, Nairobi, 28 December, 2003, p. 9.

(7) The Daily Nation, Nairobi, Tuesday 6th July, 2004, p. 1.

## CHAPTER III (A)

# Carrot Diplomacy and Good Leadership

### (1) The meaning of Carrot Diplomacy

According to the ***Webster's Seventh Collegiate Dictionary***, "a Carrot" is defined as "a biennial herb with a usually orange spindle-shaped edible root". And is also defined metaphorically as "a promised often illusory reward or advantage".

In this regard, by the concept "Carrot Diplomacy" as so used in this Chapter is not used meaning an edible root but solely in a metaphorical context meaning a reward often promised by X to Y for the purpose of X getting Y do for X what X feels unable to do directly unless Y is involved as a conduit.

On the other hand, the concept "Diplomacy" is also defined by the same Dictionary as "the art and practice of conducting negotiations between nations" in political life; and also as a "skill in handling affairs without arousing hostility: a tact". The latter meaning fits our intention. Whereas the usage in this book does also recognize the Dictionary's first definition, the book is more interested in the second than the first definition by virtue of the former's generality and universalism in life which is not as limited as the first definition is to political life only.

In the final analysis, the concept "Carrot Dimpolacy" herein is used to refer to the manner or strategy by which one skillfully handles his approach to the other party with a view to achieving what or she seeks without arousing hostility to the other party in his capacity as a homo diplomaticus. The key salient ingredient in this strategy which is not found in all other strategies is "tact" which is gentle care (gentility. It is gentle by virtue of its tender sensitive hands that allows one to handle every matter with greatest care and compassion without causing or increasing further anger to the other party.

## (2) Problem of Its Usage

But, whereas this is the reality of the concept "Carrot Diplomacy", unfortunately, the concept is often misunderstood and mistaken by many to a political strategy used solely by nation-states and political leaders against other for selfish interest. A vivid example of this holds true during President Daniel T. arap Moi's leadership in Kenya (1978-2002) whereby the strategy was always associated with Moi due to his habit of using it for his political survival throughout his leadership tenure by misusing public money, land and other assets to bribe his potential opponents to stop their acts against him or to support his non-rational policies and acts whether or not they were injurious to national interest as it is now being exposed by the Goldenberg Commission of Inquiry evidences by Kamlesh Partin who is the Principal State witness in this inquiry.

But as will be noted in the following analysis, such assumption is false and myopic. Carrot Diplomacy exists everyhwhere and is very vivid in every aspect of human life. And, the fact that it is also common in every human family globally, it is, therefore, neither unique to nation-states and political leaders nor to a few of them only.

## (3) Its Role in Non-Human Members of The Animal Kingdom

Interestingly, although on a very small scale, this Diplomacy is also very common among certain species of wild animals. A very good example is the frivolous mass chicken-killer called *esimba nialala* in a Samia language of the Samia people of Funyula Division, Busia District, Kenya. This predator effectively uses this Diplomacy by first stuffing a handful of termites into its rectum and then moving closer to where chickens are. On reaching closer to them, it quietly makes about-turn and then displays its termites cargo to them by forcing its rectum wide open infront of them with a view to attracting and luring them to come closer for a good feast on these termites (manna).

But, the moment these chickens begin to joyfully scramble for the wonderful manna, their cunning manna-provider suddenly makes a quick about-turn and then grabs one of them for a meal.

In this regard, Carrot Diplomacy is a very intriguing means. It is metaphorically referred to as "Carrot" because of the nature of its cunning motive by which one used it in order to influence another to do for him or her what one knows perfectly well that one cannot do it on one's own due to certain logistical complications. Such complications may be physical, legal, political, religious, economic, military, public opinion, etc.

## (4) Its Role in Political Life

In the history of American politics, this strategy is known as the "Dollar Diplomacy",—a means by which American Leadership has always used to influence other leaders globally by bribing them to do for America what the latter finds unable to do by itself unless it does so by way of proxy using a third party. This method intensified so much during the Cold War (1945-1988) that it caused untold sorrows to mankind particularly to targets of this strategy in Africa and Asia due to their abject poverty forcing them to accept bribes.

But as to what type of resources and who out of one's many friends and enemies alike that one may reliabily use this means in order to get one's job done for one's own interest are usually the two most fundamental challenging strategic questions inherent in this means which always put every decision-maker into a serious dilemma and sorrows whenever one discovers, in the end, that one's decision was a mistake.

A vivid example of this dilemma is the 11th Sep. 2001 New York and Washington DC terrotism tragedy in which the USA leadership suddenly came to find itself in terms of what resources it had to; and with whom out of its many friends and enemies alike it could successfully contact and account on without making a foolish mistake in the decision.

Inspite of its own military might at hand, the USA Leadership had to first swiftly recognize this problem. Accordingly, swiftly it saw the strategic importance of immediately revoking its previous ban on foreign aid to both India and Parkistan so that, like a carrot, the aid could swiftly manage to attract the co-operation of both countries on the USA side that it now desperately wanted against the Hamas, Hezbollah and Islamic Jihad who USA thought were the principal architects and builders of international terrorism network in collaboration with certain strange individuals such as Osama bin Laden.

Therefore, on the question as to who out one's friends and foes alike that a desperate person must now approach to influence, using the carrot, the decision by the USA Leadership to lift its ban on both India and Parkistan is definitely a classic answer. The decision shows that as to who one must approach against a looming dangerous enemy is never limited to one's friends only. One may choose an old friend such as Parkistan or an old enemy such as India that had not been very close to the USA because of the prevailing USA co-operation with Parkistan which is India's archi-enemy.

However, such decision usually depends on the pressing needs of each side between the seeker and the one being sought. For instance, in general human life, if one is an old enemy but is known to be badly in need of something which is essential for oneself in order to make one's ends meet, such a needy person, leader or country is an obvious potential easy catch for one's good use using this carrot.

Similarly, in International Relations, the USA decision to lift the ban on India was a vivid ramification of the fact of life that in the evernt of an extenuating existing situation forcing a person, leader or country to seek assistance of an old enemy, that person, leader or country would definitely use every carrot available within one's reach to obtain the co-oepration of that old enemy.

Also, it is easy for an old enemy to demand and easily receive all it wants from an old endangered enemy in exchange for its co-peration with that old enemy against an existing potential danger in the same manner India easily did in order to have her foreign aid restored to her by USA in exchange of India's co-oepration with USA against terrorism.

But given that this were real logic and rationale of Carrot Diplomacy, why then did it not work in the case of an acutely desperate Kenya during the Moi regime which had been denied aid by IMF and World Bank to acquire that Kenya should first meet those set-conditions? How can this be explained?

Unlike both India and Parkistan whose geographical position on the World Map empowers them with a logistical proximity to both Afganistan and Iraq useful to the USA for the latter's achievement of its aims against the sources of terrorism, Kenya's geographical position denies it such golden opportunity to enable it qualify as India did.

However, the other intriguing behavioural phenomenon in this Carrot Diplomacy stategy is that its motives are not all similar. Some are safe and some evil. Unlike the safe one, the evil one is naturally dangerous to the recipient. This is the reason why every recipient of such offers must first and foremost be always alert, skeptical and meticulously analystical before accepting any of it. Accordingly, a safe motive is righteous while an evil oriented is unrighteous as follows:

In a righteous or positive motive Carrot Diplomacy, one's sole aim is to use one's resource(s) with a just and honest view of influencing another party to continue (keep up) with one's commendable policy or performance. Such policy or performance may either be people-oriented (conscious)in keeping with the Universal Declaration of Human Rights; or a pressure in good faith aimed at forcing a certain leader or regime to rescind from its on-going or existing bad policy that may be terrorizing the general pubic through political harassment, detentions, etc. A vivid example of this righteous motive Carrot Diplomacy is the Donor Community's stand to promptly release foreign aid to those needy countries deemed of having demonstrated commendable human rights records, and to sternly withhold aid to those needy countries but having very poor human rights record with a view to psychologically forcing them to stop socio-economically suffocating their general public through human rights violations and other forms of Bad Governance characterized by management crisis, financial mismangement and election riggings in most African Countries.

But in an unrighteous or ill-motive Carrot Diplomacy, one's aim is to use the carrot with a negative aim to make the other party do what one wants to be done for one's own selfish good regardless of the injurious consequences to the recipient of the carrot, environment or total Humanity.

Vivid examples of this reality abound in the history of the Cold War (1945-1992). During that time, most politically young nation-states with a fragile socio-economic and military strength were, deliberately exploited and used at will as "puppets" by their counterpart who were already politically mature with a most powerful socio-economic and military might they were lured into hineous crimes, to Humanity, e.g., detaining without trial and assassinating their own fellow national leaders in return for the Carrot (material gains). These gains include cash money and military protection against opposition in the pretext of foreign aid.

## (5) Its Tragedy to Culture & Total Humanity

But what is the evil nature of this Carrot Diplomacy? Is it inherent in Human Life? Is it as old as our own Humanity? Is it new? Or is it man-made?

From the Old Testament of *The Holy Scripture1*, for example, which is also called *The Torah* in Judaism, we note that this is exactly the same strategy that Blair (Satan) employed to deceive and put not only our Patriarchs Adam and Eve but also all our entire Humanity into the on-going perennial untold sorrows we are now in characterized by abject poverty, miserable hunger, diseases, stupidity and ignorance, death and the search for salvation. Blair cleverly used this evil motive Carrot Diplomacy by lying to Adam and Eve that they would gain superior knowledge and wisdom equal to that of God only if they did co-operate with him and do what Satan wanted them to do while this very Satan knew perfectly well that he was actually lying to them and that if they ever did so they would be doing him (Satan) a great deal of good.

Similarly, from the New Testament[2], of the same Scripture, we also note this striking related danger. We learn that it was exactly this same evil motive Carrot Diplomacy that Satan cunningly tried to use on Jesus Christ with a view to not just tempting Him but actually destroying The Kingdom of God for Satan's own selfish good. According to the **Scripture**, Satan foolishly offered Him half of Satan's Earth's wealth if Jesus Christ could accept to do what Satan wanted Him to do (i.e, to worship Satan) for Satan's own good. Though the same Satan knew very well from **The Scripture** that he was not supposed to do so to Jesus Christ since the latter was his God, Satan was not ashamed to do so.

But that is not all. We also learn from the same **New Testament** that it was the same evil motive Carrot Diplomacy that the Pharisees, Sadducess and all other Jews headed by the Sanhedrin (Supreme Council of the Jews) collectively employed as their **sine qua non** means to lure and then use the Minister of Finance, Judas Iscariot, of Jesus Christ's Twelve Member Cabinet to lead them exactly where they could find and arrest Jesus Christ.

In view of all these prima facie facts adduced herein above, Carrot Diplomacy is indeed a complex and complicated weapon habitually used for two exhaustive and mutually exclusive aims namely: a righteous aim and an unrighteous aim. Although its user(s) may or may not know very well its illegal, unethical or immoral implications, the user(s) never feels ashamed of using it for one's selfish ends. Thus, the tragedy of this strategy.

However, it may be a very useful instrument in various ways for one's ends. Whereas, it could also be a very dangerous weapon if not watched and used in a proper and prudent manner. This is so because during Africa Independence struggle against Colonialism empirical evidences show that originally, African national leaders were not corrupt. They were not corrupt by virtue of their respective orthodox disciplinary cultures. For example, by virtue of this inelastic culture, cattle, goats and sheep are safely left alone at nights sleeping on highways in Baringo and Nandi Districts without any theft problem. Everyone is aware that any attempt to steal any of them would be cursed to death. But immediately after independence in Kenya, this culture is now rapidly changing because of pollutions brought about by foreign viruses. Moi who himself is a Kalenjin member is a vivid example of the victims of the viruses as also evidenced by the on-going revelations of his role in the Goldenberg scandal during his tenure as President of The Republic of Kenya (1978-2002).

Because of their orthodox (hard-line) disciplinary cultures, most African leaders at Independence neither know what leadership corruption was like. Nor understood the real dangers of this evil motive Carrot Diplomacy which was now the heart of the foreign policies of both the Eastern and Western rival blocs during the climax of the Cold War which had began at the end fo World War II in 1945.

As a result of this ignorance, both African leaders and the general public suffered terribly. Innocent blood was shed and unquantifiable property destroyed. Most Africa was so butchered and wretched by the said warring blocs that up today, the Continent is still nursing her wounds. She has not yet recovered! And, nobody can tell as to when she will be fully recovered from these wounds.

Leaders such as Mobutu Sese Seko for example became so much confused by this evil motive Carrot Diplomacy epidemic that killing their own fellow African leaders for the sake of a bribe from their foreign bribers during The Cold War became just as simple as killing a housefly or cockroach. To them, a leaders's normal duty which is to provide goods, and services to all citizens as a mandatory requirement for one's leadership tenure security was hopeless and vanity. They cared less since they already had the assurance from the source of this evil motive Carrot Diplomacy that their tenure of office was for "Life" that at no time any opposition would be able to remove them from office, and that whoever tried to remove them would be crashed to pieces. In fact, this is exactly the reason why most African Leaders gave to themselves strange titles of "Life President"! Such strange behaviour was not African; but a function of strange foreign ill motives of Carrot Diplomacy generated by and during the Cold War dynamics.

Whereas some of them such as Mobutu Sese Seko used this God father protection to suppress their opposition, at the same time, they used this abnormal protection to accumulate more wealth beyond what their own countries actually owned (GNP). And others such as B. Bokassa of the Central African Republic and Banana of Zimbabwe became so psychologically abnormal due to this virus that they unconsciously slided into cannibalism and homosexualism respectively. These are other types of wounds that AFrica was forced to nurse by the impact and effects of the Cold War and the latter's architects (USA and the USSR, the fathers of Capitalism and Communism respectively)

In the final analysis, because of these and many other critical dangers inherent in the use of Carrot Diplomacy as Joseph did in Egypt, etc those who do not have enough or sufficient socio-economic strength but who must therefore beg from the haves in order for the have-nots to make their ends meet are perpetual hostages of the haves and the latter's dictates. In order to avoid such traps, immediate self-awareness of who they actually are; and what they msut then do in life for themselves other than depending on the evil-motivated God fathers would be their only remedy.

This is exactly what Our Lord Jesus Christ did vis a vis all ill-motivated offers that Satan had mischieveously sought to give to Him. Similarly, this is exactly what Patriarch Joseph also did in Egypt in order for him to fend off the Egyptian woman's evil motive Carrot Diplomacy which could have immensely raptured the seal of Joseph's continence and chastity.

In this final analysis, had our Patriach Adam and Matriarch Eve been equally cautious to Satan's evil motive Carrot Diplomacy, they could not have plunged our Humanity into this perpetual mess we are in today. And had all political leaders of Africa and other politically young countries with a fragile socio-economic strength been as alert as a serpent to the dangers of this evil motive Carrot Diplomacy during the Cold War and thereafter, they would be immune from the virus. Their leadership tenure and succession would have been safe from the on-going perennial turmoil; the African Socio-economic glory could have been firmly sustained;; and rampant perennial culture of civil-strife and corruptive elections would no longer be used as tools for leadership acquisition, leadership tenure protection and leadership succession as is the habitual practice in Africa.

The nature and trend of this phenomenon in terms of its impact to our civilization since antiquity to the present, may be well understood and appreciated on the strength of the following two data: (1) It's Impact on President Kibaki's Leadership behaviour during his tenure that Kenyans had hoped with enthusiasm, that it was going to give them a long over-due salvation from a 40 year KANU leadership megalomania and paranoia but which now turned out to be a total embarrassment and nausea to them; and (2) A nosology of its genesis and impact to Humanity.

## (6) Its Impact on President Kibaki's Leadership in Kenya

(A) In its commentary titled "Corruption: Address Donors' Concerns Now" on Wednesday, 7th July, 2004, The East African Standard (which is one of the topmost renown sources of daily news in Kenya and the African Continent), vehementaly laments about an embarrassing confusion President Kibaki Leadership has now put all Kenyans in. In its own words, the paper note that:

> "Only 18 months ago, this regime was promising good governance and prudent management of public resources. Now, the champion of these ideals is in trouble with donors for abetting corruption.
>
> Britain, Canada, the USA, Switzerland, Japan, Germany, Sweden and Norway issued a critique on Monday" [July 5, 2004 bitterly demanding for an answer from the Government or else they withhold their aid to Kenya].
>
> (C ) And, in its daily of Monday, 12th July, 2004, The East African Standard also gave a lengthy, loud and dear appeal to President Kibaki to show Kenyans the way forward against corruption. Drawing its strength from warnings of other national leaders across the Country, the paper brings in a former Assistant Minister Dr. Joseph Misoi's warning to the President that unless the President hearkens to the on-going nauseating situation now terrorizing Kenyans psychologically, history would judge his leadership very harshly if

he, for example, continued to suppress the wishes of many Kenyans as the former Kenyatta-Moi leaderships had already done to them for the last fourty (4) years from 12th December 1963 to December, 2004. Referring to the ex-Assistant Minister's warning contained in a letter addressed to President Kibaki (dated Sunday, 11th July 2004:4) the daily reveals that, likemany other Kenyans, Dr. Misoi regretted that the country lacked a sound leadership based on the obvious clear signs; that for this very serious reason, unless the President evolved and invented right strategies to deal with national matters, obviously Kenya would be doomed; and finally that it was crystal clear that whereas most Kenyans were yearning for a bright future for their Nation, some of Kibaki government leaders were holding the Nation backwards into a Kingdom of Darkness. For instance, they are well known of holding the people-driven Constitution Review at ransom, thus trying to have Kenya drift backwards into a single-party Dictatorial Culture of Bad Governance and Constitutonal Disorder.

Like Dr. Misoi and majority Kenyans (based on the common sentiment across the Country), the East African Standard appealed to the President and his esteemed leadership to arise and take charge of the Nation so that, like the Biblical Joshua after Moses, may have wisdom and courage and lead Kenyans to The Promised Land.

## (7) A Nosology and Etiology of Its Genesis and Impact on Humanity Since The Generation of Our Patriarch Adam to Our Own Generation (2004 AD).

### A MODEL OF CARROT DIPLOMACY: SELECT CASES OF ITS SERIOUS ADVERSE EFFECTS ON HUMANITY SINCE PATRIARCH ADAM TO THE PRESENT *(A MANIFESITATION OF ABRNOMAL POLITICS)*

| The Briber | The Target (Bribed) | Action Needed By The Briber To Be Done By The Bribed | Adverse Consequences To Humanity |
|---|---|---|---|
| **DURING THE B.C GENERATION** | | | |
| (1) Satan | Eve against Adam | - To convince her husband Adam to ignore and disobey God's commandment and then do what God had forbidden Adam so that Adam and Eve may become as wise as God<br>- To do so in order for Satan to get Adam and Eve dislodged from The Garden of Eden and then join him in his perpetual predicament life subjected to by God after having been thrown out of Heaven to the Earth due to his un-Godly behaviouir and attitude | - Misled Adam and Eve to breach their Pacta Sunt Servanda with God<br>- Laid a perpetual foundation for Adam's seed's disobedience to God's commandment<br>- Subjected Adam & Eve to a perpetual punishment by God as follows:-<br>- Adam & his offspring to suffer diverse illnesses, death, etc for ever<br>- Eve to suffer the same<br>- Eve and her kind to suffer monthly menstruation and maternity labour pains for ever.<br>- Adam and his seeds were dislodged from the Garden of Eden because of their disobedience |

| | | | |
|---|---|---|---|
| (2) Satan | Cain against his brother Abel | - To murder his brother (Abel) in order gain a total monopoly over all blessings from his parents and God<br>- To do so in order to lose God's love and then join Satan in Satan's miserable life | - Ignited an instinct of homicide, genocide, etc in Human Life<br>- Initiated intra-family envy, false accusation, grudge, etc as a source of conflict. |
| (3) The Philistines | Delilah against Samson | - To entice Samson and find out where his strength lies and by what means these Philistines may prevail against Samson and kill him.<br>- To do so for them at a cost of 1,100 pieces of silver from each Philistine. | - Like Adam, Samson succumbed to the evil tendencies of the woman.<br>- Like Adam, Samson lost the free gift of God.<br>- His murder created a servere punishment of genocide to his murderers (Judges 16:5-20).<br>- His fall from God's grace because of a woman was also repeated by King Solomon's fall. |
| **IN THE A.D. GENERATION** | | | |
| (1) King Herod Mathew 2:1-18 | To the Magi (a team of Three Wise Men from the East) aginst the Infant Jesus Christ in Betheleem | - Subtly deceived the Magi to go and locate in Bethelehem exact where about the Infant Jesus Christ on pretence that he also watned to go and worship the Infant.<br>- But the Magi were fortunately directed by God through The Holy spririt not to go back to Herod after seeing the Infant as Herod had a hidden dangerous agenda against the Infant. | - Was so much obsessed with the glory of power of his leadership as a King of Judea that he (Herod) sought to kill the Innocent Infant Jesus Christ albert Herod had been fully bried by the people's chief prists and teachers of the law that the Christ's birth had no potential thereat to his(Herod) leadership (Mth.2:1-10). |

| | | | |
|---|---|---|---|
| | | - The Magi returned to their Country in Persia using a different route.<br>- They did not go back to Herod.<br>- Hence the safety of the Infant Jesus Christ for a megalomania leadership of King Herod and manifestation of how and why leaders always fail in her art of leadership as a custodian of justicice. | - Inspite of this honest advice, Herod ordered a summary killing of the Innocent Infant Jesus Christ.<br>- But when the Infant Jesus could not be found and killed, Herold became so enraged that he ordered child genocide of all children in Judea below 3 years old, on a megalomanic assumption that the Infant Jesus Christ would also be eliminated. |
| (1) King Herod (Mark 6:14-28) | To Herodias and her daughter against John The Baptist. | - Had himself given orders to have John arrested, bound and put in prison simply because John had advised him not to marry his brothers's (Philip's) wife "Herodias", as it was not lawful to do.<br>- Though Herodieas nursed abnormal hate against John for this advice, Herod had all the powers not to follow Herodia's advice which misdirected him to have John to be beheaded and give the head to Herodias' daughter as a reward for her impressive dance for the King's guest at the banquet in the palace. | - Ordered John to be beheaded in prison and his head brought back on a platter as a gift for the girl. (daughter).<br>- Hence a clear menifstation of a leadership megalomania rampant throughout all generations, e.g, that of King Henry VIII against Sir Thomas More (1478-1535) in England; President Jomo Kenyatta vis a vis J.M. Kariuki and Tom Mboya; President Daniel T.arap Moi vis a vis his Foreign Minister, Dr. Robert Ouko, in Kenya, during our own generation today;etc. |

| | | | |
|---|---|---|---|
| | | | - This is not only rampant in political leadership. It is equally rampant in religious leadership, e.g, the cases of Chief Priests in Jerusalem against Jesus Christ; Pope Leo X in Rome against Dr. Martin Luther, etc. |
| (3) Satan | Jesus Christ Against Himself and HisKingdom (Mathew 4:1-11) | - To miraculously change stones into bread since He was The Son of God<br>- To cast Himself down from the Pinnacle (Summit) of The Temple without fear as His security was fully assured by the presence of Angels.<br>- To worship Satan so that Satan may give Him all the Kingdoms on the Earth and their glory | - A clear manifestitation of Satan's megalomania and paranoia diseases against The Kingdom of God also common in all principalities and men of Darkness and Unrighteousness by virtue of their bankruptcy in righteousness and fear of The Lord, God, in the latter's capacity as Creator of The Universe and all living and non-living things herein. |
| (4) Chief Priest & Elders of The Jews in Jerusalem | Judas Iscariot against Jesus Christ | - To lead the soldiers to the whereabouts of Jesus Christ so that then may arrest Him (Jesus) at a bribery of 30 pieces of silver.<br>- To identify Jesus Christ with a kiss on reaching His whereabout so that the soldiers may arrest the true person. | - Proved man's bankruptcy in the concepts of gratefulness and knowledges of his Saviour. |

| | | | |
|---|---|---|---|
| (5) Pontius Pilate | Jesus Christ against His Kingdom | - To honour him (Pilate) by humbly answering his questions as so asked if Jesus wanted to be freed by Pilate from the Jews demand that he be crucified.<br>- To show to Pilate that Pilate indeed had the power to release Him to freedom or to crucify Him as so demanded by His Jew accusers. | - Confirmed man's leadership megalomania and paranoia against:-<br>- God's Kingdom, Power and Glory<br>- The concept of Justice. |
| (6) Simon (Acts 8:17-24) | Apostles Peter and John in Samaria against The Holy Spirit with the ill-hope that The Holy Spirit was a purchasable commodity | - On seeing that through laying on of the Apostles' hands, The Holy Ghost was given to whoever that was baptized, Simon offered these Apostles money saying "Give me also this power that on whomsoever I lay hands, may receive The Holy Ghost".<br>- But when both Apostles refused and rebuked him for such an assumption that God's gifts are or can be purchased using money, Simon begged them to pray for him so that he may not land into God's punishment | - As both Apostles witnessed, the Earth is full of such sinful persons like Simon who:-<br>- Assume that The Holy Ghost and God's gifts are on sale like commodities in the market place<br>- Use lies on congregations using false doctrines to exhort money from the faithfuls<br>- Thrive on such behaviour on false pretense that they are serving God. |

| | | | |
|---|---|---|---|
| (7) Pope Leox | (a) The Diet of Ausgburg (October, 1518) composed of The Dominion Order led by The Monk Tetzel<br>(b) The Diet of Worms (April 1521) composed The Assembly of the Germany Emperor (i.e., Nobility and Prelates) | - To fiercely attack and force Martin Luther to immediately rescind from his opposition to Rome's Doctrine of Indulgences if he was to be safe from eminent excommunication by Rome<br>- To hearken to the directives of The Diet of Ausgburg (October, 1518) if he was to protect himself from excommunication by Rome. | - Luther's stern refusal to change his opposition stand on the doctrine fueled Protestantism war against Catholicism and its un-Godly doctrine.<br>- Luther's assertion that Pope could also err in matters of faith made the situation worse against Catholicism.<br>- Luther's reiteration of his refusal in April 1521 at The Diet of Worms exacerbated the war against leadership megalomania and paranois in Rome. |
| (8) King Henry VIII | Sir Thomas More, Chancellor The Exchaquer in Britain from 1529 till 1532 | - To support King Henry VIII's demand to divorce the King's late brother's widow (Cathrene of Aragon) and then marry Ann Boleyn with whom the King had already become enamored—but a request more refused as it was against the Roman Catholic Canon in Rome | - More's refusal enraged the King so much that he ordered More to be beheaded<br>- More's execution equally enraged England so much that the act was seen as indictive of leadership megalomania and paranoia that have no regard for Justice. |

| | | | |
|---|---|---|---|
| (9) King Henry VIII | Prince Richard against Sir Thomas More (1478-1535) English statesman; author; and Chancellor of The Exchequer in The King Henry VIIIs Cabinet. | - In order to gain victory in his framed treason case against Sir Thomas More before The Privy Council, King Henry VIII prayed to Prince Richard to coin a false case against More in that the latter had confided into Richard that more's refusal was deliberately mean to influence entire England to also reject the King's demand to marry Ann Boleyn.<br>- Prince Richard agreed to do so on promises of a promotion and other royal rewards by the King. | - Like The Most Innocent Abel The Innocent Sir Thomas More was also executed at the expense of man's inherent evil instinct of envey and false-hood perennially terrorizing nuclear family and Humanity in general.<br>- The act accelerated a culture of Dishonesty; The Rule of Injustice and other Symptoms of Evil in England.<br>- Because of his deliberate heinous false witness against Sir Thomas More, Prince Richard hence forth became known as "Richard The Liar". |
| (10) King Loui XVI (1754-1793) | Against his own French subjects by misappropriating their state cofer to secterly aid American Colonies' War against their Mother Country, Britain. | - Megalomanically calaimed: ***Je sui l'etat e l'etat ce mois*** (i.e, I am the state, and the state is me).<br>- Totally contravened explicit commandment "**He that rules over men <u>must</u> be just; rulling in the fear of God! (II Samuel 23:2-4)** which in turn angered his subjects against his leadership. | - Psycyologically compelled his own French subjects to such a penniless situation unable to financé their both national recurrent and development programmes.<br>- This caused so much fury in France leading to the rise of The <u>French Revolution</u> against him that conseqauetnly:<br>- (1) Terminated his life by guilloting him in 1793; and<br>- (2) Brought a permanent end to a monarchy regime in France and replaced it with a Republic (1792). |

| | | | |
|---|---|---|---|
| (11) German Chancellor and Fuehrer Adolf Hitler(1940s) | To German sectret security Forces ***(Gestapo*** and SPD) against Non-Aryan Germans in Germany particulary the Jews and Gypsies who were not of Aryan blood and whom Hittler, therefore, wanted to be rooted out of Germany for the sake of Aryan German blood purity. So he demanded! | - Was influenced by the survival of the fittest theory advanced by Geopolitics and School of Realism (of Niccolo Machiavelli, Charles Darwin and Herbert Spencer) that taught that whoever conquered The Heartland and The Peripheries (i.e, Europe and its environs including oceans and seas), would automatically be deemed The Master of the World.<br>- This dangerous theory led to the rise of abnormal politics in Europe characterized by THE SCRAMBLE FOR THE HEARTLAND AND THE PERIPHERIES.<br>- Also was influenced by the anger against the Reparation Debt of 6,000,000,000 (British Pounds); and the loss of Alsace—Lorraine district to France imposed on Germany by the Versailles Treaty; and France's rejection of Italy's proposal to reconsider The Reparation. | - Obssessed with survival of the fittest theory advanced by Pseudo-Science,<br>- (1) Hittler desperately sought to colonize total Europe first and then the rest of the World second using force.(animus dominandi)<br>- (2) Apart from his own Prussia Germany, Hittler never wanted to recognize any other nation in Europe. To him, Germany was First Class. Number One!<br>- (3) Similarity, Hitler never wanted non-Aryans in Prussia Germany. Non-Aryans wee a pollution.<br>- (4) He consequently sought to root out of Germany everyone without Aryan blood<br>- (5) He consequently annihilated over 4 million Jews and 6 million Gypsies. |

| | | | |
|---|---|---|---|
| | | - Hence the rise of the leadership madness of the Napoleons, the Hittlers, etc in Europe | - (6) This action also led him to rooting himself out of life and his own Aryan Country he seemed to love and protect at all cost at the expense of the life of those Jews and Gypsies.<br>- (7) He left Germany miserably devastated and unable to stand on its own had it not been rescued by the USA Marshall Plan's emergency humanitarian aid.<br>- (8) Hitler left his "Aryan" Germany in a shamble of utter international humiliation, shame and embarrasement for a long time.<br>- (9) Thus, the consequences of a Poor Leadership and Pseudo-Science, e.g Geopolitics, etc. to Humanity. |
| (12) USA & Belgium (1960) | Joseph Mobutu Sese Seko & Moise Tshombe (premier of Katanga Province of Congo) | - To eliminate Prime Minister Patrice Lumumba in order to stop Congo from becoming Communist.<br>- To co-operate with the Belgium settlers in the most mineral-wealthy district of Katanga to secede from Congo | - Exacerbated an acute culture of Leadership megalomania and paranoia in Congo caused by the flaming intensity of The Cold War between capitalist Camp and Communist Camp. |

| | | | |
|---|---|---|---|
| | | - To do so in order to save Belgian's Union Miniers Co. in Katanga from possible nationalization<br>- To rehementhy reject UN intervention in Katanga Province civil war on false pretence that the war in Katanga was essentially a matter of Katanga's domestic jurisdiction<br>- To support Belgian military invasion in Congo as a matter of self-preservation aimed at protecting Belgian settlers and property in Katanga Province | - Sparked off a massive blood-letting in Congo thereby licensing Africa a blood letting continent:-<br>- Prime Minister Patrice Lumumba was brutally killed on 17/01/1960<br>- UN Secretary General Dag Hammarskjold was also done so on 17/09/1961.<br>- Hundred of Thousands of other most valueable lives to Africa and Humanity were equally wasted by this culture exacerbated by The Cold War and its evil weapon of The Carrot Diplomacy by USA and Belgium falsely perceiving Lumumba as a potential conduit of Communism in Africa.<br>- Enriched President Mobutu Sese Seko so much with bribery camouflaged as foreign aid that Mobutu's wealth exceeded Congo's National total wealth, as Mobutu Sese Seko expropriated USA, Belgium and other God fathers to embezzle all foreign aid to Congo and internal national resources and siphoned them to foreign countries and banks with a total impunity due to that foreign protection. |

| | | | |
|---|---|---|---|
| (13) Jomo Kenyatta (1966) | Tom Mboya | - To conceive a reliable workable formula of how Oginga Odinga may be ousted from the Vice Presidency during a KANU Summit at Limuru Conference Centre, Nairobi in 1966.<br>- To do so for Kenyatta because:-<br>- Odinga had proved a nuisance to Kenyatta Leadership's linings with the West Capitalist Bloc in preference for the East Communist Bloc.<br>- Odinga had also built such an immense empire over the Nyanza Luo Community that Mboya and all other Luo Leaders were overshadowed by Odingaism.<br>- Mboya would also become a major beneficiary of Odingaism death. Thus, Kenyatta's bribe to Mboya against Odinga. | - Made Kenyans lose Odinga and his needed contribution to nation-building from within the Kenyatta Government in his capacity as Vice President—a post he had occupied since Independence (December, 1963).<br>- Created a dangerous beginning of an irreparable endless schism and tribal divisions and hatred between Odinga's Luos in The Nyanza Province and Kenya's Kikuyu in The Central Province.<br>- Triggered the beginning of the surge for an Opposition Party to police over the Kenyatta's leadership megalomania and paranoia.<br>- Hence the formation of Odinga's Kenya People's Union (KPU) as a people's watchdog over KANU arrogance and other vices of Bad Governance. |

| | | | |
|---|---|---|---|
| (14) Jomo Kenyatta (1969) | Njenga | - To assassinate Tom Mboya who, after Oginga Odinga's departure, had also emerged a potential threat to Kenyatta's Presidency post, due to Mboya's increasing cordial relations with the Western World particularly the USA | - Ignited a country-wide uproar and unrest against the assassination and Kenyatta's leadership megalomania and paranoia.<br>- Sparked off a worsening Kenya-USA relations that had been flourishing significantly as a result of Mboya's dealings with the USA manifested in Kenyan students' air-lifts for a USA sponsored study programme in USA |
| (15) Danile T. arap Moi | Dr. Robert Ouko (1989-90) | - To accept, endorse and support Moi's policy of a state-staged corruption in The Kisumu Molasses Plant and other foreign donor supported development projects | - On refusing to be a party to such evil act, Dr. Ouko was secretly abducted at night from his ancestral home in Koru, Kisumu District (Western Kenya); heinously murdered and his body charred beyond recognition and thrown by the Got Allilah Hill in Koru. (The body was later accidentally found by Shikuku, a herdsboy) after a few days).<br>- Like the Thomas More heinous murder in 1535 (England), this heinous act flabbergasted Kenyans and Total World<br>- It confirmed man's leadership megalomania and paranoia. |

| | | | |
|---|---|---|---|
| (16) Daniel T. arap Moi (1990) | The Rt. Rev. Alexander Muge, Bishop of The Diocese of Eldoret of The Anglican Communion in Kenya (ACK) | - To suport President Moi's official statement<br>- That The Pokot People in The Northern region of The Bishop's Diocese were not in a famine danger as so being alleged by the emerging opposition euphoria and media.<br>- That The Moi KANU regime had already arrested the famine situation with a sufficient food supply of maize, beans and other staple food-stuffs to Pokot.<br>- And to do so in order to assit Moi Leadership's anti-opposition efforts so that the Opposition may not oust Moi's Leadership. | - On Muge's refusal to support such falsehood meant to compromise Muge's sacred beliefs and work (Minsitry),<br>- Moi summarily dismantled his own Presidential Bishopric Advisory Board (consisting Bishops Muge, Okullu, etc) on national security.<br>- Bishop Muge was summarily murdered in a state staged road accident on his way home from Busia to Eldoret<br>- The Bishop's murder horrified entire Kenya.<br>- This horrible act engulfled entire Kenya into a potential state of Civil War which was quickly watered down by Government Security. |
| (17) Daniel T. arap Moi | Kamlesh Pattni (architect of The Golden-berg International Company) | - To design a cunning strategy through which Moi Leadership would be able to con and siphon national resources from The Central Bank of Kenya (CBK) and every other relevant sources of public revenue to banks in foreign countries | - Kamlesh Pattni hatched out The Goldenberg International firm aimed to fulfil Moi's Leadership's demand.<br>- Both Pattni and Moi became mutual partiners in this form at the rate of 50-50% share. |

| | | | |
|---|---|---|---|
| | | - To do so in order to assist Moi's KANU party be well prepared to finance its victory against the emerging threat of 1992 Multi-party Elections<br>- To do so at the rate 35% Commission of his Total Loot.<br>- The siphoned public resurces were also to finance inter-tribal clashes to compel tribes to agree to vote for KANU | - The Firm ransaked Kenya's Economy so much that by the year 2002, Kenya's Economy was almost grinding to a stop.<br>- The scandal forced many businesses to close down and many public and private employees to be retrenched due to lack of money to pay them salaries. |
| (18) Daniel T. arap Moi (1978-2002) | - Cabinet Ministers<br>- Assistant Ministers<br>- Judges and Magistrates<br>- Permanent Secretaries<br>- Speaker of National Assembly<br>- Provincial Commissioners (PCs)<br>- Governor of Central Bank of Kenya<br>- District Commissioners (DCs) | - To support his anti-opposition policy in Kenya.<br>- To ensure that Kenya remains a one party state for the monopoly and supremacy of his KANU Party.<br>- To ensure that KANU remains in power at all costs.<br>- To assist KANU win every Election. | - Opened a Pandora box of an unruly monster of a culture of corruption that has flabbergasted not only Kenyans but also the entire International Community on the strength of the evidences now being unearthed by the new regime of President Mwai Kibaki effective its inauguration (December 2002)<br>- The Goldenberg scandal<br>- The Anglo Leasing and Finance Scandal<br>- And Embezzled Public Assets Totaling 200,000. |

| | | | |
|---|---|---|---|
| | - Internal Security Officers (Commisioner of Police, Director of General Security Unit, Director of Special Branch, Director of Criminal Investigation Department, etc)<br>- External Security Officers (Army, Navy, and Airforce<br>- Major Business Firms | | - By using all those human resources at his disposal from all spheres of life and activities in The Republic in his capacity as its Chief Executive, Chief Finance Officer, Chief Security Officer, Chief Diplomat, Chief Policy Maker, etc, Moi ransanked the Country's economy with total impunity and siphoned the loot to foreign countries using Asian Community both in and outside Kenya as so evidenced by the roles of The Goldenberg International and The Anglo Leasing and Finance Ltd which are based abroad but totally unregisted in those Foreign countries (e.g UK). |

| | | | |
|---|---|---|---|
| (19) Daniel T. arap Moi (2002 Elections) | Uhuru Kenyatta | - To accept Moi's offer that he (Uhuru) becomes a KANU Presidnetial Candidates since he (Moi) cannot be constitutionally allowed to contest again after his 2nd Term expires in December 2002<br>- To do so in order for Moi to be able to use him (Uhuru) as a cog in his scheme to succeed himself and then be able to conceal all dealings that may be perceived as illegal after Moi leadership. | - Created a turmoil in KANU summit as Uhuru candidature meant that all senior most KANU Summit members (George Saitoti, Raila Odinga, Kalonzo Musyoka, Musalia Mudavadi, Joseph Kamotho Katana Ngala, Fedelis Gumo, Moody Awori, Oloo Aringo, etc) were unqualified material.<br>- All these decamped from KANU and joined the opposition of National Alliance of Kenya (NAK) headed by Mwai Kibaki, Michael Kijana Wamalwa, Charity Ngilu and arap Kirwa.<br>- Together, the two groups entered into a mutual bilateral pact, "National Alliance Rainbow Coalition (NARC) which became so powerful above KANU that it swiftly and easily managed to dislodge KANU in the 2002 General Election and take over as the New Ruling Force in The Republic.<br>- Had Moi not resorted to using Uhuru as his Project in his Carrot Diplomacy KANU would still be in power. |

| | | | |
|---|---|---|---|
| (20) Mwai Kibaki | The KANU Rebellious Turks | - To accept to join him in The Opposition so that the two may jointly dislodge KANU from power in the December 2002 General Election.<br>- To do so on condition that these two would share power on a 50-50% basis as follows:-<br>- Mwai Kibaki (President)<br>- Michael Kijana Wamalwa (Vice President)<br>- Kalonzo Musyoka (Vice President)<br>- Raila Odinga (Prime Minister)<br>- George Saitoti (First Deputy Prime Minister)<br>- Charity Ngilu (2nd Deputy Prime Minister)<br>- Kipruto arap Kirwa (3rd Deputy Prime Minister)<br>- Moody Awori (Senor Cabinet Minister) | - As a result of this attractive Carrot posed by Kibaki-Wamalwa-Ngilu and arap Kirwa, the anti-KANU Rebelling Turks quickly rushed for this good omen, with a hilarious joy in their hearts.<br>- They consequently ensured that Kibaki and Wamalwa win though they were both hospitalized in a London hospital.<br>- Consequently, the whole Western, Nyanza and Eastern voted en masse for Kibaki as President and ensured that Moi's Uhuru Project fails.<br>- But after the Election euphoria, the so-called good Omen became a mystery.<br>- In order to avoid and silence such sources of further headaches from The Turks demands for the Omen, The President reshuffled The NARC Government and transformed it into a Government of National Unity by bringing in his Cabinet Oppostion Members. Hence the root-cause of the political earthquakes and tornadoes now waging across the Country. |

## (8) Its Chameleon Tendencies into a Harambee Spirit

As will be noted in Chapter IV below, Carrot Diplomacy is an intriguing concept. It is a chameleon in charcter in the sense that like a chamelon, it camouflages from being a satanic collective energy motivating and mobilizing agent into a bribe by which X may cunningly use to lure and then make Y to do what X wants to be done but which X is unable to do directly unless X uses Y. A classic evidence of this is the Harambee. Spirit programme initiated in Kenya during Kenyatta Leadership (1963-1978) where the Spirit was initially used honestly to assist Kenyans in various development projects which included building schools, churches and other religious institutions, hospitals and clinics, bridges and dykes against floods, children school fees, the sick treatment fees, etc; but also adversely used to create havoc in Kenya which included political elimination of oppositions using Harambee cash or other forms of bribery in order to incite the general public or to buy off certain key members of the opposition or ethnicity where the opposition leaders are based. This misture of Godiliness and Satanism plunged Kenya into a sea of agonies.

Whereas, the primary sufferer of this Harambee Spirit, as a dangerous weapon, was the oppositions, that was not all. **The secondary sufferer** was the source of resources needed to sustain Harambee Spirit. This source included the **tax payers'state coffer** to sustain its supremacy in Kenyan politics throughout his life as President of Kenya without having to go through any single election from 1963 till his death in 1978 but also created a very dangerous political culture in Kenya of demagogy, dictatorship megalomania and paranoia, to the extent that whoever tried to utter any word against his leadership had to end up in a summary arrest, and detention without any trial. Also, he created such a culture of Afro-Asian community corruption in the Country that both his successors (Daniel T. arap Moi, 1978-2002) and later Mwai Kibaki (2002-to the present) could hardly function unless they toed their predecessor's line of this Afro-Asian Culture. This obviously is the reason why the Moi Leadership is now faced with accusations as the co-architect and owner of the on-going famous Goldenberg International Anglo-Leasing and Fincance Ltd companies as the majormost source; the Business Community chiefly Asians whose source of lifelihood is chiefly business in their capacity as whole salers and retailers throughout the Country; and finally actual politicians who were psychologically forced to see to it that they always appear at all fundraising Harambee occasions with huge contributions to give in order to sustain and promote their political image and positions against their oppositions; and aspiring politicians who also loved to use the occasion to sell themselves to the leadership of the day and the general public as potential politician needing votes to take them to either Parliament or Crime Council. This led to the development of a dangerous culture of psychophancy, anarchy and total impunity in Kenya.

As a result of all this, the Kenyatta Leadership did not only manage the present flabbergasting culture of abnormal looting and siphoning to abroad banks Kenya's public assets from the Kenya Central Bank (KCB) Kenya Commercial Bank (KCB), National Bank of Kenya (NBK), Post Bank, and other sources. These scandals were subtly began and legitimized by Kenyatta.

But the more he involved the Asian Business Community and African politicians (actual and potentials), the more he socialized them on this culture of massive corruption. And, the more he did so, the more he legitimized their corrupt beliefs and actions. Hence, the genesis and consequence of the on-going scandals in Kenya today—a culture of massive corruption with total impunity that both Moi and Kibaki leadership also owe their excuse as their teacher and advisor to believe and do the same with impunity. Had Kenyatta not initiated such culture, the latter would not have initiated by itself. In this regard, it is therefore self-explanatory that in all the on-going scandal cases, none other than the Kenyatta Leadership has a vivid case to answer. Moi only followed his predecessor's foot-steps. Besides, he had already been so much classically conditioned to this corrupt culture that by the time he took over the leadership on Kenyatta's death in October, 1978, Moi was already a too grown and mature tree to successfully bend away from the only modus operandi culture of Kenyatta Leadership in which he lived and served as Vice President to Kenyatta for a total of 12 years (1966 to 1978).

And, the same also holds true with regard to Mwai Kibaki who equally lived and served Kenyatta as a Minister and as later continued to live and work with Moi on the latter's taking over Leadership from Kenyatta in October 1978 and under whom Kibaki also served as Vice President and Minister for Finance and later as Minister for Health before he decided to break up with Moi to form his opposition party, "Democratic Party of Kenya (DP)" from 1992 to his succession to Moi as President of Kenya in December, 2002.

But, what is this Harambee Spirit in Kenya? How did it come about? What was its purpose? Is it an African concept? If not, why? And from where did it originate?

## CHAPTER IV

# Harambee Myth in Kenya

### (1) Its meaning and Genesis

The concept Harambee is not an African word. It is a two-rooted Indian word in which its first part *"hara"* means *"god"* and its last part *"mbee"* means a goddess of power.

This Harambee concept was first initiated and used in Kenya in the dawn of the 1900's by the Indian coolies who were labourers imported into Kenya from their home country, India, by the British Colonial regime in Kenya with a view to using them as a source of a free human labour for the rail construction from Mombasa to Nairobi, Nakuru, Kisumu and Butere in Western Kenya; and finally from Nakuruy to Eldoret, Tororo, Jinja, Kampala and Entebbe in Uganda.

While constructing this railways, each group leader of these Indian coolies used to yell aloud to his group "Harambee"!! and then all group members would collectively yell back "yaah!!" with an aim of psychologically mobilizing and synchronizing their collective efforts together when lifting, pulling, pushing, raising up or hoisting a heavy load of steel, stone, wood, etc so that a load may be placed in its rightful positon meant for it's purpose.

Accordingly, attracted by the aim and success of this conept, "harambee" in the railway construction by those Indian coolies, Jomo Kenyatta also resolved to use it so that he may be able to mobilize various ethnicities in Kenya against the most powerfully entrenched roots of colonialism and Neo-colonialism in the Country characterized by hungry white settlers whose meaning of Independence was that they were automatically going to lose their enormous fertile farms and other wealth which they had gotten free by usurping from the African traditional owners particularly in both Central and Rift Valley regions of the Country. To them,

Independence meant that all their wealth was now going to be confiscated and returned to their African rightful owners. This assumption developed into Uhuru (independence)—phobia which in turn became an irreversible root-cause of continued Civil War in Kenya during the Colonial Era between these White Settlers on the one side and the African community spearheaded by Mau Mau headed by Jomo Kenyatta and other freedom fighters. Had these settlers returned to their sanity and sought a mutual dialogue with their counterpart in the conflict, obviously, each side would have turned a happy beneficiary by conglomerating into a Government of National Unity free of colour, creed, or partisan. On the contrary, they instead opted to a zero-sum game of a head-on-physical confrontation with Mau Mau.

And, the more this situation prevailed with a view to making a multi-ethnicity Kenya very too cumbersome to mobilize and govern, obviously the more Kenyatta saw the need to employ the "Harambee" concept as his philosophy, doctrine and strategy with which to successfully mobilize these multi-ethnicities in Kenya against Colonialism and New-Colonialism.

### (2) Its Marriage to Carrot Diplomacy As The Actual Root-Cause of Corruption Culture in Kenya from 1963 to the Present

But whereas in the life of the Indian coolies, the latter used "Harambee" concept strictly in accordance with its original orthodox meaning in Kenyatta's leadership, Kenyatta used it as a two-edged sword. On the one hand, he used it as a mobilizing agent; while on the other, as a bribery means.

As a bribery means, Kenyatta subtly used Harambee to dish out cash and other national assets to friends and potential opposition as incentives aimed at luring the multi-ethnicity Kenya to his leadership line. And, the more he did this, the more he created a culture of scandals, assassinations and other symptoms of dictatorial leadership which, in turn, became a womb in which One Party Undemocratic Culture was born in Kenya. And the more such culture emerged and grew, the more the mode of governance and all parties to it became politically socialized on its philosophy and doctrine that each became a lover of corruption and an enemy of the Rule of Law and Justice.

This state of the political climate in Kenyatta's Kenya gave birth to election riggings, briberies using Carrot Diplomacy to voters during elections to the extent that one's election victory was no more than a direct castration of justice in the election process. And, the more this was the case, the more those who occupied the seats in Parliament in the name of honourable members were actually all hawks as they had not won elections but just used Carrot Diplomacy to buy their way to Parliament. As the Goldenberg Commission of Inquiry has now just revealed, it was not only the voters who were bribed but also all senior Civil servants starting with Provincial Commisoners to District Commisioners, Divisional Officers, Chiefs and Sub-Chiefs in the Provincial Adminsitration; and then from permanent secretaries right up to the levels of officers the Carrot Diplomacy could financially afford.

Accordingly, the following Clinical Diagnosis of the Kenyatta's use of Harambee as a Carrot Diplomacy during his tenure of the Presidency (1964-1978) followed by Moi's use of the same during his tenure of the Presidency (1978-2002) here is now necessary in order to enable us understand the correlation of the two leaderships and their role as facilitators of an enabling environment for the birth and growth of the Goldenberg International Scandal:-

(1) As already noted above in our definition of the word "harambee", we discovered that it was an Indian word used as a mobilizing agent aimed at eliciting and co-ordinating every one into a formidable collective force required to successfully manage what has to be done.
(2) Because of its usefulness in a group, society or nation, Jomo Kenyatta quickly adopted and used it as his philosophical vehicle by which to govern multi-ethnically infested country such as Kenya.
(3) And, on realizing its cost-effectiveness vis a vis Kenyans, Kenyatta also used it vis a vis all Asians particularly those who owned large businesses in Kenya as a vehicle of mobilizing them to contribute to him personally according to each one's efforts.
(4) In this process, Kenyatta invented a "Brown Bag" strategy by which these contributions were collected every Friday and remitted to Kenyatta without failure.
(5) The one responsible for this Brown Barg Collection was non other than his own Vice President, who was in this case, was Daniel T. arap Moi.
(6) Thus, all these Brown Bags were collected by afternoon from the City of Nairobi centre right up to the Industrial Era where huge Harambee Collection always came from.
(7) Imbued by this cunning strategy, his own Minister of State, Peter Mbui Koinange, also invented his own Harambee strategy of 10% on every new development project that was to be initiated in Kenya which had to be remitted to him before the project can be authorized or cleared to take off.

(8) Thus, this 10% had to be paid directly to Peter Mbui Koinange in the name of Kenyatta's Harambee idea.

(9) As a result of these undertaking, a New Culture of Corruption thus germinated and grew into such a huge tree that overshadowed the original glory of the African Culture by honesty, chastity, discreet, holiness, sincerity, compassion, justice and a strong belief and commitment to taboos that always restrained every man and woman from indulging in corruption, deceit, theft, robbery, etc.

(10) Because of the development of this corrupt culture, every political leader, public administrator and the general public became too corrupt that no one would dare to provide an essential service to the public without first receiving a bribe.

(11) This bribery habit became so much entrenched in the Kenyan mind, behaviour and workmanship that it came to be baptized as "KK" (ie. "Kitu Kidogo" meaning something small in order for one to receive a service). Others called it "Chai" (meaning some tea, as an unofficial undertable service fee).

(12) The more this culture grew and was practiced in Kenya, the more employment in Civil Service, entry into Parliament, and justice in the Judiciary were purchased by whoever had enough wealth to purchase them.

(13) And, the more this habit continued with total impunity and on the support of the leadership of the time, the more no qualified Kenyan could ever get a job comensurate to his or her professional training and qualifications.

(14) The other end-results of all this unethical practice were that Kenyan Civil Service Commission mandated to recruit new civil srvants automatically turned into a rubber stamp expected to approve whoever a politician told them to employ whether or not the person had no suitable qualifications for the job.

(15) Thus, professionalism in Kenya gradually degenerated from a superb weberian bureaucratic model of efficiency and professionalism legacy Kenyatta leadershiop had inherited from the British colonial leadershiop and administration to a Kenyattarian model of inefficiency, and unprofessionalism characterized by nepotism, tribalism, mediocrity both in Parliament and Civil Service since Kenyatta leadership was more interested in whoever was to support his way forward of corruption in both Parliament and Civil Service.

(16) Because fo this development, Oginga Odinga, Billidad Kaggia, and other political leaders in the single ruling KANU party, became so much disillusioned with Kenyatta corrupt leadership which they thought was against the original spirit of Kenyan

struggle for Independence that they decided to prove tough on Kenyatta mode of leadership.

(17) On realizing this new hostile tornado against his leadership, Kenyatta secretly decide to eradicate Odinga, Kaggia and all other robots.

(18) At a highly doctored party conference held at Limuru in March 1966, Odinga's post of Vice President of KANU party was split into seven Provincial Vice Presidents a cunning method hatched out by Tom Mboya in order to humiliate and anger Odinga so that he may resign from KANU.

(19) As so predicted by Kenyatta and Tom Mboya, Odinga got mad, resigned and accepted to be head of the newly formed Kenya People's Union (KPU).

(20) Kaggia, who was also no more desirable in KANU because of his rebellious attitude against Kenyatta's corrupt leadership, resigned from KANU after having won the election to the post of Central Province Vice President but declared void so that James Gichuru could take the post.

(21) On Odinga's resignation in 1966, Kenyatta appointed Joseph Murumbi as Vice President who served in that capacity for only six(6) months but who also resigned because of his distate of Kenyatta's corrupt mode of leadership.

(22) And, on Murumbi's resignation as Vice President, Kenyatta would no more have anything to deal with rebels who were against his corrupt mode of leadership.

(23) Canided by this attitudinal meter, Kenyatta first scrutinized all members of Parliament in terms of each's potential degree of subordination and then zeroed up on Daniel Toroitich arap Moi as the only man with that potentiality that he need to support his mode of leadership.

(24) Daniel T. arap Moi served Kenyatta for a total of twelve (12) years beginning from 1966 till Kenyatta's death in October 1978.

(25) Throughout his tenure as Vice President, Moi knew exactly what Kenyatta wanted from a Vice President failure of which he would not be tolerated by Kenyatta.

(26) Thus, Moi had to play a full sub-ordinate role to Kenyatta regardless of the corrupt nature of Kenyatta's leadership.

(27) Therefore, the more Moi served under Kenyatta the more Moi was political socialized by Kenyatta to Kenyatta's corrupt mode of leadership.

(28) And, the more Moi underwent this political socialization for all those twelve years (1966-1978) the more Moi was classically conditioned to move away from his traditional culture of purity, and perfection devoid of deceit, theft, armed robbery, murder, etc witnessed even up to today in all Kalenjin area where cattle sleep on

public roads and other open areas without being stolen as this act would be against the Kalenjin commnuty taboo.

(29) But, the more, Moi was classically conditioned to move away from the legacy of his traditional beliefs and taboos, the more he metamorophosed into a Kenyatta model politically, morally and economically salivating for material gains at all costs and from every source available.

(30) This is exactly the reason why on taking over the saddle of Kenya leadership on Kenyatta's death in October 1978, Moi had to declare that he was going to follow the foot-steps of Kenyatta in all respects.

(31) This declaration is the real meaning of Moi's "Nyayo" philosophy which he launched immediately he took over the leadership as President of Kenya.

(32) Thus, it is submitted that it was during this apprenticeship as Vice President under Kenyatta for a total of twelve years (1967 to 1978) that Moi metamorphosed from the original Moi tailored according to the Kalenjin Community beliefs and taboos against every act of evil to evolve to Moi tailored according to the Kenyatta corrupt leadership culture characterized by Brown Bag Harambees, and survival of the fittest mentality which Kenyatta used to grab all land of his neighbouring residents in Gatundu and other assets in the name of Head of State.

(33) Also, it is submitted that it was during this apprenticeship period that Moi came to be socialized and accept the theory of elimination of opponents at all costs as also evidenced in Kenyatta's assassination of Tom Mboya, a case in which Moi was prevailed on to tell lies to the effect that the assassination had been instigated by a communist state in order to divide and seize by removing the man who was certainly standing in the way of scientific socialism[1] and also in Kenyatta's assassination case of J. M. Kariuki in whereby Moi was again prevailed on to tell another lie that Kariuki was not dead but actually in Zambia.

(34) But, this is not all. Although the assassination of Pio Pinto in 1965 was executed before Moi assumed the Vice Presidency portofolio, it is also submitted that this event was an added asset in Moi political socialization process as this influenced Moi to begin realizing and believing in assassination as one of the normal aspects of leadership life.

(35) Therefore, in taking over leadership as President of Kenya on Kenyatta's death in October, 1978, Moi remembered the following Kenyattarian strategies as the only means a leader must use to retain power in a multi-ethnic Kenya:-

(i) Chameleonism, i.e, a survival of the fittest strategy using deceit and dishonesty to fool the surrounding and everything around it not to recognize any evidence of danger in the leader used by Kenyatta to fool Odinga, Kaggia, JM Kariuki and all other radical nationalists by accepting Odinga's Luo traditional head gear of leadership as proof of his original commitment to Kenyan nationalism while immediately after ensuring that he had well entreched himself in leadership, he threw away the Luo head paraphanelia and the Kenyan nationalism in favour of his own tribal Kikuyu nationalism.

(ii) Lionism (i.e, a survival of the fittest strategy using one's might to grab whatever oen deems essential to him/her with total impunity which Kenyatta used to weed out his all neighbours in Gatundu and turned their rightful portions of land into his own; grabbed public liquid and fixed assets and turned them into his own; and removed both members of Parliament and Public Administrators and replaced them with his own using nepotism, tribalism etc with total impurity without any regard to the consequences to professional ethics and merits, and the Kenya's future; and to use his security might (GSU, etc) to kill every opposition.

(iii) Foxism i.e, survival of the fittest strategy using one's cunning tactics almost similar to the chameleonism but somewhat different in that one dies not have to cumflage to influence the other party but rather to tactically steal the other party's achievements as Kenyatta did using Harambee philosophy to get put of the spoil Asian business-firms had looted from the Africans through deceitful prices with the support of the KANU government.

(iv) Territoriality i.e., a survival of the fittest strategy used by a dominantly powerful group or community of a species within the Animal Kingdom to monopolize its area of operation and to keep out all other members of the same species as Kenyatta did by monopolizing the Kenya political arena solely for KANU affair and to keep out all other political parties such as Kenya African Democractic Union (KADU) healed by Ronald Ngala as Chairman and Masinde Muliro as its Vice Chairman; and Kenya People's Union (KPU) and declared Kenya a one party state.

(v) Sexual Dimnance i.e., a survival of the fittest strategy also called Animus Dominandi used by male species to monopolize all female members in a community of group of species and to practically fight and reduce all other less powerful males to a zero-sum game so that all of them become so much sexually impotent at the expense of the sexually dominant male member as Kenyatta did by demoralizing and reducing all other leaders with good potential to challenge him such as Odinga, Kaggia, Mboya, G. M. Kariuki, and many others to a political impotence.

(vi) Worship Mania i.e; a survival of the fittest strategy used by a dominant member of a group or community of human beings to force all other members to reverence that dominant member with greatest phobia to the extent that they go as far as singing and worshiping him as a semi-god as in the case of Kenyatta leadership during which all his Cabinet Ministers, Assistant Ministers, Members of Parliament, all Civil Servants, Parastatal headers and works, and all general public were so much terrified by Kenyatta phobia that they always bursted into hymn singing and the clapping of hands in greatest awe and force for Kenyatta to hear
"OH-O-O KANU YAJENGA NCHI
OH-O-O KANU YAJENGA NCHI
KANU YAJENGA NCHI
KANU YAJENGA NCHI!
Whenever Kenyatta arrived at any public gathering.

(vii) Inciticism, i.e., a survival of the fittest strategy manifested in A's used of B to do harm on C not for B's good but largely for the good of A as Kenyatta cunningly manipulated Tom Mboya in the latter's capacity as a Luo like his fellow Luo man Odinga to mischiviously initiate at the KANU Party conference held in March 1966 a humiliating proposal abolishing Odinga's KANU party post of Vice President and replacing it with other seven provincial posts of Vice Presidents so that Odinga, who had already proved too critically radical against Kenyatta's corrupt mode of governance, may be psychologically become angry and then resign from KANU party and from the post of Vice President in Kenyatta's government—a pathetic situation that did of course happen to the hopes of Kenyatta without Mboya's slightest hint of Kenyatta's secret plan to first get rid of Odinga and then also get rid of Mboya at a later date as Kenyatta achieved this sad goal on 5th July 1969 by murdering Tom Mobya using his own Kikuyu assassin[2], without any moral regard to Tom Mboya's strenuously noble efforts together with Odinga's noble efforts to salvage him (Kenyatta from his seven years detention in Kapenguria remote prison against the will of Kenyatta's own Kikuyu community leaders who had already petitioned secretly to the British Colonial Authorities in Kenya to do away with Kenyatta while still in prison and let Odinga assume the Kenyan leaders at independence!!

(viii) Hyenism, i.e, a survival of the fittest strategy of abnormal greed and gluttony manifesited in hyena's behaviour vis a vis anything that looks or smells meat by just grabbing and swallowing everything including gravels with impunity without caring of the possible real or potential danger thereafter and to try to chase away every other hyenas and scavengers which Kenyatta also used during his leadership to loot and convert the spoils to his own property with impunity without any sense of prediction of possible real or potential future repercussion against him and all beneficiaries of his loot.

(ix) Nepotism, ie, a survival of the fittest strategy aimed at monopolising key strategic areas in one self by using one's own relatives, friends and other supporters in order to close all doors and windows to all unwanted potential oppositions as Kenyatta did by monopolizing most key strategic positions in his government and strictly restricting them to members of his house of Mumbi Gikuyu community noted in the following table:

**Table 1: DISTRIBUTION OF KEY LEADERSHIP PORT-FOLIOS PER DISTRICT AND TRIBE DURING KENYATTA MOI REGIME IN POST-KPU ERA (1966-1978)**

| DISTRICT | NAME | PORT FOLIO |
|---|---|---|
| 1. Kiambu (Kikuyu) | Jomo Kenyatta | President & commander in chief of the Armed Forces |
| 2. Kiambu (Kikuyu) | Peter Mbiyu Koinange (Kenyatta's brother-in-law | Minister of State in Office of The President |
| 3. Kiambu (Kikuyu) | Dr. Njoroge Mungai (Kenyatta's cousin & Personal doctor) | Minister for Foreign Affairs |
| 4. Kiambu (Kikuyu) | Charles Njonjo | Attorney General |
| 5. Kiambu (Kikuyu) | James Gichuru | Minsiter for Defence |
| 6. Nyeri (Kikuyu) | Mwai Kibaki | Minister for Finance and Planning |
| 7. Murang'a (Kikuyu) | Dr. Julius Kiano | Minister for Local Government |
| 8. Embu (Kikuyu). | Jeremiah Nyagah | Minister for Agriculture |

| | | |
|---|---|---|
| 9. Meru (Kikuyu) | Jackson Angaine | Minister for Lands and Settlement |
| 10. M | D. Ndegwa | Governor for Central Bank of Kenya (CBK) |
| 11. . . . . . . . | B. M. Gecaga | Managing Director of British American Tobacco Co. Ltd (BAT) & Chairman of The University Council |
| 12. Akamba | Paul Ngei | Minister for Housing |
| 13. . . . . . . | Ndolo | Chief of Staff of Armed Forces |

(g) Nyayoism: A total commitment by Moi to closely follow his mentor's foot-steps in all aspects of political leadership. Thus, Moi pledged to see to it that whatever he learnt while seving as Vice President under President Kenyatta, he will have to closely sustain. Thus, every good (righteous) and evil (unrighteous) policies and aspirations and other legacies of President Kenyatta, Moi was fully determined and committed to do. And, so long as Kenyatta loved corruption by virtue of using Carrot Diplomacy to lure support to his policies whether good or bad, so was Moi also determined to do the same; so long as Kenyatta used nepotism to keep the regime and its national cake in the hands and mouths of his Kikuyu enthnicity so was Moi also determined to do the same. So long as Kenyatta loved lionism and hyenaism by grabbing even what did not belong to him as a private lands in Gatundu and plots, premises, cash in the Republic so was Moi also determined to do the same; so long as Kenyatta was so dictatorial and obliviant to wise advices that he killed multi-party Democracy in Kenya and replaced it with one-party Undemocracy, so was Moi also determined to do the same; so long as Kenyatta used Asian Community to give him cash so that he may use the same as Carrot Diplomacy to lure Kenyans to follow whatever he said, wanted (to dance to the tune of the music of his own choice), so was Moi also determined to do the same; so long as Kenyatta used assassination and other elimination means against his opponents without any regard to the Rule of Law and Justice, and to his own role as Chief Custodian and Guardian of The Fundamental Human and Civil Rights of every Kenyan in the latter's role as his subjects, so was Moi also fully determined to do the same; etc.

This obviously now explains the actual reasons why:-

(1) Many assassinations had to take place during Moi's leadership tenure (1978-2002) eg. assassinations of The Rt. Rev. Bishop Alexander Muge and Dr. Robert Ouko, whose nature and circumstances resembled those of the assassinations of JM. Kariuki, Tom Mboya 91969), Argwings Kodhek,—Pio Pinto (1965) etc. during the Kenyatta leadership (1963-1978).
(2) Moi's use of Asians intensified during his tenure as is now being revealed (a) by The Goldenberg Commission of Inquiry on the Goldenberg scandal involving Moi himself as 50% share holder with Mr. Kamlesh Pattni—a scandal that left Kenya totally bankrupt as most public wealth to the tune of Kshs. 13 billion was siphoned abroad and hidden in foreign banks. (b) By publication on The Anglo-Leasing and Finance Ltd also owned by Asians which had duped The Treasury, The Ministry of The President and Home Affairs, The Attorney General Chambers, etc to receive over Kshs. 20 billion for Passports, etc—a fact which also means that both Moi and these Asians involved in Anglo Leasings & Finance Ltd have for a long time been colluding in corrupt business for a very long period during his tenure as President just as his predecessor, Kenyatta used to do to finance Harambee activities in order to empower the latter to also sponsor the Carrot Diplomacy activities.
(3) Consequences of Harambee Spirit and Carrot Diplomacy Activities to Kenya's Destiny

The activities of the Carrot Diplomacy and its business partiner, harambee, have left Kenya in a serious degree of socio-economic and political decay. Economically, they ruined the infrastructure and investment morale from within and outside Kenya; socially, they ruined the social morality and all other fabrics of Kenyan cultural legacy of self-love and self-respect as a people; and politically, they ruined the Kenyan national pride and dignity locally and internationally with particular reference to its leadership and sovereignity in the Community of other Leaders and Sovereigns in various countries of The International System.

The most affected of all spheres of Kenya as a nation was the Kenyan economy. The latter was terrorized so much that the Country was almost collapsing soci-economically as most of its liquid and fixed assets were secretly translated into foreign currencies, siphoned abroad and hidden in foreign banks and real estates. As a result, the Country became so insolvent in the 1990's and 2000-2002 that she could neither manage to pay salaries to civil servants nor manage to provide essential services to most Kenyans as she had always done during the 1960s, 1970s and the 1990s.

In its attempt to save the already endangered Kenyan economy which was in the brim of sinking, the governing apparatus in the name of the Kenya African National Union (KANU) headed by President Daniel T. arap Moi resorted to mass retrenchment of innocent Kenyans working in civil service as a possible solution. But, this action could neither make the nation afloat nor pay all terminal benefits of those victims of retrenchment policy. As a result, while some resorted to suicide, chang'aa intoxication, etc; and some resorted to separation and divorce as they could no longer afford a peaceful marriage life any more; some resorted to theft, armed robbery and other heineous acts fo criminal nature against their will but which they had to do in order to survive.

However, this situation in the Country was just a tip of the voluminous mass of the real iceberg. The whole nation was in a total mess economically, religiously, philosophically, morally and culturally. Kenya as a nation was already in her death bed. Medically, she was in an Intensive Care Unit (ICU). Her life was in such a danger that her future was no more certain. Nairobi, Mombasa and Kisumu cities includes all towns were in a total decay to uncollected stinking gabbage with oozing swarms of flies and maggots as a justification of the criticality of the decay situation in the cities and towns throughout the Country, while hospitals and all other health security centres were insolvent that they had to resort to an austerity measures of cost sharing service fees to sustain themselves, most patients lost their life as these centres could not afford some needed medicines. In the road-network infrastructure, most roads became so full of pot-holes that they automatically became impassible or safe for most motorists especially with sleek saloon vehicles.

In the area of water supply service, many Nairobians (Nairobi residents) hardly received water form the City Council in its capacity as the source of this essential commodity. They had to get from ponds.

A list of these multi-micro-indicators of the state of decay in Kenya as a result of the Goldenberg and other scandals against Kenya's economic strength is obviously endless, painful and embarrassing indeed to most Kenyans.

4. Effect of Kenyatta-Moi Harambee Spirit and Carrot Diplomacy Culture on The Newly Formed Kibaki Government (Janurary 2003 to the Present)

Despite its often-stated commitment to its zero-tolerance war against corruption and all forms of Bad Governance in Kenya, the Mwai Kibaki leadership has been rocked by scandals after scandals running into approximately Kshs. 20, billion of tax payers' money as at June 17, 2004.

This amount arises from Kshs. 12.3 billion crude plan to buy untested jets from Aero Vodochocy of the (Zech Republic by KANU Government for Kenya military but also adopted by the new Kibaki Government) in May 2003 only five months in office after taking over the leadership in December 2002, from the then President Daniel Toroitich arap Moi; and also two scandals involving an assumed United Kingdom based firm called Anglo Leasing and Finance Ltd totaling Kshs. 6.7 billion.

The Kshs. 6.7 billion arises from the passport deal worth Kshs. 2.7 billion, and the building and equipping the three CID headquarters laboratory deal worth Kshs. 4.0 billion of which Kshs. 224 million had already been pre-paid as far back as a year ago (June, 2003) for these laboratories which as at June, 2004 has not yet even been started when this scandal was unearthed in Kenya.

But who owns and administers Anglo Leasing Finance Ltd? And what is this firms components?

Anglo Leasing and Finance Ltd, which is the architect of the passport scandal in Kenya is headed by a Mr. Colin Flynn, who is also an Accounts Manager of an associate firm called Saagar Associated. Both firms are based in the United Kingdom and are associated with a Mr. Powell Forman Kelly in his capacity as their company solicitors.

The Saagar Associates is owned by a Ms. Sudha Ruparell in her capacity as its only director and a wife of a Mr. Ashwin Ruparll of Liverpool Properties in the United Kingdom.

Sudha Ruparell also linked to a Kamsons Company Ltd firm in her capacity as its non-shareholder director, and daughter of a Mr. Chamanial Kamani, a resident of Kenya.

This Kamani is also a father to a Mr. Deepark Kamani of the Dar-es-Salaam Road-based Kamsons Ltd.; a firm that sold the Indian-made "Mahindra Jeeps to Kenya Police during the Moi Leadership (1978-2002).

The most intriguing phenomenon about this Anglo Leasing Finance Ltd which is at the centre of the Kshs. 2.7 billikon passport scandal that has dented the good image of the Kibaki Leadership in The National Alliance Rainbow Coalition (NARC) which, during its inauguration in December 2002, had launched its policy of Zero-tolerance against corruption, is that the company lacks a physical address. Thus, it is a non-existent entity though it theoretically exists on paper. Because of this reason, all attempts to contact Anglo Leasing and Finance Ltd have been futile as nobody seems to know its existence including the Post Office and Security Services in the United Kingdom.

A further flabbergasting phenomenon about the mystery surrounding this Anglo Leasing and Finance Ltd is that most Kenyan Government officers who were expected to know this firm on the strength of their correspondences with it on the passport deal, have all denied knowledge of it, though the suspended Treasury Permanent Secretary Joseph Magari, acknowledged that the Kenya Government had transacted business with it before. Similarly, a Kenyan National Security Minister Chris Murungaru as well as the Office of The President Permanent Secretary, Mr. Dave Mwangi, who were expected to have knowledge of this firm by virtue of their office as custodians of the national security, also denied knowledge of it totally.

In its communications with the Treasury on the passport deal, the Anglo Leasing and Finance Ltd firm had listed a physical address as being Alpha House, 100 Upper Parliament Street, Liverpool, UK. But, on checking this addres in order to verify its whereabout at the said building by the Kenya Governmetn when this scandal was unearthed in May-June, 2004, revealed only the offices of the Saagar Associates owned by Ms. Sudha. All calls made to Kamani's listed telephone numbers were answered by a lady who said that Kamani had since moved out though they stil owned the premises.

> "The Liverpool Post Office quated a British law firm, Powell Forman Kelly, as one representing Anglo Leasing and Saagar Associated. And, that this law firm had indicated that the Liverpool office was only a representative office dealing with businesses in English-speaking areas"[3]

Another shocking revelation about this Anglo Leasing and Finance Ltd is that a certain prominent Lawyer in Nairobi, Mr. Fred Ojiambo, who seemed to know something about this firm in its capacity as his client, refused to give needed information on the firm to the Kenya Government when called upon to do so. Consequently, he was taken to court in the week of 7th-11th June, 2004 for failing to appear before the anti-corruption police who wanted him to answer to police's questions pertaining to his statements he had issued on behalf of this firm, Anglo Leasing and Fiannce Ltd.

And, in the week of 14th-16th June, 2004, Treasury emerged with an astonishing report to Parliament by the Finance Minister, David Mwiraria, saying that this firm had wired back to Kenya a total of Kshs. 300 million on apparently learning that questions were already in the air about the exorbitant nature of the passports tender and the adverse consequences that might be soon coming to the firm; and knowing that the same scandal had already costed some Government officers jobs as Presidnet Kibaki had been forced by the scandal to suspend Finance Permanent Secretary (Joseph Magari) in charge of The Treasury, The Home Affairs Permanent Secretary (Sylvester Mwaliko), the Internal Security Permanent Secretary (Dave Mwangi) the Director of Government Information (Wilsonton Sitonic) and the Chief Litigation Counsel (Miss Dorcas Achapa) at the Attorney General Chambers who prepared legal documents pertaining to this scandal.

At the out-set, Anglo Leasing and Fainance Ltd has possed as a French company able to assist Kenya with a borrowing facility of Kshs. 2.85 billion that was at that time of transaction in 2003 required from Kenya Government to finance the passport deal. This facility offer emerged when the firm was approached to fund the deal after the Francis Charles Oberthur Fiduciare had won this passport tender, but the Kenya Governement proved financially unable to meet this Kshs. 2.85 billion deal. But, the Ethics and Governance Permanent Secretary (Mr. John Githongo) sounded the alarm against this Anglo Leasing and Finance Ltd firm on sensing that the firm never actually existed. Before him, Member of Parliament Maoka Maore (of Ntonyiri Cosntituency) was the first to blow the whistle on this passport scam. Lamentingly, he could not accept any exuse from the Office of The President and Treasury that neither of them ever know anything about this Anglo Leasing and Finance Ltd firm and yet "These people have traded with the company for over 10 years. How can they not know who is involved?" According to Maore, this Office of The President was just shielding the identity of local personalities fronting for Anglo Leasing[4]. Gun Lord Dealer and Others in The Anglo Leasing & Finance Ltd.

In search of the actual suspects owning Anglo Leasing and Finance Ltd, the East African Standard unearthed a top Kenyan Security official and an international arms dealer (whose name could not be revealed for security purpose) but is said to have transacted business with the previous Kenyan KANU Government for a period of time. He is thus said to have in the past procured radar and other military kit for the Government. He has had links with Moi Government prominent figure such as a prominent Cabinet Minister who has also been investigated for corruption in the past. He has had associations with Kenyans in the military and intelligence circles whom he also helped to open business overseas. And, now, he is also reported of formulating a new contract to supply naval equipment to Kanyan Government Navy.

Another figure the East African Standard unearthed as being connected with this Anglo Leasing and Finance business is a contractor (also name withheld for security purposes) now involved in procurement of security geers of US $ 200 million in value.

Also, unearthed figures is a tycoon with a vast interests in industry; another tycoon associated with a Nigerian Cabinet Minister.

Further, the East African Standard discovered that this arms dealer already has a decade-long association with Kenya, specializing in defence and security procurement. And that he had been a close friend of former powerful Internal Security Permanent Secretary (Hezekiah Oyugi).

A further revelation about this threatening vice is that a new corruption elite of both new and old governments has emerged and a new corruption cartel. Like an Octopus it has it tentacles on these three spheres of Kenyan national life:—Politics, business, and civil service. And, that this international arms dealer is their engine of this corrupt business effective the Moi KANU leadership.

Because of this strong culture in Kenya today, a passport deal which the new Kibaki NRC Government had initially expected to contract at a price value of Kshs. 850 million was hijacked and over-priced at Kshs. 2.7 billion with total impunity by the members of this corrupt cartel with full awareness of the huge profit of almost Kshs. 2 billion in their pockets at the expense of poor Kenyan tax payers[5].

## Footnotes

(1) The East African Standard, Nairobi; 14th July, 1969
(2) Ibid; also Colin Leys, Underdevelopment in Kenya: The Political Economy of Neo-Colonialism, University of California Press, Berkely, (1975), p. 235.
(3) The East African Standard, Nairobi, Wed, June 16, 2004, p.3.
(4) Idem.
(5) Ibid, Thursday, June 17, 2004, p. 2

## CHAPTER V

# Terrorism

### (1) Problem

Since the terrorism tragedies in Nairobi and Dar-es-Salaam in August, 1998 followed by a series of other tragedies on 11th September 2001 in New York and Washington, D.C. (USA),[1] endless concern have arisen and questions asked globally by the youth and adults alike seeking to know and understand better what this terrible thing called "terrorism" actually is or means; who or what kind ro type of person(s) that usually get involved in such agonizing violence against Humanity; whether or not terrorism is only associated with Dar-es-Salaam, New York and Washington DC; and above all, whether or not this most devastating thing can be prevented and possibly eradicated totally from this planet.[2]

### (2) Purpose

Because of this agonizing concern and challenging questions, the following definition and explanation about "terrorism" is definitely in order and justified indeed so that this destructive thing may be thoroughly understood in its entirety in terms of its meaning, genesis, role in human life; its dynamics; and more so, its usefulness to its architect i.e. the reason(s) why it exists or used at all by the user.

### (3) Findings

#### (a) Meaning of Terrorism Concept

Terrorism is a concept derived fromt the word "terror" which means use of coercion or force as one's rational tool for achieving what one canot possibly get using peaceful means. It is an act of either explict or implicit (tacit) coercion[3] or force meticulously and systematically designed or planned and executed by its architect with a sole aim of forcing, compelling, inducing or simply influencing the target (or the terrorized) to psychologically listen, understand, appreciate and possibly agree, accept or comply with the wishes, demands, complaints or grievances of the source of terrorism (i.e., the terrorist).

Terrorism is universally used by both weak and strong individuals, groups and nations against their enemies as in the era of the Cold War (1945-1980s) where main parties to this Cold War (USA and USSR) ideologically and financially terrorized weaker nations such as Kenya, Congo, etc with a view to influencing them to become supporters of their ideologies, and to assassinate or frustrate their leaders whenever the latter tried to resist such temptations. This is the reason why Prime Minister Patrice Lumumba was assassinated in Congo in 1960 and Congo became a wretched Country.

However in most cases terrorism stand out to be the most favorite tool or instrument of coercion to the relatively weaker or smaller actor(s) in every group or community of individuals and nation-states alike against the relatively most powerful actor(s) (giant) simply becauSe OF the power imbalance between the two.

In this regard, terrorism is both an explicitly and implicit (tacit) bargaining or negotiation means or tool by which a weaker or smaller actor A" usually uses or resorts in order to influence a relatively more powerful actor "B" to do what "A" actually wants "B" to do for "A" but which obviously "B" may not or could not have otherwise done or wished or liked to do freely if "A" had not used that means of coercion.

In this case, in view of this real fact, terrorism is, therefore, a rational instrumental stimulus by "A" on "B" categorically and mathematically calculated to aim at soliciting, gaining or seeking a desired positive response from "B" in accordance or conformity with the wishes or demands of "A"[4].

But, why and how is terrorism explicit or implicit?

Terrorism is explicit when it is open, clear or vividly known or understood to/by the target and the general public withregard to its source and actual aim(s) as in the case fo the famous Boston Tea Party on 16th December, 1773, when the rebel leaders of Thirteen American

Colonies raided three British ships in the Boston Harbour carrying a large quantity of 340 chests of tea cargo and totally set everything on fire with a view to forcing or compelling Britain to stop taxing them on their commercial goods to European markets since they were not being represented in the British Parliament. Another prima facie evidence of explicit terrorism is the Japanese attack on the American Merchant Ships in the Peal Harbour[6] on 7th December 1945 with a view to forcing America to accept Japanese supremacy/dominion over China and the entire East Asia. Today this is manifested in the on-going terrorist attacks on American, British, Italian, Turky, Pakistan, German and other forces of the co-alition in Iraq by the anti-coalition Iraq with a view to forcing there coalition members to leave Iraq alone for Iraq to determine their own future.

And, terrorism is implicit when its source is unknown, secretive or implicit. In this case it acts in two ways: (1) Through underground (or undercover) as in the famous case of The Walk-Over catastrophe Old Egypt by the Israelis on the eve of their escape and Flight (Exodus) from Slavery Plight in Egypt to Liberty in Cannan with a view to forcing The Pharaoh in Egypt to understand their grievances that they would no longer afford their slavery affliction;[7] and also (2) Through a third party (proxy) in order to cause hell on the target as in the case of the Cold War when the two warring parties (Capitalist Bloc and Communist Bloc)headed by the USA and the Soviet Union respectively, secretively used small powers or countries such as Kenya as proxies or puppets through which the two warring Blocs inflicted terror on each other with a view to psychologically and physically containing each other's ideological expansion without having to do that directly by themselves.

### (b) Dynamics of Terrorism

However, the most tasty flavor or ingredient of terrorism as a subject of Scientific Inquiry in Behavioural Science lies in its definition or damage/havoc it usually inflicts on the target but in its dynamics[8]. For example whenever the expected response by "B" (the terrorized) to "A" (the terrorist) does not turn out to be in agreement with the expectations of the first stimulus from "A" by not proving congruent or able to meet the actually intended demands or wishes of "A", obviously "A" is subject to be psychologically forced to go back on his or her drawing board to re-think and decide on what to do next in order to make "B" reciprocate accordingly and appropriately as a "A" may thus wish "B" to do.

Empirically, there are always two options "A" may resort to decide from," (1) Either to quit and abandon the whole business regardless of the cost already invested therein and the side-effects to arise there from due to the failure of the terrorist's original plan; or (2) to re-design the original strategy all over with full determination of not surrendering at all even if this aluta continua may mean total death for both the architect of this terrorism and all supporters of the idea.

Propelled psychologically by this aim (that often lead many terrorists to even slide into suicide terrorism (as a demonstration to the target and the public opinion alike), such hardliner terrorists usually keep on increasing the intensity of their original strategy until their original goal is achieved.

Accordingly, and in view of this reality, then The Behavioural Law[9] of Terrorist Dynamics is simply that in order to achieve one's goal, a determined terrorist, always increases the intensity of its stimulus in order to force or compel its target or victim to quickly comply or co-operate with the terrorist's demands or wishes.

This Behavioural Law is vividly explicated (simplified) here below in Model One and Model Two.

**MODEL ONE:**

**AN INCREMENTALISM MODEL OF TERRORISM STIMULUS ON THE TARGET**

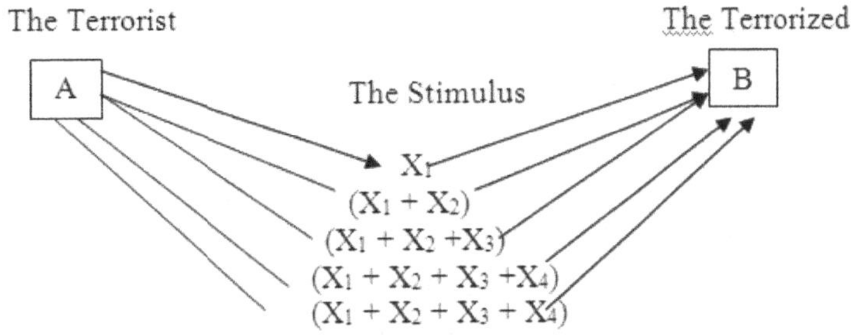

**MODEL TWO**

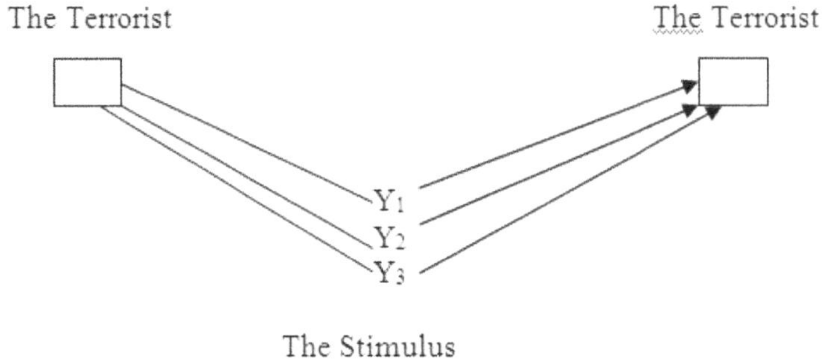


As Model One depicts, whenever "A" (or the terrorist) seems or notices that he/she has actually failed to gain a positive response from the first stimulus X1 "A" may choose to increase the intensity of his/her first stimulus (X1) to a new Stimulus (X1) + (X2) And, may keep on increasing the stimulus using his/her mathematical incremonialism as follows:-

(X1) + (X2) + (X3) + (X4) + (X5)+ (X6) etc, until "A" feels satisfied that "B"s response now proves or shows that "B" has now understood "A"s demands and is therefore able to reciprocate and co-operate with "A".

And, as per Model 1 "A" (i.e., the terrorist) who is determined to achieve his/her goal at all costs, may also use other strategies apart from the mathematical incrementalism. He/she may resort to the use of different options by dropping option Y1 and adopting option Y2. And "A" may continue changing these options indefinitely until A comes to the one that he/she will accept to the satisfying end.

But, terrorism is neither a new phenomenon in our human life which has it limited to political life as one MAY assume. It is spatio temporal free and universal in the sensE that it is as old as mankind and does exist in all aspects of our human life as also evidenced below as follows:-

1. In Economic life, it manifests in both trade and commerce whereby business "X" may use its price as a toll of either driving its business competitor "Y" out of business or simply forcing "Y" to comply with the wishes of "Y" which may probably be the latter lowering down its commodities or goods that it feels that "Y" critically depends so much for its business survival. This form of terrorism is obviously "ECONOMIC" or

"TRADE TERRORISM:, and is totally unique in its own rights form all other forms below from (2) to (7).

2. In the Social Life. Terrorism also does exist between and among individuals. For examples, Individual "A" may use his/her tactic or strategy "X" as his/her bargaining tool by which to influence individual "B" to comply and behave as so wanted by individual "A". This type of conduct is obviously also terrorism. And, it is therefore called "SOCIAL TERRORISM" because of its social character; and subject to occur also between and among groups of individuals.
3. In Religious Life, a religious group or Church "M" may wish to use its tactic or strategy "X" with a sole view to either forcing another religious group "N" to comply with "M" wishes whether "N" wants it or not. This is obviously also "terrorism". And, is therefore known as "RELIGIOUS TERRORISM" by virtue of its religious orientation.
4. In Science, intra-disciplinary scientists in one way or another do encounter various intra-disciplinary terrorism particularly in their research discoveries and inventions where by researcher "A" may steal the findings of researcher "B" thereby forcing research "B" to totally lose his efforts to researcher "A". this form of terrorism is called SCIENTIFIC DISCOVERY TERRORISM.
5. In Technology, also invention theft is also very widespread between inventors. Inventor "A" may lose this invention to inventor "B" if that invention were not yet patented. This form of theft in technology invention is called TECHNOLOGY INVENTION TERRORISM.
6. In Architecture life, we also encounter various incidents of architectural designtheft particularly of new ideas by architecture "A" from architecture "B" thereby forcing architecture "B" to lose all his talents to architecture "A". This form of theft is called ARCHITECTURAL TERRORISM.
7. In intra-family life, terrorism acts abound and are more often than in any other form of life, particularly between husband and wife and also among the children. This behaviour is more among wives than it is among husbands in various ways ranging from manipulating food in the kitchen in a manner aimed at either persuading or forcing the husband to listen to her position she may be having. Her position may either to purchase a certain attire, shoes, perfume, jewelry etc for which she wants her husband to agree and give her the money to purchase positively, she may prepare a best meal possible for her Husband in order to influence him; and if he appears reluctant, she may now resort to a negative stimulus by preparing him a nasty food

which is either too salty, half-way cooked or simply cooked very roughly with a view to punishing him so that he may now agree to change his mind and comply to her wishes. This form of behaviour between wives and husbands is called FEMININE TERRORISM[10].

8. And, in Political Life, acts of terror are the worst of all acts of terror in all other forms of life. They are so because they are the most dangerous of all by virtue of their degree of destruction on the target. The most memorable ones are, in fact, innumerable. But for the purpose of our understanding and appreciating its devastation here, mention of the following may be much in order:

    (a) The ten years French Revolution of 1789 to 1799 which devastated France so much that by the time of its end in 1799, France was not only too bloody and full of corpses of the dead of King Louis XVI, the Queen and the Clergymen who had been used to living a filthy wealthy luxury life at the expense of the overwhelming majority poor French peasants but also no longer a monarchy;[11].
    (b) The assassination of King Alexander of Yugoslavia in France on 9th October, 1934 by terrorism which did not only anger France but also forced her to try to pursue a possibility of forcing the League of Nations to bring about an international convention for the prevention and punishment of political terrorism[12].
    (c) The Vietcong Tet Offensive of 1968 which infiltrated main South Vietnamese cities and district capitals devastated South Vietnam so much by executing even innocent villagers with a view to forcing every one to co-oeprate with them but not with the enemy that such executions undermined the confidence in Saigon government of the United State and the World Public Opinion[13].
    (d) The Mau Mau Rebellion against the British Colonial Regime in Kenya which took place from the early 1950s to the beginning of 1963,left the British Colonial Regime and the White settlers in Kenya so confused and worried of their skin that they had to yield to the Rebellion's demand for independence on the terms of these terrorists[14].
    (e) The American War of Independence against their Mother Country, Britain, also so much confused and worried their Colonial Master that the latter had no other alternative but to yield to these terrorists' demand for independence which was then granted and put into force on 4th July 1776[15].
    (f) The 1998 Terroristst bombings of American Embassies in both Nairobi, Kenya and Dar-es-Salaam, Tanzania with a view to forcing the International Community

to co-oeprate with the demands of the terrorists did not only surprise the Community of its demands but also left untold sorrows of irreparable emotional scars in both Kenya and Tanzania whose costs cannot be satisfied by any monetary payments, reparations or compensation[16].

7. And the most recent series of terrorist attacks in New York City, Washington DC, and other parts of the United States of America particularly on 11th September, 2001 which devastated not only the infrastructure but also the morale of both the American government and people so much that the victim had also to retaliate against the source of that terrorism[17].

## Conclusion

In the final analysis, the concept "terrorism" is universal and spatio-temporal free. Also it is not limited to political life alone. It exists in all forms or spheres of life, where it is universally used as a bargaining, negotiation or coercion tool by one individual, group, community or nation-state against another for the purpose of influencing or seeking to influence, or to gain co-operation or compliance of/from the other party.

When used positively, terrorism is normally harm-free (harmless) and injury-free. In this way, terrorisms is normally used in the form of enormous positives rewards, gifts, super service as a tool by which to influence the target to co-operate and give out what is needed of it. But when negatively used, terrorism is definitely very harmful and injurious indeed as so manifested in those various seven prima facie evidences indicated above.

Because of this real and obvious reason, terrorism is both an inter-subjective bargaining, negotiation or coercion tool globally as well as an integral part and parcel of human life. And because of these two reasons, it is also spatio-temporal free of one's possessional values, goal or treasures at home (e.g territorial independence and integrity; human rights, liberty and freedom, etc); and in pursuit of one's milieu values, goal or treasures that one may be having at home but wishes to legitimately acquire from outside one's own home or jurisdiction.

In this regard, and as we have already noted from all those seven (7) prime facie evidences of terrorism in this paper above, terrorism may be injuriously devastating. However, it all depends on what its goal is. For this very reason, it may be a just or an unjust act all depending on its aim(s). And, this is, therefore, the most compelling reason why each act of terrorism must be first and foremost clinically diagnosed very meticulously before a verdict is delivered against it whether it is a just of unjust. This action is essential because like many other instruments of war, terrorism is also a customary instrument of war recognized by various scientists of war and peace from both Political Science and Jurispudence (International Law). This recognition is not simply because of its present devastating acts and results on humanity globally but because of its important character as a spatio-temporal free instrument of war from Antiquity to the Present Civilization.

Political Scientists especially those specialized in Strategic Studies are also of the same view arising from their research findings[18]. The same is also supported by leading jurists such as Professor L. Oppenheim and many other experts of International Law. In his celebrated master piece, International Law: T. Treatise (1967)[19], Professor Oppenheim traces its genesis and form, he also confirms that terrorism is a customary instrument of war from Antiquity to our own Civilization—a fact which, therefore; confirms that terrorism is indeed an integral part of human behaviour which can only be understood better and judged whether it is Just or Unjust by first and foremost understanding its goal, objective or aim and dynamics. And, this can only be achieved by using pure Science but not pseudo-Science saturate, motivated and driven by attitude and human emotions which are also ways a habitual enemy of every scientific investigation in Academica, because of their antithetical or antagonistic character against Truth, Reality and Justice. Unlike pure Science, pseudo-Science thrives on falsehood and economic benefits arising from such falsehood that reality is always turned upside-down into falsehood and falsehood into reality thereby ending with reality in jail!! Thus, the tragedy of Social and Behavioural Sciences as compared to both Physical and Biosciences which always honour and thrive on pure Science only.

Finally, on the questions as to How terrorism can or may be prevented in order to save Humanity from those nasty recurrent agonies terrorism always afflict on Humanity from time to time, and as to Who can or may possibly do so, the questions is somewhat complicated but actually very simple. Terrorism is a man-made phenomenon. It is not that natural and therefore beyond the reach of the human capabilities.

If it has to be prevented in order to save Humanity from the agonies caused by the terrorist havoc, the same Humanity is duty-bound to agree to first and foremost rehabilitate itself from its present life style—its wicked culture saturated with a total disregard to Justice, wisdom,

Temperance and courage on the one hand; and perfection and Holiness on the other which almost non-existent in the life of each individual, group, society, country, etc because of the universal belief and attitude of the "Survival of the Fittest" mentally most particularly in political life, business life, and in many other aspects of life including Religion.

Every person and country alike is obssesed with "me" against "them". Most do not have a suffieicnt understanding between doing good and doing evil to another. The individual and national interest alike are the order of the day that drive most people in their relations and interactions with others.

Therefore, the only remedy to terrorism is a comprehensive self rehabilitation also known as "to be born-again" in the Spiritual Life, so that Humanity may create a new Culture of a Hybrid that is not characterized by corruption, dishonesty, looming injustices, acute self-seeking mentality totally disregarding the welfare of the overwhelming majority. Which have always the root-cause of terrorism in every case of terrorism recorded so far in ouir Human History. It was the root-cause of the Israel Rebellion and Pass-over catastrophe against their oppressive Pharoah and the latter's people of Egypt; it was the root-cause of the thirteen North American Colonies Rebellion agasint their King George and his Colonial Policy in those Thirteen Colonies; it was the root-cause of the French Revoluton that ended the monarchy in France because of the insensitivity of the monarchy to the affliction of the overwhelming majority of the French peasants; it was the root-cause of the Kenyan Mau Mau Rebellion against the British Colonial Rule that had proved naked of the Human Right; and it was the same root-cause of various other acts of coercion from the Antiquity to our Present Civilization.

In a nut-shell, each individual, society, community or nation-state must be willing to move out from this existing rotten and danger and culture of injustices and other wicked ways in to a Hybrid Culture free of those Virii (Viruses) as the only rational way forward from terrorism and its existing culture.

It is only through this existing culture of terror. In other words, Humanity must be willing to accept to undergo a Conflict Vaccination metamorphosis—a process to complete re-education of society vertically and horizontally. Thus, a possible antidote of the existing culture for terrorism and other symptoms of conflict.

CHAPTER VI

# War

## (1) A General Nosology of War

The concept "War" in general entails a phenomenon of real conflict between two or more living entities. It exists in all spheres or forms of life. For example from an interdisciplinary approach, the data show Angel Michael's War against Lucifer as a War of the Men of Light against the Author of Darkness, etc. In Economy, economists policy-makers and implementers alike talk of a war against poverty. In politics, leaders talk about a war against corruption and all root-causes of Bad Governance and National Decay. In Law, jurists talk about a War against injustice (or the Rule of Law and Justice). In Health Care, clinicians and nurses alike talk about a war against diseases (e.g a war against polio, malaria, typhoid, ebola, HIV/AIDS, luekemia, meningitis, tetanus, small pox, mad cow disease, etc). In education, educators talk about war against ignorance, illiteracy, stupidity, etc. In Agriculture, farmers in general talk of war against weeds and weeves. In academia, researchers talk of war against falsehood and piracy of data and discoveries. In culture, the general talk is about a war against immorality such as a war against homosexualism and homosexuality, gayism, and all other behavioural tendencies not in keeping with moves and folkways of one's societys' culture. And, in all types of profession or work, the common global doctrine is a war against laziness and carelessness.

In this regard, it is self-evident that the war is such a universal phenomenon in Human Life that it is not only part and parcel but also as old as the Human Life. Thus, it is so spatio-temporal that a list of its types is quite endless.

## (2) A specific Nosology of War

In as much as there exists an endless list of the types of War, all these types fall into two specific, exhaustive and mutually exclusive categories of War. These categories are

(1) Hot or Physical War and (2) Cold or non-physical War as follows:-

### (a) Hot War

A Hot War is characterized by direct physical confrontation with the use of all sorts of weapons, (e.g, teeth, horns, fists, kicks, heads, etc) by which each party is naturally endowed with against its adversary. But, apart from this biological type which is applicable to both man and other animals, in human life alone, man is endowed with a physical type characterized by use of stones, clubs, spears, bows and arrows, firearms (which include pistols, rifles, canons, handgranades, surface to surface missiles, air to air missiles; etc) and biological weapons. Unlike Cold War, a Hot War is extremely devastating to both human life, and infrastructure, e.g., buildings, roads, railroads, airposts, harbours, beaches, learning and religious institutions, etc.

In human life, however, the might of war is totally non-bias as to who and what to kill or not. It is virtually indiscriminatory.

Vivid examples of a Hot War today abound. These include the recently concluded Sudanese Civil War which has been raging in and tormenting Sudan for the last fourty years since that Country's independence on 1$^{st}$ January, 1956 to the present (May, 2004) between the heavily Islam influenced Government based in Khartoum in the Islamic Northern Sudan and supported by the same by virtue of their Islamic faith, on the one hand, and the Christian Southern Sudanese population supported by their military wind, "Sudanese People's Liberation Army" (SPLA) headed by Dr. John Garang on the other. This War ended in May 2004, brokered by Kenya and the Inter-Governmental Agency for Development (IGAD). As one of the strategic conditions for the Naivasha Peace Accord, the SPLA Leader, Dr. Garang, was co-opted into the existing to the rank of First Vice President in the New Government of National Unity.

On the International Scale, vivid examples include World War 1 (1914-1918) and World War II (1938-1945) the later archtectured by Germany supported by its Axis members viz:Italy and Japan against the allies viz: the United Kingdom, France, and the Union of The Soviet Socialist Republic of Russia (USSR) now called "Russia" supported by the USA. This World War II, devastated Europe so much and left behind so many casualties to the tune of four to six million dead particularly the Gerrman Jews, Gypsies and other non-Germans not belonging to the German Aryans who were considered untouchables on the allegation that they had pure German blood that the Allies were terribly horrified. As a result of this horror, they were psychologically forced to see to it that they resuscitate the dying League of Nations and then transform it into a much more powerful world body, The United Nations, with a stern vow, as also vividly witnessed in The Preamble of The UN Charter swearing to their maker that from then henceforth, they were not going to let any further war to take place during their life due to its terrible damage both World War I and World War II had individually inflicted on Humanity and the infrastructure in Europe.

In the final analysis, a Hot War is an extremely dangerous virus. It kills, maims and psychologically drives the innocent crazy particularly refugees; it destroys all man's development efforts particularly infrastructures, e.g., roads, rail roads, bridges, harbours, airports, buildings, etc.

### (b) Cold War

Unlike a Hot War, a Cold War is basically a verbal war between the two warring parties. It may either be a beginning or an ending stage of the Hot War. Before, a Hot War begins, there must, first and foremost, be a verbal mutual enemies, each calling the other all sorts of nasty names; acusing each other of various crimes some of which may either be right or wrong but deliberately and forcefully own interest against the other and to show the general public that one is the only one who is right but the other wrong. In this case, verbal self-justification and self-glorification is the only visible principal weapon In this category of war. A physical weapon in this category is totally invisible and still silent until a right opportune time comes about when one of the quarrelling parties initiates direct confrontation using such weapon in addition to a verbal weapon. But, at first verbal insults and counter-insults; accusations and counter-accusations are the main sine qua non instrument of Cold War.

A most vivid example of this category of war include, for example, the recently ended (in the early 1980s) famous Cold War which began in 1945 between the capitalist Camp headed by USA, UK and France also called the "Anti-Communist Camp" on one side and the Communist Camp headed by USSR, People's Republic of China, North Korea and Cuba also called the "Anti-Capitalist Camp",—a war in which the two camps' mutual goal was total extermination of the other for reasons and justifications perceived by each.

Although this category of war may not be as physically devastating to the mutually warring parties it is as equally devastating to each party psychologically just as the other category (i.e., Hot War) usually does. But although it is non-physical in character while its counterpart (i.e., Hot War) is, it is as equally inciting to non-partisants as its counterpart in that it also induces each conflicting parties to bribe non-partisans to fight for them a proxy war against their adversaries. An illustration of this phenomenon is the manner in which the capitalist Camp and Communist Camp were each psychologically influenced to bribe newly independent countries in Africa beginning with the Democratic Republic of Congo (DRC) at its independence in 1960 so that it could be used as a puppet by each of these two mutual enemies against each other—a situation that resulted into such devastating civil war in that Country that lots of innocent lives and property were put to a total waste for the good fo the cunning/dishonest self-seeking parties to the Cold War as also evidenced by the following horrors of The Congo Civil War of 1960/61 an example:-

## (3) The Horrors of War: The Congo Civil War of 1960/61 Due to The Cold War Between the USA and the USSR

### (a) Introduction

Whereas the common and obvious reason is that the United Nations was created as an international instrument for world peace and security, as evidenced in article 1, paragraphs 1-4 of the United Nations Charter, its efforts to execute these duties, however, have been disparaged by some of it own Member States' and criticized by certain authors who for totally unknown valid reasons contend that the United Nations is either exceeding its jurisdiction or not exercising it when necessary. Consequently, doubts have been vehemently raised about the legality of the United Nations intervention in the Congon Crisis of 1960[2]—an argument that consequently forced the UN to leave that Country at the mercy of the scourge of continued War from 1960 to the present (2004), and a waste of human lives such as the most recent life of President Joseph Kabila. For instance, E. M. Miller[3] contends that despite a series of resolutions passed by the Security Council concerning the situation in the Congo (now Zaire), "neither . . . [the first] resolution nor any subsequent resolutions . . . expressly provided for a United Nations Force;" and that none of these resolutions authorized "the Secretary-General in explicit terms to establish a force."[4] Miller further contends that the manner in which the United Nations Force in the Congo was established represents a departure from previous methods employed, especially in Korea.[5]

A similar vehement argument, with different dimensions, has also been raised in Academia by D. S. Wijewardane, who contends that the United Nations Force in the Congo, though essentially peace-keeping, did not resemble the "enforcement" forces originally contemplated in Chapter VII of the Charter.[6] Both arguments obviously intimate that the establishement and dispatch fo the United Nations Forces to the Congo in 1960 lacked legal provision under the Charter, a most flabbergasting argument indeed against the UN's noble duties; which damaged the UN's spirit and enthusiasm in that Country so much that no peace has ever been found there since 1960 to the present.

However, if the United Nations Force in the Congo was designed to "perform a number of tasks thoughout a vast territory [the Congo] in order to fulfill its mandate . . . *to prevent foreign intervention in the form of men, arms or military supplies, and to prevent civil war*"[7] (emphasis added), then one wonders why Miller and Wijewardane allege that the nature fo the United Nations Force in the Congo lacked a genuine legal provision under Chapter VII of the Charter.

Further, there arises the question why the United Nations Force in the Congo was finally used under Secretary-General U Thant's direction against the seceding Katanga a renamed Shaba Province while such action had been ruled out previously by his predecessor, Secretary-General Dag Hammarskjold. Although both Hammarskjold in late July 1960 claimed that the United nations was "prepared to maintain the United nations Force in the Congo until such time as it deems the latter's task to have been fully accomplished."[8] when the Prime Minister requested that the Force be used against Katanga's secession to eliminate the primary source of civil disorder, Secretary-General Hammarskjold refused to allow United Nations Forces to enter Katanga on the ground that such action would constitute a violation of Katanga's right of Domestic jurisdiction enormous proportions that the two leaders became victims of it. Lumumba was seized and ruthlessly murdered by supporters of seceding Katanga Province on

January 17, 1961, and Hammarskjold died in a plane crash in Ndola (Northern Zimbabwe) on September 17, 1961, while seeking a resolution to the problem. Not until U Thant succeeded Hammarskjold as the United Nations Secretary-General was the policy of the United Nations Force in the Congo toward Katanga altered and the Force was authorized to enter Katanga. Lumumba's appeal to the United Nations for military assistance was not realistically fulfilled until December 5, 1961 (eighteen months later). By that time, the lives ofboth Hamarskjold and Lumumba as well as other individuals in the Congo had been wasted simply because of United nations inaction.

Thus, the history of the Congo Crisis of 1960 raises two pervasive and crucial questions, the answers to which may have a determinative effect upon the destiny of African nations. First, to what extent is the United Nations ready to come to Africa's rescue in case Africa is in danger of foreign aggression? Secondly, what precautionary measures must the African states take against external threat such as that of 1960 Belgian threat instead of relying completely on the United Nations?

### (b) A Prelude to the Congo Civil War of 1960/61

In order to answer these and similar questions of greatest importance to our understanding this perennial predicarment of recurrent War Africa has always been faced with ever since she achieved her independence in the 1960's, let us first and foremost examine her political history from pre-independence to independence as a prelude.

For 85 years, the Belgian colonial rule in the Congo perpetuated slavery and abuse of the Congolese people in repudiation of articles VI and IX of the Berlin General Act of 1885.[10] Thus, Belgian acts in the Congo, which in turn drove the Congolese to extreme anti-Europeanism, constituted a direct violation of the Berlin General Act and, thus, of international law.

Because of this hostility to Europeans, Patrice Lumumba, representing an extreme anti-Belgian viewpoint, became the spokesman of the 126 Congolese delegates at the 1960 Brussels Conference, received 80 percent of the Stanleyville vote in the December 1959 election, won a majority in the National Chamber in the May 1960 elections, and received a 95 percent vote of confidence from the Congolese Senate in September 1960 against Kasabubu's attempt to dismiss Lumumba from the Premiership. However, since this extreme anti-Europeanism did not occur in the British and French African colonies upon their independence, it is submitted that the Congolese anti-Europeanism—in the Congo alone—must have been generated by Belgium's unduly negligent and inhumane behaviour in the Congo.

After nearly a century of Belgian colonial rule most nationa leaders, especially Patrice Lumumba—the most prudent, eloquent, prophetic, and courageous African politician[11]—emphatically demanded Congolese independence. Consequently, the Belgian Government called for the Round Table Conference with the Congolese nationalists, headed by Patrice Lumumba, Joseph Kasavubu, and Moise Tshombe, in Brussels in January 1960.

During the Conference both parties assured each other, in good faith, of their respect for the fundamental principles of human rights, and their desire for the independence and territorial integrity of the Congolese people.[12] Lumumba assured the Belgian delegation:

The fact that Belgium has liberated the Congo from the colonial regime we were no longer prepared to accept, has won her the friendship and esteem of the Congolese people. We desire this friendship to be enduring and free of all forms of hypocrisy. We shall thus prove to the World that the principle of friendship between nations is one of real significance . . . As for the Europeans living in the Congolese State . . . . We need their help . . . It is with their collaboration that we wish to create the Congolese nation, in which all will find their share of happiness and satisfaction.[13]

After the Brussels Round Table Conference, the Congo finally was restored to self-rule on June 30, 1960. The new government was headed by Joseph Kasavubu (President) and Patrice Lumumba (Prime Minister). Below were the Provincial Premiers, such as Moise Tshombe as Premier of the Katanga Province—the same Tshombe who had grown rich through these dealings with the Belgians during the colonial period as a strong pro-Belgian.[14] Thus, the Congolese leadership held political views covering the entire spectrum from Lumumba's uncompromising anticolonialism to Tshombe's pro-Belgian sentiments.[15]

With these discrepancies among Congolese leadership, the new government fell into a series of civil wars and disorders immediately after the Declaration of Independence. Both civilian government employees and the Army demanded more employment, Africanization of officers and noncommissioned officers, and expulsion of all Belgians holding key Army posts.[16] To achieve this goal, they mutinied and attacked or threatened Belgians and other Europeans in the area; the country was in chaos, with most Europeans in an unspeakable panic. Tsombe exacerbated the deterioration of order by declaring on July 11, 1960, that his Katanga Province had seceded from the Congo Central Government to form a new and separate state in alliance with Belgium.[17] With belief in African Unity, which he preached on the grounds that "divisions lead to the suicide of Africa,"[18] Lumumba viewed Tshombe as a threat to African Freedom. As a result, the Congo Central Government immediately announced its intention of using force against the seceding Katanga Province.

Collaborating with Tshombe, Belgium intervened with her troops under the claim that intervention in the Congo was necessary to protect the lives and property of the Belgian settlers in Katanga. The Congo Central Government strongly denounced the return of the Belgian armed forces as aggression, and called on the United Nations for military assistance.[19] Suspicious of United Nations inaction, Lumumba requested military aid from the United States but President Eisenhower replied that any help to the Congo had to come from the United nations and not through unilateral United States intervention.[20] Consequently, Lumumba turned once again to the United Nations for help.

### (i) United Nations Involvement to end this War

Under Chapter IV, art, 35, para. 2 of the United Nations Charter, "A state which is not a member of the United Nations may bring to the attention of the Security Council or General Assembly any dispute to which it is party . . ." In conformity with this provision, President Kasavubu and Prime Minister Lumumba, in the name of the Congo Central Government, brought to the attention of the United Nations the existing situation in the Congo on July 12, 1960, and pleaded with the Secretary-General for immediate assistance against Belgian aggression. In their cable, the two Congolese leaders stated:

> The Government of the Republic of the Congo requests urgent dispatch by the United Nations of military assistance. This request is justified by the dispatch to the Congo of metropolitan Belgian troops in violation of the treaty of friendship signed between Belgium and the Republic of the Congo on June 29, 1960. Under the terms of that treaty, Belgian troops may only intervene on the express request of the Congolese Government. No such request was ever made by the Government of the Republic of the Congo and we therefore regard the unsolicited Belgian action as an act of aggression against our country.

> The real cause of most disturbances can be found in colonialist machinations. We accuse the Belgian Government of having carefully prepared the secession of Katanga with a view to maintaining a hold on our country. The Government, supported by the Congolese people, refuses to accept a fait accompli resulting from a conspiracy between Belgian imperialists and a small group of Katanga leaders. The overwhelming majority of the Katanga population is opposed to seccesion, which means the disguised perpetuation of the colonialist regime. The essential purpose of the requested military aid is to protect the national territory of the Congo against the present external aggression which is a threat to international peace. We strongly stress the extremely urgent need for the dispatch of United Nations troops to the Congo.[21]

The United Nations reacted slowely at first. The Soviet Union's suggestion to condemn the "armed aggression" by Belgium was vetoed by the Western Powers in the Security Council. Unofficially, Belgium was asked by the United Nations Security Council to withdraw its troops from the Congo,[22] but the Belgian Government would neither comply with this request nor accept mediation;[23] instead, Belgium insited that its troops were to stay in the Congo indefinitely. President Kasavubu and Prime Minister Lumumba then jointly dispatched another cable to the Secretary-General reiterating the need for military aid.[24] Like the first cable, this cable strongly emphasized that military aid was not needed against internal but against external aggression. In addition, it stated that unless the United Nations responded immediately, the Congolese Government would be forced to seek other assistance, especially from the Bandung Treaty Powers.[25]

However, on July 14, 1960, the Security Council unanimously adopted[26] a resolution[27] authorizing the dispatch of military aid to the Congo and formally calling upon Belgium to remove its troops from the Congo. Nationalist China, France and Britain abstained,[28] upon the failure of the French attempt to veto United Nations intervention by resorting to article 2, paragraph 7 of the United Nations Charter, which prohibits United Nations intervention in a State's domestic jurisdiction.

On the following day (July 15), before the United Nations Force had been dispatched to the Congo, Lumumba, in repudiation of a sixteen-day old Treaty of Friendship with Belgium, declared a state of war with Belgium. On July 18, Hammarskjold reported to the Security

Council that the United Nations Force of 3,500 troops[29] had arrived in the Congo and that more would be sent soon.[30] One day late, Belgium accepted a truce and agreed to remove its forces from "leopaldville" to their original bases within four days.[32]

### (ii) Application of Article 2(7) of the United Nations Charter: A Problem of Domestic Jurisdiction to the UN.

Was it illegal under the domestic jurisdiction provision, article 2(7) of the Charter, for the United Nations to intervene in the Congo? Was it essentially an internal problem of the Congolese Government? Was it a unilateral action of the United Nations to intervene in the Congo or was it through the invitation of a legitimate governement? These are the fundamental questions that should be examined to understand fully the legality of the United Nations action in the Congo.

According to article 2(7) of the United Nations Charter; "Nothing contained in the present Charter shall authorize the United Nations to intervene in matters which are essentially within the domestic jurisdiction of any state or shall require the members to submit such matters to settlement under the present United Nations Charter; but this principle shall not prejudice the application of enforcement measures under Chapter VII." (Emphasis added.) In view of this provision, should we still insist that the United Nations violated its obligation by intervening in the Congolese domestic jurisdiction? It is submitted that this question should be answered in the negative.

Despite the presence of article 2(7), in his opening statement to the Security Council, Secretary-General Hammarskjold emphasized that his request for an immediate meeting of the Security Council was made under article 99 of the United Nations Charter,32 which empowers "[t] he Secretary-General [to] bring to the attention of the Security Council any matter which in his opinion may threaten the maintenance of international peace and security." Thus, when Belgium refused to honor two previous Security Council resolutions—U.N. Doc. S/4387 and U.N. Doc. S/4405, respectively-in repudiation of its obligation under articles 25 and 49 of the United Nations Charter, which require all Member States to accept and carry out decisions of the Security Council, Hamarskjold found it necessary to press the Security Council for a third resolution against Belgium.[33] Consequently, on August 9, 1960, the third resolution(S/4426) was adopted; it called upon all Member States to accept and carry out the measures decided by the Security Council in respect to the Congo and in accordance with the United Nations Charter.[34] Since it incumbent on Belgium to honor the first two resolutions fo the Security Council, the question arises why it was necessary to pass a third resolution.

To explain the necessity of the third resolution, the Secretary-General emphasized that whereas the first and second resolutions had made no explict reference to the Charter provisions upon which the Security Council was acting, the third resolution called to the attention of the Katanga provincial authorities articles 35 and 49 of the Charter, which provide, respectively, that both Members and non-Members must join in mutual assistance carried one by Nations and that Members must join in mutual assistance to carry out Security Council measures.[35] Hammarskjold emphasized:

> The [first and second] resolutions of the Security Council of 14 and 22 July were not explicitly passed under Chapter VII [of the Charter], but they were passed on the basis of an initiative under Article 99. For that reason, I have felt entitled to quote three Articles under Chapter VII, and I repeat what I have already said in this respect: in a perspective which may well be short rather than long, the problem facing the Congo is one of peace or war—and not only in the Congo.[36]

Although the Secretary-General did not refer to article 39, which authorizes the Security Council to determine the existence of any act of aggression, it is evident that there was a more immediate demand for the use of Chapter VII of the United Nations Charter than that of article 39 per se.[37]

### (iii) Legal Principles Authorizing the United Nations Intervention in the Congo Civil War

To ascertain whether the actions of the United Nations Force in the Congo were consistent with the United Nations Charter, it is necessary to compare article 2(7) with United Nations action pursuant to articles 41 and 42 as well as the resolutions of the Security Council and the General Assembly. Provisional measures under article 40 of the Charter designed to prevent a potential threat to world peace and security can be taken only if such measures do not entail "matters which are essentially within the domestic jurisdiction of any state"[38] (Emphasis added). Consequently, in reconciling these conflicting obligations—maintanance of world peace and respect for Congolese domestic jurisdiction—the Secretary-General did not base the intervention of troops in the Congo on articles 39 and 40 but on articles 41 and 42.[39] To justify his position Hammarskjold said "[1] in the light of the domestic jurisdiction limitation of the Charter, it must be assumed that the Council did not authorize the Secretary-General to intervene with armed troops in an internal conflict, when the Council has not specially adopted enforcement measures under article 41 or 42 of Chapter VII."[40]

Further, to understand Hammarskjold's action and, therefore, the legal grounds for the United Nations Force in the Congo, one must also examine the texts of the following documents: (1) the reports submitted by the United Nations Secretary-General to the Security Council;[41] (2) the communiqué between the Congolese Government and the Secretary-General of the United Nations;[42] (3) the views of Government expressed in the proceedings of the Security Council;[43] (4) the resolutions passed by the Security Council;[44] (5) the views of the Governments expressed before the General Assembly; [45] and (6) the General Assembly's resolutions.[46]

Of great significance were the resolutins passed by the Security Council pursuant to an official plea from the Congo that had been received on July 12, 1960[47] Two resolutions[48] were passed immediately. The operative clause of the first resolution (S/4387) on which the United Nations Force was established stated that the Security Council, decides to authorize the Secretary-General to take the necessary steps, in consultation with the Government of the Congo, to provide the Government with such military assistance, as may be necessary, until, through the efforts of the Congolese Government with the technical assistance of the United Nations, the national security forces may be able, in the opinion of the Governement, to meet fully their taks.[49]

Therefore, E. M. Millers argument that none of these "resolutions of the Security Council expressly provided for a United Nations Force (or authorized) the Secretary-General in explicit terms to establish a force"[50] must be open to question. Further, if Miller contends that the Secretary-General's implementation of the Security Council's resolutions and dispatch of the Untied Nations Force into the Congo was a violation of article 2(7) of the United Nations Charter on the grounds that nowhere in the said resolutions exist "explicit terms" authorizing the Secretary-General "to establish a force"[51] then this argument must be inconsistent with that proportion of paragraph 2 of the Security Council's first resolution, which explicitly authorizes the provision of military assistance as maybe necessary.

In implementing the Security Council resolutions, the Secretary-General consulted and entered into agreement with Prime Minister Patrice Lumumba when he came to the United Nations headquarters to address the United Nations in late July 1960.[52] As a result of that meeting, the Secretary-General prepared and submitted the following agreement to the Security Council:

1. The government of the Republic of the Congo states that, in the exercise of its sovereign rights with respect to any question concerning the presence and functioning of the United Nations Force in the Congo, it will be guided, in good faith, by the fact that it has requested military assistance from the United Nations and by its acceptance of the resolutions of the Security Council of 14 and 22 July 1960; it likewise states that it will ensure the freedom of movement of the Force in the interior of the country and will accord the requisite privileges and immunities to all personnel associated with the activities of the Force.
2. The United Nations takes note of this statement of the Government of the Republic of the Congo and states that, with regard to the activities of the United Nations Force in the Congo, it will be guided, in good faith, by the task assigned to the Force in the afore-mentioned resolutions; in particular the United Nations reaffirms, considereing it to b ein accordance with the wishes of the Governement of the Republic of the Congo, that it is prepared to maintain the United Nations Force in the Congo until such time as it deems the latter's task ok have been fully accomplished.
3. The Government of the Republic of the Congo and the Secretary-General state their intention to proceed immediately, in the light of paragraph 1 and 2 above, to explore jointly specific aspects of the functioning of the United Nations Force in the Congo, notably with respect to its deployment, the question of its lines of communication and supply, its lodging and its provisioning; the Government of the Republic of the Congo, confirming its intention to facilitate the functioning of the United Nations Force in the Congo, and the United Nations have agreed to work together to hasten the implementation of the guiding principles laid down in consequence of the work of joining exploration on the basis of the resolution of the Security Council.
4. The foregoing provisions shall likewise be applicable, as appropritate, to the non-military aspects of the United Nations' operation in the Congo.[53]

Further, in the second resolution,[54] the Security Council maintained that "complete restoration of law and order in the Republic of the Congo would effectively contribute to the maintenance of international peace and security."[55] The most explicit expression of the legality of continued presence of the United Nations Force in the Congo is envisaged in the third resolution adopted by the Security Council on August 9, 1960. In this resolution the Security Council called upon "all Member-States, in accordance with articles 27 and 49 of the Charter, to accept and carry out the decisions of the Security Council [with regard to the Congo and authorized] the Secretary-General to implement this resolution and to report further to the Security Council as appropriate."[56]

In view of the foregoing, the legality of United Nations actions in the Congo is well supported. Furthermore, although the Republic of the Congo had not yet become a member of the United Nations, the Republic's appeal to the United Nations under chapter VII, article 49 of the United Nations Charter constitutes supplementary evidence of the legality of the United Nations intervention in the Congo.[57]

On the other hand, the legality of Hammarskjold's denial of Prime Minister Lumumba's request for United Nations intervention in the Katanga Province to restore law and order in the Republic of the Congo as agreed upon in the second Security Council resolution—No. S/4405), paragraph 2 and 3—is questionable since Hammarskjold' allegations that the United Nations Force's entry in Katanga would be a violation of Katanga's right of domestic jurisdiction were inconsistent with his pledge to maintain the United Nations Force in the Congo until such time as it deemed the task of restoration of peace completed.[58]

None of the pertinent United Nations documents explicitly bar the United Nations Force in the Congo from intervening in Katanga Province. Indeed, in its third resolution, No. S/4426, the Security Council noted "with satisfaction the progress made by the United Nations in carrying out the Security Council resolutions in respect of the territory of the Republic of the Congo other than the Province of Katanga."[59] (Emphasis added). As evidence of what the United Nations had accomplished so far in the Congo and what remained to be done, this implies that the Security Council expected intervention in Katanga. Thus, Hammarskjold's presumption that intervention in the seceding Katanga Province by the United Nations Force would be a violation of article 2(7) of the United.

It should also be added that, on the basis of the early experience of the United Nations Emergency Force in Korea, Hammarskjold constructed some "basic principles and rules" designed to provide "an adaptable framework for the later operations"[60] of the United Nations

Force in the Congo. These principles include: (1) The United Nations cannot station units on the territory of a Member state without the consent of the government concerned. (2) It is for the United nations alone to decide on the composition of any force, taking fully into account the views of the host government. (3) United Nations Forces should not include units from any of the five permanent members of the Security Council or from any country that might be considered as having a special interest in the situation (4) United Nations Forces should have full freedom of movement and all facilities necessary for their tasks. (5) The personnel of the Unied Nations Force should be loyal to the aims of the Organization and the Force should be directly responsible to one of the main organs of the United Nations. (6) United Nations personnel cannot be party to any internal conflict, and the United Nations Force should not be used to enforce any special political situation or to influence the political balance, (7) Since the United Nations Force is an instrument for mediation and conciliation, it cannot engage in combat activities, though it may respond with force to an armed attack. (8) The cost should be allocated among Member States according to the normal scale of budgetary contributions.[61]

To the contrary, however, Hammarskjold did not adhere to his own "basic principles" when composing the United Nations Force in the Congo. Executing only principles 1,2,4,5,6 and 8, he failed to honor principles 3 and 7. For instance, although he excluded units from the Permanent Members of the Security Council in conformity with the first clause in principle 3, he did not stick to his position as envisaged in the last clause of the same principle. Thus, in composing the United Nations Force the Secretary-General drew most of the Forces's units from African nations,[62] countries with utmost interest in the Congo because of their Pan-Africanism.

Furthermore, the United Nations intervention in Katanga Province was neither a violation of principle 7 nor of article 2, paragraph 7 of the United Nations Charter, since it was this secession that had triggered the national trouble in the Congo and had invited mercenaries from Belgium, South Africa, Rhodesia, etc., to proceed against the national government. One critic of Hammariskjold's position writes that "the decision to maintain the unity of the Congo in the face of separatist activities eventually required U.N. officials to take action which had, or could be interpreted as having, internal political implications. While the United Nations exercised restraint in using force (principle 7), the Security Council did in the end authorize the use of force when necessary, as a last resort . . . ."[63] Thus, the Secretary-General's presumption that the penetration of the United Nations Force in the Congo (ONUC) into Katanga Province would constitute a violation of the obligation of the United Nations to respect domestic jurisdiction within the framework of article 2, paragraph 7 lacks legal foundation.

The Secretary-General insisted, however, that his interpretation involved these four points: (1) The United Nations Force cannot be used on behalf of the Central Government to follow a specific line of action. (2) United Nations facilities cannot be used to transport civilian or military representatives of the Central Government to Katanga against the desire of the Katanga Provincial Government. (3) The United nations Force has no duty, or right to protect civilian or military personnel representing the Central Government beyond what follows from its general duty to maintain law and order. (4) The United Nations has no right to prevent the Central Government from taking any action which by its own means, in accordance with the purposes and principles of the Charter, it can carry through in relation to Katanga.[64] Hammarskjold also insited that these were the four elements that "would necessarily apply mutatis mutandis, as regards to the Provincial Government in its relations with the Central Government".[65]

If these four points did constitute the legal position of the United Nations with respect to the Congo, then the Secretary-General was correct, of course, that the United Nations Force had no business intervening in the seceding Katanga Province, or interfering with Katanga's form of action.

(Strange contradiction Between the Decisions of Hamarskjold and U Thant with Respect of Seceding Katanga Province to End Hostility)

If, however, one accepts Hammarskjold's four elements as the definitive legal bases for United Nations action in the Congo, there arise serious discrepancies between the United Nations position in the Congo and the rationale for that position under the administrations of Hammarskjold and U Thant. If, as viewed by Hammariskjold, the United Nations lacked legal authority to intervene in the situation between the Congolese Central Government and the seceding Katanga Province, then it should have been legally inconsistent for the United Nations under U Thant to deviate from Hammarskjold's position and resort to military force against Katanga's secession. Since the two Secretaries-General made opposite decisions with respect to Katanga's secession and since, in making such decisions both leaders were supposed to be governed by the directives of the United Nations Charter and Security Council

Resolutions, one wonders what factors might have contributed to their respective decision-making.

It is submitted that the socio-political environment (country of citizenship, educational experiences, and professional experience) of Hammarskjold and U Thant was a key factor in their respective decision-making process with respect to Katanga.[66] (See Appendix). Both Hammarskjold and U Thant were approximately the same age. Before they were appointed Secretary-General to the United Nations, both had read widely, held different responsible administrative positions in their respective governments, and represented their countries at both regional conferences and the United Nations. Regionally, Hammarskjold had served as: Sweden's chief delegate to the Paris Peace Conference on the Marshall Plan (1947), Sweden's representative at the Organization for European Economic Cooperation (OEEC), a member of the OEEC Executive Committee, and delegate to the new Council of Europe. Because of Hammarskjold's intensive involvement in inter-European cooperation, it is submitted that it is possible that Hammarskjold's Europhilia, which he acquired in the course of his education and experience in Europe, must have been a factor in his decision with respect to the Katanga question, especially since Belgium was a key participant in the Katanga secession. Since a severe action in the form of intercession by the United Nations Force against Katanga's secession would have been inconsitent with Hammarskjold's European-oriented attitude toward Katanga, he refused Lumumba's request for the United Nations Force to proceed against Tshombe's Katanga to avoid dissonance.[67]

U Thant, before becoming Secretary-General in 1961, had had some regional apprenticeship with the African-Asian Conference held in Bandung in 1955, which, like Hammarskjold's regional apprenticeship, must have been a major factor in his decision. Thus, unlike Hammarskjold's decision, U Thant's decision to take action against Katanga's secession—a decision that was welcomed by most African countries—must have been motivated, at least in part, by his Third World sympathies as well as his views as to the significance of chapter VII of the United Nations Charter. It was his positive attitude toward the Afro-Asian bloc, of which his own country is a member, that determined the decision U Thant made. Had U Thant been from the West, it is more likely that his decision would not have deviated from that of Hammarskjold. This theory of country-of-origin bias is also evidenced by: (1) the Western attitude in the 1966 International Court of Justice decision with respect to the South West African Case[68]—a decision that was absolutely political, and (2) the unconcerned attitude of the Western powers in the United Nations with regard to (a) apartheid problems in South

Africa, (b) the Smith regime in Zimbabwe, (c) the Namibia Question, and (d) the annihilation of the African population in Angola, Mozambique, and Guinea-Bissau by Portuguese colonists before the new Portuguese regime decided, in late 1974, to grant independence to these three territories.

## (c) Summary

With these experiences, it is, therefore, hoped that African states will be more conscious of their status in the world today. Further, it is hoped that African states will begin to reevaluate their Africa Union (AU) in terms of its strength and cohesiveness in common defense and cultural backgrounds. To be masters of themselves instead of relying on the United Nations or foreign powers for help, it is imperative that the African states, through AU, strengthen themselves militarily to contain further foreign aggression. This must be done because the United Nations is composed of some Member States and persons with different backgrounds and attitudes, which militate against African sympathies. Although the General Assembly has a majority of Third Word Nations, most of the key personnel are still from the West. For instance, three of the four Secretaries-General have been from the West.[69]

Although the use of force other than in self-defense or collective defense is illegal, other states have repeatedly used it to achieve their perceived ends; for instance the United States in Korea (1950-51) (the United Nations entered Korea after the United States was already in the area), Vietnam (1954-73), the Bay of Pigs (1961), and in the Cuba Missile Crisis (1962); the Soviet Union in Czechoslovakia (1968), and in Hungary (1956); and the United Kingdom, France, and Israel in the Suez Canal (1956). Neither this past experience nor the concept of self-defense as "inherent in every sovereign state and . . . . [explicit or] implict in every treaty,"[70] should be ignored by African states, which should reconsider their international status. Regardless of the Charter provision of article 2, paragraph 4, which prohibits every Member State of the United Nations from resorting to force as a means of settling disputes, under this same Charter, article 51, African states are also free at all times to defend their territories from foreign attack or invasion. Indeed they alone are rationally and legally competent to decide whether circumstances require recourse to war in self-defense.[71] According to the prevailing customary right of self-defense under the framework of International Law, the resort to physical means of self-defense is legitimate when resorted to solely for the protection of those interests that collectively comprise the nation's security and, therefore, its total political independence.[72] Furthermore, like all other dejure states elsewhere, the African states are the only ones that are rationally and legally competent to determine when they should resort or not resort to war because world history explicitly shows that we still live in an amorphous and acephalous world whose law and order, therefore, relies significantly on the 'conduct' of a constellation of sovereign political entities called nation-states. According to history, up to now, we still live in a world of anarchy-a world without any central governing body or agency above individual state(s) with a higher authority and power to make binding decisions upon nation-states and the latter's conduct.[73] Of course, states are not only homo politicus but also homo juridicus; hence, they are competent to make commitments and treaties within the framework of pacta sunt servanda as also envisaged in the United Nations Charter. However, the African nation-states must also realize that unlike individuals who must comply with the dictates of their respective sovereign states or else be punished by their respective municipal laws for usch misconduct, an endless list of empirical evidences over time (1945-2004) states do not have to comply with anyone including their own commitments and treaties whenever their truth threatened by external aggression so long as there exists no higher authority above the sovereignty of the state, which can punish any state for non-compliance. In a sense, whereas International Law sui generic is still in its infancy as it is still too primitive and, therefore, a very unreliable instrument or weapon for world order and security it empowers every state in the latter's capacity as its dejure subject, to always do not hesitate to resort to a use of force to repel off any external aggression provided that such act are strictly just for the purpose of self-preservation and self-help. Thus, given this reality, African states individually and collectively in the OAU must not ignore the alternative of self-help when United Nations decisions-based on Western attitudes and concepts-are antithetical to the best interests of Africa, ever since 1960 to the present (2004) that have consequently forsaken Africa to a sea of perennial agonies of sufferings particularly refugees madly rushing here and there in search of a safe haven for their dear lives.

## (4) Conclusion

In the final analysis, the World culture today is a function of the impacts of these two catergories of war in political, social, economic, science and scientific spheres of human life.

The history of The United States of America (USA), Europe, Africa, Asia, China, Japan, Vietnam, Laos, North Korea, South Korea, India Pakistan, etc and the Arab World (Saudi Arabia, Iraq, Afganistan, Iran, Jordan, Syria, Lebanon, etc) is full of examples of War the latter serving as a sin qua non instrument of man's selfish interests, though war has often been justified by its architect as one's means to restore or maintain law and order in the International System or in one's domestic jurisdiction. In the Anglo-Prussian War of 1870/71; World War I (1914-1918) and World War II (1938-1945), Prussia Germany which was the chief architect of all these was justified war on the grounds that it was its sine qua non instrument with which to defend its national interest (most the socio-economically richest district of Alsace Lorrain District usurped by France against Prussia Germany's wishes). In the USA history, we also note the same argument. The Thirteen North American Colonies! War with their Mother Colonial Master (The United Kingdom), each party advanced the same arguement in support of its own side, though the colonies further argued that their master was trying to relatively deprive them of their rightful needs since they were not being represented in Parliamentof their master. In the World Wars I the United States Leadership under President Woodrow Wilson justified USA's intervention in the War against Germany with the assertion "War to end War", which, therefore, meant that to him and his country (the USA) war was a sine qua non instrument for law and order whenever an enabling environment is disturbed. The USA used the same rationale to justify its entry into World War II on the side of the Allies against the Axis (Germany, Italy and Japan); and also to engage in the Cold War against the USSR and other Members of Communist Bloc.

A most recent shed of light on the role of War in the USA history as sine qua non instrument or law and order is the on-going war in Iraq and Afghanistan where the USA unilaterally initiated and has gladly continued financing its operation including changing of the sitting legitimate leaderships there with a total impunity from the UN Security Council Decision against such action. To justify its cause, the USA President George Bush argued that he no more saw any need to listen to the UN Security Council Decisions as this World Body had already proved to him that it had already out-lived its original usefulness, as a World Peace-Keeper.

A further clinical diagnosis of the USA history shows that in the economic life, the USA's behaviour is indictive of the fact that she is the Worldmost major player. She uses both International Monetary Fund (IMF) and the World Bank (WB) as her sine qua non instruments of war against to those needy but wasteful countries which depend on these financial institutions for their balances of payment by ordering them to either to USA's line or be denied the aid. Because of their waste fulness due to their lack of transparency and accountability in their use of aids coupled with their belief in dictatorial mode of governance that is totally obliviant to the Rule of Law, Natural Justice and Principles of Democracy on the one hand; and their deafness to professional guidance from IMF and the World Bank, USA Leadership has been very quick in resorting to the economic war as its sine qua non weapon with which to discipline, such undemocratic leaders with a good hope that the action would weed out the viruses of undemocracy.

In the African history, we have already noted the Congo Question in detail as a paradigm for our understanding the manner in which most African Countries have been misused and therefore subjected to untold sorrows of civil strifes and loss of innocent lives by the Super Powers most particularly during the Cold War (since 1945).

In the Asian history, War has always been the sine qua non instrument for self-love and self-respect by the relatively deprived colonial peoples against their colonial masters in the same manner both Thirteen American Colonies did in the 18th Century so as to achieve their Independence in 1776; and also all African Colonies did in the 20th century so as to achieve the same from their Colonial Masters. For example, India used War to achieve her Freedom in 1947.

And finally, in the Chinese history, we note with amazement man's inhumane instinct of using war not as a sine qua non means toward a just cause but rather as a man-killer weapon for one's own reckless self-seeking goal. A vivid example of this is the Opium War used by Europeean Countries with a specific aim of exterminating the Chinese nation as a rational way of alienating or denying them of their concept of self-love and self-respect which naturally were their rightful means of sustaining their rights to/for survival as a living entity.

Hence, man's terrorism instinct translated into a war against humanity but cunningly dressed as a sinqua non instrument for law and order.

## Foot Notes

1. One major criticism by some Member States is that the United Nations is by-passing its jurisdiction in repudiation of Internatonal Law under the Charter. For a discussion of (a) the Netherlands position in the United Nations concerning the Indonesian Question (1947); (b) the Iranian position in the International Court of Justice concerning the Anglo-Iranian Oil Co. Question (1951); (c) the French arguments in the United Nations concerning the Algerian Question (1955); and (d) the positions

of the United Kingdom, France and Israel in the United Nations on the Suez Canal Question (1956) see AUMA-OSOLO, The law of the United Nations as applied to intervention within the framework of article 2(7) of the U.N. charter, a comparative analysis of selected cases 35-125 (1969) (an unpublished thesis, Univ. North Carolina). See also cases on united nations law (l. sohn ed. 1956); M. RAJAN, United Nations and domestic jurisdiction (1958), Some Member States allege that the United Nations is not, under international law, doing enough with respect to what it was created to do. For example, on Dec. 12, 1960, former Indian Prime Minister Nehru protested the arrest of the Congolese Prime Minister, Patrice Lumumba, by Kasavubu-Tshombe's forces. Disappointed by United Nations action in the Congo, Prime Minister Nehru demaned the immediate release of Lumumba and vehently charged that the United Nations Force was too passive with respect to Katanga. 4. W. JOSHUA, United Nations peacekeeping in the Congo 1960-1964 20(1966). Also, the Afro-Asian and Warsaw Pact blocs were disappointed when their proposal that Belgium be charged with aggression against the Congo was vetoed by the Security Council.

2. See, e.g., Miller, Legal Aspects of the United Nations Action in the Congo, 5 AM. J. INT'L L. 10 (1961) [hereinafter cited as MILLER)
3. MILLER at 10
4. MILLER at 10
5. MILLER at 10
6. Wijewardane, Criminal Jurisdiction over Visiting Forces with Special Reference to International Sources, 41 British Year Book OF International Law INT'L. 122, 178(1965-1966).
7. Seyersted, United Nations Forces, Some Legal Problems 37 British Year.Book of International 351, 396-97 (1961).
8. U.N. Doc S/4389/Add.5 (1960)
9. See R. CASEMENT, the black diaries of roger casement (1904); L.CLARK, through African eyes 42-63 (1970); R. DAVIS, the Congo and coasts of Africa (1970).
10. Berlin General Act of 1885. See R. Buell, the native problem in Africa 891-907 (1928); CASEMENT, Supra note 9.
11. The Times (London), Feb. 4, 1961. See also ROYAL ANTRHROPOLOGICAL INSTITUTE, Congo tribes and parties 44-45 (1961); L. TONDEL, the legal aspects of the United Nations actions in the Congo 10 (1963).
12. La Crise Congolese, 13 chrinique de politique etrongere No. 406 (Institute Royal des Relations Internationales, Bruxelles, 1960) 630-31, 635-37, English translation in A.

MERRIAM, Congo, background of conflict 352-54 (1961). See also TONDEL, Supra note 11, at 10.

13. The Round Table Conference, Brussels, Belgium, Jan. 1968. See Colin Legum, The Life and Death of Patrice Lumumba in P. LUMUMBA, Congo, my country xii (1962).
14. J. STOESSINGER, the might of nations: world politics in our time 137-38 (1961). According to Professor Stoessinger, ther is no doubt that Tsombe was a Belgian puppet. This is evidenced by the substantial amount of money Tshombe received from the Belgians in exchange for protecting Belgian property in Katanga Province.Id. at 127-28.
15. Id. At 138
16. There were approximately 25,000 Congolese in the National Army but none of them held any respectable office. On the whole, this was the error of the Belgian Government that had failed to train and therefore prepare the Congolese for their independence. As a result, it was questionable what the common Congolese could expect from independence. For instance, one Congolese asked: "Does independence come wrapped in paper or do we get it at the bank?" See id. 137.

    Also, this same feeling was reported to the United Nations General Assembly on Feb. 2, 1962 by Aduola, the new Prime Minister. Accusing Belgian colonial rule, had only a few university graduates and very few technicians and qualified officials." See 9 U.N. REV. 19 (March 1962); TONDEL, supra note 11, at 2.

    Secondly, it should be borne in mind that Lumumba was strictly determined to adhere to the Brussels Round Table Agreements of January 1960 by maintaining the high-ranking Belgian military officers in their positions, although he accepted the demands of the Congolese troops for promotions and pay increases. But, as the Belgian commanding officers in the Congolese Army abused and refused to accept the Belgian Government grant of independence to the Congo, the African troops mutinied and demanded that Lumumba expel all Belgians. Lumumba tried to resist, but as the situation deteriorated, he finally gave in. On July 8, he agreed to dismiss them all. On July 10, he appointed former Sergeant Victor Lundula to General of the Army and Joseph Mobutu, Chief of Staff.
17. Most Belgian settlers fled into Kenya from the Congo. These refugees were helped into Kenya by the East African Railways and Harbours enroute to Brussels. On their arrival at the Nairobi Railway Station, they were helped with various supplies pending their deportation to Belgium. For further details see C. LEGUM, CONGO

DISASTER (1961). In his book, Legum estimates that "20 Europeans in all were killed during this uproar, but the raping of women and mistreatment of men were far more frequent as a concert of humiliations of the Aggressor." Id. 113.

18. A. ZOLBERG, creating political order: the party-states of west Africa 50 (1966).
19. U.N. Doc. S/4382 (1960).
20. Most African nationalists were very skeptical about the reply. They, in fact, took it as "kitchen-diplomacy" business, since Belgium and the United States are both members of the North Atlantic Treaty Organization. They also expected something constructive and more active from the United States than from any other country. Therefiore, Eisenhower's reply was a great shock to most of them.
21. U.N. Doc. S/4382 (1960). See also 15 U.N. GAOR, Supp. IA, U.N. Doc. A/4390/ Add.1(1960).
22. U.N. Doc. S/4382 (1960)
23. Dr. Ralph Bunche (a United States national and United Nations Under-secretary for Special Political Affairs) had been in the Congo since Independence. He spent the whole of July 12 mediating in the Congo-Belgian troop clashes in vain.
24. U.N. Doc. S/4382, at 2 (1960).
25. According to the STAFF OF HOUSE COMMITTEE ON FOREIGN AFFAIRS, 86TH CONGRESS 2D SESSSION staff memorandum of the Republic of the Congo 11 (1960) Prime Minister Lumumba cabled Prime Minister Nikita Khrushchev informing him that "we may have to ask the Soviet Union's intervention should the Western camp not stop its aggression." In this same document, it is also reported that Khrushchev replied that his country "will not shrink from resolute measures to curb aggression." See also 1. CLAUDE, swords into plowshares: the progress of international organization 228 (1967).
26. Voting for the resolution were Argentina, Ceylon, Ecuador, Italy, Poland, Tunisia, the United States, and the Soviet Union. See also CATHERINE HOSKINS, the Congo since independence, 484-86 (1965).
27. The adopted resolution read as follows: The Security Council, considering the report of the Secretary-General on a request for the United Nations action in relation to the Republic of the Congo, considering the request for military assistance addressed to the Secretary-General by the President and Prime Minister of the Republic of the Congo (Document S/4382).

1. Calls upon the Government of Belgium to withdraw their troops from the territory of the Republic of the Congo.
2. Decides to authorize the Secretary-General to take necessary steps, in consultation with the Government of the Republic of the Congo, to provide the Government with such military assistance, as may be necessary, until, through the efforts of the Congolese Governmetn with the technical assistance of the United Nations, the national security forces may be able, in the opinion of the Government, to meet fully their tasks:
3. Requests the Secretary-General to report to the Security Council as appropriate." U.N. Coc S/4387 91960).

28. Id.
29. Egypt, Ethiopia, Ghana, Guinea, mali, Morocco and Tunisia.
30. U.N. Doc. S/4339 (1960).
31. U.N. Doc. S/4389/Add.1 91960).
32. 15 U.N. SCOR 873rd meeting 7 91960). See also MILLER, supra note 2 at 2; TONDEL, supra note 11, at 14.
33. U.N. Doc. S/4426 (1960).
34. Id.
35. U.N. Doc S/4417, at 5 (1960). Both Members and non-Members of the United Nations can bring their dispute to the United Nations (art.35). Member States must join in mutual assistance to carry out the Security Council's measures (art. 41).
36. 15 U.N. SCOR, 884th Meeting 5 91960).
37. See 2 repertory of practice of u.n. organs 338-41 (1955). The Security Council shall determine the existence of any threat to the peace, breach of the peace, or act of aggression (art.39).
38. U.N. CHARTER art. 2(7).
39. Both articles 39 and 40 of the United Nations Charter are weak legal instruments in the event of a situation potentially threatening to world peace and security. Article 39 requires the Security Council to determine the existence of any threat to the peace, breach of the peace or act of aggression, and to make recommendations as to what should be done in the event thereof. Article 40 requires the Security Council to recommend to the parties concerned to comply with the Security Council's decisions as per article 39.

Both articles 41 and 42 are, on the other hand, the only decisive legal instruments that the Security Council can effectively implement to stop an actual threat to world peace and security. Article 41 calls upon the Security Council to decide what measures to pursue—complete or partial interruption of economic relations and of sea, air, postal, telegraphic radio, and other means fo communications, and the severeance of diplomatic relations. Article 42 calls upon the Security Council to intervene with armed forces by air, sea or land as may be necessary to maintain or restore international peace and security.

40. 15 U.N. SCOR, 887th meeting 10 (1960).
41. U.N. Doc. S/4417 (1960); U.N. Doc. S/4417/Add.1/Rev. 1 (1960); 15 U.N. SCOR, 884th meeting (1960); 15 U.N. SCOR, 887th meeting (1960); U.N. Doc S/4482 1-4 (1960); U.N. Doc S/4389 (1960); 13 U.N. GAOR, Annexes, Agenda Item No. 65, at U.N. Doc. A/3943 (1958). See also 8 U.N. Rev. 16 (May 1961); 9 U.N. Rev.7 (Jan. 1962); 9 U.N. Rev. 5 (Feb.1962); MILLER, suprea note 2, at 10; N.Y. Post, March 30, 1962 (editorial).
42. U.N. Doc. S/4414 (1960); U.N. Doc. S/4382 (1960); U.N. Doc. S/4949/Add. 14 (1961); U.N. Doc S/5038 (1961).
43. U.N. Doc S/4414 (1960) (letter from Prime Minister Patrice Lumumba to the Security Council dated July 31, 1960); U.N. Doc. S/4415 (1960) (comments by the Representative of Ghana); U.N. Doc. s/4416 (1960) (comments by Representative of the soviet of Union); U.N. Doc S/4417/Add.1/Rev.1 (1960) (comments by Representative of Guinea); U.N. Doc. S/4516 (1960) (U.S. Draft solution).
44. U.N. Doc. S/4387 (1960) (adopted at 873rd meeting, July 13, 1960); U.N. Doc. S/4405 (1960) (adopted at 879th meeting, July 22, 1960); U.N. Doc. S/4426 (1960) (adoptedat 886th meeting, Aug. 9, 1960); U.N. Doc S/4741 (1961) (adopted at 942d meeting, Feb. 20-21, 1961).
45. U.N. Doc. s/4453 (1960); U.N. Doc. 4503 91960); U.N. Doc. S/4985/Rev.2 (1960); U.N. Doc. S/5002 (1960).
46. U.N. Doc. A/Res. 1474 (ES-IV) (1960); G.A. Res. 1583, 15 U.N. GAOR Supp. 16, at 52; G.A. Res. 1590, 15 U.N. GAOR Supp. 16, at 57; G.A. Res. 1595, 15 U.N. GAOR Supp. 16A, at 13.
47. U.N. Doc. S/4382 (1960).
48. U.N. Doc. S/4387 (1960)l U.N. Doc. s/4405 (1960).
49. U.N. Doc. s/4387 (1960).
50. MILLER, supra note 2, at 10.

51. Id.
52. U.N. Doc. S/4339/Add.5 (1960)
53. Id.
54. U.N. Doc. S/4405.See also U.N. Doc S./4404 (draft resolution by Ceylon & Tunisia); U.N. Doc S/P.V. 878 (Security Council debate on Resolution), at 32, 37; U.N. Doc. S/P.V. 879 (meeting transcript adopting the Resolution), at 42-44.
55. U.N. Doc. S/4405 (1960).
56. U.N. Doc. S/4426 (1960).
57. U.N. S/4417/Add. 3 (1960).
58. U.N. Doc. S/4389/Add.5 (1960)
59. U.N. Doc. s/4426 (1960)
60. S. BAILEY, the United Nations: a short political guide 60 (1963).
61. Id
62. Ghana, Ethiopia, Guinea, Mali, Morocco and Tunisia
63. BAILEY, Supra note 60, at 62
64. MILLER, supra note 2, at 16; U.N. Doc. S/4117/add. 6, at 3-4 (1960)
65. MILLER, supra note 2, at 16; U.N. Doc. S/4117/add. 6, at 3-4 (1960)
66. See generally P. BERGER 7 T. LUCKMAN, the social construction of reality: A treatise in sociology of knowledge chs. II&III (1970); D. EASTON & J. DENNIS, children in the political system, origins of political legitimacy (1969); S. GOLDMAN et al., the federal judicial system (1968); H. JACOB, urban justice: law & order in american cities (1973); H. JACOB, justice in america:courts, lawyers & judicial process (1965); R. LUCKHAM, the nigerian military, a sociological analysis of authority and revolt 1960-1967 (1971); J. PELTASON, fifty-eight lonely men, southern federal judges and school desegregation (1961).
67. For further details on this theory of goal-perception, situation-perception, and decision-making with respect to that goal in order to avoid one's dissonance (self-blame) see L. FESTINGER, a theory of cognitive dissonance (1957); New-comb, An Approach to the Study of Communicative Arts, 50 psychological review No. 6(1953); Osgood & Tannebaum, The Principles of Congruity in the Prediction of Attitude Change, 62 psychological review. No. 1 (1955).
68. In the South West African Cases (1966), the International Court of Justice dropped the case against both Ethiopia and Liberia (plaintiff) with the allegation that the plantiff did not have any legal right or interest in the subject matter of their claims.

South West Africa Cases, [1966] I.C.J. 4. See also G. MANGONE, the elements of international law 477, 501-25 (1967).

69. Trygve Halvdan, 1946-53 (Norwegian); Dag Hammarskjold, 1953-61 (Swedish); U Thant, 1961-71 (Burmese); and Kurt Waldheim, 1971 to the present (Austrian).
70. G. SCHWARZENBERGER, a manual of international law 318 (1967).
71. W. BISHOP, international law, case and materials 776 (1962).
72. See also J. BRIEFLY, the law of nations 414-32 (1963); H. KELSEN, principles of international law 73 (1966); H. LAUTERPACHT, the development of international law by international court 317-18 (1958); L. OPPENHEIM, international law, a treatise 297-304 (8th ed. 1967).
73. International politics, anarchy, force, imperialism 3-9 (R. Art & R. Jervis eds. 1973).

# PART ELEVEN

## LEADERSHIP GENETIC ENGINEERING FORMULA: A Test for a Hybrid Culture, Good Governance, Peace and World Prosperity for All

# A PREAMBLE

This Volume Two book is succinctly the final stage of our intellectual marathon safari that began in Volume One book due to our quest for those mysteries which on the one hand have always hindered manking from getting closer to the realities of Good Leadership qualities that are a pre-requisite for World Peace and properity akin to that Peace and Prosperity that existed in the Ancient Egypt 3000-100 BC; and yet on the other hand, have proved extremely difficult for researchers to recognize them (those mysteries) lest they are eliminated.

By going through various types of land scape difficulties during our research expedition from Volume One to this Volum Two, we are pleased that we have, at last, been able to come closer to these mysteries. Our eager and perseverance have been able to lead us to their true nature characterized by the ambiquity of human life which on the one hand harbours man's abilities to understand these myteries hindering his progress to peace and prosperity and which on the other hand, harbours his disabilities blinding him from achieving these extra-ordinary ends thus leading total manking to a total disaster of confursion between man's consept of war and peace and what, therefore, to do about the two.

This confusion is further exacerbated by the fact that the same man who eagerly produces (manufactures) warfare weapons and profits heavily from their sale to fan warfare is the same mane who becomes very bitterly concerned about the horrors of war and, therefore, eagerly calls for peace and elemination of war weapons.

But these war weapons are not and cannot be ends in themselves. They do not put themselves to use in warfare. It is the same mankind and its war attitude that first prodcudes the weapons and then uses them for conflict by man against his fellow man. Therefore, elimination of war weapons alone is of no consequence at all. It is man's warfare love attitude which is the heart of the issues we must now deal with. It is this man's animus dominandi attitude envisaged in Cain's ralationship with his younger brother Abel that led Cain's murder of his innocent brother for no other valid reason apart from the fact that Cain was jealous of Abel's success in life. Cain felt that the only way he could achieve a monopoly of their parents (Adam and Eve) was to eliminate Abel by killing him. He felt that by doing so he would enjoy Abel's total absence from their parents' home, and would now become the only heir of the family's wealth. Hence the leading virus that always causes conflicts at both inter-personal and international levels.

In view of this discovery, the object of this book is three fold:

1) To show how this <u>animus</u> <u>dominandi</u> virus was eliminated in Ancient Egypt in 3000 BC using Conflict Vaccination that concequently led that Country to rise up to an extra-ordinary degree of peace and abundance in all sectors of life; (SEE **PART ELEVEN (A)**

(2) to show

   (a) how the same virus is being eliminated in Bio-Science by Geneticists using a Genetic Engineering methodology;
   (b) how the same methodology could also be successfully applied in Social Sciences; and
   (c) the positive correlation between Genertic Engineering and Conflict Vaccination; (see PART ELEVEN (B)). and

(3) to prescribe the same fomula that this Ancient Country of Egypt used to achieve this goal for our own application globally today.

In this regard, PART ELEVEN of this book deals with the first two issues (tasks); and PART THIRTEEN deals with the third.

# PART ELEVEN (A)

## HOW ANIMUS DOMINANDI VIRUS WAS ELIMINATED BY ANCIENT EGYPT USING THE AFRICAN MYSTERIES SYSTEM OF THE GRAND LODGE OF LUXOR'S METHODOLOGY OF CONFLICT VACCINATION

# CHAPTER 1

## (1) The Genesis, Scope and Role of The African Mysteries System

The African Mysteries System of The Grand Lodge of Luxor was a centre of a unique advanced learning and research on the nous (i.e. a rear wisdom and knowledge) which one could not only hardly find else where but also which one could never be able to teach or to be taught in any part of the World save solely in the Ancient Egypt where all experts on the mysteries of life could be found or existed. It existed as far back as 7000 BC and lived up to approximately 332 BC the year that Egypt was invaded and conquered by Alexander The Great of Macedonia and Greece whose ulterior motive was not just to conquer it for empire expansion purpose as such but solely in order to plunder its nous and its all legacy by a hybrid culture and civilization hardly found elsewhere in the World.

The African Mysteries System of The Grand Lodge of Luxor was named as such because it was the headquarters of all Lodges object and rule was to oversee all these other Lodges eg. in Mephis (Egypt) in Nineveh (Assyria) and in other parts of Asia Minor. Those at Nineveh and other parts of Asia Minor were opened during the Egyptian conquest and colonization of Asia Minor from 662 BC to 626 BC. under the guidance of their Egyptian most able leader, King Ashurbanipal.

But no sooner had this most able leader died in 626 BC than Egypt's new leader proved too much unable to over-see such a large realm from Egypt to Asia Minor left behind by A Shurbalnipal. And the more he proved too weak to do so the more he attracted a more able Persian leadership under the late King Cyrus' son, King Cambyses II, to invade and conquer Egypt in 525 BC thereby weakening the legacy of the Egyptian most reputable mode of governance which had been made possible by that Country's unique hybrid culture, second to none world-wide in those days of antiquity.

However, at first Egypt did not in any way lose this legacy because of their defeat and dominion by Persia. The fact is that because of Persia's prudent and immaculate conservationist policy not to destroy the legacies of those they ever conquered whenever they realized such legacies were of some reasonable welfare (Value) to them, this uniquely valuable Egyptian treasure was left totally intact by the Persian military force in Egypt throughout the Persian occupation and dominion effective 525 till 332 BC when this foreign authority militarily changed hands from the Persian to the Greek under Alexander The Great when the latter conquered both Persia and Egypt in 332 BC. The flabbergasting disaster to both Egypt and Persia as a result of this change of hands is that this immaculate legacy to mankind was not the only one that perished at the bloody primitive hands of a non-conservationist leader. Also, this leader forcefully compelled the already subdued and humbled Egypt to bow to the unbelievable henies demand. Under duress, Alexander the Great forced them to surrender to him and his Greek forces all their scientific and technological discoveries and to immediately honour him as their "pharaoh" by accroding him that title and all divine honours customarily accorded to their own leaders only.

All this and other account on what Alexander the Great did on occupying Egypt in 332 BC till his death in Babylon in 323 BC is fully documented in, for example, this most hardly found book in libraries: Stolen Legacy: The Greeks Were not the Authors of Greek Philosophy, but the People of North Africa, Commonly called the Egyptians, by George G. M. James, Philosophical Library, New York (1954). In addition, one may also benefit further from The African Origin of Greek Philosophy: An Exercise in Afrocentrism by Innocent C. Onyewuenyi, University of Nigeria Press, Nsukka, Nigeria (1993).

From the two sources in particular one would be flabbergasted to discover, for instance, how Alexander the Great cunningly and mischiviously looted and usurped all Egyptian books authored by Egyptians containing mysteries of Egyptian scientific discoveries unknown to the rest of the World save only scientists based at The African Mysteries System of the Grand Lodge of Luxor, Egypt and how he then turned to Aristotle all of them together with all their Egyptian authors, who by virtue of their unique scientific work, were required to live in seculation at the lodge. Also, these sources vividly show in depth how Alexander shockingly authorized Aristotle to change the authorship of these books to Aristotle's name—an act which did not only make Aristotle to come up as an unique author of up to 1000 books in not only one scientific area but, in fact, in diverse scientific areas; and how this act has consequently misled the entire Academia to a false belief that Aristotle was their author! Thus, the fatal disaster to the immaculate legacy of the Ancient People of North Africa commonly called the Egyptians.

### (2) Its Site and Mision Goal

The African Mysteries System of The Grand Lodge of Luxor existed at what is now called Alexandria. It's goal was to cultivate, using all creative ingenuities and other necessary means available within man's reach, and bring about an enabling environment of a hybrid quality able to produce and provide the greatest good and happiness possible to every individual in Egypt, which due to its geographical location, was faced with various difficulties and insecurities such as food and drinking water scarcity (as a large part of Egypt lies in the Sahara Desert); diseases especially tropical diseases which included malaria, sleeping sicknesses, bilharzia, etc; and many other insecurities.

### (3) Its Methodology

In order to successfully combat these myrad of insecurities, The Grand Lodge's first step was to first and foremost organize itself into specific specialisations namely, Agriculture and Mechanical Technology, Health and Medicinal Technology, Political Philosophy and Leadership Technology, Archtectural and Civil Engineering (or Building Construction) Technology, Transport Mechanical Technology, Astronomy, Mathematics, and more so Ethics and The Concept of Salvation—as a first step forward.

The second step of the Grand Lodge was now to engage each of these disciplines into a bee-hive business. Each was now to begin not playing but seriously thinking, pondering, meditating and cogitating what to the maximum of his creativity and ingenuity with regard to the Question: ***"what must now be done in my own rights to combat this difficulty on the behalf of my Egyptian people?"*** To what extent must I assist society in order to qualify for salvation so that my soul and body may not taste corruption (i.e decay)?

Consequently, in search for the answer to each of these and other related questions, each Egyptian member of The Grand Lodge gladly resolved unilaterally to give up his life to the

Lodge until he gets ways and means to these puzzles. This is also exactly, the reason why The Grand Lodge's work was named/called "The African Mysteries System" meaning a centre of unlocking these myrad of difficulties facing and surrounding the Egyptian people of the time. And, by so doing, the Grand Lodge gradually metamorphosed from a social organism into an amazing scientific monastry of greatest thinkers or brain storming dedicated individuals akin to the bee-hive and its members whereby each must show its worthness daily failure of which one had to be shown the door.

The third step forward was for political theories and art of governance engineers to forge out ways and means by which an amorphous community may be re-structed into a governable political community; and by which an acephelous community may also be re-structured into a hierarchically political structure able to steer the whole community toward a common goal, and thus do away with the existing life of the law of the jungle and replace it with a life of the law of natural justice; the existing life of living by mere luck and chance with a new well-safe-guarded and guaranteed life assured to each individual; an existing life of hunger and thirst insecurity to a new guaranteed life of food-security; an existing difficult life of health insecurity to a new guaranteed health security; etc. Hence, the efforts of The African Mysteries System of The Grand Lodge of Luxor to forge out a new constructive way forward to creating a hybrid political machine (government) entrusted with this noble responsibility empowered to cater for all these multi-needs which a single individual would hardly manage to achieve on one's own due to the existence of an unenabling environement of various scarcities, and other insecurities.

But, what are these entities called political community, a hybrid political community, and a hybrid political culture that the African Mysteries System of The Grand Lodge of Luxer sought and was therefore able to create in Egypt; And, what was their significance to the Egyptian people?

## CHAPTER II

# Political Community

### (1) Definition of a Political Communty and its Virtue

A political community is a hierarchical organic structure of a people in a given geo-political area or country and large enough in size to warrant being deemed a nation, having and enjoying their full sovereignty and political independence from all other communities or people; and having a well defined common goal of identifying and combating their myrad of insecurities which include food and water insecurity, health insecurity; river, lake, sea and ocean pollution insecurity, shelter insecurity, economic insecurity, peace insecurity, justice insecurity, business insecurity, education/learning insecurity, family insecurity, environmental insecurity, air insecurity, etc.

Because of this essential health reason, the African Mysteries System of The Grand Lodge of Luxor sought and finally created this political community out of their amorphous chaotic and anarchical structure which had existed from as far back as 7000 BC.

But, according to their judgement, this achievement alone was not enough and could therefore hardly function and achieve this myrad of needs from all the people without them first and foremost also creating another lean and more systematic political structure out of the already existing whole, and then mandate it to specifically deal with ways and means of achieveing these needs on behalf of and for the whole.

### (2) But what is a "Political Machine"?

Consequently, out of this whole, The African Mysteries System of The Grand Lodge of Luxor created a lean and systematic organism called "The Political Machine" which in our today's language is now called "Government", and charged it with its own unique duty of dispensing solutions or remedies to those multi-insecurities affecting its Political Community, i.e., The Citizenry, or Nation.

This mystery was solved by first grooming persons perceived by The African Mysteries System of The Grand Lodge of Luxor as having some sufficient signs or symptoms of leadership potentials by way of educating and training them fairly well on the concept and art of governance or leadership. After this, the next step was to expose them further by way of subjecting them to a dynamic training akin to a Monastry's methodology. By this methodology, each perceived potential leader was re-educated very vigorously and thoroughly from one's "ignorant-self" into a "philosopher-self". This was deemed imparative to be done due to the fear that an "ignorant-self" was as deadly poisonous to humanity as an Egyptian vicious cobra was to Egyptians. And, that as a woman must prove her fertility to qualify as a woman so must a leader also prove his/her leadership fertility or worthiness before being accredited with a leadership responsibility.

But, breaking through this mystery was not that easy for the African Mysteries System of The Grand Lodge of Luxor. The Mystery was as difficult and cumbersome as their search for knowledge about their God whom they kept on speculating about without any success until they, one day, in the year 1 AD, managed to do so by stumbling on The Infant Jesus Christ and His Parents on the latter's arrival in Egypt in search for a safe haven while fleeing from King Herod in Judeah who sought to kill The Infant Jesus Christ[1].

## (3) Creation of A Hybrid Political Leadership Culture Using a Political Leadership Genetic Engineering Formula

As a result of this acute hunger and thirst for a way forward for creating a political leadership that would in turn, also create a needed enabling environment requisite for the achievement of all these needs sought by the whole political community, i.e, The Citizenry.The African mysteries System of The Grand Lodge of Luxor fortunately managed to hutch out a unique technique called a Leadership Genetic Engineering which, in turn turned out to be a most reliable formula for transforming one with bad leadership potentials into one with good leadership potentials. They arrived at this flabbergasting break-through by first conceiving a unique idea of salvation. They argued that whereas, like all other living entities, man was equally a creature of some unseen Supreme Being whom man or any other creature had not been able to discover and understand his creative technique, man had an inherent duty to positively relate to this Divine Being and Creator by way of submitting one's total self to Him by honouring and respecting Him both in one's thoughts and deeds. Thus, they argued that it was one's mandatory divine duty to do so if one were to qualify to see This Divine Being and Creator and His Salvation at a later date. If not, then one could definitely be denying one's golden opportunity seeing and getting that free salvation. Thus, one would therefore not be able to see and live in Eternal Life with one's own Creator.

Accordingly, The African Mysteries System of The Grand Lodge of Luxor posited this Salvation condition to each potential leader as a mandatory dose requirement. Thus, each leader had also to play his part in the search for this salvation in as much as an ordinary Egyptian was also expected to do in order to enter The Eternal Life.

In this regard, a leader was required to be the first and foremost **to set up a good example to an ordinary Egyptian citizen by doing what was considered righteous not only to the self but also to those that he governed**. And, he was to do this not only to set a good example to the citizenry but also to please his Divine Creator who has chosen and blessed him into the position of a leader of other persons that did not have the luck of being chosen and blessed as such.

Thus, a political leader and his political machine or government were to be seen playing a perfect and holy role reflecting their virtious responsibility as custordians of the multitude on behalf of The Unseen Sovereign Divine Lord.

But, this mystery could not just come about out of no where or from varnity short of some dose into their psychic, given the fact that they were just as human as every other human beings were with a myrad of inequities, desires, etc, which may not be in line with the Rule of Law and Justice, and the expectations of both the general public and their Divine Creator, The Sovereign Lord, God.

In this regard, and in order to break through this challenging mystery, The African Mysteries System of The Grand Lodge of Luxor conceived a solution of making this fact to work. They conceived and formulated an idea of Theocentric Humanism Philosophy characterized and governed by a two-tiered virtues of Perfection and Holiness which had to be instilled like a dosage into the mind and life of every leader and non-leader in Egypt.

By virtue of this philosophy, each Egyptians's life was to be guided by these two virtues at all times in one's both thinking and deeds. Thus each had to live, behave and work within the framework of the two virtues. One's work and attitude was consequently guided by Perfection and Holiness, if one was to qualify for Salvation and finally The Eternal Life.

But, this was not expected to be a sufficient dose. It was argued that the dose should be further reinforced with an additional dosage of The Dictrine of *Summum Bonum* which in the English language ment The Greatest Good or The Greates Happiness of all Egyptians, regardless of one's gender, age, social economic status, marital status, etc. This Summum Bonum Doctrine was characterized and governed by a number of virtues the main five of which were: Justice, Wisdom, Temperance, Compassion and Courage. These virtues were used to develop society into a Hybrid Culture as follows:-

*By Justice*, every one was first taught and then expected to think and do only all that pertained to fairness, righteousness, truthfulness, right and transperancy and accountability.

*By Wisdom*, every one was first taught and then expected to think and do only those that were governed by prudence i.e those that were deemed right by prudence. Thus every one was expected not to be guided or governed by emotions but solely facts and these facts were to be right and correct to be deemed good facts; and one's judgement was to be solely a function of wisdom but not naked foolishness that always lead leaders and non-leaders into a myrad of corruption that in the end leads them into a suicide socially and professionally.

*By Temperance*, every one was taught and then expected to always remember to have brakes in one's thinking, utterances and total acts. Every one was supposed to have a sufficient amount of self-control—an element which often tend to miss among most people and thereby lead them into unnecessary trivial conflicts with thieir fellow men/woman without any valid cause and gain.

*By the virtue of Compassion*, every one was taught and then expected to always be mindful of other people's welfare. Thus, it was a virtue aimed at rehabilitating everyone from a hyena-character into a gentlemanship or ladyship character—a character of discency governed by humbleness, humility and fairness to oneself and to all others.

*And, by Courage,* everyone was taught and then expected to have a good stamina to withstand all sorts of evil temptations and the like aimed at fooling and then misleading him or her into engaging in non-cost-effective undertakings such as corruption and other symptoms of abominations of detestable results. By courage, every one in Egypt was expected to contain not only others from doing harm and other evil but also to contain the self from doing those detestable things.

**In the final analysis,** by inventing and propagating this Theocentric Humanism Philosophy and The Doctrine of *Summum Bonum*, The African Mysteries System of The Grand Lodge of Luxor did manage to break through this mystery of a virus leading one into unrighteousness of corruption, murder, robbery, assassination, arrogance, dictatorship, totalitarianism, and all other symptoms of Bad Leadership and Bad Governance in Egypt of Antiquity Grilization.

They did so by using this philosophy and the doctrine as their socializing dosages to produce a well refined political machine or mode of governance with a suffient energy, power and the will to do all those that pertained to the needs of all their Egyptian folks which were collectively **The Greatest Happiness for all** as also evidenced by the following prima facie multi-proofs of needs.

Because of this solid assurance, each leader and the governed endeavoured to the top of their will and efforts to prove perfect and holy though self-control in all their inter-persoanl interactions and all other undertakings.

This spirit was further enhanced by the public declaration to construct pyramids as a place for preserving dead bodies of the members of the royal family since everyone was assured that any perfect and holy individual never dies but only sleeps and rest while awaiting the soul's return to reunite with its body to Eternity.

Therefore the more this certainity was assured to the general public from the top to the bottom and vice versa, the more every Egyptian person excelled and accelerated in perfection and holiness in both theory and practice. And, the more this process continued and accelerated, the more the whole Egyptian Community melted into what came to be known as a HYBRID CULTURE of Hybrid political leadership and a Hybrid political community—a highly productive people of a unique sense of purpose and zero tolerance to every symptom or sigh of iniquity or corruption that we see all over Africa and the rest of the World today. A prima facie evidence of this reality of the amazing productivity of the Egyptian Hybrid Culture and Leadership, is borne out by the following empirical evidences, in Science and Technology discoveries and inventions:-

(a) In Medicine, Africa Spearheaded by Egypt became the first Continent to advance immensely in both preventive and curative medicine by the extra-ordinary ingenuity of her son called Imhotep (the first Egyptian physician and architect) that lived about 2980 BC. Imhotep lived two thousand years (2000) before Hypocrates (460-377 BC) who is erroneously called the father of medicine. In fact, it is a historical irony that even African historians and medical doctors are still ignorant of this truth most particularly the African historian who continue enjoying seeing his African doctors being misled to take an oath of Hypocrites and to display it in their practice clinics as their Bible! What a shame to African historians! But if the Greek Historian called Herodotus (5$^{th}$ C. BC) who studied in Egypt and confirms his amazement of what he actually encountered in Egypt regarding Africa's knowledge of Health Science and Medicine including Surgery and mummification which the Greek Hypcrates had also to learn before he could qualify as a physician, then what right does the Greek Hypocrates have over the African Imhotep? Is this not a daylight theft of African legacy by robbing Peter to pay Paul? Besides, even if Hypocrates did qualify from Egypt as a doctor, and transferred these skills to his mother country (Greece and Macedonia), how competent are his descendants in the area of mummification and total medicine? None!

(b) In astronomy, the same Herodotus confirms that the same Africans of North Africa (Egypt) were the first to excel in Astronomy because of their clear sky compared to the too foggy sky of the Greece and Macedonia to allow Astronomy.

(c) In Agricultural Engineering, it is also self evident that Africa spearheaded by Egypt also became the first to excel so much in increased food production and security that famine was not always a real threat. And that it was due to this reality that the Israelites (Jacob and all his children) had to abandon their Arabian homeland and come to North Africa in search of food. And so was their grand father and mother Abraham and Sarah also driven by famine to Egypt for food security. And finally, that North Africa was the first to invent and advance in irrigation technology e.g. shadoof which other nations also came to copy.

(d) In Mechanical Engineering, it was again Africa that spearheaded by Egypt that became the first to invent and advance in chariots before any other nations knew what the hell machines were all about. It was these strange machines that the Egyptians used in pursuit of the fleeing Jewish slaves from Egypt. (1447 BC).

(e) In Civil Engineering and Architecture, again it was Africa spearheaded by Egypt that proved to the World Civilization a total amazement due to her amazing knowledge in pyramid construction that required an extra-ordinary wisdom and knowledge in Geometry, Trigonometry and Mathematics.

(f) In Philosophy and Ethics, it was again the same Africa spearheaded by Egypt peoples from whom the Greeks, the Persians, the Ionians and other Mediterranean folks of Asia Minor came to learn. These included first and foremost Thales (624-550 BC), Pythagoras (582-497 BC), Socrates (470-399 BC), Plato (427-347 BC) and finally Aristotle (385-322 BC). In other words, all Ionian and Greek philosophers studied in Egypt. And, their philosophy was purely and totally Egyptian. This is the reason why all of them were either executed, imprisoned or forced into exile on the accusation that their philosophy was too foreign against the Greek gods, children, culture, traditions and beliefs in the survival of the fittest beliefs which has metamorphosed into the present mafia culture in Greece, Mecadonia and Italy.

(g) In International Relations and International Law, it was the same African headed by Egypt who initiated the two concepts as also empirically evidenced by their Egypto-Hittite Treaty of Non-Aggression signed between Egypt and The Hittites in Babylon in the year 1284 BC by which the two pledged to maintain a mutual peace between them free from aggression; and to aid each other during external aggression. This Treaty is the first and the beginning of International Law and the concept of *pacta sunt servanda* in Jurisprudence in our Civilizaiton today.

But, given that Egypt had all these amazing technology that no other country or people globally ever had, then what was its strategy in bringing about those multineeds such as food security, etc for the general public which all nations or peoples were unable to do due to lack of this rear technology that Egypt had discovered invented?

**(i) Food Security**

The first cardinal aim or goal of the Political Machine was to deal with the problem of food insecurity. It was to solve the problem of sufficient food supply for everyone—a problem which had been haunting and forcing everyone to wander from one place to another in search of food for his existence. The political machine was therefore aimed at designing and drawing up well-planned exogeneous and endogenous developmetnal strategies—Master-Plans that no single man could possibly manage on his own.

### (ii) Economic Security

The Mysteries System of The Grand Lodge of Luxor also aimed at fighting economic insecurity. This was in the sense that man was so poor and his living standards were too low and weird. The hybrid political culture was supposed to be of people with high economic capabilities and improved standard of living. The political machine was aimed at coming up with different ways and means by which man could innovate to improve his standards of living.

The life of man at the antiquity before the Mysteries System was so poor and so low with no development. The living conditions were low, poor and uncomfortable. This prompted the mysteries system to come up with a political machine to improve the economy of the people for a hybrid political community and a hybrid culture.

### (iii) Health Security

The Mysteries System also aimed at solving the problem or health insecurity that was rampant to people in the antiquity. The political machine was supposed to solve the existing health problems.

There were many diseases such as leprosy, small pox, malaria and many other host or diseases which also threatened man's life. The political machine fought these diseases for the improvement of the health political community. Men in the antiquity often suffered from many diseases which needed a political community which would jointly fight these diseases.

### (iv) Peace and Stability Security

The political machine that was moulded by the Mysteries System of the Grand Lodge of Luxor was also aimed at finding lasting solutions to the perennial problem of instability in men in the attacks from others since there was no rule to be followed. The rule of the jungle was the daily menu. The Mysteries System brought law and order for the promotion of peace and stability in Egypt.

Hammurabi, the law maker (1792BC-1750BC), the king of Mesopotamia, was the first man to codify a set of rules to be followed. Hamurabi copied this example from Uranum, his predecessor, who had acquired his knowledge from the Mysteries System of Egypt. They had copied the Egyptian system of law and justice. Long before Europe emerged from barbarism, men in North Africa at the Mysteries System had reached high degree of peace and stability. Before 1648 during the Peace of West—Phalia, Europe suffered much violence, lawlessness, chaos and instability due to the absence of a well established political machine to preserve law and order. There was intensive and extensive loss of lives and damage of property day in day out.

This is even evident when Thomas Hobbes, Marx, Weber, William Hegel, and Edmund Burke in the 16th century advocated for the quelling of the infamous chaos through the establishment of an absolute authority governance. However, in Egypt, security and peace was long established by the African Mysteries System of The Grand Lodge of Luxor.

**(v) Nuclear Family Security**

The political machine according to the Mysteries System was also geared towards coming up with a marriage and total nuclear family security. This was aimed at creating conducive environments so that people could engage in family lives with settlement.

This was aimed at enabling people to marry, have children and settle down with their families. At the antiquity, people led a life that was disorganized and awkward. This reason compelled the Priests and Hierophants based in the Mysteries System to create a political machine that would enhance family life for man's satisfaction.

**(vi) Wisdom & Knowledge Security**

The African Mysteries System of the Grand Lodge of Luxor aimed at creating a hybrid culture which was bright, intelligent and wise. The Priest/Professors sought to bring about a culture of a people who knew themselves well and who were therefore free of ignorance. They aimed at eradicating all forms of ignorance and pomitivity. They believed in Wisdom and Knowledge as a man's siqua non tool for his happiness in life. In other words, they believed that Wisdom and Knowledge were the cardinal key to the Greatest Happiness, and that man must therefore be given the best knowledge and technology to enable him fit in a hybrid political community.

A lot of Arts and Sciences were taught to men in the political community so that they can be full of scientific knowledge for a hybrid political culture. The African Mysteries System a centre of higher learning producing a hybrid culture of wise and intelligent men who would mutually co-exist with others in the community well and prosperously. The Political Machine brought about by the Mysteries System was mandated to spearhead campaigns for the civilization of man from pomitivity, ignorance, foolishness and stupidity to wisdom and knowledge. Hence, the Egyptian Traditional Motto: "Man Know Thyself!"

The African Mysteries System of the Grand Lodge of Luxor also aimed at constructing a superior leadership formula which would enable every man to get better goods and services and forge ahead confidently in life. This leadership formula was guided by the Theocentric Humanism Philosophy toward Leadership of Excellence rooted in the Holiness, Perfection and Godliness virtues as follows:

## (4) Its Theocentric Humanism Philosphy was grounded on these virtues:-

### (a) Holiness:

The virtues of being holy, one was expected to act in a righteous way and with reverence. One was required to move in Godly ways and be able to do holy acts and discard all evil deeds. A holy leader was a person whose activities were well and positively reflected in what he was doing. He was a leader who acted in the ways and powers accorded to him by the law and within the preference of his people. The virtue of being Holy ensured that man was acting in accordance with God's requirements and a leader was serving the governed as they deserved. His acts were, therefore in a total agreement with God's commandment that "He that rules over men must be just; ruling in the fear of God" (II Samuel 23:2-4)

In the antiquity, before the Theocentric Humanism philosophy, life was amorphous, there was no leader nor organization. The mysteries systems therefore brought the virtue of holiness so good leaders could serve the community committedly and diligently.

### (b) Perfection:

The Theocentric Humanism Philosophy's virtue of perfection was also aimed at producing excellent leaders. A leader was supposed to be perfect in whatever he is doing. The African

Mysteries Systems were aimed at producing hybrid leaders who were perfect in what they were doing. Perfection enabled a leader to do the right thing at the right time and in the right manner. It enables one to think critically and make wise decisions. When other leaders in various other corners of the world were characterized by imperfection and lack of leadership strategies, North Africa, through the mystery systems enjoyed quality leadership in temples political communities due to the high-tech training at the Egyptian centre of knowledge and excellence.

### (c) Godliness:

This was a virtue that leaders were supposed to adhere to at the African Mysteries Ssytem. This virtue aimed at producing leaders who were Godly and acted in the right manner. At the African mysteries system, they believed in God, and believed that God was the supreme person over all things and thus tended to follow the powers within their capacities. This was contrary to such as Greece who believed that man has power over things, and not God. The African Mysteries Systems therefore aimed at bringing about leaders who acted in good behaviour, those who feared God and those committed to the political community they are serving.

But in order to enhance promote and boost Theocentic Humanism aims, The African Mysteries Systems of the Grand Lodge of Luxor further invented the following doctrine as a vehicle toward that end:-

## (5) Its Doctrine of SUMMUM BONUM (Greatest Happiness for all) was as follows:-

The African Mysteries Systems of the Grand Lodge of Luxor in Egypt's sole aim was to bring about a quality leadership by the application of the Doctrine of SUMMUM BONUM. This Dcotrine of SUMMUM BONUM aimed at bringing about Supreme Good or Greatest Good in the political community for all. This was a doctrine that was supposed to bring about the greatest happiness in the community. The political machine in North Africa was aimed at creating an atmosphere in which all people would have absobute happiness devoid of obvious problems, harsh conditions or difficulties that are associated with poor governance, violence, injustices and evil within a political community, endemic to our generation in Africa and other developing countries.

The doctrine of SUMMUM BONUM was guided by four cardinal virtues viz Justice Wisdom, Temperance and Courage. These are four cardinal virtues that were imported to all students who passed through the Mysteries System of The Grand Lodge of Luxor.

These virtues were geared towards creating perfect and excellent administrators. They aimed at training or transforming one into becoming in his methods of leadership or administrative meticulous and scurplous strategies. Evil aims and action that are not in line with the lives of the majority in a political community were ostracized by the following four cardinal virtues:-

### (a) Justice

Justice as Universally known world wide, is one of the four cardinal virtues placing much emphsis on fairness. Because of this reason, the Mysteries Sytems schools groomed leaders who were to be fair and impartial in their leadership to all members of a community. Impartiality enabled leaders to deal fairly with all community members. This ensures that each and every citizen gets his or her deserved right and credits. This shows that a leader was one who was supposed to clearly divide and provide opportunities and profits equitably to all members of the community, as so commended by The Rule of Justice.

By being impartial also enables a leaders to be mindful of the weak and the under privileged. Injustice such as punishing members of the community wrongfully without any crimes committed was never allowed as it was seen as a non-virtue of a good leader at the Mysteries Systems.

Proper leaders as per the leadership formula of the African Mysteries Systems were supposed to be servants of God first and servants of the people second if they are to see the Kingdom of God on their death. Consequently, they were expected to demonstrate this virtue in their leadership by being objective when dealing with the community. A good leader according to the teaching of the 'Mysteries System' priests and professor, should be objective in tackling important issues. For a political machine to succeed well in serving the political community a leader should not be subjective, but objective in tackling issues. The Mystery Systems brought about training in which leaders were groomed to approach issue from an objective view. One should not discriminate or incite a group against others. One should not favour one and despise others, yet they are in the same political community.

Accordingly, by virtue of this assurance of The Kingdom of God of Everlasting Life so long as one does good to all equally, every leader and non-leader endeavoured to do his/her best at all costs and at all times. Consequently, each was a supervisor of his/her own work and made sure that one's work was not just good but excellent. This is exactly the reason why pyramids and mummification ideas emerged to preserve bodies of the dead as the souls were expected to be perfect incorruptable and were to return to the bodies at a later time.

### (b) Wisdom

And, as is also universally expected, a leader should be one who is wise and intelligent. He should be a highly bright person who is having a high level of intelligence and wisdom, if he is to succeed. The African Mysteries Systems of the Grand Lodge of Luxor spearheaded the fact that a leader should be a wise person indeed. This is the reason why all buildings and doors had inscriptions "MAN KNOW THYSELF" and also the reason why Socrates always talked of a "philosopher King", meaning that it was only a learned person who was fit to serve as a leader.

A leader with this virtue is able to make right decisions for his society and lead them in the right way or path. He is able to apply his wisdom in getting the most accurate and most conducive answer and solution to a problem. Difficult and almost impossible situations will be easily solved wisely without the society suffering any set backs. Like King Solomon in the Bible, who asked God to give him wisdom, a wise leader would be in a position to tell the difference between the truth and false; good and evil ideas and thus be in a good position to chose wisely for his subjects, and thus to save his nation from lots of chaos than a wreckless leader would.

The African Mysteries Systems made sure that wise leaders were produced for a hybrid political community for a smooth running of community affairs. The political machine was led by trained wise men who practiced this noble virtue as they had it with them already. The wise leaders trained at the Mysteries Systems enables a peaceful and wonderful flow of life in North Africa, specifically in Egypt, to be precise. Thus the result of Egypt's acceleration in amazing discoveries and innovations in various aspects of life than most societies of the time and our own time (2013, AD).

A wise leader was a Rational leader. Rationality was important for a leader as per the Mysteries System schools in Egypt. Rationality is the ability to think logically and come up with constructive deductive solutions. A leader was expected to come up with logical and deductive solution to problems facing the political community—a fact that is very rare even to-day in our own political leadership as at 21st Century AD!!

The African Mysteries Systems propagated the importance of bringing up leaders who would think deeply and reason meticulously and scrupulously so as to save the community from any wrong decision that would greatly hinder, stagnate or jeopardize the lives of the people within such a community.

A rational leader was needed as he/she was the one in a position to judge situations as they arise and solve them in the best possible way and manner they could on behalf of the masses. The Mysteries Systems were against poor and foolish individuals who take leadership positions either for granted or for their own stomach and thus not in a position to steer the community ahead.

A wise leaders was synonymous with prudent leadership strategies. A wise leader was one who prudently devoted himself for the good governance and leadership of his subjects for the greates good or happiness of those subjects. Prudence was a central governing tool to all leaders from the Mysteries Systems school in Egypt. The Egyptian priests and hierophants at the Grand Lodge of Luxor produced quality people who were capable of prudently leading the political community with all the knowledge, expertise, resources and technology they had at their disposal for the sake of their followers.

**(c) Temperance**

Further, the African Mysteries Systems of the Grand Lodge of Luxor trained leaders to be temperament. This was a virtue of self control which enables leaders to lead well without anger or any other malpractices associated to lack of self control. A true leader has self control and can thus resist temptations and make his own rightful choices. A leader with self control do not engage himself into under-meaningful arguments that retard the upload trend of a political machine for the developments of a political community.

According to The Mysteries Systems, a true leader should have no time and does not waste his time in looking at the attonist of man and other people or involve himself in quarrels with fearlessly and bitterness, but deals with issues with soberness by controlling himself well without engaging himself loosely.

Self control of temperance was also supposed to help a leader to resist and desist from indulging in evil vices within the community such as land grabbing, political assassinations, murders, ethnicity, tribalism or exmbezzlements of public funds and other symptoms of Bad Leadership Most of these vices were mostly committed by leaders out of revenge due to a certain past event that was committed against a person or a leader. But from the Mysteries Systems, in formula in Egypt enables one or the leaders from acting in such evil vices.

According to the formula of The Mysteries Systems of the Grand Lodge of Luxor, a temperament leader was modest meek and humble. By virtue of being modest, a leader was supposed to be not an informal, down-to.earth or a man of the people in the sense that one is expeted to be free of self glorification, arrogance, and boastfulness or conceit without implications of objectives. Thus, a leader should not be a person who boasts whatsoever of anything. He was supposed to be low to the people and live and talk just like people. By virtue of being humble, a leader was trained to shy and hate arrogance, that is, to abstain from vanity and arrogance of self-justification for one's wrong doings. A leader was expected not to be proud or haughty, and not assertive. He was expected to be low and with the people at all the times. The people looked for and at a leader to provide them with all their needs and necessities. They looked at a leader to be the guiding figure of the community, and he was thus supposed to be humble and low with the people in provision of all securities, e.g. food security, etc. A leader was expected to be a provider of the community needs and he was therefore looked upon as the head planner of societal needs. Meekness implied that a leader should not be submissive but steadfast and honest but not as deceitful and corruptive as the leaders today (2004).

Timid submissiveness was not encouraged in leaders. A leader should not be in a position to give in or submit to others so easily as such virtue would lead a leader to commit his/her nation to bogus deals cunningly drafted and placed before him/her for approval as in the present revelation in The Goldenberg International case where The Commision of Inquiry has unearthed this vice of submissiveness in the leadership as being the root-cause of the loss of billions of public funds from The Treasury and The Central Bank of Kenya which are the grannery and thus custodians of the Tax Payers Funds on the behalf of these Tax Payers

He should be tough and able to stand strong and make independent decisions, on strength of multiple constructive consultations and checks and balances as opposed to few persons with vested personal interests as in the passport tendering scandal case in Kenyan today (2004),

The Mysteries Systems schools of the Grand Lodge of Luxor also trained teachers to be tolerant. Tolerance was viewed as a virtue that enables leaders to endure or adapt to pyschologically or mentally to an unfavourable situations or accepting the beliefs, view or practices or other people which are conflicting with one's own. Therefore, a leader was trained to be able to tolerate other conditions which were or are contrary to his own views or preferences.

A leader was expected not to infringe on the rights of the opposition simply because they are against his views. He was not supposed to jail the people who are against his preferences, and he was not supposed to be injurious to other people who are not acting in the way he likes. A leader was expected to be tolerant to other peoples view.

**(d) Compassion:**

The Mysteries System also taught leaders on the virtue of Compassion. A temperamental leader had to have a sense of compassion. Being compassionate is having a sympathetic consciousness of others distress together with a desire the distressed to alleviate it. A leader was supposed to have compassion for other peopel that lived within the community. He was expected to be in a position to feel other people's problem; to be empathetic to them; and to try as much as possible to alleviate the problems facing different people under one's jurisdiction short of discrimination based on gender, religion, ethnicity etc.

By being emphathetic, a leader was supposed to have a natural feeling to participate in another's feelings and ideas.

A leader should not despise others especially those who are in need. The Mysteries Systems trained leaders to psychologically live with the people and think with them everyday. That was deemed a good leader.

Selfishness was a character synonymous with leaders at the African Mysteries Systems of the Grand Lodge of Luxor. By virtue of being selfish, a leader was supposed to share everything with people. A leader was supposed to share state property and all kinds of utilities and resources together with the subjects he is leading, so that no subject(s) dies of hunger or malnutrition. Such act was conceived as a curse and was therefore avoided at all costs by every leader.

The Grand Lodge of Luxor never trained selfish leaders who were out to amass wealth at the expense of their subjects, through looting of public property, and embezzlement of public funds and resources. They trained honest and selfishless leaders. The teachers were of high integrity and esteem.

### (e) Courage

Finally, a good leader, according to the Mysteries Systems, was trained to have courage. By virtue of being courageous, a leader was supposed to have a mental or moral strength to venture, preserve and withstand danger, fear or difficulty. Courage implies a leader's firmness of mind and will in the face of danger, or extreme difficulty.

By being courageous a leader was also supposed to have mettle. Mettleness means that a leader is supposed to have an ingrained capacity for meeting strain or difficulty with fortitude and resilience.

A leader should be able to face difficulty with fortitude and not fear anything at all.

A courageous leader should have Spirit. According to Mysteries Systems schools of the Grand Lodge of Luxor, a leader would have an exclusive quality of temperament to keep up his morale when opposed or threatened. He would not be scared when threatened, he should still have high spirits of overcoming all kinds of difficulties whether the enemy is too powerful or too strong for him. He should maintain a front-line commonder's spirit. A courageous leader would also have a resolution stress for determination by a leader to achieve his ends.

A leader is, from the beginning to the end, expected to be one with unlimited determination, hope and expectations to achieve one's ends without difficulties. He should be courageous against all odds.

The Mysteries Systems also emphasized tenacity as an added asset to a courageous leader. Tenacity adds to resolution whereby a leader was expected to have a stubborn persistence and unwillingness to admit defeat. A good leader was supposed to fight up to the bitter end and face all the consequences and repercussions of the war he is fighting or problems or difficulties he is facing. He is supposed to maintain his courage and unwillingness to admit defeat.

Courage gives a leader the power to stand unshakable for truth and keep him free or external pressure. He thus cannot be tempted into engaging in evil vices like corruption, bribery or other deviant behaviour. A leader of courage is able to defend his people from harm at all costs and keep them safe. Hence, the need and necessity of a people to entrust their lives on their leader. A leader was trained to be a reliable force to face all kinds or criticisms and tackle them head on without fear or second thoughts about any kind of a problem arising. He was trained to be a highly courageous person with high brevity intellect and morale. A courageous leader was expected to be a combatant as much as possible. This implies that a leader should be in a position that he is ready to engage in combat any time of the day with resilience and valour. A good leader should always be ready to engage in war and fight for the protection and welfare of his people or subjects within the political community. As commander of a political machine, a leader was thus entrusted with sovereignty, dignity and the likes of the people he is ruling. He was thus trained to be a fully combatant leader, always ready.

A courageous leader, as per the teaching the Mysteries Systems Schools of The Grand Lodge of Luxor, was supposed to be a redeemer. Redemption in this case implied that a leader was supposed to be in a position to liberate his people from the bondage of depression, poverty, slavery or any other kind of insecurity that his isubjects were in. He was supposed to be their total salvation, i.e., a person with the capability of saving his people from any kind of problem they are facing. Hence the ultimate goal of The Mysteries Systems schools to train leaders to be master redemptors, able to redeem their followers from any problem at any given time of the year or month.

Further, in The Mysteries System training policy, a good courageous leader was also expected to be heroic. He was needed to be in a better position to take chances and perform extraordinary deeds that are feared by ordinary people. He was instilled with a superlative courage expecially in fulfilling a high purpose against odds.

He was endowed with a valour training on the grounds that a valorous leader is one who exhibits illustrious bravery and audacity in fighting for the security of his/her people he /she governs.

A heroic leader should also have proofs in skill and bravery and indifference to danger or hardship. A good leader, as according to The Mysteries Sytems, was supposed to be gallantrous. Gallantry is a heroic character in which the Egyptian Preists/Professors argued that it enabled a leader to face trouble of problems with courage and without fear of danger or hardship in facing problems.

### (f) Sacrifice

Finally, every leader was trained on the art of sacrifice. According to The Mystery Systems schools, a good leader was supposed to sacrifice for others. A good leader was supposed to be a sacrificial lamb to his subjects and to be in a position even if it meant losing his life for his people. He should be able to give all he has and owns if the community is endangered. He should be in a position to provide all he has for the continuity of the society of his political community that he rules over should there be a dire need for it. A good leader should also go to war if he is forced to do so for the protection of his people. This is sacrifice.

## (6) Outline of its Leadership Formula

The leadership formula that was developed in Egypt at The African Mysteries Systems of The Grand Lodge of Luxor improved the lives of every Egyptian citizen so well with great assistance from the Political Machine that had been installed. The Political Machine improved the lives of the Egyptian citizen so well that many of them led an improved standard of living when most countries of the world were still lagging behind in development and utter poverty.

The leadership improved the problem of food insecurity that was rampant among the Egyptian citizens. New ways of farming and food production were invented and initiated which greatly increased the amount of food needed by the Egyptians. They further led to the availability of food security for everyone.

The Egyptians also managed to make so many discoveries and innovations. They were the first ones to develop irrigation systems which are still in used up to date. For instance, the use of a shadoof irridation really improved the growth of Agriculture in Egypt. Large farms could now be easily tilled and enough crops planted. This wisdom and courage led to the development of large scale plantations and settlements in other lands other than river banks, as was the norm.

The Egyptians were clever and bright on both sides of the coin. If attacked from North, they were good, and if attacked the from the South hoping they would be weak, they were even better! The same Egyptians who invented irrigation technology, invented flood prevention techniques. To control floods, they developed dykes, reservoirs and canals. These were techniques which they used in times when there was too much flooding in their lands. The Egyptians managed to do this at a time when in many other countries farmers had no ways of protecting their farms and houses from being washed away with water at times of flooding as is recurrently witnessed in Budalangi in Western Kenya and other parts of the World today (2008). The Political Machine at the time therefore greatly, facilitated these irrigation and flood control method.

Under the umbrella of the Political Machine, Egyptians achieved a grandeur and massiveness rarely, it ever surpassed in human history. They built amazing pyramids, which up to today, still exist, and which are one of the Seven Wonders of the Ancient World. The Egyptian Pharaohs who died were preserved in these pyramids, hoping that their souls would still be leading the country and that these souls would one day return to their sinless bodies. They also built great temples such as of Karnack, the seventy-foot Pharaoh statues. The Egyptians also exceeded in the art of portrait sculptures, art of jewelry and in goldsmith. They managed to make jewelry and tools by goldsmiths. These were things that improved the lives of Egyptians. The funnels and other tools were used to beautify surrounding homes and different houses of the Egyptians. They managed to do all these when many other nations of the earth were still behind and trying so hard but in vain to improve their living standards; and often most of these nations were busy at war against one another.

In Science, the Egyptians flourished so much in different disciplines which improved their lives a great deal. They invented medicines and the preservation of dead bodies, especially of their kings by mummification. The African Mysteries Sytems of the Grand Lodge of Luxor produced medical doctors of high reprite. The first physician of antiquity of any fame was the black Egyptian called Imhotep, who lived about 2980 BC. Imhotep was so highly thought of on his days that he was so worshipped as a kind of a god centuries after his death. He cured physical and mental sickness and even in later years people stremed to his shrine at the Imhotep Temple, dreamed of chim and went away cured.

The Egyptians, therefore, had the benefit of the science of medicine and did not suffer illness due to the presence of medical skills in their great country. The science of medicine reached other countries about two thousand years (2000) after it was started in Egypt. Hippocrates, who is erroneously referred to us as the father of medicine, lived 2000 years after Imhotep. Therefore, by referring to Greek Physician Hippocrates, who had gained his learning in medicine from The African Mysteries System as the father of medicine, is the highiest degree of the irony of history. It is a naked purgery.

Under the magnificent Political Machine that was invented by The African Mysteries Sytem of the Grand Lodge of Luxor, the Egyptians were the first to do surgery, even brain surgery. They treated tuberculosis, gall stones, arnthritis and dill dental work as well. The first ever fertility control recipe was also performed by the Egyptian, so says Yosef ben-Hachanan in the famous Ebers Papyrus of 1550 BC.

According to Professor Innocent, C. Onyewuonyi in his book, The African Origin of the Greek Philosophy: An Exercise in Afrocentrism, all these discoveries in medicine that were enjoyed by the African, reached in other countries of the world over two thousand years ago by Hippocrates. In his own words.

"A related proceduce (about sterility of a wagon), mentioned in the Carlberg Papyrus if, was designed to diagnose sterility in a woman, but this was copied word for word by Hippocrates—he was taught at the Temple of Imhoteph at Memphis where the work was conserved."

The Ancient Egyptians, therefore, enjoyed so much medical services at a time when other countries of the world were facing problems and difficulties in treating of diseases.

The technology mummification was also developed at The African Mysteries System of The Grand Lodge of Luxor. This was the technique of preserving of corpses (dead bodies) so they could last for a long period.

A case in mind, is that in 1922 the body of a former Egypt Pharaoh, Tu't-ank-Amon was found intact in its three-fold nest of coffins in its tomb. This treatments took about 70 days. Tu't-ank-Amon was an Egyptian King from 1347 BC-1335 BC. Emblamers always removed the brains through the nostrils and other internal organs except the heart and kidneys through an incision on the abdomen. The empty abdomen was filled with linene pads or saw dust. His body was placed in a natron, sodium carbonate, until tissues dried out. It was then wrapped with linene bandages and placed in a coffin. This technique of body preservation enabled the Egyptians to preserve bodies for long periods even up to these days when other countries could not manage to preserve bodies of dead people. And, although this art is being carried out in our own generation of 21st Century AD, the art is still too superficial and inferior to that of Old Egyptian experts who are the actual fathers of the art and yet it is now being erroneously credited to Greeks in order to deny Africa's achievement and contribution to the Civilization we have today.

Other developments realized in Egypt by The African Mysteries Sytem of The Grand Lodge of Luxor was the science of astronomy and mathematics. The Egyptians were the first to develop the 365-day World calendar that is still in use up to now (2013). They developed the knowledge of mathematics and even taught other Greek philosophers beginning with Thales and then Pythagoras, who is falsely credited for the formula of the square on the hypotenuse, popularly, called the Pythagorus Theorem. The Egyptians, under the Splendid political machine, enabled the people to live a luxurius happy life on being conversant with the time of the year due to the existence of their discovery of this 12 month calendar when most other nations in Europe, etc had no idea to calculate time.

Under The African Mysteries System of The Grand Lodge of Luxor, the Egyptians added to their history books by again becoming the first people ever, in the history of mankind, or the first nation ever to forge out a formal peace plan or protocols through signing of a treaty with a foreign nation in Babylon **titled Egypto-Hittite Treaty of Non-aggression in 1284 BC**. The Political Machine that existed in Egypt under the then Pharaoh Rameses II (1290 bc-1224 BC), was constantly at war with the Hittites in its bloody but indecisive battens amongst themselves.

As also acknowledged by Diane W. Darst, in her book, Western Civilization to 1648, the Egyptians were the first ones to sign a treaty of peace with their enemies, e.g., The Hittites.[3]

The Hittites were an Indo-European people who entered Asia Minor sometime around 200 BC. By 1700 BC they had formed a United Kingdom and ruled over the native population. The Hittites were a warlike nation. Around 1600 BC they ransaced Babylon but were unable to hold onto Mespotamian conquest. The Hittite Empire reached its height under King Suppiluliums (1380 BC-1340 BC). A contemporary of Akhnation, he took advantage of the Pharaoh's preoccupation with religious connections to conquer the Mitanni and extend Hittite control over the city states of northern Syria. Under the leadership of the later Pharaohs, the Egyptians engaged the Hittites in a prolonged struggle over Syria.

Finally in 1284 BC, the two nations agreed to cease their war by signing the only non—aggression pact ever known in the Ancient Near East. The pact established spheres of influence and endosed a pledge that each empire would aid the other during emergencies. It was reached by the marriage of a Hittite princess to Pharaoh", as a sign of firm commitment on the part of the Hittites to the Terms of The Treaty which in turn, became the landmark of The Law of ***Pacta Sunt Servanda*** in Jurisprudence (International Law) as a field of study and as an art of peace keeping in International Relations.

The Egyptians, therefore, excelled in the making and establishment of peace in the Ancient World that all other nations have now emulated. Their political machine was smart, superior and second to none in dealing with matters of International Relations. They were the very first ones to initiate a peace treaty that led to the development of a durable peace in their country and the Region as a whole that other countries have failed to do even in the modern world.

The African Mysteries System of The Grand Lodge of Luxor, therefore greatly, improved the life of many Egyptians under the guide of the Political Machine that was invented which fostered a Hybrid Culture of a durable peace and order using Theocentric Humanism Philosophy and The Doctrine of Summum Bonum, which collectively constituted a Leadership Genetic Engineering formula at The African Mysteries System of The Grand Lodge of Luxor.

## CHAPTER III

# Out-Come of Theocentric Humanism Philosophy and its Doctrine of Summum Bonum

As a result of this intellectual ingenuity of The African Mysteries Sytem of The Grand Lodge of Luxor to create an extraordinary reliable Political Machine which we call today "Government", the following mode of leadership emerged which according to its authors was expected to be a Hybrid Leadership Model for a hybrid yields of goods and services to all members of the governed—a leadership governed and guided by Theocentric Humanism Philosophy characterized by Holiness, Perfection and Godliness on the one hand, and by The Doctrine of Summum Bonum characterized by the cardinal virtues of Justice, Prudence, Temperance Compassion and Courage.

The following legacy of these extra-ordinary humans need also to be underscored:-

### (1) Their Correct Concept of "Philosopher King" in the Art of Leadership

The "Philosopher King" concept has been always misunderstood worldwide for centuries as no scientist has been either honest enough to properly define it in true perspective or content it was intended to mean by its author, The African Mysteries System of The Grand Lodge of Luxor.

Consequently, up to now, lots of misconceptions and confusions abound in Academia with each scientist misdefining it in his own misconceived ways.

In this regard, it is, therefore, hoped that the following conceptual and operational definitions will individually and collectively apprise our Academia on the actual (true) meaning of the concept according to its author, with a view to vividly showing not only its real meaning but also and foremost its intended utility to both the leadership and the governed.

The "Philosopher King" concept parsimoniously means a leader who has a mastery (i.e., who is well versed) on the Art of Governance that one must first and foremost have in order for him or her to wisely and properly guide the government into a right direction. In this rgard, one is expected to be versed in the laws and needs of people at large in view of the fact that a political leader is one who is expected by all to make good laws and to govern wisely without misusing his power of office. It is solely for that role that he/she is looked on for incentives for the betterment of the whole society, is consequently treated with honour and respect; and his word is always automatically respected and accepted with honour as a good law.

Drawing from his wisdom and knowledge on the Art of Governance gained from The African Mysteries System of The Grand Lodge of Luxor in Egypt during his tenure there as a student, Socrates argued on the meaning and virtues of the "Philosopher King" concept that in as much as a physician must be trained on the Art of Healing in order for him or her to treat patients well; and inasmuchas one must be also trained in his or her profession in order to do well in that profession, a leader must also be trained in the Art of Governance. Thus, a leader must be trained into "a political philosopher", in order for him or her to become an ideal leader.

For us to agree with Socrate's claim, we must, therefore, first and foremost look at the following characteristics of a "philosopher king" that one needs in order to be deemed an ideal leader.

## (2) Their Concepts of Truth

A "Philosopher King" has a passion for none other than Truth. He/she will never tolerate any falsehood. He/she is honest in all his/her dealings because he/she has a grace and a sense of propositions which leads one to seeing truth about things.

In this respect, Truth is a very essentia ingredient in a leader to help him/her in avoidance of lies and deception which a leader must not practice at all. It is his any reliable road map in his art of leadership for his survival.

## (3) Their Concept of Knowledge

A "Philosopher King's "Nous" (i.e the state of mind) is one which is full of knowledge compared to the nous of other men who are in an abstract state of belief without knowing much. A leader normally has the standards of reality and clear mind to refer to. Socrates says, "There are three highest forms of knowledge distinquished in elements of the mind, such as Justice, Wisdom, Temperance not forgetting Courage as their child".[2] These virtues thoroughly taught at The African Mysteries Sytem of The Grand Lodge of Luxor in North Africa now commonly known as Egypt which also advocated for Theocentric Humanism Philosophy and The Doctrine of Summum Bonum (i.e supreme happiness for all that led to Perfection and Holines for all) and finally to the germination and thriving of an evergreen tree of a Hybrid Culture that became an enabling environement for amazing discoveries and inventions in that Ancient North Africa.

The four virtues were deemed very essential in a leader because of the following facts:-

### (a) Justice

A political leader who is a philosopher king is normally guided by Justice meaning that he must be impartial in all his undertakings with the people whom he governs. By Justice, a leader always ensures that each citizen or alien is given due respect under the Rule of Law of Natural Justice and those other needs pertaining to one's rights and duties in the society. He is neither governed by meanness nor injustice. He is mindful of people's welfare both in theory and practice which one hardly finds in today's Civilization.

> ***This legacy correspinds very well with God's commandment documented in The Holy Bible under II Samuel 23:2-4 that "He that rules over men must be just, ruling in the fear of God. And he shall be as the light of the morning, when the sun rises, even a morning without clouds; as the tender grass springing out of the earth by clear shining after rain."***

### (b) Prudence

A Philosopher King's passion is for wisdom of every kind without distinction. Thus, a leader who is trained as such keenly and eagerly yearns and seeks above all else to be wise in decisions and actions. He is always eager to make the right judgement and decision for his state and what would lead them into the right course of governance. Difficult situations and decisions confronting the society is not led into perpetual domination from a multitude of diverse and adverse insecurities as is seen in most countries today where leaders are no more leaders other than ludicurous dictators and totalitarian human species bent on stuffing their stomachs with impunity other than serving the governed in fulfillment of their Oath of Office (vow).

For instance, it would have been wiser to first fill the potholes rather than wait for all the roads to be totally filled with or covered by potholes and eventually claim that there is no money for repairs as is the case in Kenyan roads today. If the Kenyan leaders were wiser enough they could have managed the funds available prudently in order to curb the insecurity of transport and communication network. In this, the disaster could have been evaded wisely if the leaders knew themselves and were philosopher kings. Like (Prophets Daniel, Joseph (Egypt) etc) of the Holy Scriptures, a wise leader is one who is easily able to make a clear distinction between truth and untruth, good and evil and hence lead oneself into some degree of perfection. But any wise leader no matter whether he is as wise as King Solomon of The Holy Scripture but who is not able to resit evil using his abundant prudence is also subject to fail in leadership just as King Solomon did fail terribly.

Accordingly, a meticulous wise leader would be able to tell which trends of technology are good for his state or country and which ones are hazardous. For instance, on the issue of legalizing abortion and same sex marriage, a meticulous wise leader would refuse the implementation of satanic such policy laws including condom policy or law in favour of Genetic Cultural Engineering to re-educate society on virtuous moral laws and customs of the old. Socrates argues that this kind of wisdom can only be found in a philosopher king. Hence the overiding reason of training every one who aspires to become a leader, on the Art of Governance first before one is allowd to govern.

### (c) Temperance

This is the ability of a political leader to resit temptations and make sound good choices that he/she deems righteous before the governed. A true philosopher king is guided by the virtue of temperance; and is rational in that he/she does not get into meaningless and empty decisions. One's mind is normally on higher realities; and, therefore, has no time for trivial rhetorics and non-productive squabbles guided by primitive petty jealousy, greed and bitterness that have always led nations to endless civil and international physical wars as well as cold wars.

This is always bound to happen whenever a leader is significantly deficient in this virtue of self control to keep him from petty issues. Self-discipline, humbleness, meekness, and self-control are attributes of this virtues which is, in essence, very important in a leader and his political machine (governance) for their success. They are essential for making rational discussions. Self-discipline enables a leader to be able to resist temptations like land grabbing, stealing of state coffers, and all "isms"—the vices that have bedeviled most contemporary world leaders and forced many of them to lose their leadership as in the case of President Richard Nixon and his Vice President Agnew in the USA political scandal. Daniel Toiritich arap Moi in the Kenyan political scandal; Joseph Mobutu Sese Seko in the Zairian policial scandal; etc.

It makes the way easier for the leader to achieve the set of goals and objectives because it empowers him/her to show and portray a sense of commitment also to implement the laid down policies and projects successfully for not the benefit of the self but of the Country as a whole in keeping with the Doctrine of Summum Bonum virtues and God's commandment to every leader envisages in II Samuel 23:2-4.

### (d) Courage

A leader with a 'philosopher king' attribute is better prepared and ready to face all eventualities of the state fearlessly and openly. Such a leader is able and ready to stand up for what he believes in and never flatters even if under threat to hide the truth. He protects truth in the interest of all the people under his dominion even if it means giving his own life for them. A good example being "Jesus Christ The Lord and Saviour of the whole world". He suffered and died courageously defending Truth. Courage gives the leader power to stand firm for Truth and keep him free from external pressures. Thus such a leader is never swayed off track into vices such as corruption, bribery and other deceitful behaviour. A courageous leader is able to defend his people and the Law at all cost and to keep them safe from any harm. Hence the peoples right to entrust their faith in him in his capacity as their steward.

During times of war, with a leader of such virtue, people are always fully assured that their leader would not let them down but faces the battle by its honest to save his society or state at large from the bondage of doom. Similarly with such virtues, a leader is never threatened by the present situation. He/she wisely forges forward fearlessly for the betterment of his/her society using all resources at one's disposal. And on the strength of the achievements made by his counterparts a leader with such virtues would always strive to make even a greater difference beyond the achievements of the counterparts.

### (e) Memory

A Philosopher's nature consist of a good memory. This helps him to be successful in learning and retaining various techniques and methodology of good governance he has learnt. The ability to remember enables him to apply what he has acquired in everything he does in order to make the concept of theory and practice relevant and more effective and efficient.

Thus, if the highest knowledge that can be learnt is the knowledge of the essential nature of goodness, the philosopher will be guided by the Theocentric Hummanism Philosophy and The Doctrine of Summum Bonum whose goal is "the greatest happiness" for all in his society. Memory, is therefore, very important in a leader because it enables a leader to remember and implement all that is expected of him from all that he has learnt about ideal leadership. The leader's memory also keeps him aware of the promises he makes to his people. It also gives him a guilty conscience whenever he fails to perform his duties to the standard of his ability or to the expectations of those that he governs in keeping with his promises to them.

Unfortunately most leaders these days have a tendency of forgetfulness or pretence of forgetting their promises and duties to the state and are more concerned with their own personal gains and attainment of riches, a habit that has cost many heavily by losing their jobs. When a leader fails in keeping a promise he made to the citizens of his state, he has the audacity to say he forgot about it because of the many demanding state affairs/stasks he has to handle. A philosopher king always knows that a leader must not forget that his first priority is always to the people who gave him that position and a mandate to lead them in comformity with the societal law of Pacta unionis and pactum subjectionis. Therefore, a philosopher king-type of a leader always has a good memory which he always relies on and is honest to it by being consciously committed to his word/promises and by remembering to draw and use lessons from his past experiences for the good of his leadership and people that he governs.

### (f) Intelligence

Intelligence is one of the sine quanon attributes that qualifies one to be a philosopher king. This leads a leader to the vision of absolute truth in his undertakings. Intelligence enable a leader to differentiate between reality and fiction. Thus, it enables a leader to have a solid base and a reliable confidence in himself. It helps a philosopher king to wisely judge things as they are and to deal with them accordingly rather than live in an imaginary worlds of fantasy and building of white castles in the air. His level of intelligence will lead him to either successfully or unsuccessfully pursue knowledge and all virtues that come under it, an to avoid the ways of the world inorder to strive to discover all that he can and pass it on to the next generation. An intelligent leader will cultivate and bring up a wise nation full of truth knowledge and amazing heights of prosperity and other symptoms of greatness akin to those of the Old City of Nineveh which was to the tune of a three-days walk in diameter (from one end of the city to another end)! This reality was evidenced by the Ninevian King's quick understanding of God's command brought to him by Prophet Jonah. Otherwise, the King would have refused to listen and told Jonah to quickly get lost with his foreign philosophy/prophesy as President Daniel Toroitich arap Moi always did by brushing off intellectuals' advice and even detain them withut trial in Court of Law during his reign in Kenya (1978-2002)

### (g) Breath of Vision

The African Mysteries System considered "Breath of Vision" as an added asset recipe on the list of virtues essential for a philosopher king on the grounds that it is a tenet that empowers a leader to contemplate reality and time. It empowers him to look forward ahead into the future and see the best action he can take for his people to make their future better and see the best action he can take for his people to make their future better and brighter. It is very important asset in a leader because it empowers him to focus and properly make plans in advance. For example, a leader who takes advantage of all the technology he has access to now, is subject to be ahead of other nations in scientific discoveries in a few years to come. A leader who is endowed with such an asset is apt to give his people and country a good hope as is certainly optimistic in everything he does or plans to do. He normally sees the "rainbow appearing after the rain". And, in this regard, he is sure of liberating his people and country in good time from future potential insecurities (disasters).

In short, to a leader with a Breadth of Vision, the impossibles are no more than passing clouds. There is no limit to what he and his people can collectively achieve together. Their collective energy or strength is mighty. Hence, the virtue of a Breath of Vision to a philosopher king but an alien to a non-philosopher king a demagog dictator totally naked of wisdom and knowledge chained on use of the gun as his rational choice.

### (h) Education/Training on the Art of Governance

The other emphasis by The African Mysteries System was that in as much as every professional must be educated (trained) in his/her art of professionalism if he/she is to prove a master of his/her work (profession), so must a philosophy-king also be educated/trained on his Art of Leadership. He must learn all that pertains to good leadership so as to become an Ideal Leader. According to the Grand Lodge of Luxor's Curriculum, a leader's education consisted of all scientific knowledge available in the World. One was expected to be taught all about Theocentric Humanism Philosophy and its ultimate virtues of Perfection and Holiness which he is expected to live by in the course of his duties. Whereas Education leads to new discoveries and improved appropriate technology, an educated leader is mandated to improve the lives of his people and also to ensure that education is availed to all his people due to its great significance towards improving their standard of living as is the case in most developed countries where education has led them to new discoveries and a comfortable standard of living. Although the discovery of the law of gravity by Sir Isaac Newton is of recent time, The African Mysteries Systems of The Grand Lodge of Luxor in Egypt was the first to discover the significance of Science and Technology, and Liberal Arts (described here below). It was them and them alone who, with the help of this Education, discovered the meaning and use of a SHADOOF IRRIGATION technology to help in combating Food Insecurity by irrigating and reclaiming the waste land; the so called "Pythagorean theorem" of Geometry and Trigonometry for building the pyramids; and also the art of mummifying or preservation of the dead bodies for years which has for ever remained a prima facie proof of the African pride. Education is very important for a leader because it replaces a closed mind with an open one; and an ignorant or primitive mind with a richly educated mind. A leader with an open mind is able to make rational decisions that are subject to benefit everyone in his country without biasness. He is able to see things in a broader spectrum and more critically. In turn, this helps him to possess qualities of a charismatic leader and to be open to suggestions from others which can be helpful to him and his country. Such a leader has a readiness to learn and is quick to learn. The more he is ready to learn, the more he becomes wiser and effective in the shortest time possible for the benefit of his society. This reality is evidenced by Alexander The Great's employment of Aristotle as his tutor during his reign as king of Greece, Macedonia and Persia (based at Babylon and Alexandria capitals).

A leader's thirst for learning enables him to grasp the things he is learning easily because he is doing it with a determined heart. Readiness to learn in a leader is essential becaue it makes him able to listen advices from other sources which may be an asset to him as a leader. This makes such a leader ready to learn from his own past mistakes and those of other leaders during his time and before, for the benefit of his success in leadership and prosperity of those that he leads.

Thus, he is able to ensure that the same mistakes are not repeated, and to learn more about his people's needs and what he should do to make each person in his country have supreme happiness.

But, like Socrates, one may ask: why do those people who claim to be "philosopher kings" not live up to the standards expected of them?" "Why are there bad philosophers in the world today?"

A response to such questions is that a bad philosopher turns out in that manner because of a number of reasons indicated here below:-

1. A philosopher king who does not hold up to the expected levels should blame nobody other than, the environment from whence he was brought up. In the words of Socrates, "if the ideal philosopher character is taught properly, it will develop to perfection, but if it is sown and grows on unsuitable soil, even the most gifted characters will be bad."[4]
2. The upbringing of a born true philosopher highly determines whether he will turn out to be good or bad. If a philosopher is brought up with the right education required on the knowledge of The Doctrine of <u>Summum</u> <u>Bonum</u> and its virtues of Justice, Prudences, Temperance and Courage, and on theperfection and Holliness virtues of the philosophy of Theocentric Humanism, he will certainly turned out an ideal leader,—a "Philosopher king".

3. Pressure from the crowd puts a strain on the would be true philosopher king who gets carried a way and start behaving in manner like them. Hence, the essential need for a leader to have a sufficient degree of Courage and Self-Control to resist such viruses.
4. In succumbing to influence, a Philosopher king loses his training and fails to put all that he has learnt into practice.
5. The human heart seeks approval from fellow mankind and so instead the philosopher being true to his calling he will do what the crowd wants him to do in attempts to win over their approval and affection. Thus he becomes a failure to his cause as so witnessed by, recurrent tragedies in Leadership History from Antiquity to the Present Civilization.
6. Some Philosopher King turnout to be corrupt due to temptations and tend to follow the ways of the world, in the latter's capacity as a factory and granary of unscriplous desires against The Rule of Law and Justice and God's commandment to every leader which reads as follows: "He that rules over men must be just, ruling in the fear of God. And he shall be as the light of the morning, when the sun rises, even a moring without clouds; as the tender grass springing out the earth by clear shiing after rain." (II Samuel 23: 2-4).
7. These kind of philosophers are tempted by the desire to acquire power and influence, wealth and false honour given to those whom the world loves. Despite the fact that, these are the various ways through which philosophers and philosopher kings become defective, Socrates believed that a leader must be a philosopher king. Socrates, however, laments that inspite of its humanistic virtues, unfortunately philosophy has been deserted by those who should be her true lovers and thus suffers at the hands of second rate interlopers who are worthless and wicked. These interlopers' main goal is to seek the dignity and title associated with being a philosopher because philosophers are considered to be reputable, respectable and knowledgeable. A true philosopher would make a good leader because philosophers are those whose riches conssit of not money but the happiness of a right and rational life. If public affairs are led by men who are morally improvised, then they will have nothing to contribute themselves but can only hope to snatch some compensation for their own inadequacy from a political career. Hence, an uphill stumbling block against every effort for a good government. These leaders are normally guided by selfishness and always have an attitude of survival of the fittest. They hardly think of their people's welfare but their own as also vividly evidenced by the still on-going Commisions of Inquiry in Kenya regarding the Goldenberg Anglo Leasing and Finance, Robert Ouko murder, Devil Worship, Land

> Grabbing and many other Scandals that have by now (2008) unearthed a shocking theft of a colossal billions of Kenya public funds and land by both The Former and Present Heads of State, Former Governor of Kenya Central Bank, Head of Criminal Matters, and many other leading personalities in the former Regime of Daniel Toroitich arap Moi at the expense of Kenyan Public. Whereas a true philosopher leader may not strive for richness as his ultimate goal due to his training on those virtues of good leadership, a contaminated environment may equally contaminate a philosopher king and put his vow to shame.

Political philosophers who live up to their standards will also make good leaders and an ideal political machine because they are chosen to rule, not out of their own will but because of their needed leadership qualities. A state whose leaders come to such position with a least enthusiasm is bound to have the best and most tranquil form of government. But a state whose leaders are eager to ruleat all cost using bribery become the worst. This is because the latter eager ruler usually seek to satisfy their own happiness and richeness and not the welfare of "wananchi". Their ultimate goal is to acquire power, respect, dignity and capital accumulation that comes with position of being a leader.

But persons with qualities of good leadership neither scramble nor use bribery for leadership. Their qualities automatically call and sell them to leadership and gladly exit only when nature wants them to do so as in the recent case of Nelson Mandela who honourably did so due to age limits. But unlike a philosopher king, a non-philosopher king usually fights to remain in power for life as has always been the case in most African countries where conflicts of civil war have always waged (ever since each country's independence) by leaders fo doom determined to shed every drop of blood to remain in power by force.

Such leaders always bring divisions among the people who will be forced to take sides and support their own individual favorite leaders as it is self-evident in most of the developing countries inclusive of Kenya, Angola, Nigeria, India etc. In most of these countries leaders always hang in a balance between peace and war. A durable peace is unreliable indeed. This is the underlying reason why all underdeveloped countries are in a state of perpetual poverty and bad governance since their independence to the present. Their degree of poverty is as extreme as their degree of bad governance. In this regard, it is self-evident, drawing from what we now know of the virtues of a philosopher-king, that unless a society is governed by philosophers, there may be no end to the schisms within and between states and individuals alike. All these perennial turmoils in developing countries in particular due to leadership poverty can only be overcome by a recognition of this fact that a leader must acquire a philosopher-king virtues guided by Theocentric Humanism Philosophy in order for the society to achieve its goals, objectives, hopes, and dreams to perfection. Only then. will all members of the society be catered for and at least have a sigh of relief from all these perennial agonies of civil strife and abject poverty caused largely by untrained poor leadership.

CHAPTER IV

# Amazing Discoveries and Innovations in Science and Technology as a Result of the Efforts of a Hybrid Political Machine.

## (1) Introduction

It is self evident that Africa and her Children have been recently recognized for various achievements in Athletics, Games, Literature, Music, Art and Clothing Design, and Science such as Prof. Ali A.Mazrui—(Political Science), the late Prof. Thomas R. Odhiambo—(Bio-Sciences), Chinua Achebe—(literature), Miriam Makeba—(Music), Kipchoge Keino—(Athletics), Wole Soyinka—(Literature), Nelson Mandela (Leadership and Governance) Senegalese President Duf (Agriculture and Food Security), Frantz Fanon (Literature), Ken Salrowiwa—(Human Rights), Nwankou Kanu (Olympics Football 1996), George Weah (Football 1994-1996 World's best player), etc

However, it is also self evident that Africa and her Children have been for many years marginalized, despised or simply looked down upon in everything they do. They have been regarded and characterized with all sorts of negative adjectives used as an abuse to the Continent of Africa calling it a "dark continent". Some of these characteristics include, for example, the following:-

(a) In his book titled <u>The Mind of Man in Africa</u>, C. J. Carothers notes the following from two French scientists called Gallais and Plaques with regard to their rating of the people of French colonies in Central and Western Africa:

The best known trait of the normal psychology of the African are, above all, the importance of the physical needs (nutrition, sexuality); and a liveliness of the emotions which is counter-balanced by their poor duration sensations and movements comprise the chief part of his existence. Intellectual life, evocation of the part, and projects for the future pre-occupy him but little. Separated from these regulating influences, he lives essentially in the present (in this sense like a child), and his conduct submits to influences and impulses of the passing moment and thus appears explosive and chaotic.[4]

(b) Carothers further notes from the writings of Williams about Africans of the Gold Coast (Now Ghana) and give the following abhorring assessment:

Compared with the white races he seems to lack initiative and constructive ideas, although he may be a shrewed judge of the attainement of others . . . Power of observation is astonishingly defective. They seem to be incapable of sustained effort . . . An African has little imagination and little humility. His self-esteem is often ludicrous. The qualities most in need of education are imagination and adjustment.[5]

(c) Carothers finally concludes that:

The African is conventional: highly depended on physical and emotional stimulation: lack in foresight, tenacity, judgment and humility: inpact for sound obstraction and logic: given a phantasy and fabrication, and, in general, as unstable, impulsive, unreliable, irresponsible and living in the present without reflection or ambition, or regard for the people outside his own circle[6].

## (2) Observation

These three findings on Africa and her personality reveals the fact that for many years Africans have been adversely castigated in everything they do. They are rated as uncivilized, barbarian, primitive, immature and silly without sufficient intelligence compared to that of a white man.

## (3) Hypothesis

Given the fact that an African is by nature without a sufficient amount of intelligence comparable to that of a white man, it is, therefore, hoped that the following account on what Africa actually is; what she has done to the World Civilization would support the white man's assumption/contention.

## (4) Prima Facie Evidences

### (a) On the Question of The Founding Fathers of Political Theory and all other Disciplines of Science:

i) Long before Europe emerged from its habitual culture of barbarianism in North Africa, Africa had reached highest degrees of civilization. As such, Africa (particularly Egypt) became the Founding Father of Political Theory and all other Disciplines of Science from the efforts of the first most centre of higher learning called: The African Mysteris Systems of the Grand Lodge of Luxor based at Mephis in the Ancient Egypt.

ii) The Nile Valley is one of the oldest habitations of man, if not absolutely the oldest. It thus means that, along the River's various valleys, man developed a community or association since he was faced with many insecurities e.g. drought, diseases and hunger. As this advanced and man moved forward steadily, it developed into a political community which was to be guided or regulated by a political machine. This machine was to ensure a smooth running of daily occurrences. It was also to maintain Law or Order. This machine is what have under the universal name "Government."

iii) In Old Egypt, the doctrine of Summun Bonum was applied for good governance and productive in functional existence of all. This doctrine meant supreme happiness for all and it gave birth to Theocentric Humanism Philosophy i.e. a philosophy guided by Perfection and Holiness virtues. Greek Sophists developed the opposite of this called Anthropocentric Humanism Philosophy guided by vices such as unholiness and imperfection and a dictrube called Summum Malum (supreme evil). As such, Summun Bonum doctrine and Theocentric Humanism Philosophy which were the main functions/concepts taught at the Grand Lodge of Luxor, formed the basis of theorizing and were all a product of the Old North Africa today commonly known as Egypt.

iv) Plato who is claimed to be Aristotle's teacher, was himself not enlightened with philosophy of which Aristotle had. It, therefore, seems absurd to believe that Aristotle was taught by Plato who had no knowledge in the Philosophical arena. Like Socrates and Thales, Aristotle learnt all these from North Africa and as such, this indicates the superiority of Africa in Academia at that time.

v) Around 4$^{th}$ millennium B. C., Sophisticated Iron, Copper and Bronze tools and weapons were used. Agriculture was on the increase. Dykes were developed to control the floods and reservious for the purpose of the shadoof irrigation engineering.

vi) Egyptians achieved a grandeur and massiveness rarely, if ever, surpassed in human history. Using their extra-ordinary talents in Science and Technology second to none globally, they built pyramids which stil exist today; great temples of Luxor and Karnak; the seventy feet pharaoh statue and as well flourished in portrait sculptures, arts of the jewellery and goldsmith. This is shown clearly by the jewels and furnishings found in the tomb of Tut-ankh-Amon recently.

vii) From the above evaluation, political theory and other disciplines advancements are a product of Africa. Also as shown in the following discussion, North Africa became the vortex of Civilization due to the presence of such amazing learning institution between 300 and 100 B.C.

viii)At around 500 B.C. Pythagoras having learnt triangles and trigonometry with geometry from Egypt, he compiled books on the same and has falsely been credited with the popular Pythagorean Theorem which is not actually his making or discovery. This can be proven to be not his inventions but Egyptians discovery. Therefore, Pythagoras Theorem is none but a naked plagiarism.

ix) The prima facie fact to prove this truth is that Egptians had as long as 400 B.C. years ago erected pyramids. Iti is therefore absurd and a product of unsound mind and reasoning (as it has always been the Europhalia's attitude towards Africans) to assume that pyramids would have been built without clear knowledge of both trigonometry and geometry. As such, the triangular theorem is of African originality as it was used by the architectures of the pyramids in Egypt.

x) The presence of the Africans Mysteries Systems, the latter's Lodges and the Royal Libraries (not forgetting presence of museum where mummies were kept) made the centre of knowledge acquisition. As a result, Greeks like Thales, Pythagoras, Socrates, Plato, Aristotle etc. migrated only to come and acquire the philosophical and scientific knowledge in Egypt that was not available in the home countries of Greece and Macedonia during their generation. It is said that when Greeks visitied Egypt (after the

Couquests of Cyrus and his son Alexander The Great) for initiation into the Mysteries Systems of The Grand Lodge of Luxor the Priests and Professors told them that:

"You Greeks are just children"

xi) The knowledge of Greeks could not be compared to that of Africans for the Egyptians Knowledge was more superb and too superior and sophisticated for non-Egyptian to understand short of a lengthy monastric experience.

xii) After learning of these great African Mysteries, Alexander The Great struggled day and night so as he could conquer North Africa and make all this amazing legacy his personal property and also use his tutor Aristotle the head of the Great Royal Libraries and the Lodges—an evil objective he finally achieved in 332 B.C.

xiii) Thence, Aristotle took all the materials he found in the Egyptians Royal libraries and temples removed their actual authors and credited them to himself. This is evidenced by the fact that, no matter how genius Aritotle or any other individual was, no human with a libing could have written or can write and compose more than a thousand books; and to make matter worse, in different disciplines and subjects. Secondly, when Aristotle died one could expect such amazing discoveries and innovations to continue smoothily by his Greek successors if they were indeed a genius people. But, since this did not happen, it is clear that Greeks had no natural ability to advance these Sciences. Hence the immediate shortfall of "great Greek intellect". Aristotle's scholarstic excellence or fame was a naked purgery. It was theft, and a silly one as no one can possibly manage writing over 1000 books in different subjects and disciplines.

xiv) To be accepted in the Egyptian Mysteries Sytems, a study of Political Science, Religion and Sciences (i.e. liberal arts and Sciences—Political Theory) was a mandatory condition in Egypt. These pursuits of Geology, Astronomy and the belief of Egyptian's religion put a number of Greek Citizens into trouble such as Thales, Pythagoras, Socrates, Plato and Aristotle as they were either banished, executed, exiled or sent into slavery by the Athenian Government because of their new doctrines, beliefs and education they had received from Egypt between 640 and 300 BC as these were judged as foreign and unheard of things in Asia Minor and the whole of Europe.

xv) "How then can a government which killed and exiled its great thinkers claim them to be Founding Fathers of the same Philosophy and doctrine they rejected? This abrupt about-turn or second thought of the governments in Asia Minor proves them dishonest. In this regard, it is self-evident that these doctrines were of African origin but not of Greece, Macedonia or any other country in Asia Minor!!

xvi) In his book, The Stolen Legacy, G. James notes that:

The seven liberal Arts, which formed the foundation training of all Neophytes and Initiates included: Grammar; Arithmetic; Rhetoric, Dialect (i.e Quadrivium) and Geometry; Astronomy; Politics and Music (i.e Trivium)[8].

He also added that:

> The Priest of Egypt were also Judges, Lawyers, Official of Government, Business men and Sailors. The above confirms that political theory and other disciplines began from and in North African Egypt between 3000 B.C. and 1000 B.C. when the whole world was still behind the curtain as history.

### (b) On the Question of Amazing Discoveries and Innovations in Science and Technology

The Ancient Egypt's valuable contribution to the world can be traced in many fields of Innovations and Discoveries be it scientific, historical, economical or philosophical discoveries.

One of the most remarkable discoveries made by Egypt was in the field of economics. At the end of Neolithic period around 5000 B.C., the Ancient Egyptian gradually transformed the Nile Valley leading its inhabitants to progress from a food gathering economy to a food producing economy. And by this important transition in human development, the Nile Valley impacted on Africa great consequence, material as well as moral. For the discovery and growth of Agriculture, this extra ordinary progress made it possible for ancient Egyptians to adepot a settled integrated Village life and this development, affected her social and moral development not only in pre-historic time but also during the dynastic periods.

In developing agriculture, she also established the principle of Co-operation within the community for without such Co-operations among the people of the Village Agriculture production would have been limited.

It is worth noting that Ancient Egyptians' civilization of historical time had two main legacies that led to current civilization of the whole World. The first is the material legacy. The second also descended from the most distant past is the most abstract cultural legacy. The material legacy (i.e discoveries and innovations) included Craft and Sciences (geometry, astronomy Chemistry), applied mathematics, medicine, surgery, and artistic production. The cultural legacy side covered religion, literature and philosophic theories for romantic satisfaction (romantism).

### (c) On Their Contribution in Crafts

The ancient Egyptian (North Africa) contribution in the Craft can be traced in stone, metal, glass, ivory, bone and many sculptures. For long period and even during historical times the tools and arms inherited from the Neolithic period continued to be used his successors. Nile was rich of flint of large sizes and excellent qualities which the Egyptians continues to have after the discovery of use of the copper and bronze.

Egyptian metal work techniques were confirmed to the use of gold, silver, copper and copper alloy as bronze and brass. The ore of copper have been found on Mt. Sinai as well as Mibai.

As ancient as the early dynastic period of 3000 B.C., the Egyptians—(North Africans) discoveries and employed in making their copper tools, all the basic techniques of metal work, such as forging, hammering, casting, stamping and soldering techniques which they mastered very rapidly.

North African men have indeed nourished the world with discoveries and innovations used by craftsmen. In the workshops depicted in painting or bar-releif on the tomb's walls both above and below the ground, one could see for example, carpenters, cabinet-makers at work making furniture and the tools used were saws, drills. Axe, chisel and wallet. In making of the jewellery, they used gold, silver and precious stones such as feldspar, lapis, lazuli, turquoise, amethyst and cumehan fashioning and furnishing them with remarkable precision into crown, necklace and other items of adornment.

The cultivation of flax rapidly led to great ability in hand spring and linen making. The latter was known from the start of the Neolithic period 5000 B.C. The women spun the flax, doing so with great skills since they frequently handled two spindle simultaneously. They used the looms which were first horizontal and then the vertical looms which enabled them produce long fabrics required for the loose—fitting everyday clothing as well as ritual Mummy wrapping and shrowd.

The wood, leather, and metal industries were also a discovery and innovation of North Africa, they were perfected and the product of these industries have survived in good conditions to the present day. The objects produced by the Egyptians craftsmen include silver vases, wooden coffins, combs and decorated ivory handles. They had spinal talents for weaving wild reeds into mats and spun fibres of the palm tree which made it easier to produce the production of study nets and ropes. Pottery was also a brainchild technique of Egypt, its manufacture developed into finer red and blackrimmed pottery and then were polished by incision and through baking. Most of the storage of various materials while some were for the decorative purposes.

Egypt in North Africa contributed also in the invention and distribution of glass making techniques to the whole world's civilization. The Phenomenon of convergence and that of glass making was discovered independently in the Nile Valley. Glass was used for beads and vases of great variety of shapes from graceful steamed chalices to vases in the farm of fish. They were usually polychromatic and always opaque. Transparent glass made its appearance under Teaukhamon (1300 B.C.). In the latter period, hieroglophic sign moulded in coloured glasses were set in wood and stone to make inscriptions. When Alexander the Great conquered Egypt he become the king and made Grand Lodge of Luxor (which he changed its name to Alexandria) it the main centre of the manufacture of glassware, exporting its products as far as China.

One of the most important industry was that of the production of papyrus which was invented by the Ancient Egyptian. No plant played a more significant role in Egypt than papyrus reeds. Its fibres were used for baot-making and cawking of the wicks of oil lamps for mats baskets, ropes and hawsers.

Over and above all, papyrus fibres was used for to make "Papyrus" from which the word "paper" is derived. Papyrus was made by placing crosswise successive layers of fine strips taken from the stem of the plant which after pressing and drying formed a large sheet. Twenty sheets of papyrus joined together while they were still moist formed a scroll of three to six meters long.

It was this scroll that constituted Egyptian books. Papyrus was used in the Egypt from the time of the first Dynasty (300 B.C.) until the end of Pharaonic period, later, it was adopted by the Greek, the Romans, the Copts, the Byzantines, the Aramears and the Arabs. Its stated that Papyrus was one of the most principal exert of Egypt—North Africa.

The technical contribution of the Egyptians to the world were their industrial and stonemansory ability.

The quarry from which the diorite came from was the famous statute of ehephren in the Cairo Museum 2800 B.C. The stones were used in building the tombs planned as the dwelling place of the dead between 3000 B.C. and 2400 B.C.

The Egyptian expertise in woodwork was brilliantly manifested in their ship building. For example the cheops' boat had no Karl and was flat-bottomed and narrow, it had no nails. Pieces of wood were held together solely by use of the tenou and mortise joint.

### (d) On Their Contribution to World Science and Technology

The Egyptian contribution to science and applied mathematics did leave valuable legacy in the innovation arena of Physics, Chemistry, Zoology, Geology, Medicine, Pharmacology, Geometry and Applied Mathematics. In fact, the Ancient Egyptians gave to humanity a large store of experiences in each of these fields. Some specific project areas follows:

### (i) Mummification Scientific Technology

One of the most outstanding scientific discovery and innovation of the ancient Egyptians is Mummfication—a discovery which has buffled all our scientists today as they cannot imagine how this can be done. It shows their mastery of a number of sciences including Physics, Chemistry, Medicine and Surgery. Their ability in each branch was an accumulation of long experience. For instance they exploited their discovery of the chemical characteristics of nation which was found in certain areas of Egypt, particularly in the wadi-el Natum by using the chemical attributes of those substances in the practical fulfillment of the demands of their belief in life after death. They believed in the continuity fo life of one lived righteously pertaining to the doctrine of summum bonum and Toheocentric Humanism Philosophy belief. This was emphasized by devising a technique of preserving human body for larger periods lying in wait for the Soul to come back from a long journey as they considered it to be. The compounds of times as mixture of sodium-bicarbonate, sodium carbonate, salt and sodium sulphate—(This was the chemical used for preserving the Mummies). The Ancient Egyptian, therefore, was aware of the use and misture of chemicals in right proposition and their administration. This was also a discovery of North Africa people. In the process of mummification the body was soaked in natron (as described above) for seventy days. The brain was drawn from the head through the nostrils and also removed the intestine by hand incision made in the side of the body. Such operations as these necessitated an accurate knowledge of anatomy and high quality process and method of preserving the dead bodies—(mummies). This a clear evidence that the development of morturies began back in Egypt.

### (ii) Surgical Inventions

It is undoubtedly, the knowledge acquired from the processes of Mummification that enabled the Egyptians to develop the Surgical techniques at a very early period of history. The good knowledge of Egyptian surgery, infact "thanks to smith Papyrus" a copy of the original work, which was composed under the old kingdom between (2600-2400 B.C.). This papyrus is virtually a treatise on bone surgery and external pathology. Forty eight (48) cases were examined systematically. In each case the author of the treatise began his account under a general heading; "Instructions concerning such and such a case" followed by a clinical description from the observation of various symptoms. The descriptions were always precise and incisive. They were followed by diagnosis. If the surgeon was to treat the patient then the treatment to be administered was described in full details. Finally the examination of mummies have revealed traces of surgery for example the jaw dating from the oldest kingdom which has two holes bored to drain an abscenss or the skull fractured by a blow from an axe or sword and successfully reset. Moreover, it is known that foreign sovereigns like the Asia prince of Bakhtans, Bacteria or cambyses himself brought into Egypt doctors such like Hypocrites who had access to the library of the Imhotep Temple at Memphis and that other Greek physician later followed his examples.

### (iii) Medicine Invention

In the history of man, ancient Egypt in North Africa made the first and most amazing contribution in medicinal Arena. Historical documents show in details the titles of Egyptian physicians and their different fields of the specialization. One of the most significant personalities in the history of medicine is Imhotep, the vizear architect and physician of king Zozer of the 3rd Dynasty. His fame survived throughout Egyptian ancient history to Greek times. Defied by the Egyptians under the name "Imouths," he was identified by the Greek with "Askelepious", the god of medicine. Infact the Egyptian influence on the Greek world in both medicine and pharmacology was easily recognizable in remedies and prescriptions.

Some medical instruments used in surgical operation have been discovered during excavation in North Africa crediting it with the innovation of the same. Other written evidences of the ancient Egyptians discoveries in medicine are the medical documents such as Ebers Papyrus, the Berlin Papyrus, the Edwin Smith, Surgical Papyrus and many others illustrated the techniques of operation and details that prescribed cures. Among the ailment identified and completely described and treated by Egyptian doctors were gastric disorders, stomach swelling, skin cancer, coryza, laryrogith, againa pectoris, diabetes, constipation, hemorrhoids, bronchitis retention and nicontinue of urine, bilharzias, opthalmia of which have to be combated by medicine.

The Egyptian doctors treated their patients by using suppositories ointments, symps, potious, oils, massage, enemas, poultices and even inhasents, whose user the Egyptians taught the Greek who latter claimed to be the light of the world blindly and fallaciously forgetting that their brainchild and masters were Africans in Egypt. Also among the Egyptians specialist there were veterinarians.

### (iv) Mathematical (Arithmetic, Algebra and Geometry) Inventions

The Egyptian method of numeration, based on the decimal system consisted of Repeating the symbols for number (ones, teashondueths, thousandths) as ½, ¼, 1/3 originated in the myths of the Horus and Seth. Egyptian mathematics may be catogorised under three sub-titles as, arithmetic, Algebra and Geometry. The Greek writers Herodotus and strabo Conari had the view that geometry was calculate the area dof land erode and addition of each year by the flooding of the Nile apparently led them to thie discovery of mathematics. In ancient treatises, the task was first and foremost to provide the scribes with formula that could enable him to find rapidly the are of the fields, the volume of grain in silos or number of bricks required for building projects. The Egyptians perfectly mastered how to calculate the area of triangles of circles, the volume of cylinder of pyramids or trancated pyramids, and that of the hemsphere. The greatest success was the area of a circle.

Knowledge of Geometry proved beyond reasonable doubt in the survey of land which played a significant role in Egypt. There are very many tombs with panitua showing teams of surveyors busy checking the boundary-stone of the fields such that they are no shifted and then measuring with a knotted cord, the fore-runner of our surveyor's chain, the area of the cultivated land.

**(v) Astronomy**

The Egyptian calendar year was divided into three seasons of our months, each having thirty days; the these the whole year had 360 days, five days was added to the end of each year. The Egyptians had corps of astronomers, working under the authority of vizear, whose job was to observe the night sky, to the vising of the stars especially sivius (sothis). To determine the day time hours, which also varied according to the season, the Egyptians need a ghomon, a simplerod planted vertically on a graduated board with a plumbob-line attached. This instrument served to measure the time spent on the irrigation of the fields since the water had to be distributed impartially. They had also water clocks which were placed in their temples. This unfortunately, water links were borrowed and perfected by the Greeks and are the clepsydias of antiquity (MOKHTAR G. 19190).

**(vi) Architecture Invention**

A new phase was started in Third Dynasty (2700 BC-2200BC). This was a period of vital development in the history of Egyptian architecture for it was during this period that the construction of the first complete building in stone was done. This is step pyramid at Sakkara (Saggaars) which forms a part of the huge funerary complex of king Zuzer. Construction of the ascending corridors. The technical knowledge acquired by the Egyptians in construction and irrigation as the result of digging canal and building dykes or dam as manifested itself in other field allied to architecture. The garden design and town planning are other aspects of Egyptians architecture carried out during this period. They had a great zeal for gardens.

**(e) On Their Contributions to Culture**

These include Egyptians contribution in the fields of writing, literature, art and religion. The Egyptians development in hieroglyphic writing in which many of the symbols came from their African environment. They first expressed themselves in pictorial ideograms which were soon formalised into symbols reflecting phonetic sound which in their abbreviated form could be considered as a step toward an alphabetic script.

### (i) Art Invention

In the field of art, the ancient Egyptian expressed their creative ideas in a great many techniques including sculpture, painting relief and architecture. They combined worldly affairs and activities with hope for the after-life and there were particularly expressive in that each was a representation of their belief, that were deeply held.

Statutes and statuettes had relief and tomb painting. They also produced very large numbr of amlets, scavla and seals. Ornamental objects and jewellery were also their innovations.

### (ii) Religion

Religion was one of the philosophical contribution of Egypt to the Modern Civilization. Egyptians in their religion developed a number of theories concerning the creation of life; the role of the natural power; response of the human community toward them; the role of gods and of the kingship; the role of the priesthood in the community; and the beliefs in eternity and life in the world. The particular apparent to the historians is the Egyptian a religion influence in certain Greco-Roman religious objects as can be seen by the popularity of the goddess Isis and her cult in classical antiquity.

In the final analysis, had it not been for the falsehood drama of Greek people and their philosophies, the African Continent would have had a different reputation and would have enjoyed a status of respect among the nations of the world.

What is significantly clear, however, is ther belief in life after death and the concept of judgement of the dead to either go to salvation or to hell all depending on the deed's account when one was alive. A positive correlation between this belief and our Christian belief is intriguing indeed.

A meticulous examination of their philosophy of Theocentric Humanism shows that they believed in Holiness and Perfection. By those two virtues, the Egyptians in The Supreme God without knowing enough who this supreme being was. In doing so, they believed that everyone had a duty to adore and worship his Supreme God and to live and do all that pertains to rightousness if one were to qualify for an everlasting life after death. In addition to this philosophy and its two tied virtues, Egyptians also had a Doctrine of Summum Bonum meaning The Greatest Happiness or The Greatest good based on these four principal virtues viz: Justice, Wisdom, Temperance and Courage, which also dictated every Egyptian to live a holy and perfect way by doing and believing in excellence in all one's undertakings, on the grounds that one's undertakings, on the grounds that one's admissibility to everlasting life will be judged as per one's performance while alive. And that a qualified one would die but one's body would not taste corruption as it would remain intact till the soul comes back after death. This is exactly the reason why pyramids were constructed and leaders treated the governed with full Justice, Wisdom, Temperance and Courage in order to please The Supreme Creator of all.

A leader was always conscious and terribly worried of making any mistakes that would anger The Supreme God and disqualify him from everlasting life.

In her most extensive and intensive study of the global cultures and religions with particular reference to this phenomenon in Egypt, Diane W. Harst <u>Western Civilizaton to 1648</u>, An American Book Works Corporation Project McGraw-Hill Publishing Co. New York (1990) shed the following important light for our better understanding and appreciation of the significant correlation between Christianity and The Old Egyptian religious beliefs:

> "The most significant changes occurred in the realm of religion. The prominence of Thebes led to the ascendancy of its city god, Amun who was merged with RE and worshipped as Egypt's national deith, Amun-Re.
>
> The Egyptians came to believe that a happy after-life was within the reach of everyone. Osiris, the dying and rising fertility god whose rebirth held out the hope of mortality for all, was transformed into the judde of those who could enter the "Field of the Blessed". Moral behaviour and good deeds became the criteria for SALVATION. In general, the lot of masses improved under the Middle Kingdom"

By virtue of this clarity to both the leader and the governed, each leader and non-leader was individually determined to fulfil one's holiness and perfection virtues by doing everything perfectly well in conformity with the virtues of Theocentric Humanism Philosophy and The Doctrine of Summum Bonum.

In other words, each leader and the governed was one's own police and supervisor of one's own behaviour and performance in one's own role, since one was eager to qualify entry into Heaven.

But, a meticulous examination of The Christian Philosophy and Doctrine, we not that each believer is expected by The Holy Scriptures to believe and behave in a manner befitting Holiness and Perfecetion is the one to qualify entry into an everlasting life in The Kingdom of God The Father, God The Son and God The Holy Spirit. This is exactly the sum total of The Teaching of Jesus Christ in conjunction to all prophesies and teaching of Prophets and The High Priests and all other saints (believers) in The Christian-dom.

Therefore, since the two faiths have the same goal though from totally diverse source, the fact is that they are both congruent.

It is, however, very much submitted that the two are diverse from each other from the source point of view, but all this was only due to the fact that Christianity is much more modern and learned than the Egyptian religion of Old Generation.

Because of this age difference, it is self-explanatory why the Old Egyptians worshed idols, while Christianity does not. When Christianity first entered Egypt in the year 01 AD by the entry of The Infant Jesus Christ and His Mother Saint Mary and Joseph insearch for a safe haven in Egypt on The Command of God to His parents, on fleeing from Judea where King Herod wanted to kill Him, the following revelation came to light in Egypt for the Egyptian to begin knowing the essence of The Supreme God they had been yeanning to know but had not yet known and had therefore to remain a hostage to believing in idols:

(1) On entering Egypt and securing an inn for the might, an Egyptian idol that they worshiped happened to be closer to where the inn was. This idol had an Egyptian priest who ministered to it and who, as often as Satan spoke out of it, related the things Satan said to the Egyptians and the neighbouring countries.
(2) But when The Infant Jesus Christ and His parents entered that inn, the town trembled as if there was an earthquarke. For this reason all magistrates and priests of the idols

assembled before that chief idol to inquire into what was the meaning of the quake and whether there was going to be dread or what?[1]

(3) The idol answered them that:

> "The unknown God is come hither, who is truly God; nor is there any one besides him, who is worthy of divine whoship; for he is truly the Son of God."
>
> "At the fame of him this country trembled, and at his coming it is under the present commotion and consternation; and we ourselves are affrightened by the greatness of his power.
>
> And at the same instant this idol fell down, and at his fall the inhabitants of Egypt, besides others ran together"[3]

(4) But the son of the priest immediately ran into the inn; and on finding there the parents whom all others had left behind and forsook due to the fear, this son took one of the infant Jesus Christ's swaddling clothes and put on his head. And presently, the devils came out of him thorugh the mouth and flew away in the form of crows and serpents. Immediately the boy was healed.

(5) And when the father of the of the healed boy saw this miracle, he was exceedingly rejoiced and believed in The True Living God who made the Heaven and The Earth.

Hence, was fulfilled the prophecy which says that

> "Out of Egypt, I have called My son!"[3]

And, hence the beginning of Egypt to first know and believe in The True God to this day; and thus, a significant relationship between Egyptian religion and Christianity and The Modern World Civilization. Obviously, had there not been such potential relations between the two, it is possible that The Infant Jesus and His Parents would not have been commanded by God to flee from Judea and go to Egypt in Africa. God would have to possibly commanded them to go elsewhere. But, since God chose Egypt (Africa) out of all other Countries in the entire world especially those which were very close neighbours to Judea such as Greece, Macedonia, Italy, Syria, Turkey, Saudi Arabia, Iraq, Afganistan and Iran, but instead commanded them to go all way to Egypt which was too far away and where they had to first cross the huddles of

The Red Sea and The River Nile Delta before entering Egypt, it is self-evident that certainly Egypt had something of significant value in The Eyes of God that made our LORD God to zero to Egypt as suitable safe haven for The Infant Jesus Christ and His Parents. And this must be the valid reason why The Sovereign LORD God says:

> "Out of Egypt, I have called my Son!"[4]

But, supposing that this assertion is defective, a nagging question at hand is, "why then did The Sovereign LORD God choose Egypt as a safe haven for the Infant Jesus Christ and His Parents other than any other convenienthy available neighbouring countries to Judea? If The Sovereign LORD God did not see anything of value in these nearby neighbouring countries to Judan, Them to Europe or India which would have been more easily accessible to The Infant Jesus Christ and His Parents than Egypt due to the latter's longer distance and various other constraints? Where were the so-called famous Greece and Macedonia which are all now being cherished as "The Fathers" and "Mothers" of our World Civilization while scientific evidences confirm that all famous Greeks and Macedonians such as Thales, Pythagoras, Socrates, Plato and Aristotle were students of Egypt from where they gained all their learning in Philosophy, Astronomy, History, Biology, Medicine, Political Science, Archtecture, Mathematics, etc. And, that it was soley because of this foreign nous (wisdom and knowledge) which they had gained from this foreign country that put them into trouble on their return back home in Greece and Macedonia where this nous was found and declared antithetical or a nuisance to the culture and religion of these two countries. Thales, Pythagoras, Socrates, Plato and Aristotle had to be put to punishment because of their foreign nous.

But, given that all this account is spurious without any valid scientific content, then the nagging question is why did Greece and Macedonia punish each of these so-called "Fathers" and "Mothers" of Civilization? And, why did the same Greece and Macedonia declare their nous a nuisance and a poision to the culture and religious beliefs of their people.

Further and foremost important, World History reveals that Alexander The Great of Greece and Macedonia came to learn of the amazing hybrid culture and nous of the Egyptian people which had produced his famous nationals such as Thales, Pythagoras, Socrates, Plato and Aristotle during their studentship in Egypt, albeit Thales, Pythagoras, Socrates and Plato had been disowned and punished by Greece and Macedonia due to their love for the foreign nous they had acquired in Egypt.

Alexander had learnt from history, on ascending to leadership of a dominion covering Greece and Macedonia, that it was solely because of this amazing hybrid culture and achievements in science and technology that had attracted the Persian leadership to invade and conquer Egypt. In the words of Diane W. Darst,

> ". . . . At the beginning of the fourteenth century, Egypt was the wealthiest Kingdom in the Near East. Its agriculture, commerce, and crafts thrived although slavery also increased. Its influence extended as far as Cyprus and Crete. Its palaces, temples, obelisks, and tomb paintings were of high quality. The literature of the New Kingdom, such as the magic spells of The Book of the Dead, hymns to the sun, and tales of adventure, was equally distinctive"[9]

Darst further shows that immediately Egypt revolted against its foreign conquest by Assyrian leadership under King Esarhadden who had conquered Egypt in 671 BC and successfully restored its sovereignty and independence from Assyria in 662 BC during the Egyptian leadership of King Ashurbanipal (who is credited as a well brained leader), Egypt did not only restore its independence but also conquered colonized and significantly

> ". . . . advanced Assyria culturally. His fabulous library at Nineveh contained ancient works from all over Mesopotamia.[10]

Thus, it was Egypt's immense leadership and scientific excellence that built the famous old Neneveh City whose diameter was so great that it needed one to walk to the tune of three solid days from one end of the City to another end.

But how did Egypt then fall out of sight in Assyria? Why did it become a victim to Alexander The Great's conquest?

In her own words in response to such questions, Darst notes that first Egypt fell out because of

> ". . . The problems of overseeing such a large realm [for Egypt] increased in magnitude after Ashurbanipal's death (626 BC).[11]

And that no sooner had Egypt fallen out of Assyria due to King Ashurbanipal's death (526 BC) than the Assyrian Empire also fell to a coalition of the Chaldeans and The Medes

Leadership of King Nabopolassar who 14 years ago had liberated the Chaldeans from the Assyrian domination on King Ashurbanipal's death.

The history data further shows that King Ashurbanipal's death in 626 BC, left a too weak leadership in Egypt to manage affairs of a vast empire all way from Egypt to Assyria. This weaknes created too wide open doors and windows for foreign invasion and conquest of Egypt and Egypt's post-colonial spheres of influence in Assyria.

Hence the plot by King Nabopolassar of The Chaldeans to teamup with The Medes to overthrow Mesopotania, Syria and Egypt in 612 BC. And, after that conquest, both Chaldeans and the Modes enjoyed supremacy and a vast wealth of the spoils of their victory from Assyrian, Egyptian and Mesopotamian culture and art.

A century late, The Persian Empire was created by King Cyrus The Great who kept on conquering one nation after another beginning with the Medes, the Lydians 9540 BC in Asia Minor, western coast of Asia Minor, India in Asia and finally Babylon in 538 BC.

After Cyrus death, his son King Cambyses II, added to this Persian Empire Egypt and all parts of North and West Africa by the year 525 BC.

On the death of King Cambyses II in 521, King Darius I, the Great ruled from 521-486 BC. Before his death, King Darius II expanded his Persian Empire to the Far East and maintained his empire's hold over Egypt and the rest of North Africa.

Before Darius death, the Greeks had already noticed significant value of the Egyptian legacy having been the reason why King Cyrus had decreed to his army to be kept intact, which was a departure from the customary practice of military treatment of spoils of the conquered peoples.

Consequently, on defeating the Persian army in 331 BC, Greco-Macedonian army under the leadership of Alexander The Great, the latter's eyes were focused on Egypt first and foremost because of Egyptians' amazing spoils of wealth which the Persians had been lavishing on.

Because of this burning desire for Egyptian cultural glory, Alexander The Great fulfilled his goal by marching into Egypt and conquering it in 332 BC.

But, before the death of King Darius II in 330 BC who had taken cover the leadership then King Darius I The Great on the latter's death in 486 BC, constant schism and blood-letting ensured and prevailed from time to time within the leadership, thereby creating an automatic achilles' spot in the Persian leadership for Alexander The Great to exploit and overthrow its supremacy in Asia Minor.

As a result of all these symptoms of internal political decay in the Persian leadership, Alexander The Great easily attacked and brought the Persian Empire to its end in 331 BC after having done the same to Egypt and total North Africa in the previous year (332 BC).

The most flabbergasting point have to be underscored with regard to Alexander The Great's behaviour upon taking over Egypt and her hybrid cultural legacy is that whereas on taking over Babylon and making it his New Capital for his New Empire consisting of Asia Minor, North Africa and Mesopotania,

(1) He sought and was granted to be crowned as a pharaoh of Egypt, as a sign of his heartfelt appreciation for their extra-ordinary hybrid cultural legacy he had never experienced in all his life.
(2) And, further, on his death on 323 BC in his Capital of Babylon from a short illness of malaria, Alexander The Great left a will sternly demanding that his body must neither be buried in Babylon nor back in his home-country of Greece-Macedonia but strictly in Alexandria, Egypt, (North AFrica)—where his body was carried to and buried according to his own will.

Curiously, one may therefore ask why in Alexandria, Egypt but not in his own mother country of Greece-Macedonia or in his capital of Babylon? And, why washe crowned as a pharaoh of Egypt while he was not an Egyptian?

A succinct answer to all these questions is that his desires were a function of his heartfelt appreciation and esteem of the Egyptians' amazing legacy second to none according to the best of his personal and professional judgement as a World Leader. Hence the significance of Africa to our World Civilization today.

The dishonesty in the publication movement of Greek philosophy become very glaring when we refer to the misconceived fact by foolishly calling the theorem of the Square on the

Hypotenuse a Pythagorean theorem this is to conceal and totally of a right angle triangle being equal to the sum of the squares of the two opposite sides murder truth. It is this and similar acts of purgery that have enslaved Science from advancement for centuries ever since Antiquity as one cannot imagine how the Egyptians could teach Thales, Pythagoras, Socrates, Plato and Aristotle and then, turn around, to be students of their students. It is an illogical.

But as the Bible assures the believers "know the truth and truth will set you free", so, it is the highest time that Humanity is enabled to know the truth about Africa's contribution to the World Civilization as so documented herein in order to liberate Science from the bondage of deceits and purgery.

# CHAPTER V

# Conclusion

This Marathon study brings us to the following wisdom:-

1. It confirms our original working hypothesis gained from Prophet Isaiahs prophesy that the whole earth or Humanity is indeed a perpetual hostage to a thick darkness ever since the time of our patriarch Adam and Eve. (Isaiah 60:2); and that this is why all leaders are also a perpetual hostage to Transparency and Accountability Deficiency Syndrome (TADS)
2. Because of this perennial bondage:-

    (a) Leaders are rebels against their own Maker, The Sovereign Lord who actually chooses and annoints them to their leadership by virtue of their Oath or Ofice and Terms of Reference
    (b) Like these leaders, total Humanity is also a rebel to its Maker
    (c) Unlike an ox or dog that knows, honours and sincerely loves its master; and, unlike an ass which knows and honours its master's crib our conduct, effective Adam's and Eve's generation to our own generation confirms that whereas they verbally claim to be true children of God and that we definitely know and love Him very much, we actually don't ot as per (c) below.
    (d) In as much as we are an offspring of evil leaders and sons of corrupters, our behaviour also confirms that we are also the fathers and architects of the same evil and corruption against our Maker who chooses and annoints our leaders to their respective positions in our political life.
    (e) By virtue of our own acts, we are indeed a people so laden with an instinct for corruption, injustice, murder, self-glorification, self-justification, self-seeeking and all other manifestations of inquity and Bad Governance that we are not indeed

qualified enough to be a worthy homage or clean vessel through which our Creator may love or wish to manifest His Glory on earth. Thus, we are a dry wood, a corrupt planting unfit to be God's planting.

3. The above two compex and complicated constraints in (1) and (2), constitute the backbone root-causes of the perpetual Bad Governance and leadership failures from Adam's generation to our own generation. Also, they are prima facie grounds on (a) why leaders in our generation are intolerant and sometimes hostile against criticisms whenever they are advised that what they are doing is non-productive to the nation; (b) why like Heroid vis a vis the birth of The Infant Jesus Christ in Bethlehem, every political and religious leader automatically becomes paranoid and ready to kill much the opponent whenever he hears or sees any one wishing to stand against them in elections for they love the praise of men in streets more than the praise of God (John 12:43) (c) Why the elightened few whom Socrates called the "Philosopher King", have always encountered serious difficulties including tortures to death from their leaders as it did happen to the same Socrates and Sir Thomas more to enlighten the leaders better on the virtues of Good Leadership and Good Governance.
4. The above constraints are prima facie pointers to the root-causes of not only leadership failure in political life but also of the looming world-wide poverty, diseases, wars, refugee agony, floods, hurricanes, tornadoes, genocide, massacres, and the present Aids epidemic which has not only proved an impossible mystery to all human science but also a major lesson to humanity that our iniquity to God may be so much that we no longer desire any further Grace and Love from Him. This could be the reason why He has locked up that mystery from our possible comprehension otherwise, one must question why, with all this most sophisticated science our generation now has, we have totally failed to understand this mystery of AIDS and its cure!
5. A solution or cure to this darkness is succinctly the aim and justification of the above recommended remedies drawn from the Ancient Egyptian Leadership Genetic Engineering Formula.
6. However, all these remedies should not be misconstrued as strictly good or meant for political leaders only. They are universally good for all of us in our individual life and positions and rights given to usas a free gift by our Almighty Lord, God for it is natural that not all of us have the same positions and talents.
7. Accordingly, it is to each individual to recognize and remember at all times that whatever one does is a manifestation of God's Glory through him or her.

8. In as much as Noah's self-adherence to these remedies qualified him before God as a perfect, honest, faithful, obedient and righteous man worthy of God's abundant Grace to become head of God's chosen remnant of Humanity during the Flood and then God's seed of our present Humanity after the Flood so must it also be equally true that a similar God's Grace to each of us is fully assured provided that we also emulate Noah's paradigm of an exemplary leadership in theory and practice in our life, beginning with both spiritual and political.
9. As God did not compel Noah to believe and carry out evils, no more should a leader attempt to assume that by compelling his followers to do what he knows is not right, he is doing it to the Lord God Himself who gave him the right to life and anointed him to the position he holds. By detaining or killing an innocent person for a just cause of human or civil rights, the leader is doing all that evil to The Sovereign Lord and not to that visible person.
10. Similarly, each individual should also remember that by doing good to others in his position, he is ultimately pleasing nobody but God; and that by doing evil, he is ultimately aggravating nobody but God who gave him a free gift of life and the position in which he is thus acting as a parent, teacher, doctor, professor, fisherman, preacher, lawyer, judge, etc. What our leaders and entire Humanity have been unable to recognize and honour is this existing fact that God has a Covenant with each of us from conception to birth and thoughout our life a covenant of life, peace and success but not a covenant of death, chaos and failures.
11. This covenant is entrusted to each of us in good faith with a view and good hope that we will utilize it well, with dignity, humbleness, loyalty, God-fearing and in keeping with the good judgement in our God given gifts of individual capacities in order to enable our Holy Heavenly Father to gladly manifest on earth the Glory and Power of His Mysteries through us so long as we make ourselves qualified for that noble, duty. But, in reality, are we really qualified as vessels for this Glory?
12. The covenant is not meant to let our Heavenly Holy Father down but to exalt His Glory through our various individual gifts of statuses and talents. Consequently, our failure in our acts to make ourselves justified for their gifts is our own making. It is due to our marginalization of this reality and our arrogance and self-pride by trying to exalt ourselves to God's level.

# PART ELEVEN (B)

## HOW A SIMILAR HUMAN DEFECT IS BEING ELIMINATED TODAY BY BIO-SCIENCE USING GENETIC ENGINEERING METHODOLOGY

In order for one to understand and appreciate well the need and significance of a "Leadership Genetic Engineering" formula in Society, Community, Nation, Country and our Total World today, which is the subject of this book, let us, first of all, understand the meaning and significance of "Genetic Engineering in Man" as a prelude. This will lead us to an easier comprehension and digestion of this subject matter as a starting point in our intellectual safari to our destination.

# GENETIC ENGINEERING IN MAN AS A PRELUDE TO LEADERSHIP GENETIC ENGINEERING

The concept, "Genetic Engineering in Man" refers to a natural process which always takes place (and must actually do so in all normal circumstances) in every human being's life-time. The process begins from one's conception in a mother's womb to one's birth; and continues throughout his/her life time uninterrupted.

A diagnosis of this process shows that the process is a sum total (or a product) of two distinct (exhaustive and mutually exclusive) but positively interdependent sub-engineering processes viz: Biological and Socio-logical Engineering.

While the former is the first of the two and begins before one's birth right at one's conception in the mother's womb and continues throughout one's life time after one's birth in accordance to/with the biological (natural) dictates or constitution inherent in the Law of Nature, the latter (the Socio-logical) one, on the other hand, starts immediately after one's birth by one being introduced to various basic needs essential for one's survival. These needs include baby food (milk) and motherly caressing, etc. as a starting point of the socialization process which, like its counterpart (i.e, Biological Engineering), also continues to take place throughout one's life time. The nature and dynamics of each of the two is detailed below.

## (1) Biological Engineering Process

A Biological Engineering process is a systemic growth/development inherit in one's life in a total compliance with and is constitutionally fixed by the natural dictates of one's Maker. It is inherent, fixed and governed by the Law of Nature. It is completely outside one's personal wish, preferences and powers to alter what has already been biologically determined for him/her to become in Life by that Law. If one has to become a male or female, that fact is already a must. It has already been biologically fixed and, therefore, one has no powers of his/her own to change reality of this biological fact. One's Maker who is also The Supreme Commander of the Total Universe is the final determinant of all Creation. The same Biological Engineering command/dictates also applies to one's race, body, body size and other characteristics relative to the characteristics of other members of one's society. For example, if one is already determined by the Law of Nature to be born white, black, yellow or red, that is already a Must! One has to be born so! It is an already foregone conclusion! It is beyond any one's powers or wishes to change it. And no single soul has any means to alter that given fact! This given is one's sole right totally reserved for one's Maker who is The Supreme Maker of The Total Universe (God). Therefore, any one's presumptuous attempt to tamper with this already biologically given would be a total vanity; and shall be an insult to one's own sanity and wisdom given the fact that this matter is totally restricted to God, and is beyond the province of not only Mankind but also the province of God's Angels.

In sum, this is what is known from the ***Geneticists*** (scientists specialized in genetics) as heredity (i.e., transmission of likeness) in all species whereby each species must beget its own kind in compliance with the Law of nature. It is an automatic bio-genetic engineering process totally free from man's participation. It is a naturally self-executing phenomenon inherent in every species aimed at sustaining a permanent/constant heredity of each species.

However, this does not mean that man cannot and should not attempt or contemplate manipulating this process for positive goals. Man is free to do so provided that and so long as his intervention is not aimed at changing what has already been biologically fixed/determined to become. His freedom to do so arises from and is sustained only when his intervention is to assit in correcting a deformity. Unlike the automatic bio-genetic engineering process governed by the Law of Nature, this is a man-made bio-genetic engineering process by human intervention.

For example, if a couple who may be experiencing difficulties in getting or conceiving a baby, man is free to exploit his Bio-science to assist this couple to conceive in accordance with the following God's commandment contained in the Book of the Genesis chapter 1:26-28:-

> *"And God said, let us make man in our image, after our likeness: and let them have dominion over the fish of the sea, and over the fowl of the air, and over the cattle, and over all the earth, and over every creeping, thing that creeps upon the earth." (Verse 26)*

*"So God created man in his <u>own</u> image, in the image of God created*

*He him; male and female created He them." (Verse 27)*

*"And God blessed them, and God said unto them, Be fruitful, and multiply, and replenish the earth, and subdue it, and have dominion over the fish of the sea, and over the fowl of the air, and over every living thing that moves upon the earth." (Verse 28)*

*"And God saw everything that He had made, and, behold, it <u>was</u>*

*Very good . . . . (Verse 31).*

Thus, in conformity with/to this God's commandment by which man has been blessed above all members of the Animal Kingdom to which man is also one, man's duty has been to first develop his skills in Science and Technology. Using Science, Man has God's blessings <u>to discover the laws of nature</u> that may enhance or empower him to know what to do in life in order to correct a deformity or eradicate a disease and free his Mankind from captivity of this disease.

And, on having achieved this stage of discovery, man now moves on further to stage two, the implementation stage, to exploit this discovery in order to achieve his ultimate goal of life saving stage which is <u>Technology</u>.

These two (Science and Technology) are the only means by and with which man is blessed to use for his survival and intervention in matters of God's province provided that this intervention is solely for correcting a deformity in one's creation or for counteracting a malady (disease) posing a real or potential threat to Human life as is the empirical case today where man is now seriously engaged in scientific research exploring all sources from which a valid and reliable cure of HIV/AIDS disease, that is now terrorizing and killing uncountable number of Human species globally with a total impunity, **may be found.**

Therefore, as we now begin to understand in detail man's Biological Creation which is the first stage of the Genesis of his life, it is very necessary for us to first register one's appreciations to Bio-science experts for their amazing extra-ordinary contributions to Human wisdom and knowledge of this subject, e.g., by Dr. John Brumbaugh, Genetic Engineering: Back To The Bible (1991).

By virtue or on the strength of their useful discovery, we all now scientifically know with joy that man is a product of the union of a sperm and egg cells which, on contact of these two cells, slowly and systematically develop into continuously growing nulti-building bricks-like blocks akin to those blocks used in masonry. These cells are of various types. Each type has its own function. For example, whereas the flat cells resembling tilapia fish scales and mosaic tiles are the ones responsible for the making of our blood vessels called arteries and veins, the cells responsible for making liver, lungs and spleen are totally different. These are normally cube-like cells resembling a sponge and honey bee comb. And, the most intriguing cells are those which are responsible for making our brain.

This type of cells is very unique. The cells are akin to a spider's cobweb consisting of a net-like structure of cells spread out all over our bodies. In the same manner that in the center of a spider's net there is always a spider house in which it (the spider) lives while all around it is a net-work of multi-threads netted together like a fish-net for the purpose of serving that spider as its trap by which it catches its preys for food, the same structure holds true with these net-like cells in our bodies that collectively form the nervous system of our bodies.

But, unlike in the spider-nets system, where each net is independent of the other, in our body system, the nervous system is composed of and is a sum total of a multitude of multi-units of these spider-like nets. Each spider net-end is also connected to the net-end of another spider-like net thereby forming a sum total of multi-billion or trillion spider-like nets with each net originating from one spider-like entry called nucleus. This nucleus is the key to the normal functioning of the nervous system in that it is the governor and director of its net-like ends from itself to the net-like ends of its other neighbor(s) or nucleuses. Consequently, a mutual harmony between and among these multi-neighbouring nucleuses or nuclei is extremely necessary for the normal functioning of our nervous system. Failure of this mutual harmony, obviously an individual's behaviour begins to manifest into a certain abnormal symptom. Many types of such symptoms include madness, foolishness, arrogance, unnecessary outbursts, dictatorial commands, insults, irrational decisions, interference in matters outside one's jurisdiction greed, usur-pation of what actually belongs to others, etc. Under a high power microscope, this network of multi-spider net like cells also resemble long-legged spiders mutually connected to each other using their long-legged ends. This unique biological arrangement throughout our bodies biologically empowers an individual's body to be constantly sensitive and able to feel, discern and tell very well the nature of each object that comes into contact with his body. The individual is, therefore, able to tell whether the object is cold or hot; friendly or unfriendly, hostile or not hostile, peaceful or injurious, lovely or not lovely etc. on the strength of this biological arrangement.

Each long-legged spider-like cell contains a living entity of the individual's life called **nucleus**. This nucleus is embedded in each cell. It is systematically and sensitively wrapped inside each cell. The cell is a container of this nucleus.

A further meticulous examination of the actual material in which this nucleus is wraped shows that this material is a thin thread-like substance or piece christened as DNA (i.e., deoxyribonucleic acid) The examination shows that this DNA is not just one piece or substance. It is a sum total of 46 pieces of different lengths as follows: 23 of the same type and length and 23 also of the same type and length. In other words, each DNA has a total of 23 pairs called <u>Chromosomes</u> in Bioscience.

These chromosomes are a cassette-like materials biologically constituted to work as governors and directors of the development of each fetus. Also, they are biologically constituted to direct the normal functioning of the individual's body from one's infancy to one's adulthood (i.e. throughout one's life time).

But, chromosomes are not biologically empowered to make the information contained in them (like cassette tapes) to come out or materialize or govern or direct the making of an individual. This work is biologically reserved for/to another biological substance in the DNA called **<u>Cytoplasm</u>**. It is this cytoplasm which is empowered to make what is contained in the chromosomes to manifest.

Thus, like a tape recorder, the cytoplasm reveals the contents of the chromosomes public by announcing what the union of the sperm and the egg will actually or supposed to become. It makes manifest whether the union is to be female or male; white or black; tall or short; blond or black hair; etc.

It is this cytoplasm which brings forth or determines various chemicals that make up an individual's body. And, it is these chemicals that biologically direct an individual's behavioral patterns including personality.

The significance of cytoplasm in one's life is that these chemicals emanate from the union of one's father's sperms and one's mother's egg. The father's sperm consists of three (3) feet long thread-like substances called DNA; and the mother's egg also consists of same length of three (3) feet long thread-like substances called DNA.

Both pairs of DNA totaling a six (6) feet long taped substance are stored in the nucleus; and the union of the sperm and egg (i.e. the fertilized egg) always begins to develop into its own unique DNA having copies of some DNA characteristics of both the father and the mother.

As a result of this copying of DNA from both parents, an offspring is born with some appearance and behavioral patterns of both parents. However, the degree of this appearance and behavioural patterns is always determined by the degree of DNA characteristics gained from each parent.

If the offspring's DNA has more DNA characteristics from one of the parents e.g., the mother, the appearance and behavioural patterns of the offspring will automatically also be more akin to those of the mother than of those of its father.

But should the DNA characteristics copied from both or any of the parents prove not that significant compared to the amount of DNA characteristics of the fertilized egg, the offspring's appearance and behavioural patterns will automatically be unique or different from its parents' appearance and behavioural patterns. Thus, whenever the copying of the DNA at fertilization period from the mother is more signinficant than DNA copied from the father, the offspring's appearance and behavioural patterns will also be significantly similar to the mother's appearance and behavioural patterns.

The offspring's appearance and behavioural patterns will only resemble those of the father when the amount of DNA characteristics copied from the father during fraternization is significantly more than DNA characteristics copied from elsewhere.

In the final analysis, it is these DNA chemicals manufactured by the cytoplasm in an individual offspring at the inception (sperm and egg union) period that are biologically responsible for or constitute the making, or the genesis of that offspring's appearance and behavioural patterns in society. They determine the offspring's facial appearance, voice, attitude, expressions, gestures, public relations, etc. Also, they are responsible for the making of that individual's temperance including its level of intelligence, justice, prudence, response (obedience) to one's accepted code of good moral conduct called customs and taboos, transparency and accountability in one's society.

But this process is solely biological without any external influence from one's society. The process is totally and completely nitrogenous. And, it is nitrogenous in that it is governed by the biological constitution also known as the law of nature.

On the other hand, whenever there exists a presence of an external influence, the process ceases to become nitrogenous. It now becomes extrogenous as will be noted in the following social engineering process discourse.

## (2) Sociological Engineering Process

A Sociological Engineering is simply a social creation strictly inherent in Mankind only since unlike in all other members of the Animal Kingdom where each is born with all know-how (technology) on how to survive in life, e.g. how to construct a house, etc, man is born totally ignorant. He has to learn all this from his fellow man. This process is the second stage immediately after the first stage (Biological Engineering). It begins immediately after one's birth continues throughout one's life time through a process called socialization. This process uses various means called Socializing Agents that first start with one's mother and thereafter followed by one's father, baby sitter, peer groups, educational and religious institutions, etc. It is through these agents that one always becomes an intersubjective member of one's society, community, or country in that it is through them that one learns one's language, type of food, eating habit, music, customs, etc. collectively called tradition.

However, in order not to leave any stone unturned, this study employs an Interdisciplinary Approach methodology which consequently enables it to bring into play every relevant discpline that may assist it to unearth everything that must be done so for analysis. By so doing, the book recognizes the significance of Theology to this etiological exploration of leadership failure that has always plunged the innocent Humanity into a sea of agonies.

With the aid of this Theology, the book notes under the Book of the Genesis in Chapter 1 verse 28 of The Holy Bible, that man is the only one out of all other members of the Animal Kingdom who is blessed and empowered by his Creator to

> "Be fruitful and multiply and replenish the earth and subdue it: and have dominion over the fish of the sea, and over the fowl of the air, and every living thing that moves upon the earth."

Further, the book also notes from The Book of The Prophet Hosea under Chapter 4 verse 6 that our Humanity is to blame for all failures and agonies because we seem to be too proud and stubborn by refusing to hearken and make use of the wisdom and knowledge readily availed to our use by our Creator; and finally that this is succinctly the reason man always perishes from even minor and easily preventable curable insecurities.

But in cognizance of these blessings and warning, man has engaged in Science and used it to discover various useful ways and means of enhancing his security over various insecurities in all sectors of life. Also, he has used Technology to translate whatever scientific discoveries he has into some useful tangible and intangible technological goods and services for society as follows:

### (A) In Physical Science

Man's advanced knowledge in Physical Science has aided him very immensely in enhancing himself against various forms of disaster that could have arisen against his chance of survival. Today, the modern man has gained significantly from his scientific and technological revolution that has proved him not only an able creature but also an able creator. His advancement in these two areas for the purpose of his security position in life has advanced him immensely in dignity above the dignity of his counterpart in the Ancient generations and dignity of all other members of the Animal Kingdom. This advantage has also been aided by the on-going increasing advancement in Information Technology (IT) which, has, in turn, also advanced his interdependence between himself and both his nearby and distant neighbors at the end of the earth. It is this revolution in man's life that places the modern man in a high superior position above that of his Ancient counterpart and all other Members of the Animal Kingdom.

In this regard, due to this rise of genetic engineering Era in Physical Science, the modern man is now no longer a village man. He is no more akin to his ancient counterpart who was virtually an island to himself before the modern global communication revolution emerged with the invention of an aeroplane, radio, television and mobile cell phone technology which has, in turn, made it easier and faster for the modern man to communicate with his counterpart at various distances and points than his ancient man was possibly able to do or dream of.

Also, through this obedience to his Maker's blessings contained in The Book of the Genesis in The Holy Bible, the modern man has further exploited his Physical Science talent to advance his victory over various insecurities.

These include, for example, road, sea and aerial transport insecurities that the ancient man was totally unable to manage because of the absence of this science and technology in his life time.

**(B) In Bio-Science**

In Bio-Science like in Physical Science, we also note an amazing victory of the modern man against various biological insecurities. Unlike his counterpart in the Ancient generation, the modern man has advanced immensely in Biological discoveries in total obedience to God's blessings documented in The Book of The Genesis. Chapter 1 verses 26-29. We see the modern man a victor of various man-killer diseases such as Polio, etc. in response to his obedience to God. Today, the modern man has gone into too far heights to create genetic engineering methodology to empower man and woman who are not biologically able to bear children to do so. This methodology was alien to the ancient man, though the latter was able to respond to God's command in the little way he could possibly manage. But, today the modern man has extremely benefited and advanced using this new technology that his counterpart in the ancient times did not have at hand. In his booklet, Genetic Engineering: Back To The Bible (1991), Dr. John Brumbaugh, presents the pros and cons of Genetic Engineering formula used in Bio-Science and how the modern man has extremely benefited from it.

And, in as much as Genetic Engineering has proved an astonishing medical breakthrough with remarkable technological advances occurring at a very fast-paced rate, today this has only been possible by the will and determination of the modern man. He has paid a close attention to God's command contained in the Book of The Genesis directing him to do all that pertains to his abilities to overcome his insecurities. Hence, man's tremendous success in genetic engineering, cryobiology, surrogate motherhood, sperm bank and other many scientific techniques used today by the modern man which have, therefore, given a remarkable relief to mankind in reproductive technology beyond the heights of the ancient man's technology.

And, hence our will and determination in this study to also follow the same path of Bio-science and Physical science counterparts in our efforts to combat the mysteries surrounding Bad Governance which have always led Mankind to untold sorrows of agonies from various forms of conflict such as cold and actual war, terrorism, strikes, etc. that have always erupted as a reaction to Bad Governance as so documented in the World History books, etc.

But, what is Genetic Engineering so far? What does it actually mean? And, how can it also be of some benefit to Humanity in Social Science as it has done in both Bio-Science and Physical Science where the latter has flabbergasting shocked our generation with an amazing revolution in information, transport, weaponry and other various technologies? Can man also benefit from the same particularly in the art of Leadership which has persistently remained a breeding ground of/or wars and other source of blood-shed?

## (3) Genetic Engineering in Social Sciences

Before we understand the concept and its function or utility in Social Science to man, let us first understand it in Bio-Science, where it first originated and how and why it has successfully proved very useful to Mankind from one generation to the other.

### (A) Genetic Engineering Concept

The concept "Genetic Engineering" is a Bioscience discovery or invention. In Bioscience, it is understood as both a phenomenon and a process. As a phenomenon, it is a man's discovery in Bioscience by Scientists for the purpose of mankind an improvement of life. And as a process, it is the cutting, mixing and splicing of DNA to produce a desired effect in a micro-organism, plant, animal or human being.

The DNA is an abbreviated word or name of/for another discovery in Bioscience known in full as "deoxyribonucleic acid." It is a computer-like tape of all living things that govern or directs the development, growth, function and dynamics of an organism. It is the power-house or simply acts as a store house of the nature and manner of the normal functioning of every living organism.

By virtue of its inherent duty according to its biological constitution, it is the sole determinant of whether an organism must be male or female, and its colour, size, etc. In human nature (being) DNA determines and directs one's form whether one must be tall or short, slim or obese, blond or dark-haired, blue or bad eyed, long or short nose etc. DNA role does not stop at those physical characteristics or nature of an individual. It also determines and directs the individual's behaviour and attitude. For example, it determines and directs whether one is/must be humble or not, arrogant or not, a liar or not, dishonest or honest, just or unust, a thief or not, hot tempered or cool tempered, loyal or disloyal, friendly or unfriendly, loud mouth or discent, hyena-like or mindful of other's welfare, etc.

As a result, Genetic Engineering methodology has proved a great gain to man globally in various sectors of life by the aid of Bioscience as so noted above. It has benefited Humanity in various ways, e.g. in food production by increasing quality and quantity of food and food supply against hunger insecurity; in genetic disease detection, production and treatment using genetic engineering tools; in reproductive manipulation in order to genetically correct infertility problems; and in many other areas yet to emerge.

However, all this has been as a function of man's positive response to God's blessings availed to him to the effect that he shall be dominant over all other living and non-living creatures on Earth and freely exploit his faculties so that he may become fruitful, multiply and replenish the Earth for the purpose of his own survival (Genesis 1:26-28). And most important of all, this discovery in this study has also been made possible solely because of the study's efforts to resort to an Inter-disciplinary Approach as a methodology which, in turn, has led it to this end. Otherwise, this successful end would not have been a reality.

### (B) Role of Genetic Engineering in Social Sciences

The above account proves beyond any reasonable doubt that in both Physical and Biological Sciences, Genetic Engineering has performed extra-ordinarily well to the advantage of

Mankind. It has served as a reliable and valid vehicle by leading the modern mankind to flabbergasting horizons of achievements, relief and jubilations which the ancient mankind was unable to dream of in those old days. These achievements of relief and jubilations include, for example, victory over various diseases such as ***Hemophilia*** (a hereditary tendency to uncontrollable bleeding) which has by now been well identified, understood and effectively controlled manageably in human beings by genetically engineering the defective blood clotting chemical among the clotting chemicals called **Factor III** so that a defective blood chemical may once again begin functioning normally.

In view of these facts in both Physical and Biological Sciences, and whereas Social Science is also a Science sue generies in Academia, it is self-evident that Genetic Engineering methodology in Social Science is also possible. If applied, it can transform the existing Leadership Culture genes that do determine and control/direct the nature, functioning and dynamics of that leadership culture from its existing defective abnormal nature **of Malleadership (Malgovernance)** characterized by Anthropocentricism and Summum Malum (Happiness of only The Fittest (i.e., the haves at the expense of the multitude Have-nots) to its corrected normal nature of Good Leadership (Good Governance) characterized by Theocentricism and Summum Bonum (Happiness of all in Society, Community or Country).

Thus, since Leadership in Humanity is consequently a human attribute in that it is a role played by a human being, it, therefore, also follows that leadership is a human nature made of human character. And the more it is also human in nature, then it is also determined and directed by a computer like tape called DNA that determines and directs development, functioning and other natures of leadership in society.

In this regard, it is up to those social chemicals biologically inherent in an individual playing the role of a leader over others that also determine and direct him and all his decisions, policies and policy-making and inplementation processes.

Consequently, whenever one of a leader's social chemicals which are directly responsible for his normal functioning of his official duties, e.g., in policy decision making and implementation is for some reason or another defective, e.g because of the absence of a sufficient degree of rationality, obviously that leader's acts in those functions will also be defective. This situation is called "**mal-leadership**" meaning that the leader's behaviour in those processes is not normal. It lacks rationality. And, when it lacks rationality then it must be devoid of justice and all wisdom likes to lead it to justice in keeping with God's commandment contained in II Book of Samuel Chapter 23 verses 2-4: ***"He that rules over men must be just; Ruling in the fear of God . . . ."***

A Clinical Diagnosis of such situation (or mal-leadership) is subject to show pathological symptoms of angry outbursts, arrogance, name-calling on one's subordinates; dictatorship manifested in the leader's tendency to force his/her decision or wishes down the throat of evey one without any regard to their intellectual contribution and human rights as also officers entitled to providing suggestions or criticisms; and boisterous boastings that one is everything and all others are nothing to his/her; etc. Any question by a subordinate to seek a candid explanation on a matter is shouted at and quickly shot down or placed under the carpet; any criticism to such leader's directive is quickly judged wrong, malicious and therefore worth an arrest and detention order to the author on spot. The author may as well be hanged without trial. And if with trial, the trial must be a Kangaroo one totally naked of justice since any attempt to use a just trial may lead to acquittal of the accused.

Empirical cases in support of this mal-leadership problem abound globally and are found in every generation. The most classic ones include, for instance, the King Henry VIII case against Sir Thomas Moore (1478-1535)—an innocent English statesman who was mercilessly apprehended and put through a Kangaroo trial by King Henry VIII who finally put that statesman to death without any iota of a just case against him (Sir Thomas Moore). But an Etiology of the King's pathological state confirms beyond any reasonable doubt that the King was not mentally sound. And that whereas it was neither a secret nor malice against his pathological state no one in his dominion (England) was able to remove him from the throne since hereditary mode of leadership is also controlled by a Kangaroo leadership selection. This defect consequently led to leadership poverty disaster in that country. The data on the case is loud and clear against the King and the nature of his leadership. Because of his mal-leadership, the King was acutely angry with Sir Thomas More simply because of the latter's refusal to support/endorse the King's wishes to divorce his matrimonial wife and marry a widow of his brother who had just passed away, while the King knew very well that his wish was against the Roman Catholic doctrine to which he and the whole England also prescribed in those 15th Century days.

But, had this Genetic Engineering dose been known and administered to the King, obviously Sir Thomas More's life would have been saved. The King would have seen the light and realized his faults, mistakes or wrong doings against both the Roman Catholic doctrine and Sir Thomas More's stand (refusal to support the King). But this mal-leadership disease was not unique to King Henry VIII. It also holds true to most leaders effective the time of our Patriarch Adam and Matriarch Eve to the present.

This is why most leaders of the Kingdom of Ancient Israel also failed. And, the same situation also held true with respect to all failed leaders globally. These include Napoleon Bonaparte (1769-1821); Adolf Hitler (1899-1945); Benito Mussolini (1883-1945); and leaders of Independent Africa whose promises on oath during the struggle for independence later came to mean absolutely nothing of value to them Leaders such as Jomo Kenyatta, Daniel Toroitich arap Moi and Mwai Kibaki in Kenya are classic examples of this paradox. They (together with many others such as Moise Tsombe, Joseph Kasavubu and Mobutu Sese Seko in Congo for example) became betrayers of their own Continent by ignoring their vows on oath all trashed away their vows into the dust bin and began engaging in corruption and dictatorship to satisfy their greed and animus dominandi by even killing their critics in order to remain free and maximize their greed at the expense of the poor tax payers. This is exactly the reason the Continent of Africa is still embedded in a cobweb of agaonies of conflict, coups 'd etat, terrorism and many other symptoms of underdevelopment and dependency.

### (C) Correlation Between Socio-Genetic Engineering and Bio-Genetic Engineering

Whereas the ultimate goal of Bio-Genetic Engineering is to save life by undertaking every scientific and technological discovery incention and innovation to cure and prevent a defect problem in life, so is the same goal for Socio-Genetic Engineering. In the preceding discourse, we have noted with concern how the most innocent Sir Thomas More (1478-1535) who was later consecrated into a Saint was executed by King Henry VIII for no valid reason other than due to the King's pathological state of mind that no one in his dominion of England was ready to recognize, and oppose in order to save the life of the innocent but helpless defenseless statesman that was later anointed as a Saint by the Church.

An on the strength of our Interdisciplinary Approach adopted for the sole purpose of this Study, we noted that in order for the Study to prove exhaustive and thorough, it must also employ Theology among other disciplinary methods such as Psychology, Sociology, Socio-Psychology, Psychoanalysis, Psychiatry, Abnormal Psychology, Abnormal Politics, etc.

In this regard by using Theology, we come across a famous Biblical case of Nineveh. When that country had proved too filthy and, therefore, totally intolerable to God due to its wicked ways of Homo Sexualism and Homosexuality, God also resolved to destroy it from the face of the earth in the same manner He had done to the two Ancient Palestinian Cities of Sodom and Gomorrah in the plain of Jordan during the generation of our Patriarchs Abraham and Lot and Matriarch Sarah between the year of 2000 BC and 1950 BC.

But, the data further shows that when this flabbergasting threatening new reached both the King and his Ninevian subjects from God's messenger Prophet Jonas, whom God had by virtue of His Law of Natural Justice, sent to warn them on the matter, all of them were overwhelmed with awe; and desperately decided to repent and renounce their wicked ways. They did so en mass so that they may be saved from this real danger that they knew had in the past already destroyed Sodom and Gomorrah cities from the face of this Earth planet.

The Holy Bible. Which is the primary source of the data on this situation, further shows us that as a result of this en mass act by both the King and his subjects, certainly they were all forgiven and their City was never destroyed. The City was saved and spared.

The key lesson learnt from this situation worthy our objective in this Study is the action of the King, in his capacity as the leader of the people of Nineveh. Like his own subjects, he was also engaged in wicked ways. Consequently, his leadership was dented, dirty and, therefore, naked of justice and all other virtues of good leadership in Nineveh. It disobeyed God's commandments envisaged under II Book of Samuel Chapter 23:2-4 which stipulates that "***He that rules over men must be just; Ruling in the fear of God***".

But since the King was rational and observant enough to discern the forthcoming danger, he immediately agreed to correct his mistakes as soon as he learnt of this warning from God through the Prophet that he must repent and get out of his unjust ways if he were to survive. By so doing, it is self-explanatory that the King's acceptance to undergo this self-social transformation was, in the final analysis, a Socio-Genetic Engineering process.

It was only because of his willingness to undergo this process that he was able to save both his life and the life of his leadership in Nineveh.

But Genetic Engineering in Biological Science means cutting, mixing and splicing of DNA to produce a desired effect in a micro-organism, plant, animal or human being.

Therefore, in Social Science, this repentance by both the King and all his subjects in Nineveh must also have been none other than an explicit act of Genetic Engineering in Social Science. It must have been so because, like Genetic Engineering in BioScience already detailed above, the act of repentance alone led to a healing and recovery of the King's nation of Nineveh from its defects and likehood of utter destruction by God. **This healing and recovery must therefore have been a function of a social surgical cutting, mixing and splicing of the defective character of the King and his subjects with a view to removing the defective part(s) and replacing these parts with totally new good (normal) part(s) onto the whole social character of both the King and his Ninevian subjects.**

Therefore, the meaning and significance of this process is simply that it is a social chemical in a Socio-Genetic Engineering process designed to provide a desired surgical remedy to one's ill/defective social character so that one may now begin to live a normal life (behaviour) in the same manner a **biological chemical** is also expected to do to an individual's defective life in Biological Engineering process.

Similarly, in another famous case already noted above between King Henry VIII of England and Sir Thomas More, it is also evident that by virtue of the latter's innocence, he should not have been sentenced to execution by the King. He was executed simply because the King was psychologically defective. But, had the King been able to have an access to this Socio-Genetic Engineering process using, psychiatry or any other relevant Social means, this action would have saved the King's leadership from this unjust decision. It would have healed the King's leadership by surgically removing the defective part of the King's social chemicals and replacing the defect with a correct (normal) one. This would, in the end, have corrected the King's social chemicals and character in decision-making. And, the King would, therefore, have been made by this process to be born-again and begin right away to discern correctly what is just and what is unjust in his leadership with regard to the case of not only Sir Thomas More but also to all other cases. Sir Thomas More would not have had a case to answer.

A further examination of the role and goal of the law enforcement entities such as the Judiciary, Police Force, Prisons, Prosecution, etc, using Criminology as means, shows a common denominator with the role and goal of social Genetic Engineering process. Each is aimed at cutting, mixing and splicing of the whole social chemicals in order to produce a desired effect in an individual by removing the defect(s) from the social chemical of that individual and replacing it (them) with the correct, normal part(s).

As a sociological study of the nature of crime, criminals, and the punishment that society used to curb criminal tendencies in society, Criminology does not only enable one to understand well these phenomena. Also, and, in the main, it enables one to understand and appreciate the commonality between the role and goal of the Law Enforcement in society on the one hand and the role and goal of Socio-Genetic Engineering processes on the other which is to bring about a correction of systemic defects in a society or individual. And since both Law Enforcement and Socio-Genetic Engineering mean the same thing with regard to their ultimate aim, then their significance to life in society is as extremely essential as the significance of a Bio-Genetic Engineering is to life in Society. Both are related forms of genetic modification since they are specifically concerned with genetic defect corrections from an abnormality to a normality which is, therefore, totally different from the other forms of genetic modification such as genetic transformation and counseling of one who is interested in being genetically changed from a certain form in life such as a male gender to a female gender, and also mentally changed on how to live in peace with such new life.

In this regard, the form of Genetic Engineering that is relevant to our ultimate goal in this intellectual expedition in search of Leadership Failure correction, is succinctly a Socio-Genetic Engineering because of its abilities to surgically remove those defects inherent in our Society's Social chemicals responsible for misleading a leader to engage into unjst tendencies that consequently conflict with standing policies and laws expected to protect and promote sanctity of life of every individual in keeping with a leader's oath of office and terms of reference bestowed upon him/her during his installation in the Leadership (as a leader) by his people; and also in keeping with God's commandments envisaged under II Book of Samuel 23:2-4 that stipulates as follows:

**"He that rules over men <u>must</u> be just, ruling in the fear of God.**

**And he <u>shall</u> be as the light of the morning, when the sun rises, <u>even</u> a morning without clouds; <u>as</u> the tender grass springing out of the earth by clear shining after rain."**

However, this does not mean that Genetic Engineering efforts condone what the disciples of Capitalism believe in and are always obsessed with for the purpose of their capital accumulation at the expense of the have-not's by exploiting Bio-science to manufacture for them marketable destructive chemicals such as Phthalates found in vinyl flooring, plastics, soaps, toothpaste; Bisphenol found in babies' bottles and food can linings, mobile phones, computers and pesticides such as pyrethroids, liuron, vinclozin and fenitrothion; etc. so that they may use their proceeds to become filfthy wealthy without any due regard to the immoral consequences of such chemicals.

From the recent study findings by a leading Bio-technology researcher, Prof. Richard Sharpe, based at Britain's Medical Research Council, London, immoral consequences of such chemicals include soaring rates of birth defects, testicular cancer and falling sperm counts. According to this scientist, "some cosmetics and soap used by pregnant women have the potential to 'feminize' male fetuses during the formative stage in the world". He further adds that "Chemical cocktails [do] block the male sex hormone testosterone, or [simply] mimic the female sex hormone oestrogen". Thus, although Mankind is protected by nature, obviously nature cannot tolerate such misconduct by man!

Astonishingly further, other related studies also add that whereas "lead is not banned, World Health Organization (WHO) allows certain levels of lead substances to be legally used in cosmetics knowing very well that lead and mercury used in cosmetics for skin lightening not only lead to a real danger of kidney destruction but also to a potential danger to women's children life. The same danger is also real in pesticide and herbicides chemicals leading to serious abnormalities particularly in male reproductive health with obvious symptoms of penis malformation and testicular cancer disease. (Elizabeth Mwai "Why Baby Boys Are Turning into Girls" ***THE STANDARD***, Nairobi, Friday May 15, 2009).

Such irresponsible misuse of Science and Technology such as using hormone disrupting chemicals for a mere selfish purpose of making oneself filthy wealthy with a total impunity of World Leadership is contrary to the ethical concept of Science and Technology being appealed to/for in this Study to assist Mankind with a solution to the on-going global danger of Leadership Failure.

Obviously, this dangerous application of Science and Technology with a total impunity of the World Leadership which is expected to be a Custodian of Humanity is an insult to the unique blessing bestowed unto man alone by his Creator explicitly documented in The Book of The Genesis in The Holy Bible, Chapter 1:29 which empowers man alone to use all other members of his Animal Kingdom as well as all members of the Plant Kingdom for his food and other purposes of his survival. But no where do we find any source of data blessing man to exploit Science and Technology for the purpose of his self-destruction as so erroneously purpoted by the proponents of Political Realism beginning with Niccolo Machiavelli, Charles Darwin et al. Hence the urgency of this call for a Leadership Genetic Engineering Formula contained in this Volume II.

## References

Anderson, Kriby, Genetic Engineering: The Ethical Issues, Zondervan Publishing House, Grand Rapids, Missouri, USA (1982).

Brumbaugh, John, Genetic Engineering, Back to the Bible, Lincoln, Nebraska, USA 68501, (1991).

Sanxhez, Vincente and Juma, Calestous, eds. Biodiplomacy: Genetic Resources and International Relations, Acts Press African Centre for Technology Studies, Nairobi, Kenya (1994).

Kipkorir, B.E., Imperialism and Collaboration in Colonial Kenya.

Achebe, Chinua, The Good, The Bad And The Greedy.

Ramsey, Michael, Ethics, Governance and Reasoning, Fountain Publishers, Kampala (1963).

# PART TWELVE

## CONFLICT VACCINATION FORMULA: A Path to a Hybrid Culture of Peace, Democracy and Good Governance and Accelerated Socio-Economic Recovery and Development in Africa and Total World.

# A PREAMBLE

The aforegoing research marathon efforts envisaged in Volumes One and Two is an etiology of the mysteries which according to the findings, have always been responsible for continual failure in the art of leadership effective the generation of our Patriarch Adam and Matriarch Eve to our own generation.

Throughout this marathon, the research ultimate goal has always been to do all that pertains to what must now be done in order to save this and our succeeding generations from the scourge of various forms of man-made disasters and shame caused by man's endless failure in his art of leadership globally.

In order to do so, it was necessary to resort to and use an interdisciplinary approach on the strength of its high power lens and batteries able to shed enough light on those mysteries for this researcher than what unidisciplinary approach is capable of doing due to its lower power lens and batteries.

Hence, the discovery and submission of this CONFLICT VACCINATION FORMULA in this Phase Thirteen for the benefit of our World Community that has always been besieged and terrorized by conflict, poverty, kleptocracy, dictatorship, totalitarianism, and other various symptoms of Leadership Failure disease that has always besieged and terrorized Humanity from the Antiquity to the present.

Its vision is succinctly to serve our Humanity in its capacity as an axis of wisdom and knowledge towards a genuine lasting peace and stability which is a prerequisite condition for an assured socio-economic recovery and accelerated development needed by Humanity.

Its vision and mission is to prove to Humanity that it is a valid and reliable roadmap toward a prosperous destiny of abundant milk and honey akin to the Biblical Canaan.

And, its justification is manifested in the fact that it is not a newly invented idea without any prior prima facie evidence of success. Rather, it is to prove beyond any reasonable doubt that it is a discovery of an already existing discovery of the Ancient Egyptian Peoples who first discovered and successfully used it over 3000 BC to lead their Country into a Hybrid Culture characterized by empirical evidences of various areas of abundant security in food, health care, intellectualism, science and technology, good leadership, etc.

As a result of their individual and collective obedience to this Formula from top-bottom-top (i.e., vertically and horizontally) without any qualms by any one due to one's socio-economic or political status, these People of Ancient Egypt found themselves in a destiny of a flabbergasting abundance of prosperity in every sector of life. And, due to this new development and because of their obedience and use of this CONFLICT VACCINATION FORMULA, the Ancient Egyptian People became so extra-ordinarily shining, splendid and immaculate over all others in both the Mediterranean and Asia Minor Regions in all areas of life that they were regarded by their neighbours in those regions as a flabbergasting rare species.

Because of this, a formula, these actual amazing developments emerged:-

(1) Their Country became a safe haven for a host of desperately starving foreigners fleeing their famine stricken countries. These included, for example, our Patriarch Abraham (2000-1850 BC) and his wife Sarah; and his grand son Jacob (1800-1700 BC) and Family who followed on later after Abraham's death in 1850 BC.

(2) Their Country became a safe haven for foreign students from the Mediterranean and Asia Minor Regions in search of the most extra-ordinary rare wisdom and knowledge that had become evident to those Regions. These students included, for instance, Thales (640-546 BC), Pythagoras (582-497 BC), Socrates (427-399 BC), Plato (427-347 BC), Aristotle (385-322 BC), to name but only a few.

(3) Also, their Country became such a darling of all in those two Regions. For instance,

    (a) The Persian Leader, King Cyrus the Great (600-529 BC) desperately sought to have it after occupying the entire Mediterranean, Asia Minor and India but died in 529BC before making his ends meet.

    (b) His son, Cambyses II, who took over the leadership from his father also so craved for the same Egypt and its amazingly immaculate legacy that he eventually managed, to succeed in 525 BC but was, however, summarily slained three years later while on his way home in Babylon Capital from Egypt.

(c) His successor, King Darius, also hardly prevailed before he was toppled in 332 BC by another power hungry Greeco-Macedonian Dominion under Alexander The Great, son of King Philip of Macedonia, who, after occupying Egypt and its legacy, completely defeated Persia and took over the latter's Babylon Capital, in 331 BC.

(d) Obsessed and overdriven by a hyper-appetite for this most amazing Egyptian legacy which he had never heard of before, Alexander the Great proved so hungry for these legacies that he was like a hungry hyena. For instance

(i) although, by virtues of having inherited the throne of his father (King Philip) as King of Greeco-Macedonia Kingdom, and was accorded the Greeco-Macedonian traditional divine title of "SON OF PHILIP" the King, Alexander The Great renounced that title on occupying Egypt and forced the People of Egypt to grant him their traditional divine title of "SON OF AMMON" the priestly title of Pharaoh, which was equivalent to a name of a little god that had to be worshed by all in Egypt.

(ii) Also, Alexander The Great did away with his Greeco-Macedonian royal attire and began wearing the Egyptian attire used by the Pharaohs. Thus, he was no longer a Greece-Macedonian but an Egyptian.

(iii) And, as that was not enough, Alexander The Great moved his father's Royal Palace from Macedonia to both Babylon and Alexandria, respectively; and, hardly went back home in Greece and Macedonia. Thus, he fell in love with Egyptian Hybrid Culture that he became married to it and forgot his Greeco-Macedonian Motherland.

(iv) And becaue of this rare legacy of a Hybrid Culture character, Alexander The Great made a vow that whenever and wherever he died, his body must be carried all way to Alexandria and buried there. This was done so; and his tomb lies not in Greeco-Macedonia or Babylon but in Alexandria as a result of the effect of the CONFLICT VACCINATION FORMULA on the Ancient Egyptian People which had transformed them into a people of an extra-ordinary legacy that flabber-gasted not only Alexander The Great but also every one in the Mediterranean, Asia Minor and Persia Regions in those Ancient Days.

In the final analysis, the above prima facie evidences of the significance of CONFLICT VACCINATION FORMULA to a people, country or nation is not all. They are just a tip of the iceberg. A list of its significance is quite endless; and would require volumes of books to exhaust them all. For example, the Hybrid Culture led to its development gave birth to a host of unbelievable unique amazements. The culture gave birth to a most rare physician called IMHOTEP who The World Book Encyclopedia, Vol. 10, p. 67 calls

> "an Egyptian physician, honoured in medicine as the first physician known by name. He lilved about 2700 B.C., and served as vizier (prime minister) to King Zeser of the third Egyptian dynasty. His name became so great that after his death, the Egyptians elevated him to the status of a god and worshiped him for his healing powers. The Greeks indentified him with their own god of healing, Aesculapius. Temples were built to Imhotep, and bronze statuettes of him have been preserved. A statue of him stands in the Hall of Immortals in the International College of Surgeons in Chicago, [USA]".

Obviously, *The World Book Encyclopedia* cannot tell tales. Dr. Imhotep was so much gifted and trained by The African Mysteries System at The Grand Lodge of Luxor using CONFLICT VACCINATION FORMULA that he emerged as the most unique black Egyptian physician the World at large had ever witnessed. And, the evience by *The World Book Encyclopedia* confirms that he lived over 2000 years before the Greek doctor, Hippocrates, ever lived. In this regard, the evidence confirms the truth that Hippocrates is not the actual father of medicine as the Academia has always purported[2]. Also, the evidence proves what is written in the *Book of Hosea* at 4:6 that mankind always perishes not only because of his lack of wisdom and knowledge but also because of his disobedient attitude towards any truth. Man has a notorious attitude to despise and reject wisdom and knowledge.

Thus the tragedy of man. His notorious tendency to conceal such a useful formula from his Humanity throughout the ages up to today has, in the final analysis, enslaved Humanity to a sea of agonies of a perpetual underdevelopment.

However, this tragedy has neither been unique nor a work of the ordinary unlearned. It has always been a function of a mischief of the learned having a notorious intent of deliberately concealing every truth that must be concealed at all costs. This is also evidenced by the concealment of inter alia the true authorship of those 1000 books claimed in the Academia to have been authored by the tutor of Alexander The Great, Aristotle—the books he did not actually author according to prima facie facts[3] available in Academia but totally ignored thereby forcing Humanity to believe in myths as evidenced by the issue of the case as who between Imhotep and Hipocrates is the true "Father of Medicine". And, as that was not enough, other endless efforts have always been exerted to mercilessly attribute or credit the ancesterial roots or links of the Ancient Egyptian to Europe with an argument that this Ancient Egyptian was of a caucasoid but not of a Negroid nature. The ulterior aim has always been to conceal truth, since Africa has always been too under-rated to be allowed to be known as a mother of such legacy.

At this point, one may now rightly and correctly ask where this legacy went; and who may, therefore, be responsible for this disaster.

In the aforegoing account, we have demonstrated with prima facie facts how the legacy so much attracted every one in the neghbouring Regions of the Mediteranean, Asia Minor and Persia. And, how these neghbouring Regions reacted to Ancient Egypt and its legacy.

Therefore, on the questions where the legacy is today; and if dead, what may have caused its death, the following account is in order.

Persian invasion of Ancient Egypt followed with by the Greeco-Macedonian invasion in 333 BC-331BC, each scrambling for the famous Egyptian glory did not end with Persia-Greeco Macedonian scramble. The scramble also attracted the Romans, who, as will be noted here below, became responsible for the demise of the Ancient Egyptian legacy.

In order to gain enough military capability to oust Greeco-Macedonian supremacy over Egypt so that Rome may become the new master of the legacy, the Romans first unified the Italian peninsula into a confederation of allies. Then, as a united force, and in a seires of wars, Rome conquered Sicily, Sardinia, Corsica, Spain, Macedonia, Greece and parts of North Africa and Asia[5]. Specifically, in 146 BC Macedonia and Greece were added to the Ancient Roman Empire thus giving Rome the military right of possession over the Ancient Egypt and its glory. But through the imperial edicts of this Ancient Roman Emperors viz: Theodosius in the $4^{th}$ century, AD, and Justinian in the $6^{th}$ century A.D,[6] Ancient Rome abolished the author of CONFLICT VACCINATION FORMULA, The African Mysteries System of the Grand Lodge of Luxor, which had discovered and promoted this formula that led Ancient Egypt to the development of its Hybrid Culture of this flabbergasting legacy. Rome took this action against the Mysteries on the excuse that the mysteries was promoting a Hybrid Culture using a Theocentric Humanism Philosophy that emphasized the virtues of Perfection and Holiness for every Ancient Egyptian to recognize and use in one's daily life from the Pharaoh's leadershiop right up to the ordinary common man. As a reinforcement to this Theocentric Humanism Philosophy, the Mysteries had also developed a doctrine of *Summum Bonum* that ment "the greatest welfare for all in society. The doctrine had inter alia the following virtues: Justice, Prudence (wisdom), Temperance and Courage which every Ancient was always expected to adhere to throughout one's life and undertakings.

Each was sensitized on the significance of this Philosophy and Doctrine vertically and horizontally (from the Pharaoh leadership to the Grass-roots) by the Author of this Philosophy and Doctrine. The African Mysteries System of The Grand Lodge of Luxor; and encouraged to accept and believe that by living such a life one would automatically qualify for a rite of passage to Eternity upon one's death. Both the Pharaoh and every ordinary Ancient Egyptian had this common belief/faith. And, it was becaue of this faith that pyramids were constructed in Ancient Egypt and publicly used as royal safe havens for the bodies of dead Pharaohs awaiting return of their souls at a later date. And, each Pharaoh and his royal family members did all they could to keep themselves perfect and holy. The Pharaoh in particular morally and spiritually disciplined himself so much on the requirements of the virtues of that Philosophy and Doctrine that his acts were conceived divine. This act was so perfect and holy that he was perceived as a god by his Ancient Egyptian subjects. He was therefore, universally accepted as an intercessor between them and their sun-god "Ra" also known as "Re". In the final analysis, both the Pharaoh and his subjects had a national duty to undergo this process of DEITIFICATION OF MAN in order to be deemed Egyptian.

Hence, the anger to Rome to dismantle that faith which, according to Rome, was antithetical and therefore a threat to the Toman Catholic Faith, in which the Pope is spiritually believed to be the real intercessor between the believer and God.

And, as a result of these two imperial edicts of Emperor Theodosiks in the 4$^{th}$ Century AD and Emperor Justification in the 6$^{th}$ Century AD., the CONFLICT VACCINATION FORMULA and its two vehicles viz: Theocentric Humanism Philosophy and The Doctrine of *Summum Bonum* were officially terrorized and forced to wither away. And the more the Formula and these vehicles withered away, the more the Ancient Egyptian HYBRID

CULTURE of a rare legacy that the neighbouring countries of the Mediterranean, Asia Minor and Persia Regions had never heard of before, also withered away on the face of North Africa. Thus, a disaster to mankind's roadmap to a HYBRID CULTURE of an immense prosperity that had been discovered by man's creativity in North Africa during the Antiquity,[7] and which is therefore being strongly prescribed to our generation by this Volume Two.

## FOOTNOTES

1. R. Lane-Fax, The Search for Alexander, Little Brown, Boston (1980), p.388, and p. 408;and Diane W. Darst, Western Civilization to 1648, McGraw-Hill's College Review Books, McGraw-Hill Publishing Co., N. Y. 91990), p. 98. also, see Innocent C. Onyewuenyi, The African Origin of Greek Philosophy: An Exercise in Afrocentrism, University of Nigeria Press, Nsukka, Nigeria 91993) pp. 155-156.
2. Innocent C. Onyewuenyi, op.cit p. 51. Also, see: George G. M. James, Stolen Legacy: The Greeks Were Not the Authors of Greek Philosophy But the People North Africa Commonly called the Egyptians, Philosophical Library New York, 1954; and The World Book Encyclopedia, Vol. 10, p. 67.
3. William T. Stace, Critical History of Greek Philosophy, St. Martin's Press, New York (1969), p. 253.
4. Innocent C. Onyewuenyi, op. at. Pp. 70.82.
5. Diane W. Darst, Western Civilization To 1648, McGraw-Hill's College Review Books, McGraw-Hill Publishing Company, N. Y. (1990), pp. 112, 147.
6. George G. M. James, op. cit., p. 154.
7. But, given from the aforegoing account, that it was black African who invented the idea of putting up an African Mysteries System of the Grand Lodge of Luxor during the Ancient Egypt which turned out to be the ony existing institution of higher learning during those days, and which, in fact, became a man's vehicle for transforming the Ancient Egyptian people into a people of a HYBRID CULTURE of an unique immaculate legacy that every one in the neighbouring Regions of The Mediterranean, Asia Minor and Persia began scrambling for, how can it be possible that the same inventive African of all times can be judged "DAFT" as a Nobelist and pioneer gene scientist, Dr.James Watson, so contends (The Sunday Nation, Nairobi, November, 4, 2007)? If he were that daft, who was this IMHOTEP, the only celebrated world physician of all times? Was he not a black African too? But, Watson is not the only one. He is just one of those with such negative attitude about an African.

An 18th Century German romantic philosopher, George Wilhelm Friedrich Hegel (1770-1831) is also another one on an endless list. Although he never set foot in Africa but only gained his view about Africa from missionaries, also contends that

> "The Negro . . . . exhibits the natural man in his completely wild and untamed state . . . . There is nothing harmonious with humanity to be found in this type of character [African]. (Hegel, The Philosophy of History, Willey Book Co. N. Y. (1944), p.a.)

And, from among those missionaries that were a source of Hegel's account about an African, Rev. W. N. Bently, we also find the following similar judgement:

> "An African whether Negro or Bantu, does not think, reflect or reason, if he can help it. He has a wonderful memory has great powers of observation and initiation, much freedom of speech, and very many good qualities; he can be kind, generous, affectionate, unselfish, devoted, faithful, brave, patient and perservering; ***but the reasoning and inventive faculties remain dormant.*** He readly grasps the present circumstances, adapts himself to them and provides for them; but a careful thought-out plan or a clear piece of induction is beyond him". (Bently, Pioneering on the Congo (1900), p. 256. Also, in Lucien Levy-Bruhl, Primitive Mentality, A. M. press, Inc., N. Y. (1978) pp. 27-28.

Therefore, if this were so as Hegel, Bently, Dr. Watson and many others with such negative judgement about an African, the nagging question to be answered by the same judges, is **how on earth was the same African able to create a Hybrid Culture with those amazing unique glory in the Ancient Egypt since, antiquity till it was officially terrorized and finally exterminated from the face of the Earth by the imperial edicts of the Roman Emperors viz: Theodesius in the 4th century and Justinian in the 6th century A.D.?**

# CHAPTER 1

## 1. INTRODUCTION

## 1.1 DEFINITION OF CONFLICT VACCINATION

1.1.1 Conflict Vaccination is a new scientific methodology in our Civilization today aimed at paralyzing all conflict viruses present in the body politique of a country that has these viruses, and conferment of immunity to countries yet to be infected.

1.1.2 In this regard, Conflict Vaccination is a brand new concept and innovation in Humanities, Science and Technology

1.1.3 This innovation has come into being as a result of the author's thirty three years of intensive research in both Conflictology and Conflcit Vaccinology defined in 1.1.4. below

1.1.4 Whereas Conflictology herein entails a systematic clinical diagnosis and prognosis of conflict with a view to clearly identifying its pathological root-causes (i.e viruses) and the latter's effects on a society, country, nation or people, Conflict Vaccinology is a study of how these viruses and their pathological effects can be cured and or prevented with a view to restoring the already affected society, country, nation and people from a dysfunctional (abnormal) state to a eufunctional (normal) state.

1.1.5 And, Nosology of Conflict is a scientific classification of conflict into its different specific types as a disease sue generic.

1.1.6 The two are individually and collectively an added indispensable asset to the Conflcit Vaccination process in an effort to transform a pathologically ill society, country, nation or people from conflict infected culture into a Hybrid Culture (defined under 1.4.2 below)

1.1.7 But what is a Conflict sue generic? And, how can we scientifically understand it so that we may also be able to know how to sussessfully eradicate or prevent it globally and with what scientific strategy?

## 1.2 Definition of Etiology and Nosology of Conflict

1.2.1 **A conflict** is a friction between two or more living or non-living entities; whose pathological cause(s) can only be established using an Etiology of Conflict (i.e., a scientific (clinical) diagnosis of the friction in question).

**1.2.2 Its Nosology, (i.e., its scientific classification as a disease in its own right into** various types based upon their different root-causes and requisite remedies) shows that it falls into these three specific, exhaustive and mutually exclusive forms viz: Conflict in The Animal Kingdom, Conflict in The Plant Kingdom and conflict in The Non-Living Entities as follows:

### 1.2.2.1 CONFLICT IN THE ANIMAL KINGDOM

(1) In **the Animal Kingdom**, Conflict is a friction between two or more living organisms or entities caused by a disagreement, discord, disharmony or displeasure, etc, on an issue, value, objective or goal which may either be possessional or milieu.

(a) A possessional goal is that goal which is already in one's possession or responsibility, e.g. one's lover, money, land, job, food or any other property including one's leadership position.

(b) And, a milieu goal is that which is distant, i.e. not alredy in one's possession but only perceived and needed; and which one, therefore, makes an effort to achieve using whatever strategy he or she may deem appropriate for achieving it.

(2) And, in the Animal Kingdom, Conflict further falls into a set of two specific, exhaustive and mutually exclusive forms viz: THE HUMAN CONFLCIT AND THE NON-HUMAN CONFLICT as follows:

(A) THE HUMAN CONFLCIT (which is our main subject of diagnosis and prescription in this PROPOSAL) may EITHER BE intra-state OR inter-state AS FOLLOWS:-

(a) An Intra-state type of Conflict includes all forms of conflicts found within a state or country e.g

(i) **A Social Conflict**, e.g a friction between two or more persons on purely social grounds such as in the case of intra-family squabbles, etc.

(ii) **A Political Conflict**, e.g an intra or inter-political party friction on purely political reasons.

(iii) **An Ideological Conflict**, e.g a verbal friction between state authorities and the insurgent movements purely on ideological grounds motivated by different images and stereotypes.

(iv) **A Tribal Conflict** e.g the on-going perennial tribal conflict between the majority Hutus and Minority Tutsis in both Rwanda and Burundi which in 1994 culminated into Africa's most heinous catastrophe closer to the 1945 Nazi Germany catastrophe.

(v) **A Philosophical Conflict**, e.g an epistemological squabbles between various thinkers and believers as well due to their differences in understanding of certain phenomenon because of their different source of orientations.

(vi) **A Racial Conflict**, e.g the ugly racial tension during the Apartheid era in South Africa which had been deliberately institutionalized and orchestrated by the then minority white regime against all non-white races in that Country; and also another ugly racial situation during the Nazi Germany against the Jews and Gypsies by the Aryan race, that culminated into the World's most flabbergasting catastrophe in 1945.

(vii) **A Religious Conflict** characterized by both intra and inter-spiritual frictions witnessed in many countries all over the world.

(b) **An Inter-State Type of Conflict** falls essentially into the following two broad categories:-

1. **A Political Conflict Type** is characterized by frictions which are purely poltical by nature, e.g., the on-going political friction between the State of Israel and the State of Palestine in the Middle East Region where each side is firmly armed and determined to subdue the other for its own national interest defined in terms of economic, territorial, natural resource, military, and other powers (gains or victory).
2. **An Ideological Conflcit Type** is characterized by verbal tensions, e.g the most famous Cold War of our generation witnessed between the Capitalist Camp on one side spearheaded by the USA and the Communist camp on the other spearheaded by the USSR

with firm determination to exterminate the other at all costs for their own national interest defined in terms of psychological power (victory) . . . a heinous situation that resulted into a host of megacides world-wide through assassinations of political leaders in Africa, Asia and other Third World Countries solely at the expense of those two warning camps.

3. **An Economic Conflict-Type** e.g, in the recent World Trade Organization (WTO) negotiation that led to the collapse of the noble initiative due to the absence of pacta sunt servanda (i.e.) a firm mutual honour, trust and commitment) which is always an essential natural ingredient for success fo every negotiation, co-operation and partnership in our International Community.

## (B) CONFLICT IN NON-HUMAN ANIMALS

(1) By their very nature that constitutionally limits all non-human animals from advancing to that high powered faculty strictly reserved for human beings conflict in all non-human animals is strictly biological i.e innate but not learned as it is the case in human beings.

(2) However, inspite of this biological constitutional set-back against all non-human animals, a conflict between and among them is almost similar to that of human beings in the sense that it is also caused by the same two specific, exhaustive and mutually exclusive goals viz:-

(a) It may be caused by an entity's NEED and also BELIEF in the same Natural Law of Individual Rights and Justice for an entity to rightfully defend and protect its possessional goal, values or legacy viz: its shelter or home security, territorial independence and integrity security, food security, community life security, individual life security, love security, and other legacies whenever that entity senses, sees or believes them to be under a potential or real threat of aggression by an intruder.

(b) And, it may also be caused by an entity's NEED and BELIEF in the same Natural Law and Justice to defend its individual rights of acquiring a milieu goal or value e.g. food from the world around it (i.e ecosystem) which it badly needs for its survival because it does not have at home but which it is being denied by an enemy from getting.

### 1.2.2.2 CONFLICT IN THE PLANT KINGDOM

Conflict does not exist in the Animal Kingdom only but also in the Plant Kingdom as follows:-

(1) It manifests itself in the form of a scramble between two or more plants or plant species in an ecosystem competing for food i.e sunlight from the sun above and nutrients from the soil below.
(2) Because of each plant's natural scramble for such food, an environment is created of aggressiveness, aggression and antagonism that collectively constitute a virus of survival of the fittest against each other.
(3) Due to this virus, friction is ensured, and could be very dangerous indeed
(4) Because of this invevitable friction, conflict between the two or more plants aggressively competing for food and survival in general, arises.

### 1.2.2.3 CONFLICT IN THE KINGDOM OF NON-LIVING ENTITIES

Conflcit also exists between and among non-living entities; for instance, between two or more mechanical parts of a bicycle, motor vehicle, aeroplane, train, etc., as follows:-

(1) Whenever these parts aren't fitted and tightened as properly as they are required to be done by the mechanical principle, a conflict between them naturally occurs though such a phenomenon is generally called 'a friction".
(2) But because of the bodly damage caused on each part by this friction between the two, this action is a conflict.

### 1.2.3 A SUMMARY

#### 1.2.3.1 In the final analysis:

(a) A conflict among human beings may be psychological, verbal or physical friction between two or more persons (individuals); or between groups of individuals such as ethnicities (or tribes), political parties, clubs or religious faiths; or between a Government and the Opposition (or Rebels).

(b) A conflict between a Government and the Opposition in particular, usually arises from the Opposition's disenchantment against perceived Government's intolerably bad policy or conduct which may be deemed by the Opposition as injurious to the common man (the grass-rrots) politically, socially and/or economically, e.g.,:-

(i) Government's perceived dictatorial policy and lack of Transparency and Accountability;
(ii) Government's perceived disrespect for the Rule of Law and Justice;
(iii) And all other perceived symptoms of viruses in Governance which collectively constitute a Government's perceived CULTURE OF WICKED WAYS, i.e a culture of Bad Governance which is saturated with corruption; devil worship; management by crisis; inefficiency and incompetence caused by job acquisition throught nepotism, bribery and tribalism but not through merits and other professional criteria; and total dependence on bribery and coercion using security forces to legitimize one's policy and leadership and to receive compliance of the grass-roots who may be opposed to the policy and leadership.

## 1.3 SYMPTOMS AND DANGERS OF CONFLICT VIRUSES: (A Pathology of Conflict)

1.3.1 A conflict virus is the most dreadful and contagious of all viruses to Humanitry such as polio, Ebola, small pox, cow pox, Aids, leprosy, typhoid, sickle cell anaemia, etc because of its most flabbergasting and devastating impact and efficacy on Humanity manifested in its intensity in speed and the magnitude of the scope it usually covers in every society or community that it erupts in and covers with an amazing speed by mobilizing every one into the uprising or fight and by indiscrimantely affecting, maiming and completely destroying both human life and the infrastructure at will—a situation which does not arise at all from all other contagious and non-contagious viruses in the history of mankind.

1.3.2 A vivid empirical example of this dreadful virus is corruption which attracts and affects not only one or two persons but many. For instance, regardless of one's clear awareness of the existence of The Rule of Law and Enforcement, and the Degree of

Punishment commensurate to corruption, man has a notorious tendency to ignore all that and collude with one another.

1.3.2.1 To sneak into risky establishments such as banks with an AK 47 or other sophisticated weapons to rob that bank regardless of the dangerous consequences to him;

1.3.2.2 To mislead the electorate with false promises during the elections with a view to gaining votes from them by false pretences while knowing very well that he is not going to fulfill those promises and thus putting the electorate to wrath and perpetual conflict against him/her.

1.3.2.3 Or to set bombs or fire on property aimed at terrorizing or initiating terrorism, guerrilla warfare or a full fledged war such as a civil war or global war.

1.3.3 This virus is prevalent:-

1.3.3.1 In a culture of a Political Community and Leadership which is not firmly grounded in and guided by the Philosophy of Theocentric Humanism which is characterized by everyone's firm belief in Holiness, Perfection and Godliness and the Doctrine of Summum Bonum characterized by the following cardinal virtues requisite for every Leadership of Good Governance: Justice, Wisdom, temperance, courage compassion, excellence and dignity (self-love and self-respect).

1.3.3.2 In a Culture of a Political Community and Leadership which does not respect, honour and live by the principles of Transparency and Accountability—a culture characterized by a massive financial mismanagement of all fixed and liquid assets of the nation not only in the public sector but also in the private sector through looting and vandalizing these assests with impunity thereby rendering the nation too poor to:

(a) Sustain its recurrent and development programmes and activities for the wellbeing of its citizens, and

(b) Thus making those programmes and activities to stand like ghosts or white elephants in the country.

1.3.3.3 These fixed and liquid assets are as follows:-

(a) A nation's fixed assets include, for example, public land and all public natural resources within their geo-political jurisdiction (boundaries).
(b) Liquid assets include all revenues collected from the taxpayers and all other sources of tax such as customs and excises.
(c) The liquid assets may also include the donor aid received from the donor community and all assets of private companies and religious institutions in their capacities as inter-subjective members of the whole National System (Nation).

1.3.3.4 In a culture of a Political Community and Leadership which does not honour, respect and live by the Principles of Human Rights of its People because of its dreadful acts of intolerance by the Regime or Government totally denying certain group or groups of people from:-

(a) Freely and cheerfully participating in the political processes of their country of citizenship such as voting and other relevant activities in accordance with their legitimate Human and Civil Rights; and
(b) Freely and Cheerfully Enjoying Goods and Services provided by that Regime in that Country on equal footing with other citizens possibly becaue of their different race, religion, region, tribe or ethnicity, gender, educational background, line of profession, political party affiliation, etc. which include, for example, one's rights:-

(i) To participate in the electoral processes of his/her Country in one's rightful capacity as a bona fide citizen of that country.
(ii) To participate in all employment opportunities and to get every job of his or her choice based purely on merit but not on nepotism, tribalism, skin colour, genderism or other corruptive criteria.
(iii) To initiate, carry out or engage in any business of one's choice and talent anywhere one wishes to do so in his or her country of Citizenship without being discriminated against by being labeled as a "foreigner" or "untouchable", and also being intimidated, antagonized and harassed day and night with arsonism and other

death threats with a view to forcing him or her to flee back to his/her place of origin while paradoxically they (the perpetrators) are always welcomed and freely allowed to initiate and carry out their private businesses everywhere in other tribal or ethnic regions without such threats they habitually inflict on others from those other regions; and

(iv) To use the utilities or facilities such as recreation centres, hotels, toilets, shopping centers and markets, churches, schools, games, buses, trains, etc. without being denied the right to use such facilities because of one's tribe or ethnicity, gender, or other biased institutional criteria, etc.

**Nota Bene 1: Global Significant Empirical Evidences of those Symptoms and Dangers of Conflict Viruses to Humanity.**

Whereas this problem is prevalent in Africa and is one of the critical root-causes of the Culture of Bad Governance and Conflict on the content, the following significant empirical evidences confirm that the situation is global, and, therefore, that our Remedial Measure recommended herein against this disease are also globally needed:-

(1) The on-going oppression of certain group(s) of people in India who are derogatively labeled or referred to as "UNTOUCHABLES" by their fellow Indians and the Indian Regime because of the unfortunately institutionalized Caste System whose traditional aim is to illegally rob them (the Untouchables) of their Human Rights and Civil Rights endowed to them by God vividly documented in their own Mother Country's Constitution.

(2) Continued disenchantment among most Minority Black Americans in the United States who, by virtue of ius solei are bona fide citizens of that Country but who still feel that they are not being recognized and treated with full human dignity on equal footing with their fellow white Americans as has been evidenced by the year 2000 Presidential Election Voting Controversy in Florida which led to the revelation of the centuries hidden secret that their (Black Americans) participation rights and vote have always not been handled/treated as fairly and justly as those of their white counterparts in all elections simply because of their historical slavery background. Albeit the FIRST

and FOURTEENTH Constitutional Amendments did outlaw such illegal practices throughout the Country as far back as 25th September 1789 and was dully ratified and adopted by the same Coutnry on 15th December, 1791, the viruses still persist in the blood and mind of most white majority Americans.

(3) Still Existing Fresh Scars of Oppression which the overwhelming majority Blacks in South Africa suffered from the blooded-hand of the Minority White Apartheid Regime racial policies which was aimed at denying all Blacks of their rights to freely participate in the electroral processes in a similar manner Minority Black Americans used to be mistreated in the United States of America by their White Counterparts before those Constitutional Amendments were instituted against such practices.

(4) The Oppression Scars which the Colonial Peoples of the then Thirteen African Colonies in North America, Indian and Africa, also suffered from the blooded-hand of the Colonial Rule by the latter's wicked way of taxing them; and plundering their natural resources and free or cheap labour; and denying them their participation rights in electroral processes that consequently forced those colonized Peoples to revolt against that Regime and to shed blood in search of their liberty and Human Dignity from that Oppressive Rule.

1.3.4 In the final analysis, such a country is one that is culturally and morally ill in that:

1.3.4.1 its viruses are manifested in its moral and socio-economic wicked ways

1.3.4.2 Its culture is wretched, corroded and on the verge of collapsing, And falling apart due to rampant corruption and all other symptoms of a Culture of Bad Governance in all sectors of that Country. It neither believes nor honours the principles of Justice, Honesty and Self-Esteem (Dignity).

1.3.4.3 It believes in and practices dishonesty, falsehood, bribery, cunnings, idolatry, devil worship, murder, disrespect to the Rule of Law and Survival of the fittest mentality rooted and enhanced by Anthropocentric Humanism Philosophy and the Doctrine of Summum Malum characterized by a culture which believes and lives by those wicked ways, totally opposed to the Hybrid Culture guided by Theocentric Humanism Philosophy and the Doctrine of Summum Bonum.

1.3.4.3.1. And, it thus uses and lives on these practices as a means for its daily survival and acquiring wealth over wealth.

**Nota Bene 2: Further Significant Global Empirical Evidences of those Symptoms and Dangers of Conflict Viruses already defined above:-**

(1) That whereas the above problem constitutes another significant type of virus (or root-cause) of rampant conflicts in Africa, the following global evidences also confirm that the problem is global and that the total World also requires Conflict Vaccination Remedy:-

(a) To-date, global drug addiction and drug trafficking disease is already at its increase daily, with Mafia as its main engine based in Italy and South America and is likely to drift total World Humanity into an Intensive Care Unit (ICU) unless a prompt remedial measure is taken to contain it.

(b) The Increasing Global Espionage and Terrorism virus is another threat to Humanity due to its World-wide base and fatal activities which also are likely to lead Humanity into an ICU if no immediate care is taken to contain it.

(c) The Increasing Wide-spread of Devil Worship and Children Sacrifices are also another dangerous global contagious virus so much threatening Humanity World-wide today that an immediate measure is also necessary to eradicate this emerging wicked culture and to replace it with a new culture called a HYBRID CULTURE which is not only free but which is also resistant, resilient and robust to those viruses in (1), (2), (3) and (4) above which are likely to destabilize and destroy TOTAL Humanity in our endangered Civilization.

**Nota Bene 3: Empirical Evidence of Intensity of Human Conflict Today**

As has been noted above and as will be noted in the entire text of this PROPOSAL, Conflict is much more lethal to Humanity than all other sources of democides, e.g., Aids, earthquakes, etc. For example:

(1) In 1945, World War II exhibited to Humanity such flabbergasting and frightening genocide of over 6,000,000 Jews, Gypsies and other persons of non-Aryan blood by forced suffocation in gas-chambers of the Nazi German regime due to that regime's hyper-hate spirit against non-Aryan race in Germany that the victorious Allied Forces (of the United States, the United Kingdom, the Union of Soviet Socialist Republic of Russia, the Republic of France, and the People's Republic of China) became so much nauseated by THE HORRORS WAR that they had to take the following MUTUAL VOW which, in turn, became THIS PREAMBLE OF THE UNITED NATIONS:

***We the Peoples of The United Nations are determined***

- To save succeeding generations from the scourge of war, which twice in our lifetime has brought untold sorrow to mankind, and
- To reaffirm faith in fundamental human rights, in the dignity and worth of human person, in equal rights of men and women and of nations large and small, and
- To establish conditions under which justice and respect for the obligations arising from treaties and other sources of international law can be maintained, and
- To promote social progress and better standards of life in larger freedom, and to these ends
- To practice tolerance and live together in peace with one another as good neigbours, and
- To unite our strength to maintain international peace and security, and
- To ensure, by acceptance of principles and institution of methods, that armed force shall not be used, save in the common interest, and
- To employ international machinery for promotion of the economic and social advancement of all peoples

**Have resolved to combine our efforts to accomplish these aims:**

**Accordingly,** our respective Governments, through representatives as assembled in the city of San Francisco, who have exhibited their full powers found to be in good and due form, have agreed to the present Charter of the United Nations and to hereby establish an international organization to be known as the United Nations.

(2) BUT NO SOONER had dust, coupled with the chocking gun-smoke and man's fresh conflictophobia (i.e., fear of conflicts and wars) settled down from the just ended World War II in 1945 in order to allow The UN-Founding Fathers' VOW to take root and bear them the expected fruit THAN our Humanity AGAIN found itself being compelled to go back to its knees desperately supplicating for it's Almight Creator's divine intervention against a new wave of fresh wars that had taken hostage of a total of 52 countries between 1946 and 1975; being fueled by rise of a fierce Cold War between the capitalist camp headed by the USA and the Communist camp headed by the Union of Soviet Socialist Republic (USSR). This unexpected flabbergasting tragedy first begun with some least bothersome sparks of conflict in Syria-Lebanon (1946), Greece (1947) and then Berlin (1948). However, these new sparks in Korea (1950), Kashmir (1950) and particularly in the Suez Canal Crisis (1956), the Congo Crisis (1960), the Cuba Missile Crisis (1962) and in more others globally as so fully documented in detail in this author's article, "UN Peace-keeping Policy: some Basic Sources of its Implementation problems and Their Implications", CALIFORNIA WESTERN INTERNATIONAL LAW JOURNAL, Vol. 6, No. 2 (1976), p. 350. THE INTENSITY of this new global development obviously buffled both the UN Founding Fathers and the Total International Community so much that none of them could now possibly explain the real meaning, essence, significance and rationale of THE VOW which had now become THE FOUNDATIN OF THE UNITED NATIONS as so witnessed by the content of THE PREAMBLE OF THE UN CHARTER stated above in (1) whose Founding Fathers had just formulated and ratified in 1945. Accordingly, due to the intensity of this new development which was not only a challenge but also an embarrassment to the VOW's ARCHITECT, the latter were obviously in a terrible psychological pain trying to understand and possibly explain whether their new plan efforts for A LASTING PEACE against all future wars, as so empirically evidenced by their sentiments contained in THE PREAMBLE OF THE UN CHARTER, had now proved a zero-work, a total waste of time or just a joke to them and the entire World Community which they had sought to save from further scourge of wars!! This concern became an obvious agonizing mental pain to them. Hence, the rationale of this' intervention by this CONFLICT VACCINATION PROPOSAL.

(3) Similarly, in 1994, The Rwanda Civil War catastrophe cost Humanity another acute mental pain of conflictophobia arising from a death toll of over 1,000,000 Hutus and Tutsi together due to their perennial mutual tribal hate spirit in that Country.

(4) And, as per the recent Conflict research findings by Professor Rudolph J. Rummel of the Univeristy of Hawaii, also supported by Professor A. Schmid in the latter's recent article, "Twentieth Century published in the Megamurders: Determining the Extent of Demicide" PIOOM Newsletter and Progress Report, Vol.3, No. 1 (summer 1991),

(a) It is self-evident that our Humanity is at a much more risk of conflicts than ever before.

(b) Conflict has to date cost Humanity to the tune of a total of 143,160,000 deaths of helpless citizens and foreigners through shootings, beatings, tortures, knifes, burnings, crushings, hard labour, buried alive, drawings, hangings, bombings, poisonings and many other myriad of ways master-minded by the blood-thirsty regimes globally—a most flabbergasting figure equivalent to the entire population in both Eastern and Central Africa Region! And, also a figure closer to 50% of the total USA population today!

(c) Our Humanity is indeed already in the INTENSIVE CARE UNIT (ICU) desperately calling for an EMERGENCY INTERVENTION!! By Science and Technology.

(5) Hence, THE NEED FOR this Conflcit Vaccination.

## 1.4 THE AIM OF CONFLICT VACCINATION TO HUMANITY

1.4.4.2.1 Like the aim of all vaccines such as the polio vaccine in Bio-Science developed in 1955 by Dr. Jonas E. Salk of the Univeristy of Pittsburgh and later improved on in 1961 by Dr. Albert Sabin of the University of Cincinnati to help Humanity against the mass killer polio disease,

1.4.4.3 Conflict Vaccination's aim also is to assist Humanity against the Conflict viruses in Kenya and the entire African Continent as follows:-

(a) **By paralyzing those viruses found in the affected body politique culture** using the vaccine dose as so detailed in the Methodology Section 1.6 below.

(b) **By rehabilitating the affected body politique culture** from its ailing or abnormal state to its health or normal state thus, reversing the sick body politique culture from its dysfunctional state to its eufunctional state.

(c) And, **by conferment of immunity against future infection**

1.4.4.4 Conflict Vaccination is, therefore, real in that it seeks to scientifically free the endangered Humanity from all agonies caused by conflict, e.g., dismantlement (dislocation), exodus and other acute sufferings of refugees, self-annihilation; rampant abject poverty; malnutrition; infrastructure destruction; and all aspects of socio-economic retardance in a country.

## 1.5 SUMMARY OF CONFLICT VACCINATION PROGRAMME AND ITS ULTIMATE GOAL TO HUMANITY

1.5.1. In the final analysis, Conflict Vaccination is a Cultural Engineering Process aimed at healing, saving or resuscitating an endangered Country from the agonies of the mass killer Conflict virus.

1.5.2. Its ultimate goal to Humanity is:-

1.5.2.1. Eradicate all root-causes of conflict and poverty characterized by massive national financial mismanagement, bribery and all other symptoms of massive corruption such as devil worship, falsehood, injustice, assassination, terrorism, election frauds, drug addiction and drug trafficking, managerial and administrative inefficiency, professional poverty or deficiency, depleted road networks, massively destroyed or decaying environment, stinking cities and towns, contradiction in leaders' theory and practice, arrogance, dictatorial rule, misuse of one's office for one's corruptive ends, wide spread pollution of rivers and lakes, wide spread general public outcry against oppressive leadership, and segregation in schools and other public institutions against certain groups of people as in the case of the former Apartheid Regime in South AFrica before the Era of the Mandela

Government Black Segregation in the United States of America before and after the FIRST and FOURTEENTH Constitutional Amendments out-lawing Segreation in that Country had been put in place; and the Caste System in India up today. All these are individually and collectively prima facie evidences of tangible viruses in a Culture of a Country of Bad Governance and endless conflicts of various types.

1.5.2.2. And to create a HYBRID CULTURE of Good Governance essential for Accelerated Socio-Economic Productivity.

1.5.3 Definition of A Hybrid Culture:

1.5.3.2. A Hybrid Culture is a culture that is highly immune to conflicts in the sense that it is a culture which has been scientifically treated or vaccinated with a view of making it FREE, RESISTANT, RESILIENT AND ROBBUST to those symptoms of wicked ways which always cause Conflict to occur in a society.

1.5.3.2 And, it is a Culture which is based on, rooted in and guided by Theocentric Humanism Philosophy characterized by its society's firm belief in Holiness, Perfection and Godliness and the Doctrine of Summum Bonum also characterized by the virtues of Justice, Prudence (Wisdom), Honesty, Temperance, Courage, Excellence and Dignity of man (Self-Love and Self-Respect)—a fact which, inturn, confirms that this is the only reliable culture with the necessary capacity to bring about Good Governance, a Durable Peace and an Accelerated Socio-Economic Recovery and Development in our edangered:

(a) Kenya

(b) All Africa

(c) And the Total World

1.5.4. And, by virtue of its guaranteed stable ecosystem, a Hybrid Culture shall yield to Kenya and each of the other African Countries needed enabling environment for a highest achievement in Science and Technology which, as of now, they do not have and which they therefore need first and foremost in order for them to achieve a beter standard of living from their God-given minerally rich Continent which is next to none on this Planet.

## 1.6 METHODOLOGY OF ADMINISTERING CONFLICT VACCINATION TOWARD A HYBRID CULTURE

1.6.1 Operational Definition of Conflict Vaccination Dose And How This Dose Should Be Administered:-

(a) Conflcit Vaccination dose is composed of the following macro-ingredients:

(i) FORMAL PEACE EDUCATION, i.e Structured peace education policy promoted by innovative means of teaching, seminars, workshops, conferences, etc. for both Leaders and the General Public in society; and

(ii) INFORMAL PEACE EDUCATION i.e., unstructured peace education through informal conversations or discussions and counseling during interpersonal interactions at informal social-settings.

(b) These macro-formal and Informal Peace Education Ingredients are, in turn, composed of the following micro-ingredients:

(i) AWARENESS OF GLOBAL ANTI-CONFLICT SENTIMENTS, e.g., awareness of all historical declarations of war as worst/dangerous means for settling disputes; and awareness of Corruption and Autocracy as a Fatal Disease to the art of Good Governance and People's Peace, Unity and Prosperity.

(ii) AWARENESS ON GLOBAL SOCIO-ECONOMIC ADVANTAGES OF PEACE, LOVE AND UNITY such as accelerated socio-economic, scientific and technological advancement normally brought about to a society by the presence of those triangular micro-ingredients (i.e., Peace, Love and Unity) that would, therefore, be realized in/by each Country if Peace, Love and Unity were allowed to prevail and flourish globally.

(iii) AWARENESS OF GLOBAL SOCIO-ECONOMIC DISADVANTAGES OF CONFLICT such as devastating destruction of human life and infrastructure; increased refugee agony; and promotion to national socio-economic retardance normally brought about to society by greed, hate, national disunity and all other various viruses of conflict, globally manifested/witnessed during World

War I and II respectively as well as in Civil Wars, e.g., Rwanda, Somalia, Bosnia, etc.

### 1.6.2 The Vaccination Programme

These ingredients should be administered to a society as follows:-

(a) There must first and foremost be a Government policy and enforcement means in place to enforce the programme to every individual in both urban and rural settings; and in all public and non-public but strategic institutions such as schools, universities and religious fora.

(b) For the programme to work effectively, each individual must be led to accept and promote it at all costs, place and times through formal and informal interpersonal interactions from the nuclear family level to larger social settings such as bars, restaurants, hotels, clubs, etc.

(c) The process must first and foremost begin with the society's leaders (ELITE) before it is ministered to the general public (GRASSROOT) as follows:-

  **(i) ELITE CONFLICT VACCINATION**—i.e., a Vertical Vaccination process aimed, at re-educating the Leaders on the concept and disadvantages of peace, love and unity to a Country or Nation, on the one hand and the serious disadvantages of conflict, hate and disunity to a country on the other.

  **(ii) GRASS-ROOT CONFLICT VACCINATION** i.e., a Horizontal Vaccinaton process aimed at re-educating the general public on the same SIDEWAYS i.e from one corner to another corner of each country.

### 1.6.3 The Instruments that must be put in place in order for Conflict Vaccination to Suceed.

In order to succeed, Conflict Vaccination Programme would require the following instruments:-

(a) Structural mobile face-to-face seminars, workshops, conferences, religious crusades, teaching institutions; and other avenues that may be deemed strategically useful in re-educating the general public and their respective leaders (elite) on the concept and strategic importance of peace and stability to socio-economic, political, scientific and technological progress of a society.

(b) Distant electronic media especially Radio, Television, Video, Internet, etc. which currently are the most strategic instruments next to none in reaching and re-educating both the literate and illiterate in both urban and rural areas at the fastest speed and cheapest means.

(c) Both live stage and electronic drama which is also an additional most instrumental tool in re-educating both literate and illiterate at the fastest speed and cheapest means on an existing situation as also witnessed by various stage plays throughout history such as those of Shakespeare, etc.

(d) Both live and electronic music which is another fastest and most effective means of re-educating both literate and illiterate as also evidenced by our overtime global behaviour using psalsms, lyrics, lamentations, eulogies, etc.

(e) A formal Government policy legalizing this Vaccination process as a mandatory requirement to be honoured by all for the betterment of all.

## II. JUSTIFICATION OF CONFLICT VACCINATION

### II.1 Existing Global Conventional Conflict Resolution programmes

#### II.1.1 The existing global conventional methodologies of peace or dispute settlements:

(a) From time immemorial (Antiquity) to the present, numerous methodologies abound which have always been invented to assist Humanity in bringing about peace whenever and wherever that peace was disturbed by cold war or real war.

(b) These include, for example, Peace Negotiations also called "Round Table Peace Negotiations or Conferences", e.g., The Egypto-Hittite Treaty of Non-Aggression of 1284 B.C. which aimed at restoring peace and order between the Old Egypt and Babylon (in the Antiquity) Constructions of Treaties, Laws (which include Municipal Laws and International Laws also known as Jus Gentium in Jurisprudence), Pacts, Accords, Law Enforcement Instruments (such as Police, Courts and Jails), etc. spelling out principles, statutes and articles **outlawing** an unjust war as means for settling disputes and principles **authorizing** a just war to be used solely for self—defense against aggression; Regional Defence Organizations such as North Atlantic Treaty Organization (NATO); Initiation and promotion of scientific, technological, cultural, and education, educational, exchange, co-operation or collaboration as means for fostering mutual peaceful co-existence between and among individuals, groups of persons and nations; formulation and management of Truth Commissions; etc.

### II. 1.2. Inefficiency and Ineffectiveness of the existing Global Convention Conflict Resolution Methodologies

(1) However, a Balance Sheet of all these convetional efforts reveals that the outcome of all these efforts has always been either marginal or a zero work as most of these treaties, pacts and laws have been broken, ignored, manipulated, with total impunity etc thus giving freedom to conflict to erupt at will, e.g, the peace of Westphalia (1648), The Warsaw pact (1955), The Berlin General Act (1885), The League of nations Covenant (1918), The Brian—Kellogg pact (1928), The Washington Naval Arusha Peace Accord (1993), etc.

(2) Consequently, there exists no concrete Global Conflict Vaccination Progamme(s) either at National or Global level for this <u>dose</u> exercise a part from a world—wide reliance on flimsy programmes which have often proved miserably unreliable, e.g.: Round Table Peace Negotiations; Peace Convetions, Conferences, etc.; peace Treaties, Accords, pacts etc.; Enactment of laws and law Enforcement Systems which, of cause do work only at national level but which have always proved very ineffective and hence very unreliable indeed at the global (international level as already evidence by the difficulties suffered so far by both the Permanent Court of justice (1945 to date); National Self—Defence Systems; Regional Self—Defense System of which only the north Atlantic Treaty Organization (NATO) is the only which has proved successful and hence reliable; the UN Defense System envisaged Under chapters VI and VII of The UN Charter but which has been often crippled by the same UN Self—Seeking States on the strength of their defended principles of equal Sovereignty and Domestic Jurisdiction Right under Article 2 paragraph 7 of the same Charter; Inter—Cultural Exchange; Scientific, Technological, Economic Educational, Social and other Co—operation: <u>Inter alios</u>

(3) **The root—cause of this virus.** Has always been due to the following facts:

   (i) Instead of focusing on the head which is the actual root—cause of the conflict being dealt with, these efforts have always been wasting time on myopic part of the conflict which is equivalent to the the segment of the tapeworm but not its head.

(ii) This oversight is exactly the actual a reason why all these conventional efforts have always failed to yield any lasting peace thus giving total freedom to the conflict virus to prevail and multiply at will in Africa against Humanity.

(4) **In view of this Scientific reality**, it is self—evident that in order for any effort against Conflict Virus (es) to yield a lasting peace, one must, first and foremost, focus on the head of a conflict, i.e, its actual root-cause or its viruses, but not its symptoms. In order to identify these viruses, one must first and foremost get hold of the culture of the parties to the conflict being examined or settled and clinically diagnose it very meticulously **using Conflictology** and **Conflict Vaccinology** whose meaning and mechanics are provided herein (see Glossary Nos. 9 and 10)

## Existing Methods of Administrering Conflict Resolution in Africa Today

(1) Existing Instruments of Conflicts Prevention in African

(a) Again, as already indicated in (II.1) above, there still exists no formal public instruments in Africa at either national or continental levels mandated to do this exercise.

(b) The only instruments available now are those ones cited in II.1.(2) above which are, in fact, not effective as experience of recurrent perennial civil and international wars also show that Peace Treaties, Pacts, Accords International Law, Continental Organization such as the newly created African Union (AU) and its predecessor the OAU, etc. all have failed to prove as a reliable insurance to Africa against both civil strife e.g. Somalia, Sudan, etc), and inter-African state war (such as the on-going war in the Democratic Republic of Congo (DRC), Somalia, etc.

(2) Inefficiency and Ineffectiveness of these Conventional Instruments in Africa

(a) All Conventional Instruments which are mainly International Law, Peace Treaties, Accords and pact (such as The Arusha Peace Accord of August 1993) which had aimed, in good faith, to solve, once and for all, the perennial civilian conflict virus, for example, in a country such as Rwanda which had been devastating that country ever since the civil war of 1959, totally failed to save that country. Instead, it left the said country to slide into a holocaust of untold civil war whose agony has not simmered down up to today.

(b) Similarly, like the unfortunate Peace Treaties, Accords and Pacts, International Law has equally failed as a reliable anti-biotic pill against conflict sicne it has failed to win recognition of African nation-states to honour and respect the concepts of sovereign equality, territorial independence and integrity of their own sister states in the Continent on the one hand; and the Law of Original Responsibility as well as the Law of Vicarious Responsibility on the other which collectively constitute a full proof of the failures of International Law as a reliable instrument of a durable World Peace and Security.

(c) And, like the two conventional tools in (1) and (2) above, Diplomacy—or Statesmanship has similarly failed very terribly due to a perennial culture of dishonesty and self-seeking attitude all over the Continent—also a litmus test confirming that Diplomacy is also not a reliable instrument of a durable World Peace and Security.

Efficiency and Effectiveness of The Novel Conflict Vaccination Methodology Prescribed Herein:

11.2.1 But, to date, the following programmes which could have been recognized, harnessed and then exploited to enhance effective and successful administration of this dose globally have unfortunately not been effected. These include:-

(1) Formal Peace Education Programme which each African Country could have recognized and then adopted as a substantive mandatory Government Policy by which to educate its people/National on the concept, essence and significance of mutual Peace and Stability for their Accelerated Socio-economic Recovery and Development using all teaching institutions; all public and private offices; all leaders' public rallies; all media/the press; all religious institutions etc; that each Country may deem necessary and appropriate to use for this particular purpose.

(2) Informal Peace Education Programme which, in addition to the Formal Peace Education Programme as mandatory Government Policy by each African Country, could, also have followed suit and then become an obvious added

asset to that country in promoting Peace and Stability as a prerequisite for an Accelerated Socio-Economic Recovery and Development.

(3) Elite Conflict Vaccination, i.e An Action of Leaders from all walks of life and profession which could have been put in place so that these leaders may freely and willingly exploit their leadership role to educate each other and all their Grass-Roots on the concept, essence and significance of Mutual Peace and Stability as a prerequisite for an accelerated socio-economic recovery and progress of their country and as a dose with which to eradicate their poverty and other sources of suffering.

(4) Grass-Roots Conflict Vaccination, i.e., An Action by the general public at the grass-roots level in both urban and rural areas which could also have been put in place so that these grassroots may freely and willingly exploit their important role in their capacity as the overwhelming majority and center of democratic power into their respective home of domicile to educate each other at all levels of interaction on the meaning and importance of Mutual Peace as a necessary stimulating agent (or catalyst) for them to accelerate in their socio-economic initiatives, improvement in their standard of living, and poverty eradication.

11.2.2 This novel approach against Conflict Viruses is new, different and very important in that unlike the conventional approach which always aims at the tail of the virus, it aims at destroying the head, which is the root-cause of the virus of Conflict once and for all so that every peace treaty or accord may be a lasting one.

11.2.3 Its ultimate goal is to facilitate and promote development of a Hybrid Culture in a society as so detailed below in 11.2.4.

11.2.4 Conflict Vaccination Towards A Hybrid Culture in Society (1) In order to achieve A Hybrid Culture in Africa, Conflict Vaccination shall be administered vertically and horizontally using these specific dosages:-

(A) VERTICAL CONFLICT VACCINATION DOSAGE which is an Elite Conflict Vaccination Dosage Designed to be administered from Up down and Down up, targeting the following elite members:-

(a) Political Leaders consisting of Heads of State and Government, Cabinet Ministers, Assistant Ministers, Members of Parliament or National Assembly (which ever shall be deemed applicable) and Civil Leaders.
(b) All Heads of Political Parties
(c) All Political Appointees
(d) All Civil Service Heads
(e) All Heads of the Provincial Adminsitration including Chiefs and Sub-Chiefs
(f) All Heads of Religious Institutions
(g) All Heads of Private Business Companies
(h) All Heads of Academic Institutions
(i) All Heads of Civil Societies such as Clubs, Associations and Cooperatives
(j) And, all Village Heads (Ligurus)

**Nota Bene 4:** Because of their natural strategic role in the body politique not only as leaders of a society but also as the most influential persons to the masses (Grass-root) in that society, the Elite shall serve as:-

(a) The most powerful socializing agent to effectively educate and re-educate society with maximum net gains on the concept and significance of Peace, love and Unity in Kenya and Total Africa.
(b) The most rightful agent in influencing its followers from TOP-DOWN and DOWN-TOP in society with total efficiency and effectiveness on those three concepts and their significance.
(c) The most reliable tool for the Conflict Vaccination Program in educating and re-educating the grass-roots on the concept and significance of Transparency and Accountability, Holines, Godliness, Perfection—virtues extremely essential for every body's daily life in society as the only path to a HYBRID CULTURE which is also a prerequisite to this long over due mode of Good Governance, Durable Peace and a Rapid Socio-economic Recovery and Development Africa is eagerly looking for.

(B) HORIZONTAL CONFLICT VACCINATION DOSAGE is a Grass-Roots Vaccination dosage to be administered sideways (horizontally) targeting the entire general public particularly the common man in both urban and rural areas, i.e., from the Left to the Right and vice versa in the Country.

**Nota Bene 5:** (a) Because of the amorphous and over whelming scope and role of the majority Grassroots more than the scope and role of the minority Elite in every society, the Grass-roots Conflict Vaccination shall be very essential for the total society in order for a Complete Conflict Vaccination to succeed and take a firm root in an ailing Country under treatment and to confer lasting immunity.

(b) And, because of its immense scope from one end to another in society, Horizontal Conflict Vaccination shall be the only strategic method in order to effectively and successfully reach every person in an ailing society.

### 11.2.5 Reliability of the Roles of Elites and Grass-Roots in Administration of this Conflict Vaccination dose

(a) In this regard, both The Elite and the Grass-roots shall be the most reliable agents in the Administration of this dose to each other.

(b) Since the Grass-Roots also play a very significant role in influencing the Elites in both policy formulation and policy execution and since the Elites always listen to them keenly lest they risk their Grass-Root support to their political positions in their Countries, the Grass-Roots shall serve as a most strategic Conflict Vaccination tool to the Elite in each Country.

(c) Apart from the Elite and the Grass-Roots as a most powerful Conflcit Vaccination agents, the following tools of Conflict Vaccination shall also be used in order to effectively sensitize Kenya and the Total Africa on the seriousness of the existing morally decaying culture and to disseminate the OBJECTIVES and ADVANTAGES of this Programme:-

(i) Electronic media, e.g radio, television, internet etc.
(ii) Public rallies, seminars, workshops, Churches and other Religious Institutions, etc.
(iii) Written literature, e.g. pamphlets, fliers, posters, Press release, etc.
(iv) State Music and Drama due to their long traditional evidences as effective means in human communication, education, mobilization and psychological message.
(v) In-service certificate and Diploma Courses.
(vi) Undergraduate and Postgraduate Teaching and Research

## 11.3 EFFICACY AND ADVANTAGES OF CONFLICT VACCINATION TO KENYA AND TOTAL AFRICA

11.3.1 Kenya and Total Africa shall Consequently:-

(a) Be relieved from the existing dreadful viruses of conflicts which have always wrecked and seriously maimed thereby rendering them politically and socio-economically, perpetually less effective and less competitive in the International Community though they are covered by the Principle of Sovereign Equality enshrined in the UN Charter, AU Charter and also in our God given Natural Law (jus naturale) which automatically empowers them to be also recognized, accepted and treated on an equal footing with all other Sovereign Entities at all times in that Community.

(b) Begin to prudently invest their tangible and intangible resources, in rational activities for socio-economic recovery and development and immensely accelerate in those activities other than repeating their old perennial mistakes of investing in armaments for self-destruction.

(c) Begin to enjoy the fruits of their Hybrid Culture characterized by Good Governance, a Durable Peace and a Rapid socio-Economic Recovery other than wasting all their time and resources to the existing culture of Bad Governance, Conflicts and Abject Socio-Economic Poverty that has kept Africa a hostage for decades.

11.3.2 Social Scientist and their Social Sciences shall now consequently begin to prove instrumental to Humanity in problem solving as their counterpart in both Bio-Science and Physical Science have demonstrated and are still so doing for centuries effective the time the idea and role of Science was initiated in 7000 BC by The African Mysteries System of the Grand Lodge of Luxor now known as Alexandria, Egypt.

## 11.4 WHAT KENYA AND HER SISTER AFRICAN COUNTRIES SHOULD THEREFORE DO TO EMBRACE THIS PROGRAMME AGAINST CONFLICT VIRUSES IN AFRICA

11.4.1 Like His Excellency President Daniel Toroitich arap Moi, The Head of State and Government of The Republic of Kenya, who, in his challenge to African Leaders in Lusaka, Zambia at the COMESA Summit held in October, 2000 and who has also repeated the same challenge to Universities and the Donor Communities alike during his speeches at the Association of African Universities, (AAU) meeting at Safari Park

Hotel, Nairobi (on 6th February, 2001) and also to the UN Environment 8th February, 2001) respectively, strongly gives credence to conflict as Enemy Number One to Kenya and Total Africa which must, therefore, be collectively contained first and foremost by all African Leaders and Universities as a prerequisite to successfully tackling socio-economic problems, it is here hoped that all other Heads of State and Governments and Universities in Africa would equally do the same and collectively support this Conflict Vaccination Programme against this Dreadful enemy.

11.4.2 This action is necessary because:-

11.4.2.1. In the absence of peace in Africa no foreign and local large scale investors will be attracted to come and invest in the Continent

11.4.2.2. In the absence of such investments in Africa:-

(a) No significant socio-economic recovery and accelerated development can be realized

(b) And, most national resources in each African Country are subject to continue to be wasted on armaments for self-annihilation as the situation has always proved to be since independence in most Countries on the Continent.

11.4.2.3. But in the presence of a DURABLE PEACE

(a) Significant influx of FOREIGN INVESTORS is assured to enhance national socio-economic recovery and development because of this assured security.

(b) Nationals who are hoarding their savings in foreign banks outside Africa will also be encouraged to return the savings back home.

11.4.2.3. And like all Great Leaders from Antiquity to the Present such as the Egyptian Pharaohs (who founded and enhanced The African Mysteries System of the Grand Lodge of Luxor which in 7000 BC developed all Disciplines of Science that we now have in our Civilization today to sustain Humanity in complex society-problem solving); Alexander The Great (336-323 BC); and King Solomon (971-931-BC) (who like their Antiquity Counterpart, also became great leaders because of the support they gave to Science Development and the support they also received from this Science), it is here hoped:

14.4.3.1 That The Heads of State and Government of African Countries would do the same by giving sufficient support to Science development for the sake of their leadership and the welfare of their peoples against this man-killer conflict disease.

14.4.3.2 That they will also emulate the exemplary model of the 23rd American Presidnet Franklin D. Roosevelt (1882-1945) who, himself a victim of partial paralysis of polio, also emulated those great leaders and consequently enabled the following amazing achievements for Humanity in our civilization:-

a) In 1927, he founded The Georgia Warm Springs Foundation which became the first institution in the history of Mankind to fight against the polio disease agony in America, and in our Civilization.
b) And in 1938 he encouraged the establishment of the National Foundation for Infantile Paralysis which is now called THE NATIONAL FOUNDATION and which later generously provided all financial needs for further research that resulted into the discovery of POLIO VACCINES by Dr. Salk and Dr. Sabin in 1955 and 1961 respectively in defense of Humanity against the danger of this polio virus.

11.4.4. Similarly, all institutions particularly Universities may also need to emulate such lessons particularly the exemplary model of Harvard University which in 1949 strongly supported its scientists such as the following bacteriologists: Dr. John E. Enders, Dr. Fredrick C. Robbins and Dr. Thomas H. Weller who, because of this financial and moral support, managed to:-

(a) Develop and apply a practical way of growing polio virus outside the human body for the first time in the history of medicine in our Civilization;
(b) And open a way for further research which also later aided the success of Dr. Salk and Dr. Sabin in the discovery of the present POLIO VACCINE now being used globally against this killer virus though it is not as dangerously contagious as the Conflict Virus is to Humanity's life and national development.

11.4.5 It is hereby equally hoped that all Political Scientists and their fellow Socio-Scientists will take time to pay heed and also emulate the noble role and contribution of both Bio-Scientistis and the Physio-Scientists to Humanity e.g:-

11.4.5.1(In Bio-Science)

(a) The amazing life saving polio vaccine discovery in 1955 and 1961 against the dreadful man-killer polio virus by both Dr. Salk and Dr. Sabin respectively.
(b) The amazing life saving penicillin and Antibiotics discovered by Sir. Dr. Alexander Fleming in 1929;
(c) And the amazing life saving inoculation discovery by Professor Louis Pasteur (1822-1895) against rabies from mad dog bites and the discovery of food preservative against food decay through a pasteurization process named after him.
Although Prof. Pasteur discovered this phenomenon in 1864 while still as young as only 26 years old, his efforts did not only give a breath of relief to mankind against such dreads but also placed Bio-Sience into the highest Orbit of Scientific Prestige and Glory that Behavioural Sciences have not yet managed to reach and should therefore also endeavour to do so.

11.4.5.2 And in Physical Science the following man's advancement in his understanding of nature around him using:-

(a) The laws of gravity and motions discovered by Sir Dr. Isaac Newton in 1666 on how the Moon actually revolves around the Earth; and how this Earth and all other planets also revolve around the Sun; and how all these phenomena could be explained and understood better by use of calculus;
(b) Galilei Galileo' stern emphasis on a combination of both observation and experimentation as the only way of understanding nature arising from his own scientific experience and discoveries in as far back as 1585 when he was only 20 years of age;
(c) And finally, the amazing wisdom of the greatest scientist of modern time, Prof. Albert Einstein (1897-1955), whose scientific discovery of relativity saved mankind from the mist of darkness and ignorance by leading us to a better understanding of our universe.

11.4.6 And, also like The World Bank which has already expressed its interest in financial supporting this NEW and UNIQUE INITIATIVE aimed at assisting the Governments of Kenya and all other African Sister States in The Continent to find scientific ways and means of eradicating or reducing this dreadful man-killer disease called "CONFLICT", IT IS HEREBY HOPED:-

(1) That all other members of the Donor Community who are equally concerned about this dreadful disease SHALL JOIN HANDS together with both the World Bank and all African Governments and Peoples in the Continent to SUPPORT THIS INITIATIVE for the Greatest Good of the People of Africa in total as a paradigm for a global war against conflict and poverty.
(2) And, that with this consorted effort, Kenya and the entire Continent of Africa shall, in no doubt, be relieved of this dread so that they may now begin to properly utilize their Donor Aid and National Resources as so expected of them in order for them to easily attract more foreign investors to come to Africa and assist them in their respective National Socio-Economic Recovery and Development.

## III. ESTABLISHMENT OF THE INSTITUTE OF CONFLICT VACCINATION IN AFRICA: A path to a Hybrid Culture of Peace, Democracy, Good Governance and Accelerated Socio-Economic Recovery and Development in Africa.

### III.1 OBJECTIVE

III.1.1 To eradicate the existing root-causes of civil strife and the agony of refugee exodus and other symptoms of human catastrophe caused by such strife.

1.1.2 To bring about a Hybrid Culture of Peace, Good Governance and democracy in the Continent of Africa as a prerequisite for accelerated socio-economic recovery and development in each Country.

1.1.3 To restore the Glory and Dignity of the Peoples and Governments of Kenya and Total Africa by assisting in eradication of the existing decaying culture as a prelude to doing the same for the Total World.

1.1.4 To facilitate the reorganization and enjoyment of the strategic role and utility of Behavioural and of Social Sciences in socio-economic problem solving in the same spirit that both Bio-Science and Physio-science have individually done and are doing to Humanity.

1.1.5 And, to create, develop, facilitate and promote CONFLICTOLOGY, CONFLICT VACCINOLOGY and CONFLICT VACCINATION in Africa and Total World with a sole aim of providing a requisite PREVENTIVE CAPACITY against future scourge of conflict which has, for centuries, always brought untold sorrows of destruction to Humanity in Africa and the Total World.

## 1.2 LOCATION (SITE)

111.2.1 The Institute of Conflict Vaccination shall be located in Kenya to serve as the nucleus of the Programme for the entire Continent

111.2.2 In pursuance of the Objectives indicated in 111.1 above, The Institute shall establish regional linkages in the African Continent and Total World to collectively assist in the execution of this Conflict Vaccination Programme.

## 1.3. METHODOLOGY

111.3.1 The Institute of Conflict Vaccination shall use a Cultural Engineering Methodology as a vehicle; and shall do so beginning with Kenya or any other African Country with sufficient logistics to facilitate success of the Institute's efforts as so prescribed here below in 111.3.2.

111.3.2 In its efforts to realize the objectives stated in 111.1 above for The Peoples of the entire African Continent, The Institute of Conflict Vaccination in Africa shall use the following strategic methodology:-

111.3.2.1 Structured mobile face-to-face seminars, workshops, conferences, crusades, religious institutions and other avenues that shall be deemed strategically useful for senzitizing all Kenyans and nationals of all other Sister African Countries at both elite and Grass-root levels on how the existing culture of corruption and other forms of wicked ways actually works in all public and private business offices and the agony and shame this culture is causing the Kenyans and all other African Peoples throughout the African Continent.

111.3.2.2 Distant electronic media namely Radio, TV, Video, Internet etc, as the most appropriate strategic tool for easily reaching and sensitizing both literate and illiterate masses in both rural and urban environments.

111.3.2.3 Both live stage and electronic drama as an appropriate and reliable means of communication in the shortest time possible to the masses whose level of literacy is not reliable for the overall objective.

111.3.2.4 Both live stage and electronic music as a fast and effective means towards helping the public in understanding the subject matter being conveyed to them.

111.3.2.5 Clinical Diagnosis and Prognosis of Conflict using Applied Peace Research of the Interdisciplinary Approach with a view to identifying possible hidden root-causes of conflict and to providing an appropriate cure.

111.3.2.6 Meticulous in-depth analysis of such data with a view to identifying relevant curative or preventive doses for a conflict at hand.

111.3.2.7 Joint inter-university teaching and research venture in pursuance of the goals as follows:-

(a) Initiating and promoting in the Republic of Kenya and each Sister African Country and The Total World CONFLICTOLOGY and CONFLICT VACCINOLOGY using:-

(i) Clinical Diagnosis and Prognosis of Conflict also called "Applied Peace Research" with a view to identifying root-causes of each conflict embedded in a country's total culture and in providing curative or preventive measures against that conflict in a scientific manner.

(ii) Training in Peace and Conflict Reconcilliation, Conflicts Vaccination, Refugee Resettlement and Rehabilitation and all other related Questions and Issues of Peace, war, Democracy, Human and Civil Rights, Political Theory, Political Economy, Public Policy, Foreign Policy, Diplomacy, Organizations, Theory and Practice of Inter-personal and International Relations, Art of Governance with emphasis on the Nature and Consequences of Good Governance and Bad Governance, Strategic National Security Studies, etc.

(b) Providing research and training facilities in Peace Research at both Applied Research and Theoretical Research levels for Pre-Doctoral and Post-Doctoral Fellows interested in Peace Research in African and Total World.

(c) Promoting, sponsoring and providing facilities for conferences, seminars, workshops and symposia for the purpose of enhancing:-

(i) Clinical Diagnosis and Prognosis of Conflicts
(ii) And Exchange of Knowledge with fellow Scientists and Policy-makers on the findings and proposed remedies of a conflict and all other related issues requiring Tribunal attention, but having a potential threat to peace and security at local, national, regional or international level.

(d) Providing and promoting training facilities in Peace Research Methodology and Technique for College Undergraduate, Graduate and Post-graduate Studies leading to a degree of BSc, MSc, PhD., and Diploma and Professional Certificate in Conflictology and Conflict Vaccinology.
(e) Initiating, promoting and managing in Kenya and every Sister African Country a Comprehensive Conflict Vaccination Programme vertically and horizontally using such Peace and Human Rights Education and Training Programmes for both the Governing Party and the Opposition Party (or Parties) and for students in all educational and training institutions.
(f) Training leaders (Elites) and the general public (the Grassroots) on the concept, essence and significance of CONFLICT VACCIANTION for the good of all Peoples of Kenya and the entire African Continent.
(g) Initiating, promoting and regularly evaluating or assign the efficacy of the programme using appropriate technology across the Continent.
(h) Inoculating the Spirit of Peace, Democracy and Good Governance in Kenya and entire African Continent by applying:-

(i) Theocentric Humanism Philosophy characterized by the Spirit of Holiness, Perfection and Godliness.
(ii) The Doctrine of Summum Bonum characterized by one's firm belief in Justice, Wisdom, Temperance, Honesty, Courage, Self-Love and Self-Respect, Excellence and Dignity, of every individual in Africa regardless of gender, religion, education, profession, age, marital status, etc.

(i) Doing all these in fulfillment of the Spirit of the African Mysteries System of the Grand Lodge of Luxor in the capacity as The Founding Fathers of this Theocentric Humanism Philosophy and the doctrine of Summum Bonum which they initiated and promoted in Antiquity Egypt in 7000 BC before Egypt was ransacked and the programme destroyed by the Romans under King Theodosius in the 4th Century AD and finally under Justinian in the 6th Century AD.

(j) Using the following strategic Inter-Disciplinary talent to the Programme's effectiveness:—Political Science, History, Anthropology, Psychology, Theology, Psychiatry, Psychoanalysis, Child Education, Education Psychology, Environmental Studies, Sociology, Religion, Drama and Music.

(k) Using the following languages used in Africa:-

  (a) English
  (b) French
  (c) Swahili
  (d) Portuguese
  (e) Spanish
  (f) Local African language where appropriate

(l) Using at least one University in each African Country to act as the resident contact center for the Programme in that Country, e.g., Makerere University for Uganda; University of Dar-es-Salaam for Tanzania,; Addis-Ababa University for Ethiopia; University of Ghana for Ghana; Ibadan University for Nigeria, etc.

(m) Establishing and managing linkages with regional organizations in the Continent which shall serve as contact centers and facilitators of this Programme, e.g. the African Union (A.U.), the Red Cross, East African Community (E.A.C.), Inter-Governmental Authority on Development (IGAD), Economic Community of West African States (ECOWAS), and Southern Africa Development Community (S.A.D.C).

## III.4 EXPECTED OUTCOME (Results) FOR HUMANITY IN KENYA AND THE TOTAL AFRICAN CONTINENT

111.4.1 As already vividly and candidly pointed out in the preceding definition of CONFLICT VACCINATION as a concept and as a process sui generic; and its expected INPUTS and OUTPUTS for the benefit of the Peoples of total Africa, the first and foremost key point to be under-scored here once again is:-

111.4.1.1 That drawing from our own experience of the acute agonies most African countries have already suffered so far and are still continuing to suffer from the scourge of conflicts, the Scientific Truth is:-

(a) That all this agony is a function of the existing unruly and unmanageable decaying culture of rampant massive corruption and devil worshipping in all sectors of society; and
(b) That the agony is not a function of individual leader or leaders in their capacity as persons or Africans.

111.4.1.2 That drawing from Scientific Evidences of our Clinical Diagnosis of corruption as a social problem, another Scientific Truth is:-

(a) That this problem is not African in origin
(b) That its origin has its root in the most unruly and ungovernable wicked culture which believes in and lives by Anthropocentric Humanism Philosophy of the Sophists based in the Antiquity Ages of Greece and Macedonia; the Patricians of Italy, the Huns, the Visgoths and Ostrogoths of Prussia—Germany—a culture that has now bred Mafia and Mafiaism.
(c) That this unruly and ungovernable Culture is a culture of rampant deceits, falsehood, dishonesty, militarism and survival of the fittest mentality characterized by a culture of Robin Hood the robber and The Gun Smoke in Europe and America respectively which always tormented those Countries throughout the Dark Ages till the Peace Treaty of Westphalia in 1648 that forced this culture to go underground and begin to secretly work from undercover in the vail of "Mafia" in Europe and South America; and the "Kuklux Klan (or KKK)" in North

America aimed at advocating white race supremacy against all other non-white races.

(d) That this is the same culture which, in the end of the Dark Ages, metamorphosed and gave birth to the following two other most notorious cultures:-

(i) Colonialism and Imperialism which later on spread into the Americas, Asia and Africa.

(ii) And Mafia based chiefly in Cicily (Italy) and in all Asia Minor and in Columbia in South America which could easily wreck and completely destroy the entire Humanity throughout the World like the atomic bomb on Hiroshima and Nagasaki in 1945 if Social Scientists cannot promptly recognize this potential danger and rapidly intervene to assist World Leaders against such eventualities using appropriate technology such as our CONFLICT VACCINATION technology by which this culture of a potential danger to World Peace and Security should be pre-emptively be disabled or nipped in the bud before its danger takes us by surprise.

111.4.2 In this regard, The Institute of Conflict Vaccination is expected to yield the following advantages for Humanity in Kenya and the Total African Continent:-

111.4.2.1 It shall assist Kenya and Total Africa:

(a) To free themselves from their present unruly, ungovernable and dangerous culture of wicked ways.

(b) To create for them a new HYBRID CULTURE as a basis for Good Governance, Democracy and Accelerated Socio Economic Recovery and Prosperity for our African People.

(c) To have an ensured job security for their leaders so that the latter may now begin to concentrate and perform better during their leadership tenure for the benefit of all but not for a few of the people that they lead as they are doing now thereby breeding more viruses of conflict throughout Africa.

(d) And, to begin investing their resources in ethical activities and policies instead of investing them in activities and policies aimed at initiating, promoting or enhancing viruses of conflicts between themselves and those persons, groups of persons or political party or parties that may be opposed to their leadership with a view to using such resources to kill, arrest, detain, drive the opposition into exile; or socio-economically paralyze, maim, disable or incapacitate the opposition by maliciously destroying all their God-given rights to participate, carryout or manage business for a living.

111.4.2.2 In the final analysis, this Conflict Vaccination Institute shall assist Kenya and each Sister African Country:-

(a) To restore their lost Dignity and Glory
(b) To fulfill the duty and obligation of Science to Humanity

## 111.5 ITS AUTONOMY AND LEGITIMACY REASONS

111.5.1 As already empirically evidenced in our OPERATIONAL DEFINITION of conflict as a concept sui generic in 1.2 above, conflict is a multidimensional and a most elusive phenomenon which cannot be properly understood, explained and predicted with a high degree of parsimony and confidence in Science without using an INTER-DISCIPLINARY APPROACH.

111.5.2 This Approach includes: Political Science Ethics, Psychology, Psychiatry, Sociology, Cybernetics, Anthropology, Geography, Socio-Psychology, Theology, Social Work, International Law (Jurisprudence), Child Education, Education Psychology, Music, Drama, Environmental Studies, etc, which must be harnessed together in order for this Initiative to yield or realize the intended Objective for Africa and the Total World.

111.5.3 The Conflict Vaccination Institute shall be free and safe from all conflict viruses only if it is allowed to exist as a totally INDEPENDENT ENTITY.

111.5.4 By virtue of its novel unique goal and methodology, it is reasonable that it is set up as an independent entity in the Continent in order for it to fully exercise its autonomy and to be as productive and innovative as it is thus expected.

## 111.6 ITS ORGANIZATIONAL STRUCTURE

The Institute of Conflict Vaccination in Africa shall have the following structure with the following positions and functions:

**POSITION: FUNCTION:**

| POSITION: | FUNCTION: |
|---|---|
| 1. Director General | Chief Executive and Accounting Officer of The Institute charged with the following responsibilities<br>(a) Overall supervision of all Functions and Financial Management of The Institute<br>(b) Overall Fund Raising from both local and Foreign donors<br>(c) Overall Steering of Management Committee Meetings.<br>(d) Chief Representative of The Institute at all external meetings |
| 2. Deputy Director General: | Chief Administrative Secretary of The Institute responsive to the Director General and charged with the following responsibilities.<br>(a) General Administration of The Institute on behalf of the Director General.<br>(b) General Supervision of all expenditures and payments of such expenditures on behalf of the Director General.<br>(c) General Supervision and Maintenance of all fixed and moveable assets of The Institute on behalf of the Director General.<br>(d) General Arrangement of Management and all Statutory meetings including protocol matters on behalf of the Director General.<br>(e) General Supervision of the following Junior Officers and their functions:<br>(i) Administrative Officer responsible for all Adminsitrative, Insurance and Protocol matters of The Institute.<br>(ii) Finance Officer responsible for preparation of all books of Accounts ready for Audit.<br>(iii) Internal Auditor responsible for preliminary verification (audit) of all expenditures and assets of The Institute for the EXTERNAL AUDIT. |

(iv) Security Officer responsible for all security matters of The Institute
(v) Medical Officer responsible for all health matters of The Institute staff.
(vi) Communications Officer responsible for all media, publications, and documentation.
(vii) Electronics Officer responsible for maintenance and arrangement of all electronic equipment wherever they are needed by The Institute.

3. Chief Expert in Cultural Engineering Division: Head of the said Division responsible to the Deputy Director General and charged with the following responsibilities of The Institute on behalf of the Director General aimed at rehabilitating the existing culture from its present conflict virus infested STATE to a new conflict virus free STATE called HYBRID:

(a) ELITE CULTURAL ENGINEERING whose duty shall be:

(i) To rehabilitate the existing Elite Culture in each African country from its present state of conflict virus condition to a Hybrid Culture which is free from such viruses.
(ii) To use The Institute's approved appropriate technology, e.g. seminars, conferences, workshops, religious institutions, schools, live stage and electronic music, live and electronic drama, etc with a view to demonstrating to them the need to understand:-

- The concept and significance of Peace, Love and Unity in a Nation.
- Why Leaders Actually Fail in their Leadership and consequences to their Nations and themselves.
- How Leaders can easily succeed in their Leadership Tenure and Consequences to their Nations and themselves.

(b) GRASS-ROOT CULTURAL ENGINEERING whose duty shall be:-

(i) To rehabilitate the existing wicked culture of the General Public or the Masses in each African Country which is at this time infested with conflict viruses.
(ii) To transform that culture from its conflict viruses infected state into a conflict virus free state called HYBRID.
(iii) To use The Institute's appropriate technology to realize this needed Hybrid Culture.

(c) GRASS-ROOT CULTURAL ENGINEERING EVALUATION whose duty shall be:-

(i) To assess the efficacy of the process.
(ii) To report to the Director General possible recommendation(s) or alternative option(s)

4. Chief Expert in Conflictology and Conflict Vaccinology Division: Head of the said Division responsive to the Deputy Director General, and charged with the following responsibilities:

(a) Overall Supervision of:

(i) The Division's Clinical Prognosis of Conflicts;
(ii) The Nosology Function of the Division whose duty shall be to carry out a clinical investigation of all types of Conflict Viruses coherent in Leaders of each country in Africa which have consequently made either good or bad leadership and governance.

(b) To provide appropriate remedy likely to forge out a HYBRID CULTURE essential for Good Governance and a Rapid Socio-Economic Recovery and Productivity in Africa for the present majority poor African.

(c) GRASS-ROOT CLINICAL DIAGNOSIS & PROGNOSIS OF CONFLICT whose duty shall be:

(i) To carry out a clinical search for all types of conflict viruses inherent in the Grass-root of each Country in Africa which consequently make them always susceptible to conflict in their country with particular attention to their attitude toward authority and policy of their country's leadership and the reasons thereof.

(ii) To provide appropriate remedy to such viruses.

(d) EVALUATION OF CLINICAL DIAGNOSIS & PROGNOSIS OF ELITE & GRASS-ROOT CONFLICT VIRUSES whose duty shall be:

(i) To undertake a systematic in-depth analysis of the efficacy of the Department vis a vis the overall objective of the division and institute.

(ii) To recommend its findings and recommendations to the Director for appropriate action and directive for new strategies and other needful.

5. Chief Advisor on Degree Programme and Students Admissions Department:

Head of the said Department responsive to the Deputy Director of the division and who shall be responsible for:

(a) Implementation of the approved Institute Degree Programme stated in (h) below:

(b) Assessment of the Efficacy of the programme toward the overall goal of The Institute.
(c) Submission of the same to the Deputy Director General for appropriate Management action.
(d) Assessment of new student credentials seeking admission to THE INSTITUTE'S teaching and research programme.
(e) Admission of qualified student(s) to specific Institute Degree Programme.
(f) Recruitment and Supervision of the teaching staff.
(g) Confirmation to the Deputy Director General each student that may be qualified for graduation in accordance with the Curriculum in (h) below.
(h) DEGREE PROGRAMME COURSES (CURRICULUM) IN CONFLICTOLOGY AND CONFLICT VACCINOLOGY

- Human Ecology
- Human Relations
- Political Psychiatry
- Classical & Modern Political Theory (Philosophy)
- Ethics and Politics
- Theology/Religion
- Theory and Practice
- Past and Present Theories of International relations.
- Man and the Environment
- Indigenous knowledge systems and technology
- A History of Science and Technology
- International Communication
- Cybernetics Public and Private Administration
- Policy Analysis
- A History and World Peace Keeping
- Public and Private International Law
- Public and Private

- International Organizations
- Political Economy
- Natural Resources Management and Utilization
- Strategic Security Environmental Engineering & Management
- Leadership pathology (Why Leaders Fail in Leadership)
- Nosology of Conflict

| | |
|---|---|
| 6. Professors and Lecturers of Conflictology And Conflict Vaccination | Who shall be scientists responsible directly to the Chief Expert for that Programme in their individual and collective contribution to the development of CONFLICTOLOGY AND CONFLICT VACCINOLOGY against the existing scourge of conflict in Kenya and Total Africa; and to create a Hybrid Culture in Africa. |
| 7. Expert for Elite Cultural Engineering Department: | Who shall be responsive to the Chief Expert in Cultural Engineering Division directly responsible for implementation of Elite Cultural Engineering Programmes under direct supervision of the Chief Expert. |
| 8. Expert for Grass-Root Cultural Engineering Department | Who shall also be responsive to the Chief Expert of the said Division and directly responsible for the Implementation of grass-Root Cultural Engineering Programme under direct supervision of that Chief Expert. |
| 9. Expert for Elite Clinical Diagnosis and Prognosis of Conflict | Who shall be directly responsive to the Chief Expert for the Clinical Diagnosis and Prognosis of Conflict Division and directly responsible for Elite Clinical Diagnosis and Prognosis duties in keeping with the overall goal of that Division and The Institute. |
| 10. Expert for Grass-Root Clinical Diagnosis of Conflict: | Who shall be directly responsive to the Chief Expert in Clinical Diagnosis and Prognosis of Conflict Division and directly responsible specifically for the clinical diagnosis and prognosis of the Grass-Root under direct supervision of that Division's Chief Expert in the latter's effort to realize the overall objective of the Division and The Institute as a whole. |

## DEGREE REQUIREMENTS

| Degree of Science | No.of Semesters | Units |
|---|---|---|
| Bachelors | 8 | 96 |
| Masters | 4 | 36 |
| Ph.D | 6 | 57 |

## ADMISSION REQUIREMENT

1. A minimum of a C+ High School grade shall be essential for a Bachelor's entry.
2. Admission to a Masters' and Ph.D. Degrees programmes shall be strictly reserved for those students who have already successfully completed their Bachelor's and Master's degree in both Conflictology and Conflict Vaccinology at the Institute of Vaccination since there exists no any other institution of learning throughout the World offering such academic discipline.
3. Also Admission for a Diploma or Professional Certificate training programme shall be open to Leaders and Managers of any institution who are interested in quickly grasping the essentials of a Hybrid Culture and the latter's contribution to the art of Good Governance which Africa is already lacking and would, therefore, like to get at all costs.

## 111.7. OPERATIONAL LOGISTICS

The Institute of Conflict Vaccination shall require the following equipment to carry out its activities/programmes effectively:

| EQUIPMENT | QUANTITY |
|---|---|
| 1. Public Address System................................................................ | |
| 2. Computers ................................................................................ | |
| 3. Computer Printers...................................................................... | |
| 4. Video Recorder.......................................................................... | |
| 5. Television ................................................................................ | |
| 6. Video Machine.......................................................................... | |
| 7. Motor Vans (Coaster) ................................................................ | |

8. Telephone Equipment.........................................................
9. Fax Machine ...................................................................
10. Photocopier Machine (coloured & balck and white) .................
11. Tent ...............................................................................
12. Computer Laptop...............................................................
13. Cameras ..........................................................................
14. Printing Machine ..............................................................

**APPENDIX D4 X 1**
**LABORATORY AND OFFICE REQUIREMENTS**

| NO. | ITEM | DESCRIPTION | QUANTITY | COST $ | TOTAL $ |
|---|---|---|---|---|---|
| 1 | SERVER | HP/COMPAQ, Full Multimedia 2.4 HGZ PIV, 120 GB HDD, 512SORAM with 17" color monitor, Ms windows 2000 server software | 2 | 2,500.00 | 5,000.00 |
| 2. | COMPUTER (Branded) | Full multimedia, 2GH2 P.IV, 40GBHDD 256 DDR RAM, 52x32x52 CD RE WRITER with 17" colour monitors with digital control | 60 | 1,250.00 | 75,000.00 |
| 3. | PRINTER (Lab. use) | Heavy Duty (Black & White) | 5 | 750.00 | 3,750.00 |
| 4. | PRINTER (Office use) | Light Duty (Colour) | 5 | 500.00 | 2,500.00 |
| 5. | LAPTOP | 2.4 GHZ/256RAM/ 30GBHDD/DVD+CD RW/14" TFT SCREEN 56FAXMODEM/10/100 NIC/WINXPP) | 5 | 1,250.00 | 6,250.00 |

| | | | | | |
|---|---|---|---|---|---|
| 6. | PHOTOCOPIER | Heavy Duty EPSON/ COPY CAT | 2 | 1,875.00 | 3,750.00 |
| 7. | HUBS/SWITCH | 24 Port | 3 | 375.00 | 1,125.00 |
| 8. | HP SCANNER | For Office use | 2 | 375.00 | 750.00 |
| 9. | FAX MACHINE | Standard | 5 | 20,000 | 1,250.00 |
| 10. | TRANSMISSION CABLES | (Twisted Pair (10 Base T) | 2000m | 1.25 | 2,500.00 |
| 11. | ACCESSORIES | RJ45 jacks<br>Wall outlets<br>Crimpling tool | 150<br>70<br>2 | 0.25<br>3.75<br>62.50 | 37.50<br>626.50<br>125.00 |
| 12. | COMPUTER TABLES | Standard | 40 | 125.00 | 5,000.00 |
| 13. | CHAIRS LAB | Standard | 40 | 75.00 | 3,000.00 |
| 14. | CHAIRS OFFICES | Standard | 10 | 75.00 | 750.00 |
| 15. | UPS 5000VA | | 4 | | |
| 16. | UPS 1000VA | | 10 | | |

**PUBLIC ADDRESS SYSTEM & ACCESSORIES**

| NO | ITEM | DESCRIPTION | QUANTITY | UNIT PRICE $ | TOTAL COST $ |
|---|---|---|---|---|---|
| 1. | AMPLIFIER | Integrated stereo Amplifier 45 Watts RMS output power per channel: DIN 502 per channel | 2 | 750.00 | 1,500.00 |
| 2. | SPEAKER | Column 300W PMPO | 4 | 187.50 | 750.00 |
| 3. | MICROPHONE | Cordless, transmitter frequency 174.1 MHZ transmitting range 15m, frequency response: -80 to 15,000HZ | 2 | 750.00 | 1,500.00 |

| | | | | | |
|---|---|---|---|---|---|
| 4. | VIDEO CASSETE RECORDER | 4+2 head Nicam Long Play Vido Recorder (Philips). Auto instill with date and time down load, NTSC playback | 2 | 750.00 | 1,500.00 |
| 5. | T.V. SET | Panasonic (Japan), 26" | 2 | 500.00 | 1,000.00 |
| 6. | VIDEO CAMERA (Cam Corder) | Accepting/using standard VHS Cassette | 2 | 875.00 | 1,750.00 |
| 7. | EXTENSION POWER CABLE | ANTI POWER SURGE | 15 | 12.50 | 187.50 |

1.9 PROPOSED FUNDING SOURCES

1.9.1 By virtue of the significance of the OBJECTIVE of this Programme the Institute hopes to get funding assistance from various sources

1.9.2 Momentarily, The World Bank has already expressed its interest in sponsoring this initiative.

1.9.3 And we also plan to contact other sources such as the: United States Agency for International Development (USAID), European Union (EU), Japan, The United Kingdom (UK), Germany, France, Italy, Belgium, Canada, the Governments and Peoples of Africa, Global Institution such as the UN and Multi-national Corporations, Continental institutions such as the Organizations in Africa such as the Inter-Governmental (IGAD), East African Community (EAC), the Economic Community of the Western African States (ECOWAS), Southern Africa Development Coordination Conference (SADCC) and the Common Market for Eastern and Southern Africa (COMESA).

## IV. GLOSSARY

1. "Institute" here in means an institution established to bring about or provide goods and services to Humanity which in this regard, ways and means of eradicating conflict in Africa and The Total World.
2. "Conflict" herein means an absence of peace and stability between or among persons, countries or nations at a given time.
3. "Nosology" herein means a scientific systematic classification of conflict into their exhaustive and mutally exclusive types strictly based on their causes and cures.

4. "Etiology" herein means a scientific (clinical) diagnosis of the conflict or friction with a view to establishing its actual causes and whether these causes are pathologically natural or man-made viri.
5. "Vaccination" herein means an innoculation using a scientifically discovered anti-virus dose(s) against an existing disease virus with a view to (a) curing by way of paralyzing and eliminating that virus and that may already be present in a living body; and (b) preventing by way of containing that virus wherever it may specifically be in the body from spreading in that body or from entering and spreading new normal bodies which may not yet have been already infected.
6. "Conflict Virus(es)" is a brand new scientific concept in the Academia herein meaning all anti-bodies against the normal health of a political system (society, country, Nation or Total World) and the letter's eufunction by the way it is rendered practically to acquire or achieve any significant socio-economic development and advancement for its people fostered and promoted by the same anti-bodies manifested as Bad Governance or Bad Leadership defined as Autocracy; Totalitarianism; Self-Glorification (Characterized by management crisis using arrogance and terror as a weapon against one's peers including even small persons whom, as a leader one is, in fact, obligated to respect, serve and protect against every odds in life); **Corruption** (characterized by use of one's leadership position to steal significant assets of the country that one is obligated to serve as its Leader and Servant; **Obstruction** to The Rule of Law and Justice by cunningly fostering and promoting vices for one's benefit; initiation and supporting bad policies and acts aimed at destroying other than improving the Environment and Total Ecosystem; Engaging in Devil Worship that always put God to anger as in the cases of Sodom, Gomorrah and Nineveh that led them to their own self destruction; etc.
7. "Conflict Vaccination" herein is therefore new scientific concept in the Academic meaning both **curative** and **preventive** processes against conflict viruses which may already be prevalently saturated in a society's culture with a view to scientifically and practically rehabilitating and transforming that society's culture from a conflict virus state into a new state called "HYBRID CULTURE".
8. "A Hybrid Culture" herein is also a new concept in the Scientific World meaning a culture which is free from and also resilient and resistant to conflict viruses; it arises from Conflict Vaccination Process on both the Elite and the Grass-Roots; and because of its sound peace and stability character, it is the most reliable enabling environment for a rapid socio-economic recovery and accelerated national development for the well-being of a country.

9. "Elite" herein means all types of leadership in each Country or Society which include political, religious, economic, club, village, etc.
10. "Grass-Roots" herein means the common men and women and children headed by the Elites from all walks of life in a given Society, Country or Nation.
11. "Conflictology" herein is a new scientific concept currently introduced in the Academia by virtue of the problem nature, objective and rationale of this Proposal meaning a clinical diagnosis and prognosis of a conflict with a view to scientifically and systematically searching for and identifying all its actual root-causes (viruses) for the action of the province of Conflict Vaccinology (defined in II, below).
12. "Conflict Vaccinology" herein is also another new scientific concept in Academia meaning a clinical diagnosis and prognosis of conflict vaccine with a view to scientifically identifying the appropriate cure for each conflict and administration methodology of that cure.
13. "Vertical Conflict Vaccination" herein means a Vaccination process from top-down, i.e from (or beginning with) the Elite of a society right down to that society's Grass-Roots aimed at rehabilitating that society from its existing corroded (corrupt) culture saturated with conflicts and Bad Governance to a hybrid culture free from such root-causes of Bad Governance.
14. "Horizontal Conflict Vacciantion" herein means a sideways vaccination process from one corner to another corner or a country focusing on both the Elite and the Grass-Roots of that Country aimed at doing the same as in No. 11 (above).
15. "Vertical Conflict Vaccinology" herein means a top-bottom Clinical Diagnosis and Prognosis of conflict in a society specifically aimed at first identifying the actual root-causes of conflict in a country from the Elite's stratum to the Grass-Roots structure and also how such root-causes could or may be cured (or eradicated) and contained (or prevented) from either spreading or re-occuring in future.
16. "Horizontal Conflict Vaccinology" herein means a Prognosis of Conflict in a Society specifically focusing on the Grass-Roots with a view to identifying what could or may be the actual root-cause of their conflict; an appropriate cure; and how that identified cure could or may be administered to eradicate or prevent similar root-causes from infecting the country, nation or people in question.
17. "Elite Conflict Vaccination" herein means an inoculation process focusing on the elite stratum of a society with a view to curing and also preventing that Elite from the existing conflict viruses as a first and foremost step before moving the process to the Grass-Roots.

18. "Grass-Roots Conflcit Vaccination" herein means a vaccination process focusing on the Grass-Roots with a view to also curing and preventing them from existing conflict viruses a second step of the process after the "Elite Conflict Vaccination" step.
19. "Elite Conflictology" herein means a clinical diagnosis and prognosis of the existing conflict viruses within but first beginning with the Elite as a possible suspect of conflict viruses so as to understand what could or may be their possible role or contribution to conflict in their Society, Country, Nation or Total World.
20. "Grass-Roots Conflictology" herein means a clinical diagnosis and prognosis of the existing conflict viruses within a country specifically focusing the study on the Grass-Roots as a possible suspect of these conflict viruses so as to understand better what could or may be their possible role or contribution to conflict in their Society, Country, Nation or Total World.
21. "Culture Engineering' is also another new scientific concept currently introduced in the Academia on the strength of this study meaning a scientific process of rehabilitating and transforming the existing culture from its present wicked state, saturated with various conflict viruses defined under Glossary No. 4 above, to a HYBRID CULTURE state defined under Glossary No. 6 above which any rational country such as Kenya should seek to achieve for the advancement of its people.
22. "Director General" herein means a Chief Executive and Accounting Officer of The Institute whose responsibilities are spelled out in details under Section 111.7(1).
23. "Deputy Director General" herein means a Chief Adminstrative Secretary and Aid to the Director General in all matters pertaining to General Adminstration and Financial Management of the College on behalf of the Director and who shall, therefore, always deputize for the Director in the absence of the latter.
24. "Chief Expert in Cultural Engineering" herein means a Chief Technologist or Expert in the art of Rehabilitation and Transformation of the existing culture of violence to a HYBRID CULTURE free from, resilient and resistant to conflict viruses.
25. "Chief Expert in Conflictology and Conflict Vaccinology" herein means a Chief Technologist in the art of Clinical Diagnosis and Prognosis of Conflicts aimed at scientifically identifying the actual root causes of conflict and their possible remedies for on-ward transmission or submission to the Deputy Director General for possible action by the Chief Expert in Culture Engineering.
26. "Expert in Clinical Diagnosis and Prognosis of Conflicts" herein means one in charge of Applied Peace-Research aimed at identifying conflict viruses and their curative and preventive means.

27. "Registrar for Degree Programmes and Student Admissions" herein means an Officer in charge of implementation of the programmes and processing of student applying to the programmes.
28. "Administrative Manager" herein means an aid to the Deputy Director General, Adminstration and Finance in matters pertaining to administration.
29. "Finance Controller" herein means an aid to the said Deputy Director in matters pertaining to financial management and maintenance of all Books of Accounts, institutional fixed assets, etc on behalf of The Director.
30. "Expert Assistant" herein means an aid to the Chief Expert in his respective Department to which he/she is assigned.
31. "Professor/Lecturer" herein means an expert in Conflictology and Conflict Vaccinology" and one who shall be a qualified scientist in the two to guide the junior scholar and/per the neophyte through the teaching and scientific research programme with a view to leading the student to either an advanced degree, diploma or professional certificate in the two disciplines; and to lead participating Political and other Leaders including Managers through period short-Term Intensive Training Programmes on the nature of Hybrid Culture as a pre-requisite for Good Governance and Socio-economic Recovery.
32. "Student' herein means one admitted to The Institute for an intensive and extensive professional training in Conflictology Vaccinology with a view to making him or her a neophyte for promotion of Conflict Vaccination toward a Hybrid Culture.
33. "Neophyte" herein means an advanced scholar who in the modern Academia is also known as Research Fellow, above a junior scholar level. This shall come to the Institute to do advanced research in Conflictology and Conflict Vaccinology leading to an advanced degree which, in the American terminology, means "Post-Graduate", i.e., a Ph.D degree programme). The term was first used by The Founding Fathers of Science, Technology and A Hybrid Culture called The African Mysteries System of The Grand Lodge of Luxor between 5000-3000 BC at a place in North Africa now known as Alexandria after Alexander The Great, who militarily conquered and occupied it in the year 332 BC due to its extra-ordinary eminence in Science, Technology and Hybrid Culture of Governance from the extra-ordinary talents of Professors/Priests of that Lodge. By then, a neophyte was a student of extra-ordinary scientific mastery, e.g., Imhotep (the first immaculate African Egyptian physican and architect who lived in 2980 B.C.) and Thales, Pythagoras, Socrates, Herodotus, and other foreigners who become what then became because of their enrolment for advanced study at The African Mysteries System of The Grand Lodge of Luxor.